Feasting on the Word[®]

Editorial Board

Feasting on the Word®

Preaching the
Revised Common Lectionary

Year A, Volume 3

DAVID L. BARTLETT and BARBARA BROWN TAYLOR

General Editors

WJK WESTMINSTER
JOHN KNOX PRESS
LOUISVILLE · KENTUCKY

Scripture quotations from the New Revised Standard Version of the Bible are copyright © 1989 by the Division of Christian Education of the National Council of the Churches of Christ in the U.S.A. and are used by permission. All rights reserved. Scripture quotations marked (ESV) are from The Holy Bible, English Standard Version® (ESV®), copyright © 2001 by Crossway, a publishing ministry of Good News Publishers. Used by permission. All rights reserved.

Extract from Michael Morgan, *The Psalter for Christian Worship* (Louisville: Witherspoon Press, 1999). Used by permission. Extract from Glenn Burleigh, "Order My Steps," *Praises with the Orchestra*, Glenn Burleigh Music Workshop. Used by permission.

Book design by Drew Stevens
Cover design by Lisa Buckley

First edition
Published by Westminster John Knox Press
Louisville, Kentucky

This book is printed on acid-free paper that meets the American National Standards Institute Z39.48 standard. ♾

PRINTED IN THE UNITED STATES OF AMERICA

11 12 13 14 15 16 17 18 19 20 — 10 9 8 7 6 5 4 3 2 1

Library of Congress Cataloging-in-Publication Data

Feasting on the Word : preaching the revised common lectionary / David L. Bartlett and Barbara Brown Taylor, general editors.
     p. cm.
  Includes index.
  ISBN 978-0-664-23106-4 (v. 11 alk. paper)
  ISBN 978-0-664-23105-7 (v. 10 alk. paper)
  ISBN 978-0-664-23104-0 (v. 9 alk. paper)
  ISBN 978-0-664-23103-3 (v. 8 alk. paper)
  ISBN 978-0-664-23102-6 (v. 7 alk. paper)
  ISBN 978-0-664-23101-9 (v. 6 alk. paper)
  ISBN 978-0-664-23100-2 (v. 5 alk. paper)
  ISBN 978-0-664-23099-9 (v. 4 alk. paper)
  ISBN 978-0-664-23098-2 (v. 3 alk. paper)
  ISBN 978-0-664-23097-5 (v. 2 alk. paper)
  ISBN 978-0-664-23096-8 (v. 1 alk. paper)
  1. Lectionary preaching.   2. Common lectionary (1992)   I. Bartlett, David Lyon, 1941–
II. Taylor, Barbara Brown.
  BV4235.L43F43 2008
  251'.6—dc22

                                                        2007047534

Contents

Publisher's Note

Feasting on the Word: Preaching the Revised Common Lectionary is an ambitious project that is offered to the Christian church as a resource for preaching and teaching.

The uniqueness of this approach in providing four perspectives on each preaching occasion from the Revised Common Lectionary sets this work apart from other lectionary materials. The theological, pastoral, exegetical, and homiletical dimensions of each biblical passage are explored with the hope that preachers will find much to inform and stimulate their preparations for preaching from this rich "feast" of materials.

This work could not have been undertaken without the deep commitments of those who have devoted countless hours to working on these tasks. Westminster John Knox Press would like to acknowledge the magnificent work of our general editors, David L. Bartlett and Barbara Brown Taylor. They are both gifted preachers with passionate concerns for the quality of preaching. They are also wonderful colleagues who embraced this huge task with vigor, excellence, and unfailing good humor. Our debt of gratitude to Barbara and David is great.

The fine support staff, project manager Joan Murchison and compiler Mary Lynn Darden, enabled all the thousands of "pieces" of the project to come together and form this impressive series. Without their strong competence and abiding persistence, these volumes could not have emerged.

The volume editors for this series are to be thanked as well. They used their superb skills as pastors and professors and ministers to work with writers and help craft their valuable insights into the highly useful entries that comprise this work.

The hundreds of writers who shared their expertise and insights to make this series possible are ones who deserve deep thanks indeed. They come from wide varieties of ministries. They have given their labors to provide a gift to benefit the whole church and to enrich preaching in our time.

Westminster John Knox would also like to express our appreciation to Columbia Theological Seminary for strong cooperation in enabling this work to begin and proceed. Dean of Faculty and Executive Vice President D. Cameron Murchison welcomed the project from the start and drew together everything we needed. His continuing efforts have been very valuable. Former President Laura S. Mendenhall provided splendid help as well. She made seminary resources and personnel available and encouraged us in this partnership with enthusiasm and all good grace. We thank her, and look forward to working with Columbia's new president, Stephen Hayner.

It is a joy for Westminster John Knox Press to present *Feasting on the Word: Preaching the Revised Common Lectionary* to the church, its preachers, and its teachers. We believe rich resources can assist the church's ministries as the Word is proclaimed. We believe the varieties of insights found in these pages will nourish preachers who will "feast on the Word" and who will share its blessings with those who hear.

Westminster John Knox Press

Series Introduction

A preacher's work is never done. Teaching, offering pastoral care, leading worship, and administering congregational life are only a few of the responsibilities that can turn preaching into just one more task of pastoral ministry. Yet the Sunday sermon is how the preacher ministers to most of the people most of the time. The majority of those who listen are not in crisis. They live such busy lives that few take part in the church's educational programs. They wish they had more time to reflect on their faith, but they do not. Whether the sermon is five minutes long or forty-five, it is the congregation's one opportunity to hear directly from their pastor about what life in Christ means and why it matters.

Feasting on the Word offers pastors focused resources for sermon preparation, written by companions on the way. With four different essays on each of the four biblical texts assigned by the Revised Common Lectionary, this series offers preachers sixteen different ways into the proclamation of God's Word on any given occasion. For each reading, preachers will find brief essays on the exegetical, theological, homiletical, and pastoral challenges of the text. The page layout is unusual. By setting the biblical passage at the top of the page and placing the essays beneath it, we mean to suggest the interdependence of the four approaches without granting priority to any one of them. Some readers may decide to focus on the Gospel passage, for instance, by reading all four essays provided for that text. Others may decide to look for connections between the Hebrew Bible, Psalm, Gospel, and Epistle texts by reading the theological essays on each one.

Wherever they begin, preachers will find what they need in a single volume produced by writers from a wide variety of disciplines and religious traditions. These authors teach in colleges and seminaries. They lead congregations. They write scholarly books as well as columns for the local newspaper. They oversee denominations. In all of these capacities and more, they serve God's Word, joining the preacher in the ongoing challenge of bringing that Word to life.

We offer this print resource for the mainline church in full recognition that we do so in the digital age of the emerging church. Like our page layout, this decision honors the authority of the biblical text, which thrives on the page as well as in the ear. While the twelve volumes of this series follow the pattern of the Revised Common Lectionary, each volume contains an index of biblical passages so that all preachers may make full use of its contents.

We also recognize that this new series appears in a post-9/11, post-Katrina world. For this reason, we provide no shortcuts for those committed to the proclamation of God's Word. Among preachers, there are books known as "Monday books" because they need to be read thoughtfully at least a week ahead of time. There are also "Saturday books," so called because they supply sermon ideas on short notice. The books in this series are not Saturday books. Our aim is to help preachers go deeper, not faster, in a world that is in need of saving words.

A series of this scope calls forth the gifts of a great many people. We are grateful first of all to the staff of Westminster John Knox Press: Don McKim, Jon Berquist, and Jack Keller, who conceived this project; David Dobson, who worked diligently to bring the project to completion, with publisher Marc Lewis's strong support; and Julie Tonini, who has painstakingly guided each volume through the production process. We thank former President Laura Mendenhall and former Dean Cameron Murchison of Columbia Theological Seminary, who made our participation in this work possible. We thank President Steve Hayner and Dean Deborah Mullen for their continuing encouragement and support. Our editorial board is a hardworking board, without whose patient labor and good humor this series would not exist. From the start, Joan Murchison has been the brains of the operation, managing details of epic proportions with great human kindness. Mary Lynn Darden, Dilu Nicholas, Megan Hackler Denton, and John Shillingburg have supported both her and us with their administrative skills.

We have been honored to work with a multitude of gifted thinkers, writers, and editors. We present these essays as their offering—and ours—to the blessed ministry of preaching.

David L. Bartlett
Barbara Brown Taylor

A Note about the Lectionary

Feasting on the Word follows the Revised Common Lectionary (RCL) as developed by the Consultation on Common Texts, an ecumenical consultation of liturgical scholars and denominational representatives from the United States and Canada. The RCL provides a collection of readings from Scripture to be used during worship in a schedule that follows the seasons of the church year. In addition, it provides for a uniform set of readings to be used across denominations or other church bodies.

The RCL provides a reading from the Old Testament, a Psalm response to that reading, a Gospel, and an Epistle for each preaching occasion of the year. It is presented in a three-year cycle, with each year centered around one of the Synoptic Gospels. Year A is the year of Matthew, Year B is the year of Mark, and Year C is the year of Luke. John is read each year, especially during Advent, Lent, and Easter.

The RCL offers two tracks of Old Testament texts for the Season after Pentecost or Ordinary Time: a semicontinuous track, which moves through stories and characters in the Old Testament, and a complementary track, which ties the Old Testament texts to the theme of the Gospel texts for that day. Some denominational traditions favor one over the other. For instance, Presbyterians and Methodists generally follow the semicontinuous track, while Lutherans and Episcopalians generally follow the complementary track.

The print volumes of *Feasting on the Word* follow the complementary track for Year A, are split between the complementary and semicontinuous tracks for Year B, and cover the semicontinuous stream for Year C. Essays for Pentecost and the Season after Pentecost that are not covered in the print volumes will be available on the *Feasting on the Word* Web site, www.feastingontheword.net.

For more information about the Revised Common Lectionary, visit the official RCL Web site at http://lectionary.library.vanderbilt.edu/ or see *The Revised Common Lectionary: The Consultation on Common Texts* (Nashville: Abingdon Press, 1992).

Feasting on the Word

Numbers 11:24-30

24So Moses went out and told the people the words of the LORD; and he gathered seventy elders of the people, and placed them all around the tent. 25Then the LORD came down in the cloud and spoke to him, and took some of the spirit that was on him and put it on the seventy elders; and when the spirit rested upon them, they prophesied. But they did not do so again. 26Two men remained in the camp, one named Eldad, and the other named Medad, and the spirit rested on them; they were among those registered, but they had not gone out to the tent, and so they prophesied in the camp. 27And a young man ran and told Moses, "Eldad and Medad are prophesying in the camp." 28And Joshua son of Nun, the assistant of Moses, one of his chosen men, said, "My lord Moses, stop them!" 29But Moses said to him, "Are you jealous for my sake? Would that all the LORD's people were prophets, and that the LORD would put his spirit on them!" 30And Moses and the elders of Israel returned to the camp.

Theological Perspective

This story raises theological questions about the nature of the spirit's work and the source of religious authority. Because the spirit works in two distinct— and perhaps even opposing—groups of people in this text, and because the story occurs in the context of a crisis in Moses's leadership, it is pivotal for exploring ecclesial issues that lie at the heart of the church's relationship to both spirit and authority. The first work of the spirit concerns the seventy whom Moses has gathered in the tent outside the encampment of the people. There, the Lord takes "some of the spirit" that is on Moses and "put[s] it on the seventy elders." The second work of the spirit rests upon Eldad and Medad (the Two) inside the encampment. Both the seventy and the Two prophesy[1] as a result of having received the spirit.

The prophecy of the Two might have remained unknown but for the tattletale young man who complains to Moses. The added dismay of Moses's assistant, Joshua, assumes that only the seventy ought to have the legitimate powers of the spirit, since it is Moses's own spirit that the Lord has apportioned among them. This assumes that only the known

1. Prophecy is "the power of instructing and admonishing the people with an authority that was recognized as having its source in God" (Pamela Tamarkin Reis, "Numbers XI: Seeing Moses Plain," in *Vetus Testamentum* 55, no. 2 [2005]: 222).

Pastoral Perspective

The roaring of a mighty wind, the speaking in tongues, acting as if filled with new wine, on fire with the energy and love of God—these are just some of the ways the book of Acts tries to describe the event we call Pentecost. In that description, we witness the wildness of God's Spirit that infuses both individuals and whole communities. It is an ecstatic, joyous experience and unimaginably powerful.

What then can the passage from Numbers add to our understanding of the ways God's Spirit works in the world?

Perhaps it can show us something about leadership—Spirit-led leadership.

In Numbers, the context for leadership is the wilderness. Moses, the charismatic leader, and the Israelites are still relatively new in their wilderness sojourn and are living on manna provided daily by God. A dark mood comes over some in the community, who begin murmuring about the lack of meat in their diet (vv. 4b–7).

As we know, a dark mood can come over any congregation or organization: complaints about things that are done or not done, a looking back to the past as the good old days, second guessing decisions, blaming the leader. Such complaints can infect the whole community and blind members to the

Exegetical Perspective

One of the great things about Numbers in particular, and the Bible in general, is the way that extra stories seem to break out just when we think the main story is over. In a basic way, both the exodus in the Old Testament and Jesus' resurrection in the New are "extra" stories that crop up once the main stories of oppression and power have done their worst. Even when the main story is positive, such as the ordering of the tribes at the beginning of Numbers and the apportionment of property at the end, little "extra" stories appear (about the tribe of the Levites or the daughters of Zelophehad) that may have more to tell us about God and God's people than the major story now complete. Such an "addendum" is the second half of the reading from Numbers 11.

The main story in Numbers 11 is a story about grumbling—both on the part of the people and on the part of Moses. No sooner has Israel been organized and trained for the march, than the people, then Moses, come to a halt in order to complain—the people about the quality of the fare, and Moses about the burden of leadership. God, determined, even at great cost, to keep both Moses and the people moving, proposes two gracious and/or disciplinary acts—a surfeit of quails for the rabble (sufficient to fill them up to and out of their nostrils) and a surfeit of fellow leaders for Moses (as

Homiletical Perspective

This text for Pentecost celebrates the coming of the spirit poured out on Moses, the seventy elders, Eldad and Medad, and ultimately all the people of God. A sermon could focus on one of the important themes in this narrative that connects with the celebration of Pentecost: God empowering the faith community through the outpouring of the spirit of Moses and the others.

The exigency that leads to this outpouring comes from a crisis within the community. The complaining of the people reaches a crescendo, pushing both the Lord and Moses to the brink. The Lord responds in anger, determined to severely punish these ungrateful rabble-rousers. Moses once again intervenes, this time voicing his own weariness; he is experiencing extreme pastoral burnout. He can no longer manage or respond to the demands of the people. So he appeals to the Lord's gentler maternal affections to care for the people (Num. 11:11–15).

Understanding Moses's exhaustion, the Lord tells him to choose seventy individuals among the elders of Israel to help carry the burden. God then gives these elders some of the spirit that God has given Moses, to enable them to fulfill their leadership roles (vv. 17, 25). Then, unexpectedly, the spirit falls on two other men, who begin to prophesy—much to the chagrin of Joshua. Joshua demands that Moses

Numbers 11:24-30

Theological Perspective

leader bestows appropriate powers. Accordingly, the spirit rests inappropriately on the Two. Joshua insists that Moses's authority is thwarted by having brought the seventy together, only to find that the spirit has simultaneously been working in the camp. Moses turns on Joshua, glad for the increase in prophetic voice among the people.

Curiously, the spirit works in this story in concert with the Lord and also on its own. Here, at least, "the LORD" and "the spirit" are differentiated from each other. This does not mean that they are not closely associated, only that the actions in this scene depict two different movements. Verse 25—"The LORD came down in the cloud . . . and took some of the spirit" to put on the seventy—shows the spirit as a passive actor. Regarding Eldad and Medad, we do not hear that "the LORD" has anything to do with it, only that "the spirit rested" on them. Can the spirit act on its own without benefit of "the LORD's" power? Can and do the Lord and the spirit act independently of one another? (What might such an idea say to Christians about the triune God?) From where, indeed, does authority derive? The spirit is not bound by human expectation.

That the spirit comes upon those chosen by the leader and those not chosen by the leader also represents the spirit's confounding trickster role in distinguishing the organization of the Israelites from that of a cult.[2] A succession of challenges to Moses's authority and his responses throughout the wilderness journey ultimately keeps the focus on YHWH rather than on the authority of the human leader. The struggles over Moses's leadership and such obstacles to his power as YHWH's refusal to let him enter the promised land mean that Moses will not become a messiah figure.

Not only does the spirit rest on others than those appointed by Moses, but his welcome of their prophecy undermines Joshua's corrupting sense that lives enriched by the spirit are in competition with each other. Competition is necessary only where gifts are scarce. If divine power is finite, humans will naturally fight over it. If divine power is infinite, humans need not fear finding it sown anywhere on anyone at any time. Beyond that, the spirit's gift of prophecy visits anyone, removing the need to grab at it.

In addition to unveiling human ignorance of the work of the spirit, this text also displays the depth of Moses's ability to trust the Lord. Moses has no

Pastoral Perspective

grace at hand. Negativity can also affect the leader, as we see in this passage.

Moses gets depressed. He is out of his depth. Finally, his feelings about the futility and inadequacy of his leadership surface. "I am not able to carry all this people alone, for they are too heavy for me. If this is the way you are going to treat me, put me to death at once" (vv. 14, 15). Death is better than the burden of leadership carried alone.

This humble confession points to a profound truth and the deepest meaning of Pentecost. If we try to respond to the crying needs of the world as individuals, we will soon find ourselves in despair. The Pentecost experience and the gift of the Holy Spirit mean that no one needs to carry any burden alone. For leaders, as well as all others, God's Spirit is always available to guide, always willing to lead, and always present in every circumstance.

This truth is demonstrated dramatically in today's text as God responds immediately to Moses with specific instructions on how to solve the leadership problem. He is to select seventy elders. These leaders, when stationed in front of the tent of meeting, will receive a portion of Moses's own spirit, empowering them to share in governing the community. These divine instructions are carried out, and when God's actions are complete, the seventy are momentarily seized by a frenzy of prophetic ecstasy. Furthermore, the outpouring of God's spirit flows into the camp and seizes two others, Eldad and Medad, causing the two of them to go into an ecstatic frenzy just like the other seventy. Joshua, perhaps out of jealousy or a need to control, tries his best to get Moses to squash this uncontrolled fervor of the spirit. Moses rejects this idea, saying, "Would that all the LORD's people were prophets, and that the LORD would put his spirit on them!" (v. 29).

We all know that "leadership" is a word that holds many hungers. It is often much harder to exercise than we imagine it to be. Countless books have been written to help the leader lead and leaders try everything. In a climate of unprecedented change, there are no easy answers. Leaders admit that after trying all the available tools and resources, they still feel frustrated and disappointed. Leaders are also vulnerable to the emotional ups and downs of anger, discouragement, and exhaustion in the face of daily challenges. In some situations, leaders face physical peril and threats to the safety of their families as well.

Dr. Martin Luther King Jr. told of a midnight hour of despair in the early years of his leadership in the civil rights movement. He had received many

---

2. Tikva Frymer-Kensky, "Moses and the Cults: The Question of Religious Leadership," in *Judaism* 34, no. 4 (Fall 1985): 444–52.

Exegetical Perspective

made evident by that superabundant Hebrew number, seventy; see Exod. 1:5). Both the people (by the end of v. 35) and Moses (by the end of v. 25) know the answer to the question the Lord poses to Moses in verse 23: "Is the LORD's power limited?" (Here is a general biblical rule: watch out when the Lord poses rhetorical questions!)

Then comes this little "extra" story about Eldad and Medad (vv. 24–30).

First, it is unclear whether Eldad and Medad are part of the original seventy designated for a dose of Moses's spirit. Verse 24 implies that the full contingent has already been assembled at the tent outside the camp, yet verse 26 makes clear that these two have been "registered." Thus it becomes apparent that even the narrator is a little queasy about the Lord giving out more spirit than has been promised, particularly when that spirit is given to as rancorous a species as Homo sapiens. How will we control such gifts if we cannot count and register them or, at least, their recipients?

Second, there is another deep concern about "spirit control" rumbling in this passage. As the text worries over how many people will be affected, it also worries about how long their "affectation" will last. It is curious that a story about spreading the spirit also wants to make clear that the spread of spirit is only temporary: "when the spirit rested upon them, they prophesied. But they did not do so again" (v. 25). Somebody, telling this story, is as worried about an oversupply of the spirit as about an oversupply of quail.

Third, and finally, it is even more remarkable that this little "extra" story about unauthorized spirit-sharing makes the canonical cut. While Joshua wants to stop the people, the incident inspires Moses, leading him to give one of the great speeches in all of Scripture: "Are you jealous [a loaded word, as the very God whom Moses serves has claimed some jealousy as part of this God's nature, Exod. 20:5] for my sake? Would that all the LORD's people were prophets, and that the LORD would put his spirit on them!" (v. 29). So, by Moses's intervention, this little story becomes part of the big story, and we must ask, on this Pentecost Sunday, why?

Well, in one way, this little "extra" story makes a strong statement about control. While the writers of these stories are much concerned about which gifts are given *outside* the camp and which *inside*, whether Eldad and Medad are part of the seventy or make it seventy-two, whether spirit gifts are momentary and "charismatic" or can become lifetime and

Homiletical Perspective

stop them, but Moses validates their activity and even takes it to the next level. He says he longs that all the Lord's people might be prophets (v. 29).

The perspective of Joshua often limits the ministry of the church. Joshua's jealous protection of Moses led Joshua to demand a cessation of the prophecy (v. 28). Such jealousy is often displayed in attitudes of possessiveness: "This is my turf, my ministry, my contact, and no one else has a right to intervene."

In addition, Joshua may not have wanted anyone else sharing the limelight with Moses and himself. Sometimes we believe that a leader loses that coveted public attention when others share in the leadership responsibilities. It is easy to interpret the story this way. God takes "some of the spirit" of Moses and gives it to the seventy elders (vv. 17, 25); we conclude this means that Moses loses some of his authority and power (see also 2 Kgs. 2:9).

Our culture, of necessity, calls us to measure quantitatively the material resources we possess. We know the natural resources of food, water, air, land, and minerals are limited. When they are depleted, they are forever gone. So we must cling to and even hoard what we already possess. As a result, the abundance of one nation or community leads to scarcity for another. The rich get richer and the poor get poorer. If we apply this same understanding to our spiritual resources, we believe that there is only so much to go around and therefore we must protect what we have, lest we lose it all. Such a faulty perspective destroys the power of the church, because the church becomes selfishly protective of its resources.

The gift of the spirit is better compared to a gift like wisdom. When a person shares wisdom with another, this act does not diminish the wisdom of the giver. Rather, it is like using a candle to light other candles. The candle does not lose its light because it shares it with others. Rather, the light becomes even brighter when shared.

When leaders share their skills, authority, and resources with others, they do not diminish their effectiveness, but enhance it. In turn, the value to the community grows exponentially. In the book *Undaunted Courage*, Stephen Ambrose offers an engaging history of the Lewis and Clark expedition.[1] As plans for the expedition took shape, the military, operating by their strict chain-of-command policy, made Lewis captain and Clark lieutenant. Lewis, however, was adamant about equally sharing his

---

1. Stephen Ambrose, *Undaunted Courage* (New York: Simon & Schuster, 2005).

Numbers 11:24-30

Theological Perspective

qualms about prophetic utterances popping up where he has no hand in it. Moses's acceptance of divine choice, unmediated by the community's established ordering of authority, frustrates human desire to build walls, cut off possibilities, and determine the results. The work of the Lord undermines the best of human attempts to control it.

The preacher's task in dealing with this text is to stand back from self-defense and look at it with a cold eye, for without that critical distance, it may be even subconsciously tempting for the preacher to venerate Joshua's position, eager to salvage the power of the status quo. Where and how does the preacher function like the young man and Joshua, announcing where and in what form the spirit's work is inadmissible in the church (both universally and locally)? This text will not be honestly proclaimed unless the preacher lays bare—at least to herself or himself— the troubling temptations to determine the spirit's resting places and corral the spirit's outpouring. The preacher might usefully address the walls and boundaries the community has already in place, thereby dismantling its obsession with its own self-justification, and yield a portion of the sermon to discuss fear of the unanticipated explosion of spiritual energy, among other sins. In its surprises, the spirit is revealed as the maker of holy chaos and the reordering principle of righteousness and peace that Scripture promises again and again.

A final task is to locate the spirit's relationship with authority and order in the congregation. Theologically, the spirit works within and outside the gathering. Moses and the elders could see and participate in the gathering at the tent, where the Lord promised the spirit would be working. They could not anticipate that the spirit would also pour itself out onto Medad and Eldad in the camps. The church's joy is to steward the gathering so that the spirit's work through word and sacraments is proclaimed wherever Jesus promised to be present (in the midst of two or three gathered in Jesus' name, among the "least," and in water, bread, and wine). Simultaneously, the church looks beyond itself to find Eldad and Medad, who are somewhere outside the gathering every day, also visited by the spirit of the Lord.

MELINDA QUIVIK

Pastoral Perspective

calls threatening to bomb his home. He feared for his wife and his new baby daughter. He wondered if the struggle was worth it if these precious persons suffered or died because of him. Restless and unable to sleep one night, he sat at his kitchen table with a cup of coffee and spilled out his fears, doubts, and despair to God. "At that moment I experienced the presence of the Divine as I had never before experienced him. It seemed as though I could hear the quiet assurance of an inner voice, saying, 'Stand up for righteousness, stand up for truth. God will be at your side forever.'"[1] That was enough to renew his strength and commitment to lead.

Paul says that "we live and move and have our being" in God (Acts 17:28). In other words, there is no place that God is not. In our congregations, our organizations, our families, our neighborhoods, in all aspects of our lives, God's Spirit is present and available to guide us each step of the way. Our challenge is to remember this and turn to God moment to moment.

What spiritual disciplines help you to practice turning to God? What ways of praying open you to God's guidance? Where do you find support for your spiritual journey? Who listens with you to the movement of the Spirit in your life and encourages your response to God's callings? Where is an honest, authentic spiritual community in which you can reveal your doubts and fears and deepen in your knowledge and love of God? What action in the world invites your God-given talents and engages your passion for living? Where do you find the courage to live out those invitations?

In the midst of whatever hardship we are in, we can open ourselves to God's transforming Spirit and live from the knowledge that we are not alone. We can turn to that indwelling Spirit and let it guide us through all dimensions of the day and night. We can trust in God's leadership. When we do this, our lives and our leadership are truly Spirit-led.

CAROLE A. CRUMLEY

---

1. Martin Luther King, Jr., *A Testament of Hope: The Essential Writings and Speeches of Martin Luther King, Jr.,* ed. James Melvin Washington (New York: HarperSanFrancisco, 1986), 509.

"institutional" (all concerns that later institutions of church and synagogue will take very seriously), the Lord, through Moses, is much less concerned. One of the annoying things about God's spirit in the Old and New Testament is that while we may attempt to choreograph and control it (with liturgies and licenses and limits on office), it is ultimately more like the wind than our books of order: "The wind blows where it chooses, and . . . you do not know where it comes from or where it goes. So it is with everyone who is born of the Spirit" (John 3:8).

In another way, this little "extra" story makes a stronger statement about the paradoxical nature of surfeits: some may be bad (as in quails), while some may be good (as in spirit). Could it be that God's jealousy (unlike our own) is grounded not in *possession* but in *generosity*, that God cannot abide our giving ourselves to a God whose gifts are limited? Could it be that God's power is unlimited not only in numbers, but in duration, constantly spilling over till all God's people and all the world's nations become prophets? Could it be that Pentecost, for the church, is just like the story of Medad and Eldad, for the synagogue? There has been, is, and ever will be a little "spillage" when it comes to the Spirit's gifting. The Spirit made Medad and Eldad part of the seventy. The Spirit made the church a partner to the synagogue. Who knows, this Pentecost, what the Spirit may be up to next—as long as the Spirit makes it past *our* editors!

RICHARD BOYCE

authority with Clark; he insisted they would be cocommanders. Though the military never granted Lewis's request, Lewis and Clark operated as coleaders, without the thirty men under their command ever knowing otherwise. They made collaborative decisions all along the arduous journey. This sharing of authority contributed greatly to the success of the expedition.

In the church the sharing of gifts, responsibilities, burdens, authority, and credit with others does not weaken individual leaders but strengthens them and builds up the body. When leaders share their resources and their authority through mentoring and empowering others, God's spirit is multiplied.

Spiritual resources can also blossom in unexpected places. Moses was open to sharing the spirit with those outside the conventional channels of institutional authority. From the ranks of our own Christian communities, insignificant people, like Eldad and Medad (never again heard of in the Bible), respected by the faith community and working quietly behind the scenes, continue to be summoned freely by God for responsibilities in those communities.

Abuses and misunderstandings, however, can arise from the outpouring of God's spirit on individuals. Because such spirit-led individuals stand out from others, the temptation is to make them into idolized celebrities; but there is a difference between a celebrity and a spirit-led leader. Celebrities tend to draw attention to themselves. In contrast, spirit-led leaders use their gifts not for personal gain but for the building up of the community. Moses rejects self-promotion, desiring to share the gift God gave him with as many others as possible. Thus, according to this narrative, the most gifted, spirit-filled leader is the most humble (12:3).

In addition, the purpose of God's giving the spirit to the elders is in order to help Moses with the *burden* of leadership. As D. T. Williams says, "Far from being blessed, the elders would be burdened; here it is noteworthy that the prophetic 'office' is often described as a burden (e.g., Hab 1:1), indeed one that the prophet would often love to be rid of."[2] Thus the coming of God's spirit is neither for the personal gain of the recipient nor for the enhancement of one's own public worship experience, but for the blessing of God's people.

DAVE BLAND

2. D. T. Williams, "OT Pentecost," *Scriptura* 83 (2003): 506.

Psalm 104:24-34, 35b

²⁴O LORD, how manifold are your works!
  In wisdom you have made them all;
  the earth is full of your creatures.
²⁵Yonder is the sea, great and wide,
  creeping things innumerable are there,
  living things both small and great.
²⁶There go the ships,
  and Leviathan that you formed to sport in it.

²⁷These all look to you
  to give them their food in due season;
²⁸when you give to them, they gather it up;
  when you open your hand, they are filled with good things.
²⁹When you hide your face, they are dismayed;
  when you take away their breath, they die
  and return to their dust.

Theological Perspective

I have traveled a great deal for many years. At one point, an airline's agent told me that the only greater service they could provide me was to pull the planes up to my door. What this means is that I have seen many glorious sights from airplane windows—the icy coastline of Greenland, the teeming harbors of Japan, the veldt of Africa, the humidity that visibly hangs around Atlanta, and the like. For many years, I lived in Washington, D.C., but I am now in Denver. There is something special about my current home region: it is glorious beyond words.

Just the other day, I was returning from the starkly brilliant desert of Arizona and was struck by the relatively lush greenery on the plains of Colorado. I quickly thought of Katharine Lee Bates's experience in 1893, when she came to Colorado and noticed the "spacious skies," the "amber waves of grain," the "fruited plain," and, perhaps most breathtakingly (from the summit of Pike's Peak), the "purple mountain majesties" of the Rockies. This latter experience can take your breath away.

It is this sentiment that drives the author of Psalm 104. The author's conviction is that God is the sovereign creator of what today we would call the natural order. This creation is not just a mechanism, but rather is understood as an interlocking web of

Pastoral Perspective

"God's in his heaven—All's right with the world!"[1] Whenever I read Psalm 104, I think of these words from Robert Browning's poem "Pippa Passes." Scandalous in its time because of its sexual allusions, the poem has nonetheless given us this phrase that extols God as creator and sustainer. The psalmist notes the sense of order in creation and sees behind this order a purpose for all of life, a purpose grounded in God. Theologians have, of course, debated this purpose and its meaning ever since the psalm, and one of the dilemmas of the twenty-first century is whether such a purpose (and the God behind it) even exists at all.

These twenty-first-century questions must be put in the context of the psalm; the psalmist notes the order of creation and is moved to praise God for it. In the first part of this psalm, the author praises various parts of the creation as evidence of God's power and benevolence: the sky, the rain, the mountains, the wonderful water that is such a great gift to the arid regions where the psalmist lives, the trees, and even the young lions who roar and hunt at night. In our lectionary passage, the psalmist also speaks to the deep Hebrew fears of the sea. In Genesis 1:1–2, in the sea, chaos has great presence at the beginning

1. *The Oxford Dictionary of Quotations*, 4th ed., ed. Angela Parrington (New York: Oxford University Press, 1992), 151:28.

³⁰When you send forth your spirit, they are created;
   and you renew the face of the ground.

³¹May the glory of the LORD endure forever;
   may the LORD rejoice in his works—
³²who looks on the earth and it trembles,
   who touches the mountains and they smoke.
³³I will sing to the LORD as long as I live;
   I will sing praise to my God while I have being.
³⁴May my meditation be pleasing to him,
   for I rejoice in the LORD.

. . . .
^{35b}Bless the LORD, O my soul.
   Praise the LORD!

Exegetical Perspective

Psalm 104 is an individual's hymn of praise and follows the typical structure of such hymns: an imperative to praise God (v. 1a); the reason to offer praise (vv. 1b–35a); and a renewed imperative to praise (v. 35b). Because the psalm focuses upon the work of God as creator, the psalm is sometimes called a creation hymn. The verses to be read on Pentecost are part of the final two elements of the psalm's structure and are best heard within the overall framework and thought of the entire psalm.

Psalm 104 opens with a self-command for the poet to praise YHWH with the " soul," or better, "entire being" (*nephesh*) (v. 1a). The poet paints a picture of YHWH's regal presence and work in the heavens (vv. 1b–4) and proceeds to portray the ordering of the earth (vv. 5–18). A chief part of God's ordering is the containment of the potentially dangerous waters so that they may sustain abundant life for grass, trees, and wild and domestic animals. Verses 19–23 detail YHWH's delineations between seasons and night and day. The stated reason for seasonal and daily boundaries is to allow for the peaceful interaction between predators (lions) and people.

The Pentecost reading begins with the next section (vv. 24–30), which opens with an expression of sheer wonder and awe: "O LORD, how manifold are your works! In wisdom you have made them all." It

Homiletical Perspective

The feast of Pentecost invites us as church to celebrate the presence of the Spirit everywhere, in everyone and everything God has created. Psalm 104 begins this song of praise: "O LORD, how manifold are your works!" (v. 24). The invitation expands our hearts as we see, hear, taste, and are touched by God's Spirit sent forth by the risen Christ. The gifts of the Spirit are passionately unleashed, and our world is changed, set afire, awakened! The preacher, guided by the psalmist, envisions all living things as dependent on the Creator's love energy and announces, "When you send forth your spirit, they are created; and you renew the face of the ground" (v. 30). We dare to look upon our God, who looks on us with love, and we are awestruck at the manifold works of the Spirit. Such lived experience and remembrance calls forth from every waiting, welcoming heart a song of praise, a hymn to God's creative wisdom and power.

Psalm 104 is an appropriate response to the glory of God made manifest, the source of all life and nature. It engages the congregation that has just embraced the memory of Acts 2:1–11, affirming the power of God who accomplishes God's purpose of blessing the community with order, harmony, and Spirit-driven mutual understanding.

The hearers now proclaim with unleashed tongues their deep-down desire to receive God's

Psalm 104:24-34, 35b

Theological Perspective

living relationships grounded in a discernible (though not completely fathomable) wisdom.

Such awareness has sometimes gotten us biblical folks into trouble—both with some who claim no commitment to the transformative love of God and with some who do. We can maintain, from ancient times until today, that God is an intelligent designer whose works bear clear witness to that design. However, given how words are often used as signals of politically charged agendas, we must be very thoughtful when speaking this way, so as not to make God in our own image. Others of us, upon hearing this way of talking, however, may sputter in response that this certainly should *not* be a way to understand God's relationship with creation, some even going so far as to argue that there is not a creator somehow both present within as well as transcendent of the "manifold works" referred to by the psalmist.

The modern world, at least in some circles, has moved to what some call a postmodern phase of human self-understanding. This shift has to do with how we see reality and filter it to make it intelligible. For some, truth is strictly rational; if it cannot be measured by certain metrics, then it is not true (and maybe not even real). For others, truth is what each makes of it—that is, "my" truth is what counts. It seems to me, though, that the psalmist is pointing us beyond this intellectual spat to an ancient slant on an important issue: How does meaning get made? How do I find purpose in my life?

A word that used to be in favor is one I propose we will do well to reintroduce: the ineffable. This is not a big word intended to confuse; indeed, it has been used with stunning lucidity throughout human history when we face the limits of our experience. In Christian traditions, there is a very old strand of witness that asserts it is better to say what God and the divine realm are *not* than positively to claim that we satisfactorily grasp them by the words we use. Even for some who do not profess faithfulness as some of us would recognize it, there can be a similar awareness. Perhaps it was most arrestingly put in the twentieth century by Ludwig Wittgenstein, who ended his very famous (though brief) work on the logical structure of our thinking by doing what, centuries earlier, Thomas Aquinas had done—namely, say that at a certain point our capacities to understand logically and to capture reality clearly in words are eclipsed by our experiences of the world. We are somehow taken outside ourselves and have experiences that we can never express adequately.

Pastoral Perspective

of creation; but here in the psalm, even the scary sea is seen as part of God's wise creation. The Israelites are terrified of the sea and the "creeping things" in it (v. 25), but in this psalm Leviathan, the menacing sea monster elsewhere (Ps. 74:14), now frolics in the sea (v. 26). Underneath these praises of creation is also a sacramental sense of the presence of God in a continuous and daily format, a presence that sustains all creation. Here we find no image of God the clockmaker who has taken a permanent vacation from creation but, rather, a God who sustains and engages creation on a regular basis.

From our modern point of view, we receive a new light each day because our part of the earth rotates back toward the sun, but for the psalmist we receive a new day because God calls it into existence. For all our modernity, our common language about the daily returning of the light remains the "sunrise" and the "sunset," even though we know scientifically that it is the movement of the earth, not the sun, that produces such contrasts in light and dark. This continuing tension in our own current language points us to the longing in our hearts. We have a hunger for the universe to have meaning, for our lives to have meaning, and for that meaning to be found not in the destructive chaos that we seem to experience so much but, rather, in an order created and sustained by a loving God.

We live in an age struggling to find a new center of meaning, a center previously lodged in a rational Enlightenment, where individual consciousness was ruling monarch. That center itself had replaced a universe where the God of Christendom was the center, a point of view that had become stagnant in an authoritarian, repressive approach that sought to crush individual consciousness. In 2009 the two-hundredth anniversary of Darwin's birth and the four-hundredth anniversary of Galileo's invention of the telescope reminded us of the shaking of the foundations. The ramifications of Darwin's revolutionary approach are just now being discovered: If life is only a struggle to survive, what meaning is there? Why soar to heights of love and compassion? Galileo's astounding work to stretch the human eye to the far reaches of the universe also brought with it a disturbing possibility: we could come to believe that we are only specks of sand with a bit of consciousness attached.

Though he knew nothing of Darwin and Galileo and their wonderful and visionary work, the psalmist anticipated the kinds of questions that their work raised. From long ago and far away, he asks us

seems hardly possible that there can be such ongoing divine care for the detailed workings of all parts of the world (the predominant verbs in the psalm are participles and imperfect forms, which suggest continuing action). Yet the beautiful and panoramic view projected by the psalmist suggests that this is precisely the case. Just as lions and people can safely coexist (vv. 20–23), both ships with people and the fearsome Leviathan (cf. Job 41) traverse the sea without fear of harm. Day and night, lions and people, Leviathan and ship, land and sea—"In wisdom you have made them all!"

Verses 27–30, with their references to spirit/breath (*ru'ah*), are the ones that most closely associate this psalm with Pentecost. It is striking that these verses portray YHWH's provision for all of the teeming life on earth as including both tangible food and less tangible breath. The physical and spiritual are both part of the warp and woof of the fabric of life and cannot be separated without damaging the larger tapestry. YHWH provides food that creatures "gather" when the time is right. Should God withhold divine provision (i.e., "hide your face," v. 29) the result is dust with no breath—the condition envisioned in Genesis 2:4b–6. Likewise, when YHWH sends forth the divine spirit, the face of the ground/earth (*'adamah*) is renewed (v. 30). Renewal involves both the spiritual and physical (breath and ground), which together encompass the totality of life. In this connection, the creatures who receive the "most press" in the psalm are wild animals, wild asses, birds, cattle, trees, storks, wild goats, coneys (rock badgers, v. 18), lions, sea creatures, and Leviathan. Humans are mentioned in verses 14, 15, 23, and (as we shall see) 35a, but these scant references have the effect of "decentering" people. The overwhelming focus of the psalm is the nonhuman world. The gift of divine provision—food and breath—extends to the whole of creation and not just the human community.

Verses 31–35 contain two petitions (vv. 31–32, 34–35a) and two proclamations of praise (vv. 33; 35b). The first petition is for YHWH to continue to take delight in the intricate beauty of the world the psalm has described. Although the world has been fashioned "so that it shall never be shaken" (v. 5), the psalmist knows that the power to maintain the stability of the earth lies in the hands of YHWH, who can cause the earth to tremble with a glance and the mountains to smoke with a touch (v. 32). In the face of such power the psalmist resolves to offer robust song and praise (v. 33). The second petition (v. 35a)

gifts, taking only what is needed with grateful hearts, so that they may experience the harmony that comes with a bountiful harvest that is shared with all. The preacher gently reminds those who have ears to hear that even when we misuse what God has created and given us, God continues to send forth the Spirit to the earth, and, though not without turmoil, the universe is renewed. The creative Spirit of God is ever present, and we are drawn to abandon ourselves into loving arms, ever singing God's praise while we live.

The challenge for the preacher becomes the choosing of a lens through which the congregation may look at and respond to this text. These words of praise, for the magnificence of the created world and in awe of the wisdom of the Creator, pour out of the heart of the psalmist. With careful guidance, the preacher may lead the hearers to reflect with a deep sense of global consciousness. This can be problematic for a society still somewhat resistant to the truth of the impending ecological crisis. The ecospirituality implicit in the psalm calls us to an awareness of our threatened earth and leads us to become stewards of God's covenant with all living things. Our spiritual traditions inspire us to care for, rather than consume, creation.

The ecological crisis may indeed lead us into a deeper relationship with our God and help awaken us to the true meaning of life, which is to love all that exists. The psalmist pleads for the "glory of the LORD to endure forever" (v. 31) and speaks of a God "who looks on the earth and it trembles, who touches the mountains and they smoke" (v. 32). This time in our history may be a moment of grace that will transform our lifestyles from consumerism to a life in harmony with creation.

A further possible question to ponder is how this technological world can enable us to see with new eyes, be with all our brothers and sisters despite geographical distance, and in fact give praise to our God in a new Pentecost moment, in many different languages heard as one around the globe! Our hymn of praise lifts our souls and beckons us to do more than celebrate—to savor, save, and cherish *all as gift*.

On another note, the preacher may choose to capture the imagination and sensitivity of the hearers by inviting them to see and appreciate these gifts of the Creator through the experience of a toddler's first visit to the seashore. The summer sunshine sparkles on the water. Blue sky and clouds usher in a gentle breeze. Spirit comes to life in this child of God who runs with fearless innocence to the water's edge, then dances with delight as the tide envelops tiny

Psalm 104:24-34, 35b

Theological Perspective

Pentecost points to one of these extraordinary rationality-exceeding moments. For all the words that have been written about what this moment actually looked like or meant to its original participants, we will do well to learn what we can from the efforts of others to talk about it, and to realize that the point of the Pentecost narrative in Acts illustrates the deep insight of the psalmist: we understand God as the source and giver of life (and have ratified this in some ancient creeds, especially the Nicene), the wellspring of divine wisdom, and the source of our vocation, our meaningful work, in the world. As it is with the splendid (though also sometimes raw and bloody) works of creation, so it is with human beings: we are enlivened by the gift of God's Spirit. Pentecost represents an outpouring, a filling up, of human lives with a vibrant, hope-giving, wisdom-bringing presence that conveys with it utter assurance that while we have not earned such a gift, we are nonetheless recipients of it and thus connected with the author of that gift, the God who is the creator—and re-creator—of the universe. We are made one with a reality much bigger than we are, and in that very moment given a charge to keep—a requirement that we not only utter words, but also embody behaviors showing that we can live into his identity.

The psalmist speaks to us across the ages: "May the glory of the LORD endure for ever; may the LORD rejoice in his works" (v. 31). This is not just one now-dead witness, celebrating something long ago felt to be important. No, it is a challenge to those of us today who seek to be fed by God's love and grace—that we carry on the tradition of witness as long as the breath of God is within us.

DAVID G. TRICKETT

Pastoral Perspective

to consider what even now the physicists affirm: life is a mystery, and we must take our best guess and leap. For all its powerful work, modern science cannot answer the fundamental questions of life, and the best scientists are well aware of this. Science is not built for the questions that the psalmist addresses, and this is why the paradigm of meaning is shifting in this "postmodern" age.

In our wondering and in our wandering in this twenty-first century, the psalmist asks us to consider an ancient answer to the fundamental questions of life, questions that each generation must consider and answer for itself. This psalm is not a naive, "all is wonderful" song, but rather a song at a more basic level, a song about where each of us lives. The psalmist affirms that at the very ground of all existence is a powerful and generous and gracious God. At the heart of our very hearts is the Spirit of God who knows our names. It is the same Spirit who called out those men and women to proclaim the mighty acts of God on Pentecost.

The psalmist asks us to engage this God on a personal and on a sacramental level, not so much in a sentimental way but rather in a more basic approach. The Spirit of God flows through all and in all, in ways that are both available to us on a daily basis and beyond our capacity to comprehend. The crowds who heard the proclamations of this God in the multilingual words of Pentecost asked, "What does this mean?" (Acts 2:12). We ask that question too, and the psalmist answers for us. If we have ears to hear, eyes to see, and hearts to receive, we will find God at the center of our lives and at the center of all of life. Our response? To praise God as long as we live.

NIBS STROUPE

Exegetical Perspective

is omitted from the lectionary reading, presumably because of religious sensibilities. However, the verse is crucial for an adequate understanding of the psalm, because it shows that the poet understands that the one thing that can most place in jeopardy God's intricate creation is sinful humanity. Humans incapable of discerning the beauty of the world and bent on selfish exploitation of the earth and its creatures can loosen the stability of the earth and plunge the whole into catastrophic disaster. The petition is that God will prevent such unspeakable horror. Following the petition, the psalmist moves to a renewed command to praise that takes up the initial affirmation (v. 1) and wraps the entire psalm within a stance of praise.

At least two claims made by this psalm are relevant for Pentecost. First, the psalm revels in the diversity of life on earth and contends that God's gift of breath is for the well-being of all and is not the exclusive privilege of a select few. Just as God's gift of the Spirit in Acts 2 does not eliminate diversity but enables understanding among myriad peoples, Psalm 104 asserts that divine provision of water and food, dust and breath makes possible the harmonious workings of the whole. What a powerful claim to embrace in a time when regional, political, ethnic, and hosts of other differences threaten to drive communities ever farther apart from one another! Second, the psalm's insistence on holding together dust/earth and spirit/breath as constitutive of life grounds its ethical vision. Psalm 104 will not yield to an overspiritualization that refuses to engage material concerns. The psalm evokes a human response that upholds and contributes to the beauty of God's world and refuses to usurp this beauty for exploitative and selfish ends. This claim infuses Pentecost (originally an Israelite wheat-harvest celebration) with an ecological thrust often ignored and most worthy of recovering in these times.

V. STEVEN PARRISH

Homiletical Perspective

toes. Hands clap and giggles burst forth as this little one gives praise to a God. Yes, with childlike trust we all can pray with the psalmist: "May my meditation be pleasing to him, for I rejoice in the Lord" (v. 34).

The congregation can be drawn into another revelatory scene. The elderly woman is sitting peacefully in her wheelchair outside the nursing home, facing the midmorning sun. A gentle summer's breeze is experienced as a kiss from her beloved Lord, and her eyes study the colors of a nearby rose garden. Hands, withered and shaking a bit, adjust the oxygen tube that channels air into her lungs as the words of a personal prayer are whispered to the Creator in praise of another day of living: "Bless the Lord, O my soul. Praise the Lord!" (v. 35b).

Finally, the preacher is left with the dilemma: to whom, where, and how to shape and celebrate this text. With a little coaxing, the present company might be invited to call out a favorite verse that speaks of their joy and thanksgiving. Perhaps in one voice they can repeat after the preacher these words of praise: "I will sing to the Lord as long as I live; I will sing praise to my God while I have being" (v. 33).

Then, afire with the Word and with an unnamed energy, they will experience the fervor bequeathed to them from the writers of these ancient texts. With harmonious praise they are sent as disciples into their world, speaking a new language of love, amazed and chattering as though overfilled with sweet wine. A new people will watch and listen with wonder and surprise. These eternal words flowing from their mouths will open gentle, glowing hearts that are receptive and ready to proclaim, yet again, this hymn of praise!

CONSTANCE M. KOCH, O.P.

Acts 2:1-21

¹When the day of Pentecost had come, they were all together in one place. ²And suddenly from heaven there came a sound like the rush of a violent wind, and it filled the entire house where they were sitting. ³Divided tongues, as of fire, appeared among them, and a tongue rested on each of them. ⁴All of them were filled with the Holy Spirit and began to speak in other languages, as the Spirit gave them ability.

⁵Now there were devout Jews from every nation under heaven living in Jerusalem. ⁶And at this sound the crowd gathered and was bewildered, because each one heard them speaking in the native language of each. ⁷Amazed and astonished, they asked, "Are not all these who are speaking Galileans? ⁸And how is it that we hear, each of us, in our own native language? ⁹Parthians, Medes, Elamites, and residents of Mesopotamia, Judea and Cappadocia, Pontus and Asia, ¹⁰Phrygia and Pamphylia, Egypt and the parts of Libya belonging to Cyrene, and visitors from Rome, both Jews and proselytes, ¹¹Cretans and Arabs—in our own languages we hear them speaking about God's deeds of power." ¹²All were amazed and perplexed, saying to one another, "What does this mean?" ¹³But others sneered and said, "They are filled with new wine."

¹⁴But Peter, standing with the eleven, raised his voice and addressed them, "Men of Judea and all who live in Jerusalem, let this be known to you, and listen

Theological Perspective

This extraordinarily rich text demands consideration of the role of the Holy Spirit in the church.

In this text and in the theology of Acts, the pouring out of the Holy Spirit upon the church is both the sign and the instrument of the launch of the church's mission. The disciples had been instructed by Jesus to wait to be "baptized with the Holy Spirit" (Acts 1:5) and to be empowered by the Holy Spirit to be "my witnesses in Jerusalem, in all Judea and Samaria, and to the ends of the earth" (1:8). Thus they waited—until Pentecost, when the gathered disciples experienced in unmistakable ways the promised outpouring of the Spirit.

This rush of Spirit power initially enabled the disciples to proclaim their gospel message in the tongues of the diverse peoples gathered in Jerusalem. In this text the Spirit also empowered Peter to offer the first sermon of the church era. This sermon linked that morning's outpouring of the Holy Spirit to the promise from Joel of just such an outpouring in the "last days" (Acts 2:17; Joel 2:28–29). The text goes on to indicate the success of this first preaching event: "three thousand persons were added" (2:41), and the church's mission was launched with a flourish.

The Bible does not speak with a single voice about the role of the Holy Spirit, and space does not permit a full exposition. This text from Acts does

Pastoral Perspective

The Pentecost worship services of many churches will include a time with a group of blessed and energetic kids. A majority of pastors addressing this lively bunch will introduce Pentecost as the birthday of the church. Some will even lead their charges in a heartfelt though off-key rendition of "Happy birthday to you." Within this metaphor of a birthday party, we might understand some of the pastoral issues and challenges of this Pentecostal Scripture.

First, how long has God been planning this party? The poetry of Genesis 1 describes God's creative spirit blowing over the formless void, and Genesis 2 narrates the life-giving breath of God. Later, the spirit appears in times of darkness and distress. While the one group of people of YHWH sits in exile in Babylon and others gather the pieces of the shattered world of Israel, the prophet Isaiah (11:2) promises the coming of one upon whom this spirit shall rest, the spirit of "wisdom and understanding," of "counsel and might," of "knowledge and the fear of the LORD." During the time of domination and abuse by the Roman Empire, oppression and judgment of the religious authorities, and elitism and slavery of the ruling classes, Luke records John's promise of one who will baptize by the Spirit (3:16), and Jesus later agrees (Acts 1:2).

In the extensive planning of this Pentecostal party, the spirit of YHWH weaves together the generations

to what I say. ¹⁵Indeed, these are not drunk, as you suppose, for it is only nine o'clock in the morning. ¹⁶No, this is what was spoken through the prophet Joel:

> ¹⁷'In the last days it will be, God declares,
>   that I will pour out my Spirit upon all flesh,
>   and your sons and your daughters shall prophesy,
>   and your young men shall see visions,
>   and your old men shall dream dreams.
> ¹⁸Even upon my slaves, both men and women,
>   in those days I will pour out my Spirit;
>   and they shall prophesy.
> ¹⁹And I will show portents in the heaven above
>   and signs on the earth below,
>   blood, and fire, and smoky mist.
> ²⁰The sun shall be turned to darkness
>   and the moon to blood,
>   before the coming of the Lord's great and glorious day.
> ²¹Then everyone who calls on the name of the Lord shall be saved.'"

Exegetical Perspective

In this lection the group of disciples—restored now to the full twelve—behold a vision, are filled with the Holy Spirit, and speak in foreign tongues (vv. 1–5). Reactions from inhabitants of Jerusalem follow (vv. 6–13); then Peter addresses the marveling if divided crowd (vv. 14–21). Peter's oration interprets the happening, cites relevant Scripture, and draws the conclusion: the events around Jesus Christ followed by this bestowal of the Spirit prove that the last days whereof the prophets spoke have come. The speech continues beyond the lection and culminates with a call to repentance and baptism (2:38); three thousand heed the call and form a community to communicate the fullness of what they have received.

The setting at Pentecost, the Jewish feast of Weeks (Exod. 23:16; Lev. 23:15–22; Deut. 16:9–10), connects this new revelation with the giving of the law on Mount Sinai. ("Pentecost" is Greek for "fifty," thus signifying the fifty days or seven weeks after Passover.) Originally an agricultural festival celebrating the end of spring harvest, the feast of Weeks was in the Roman period associated by various strands of Judaism with the covenant. Fire signals the presence of the Divine, hence God's self-revelation, as in the burning bush, the descent of God on Sinai, and the fiery chariot of Daniel 7. The same motif occurs in John the Baptist's prophecy that one will come who

Homiletical Perspective

"The Holy Spirit is a gentleman," the elders of the Pentecostal church where I grew up were fond of saying: "He never forces his way in, and goes only where he is invited." But the first few verses of Acts 2 seem to tell a different story. Set up by Jesus' touting (1:4–8) and by the vivid, almost lurid, imagery used to describe the scene, the Holy Spirit's entrance in Luke's story is anything but discreet. No gentleman caller, this violent phenomenon enters the room with a roar. The ruckus draws such a crowd (2:6) and causes such agitation (vv. 6–7, 12–13) that Peter has to raise his voice to be heard. In Acts the coming of the Holy Spirit is associated not with polite murmurs, white gloves, and dainty manners but, as Jesus predicted, with power—the kind of power that could knock a person into orbit, even "to the ends of the earth."

Of course the church elders were not entirely wrong about the Holy Spirit's nature. (Their metaphor of choice is lamentably male but not wrong.) The "gentlemanly" view not only speaks eloquently of the spiritual experience of many, but resonates with numerous descriptions of the Holy Spirit found in Scripture. In addition, the setting of the Acts story makes it clear that the Holy Spirit *was* being invited or at least waited for (1:4, 14).

On balance, the kinder, gentler view of the Holy Spirit may well be the more accurate one. Apart

Acts 2:1-21

Theological Perspective

give us a beginning point: the Holy Spirit is poured out by God the Father to empower the church to advance Christ's mission to the very ends of the earth. The Holy Spirit enables the disciples to preach God's Word, and to be understood even in languages they do not know. The Spirit empowers numerous awe-inspiring "wonders and signs" (2:43; cf. 4:30–31), and miracles of healing, economic sharing, and community (2:41–45). The Spirit gives the apostolic leaders courage in the face of threats and even the beginnings of martyrdom (4:8, 29; 7:55). The falling of the Spirit upon believing Gentiles confirms for Peter and other early church leaders the propriety of the transition of the gospel into the Gentile world (10:44–48). The Spirit provides guidance in major decisions, such as the commissioning of Barnabas and Saul to missionary travel (13:2) and the decisions of the Jerusalem council (Acts 15).

The apostle Paul seems to have developed an elaborate theology of the Holy Spirit, who "helps us in our weakness" (Rom. 8:26), sends spiritual gifts to equip the church for its ministry (1 Cor. 12), reshapes the character and temperament of cooperating believers (Gal. 5:22ff.), and empowers such mysterious worship and edification gifts as speaking in tongues and interpreting the meaning of such speech (1 Cor. 14:1–25), or receiving and speaking a divinely inspired word of prophecy or song (1 Cor. 14:26–32).

The early church, at least in large part, seems to have been remarkably open to a dynamic and fluid way of operating, based on its theology and experience of the Holy Spirit. Where to go, what to do, how to worship, who should speak in worship, what should be said in worship, who should lead the community, how the community should be led, how to relate to outsiders, who should relate to outsiders, what to say when under threat—these and many other matters seem to have been handled through reliance on the empowerment and direction of the Holy Spirit. The tensions inherent in this Spirit-led community life begin to be apparent already in the New Testament, as when Paul has to offer instructions in 1 Corinthians to bring the worship life of that community into some order.

Freedom in the Spirit versus structure and order—this dynamic has never disappeared in the life of the church. With Spirit-led freedom came tremendous gains in shattering received religious and cultural patterns of all types, including crossing the Jew-Gentile barrier, making advances against sexism, and moving people toward radical economic sharing

Pastoral Perspective

through a Spirit that brings life out of death, hope out of despair. Folks sitting in their pews recognize the darkness and distress of their world. As we witness the growing gap between the rich and the poor, growing manifestations of poverty and unchecked disease, growing divisions between nations and within economies, and growing intolerance of any opinion or ideal other than our own, we celebrate our glimpses of the work of that Spirit, and we await again blowings of that fresh and life-giving Spirit.

After this long period of preparation, YHWH's guest list to this Pentecostal party deserves attention. Who are the "they" (2:1) who wait aimlessly in the upper room? Is the party limited to the eleven male disciples listed in Acts 1:13? Does the party also include "certain women, including Mary the mother of Jesus," mentioned in Acts 1:14? Might other men and women who joined Jesus throughout his ministry be present? In essence, the question of God's guest list raises the question of whether these Pentecostal disciples who become apostles are a fairly homogenous group of narrow representation or whether they are a larger group who embodies much more diversity in gender and culture.

These questions become important as churches and denominations continue sometimes heated and divisive conversations about who may and who may not faithfully worship and serve in leadership positions. The interpreter's understanding of this guest list might shed light on the conversation about the inclusiveness or exclusiveness of what John Calvin calls the "priesthood of all believers."

As with many birthdays past a certain age, this one includes a myriad of smiles and joy, questions and regret by participants and observers. At the beginning of the story, one can imagine the disciples moping in their state of abandonment, not for the first time. They walk with Jesus for up to three years before the evil powers steal him on the cross. Then, through the miracle of resurrection he reappears and walks again with them, only to abandon them at the ascension. Now they wait, disappointed again.

As the story progresses, we can sense a feeling of jealousy and inadequacy creeping into the questions of the "devout Jews" (v. 5), who wonder why they are not invited guests at this party. We also understand the tension of the "crowd gathered" (v. 6), as they experience with awe and cynicism the sudden communicational versatility of these brothers and sisters. By the end, the disciples face the uncertain future of ministry in an unwelcoming world separated from one another and from the corporeal presence of Jesus.

Exegetical Perspective

will baptize "with the Holy Spirit and with fire" (Luke 3:16; see Acts 2:38).

The miraculous speech, after the vision of "divided tongues, as of fire" (v. 3) resting upon the disciples, recalls by way of contrast the tower of Babel and the division of languages then imposed. The gift of the Spirit broke down this dividing wall. So much is intimated by the responses of the international (Jewish) populace in Jerusalem when they heard their native tongues spoken by Galileans, back-country Jews unlikely to speak foreign languages. Although "all were amazed and perplexed" (v. 12), not all were inclined to accept the phenomenon as divine in origin. Some reduced the event to intoxication from "new wine" (v. 13), that is, particularly potent wine (some pagan oracles made use of alcohol). Peter refuted this possibility in his speech (v. 15) and then explained the event as the fulfillment of end-time prophecy.

The citation of Joel 2:28–32 in verses 17–21 is not quite verbatim. "In the last days" deviates from Joel's "afterward" (NRSV's rendering of the Hebrew) to adapt the quotation to the present purpose. "God declares" is an authorial addition to clarify that it is God speaking through the prophet. Key phrases of the scriptural citation showcase themes recurrent throughout Acts that proclaim the universal outreach of Christianity, the effect of God's pouring out "my Spirit upon all flesh" (v. 17). "All flesh" includes people of all ages and sexes, all humanity: "my slaves, both men and women, . . . shall prophesy" (v. 18). The latter part of the quotation details other signs of the last days, "portents in the heaven above and signs on the earth below" (v. 19). These dramatic cosmic manifestations—the darkening of the sun and the turning of the moon to the color of blood—signify a fundamental reshaping of creation that will come with "the Lord's great and glorious day" (v. 20), when "everyone who calls on the name of the Lord shall be saved" (v. 21).

The "Day of the Lord [YHWH]" in biblical prophecy is the day par excellence of God's just judgment and retribution (e.g., Amos 5:18–20, Zeph. 1:7–16). Here, however, the "day of the Lord" (v. 20) refers to the coming of the Son of Man (see Luke 21:27). Peter remarks toward the end of his speech that "God has made him both Lord and Messiah, this Jesus whom you crucified" (v. 36). God's delegation of Jesus, the victim of the violence, as "Lord" of the divine judgment, was also a key element of Paul's gospel (Rom. 2:16). Thus the "name of the Lord" (v. 21) by which people call upon God in repentance

Homiletical Perspective

from this text, there is little evidence of the Holy Spirit working in any "violent" fashion. Many Christians have become accustomed to thinking of the Holy Spirit as more of a Hawaiian breeze than a Chicago gale. However, this important passage may at least remind contemporary congregations that the Spirit does not always arrive as a still, small voice or a faint stirring in the heart. The Holy Spirit's power is not always subtle, fragile, or polite. Even today it can be electric, atomic, and volcanic. There are a number of ways a sermon might address such power and relate it to the lives of the congregation.

Spiritual Power. Sometimes the power of the Holy Spirit known in worship services resembles the vision of poet-theologian Amos Wilder: "The world is molten and hearts are sifted. The altar is like a third rail that spatters sparks. The sanctuary is like the chamber next to an atomic oven. There are invisible rays and you leave your watch outside."[1] Spiritual power can create thundering choirs, soaring rhetoric, over-the-top praise bands, and sermons that rock with joy. It can create congregations who sing with their hearts in their faces, pray without ceasing, and extend themselves for others. Many congregations can use a reminder of these facts.

A sermon suggesting the availability of ecstatic, dramatic, or profound spiritual experience represents one approach to this text. Some preachers shy away from such interpretations, thinking either that they are too obvious (take the text too literally), outmoded ("that dispensation has closed"), dangerous (lead to emotionalism), or untrue (what happened in the upper room was merely a psychological phenomenon). Misgivings about and tensions with the text must certainly be taken into account. However, a general emphasis on the magnitude, scope, and scale of the Spirit's work could hardly be amiss. No matter how you look at it, Acts 2 shows a big God with a big word at work expanding out into a big world. These are the kind of God and the kind of story that inspire listeners and create, not little people of the little word, but believers who are madly expressive.

Uniting Power. An alternate approach is suggested by the churning scene in which the story is set. Luke describes the crowds as bewildered, amazed, astonished, and perplexed. "What does this mean?" they ask (v. 12). We see them milling around, stepping on

1. Amos Wilder, "Electric Chimes and Ram's Horns," *Christian Century* 88, no.4 (January 27, 1971): 105.

Acts 2:1-21

Theological Perspective

and away from selfishness. On the other hand, it also relied heavily on a kind of trusting communal intuitionism, in which Spirit-empowered believers were given wide latitude to discern and communicate the Spirit's engagement with them just as they felt led to do so. Clearly this could be problematic.

It is clear by the later New Testament writings, such as the Pastoral Epistles, that fluid Spirit-driven freedom was giving way to a more hierarchical and structured internal communal life. Large parts of the church developed practices and sometimes a theology in which the Holy Spirit's role became much confined. It was not just that the more extraordinary gifts of the Holy Spirit to the early church, such as healing and tongue-speaking, were believed to have ceased; it was also that little emphasis was placed on any other significant role for the Holy Spirit in the church's life. Structures were established for everything, including teaching, worship, leadership, and decision making. In many churches it became a rare thing to hear any mention of the Holy Spirit.

Taken as a whole, though, the Christian church has never been without a voice for a more radical reliance on the Holy Spirit. Whether in medieval mysticism, or in the radical wing of the Reformation, or in the emergence of a full-blown charismatic/Pentecostal movement in the twentieth century, voices seeking a recovery of the primal early experience of the Spirit have not been silent. Today, the fastest-growing movement within the global church is found precisely in Pentecostalism, which has proven to be highly appealing both in the developing world and in the United States. Perhaps the semicollapse of Enlightenment orthodoxy, with its elevation of reason and science as the only paths to true knowledge of the world, has opened the door to a recovery of a kind of pre-/post-Enlightenment religiosity in which once again people are open to, and therefore experience, "signs and wonders."

DAVID P. GUSHEE

Pastoral Perspective

In the midst of the wilderness of these celebrations, these folks live the fear of transitions begun and changes realized.

Many folks in our pews know this fear. Some of them are transitioning from the challenges of childhood to a whole new set of challenges that accompanies raising families and planning for futures in a world full of unpredictable economies and unequal access. Others sit in their church realizing that while their pew does not change, their world does. They mourn the loss of the church, the community, the family, or the constant stability they once loved. Times of life transition come with promise and hope, with fear and mourning, and our congregants experience them all.

Finally, after the preparations and the guest invitations, after the mourning and sense of loss, we celebrate that at this party folks take away some incredible party gifts. Some of these disciples have been training for this time for up to three years as they learn by their mistakes and Jesus' example, through the challenge of parables told and crosses to be borne. Now this birthday party has the feel of a graduation party. The promise of the Spirit is finally fulfilled, and they receive their authentic voices, with which they will enter an unwelcoming world preaching and living the love of Jesus.

This narrative challenges our congregants to find the Spirit within them and to locate, claim, and utilize their authentic voices, gifts, and skills with which to love and serve. However, we cheapen the Spirit and her gifts if we reduce them to dwelling exclusively within the individual. This Spirit that swept through the house gifted more than those disciples at Pentecost and the disciples with whom we minister today. That Spirit has been loosed into the world, and its creative and life-giving power is now the gift of families and communities, of churches, and of nations. The relevant question becomes not just "How will *I* respond to these party gifts of the Spirit?" but "How will *we* respond to these gifts?"

DAVID M. BENDER

Exegetical Perspective

for forgiveness (v. 38) is the name of Jesus (see Acts 4:12). One does not appeal directly to the Father but to the one "standing at the right hand of God" (thus Stephen's vision of the Son of Man in Acts 7:55; see Dan. 7:13–14).

The phenomenon of tongues here described raises questions by comparison with what Paul said on the topic.[1] The author of Acts can hardly have been unaware of the glossolalia, or unintelligible ecstatic utterance, practiced by Paul and his churches (1 Cor. 12:10; 13:1, 8; chap. 14). Acts mentions tongues again at 10:46 and 19:6, portraying it as a prebaptismal and postbaptismal response to the reception of the Spirit. In neither of these latter cases of "tongues" does Luke distinguish it from the original Pentecost gift or give any indication that it might only have been the glossolalia of the Pauline congregations. Perhaps this latter phenomenon was too closely related for Luke's comfort to Greek ecstatic prophecy, where the prophetess or prophet would speak incoherently in a state of divine possession. In contrast, the Pentecost event "stresses the communicative rather than the ecstatic dimensions of their speech."[2]

The way the lectionary passage breaks the Pentecost account at the emphatic conclusion (v. 21) of the citation from Joel binds the theme of the bestowal of the Holy Spirit to the belief in Jesus as Lord. The resurrected Christ's words to the disciples in chapter 1 were not subtle: the power of the Holy Spirit coming upon them (1:8) will empower them to become "witnesses" to Jesus. Hence Luke reports Peter opening his speech by witnessing to the evidence that the tongues of the disciples and the words of the prophet bear upon the question of what kind of man Jesus is.

STEPHEN A. COOPER

Homiletical Perspective

each other's toes, faces reddening, voices rising in confusion. It is a picture of Babel. The human community described in Genesis 11:1–9, divided by God into diverse language groups, begins to be mended here. As the Spirit arrives and Peter explains, the confusions of Babel are reversed. Instead of widening confusion, there is dawning comprehension, incipient reunion. What was divided is mended as people speak languages other than their own. The Spirit-baptized are drawn together, this time in the Spirit's power, for the purposes of extending the realm of God. Whereas Babel's reach was vertical, through the story of Luke–Acts the realm of God expands horizontally. The congregation may well see themselves as a part of the widening circle begun in Acts—part of the growing momentum, building ripple by ripple toward the ultimate reunion of humankind. As homiletician Ronald J. Allen puts it, "Whenever bits and pieces of the human family are reunited, their reunion points to the final regeneration."[2]

Identifying Power. Finally, an entirely different approach to this text is suggested by the image of the tongues of fire. Commentators have had relatively little to say about the significance of the image. Links to texts such as Isaiah 5:24 seem weak, and many scholars content themselves with observing that elsewhere in Scripture fire is associated with divine presence or purification. However, the sharp peculiarity of "divided tongues, as of fire" (v. 3) is not fully addressed. One theory put forward by cutting-edge New Testament scholar Herman Waetjen[3] notes the similarity between a figure on Roman coins and the image of the text. Specifically, on a Roman coin of the first century, divided tongues of fire appear over the head of Caesar as a sign of royalty—even a sign of divinity. "Caesar is the Son of God," the symbol proclaims to the first-century world. Preachers and congregations may well ask themselves what in their lives proclaims their divine lineage. If twenty-first-century daughters and sons of God are not best identified by sticky nametags, WWJD bracelets, or denominational lapel pins, what does identify us as part of the divine family?

JANA CHILDERS

---

1. R. I. Pervo argues that Luke transformed a story he had about an "ecstatic speech" event "into a linguistic miracle," whether from "distaste for glossolalia or to expound universalism, or both" (*Acts: A Commentary* [Minneapolis: Fortress Press, 2009], 60).
2. Thus L. T. Johnson, *The Acts of the Apostles* (Collegeville, MN: Liturgical Press, 1992), 42.

2. Ronald J. Allen, *Preaching Luke-Acts* (St. Louis: Chalice Press, 2000), 76.
3. Herman Waetjen, lecture on Acts 2, given at San Francisco Theological Seminary, 1998.

John 7:37-39

³⁷On the last day of the festival, the great day, while Jesus was standing there, he cried out, "Let anyone who is thirsty come to me, ³⁸and let the one who believes in me drink. As the scripture has said, 'Out of the believer's heart shall flow rivers of living water.'" ³⁹Now he said this about the Spirit, which believers in him were to receive; for as yet there was no Spirit, because Jesus was not yet glorified.

Theological Perspective

On the last great day of the feast of Tabernacles, Jesus says to those with him, "Let anyone who is thirsty come to me, and let the one who believes in me drink. . . . 'Out of the believer's heart shall flow rivers of living water.'" The Gospel writer declares that this living water refers to the Spirit, which had not yet been given. For John, the Spirit is given only when Jesus is "lifted up," only when he is crucified (12:23, 32). The Spirit is poured out only when Jesus goes away (7:33)—only when he gives up his own spirit in death (19:30). Living water springs forth from Jesus when he is at his most vulnerable, when—as it is in old age—one must open oneself to others, for good or for ill (21:18). These are common themes in John's account of the good news of Jesus: presence through absence, life through death, power through vulnerability.

For many of us, these are paradoxes. How is someone more present to us when they leave us? How does living water spring up in us when another lets go of what they have? How does power—even the power of eternal life—come from vulnerability, opening ourselves to potential harm, even death?

Through the centuries, Christian scholars and theologians have identified John as the most mystical of the evangelists. Some mystics, influenced by the Platonic tradition, tend toward dualism, drawing

Pastoral Perspective

When Jesus cried out, "Let anyone who is thirsty come to me" (v. 37b), we all know he was not talking about people who had physical thirst. He was talking about some condition within the human spirit—some parchedness, a dryness, a lacking of the fluid of life.

We have all sat in meetings where we were thirsty. It was tedious. There was a whole lot of human rationale and reasoning, of logic and persuasion; but we were all dry. We were all thirsty. The room needed an immersion in the Holy Spirit. Something was missing. Jesus cried out, "Let anyone who is thirsty come to me."

When you look at our nation today, you wonder if we are not in an epidemic of thirst. There is a dryness in the land—a dryness in relationships, a dryness in leadership, and a dryness in dreams for the future. There are many people in our pews whose dreams have dried up. They are thirsty and in need of some Spirit. Jesus cried out, "Let anyone who is thirsty come to me."

There are people in our pews who are parched in their relationships with somebody, somewhere. A relationship is dry, it is brittle, and it is painful. It has cracked and there is no moisture in it. Such people are thirsty and in need of some Spirit. Jesus cried out, "Let anyone who is thirsty come to me, and let the one who believes in me drink" (vv. 37b–38a).

Exegetical Perspective

John 7–8 tells of Jesus' appearance at the Jewish festival of Booths, or Tabernacles, which centered on the temple in Jerusalem.[1] The first-century historian Josephus refers to this as the most important of the Jewish festivals. We read in 1 Kings 8:2 that this was the festival during which Solomon dedicated the temple. Originally a harvest festival, it came to be associated with the eschatological hope for a time when God's life-giving presence would flow out in rivers from the temple, like water from the rock in the wilderness. Celebration of the festival included ceremonies involving water and light, both of which figure in Jesus' identification of himself in these chapters, here and in 8:12.

In the Synoptics, the adult Jesus travels to only one festival. In John, however, festival scenes of revelation and conflict begin with Jesus' cleansing of the temple in 2:13–22 and regularly punctuate the narrative as it moves toward the death of Jesus at the Gospel's third and final Passover. Even the brief reference to the upcoming Passover in 6:4 occurs in proximity to the conflict concerning the bread of life discourse, which in turn leads to the announcement in 7:1 that Jesus is staying in Galilee because he is in

---

1. The name is based on the same root as the verb used in John 1:14 to speak of the Word becoming flesh to dwell, or tabernacle, among us.

Homiletical Perspective

There are two main themes in this brief passage, both of them strong sources for preaching. The first is about human need. "Let anyone who is thirsty come to me," Jesus says (v. 37), speaking directly to human yearning. This invitation seems at first to be addressed to everyone everywhere, to the whole of humanity. Who among us is not thirsty, thirsty for something? Thirsty for meaning, money, knowledge, intimacy, possessions, fame, power. To be human is to be thirsty for something more than we have, thirsty to be someone more than who we are now.

Advertisers know we are thirsty, and thus they have learned how to talk like Jesus. All advertising in our consumer-oriented society is essentially based on the pitch, "Let anyone who is thirsty, come here." Diets? "Lose the weight you want, eating the foods you love." Cars? "Don't let it pass you by." Anti-aging creams? "Correct wrinkles and fine lines before it's too late." Motorcycles? "They're all built to do one thing: get you there first." Fragrances? "Sizzles with surprising femininity, as well as a hint of sexiness." Thirsty to be thin? Young? Sexy? Exciting? Come to us, all who thirst.

Jesus' invitation is far more than a shallow bar call to a parched and thirsty generation. Jesus speaks to people who have tried what the culture has to offer and found it empty, people who are burned out

John 7:37-39

Theological Perspective

stark contrasts between opposites—the spiritual and the material, soul and flesh, light and darkness, personal and communal. However, those mystics who stay most true to those biblical patterns of thinking and most grounded in Hebrew ways of knowing think in terms of dialectics not dualisms. That is, they see a dynamic, interactive relationship between these realities.

Meister Eckhart, the fourteenth-century Dominican and spiritual cousin of the Fourth Evangelist, illuminated the way in which the quality of one's presence depends on one's absence—in a manner of speaking. To explain how that is, Eckhart used the example of human speech. He marveled at the character of speech: "It is an amazing thing that something flows forth and nonetheless remains within. Words flow forth and yet remain within."[1] We can speak words that affect others, but the thoughts that formed them stay within us. In fact, the more discipline and skill we develop in our thought processes, the more beneficial our words may be to and for others. So, to the degree that we are "absent" from them, developing a richer internal intellectual and spiritual life, the more able we are to be "present" to them.

Eckhart uses this form of human expression to describe the dynamic nature of God:

> All creatures flow forth and yet remain within. . . .
> God is in all things. The more [God] is within, all
> the more [God] is without.[2]

Creation and creatures flow out from God, but remain within God. They are distinct from God, but are not separate from God. Therefore, the more God dwells deeply within God's self, the more God flows out, in and through creatures. Transcendence and immanence are not polar opposites, just as God and the creation are not. There is both distinction and a deep unity.

Further, Eckhart describes this dynamic nature of God in Trinitarian terms. God remains within God's self, where God "gives birth to the only begotten Son." From this remaining within there is a "flowing out"—"the Holy Spirit blossoms."[3] Inherent in the nature of God, then, is this dual capacity to "remain within" and to "flow out." These two capacities are not opposed to one another but, rather, enhance, reinforce, and support one another.

1. Meister Eckhart, "Sermon 2: Creation: A Flowing Out But Remaining Within," in Matthew Fox, trans., *Passion for Creation: The Earth-Honoring Spirituality of Meister Eckhart* (Rochester, VT: Inner Traditions, 2000), 65.
2. Ibid.
3. "Sermon 6: The Greatness of the Human Person," in *Passion for Creation*, 103.

Pastoral Perspective

At some level, the people in the pew want to know how to get that drink. Do they have to become more pious? Do they have to come to church more often? Do they have to increase their pledge? Do they have to stop smoking, dancing, drinking, and cursing? Do they just have to pray?

Today is Pentecost Sunday. Do you ever feel as if mainline Protestants and Catholics in America just do not get Pentecost? They come out of the woodwork for Christmas Eve, and they still do a fair job showing up for Easter, but Pentecost is almost something the preacher pushes on the congregation. They do not really seem to understand.

I have tried asking the entire congregation to wear something red on the day of Pentecost. Twelve people remembered to do that, while everybody else either forgot it or did not want to do it. We have tried having liturgical dancers at Pentecost. That did not go over very well. We have tried having six people read the Pentecost passage in Acts in six different languages all at the same time—the Presbyterian version of speaking in tongues. We have tried trumpets, banners, and anything else we could get away with, but it never seems to work. The congregation does not latch onto Pentecost. They do not anticipate it. There are no Pentecost dinners or parties. There is no Pentecost parade. We do not send Pentecost cards to each other. Even the stores have not picked up on Pentecost.

Have you ever wondered why that is? Why is Pentecost, in most places, the lost celebration within the church? Maybe people do not want to get too close to the Holy Spirit. Maybe we do not understand it, but we do not understand Christmas or Easter either. I can celebrate the birth and the resurrection of Jesus Christ, but celebrating the coming of the Holy Spirit on all human flesh, including mine, may be too much.

Well then, take it away. Someone has said, "When a horse dies, it is time to dismount!" If Pentecost is a "dead horse," then dismount. However, what do we lose if there is no Holy Spirit involved with human flesh?

For one, I do not know why I am praying for anything. If God does not touch human life somewhere, somehow, then what good are prayers?

Secondly, how do I get and stay connected to God? If the role of the Holy Spirit is to teach us things that Christ taught us, to convict us of sin, to inspire us to love, then how does all that happen if we dismount from Pentecost?

When Paul was trying to teach the Christians in Galatia about the Holy Spirit, he made a list of fruits:

danger in Judea. On this visit to Jerusalem, the conflict with the authorities heightens in intensity, with four references in chapter 7 to the threat to kill Jesus and three references to his arrest. The references to his arrest and death occur more frequently here than in any other chapter. We also find in 7:39 the first reference to Jesus' being glorified through his death, and this festival encounter will end in 8:59 with the first attempt to stone him.

It is in this atmosphere of menace and fear that Jesus, who has initially come to the festival in secret, stands and cries out at the climactic moment of the celebration, the "great day," when a dramatic water libation would have occurred in the temple. In the context of this ceremony, he offers himself as the source of living water for anyone who thirsts. His invitation builds on the relationship he draws between himself and manna in the wilderness in 6:48–51 and is similar to the promise in 6:35; but here, where the emphasis is on drinking, we also hear echoes of the offer of living water to the Samaritan woman (4:14).

John is rife with water imagery. In his first miracle, Jesus turns water into an abundance of wedding wine (2:1–11). We see the pairing of water and Spirit in the testimony of John the Baptist (1:32–34) and in Jesus' conversation with Nicodemus (3:5). There, in 3:4, we also find the word "womb" (*koilia*), understood in 7:38 to be the seat of emotion and translated "heart." The presence of the three terms (water, Spirit, womb) in both places is suggestive. Nicodemus asks if one must enter the mother's *koilia* again to be born from above; Jesus replies that he must be born of water and Spirit. In 7:38 it is the *koilia* of believers themselves that Jesus will convert from a place of thirst to a source of abundant living water. In 4:7–26, we find another reference to living water and a conversation about the Spirit; there the water that Jesus gives becomes in those who drink it "a spring of water gushing up to eternal life" (4:14). Finally, at the moment of glorification foreshadowed in 7:39, after Jesus hands over his spirit (19:30), water and blood pour from his side (19:34).

The Scripture citation in 7:38 raises two questions for interpreters: the source of the quotation, addressed below, and the question of whose heart is intended, Jesus' or the believer's. The passage quoted by Jesus actually says, "Out of *his* heart shall flow rivers of living water." Interpreters have debated the issue since the second century, with many arguing that it refers to Jesus. The NRSV presents the other alternative, which is supported by punctuation in an important early

on the world's hollow promises and false advertising. Jesus instead summons people who have tried the fizzy, sweet sodas of the culture and found them wanting. Jesus' words are an echo of the prophet Isaiah, "Ho, everyone who thirsts, come to the waters" (Isa. 55:1), but Isaiah's subsequent words feed into Jesus' invitation as well: "Why do you spend . . . your labor for that which does not satisfy?" (Isa. 55:2). Jesus is not saying, "Whatever drives your thirst, come to me," but, rather, "When you have discovered that none of the empty promises of a seductive culture can ease your thirst, come to me and drink of the true and living water."

United Church of Christ pastor Lillian Daniel once told of a conversation she had with a young police officer after she and some other Christians had been arrested inside a government building while protesting unfair labor practices. Just before they were arrested, they had been singing hymns together. Daniel was now locked up, alone, in a paddy wagon. The policeman assigned to guard her spoke to her through a narrow window, apologizing for her undignified treatment and expressing sorrow that he had to be the one to enforce it. Daniel asked him, "Why are you in this field, if you hate it so much?"

"Just fell into it, I guess. After the military. So I retire in two years, and I'm young," he said.

Then the officer revealed a deeper thirst in his life. "But what I wanted to say to you was something else," he added. "What I wanted to say to you was that back there, when you guys were singing 'Amazing Grace,' in the capitol building, I liked that. I liked the way your voices sounded when you sang those songs. So I wanted to let you know."

"Thanks, again," she said.

"You'll get out of here soon," he said.

"You too," she said.[1]

Jesus speaks to all people who, like that young policeman, find themselves in a place that is essentially unsatisfying, who are still deeply thirsty for a life of profound meaning. Like the sound of a beautiful hymn in the midst of the world's cacophony, rises the call of Jesus, "Let anyone who is thirsty come to me."

If the first theme in this passage is about human need, the second theme has to do with the identity of Jesus, or more specifically with what happens when we respond to Jesus and take our deepest thirsts not to the dry wells of the world but to him.

1. Lillian Daniel, "Minute Fifty-four," in Jackson W. Carroll and Carol E. Lytch, eds., *What Is Good Ministry?* (Durham, NC: Duke Divinity School, 2003), 7.

John 7:37-39

Theological Perspective

To be made in the image of God, then, means that we have these two interrelated and reinforcing capacities. We have the ability to "remain in"—to act as sovereign persons, to develop the intellectual, emotional, spiritual gifts that God has given us and that the world needs from us. We also have the ability to "flow out"—to reach out, to connect to others, to offer them our gifts, and to receive from them the gifts only they can give. The more we "remain in," the more effective we are at both giving what others need from us and receiving what we need from them. The more deeply we relate to others in this necessary exchange of gifts, the richer our internal, personal resources and lives.

In this human and divine exchange, the Holy Spirit blossoms. The presence of the Spirit does not replace human agency and capacities; it encourages, fosters, and enlivens those who listen and love, as Jesus did: "I do not call you servants any longer, because the servant does not know what the master is doing" (15:15).

To believe in Jesus is to trust him and to believe in his way—to do what he did. He shared "everything that [he had] heard from [his] Father" (15:15), he loved others, and he made himself vulnerable to them and to the world. Those who trust Jesus are to do the same—"to love one another, as I have loved you" (15:12). His friends are sent into the world (17:18) to share what they have received and to go and "bear fruit" (15:16).

This love—this giving and receiving—is risky business.

> "Servants are not greater than their master." If they persecuted me, they will persecute you; if they kept my word, they will keep yours also. (15:20)

The life-giving exchange—the spring of "living waters"—of giving and receiving makes them vulnerable. To live, one must risk death; but the Advocate—the Helper—will come and prove the "world" wrong about sin (distrust), unrighteousness (the assertion that Jesus' way is not God's way), and judgment (the way of "the ruler of this world" is not the true way, John 16:8–11). In addition, this way of life leads to a joy that no one can take away (16:22).

STEPHEN B. BOYD

Pastoral Perspective

"love, joy, peace, patience, kindness, generosity, faithfulness, gentleness, and self-control" (Gal. 5:22–23a). We want to celebrate some of that. We surely need some of that. If we lose Pentecost, how do we bear those fruits? Can we manufacture them?

Sometimes we get rid of things that we do not understand but we cannot afford to lose. We do not have to understand the Holy Spirit; we just have to understand that we *need* the Holy Spirit. The Christian faith without the Holy Spirit is like a swimming pool without any water. What is the point? You have a lot of form and structure but no function. We have been in that pool.

Pentecost cannot be declared a "dead horse." We cannot afford to dismount from the celebration of the gift of the Holy Spirit, because the options are unthinkable. There cannot be a world where there is no Spirit. There cannot be a world where humans are not touched by the Divine, even if they do not understand it and cannot explain it. There cannot be a world where God does not infuse the very mind and will of God within human life. There cannot be a world without "love, joy, peace, patience, kindness, generosity, faithfulness, gentleness, and self-control." There just cannot be.

Maybe you preach this sermon by starting out saying, "Perhaps we should get rid of Pentecost." That would surely get somebody's attention. Be careful, it might get a couple of Amens or a round of applause! However, the shock factor could awaken the ears to hear what this day brings to us. What if we did not have Pentecost? What if there were a world with no Spirit? That just cannot be. Thank God it is not.

STEVEN P. EASON

Exegetical Perspective

manuscript. In this reading, the postresurrection believer becomes a conduit for the rivers of living water offered by Jesus, an image similar to the spring of water in 4:14, with both interpretations underscoring the liveliness and power of the Spirit.

The idea of the Spirit flowing not only from Jesus but also from the believer is consistent with the promise of this Gospel that the Father and Son are to be one with the believer, as they are one with each other (14:20; 17:20–23). Jesus and the Father are to make their home with those who love Jesus (14:23). The Spirit is to come after Jesus as another Advocate to abide in Jesus' own and make Jesus and the Father present to them (14:16–17, 26; 16:7). These passages also shed light on the explanatory note in 7:39 about the Spirit. According to the note, the Gospel does not suggest that the Spirit does not exist before this point, but Jesus repeatedly tells his own on his last night that he will be sending the Spirit to them in a new way after his departure.

The second point of ambiguity in the passage concerns the location of the verse Jesus cites. There is no perfect fit but a wealth of possibilities. These include passages related to the water from the rock in the wilderness (Ps. 78:15–16); the eschatological promise of rivers flowing from the temple (Ezek. 47:1–12; Joel 3:18) and from Jerusalem (Zech. 14:8); the promise of rivers in the desert (Isa. 43:19; 44:3; 58:11); Wisdom, who calls to her children to come and drink (Prov. 18:4; Sir. 24:30–33); and the beloved compared to a garden fountain, a well of living water, and flowing streams from Lebanon (Song 4:15).

With Jesus' bold invitation and promise, John 7:37–39 calls readers to remember God's faithful provision in desert places in the past, to trust in God's assurance of abundant goodness in the future, and to celebrate the gift of the life-giving Spirit flowing through them like rivers from the throne of God even now.

MEDA A. A. STAMPER

Homiletical Perspective

We might expect Jesus to say, "I am the river of life; come to me and I will give you living water to drink." What Jesus says, however, is actually far more radical. Jesus promises that if we come to him with our thirst, *we ourselves* will become rivers of life: "Out of the believer's heart shall flow rivers of living water" (v. 38b). When thirsty people come to Jesus, he does not merely hand them a spiritual beverage, momentary relief for thirst; he gives them instead the indwelling of the Holy Spirit (this is why this text appears in the lectionary at Pentecost). Through the Spirit, believers participate in the unceasing life of God, and the water of abundant life flows and flows through them.

This promise of the Spirit means that Jesus—the Jesus of history, the Jesus who walked the dusty back roads of Galilee, the Jesus who taught and healed and formed a community of disciples, the Jesus who was tried by Pontius Pilate and executed on a Roman cross—this Jesus is for believers not just a memory or a story or an idea, but a living and unceasing presence.

One way to put this is that through believing in Jesus we receive the Spirit and, in the power of the Spirit, we have Jesus always in our hearts. Immediately, though, warning flares must go up. If we imagine "Jesus in our hearts" as something sweet and highly spiritualized, we have it completely wrong. The shock of Jesus was that in him what the philosophers said was impossible and offensive had actually happened: the eternal and mysterious divine Word had become flesh, and the result was not to render the Divine vulgar but to make the material sacred. The shock of the Christian life is that the glorified Jesus has once again, through the Spirit, become flesh in the lives of believers, and the result is not that Jesus has become confined in the small space of believers' hearts, but that the lives of believers have become like his—large and life giving, "rivers of living waters."

THOMAS G. LONG

Genesis 1:1-2, 4a

In the beginning when God created the heavens and the earth, [2]the earth
was a formless void and darkness covered the face of the deep, while a wind
from God swept over the face of the waters. . . .
    [4]And God saw that the light was good.

Theological Perspective

The very opening of the biblical canon deals with
large matters that at first do not seem to ground creation in historical reality. We hear of a formless void,
darkness, a face, a wind over waters. Where and
when is the creating happening? What does it mean
to speak of "beginning" in the context of a "formless
void"? These are generalized images. Formlessness is
infinite, and the void is endless nothingness, like that
of a black hole or a bottomless well. Such limitless
lack of order we usually call "chaos," but a distinction needs to be made between the chaos of a temporary event (experienced in the midst of a street
riot, for instance) and the chaos of utter oblivion,
nullity. The chaos of a single moment returns to a
semblance of order (either a prior order or something newly ordered), whereas the chaos of the ultimate abyss describes something (or some nothing)
that cannot be expected to shift at all. Change in
time cannot occur unless both time and form exist,
unless time is ordered out of chaos.

The theological issues here deal with the identity
of time itself and the relationship between Creator
and created. Did time begin when God created the
heavens and the earth, or did time already exist
before creation? When is the beginning? Did the
beginning exist apart from God? These questions
have been probed and mined for centuries, and we

Pastoral Perspective

Trinity Sunday has been the bane of preachers for
generations. Senior pastors regularly dump the
preaching for this Sunday on their junior associates.
All Christian clergy seemingly struggle with understanding and articulating the divine mystery of the
Trinity at some point in their ministries.

Preachers are not helped by the historical documents of the church, such as *Quicunque Vult,* commonly called the Creed of Saint Athanasius. It is still
found in the *Book of Common Prayer* used in the
Episcopal Church.[1] It begins "we worship one God
in Trinity, and Trinity in Unity, neither confounding
the Persons, nor dividing the substance." Then, trying to further clarify the three persons, the creed
continues: "The Father uncreate, the Son uncreate,
and the Holy Ghost uncreate. The Father incomprehensible, the Son incomprehensible, and the Holy
Ghost incomprehensible. . . . And yet . . . there are
not three incomprehensibles, nor three uncreated,
but one uncreated, and one incomprehensible."

By now, we are all shaking our heads at the
incomprehensibleness of it all.

The Catechism, An Outline of the Faith, found in
the same book, gives a simpler answer. "Q. What is

---

1. *The Book of Common Prayer* (New York: Church Hymnal Corporation,
1976), 864–65.

Exegetical Perspective

One of the things for which an interpreter of the Revised Common Lectionary must always be alert is a missing verse in the midst of an otherwise well-defined passage. Often there will be in the omitted segment something troubling regarding God or humanity—at least, something troubling to the "modern" mind. However, what could possibly be offensive or distracting about verse 3 in this most familiar of all passages: "Then God said, 'Let there be light'; and there was light"—or verses 4b and 5 for that matter?

There are many other exegetical matters that may seem more pressing in this opening trumpet blast from Genesis. There is the loaded question of the relative clause in verse 1 ("when God created the heavens and the earth") and whether it should be relative or not (see the alternative reading "In the beginning God created"). This has deep implications for our understanding of the locus for God's past and present creative acts. Does the God of the Bible fashion order out of chaos, or life out of nothing, or both?

There is the fascinating issue of the *tohu wabohu* (the "formless void and darkness") and its context in ancient literature and for us today. How would such a phrase capture a deep part of Israel's experience if we date the final form of Genesis 1 to the chaotic days of Israel's exile in the city of Babylon?

Homiletical Perspective

Scripture is theocentric not christocentric. Scripture is about God and how God works through Christ and through the Holy Spirit. Such a perspective provides the opportunity to enter into dialogue with other, non-Christian religious bodies that believe in God but not Christ. Trinity Sunday emphasizes the oneness of God though manifesting God's self in distinct realities. The opening of Scripture clearly sets the tone for how we are to understand God. God is one. God is a universal God. God creates, sustains, orders, preserves, provides, and loves. The first creation account offers an important opportunity to speak about the centrality of God in Scripture: "In the beginning, God."

This text raises a couple of possibilities for the development of a sermon. The preacher might choose to bring to the attention of the congregation the significance of how Scripture begins. This may appear obvious, but the implications are profound. Scripture begins not with the choosing of Abraham or the election of Israel (Gen. 12). It begins with creation. This means that we must jettison any ethnic, parochial, or provincial understanding of God. God is a universal God, not a God of any one people, nation, or race. The Bible begins by announcing, "In the beginning when God created the world," not, "In the beginning when God created Israel." God's creational activity is

Genesis 1:1-2, 4a

Theological Perspective

are still at their mercy. The opening words of Genesis call us to understand time and God's relationship to time and to creation. Translations from the Hebrew, like the NRSV, establish the existence of a beginning, asserting that God was actively creating "in" the beginning. Another translation seeks to retain the feel of the language, yielding this: "At the beginning of God's creating of the heavens and the earth . . ."[1] Here the words establish that God was already creating before the hearer or reader is told that the matter of concern is what happened "at the beginning" of that creating. We might say that the more classic translations (e.g., NRSV and KJV) are grounded in the reality of time, others in divine activity.

Some recent scholarship shows that translations rendering the first word of Genesis as "*the* beginning" understand the Hebrew to be a restrictive relative clause that cannot necessarily be supported by the grammar.[2] The result is an assertion that creation had an absolute origin or moment of beginning. (What, for example, might the presence of an absolute moment of origin mean in light of the well-established scientific theory of evolution?)

We cannot resolve this discrepancy, but we can notice that, theologically speaking, the nuanced conflict between interpretations of the first word of Genesis (and there are good arguments on many fronts) assures us that ambiguity is primary, that the Scriptures may intend for us to overlay disparate understandings, and that multiple simultaneous insights—existing as they do in the very Word of God—only serve to deepen and enrich our understanding of this world and of God.

Perhaps because of their lack of clarity, the issues of time and the relationship between God and creatures become, nonetheless, real. They exist in an age that has a beginning, either because it was "in" that beginning that the creator began to work or because it was the beginning of God's work. What God created is described by ritualized language—"the heavens and the earth"—that by virtue of its formulaic, liturgical nature creates a reality previously unknown.

God engages, in these verses, both within and in time and in contact with all that exists. This means that God and creation (earth and all stars) have relationship. God acts in and upon time and space through a trembling, moving, stirring spirit or wind

1. Everett Fox, *The Five Books of Moses: Genesis, Exodus, Leviticus, Numbers, and Deuteronomy* (New York: Schocken Books, 1995), 11.
2. Robert D. Holmstedt, "The Restrictive Syntax of Genesis i 1," *Vetus Testamentum* 58 (2008): 56–67.

Pastoral Perspective

the Trinity? A. The Trinity is one God: Father, Son, and Holy Spirit."[2] A simpler answer, yes, but one that still leaves inquiring minds wanting to know. Perhaps that is the problem. We want to know, analyze, and explain the Trinity by our intellect, when what we are talking about is mystery. The early church fathers were trying to describe the indescribable, their own mysterious experience of God. Yet mystery is ultimately inexplicable and, in the end, words fail. Mystery can be known only by the spiritual heart.

So where to begin? The lectionary suggests the first verses of the first chapter of the first book of the Bible, Genesis 1. Traditionally we have understood these verses as pointing to the first person of the Trinity, God, the Father and Mother of us all, the creative energetic force of all creation. However, these verses also give us glimpses of the other two aspects of the mysterious Trinity. Those brief verses depict the immense power of the spirit of God that hovers and broods over all darkness and then offer the piercing image of the light of God that shines in the darkness and cannot be overcome by it. Genesis looks into the heart of darkness and sees something beautiful and hopeful: a creative force, a hovering spirit, and a penetrating light that cannot be overcome.

Darkness, light, and new life are all aspects of our human experience. We are creatures of sunset and sunrise, of the ebb and flow of the tides of life, of darkness and light. Within our life stories and the stories of our human history, there are dark sides that do not go away. Human suffering does not go away. Also within our human stories are experiences of new life and fresh possibility brought by the overshadowing spirit, of a creative force bringing order out of chaos, of the light of Christ that shines across the ages and beyond the grave.

Paul in his speech to the men of Athens (Acts 17:27), tries to explain why God made us. This God, he says, made us so that we might seek God, grope for God and in our groping perhaps eventually find God. When we voyage into the darkness and light of our own experience, we may encounter what we grope for, the reality that we call God, the mysterious Trinity.

Let us approach this from another perspective and consider a visual depiction of the Trinity. Perhaps the most compelling one is an iconic image of the Holy Trinity created by Andrew Rublev, who lived in fifteenth-century Russia. Through his praying with Scripture, Rublev began to understand the three messengers who visited Abraham and Sarah

2. Ibid., 852.

Trinity Sunday

Exegetical Perspective

There is the "fertile" discussion of the Hebrew word which the NRSV translates as "swept," but other translations interpret as "hovering" or "brooding." What are the semantic implications of this word, and do they point toward other biblical language that is equally charged with generative possibilities and mystery ("and the power of the Most High will overshadow you; therefore the child to be born will be holy; he will be called Son of God," Luke 1:35)?

All of these questions are good questions, and probably should be answered when this passage shows up on any other lectionary Sunday. Nevertheless, what if the preacher simply goes forward with this passage, as edited by the lectionary committee, on Trinity Sunday?

Here is an idea. It cannot be a mistake that in this passage, so edited, there are three occurrences of the word 'elohim or God: verse 1 (God creating); verse 2 (the wind or spirit from God); and verse 4 (And God saw that the light was good). This threefold structure thus links the word "God" with light in verse 3, a link that cannot help but point the reader toward a similar linkage in another creation account, in the Gospel of John: "The light shines in the darkness, and the darkness did not overcome it" (John 1:5). This linkage of light and Logos, of light and the second person of the Trinity, now makes evident the problem with verse 3: the light in Genesis 1 is a creation of God's speaking, and thus is not coeternal with the Father. Now not only the symmetry of the text but the Trinitarian theology implied in the text breaks down. What is the interpreter to do?

The first thing the interpreter must do is come clean with the problem of citing Scripture for doctrinal sermons. Genesis 1 is no more directly addressing the Trinity than Matthew 28 (which at least requires no editing to see the Trinitarian baptismal formula contained in verse 19). As Matthew 28 is primarily about the sending of the disciples, so Genesis 1 is primarily about God creating order out of chaos, back then and today. The Trinity is at best a "second order" rather than a "first order" interpretation of Scripture, and the faithful exegete on this Sunday should not pretend otherwise.

However, if the preacher decides to preach on this edited text on this particular Sunday, there are some things that this passage and this Sunday have to say about God and us.

First, there is a multiplicity to God's revelation in the world, which even (or especially) this opening prelude makes clear. The God of Scripture is just too

Homiletical Perspective

inclusive. God makes the sun to rise not just on Christians or Americans or Europeans. God causes the sun to rise and the rain to fall on all humans, animals, and plants. God blesses all creation.

It is tempting for churches to develop exclusivity and a sense of ownership when it comes to God. Israel fell into that trap. The oneness or onlyness of God came to mean the onlyness of Israel. As Walter Brueggemann says, monotheism led to monoethnism.[1] They came to believe not only that YHWH alone is God but also Israel alone is God's people; this opened the door to believing they were privileged and resulted in their abuse of power.

Another direction a sermon could take is to ask who is this God we serve? Genesis 1–2 gives the basis for responding to that question. God is the creator of the world; but the primary focus is not *that* God created the world but *why* God created the world. The reason: God loves humans. God's specialty is loving and caring for creation.

God demonstrates this love in the collaborative way in which the world operates. Genesis 1:1–2:4 recounts the six days of creation. Nothing is made for itself alone. Everything contributes to the whole of creation. The first three days God creates the *habitat*: structure and light, sky and water, land and plants. The next three days God creates the *inhabitants* to fill the habitat, which symmetrically correspond to the first three days: the light bearers, the birds and sea creatures, and finally land animals and humans. Each part contributes to the whole. God provides for the needs of all God's creatures because God's specialty is love. However, God did not make the order of creation rigid or mechanical; humans are still called upon to subdue it (1:28; 2:15). Rather, God created a flexible, dynamic, and complex world with a mind of its own—again a demonstration of God's love.

God, however, especially loves humans. One way the writer emphasizes this is by telling the creation story twice. Genesis 1:1–2:4a details the first account, which offers a wide-lens, panoramic perspective of creation that climaxes in the creation of humans, male and female. This is the curtain-call order, the order in which the actors enter the stage after the play is over to receive the applause of the audience. The final actors to enter are those who played the central characters.

The second creation account follows in 2:4b–25. This is the commencement order account of creation.

1. Walter Brueggemann, *Texts That Linger, Words That Explode: Listening to Prophetic Voices*, ed. Patrick D. Miller (Minneapolis: Fortress Press, 2000), 90.

Genesis 1:1-2, 4a

Theological Perspective

that might be a passing turbulence and invisible, except as it has an effect on finite matter: water itself.

A fruitful comparison exists between Genesis's reckoning of creation's origin and that presented in the other ancient creation stories (such as the *Enuma Elish*). In brief, the parallels include deep water, breath moving over the waters, and light coming into existence. Remarkable disjunctures have also come to light, however, and these differences are rich with distinctive attributes of YHWH. In Genesis, the creation of light is not, as in the Egyptian stories, a manifestation of the creator-god's self, but an existence generated by the command of the Divine. The creation and the Creator are, thus, not identified wholly with each other. YHWH existed prior to the creation, whereas the Egyptian creator-god came into being with the creation itself.[3] YHWH creates with a word, Marduk (a Mesopotamian deity) with a violent rending of the god of chaos.

Finally, this text offers the theological question of the value of creation. Out of nothing, something was made (*creatio ex nihilo*). Why is this important? The Creator's first pronouncement is that the creation is good. The goodness here is not an aesthetic or ethical proclamation about the nature of light; rather, goodness concerns the use to which it can be put for God's intention. We do not learn what that purpose is in these verses, but God is pleased. The light is "good." God names it.

One clue to God's purpose is that in this text we are given an image of God's own spirit (*ru'ah*) entering into a relationship with the manifestations of chaos and, by such action, transforming them into a heaven and earth in which we—whose language forms this story—can thrive. This creates not only a new order but also a new reality. The God of Genesis—whom humans have come to know in deeper ways throughout the whole of the Scriptures—is a power available to all creation.

MELINDA QUIVIK

Pastoral Perspective

and announced the future birth of a child to this aged couple (Gen. 18:1–15) as precursors of the Holy Trinity of the New Testament. In the icon depicting that scene, he draws three figures seated around three sides of a square table. There is an opening on the fourth side immediately in front of the viewer.

As one gazes on this image, one is aware of the vast silence that surrounds the three figures. They seem to be looking into each other with an unqualified dignity, respect, and loving gaze—three distinct persons, three yet one. The fourth side to the table is left open intentionally by Rublev, signaling an invitation for the person viewing the image to draw near, even to sit at the table and join in the intimate conversation taking place. In a profound sense the person viewing the icon completes the image by joining the divine circle of the Sacred Three.

Henri Nouwen, the well-known twentieth-century Dutch theologian and author, spent many hours gazing on this icon during a particular time in his life of severe depression. He writes about that journey in his little book *Behold the Beauty of the Lord*.[3] He says that gradually, over many months, through that image, he came to know the Trinity as a Community of Love, a House of Love. In that household there was no fear, no greed, no anger, no violence, no anxieties, no pain, no suffering, even no words, only love, enduring love and deepening trust. It was a house, he said, in which he could dwell forever.

One significantly different understanding of the Trinity comes from Meister Eckhart, a fourteenth-century German mystic. He wrote that God the Father laughed, and the Son was born. Then the two of them laughed, and the Spirit was born. When all three laughed, the human being was born. For Eckhart, the mystery of the Trinity was surrounded by peals of golden laughter at the heart of the universe.

What does your experience tell you about the Trinity? How would you describe the indescribable, incomprehensible mystery of the Trinity? Trust your spiritual heart to know the way. It is the only compass you need.

CAROLE A. CRUMLEY

---

3. Gordon H. Johnston, "Genesis 1 and Ancient Egyptian Creation Myths," *Bibliotheca Sacra* 165 (April–June 2008): 186–87.

3. Henri Nouwen, *Behold the Beauty of the Lord* (Notre Dame, IN: Ave Maria Press, 1987).

big and mysterious and communal to allow a single subject (*'elohim*) to drive a series of verbs (create, said, see) that thereby describe this deity as *simply* a single actor over against the creation this particular God brings about. The spirit or wind of this God is also an actor; the spirit "sweeps, hovers, and broods" over the stuff of this world in a way that hints at relationship—both inside and outside the Godhead this passage portrays.

Second, the real question in Genesis 1 is not one of what preceded what, but of who orders all. This, not the vagaries of Hebrew grammar, is what makes Genesis 1 so perplexing when we insist on asking it our own questions, questions of the preexistence of matter or the preexistence of the Son. Genesis 1 explicitly makes the claim that the ordering activity of God was present at the beginning of the story, as it is now and has been at every step along the way.

Most remarkably, and most reassuringly, for exiles yesterday and today, this creative ordering is made tangible and visible within creation through the light that still shines forth in the darkness day to day. This analogical linkage between the light spoken into being in the omitted verse 3 of our passage, and the light that is the Word in the opening verses of the Gospel according to John, is a better path toward a Trinitarian sermon from Genesis 1 than one dependent on obtrusive editing. As the faithful Jew learned to trust God's ordering power in the light that breaks the darkness every morning, so the faithful Christian has learned to trust God's ordering power through the light and life that breaks the darkness through the spirit of the risen Christ. It is the tangible and visible nature of God's ordering power in Genesis 1 that provides the surest bridge toward the gospel from this "fanfare" passage of the Bible, whether on Trinity Sunday or any other day of the year.

RICHARD BOYCE

A commencement order at graduation begins with the president, followed by administrators, then faculty, then the graduates. The second account of creation leads off with the creation of humans, once again to emphasize their central role. Among other things, these two accounts emphasize that humans are the crown jewel of God's created order. To paraphrase Paul, "You are God's masterpiece" (Eph. 2:10). God created the world because God loves people.

What confirms God's special love for humans is that they are the only ones made in God's image (1:26–27). This is one of the reasons God insists on Israel not making images of the God they worship. God's image is already placed within humans; no other kind of representation is necessary. As God's image bearers, male and female are given a responsibility: to have dominion over the created order (v. 28). Humans are given dominion, not domination; they are caregivers, not exploiters (cf. Ps. 72:8–14). We do unto creation as God has done unto us; we express love and care toward the world. Being image bearers of God is also at the heart of how we see other humans, which results in treating them with dignity, regardless of race, age, gender, social or economic status.

This opening account of creation calls preachers to help congregations broaden their vision of God's grace. The opening scene reveals its breadth and depth. God's grace is not limited to humans but is poured out on the whole universe, infused in its very essence. Without God's ever-present involvement, the world would not be able to continue, and humans would not be able to live. John Walton maintains, "Instead of proclaiming that 'the cosmos was created by God' (using past tense as if the job is done), we should rather proclaim, 'The cosmos is God's creation.' We may thus lay claim to the dynamic role of God in a perpetual act of creation."[2] God loves, sustains, and cares for the universe and all its inhabitants day by day.

DAVE BLAND

2. John Walton, *Genesis*, NIV Application Commentary (Grand Rapids: Zondervan, 2001), 105.

Psalm 8

¹O LORD, our Sovereign,
　　how majestic is your name in all the earth!
　　You have set your glory above the heavens.
² Out of the mouths of babes and infants
　　you have founded a bulwark because of your foes,
　　to silence the enemy and the avenger.

³When I look at your heavens, the work of your fingers,
　　the moon and the stars that you have established;
⁴what are human beings that you are mindful of them,
　　mortals that you care for them?

Theological Perspective

This text points us to the fullness of the divine mystery. Our ancestors accounted for this by counting three major self-presentations as God's. This kind of calculation can seem like an aspect of a stand-up routine, rather like one from the young Bill Cosby: a small child comes home, proud of having learned a mathematical feat—addition. The child's report that two plus two equals four leads family members to be pleased. Then the child asks what a two is. So with God in three persons; we have had innumerable persons articulate this notion, and still many of us scratch our heads, unsure what it means to be three-yet-one.

Though Christians have wrestled with Trinitarian issues from the days following Jesus' death and resurrection, formal doctrinal commemoration of the Trinity as a key festival came only in the fourteenth century. Speculation as to why the church acted then does not bring clarity. It may be the case that many primary texts from our first thousand years of Christian witness tended to focus primarily on the primordial creator God, or the life of Jesus as Christ, or the life-giving and revivifying presence of God's Spirit, decisively seen at Pentecost. These three focal points were often enough clumped together, but many people get confused by what this kind of "commingling" represents. Because we Christians have sometimes fought bloody battles over one or

Pastoral Perspective

From the praise of God's universal and cosmic handiwork, in last week's psalm, we now move to a more specific focus of praise and contemplation—the creation of human beings and the questions of human existence that travel with us throughout our lives. The psalm begins with praise of God for the wonderment of God's creation and then moves to the particular wonder of the creation of human beings and of human consciousness. Why did God create each of us and all of us? Why did God create us, with this consciousness of our own existence, with this awareness of our mortality, with a sense of our individual selves? Why this uniqueness for us?

These reflections imply an even more profound understanding. Out of the billions of creatures in the universe, out of the billions of human beings on the earth, we are bold to claim that God knows our names. We make this bold claim that we are children of God, not because of who we are or what we have done, but because of who God is and what God has done as Creator, Redeemer, and Sustainer. This claim is both a wondrous discovery and, at times, a frightening awareness.

This self-awareness and this ability to transcend ourselves makes us just a "little lower than the Divine," as verse 5 puts it. It leads to powerful experiences such as the joy of love, the thrill of music, the

⁵ Yet you have made them a little lower than God,
    and crowned them with glory and honor.
⁶You have given them dominion over the works of your hands;
    you have put all things under their feet,
⁷all sheep and oxen,
    and also the beasts of the field,
⁸the birds of the air, and the fish of the sea,
    whatever passes along the paths of the seas.

⁹O Lord, our Sovereign,
    how majestic is your name in all the earth!

Exegetical Perspective

Psalm 8 is a hymn, although it is distinct from others in its direct address to God. The command for the worshiping community to offer praise, which is typical of most hymns, has here been replaced by an affirmation to YHWH about the Holy One's sovereignty (vv. 1a, 9). Likewise, the reason to render praise (vv. 1b–8) is spoken directly to God rather than cast as proclamation about what God has done. One of the most prominent features of the psalm is the identically worded affirmation that envelops the text and imbues the whole with an aura of YHWH's sovereignty. This is crucial for interpreting Psalm 8.

Verse 1a boldly claims that YHWH is Lord (*'adon*). This is the language a subject uses in the presence of a superior, especially a king (e.g., 1 Sam. 24:8; 1 Kgs. 1:17; 3:17). The NRSV translation, "Sovereign," captures the essence of the Hebrew well and situates the psalm as address to royalty. The majesty of the divine name is known throughout the entire earth. To speak of YHWH's "name" is a way of affirming God's presence (immanence) while preserving the understanding of divine loftiness (transcendence).[1] God is fully present throughout the

1. See the book of Deuteronomy, for example, with its frequent references to "the place where YHWH will cause the name to dwell" (e.g., Deut. 12:5, 11, 21; 14:23). The idea is that God can dwell in the heavens but be fully present with the people at the temple where the divine name dwells.

Homiletical Perspective

We gather today to celebrate Trinity Sunday. The preacher's work is not so much to enable the congregation to understand this mystery of one God in three divine persons, but rather to acknowledge God as an incomprehensible mystery, love far beyond our ability to grasp. The message is heard throughout Psalm 8 as it gives forth the reasons for praising God.

We gather today to give glory to the Divine and to recognize that without the Trinity our Christian lives make little sense, for we draw meaning and purpose from this mystery. We are called to remember with deep gratitude and great responsibility what makes for our Christian living, that is, a sharing in the rhythm of God's own life, the life of the triune God.

Indeed, the Trinity and our participation in this loving relationship of persons are very important for our daily living. In the Trinity we discover the model of perfect love. God as Trinity is an eternal exchange of love. The love of the Father (Mother) and the Son (Redeemer) is the Holy Spirit. What we celebrate and believe is a communion of love enabling us to become the community of God's love. We know and believe that Scripture has told us the story of God, who breaks into our history sharing divine life with us. Scripture introduces us to God who creates us in God's own image and likeness (Gen. 1). In the Word we encounter God who became like us and gave us

Psalm 8

Theological Perspective

more of these three foci, it simply may have been time, by the fourteenth century, formally to call attention to a central Christian conviction: though we experience God in a variety of ways (perhaps even more than three!), the *unity and coherence* of God's full reality trumps our respective attachments to one or another of the ways we experience God.

This demands respecting difference, one of the things that Christians do not have a very good track record of accomplishing. By affirming that God is one, that God is present with us in many ways, *and* that these ways are never susceptible to our complete intellectual encompassment, we see that diversity is at the very heart of God. Respect for diversities of many kinds is therefore part of our calling as responsible persons of faith.

Our psalmist today talks about both human distance from God and our connection with God. The latter is seen as the basis for human dignity. This way of thinking is both promising and problematic; it makes a vital theological point, but its interpretation over history has come at a huge cost.

The psalmist is very good at distancing us from God. One twentieth-century philosopher talked about this kind of separation as if we and God were on opposite sides of a major river—in his illustration the Rubicon. We are led to understand ourselves and God to be on different sides of something—but what, actually? Here is a way to frame it: God is maker of heaven and earth; we are not.

It is one thing to recognize that we are not God; indeed, this is good. It is another to believe that we are so separated from God that no effective connection exists between God and us. It was for this reason that God-with-us, Immanuel, came into the picture. Jesus represents this face of God. We are connected, but still are not the same as Jesus—and yet not completely different from God either. Trying to sort out doctrine is like walking an intellectual tightrope. That is one of the reasons it is so important to celebrate the *unity-in-diversity* of God on this feast day.

Our psalmist states not only that somehow we are significantly different from God, but also that we have a particular standing in the grand scheme of things (vv. 5–8). This line of thinking, also reflected in the first chapter of Genesis, has driven a historically dominant interpretation of how human beings are responsible agents in the world, particularly in relationship with other creatures and peoples in places that we or our ancestors have perhaps invaded or colonized. As history has unfolded, many of what we today call "developed" nations have been

Pastoral Perspective

searching depth of poetry, the discovery of history and time, and the disciplined explorations of theology and philosophy. The biblical witness is also aware that this consciousness can have difficult consequences. Psalm 144:4 notes the cruel nature of having knowledge of our mortality: our "days are like a passing shadow." Job 7:16–20 is almost a parody of the wonder of Psalm 8: "What are human beings, that you make so much of them, that you set your mind on them, visit them every morning, test them every moment?"

The biblical witness is well aware of the pain and struggle that adhere to this wonderful knowledge. Our discovery of ourselves can lead to individual isolation, anxiety over our mortality, the possibility of meaninglessness, and our acceptance of lesser definitions of ourselves, and consequently the deeding over of ourselves to the lesser powers. That brings us back to the question that the psalmist raises in this passage, a question most of us seek to avoid, but also a question we will be seeking to answer, in one way or another, all of our lives: Who am I? Why do I exist? What is the purpose of my life?

The psalmist calls to us from several thousand years ago, asking us to consider the nature of our lives and to consider how we often seek to answer the questions of our lives in our twenty-first-century context. We live in a reductionistic, individualistic age. Each of us is told that we as individuals bear the burden for developing our own meaning, that the community is only oppressive and opportunistic. This emphasis has brought us great movements for justice and for the dignity of each person, but it has also left us feeling lonely and lost and alienated.

For all of his "primitive" approach, the psalmist is well aware that we cannot avoid answering this hunger for meaning. We will not be able to sustain ourselves for long as heroic individuals. We will find solace somewhere. If it cannot be in an authentic, intentional community, it will be in tribalism, in increasingly closed and repressive communities, which offer us shelter from the nagging void of meaninglessness. We have seen far too many examples of this kind of movement in the twentieth and twenty-first centuries: oppression and violence and murder and slaughter, all in the name of the lesser god that has offered us shelter from the storm of meaninglessness.

The psalmist notes an example of how we abdicated our closeness with God by allowing the lesser powers to tell us who we are. We have used the "dominion" of verse 6, stated earlier in Genesis 1:28,

Exegetical Perspective

whole earth through the name, without being contained at any single place. There are textual difficulties in the Hebrew of verse 1b that are not easily resolved, but the basic idea of YHWH's glory being upon or above the heavens seems clear. To speak of the majesty of God's name that fills the earth and the divine glory above the heavens may be the psalmist's way of using two extremes ("earth" and "heavens") to say that YHWH's majestic glory abides throughout the entire cosmos.[2] From the images of majestic royalty and heavenly heights, verse 2 shifts the focus to "babes and infants." It is a curious verse because of this image and the lack of any clear clues as to the identity of "foes," "enemy," and "avenger." Since this language occurs between the previous references to earth and heavens, and the following verses (vv. 3–8) will take up other creation images, the enemies may be understood as those chaotic forces that God reins in to establish an ordered world. In a mysterious way, the babbling of children is a source of strength ("bulwark") that helps keep hostile forces at bay and so contributes to the well-being of the created world.

Verses 3–4 contrast the magnitude of the heavens and the finitude of human beings. The psalmist's eyes turn upward toward the endless expanse of the night sky, filled with the moon and stars. Importantly, these phenomena are not just "out there," but are described as products of God's creative power—"the work of [YHWH's] fingers." This is precisely what makes the question that follows so acute. If YHWH is intensely engaged with the heavens and luminaries, how can there possibly be time to attend to human beings? Divine care toward humans is expressed through two images: God *remembers* and *visits* them ("mindful of them" and "care[s] for them," NRSV). Both words can point to God's saving and sustaining care (e.g., Gen. 8:1 and Exod. 2:24 for "remember"; Ps. 65:9 and Jer. 15:15 for "visit"). What is more, God's memory and visitation extend to all humans, not just Israel. The term translated as "mortals" is literally "son of man"—an expression that refers to flesh and blood, mortal, humans. Although the term takes on messianic and christological connotations in later Jewish and Christian thought, it originally designated a member of the human species. This again intensifies the question, What is the place, the role, of human beings in the grand scheme of the cosmos?

2. This literary technique is known as merismus, the use of contrasting parts to express the totality of a whole.

Homiletical Perspective

the divine self as the Son of God who promised to make the divine home in us (John 14:23) and send us the Spirit who will teach us everything. The whole cosmos reflects the reality of the relationship of the Trinity; yet in all of this, we only get a glimpse into the mystery we call God. We resort to talking in images, sometimes from Scripture, sometimes from our ordinary lives, in order to capture, if only for a moment, that which by faith we believe.

In the gift of psalm we now sing of the sovereignty of God and our human dignity. The words of the psalm contrast the finite nature of humans with God's infinite majesty and extol the dignity and power to which God has raised humankind. We take note of how this psalm of praise begins and ends, acclaiming God's name over all the earth. With the psalmist we are in awe at the infinite variety of God's plan and are humbled by God's generosity in making us cocreators of the earth and guardians of our planet (v. 6). We receive with gratitude the mandate to care for all God's creatures and to tend the land and the sea and the very air we breathe. We receive with gentle reverence the creative works of God's fingers (vv. 7–8)!

The preacher might invite those gathered to consider the work of their own hands. Have they ever created something, built their own home, written a poem, composed a song, painted a portrait, planted a garden? With delight we invite others to experience our creation as we cherish and share what is ours. Can they remember their awe and wonder at the birth of their own child, overwhelmed and amazed at the fruit of their mutual self-giving? Then, just perhaps, they can sing with penetrating joy the praise of a God who has created each of us and the whole world.

The preacher may also choose to focus the attention of the hearers on this gift of dominion over the works of God's hands, which beckons us to celebrate joyfully and to care for one another and all that God has created. Our gaze turning inward, we examine the way we live, the respect we owe to one another and ourselves and the earth. We might begin to understand and appreciate our role in this world, coming into awareness that creation is not yet finished. God is at work even now and remains in the world at work in all the actions of creatures. When we cooperate in carrying out God's plan for the world, a plan that involves conquering sin and evil, enabling all people to share in divine life, then we are truly God's coworkers.

If the preacher chooses to highlight the reflective question inherent in verse 4—"What are human

Psalm 8

Theological Perspective

grounded on this deep separation between human beings and our fellows-in-creation, because we have celebrated our being only a "little lower than God"—we believe we are higher than anything else.

This has contributed to a disastrous outcome, ranging from global warming to the extinction of many species of life to the commodifying of nonhuman creatures as valuable chiefly insofar as they contribute something to human well-being, and our denigration of peoples somehow not like us—including practices such as human trafficking and genocide. This view, which sees at least some human beings and God on one side of the Rubicon and all others on the other, is in need of revision. A thoughtful engagement with the *unity* of God, which is what Trinity Sunday is all about, can help us see that we are given a special responsibility to be in the world as God's servants, precisely to serve as *stewards*, not *owners*, of the world about us.

In sum, if we take seriously what Trinity Sunday is all about, and affirm with the psalmist the last line of this biblical poem—"O LORD, our Sovereign, how majestic is your name in all the earth!" (v. 9)—then we declare loyalty to a divine sovereign that we experience in many ways (including at least Creator, Redeemer, and Sustainer—the "persons" of the Trinity). This loyalty calls us to serve as thoughtful champions for—and neighbors of—all others who reside on the same side of the Rubicon with us. The real separation is between our primordial Creator and *all* creatures, not between some of us as called apart and our fellows in creation. Recognizing *that* vast oneness, respecting diversities that cross even species lines, is a truly inspiring and hope-giving way to celebrate the fullness of the Trinity.

DAVID G. TRICKETT

Pastoral Perspective

to answer our own anxieties rather than taking care of God's creation. We have greatly weakened ourselves and our ecosystem because we have allowed the power of money to tell us who we are. We all have come to believe that if we can just get enough "stuff," we will lose that gnawing hunger that seems permanently rooted in our hearts—"Who am I?"—and we will feel better. If we can just touch the hem of the products, we will be healed.

So, yes, Job's complaints about human existence resonate in us, but the author of Psalm 8 asks us to consider another answer, that we are created by a loving God who has given us "godlike" characteristics: transcendence, individual consciousness, and awareness of ourselves and others. That we are even able to contemplate the questions of human existence, that we even have awareness of ourselves, says the psalmist in her wonderful poetry here, is a gift. Yes, a gift of God—burdensome as it sometimes seems—a gift of God that carries great joy, great possibilities. I have life! We have life! We know it!

The psalmist asks us to live in gratitude and in wonder for our relationship to God. God is author of life and sustainer of life. In our time, especially, we are asked to to step out of anxiety and despair and move into gratitude: we have life, and we know it. Another psalm puts it so well: "for the wonder of your works, for the wonder of myself, I thank you" (Ps. 139:14 JB). Here in Psalm 8 we are reminded of great possibilities for ourselves, possibilities that are nurtured and grow out of the splendid gifts of God: transcendence, gratitude, loving, and compassion. Let us find ourselves and our answers to ourselves and for ourselves in these gifts of a loving God.

NIBS STROUPE

Exegetical Perspective

On the heels of this existential question, verses 5–8 affirm that the role of humans on earth is significant indeed. First, humans are also the products of God's creativity. Second, they are very special products and stand only "a little lower than God." On the one hand, this statement is a bit cryptic, because the word translated as God (*'elohim*) can mean gods—a possible allusion to heavenly beings or the divine council (cf. Ps. 82). The ambiguity frustrates precision but serves quite well to illustrate the mystery that characterizes the Divine—a point well made on Trinity Sunday. On the other hand, while verse 5 is cryptic, it is clear that humans hold an exalted position. The structure of the verse in Hebrew qualifies this position in an important way.

> Yet you have made them *a little lower than God,*
> *with glory and honor* you have crowned them.

In this chiastic arrangement, YHWH's work of "making" and "crowning" surrounds the status of humans. Just as the psalm's structure claims that humans are surrounded by the sovereignty of YHWH (vv. 1a, 9), verse 5 asserts that human status ("lower than God," "glory and honor") is totally the result of God's creativity that surrounds humankind. As J. Clinton McCann Jr. notes, human status is "derivative."[3] Human vocation, described in verses 6–8 in language evocative of Genesis 1:26, is to exercise care for other creatures in the same way that God "remembers" and "visits" humans. Anything less would be a denial of YHWH's sovereignty and an abdication of the role God envisions for humankind.

Although identical to verse 1a, the words in verse 9 take on added texture and depth. Heavens, earth, humans, and creatures are products of and responsible to the sovereign YHWH.

V. STEVEN PARRISH

Homiletical Perspective

beings that you are mindful of them?"—then we might take a journey of remembrance back to our incorporation into this divine relationship, namely, our baptism. For us who believe, our immersion into this mystery—this love relationship of Father, Son, and Holy Spirit—becomes the very source of our life and is at the heart of our faith. The image of the newborn infant, this child of God, born of love to give and receive love, is most transparent of the cocreative love relationship of humanity with Divinity and, in light of the gift of baptism, one that we can truly appreciate.

Finally, the preacher might challenge the congregation to grapple with their responsible presence to a global society threatened by a culture of death and destruction. While our hearts sing the praises of our Creator, Redeemer, and Sanctifier, our consciences are ever aware of our failure to live in their image. We are crowned with glory and honor and made a little lower than God (v. 5), yet we at times try to destroy that image of God within ourselves and in the world around us. When we do not love, we destroy God's image within us. When we hate, use violence, kill, disregard, and discard, we are destroying God's image. This psalm and this feast call us to a responsible awareness that it is God who is love who has made us in that image of God. So we must be people who love, who give of ourselves, always reaching out in praise and in love for one another and for all the earth.

CONSTANCE M. KOCH, O.P

---

3. J. Clinton McCann Jr., "The Book of Psalms," in *The New Interpreter's Bible* (Nashville: Abingdon, 1996), 4:712.

2 Corinthians 13:11-13

¹¹Finally, brothers and sisters, farewell. Put things in order, listen to my appeal, agree with one another, live in peace; and the God of love and peace will be with you. ¹²Greet one another with a holy kiss. All the saints greet you.

¹³The grace of the Lord Jesus Christ, the love of God, and the communion of the Holy Spirit be with all of you.

Theological Perspective

Paul ends this painful letter with an appeal to order, mutual agreement, and peace, qualities much needed in the fractious Corinthian community. He links the presence of "the God of love and peace" (v. 11c) to that community with their movement toward such goals.

It would be easy to miss the link between the closing exhortations and closing Trinitarian benediction. It seems clear that they are linked, in that the very qualities that are to characterize the Christian community already characterize the relations that exist within the Trinity: order, mutual agreement, and peace.

Recent decades have seen an explosion of theological work on the doctrine of the Trinity, a concept of the Deity which had so often seemed to be an incomprehensible metaphysical formulation from an earlier age. Today it has returned to the center of theological reflection among numerous leading Catholic, Orthodox, and Protestant theologians.

The rediscovery of the Trinity has been deeply affected by the urgent need to reconceive the relationality of the human person in a profoundly brutal era. The *social Trinity* has surged to the forefront of theological reflection as a paradigm for what it means to be human and to relate humanely to our fellow Christians and all neighbors.

Pastoral Perspective

The church that Paul addresses in 2 Corinthians offers the comforting assurance that today's church did not invent congregational conflict. Pastors and other church people tell frightening stories of when the congregation's governing body changed the locks on the doors while a church staff member was on vacation, of how passive-aggressive leaders of a congregation organized a telephone campaign to plan a congregational boycott, of how a congregational leadership meeting ended with one leader offering to solve his differences with another through the exchange of fisticuffs, of allegations and accusations that, regardless of their veracity or relevancy, threatened congregational unity and mission.

Similar nightmares fill the memories and the lives of too many church folks, and they filled the lives of the congregation in Corinth. Paul lived with this congregation for a couple of years, and he corresponded with them by letter on at least five occasions. After his initial stay with them, he returned at least twice. Now a rival group of "superapostles" within the congregation has challenged his authority and his competency (chap. 10). While we hear of the "superapostles" only in Paul's words, they are apparently missionaries who claim that both their eloquence and their miraculous powers far exceed Paul's own. The rival group has fractioned and

Exegetical Perspective

The conclusions of Paul's letters reveal the apostle's concerns as much as his openings. Ancient rhetoric demanded that speeches conclude with an emotional recapitulation of the whole communication. This Paul does through the exhortation (v. 11) and a closing benediction (v. 13) that coordinates grace, love, and fellowship with Christ, God, and the Holy Spirit. The final three verses of 2 Corinthians exhort the church to peace and concord, extend warm greetings all around, and sign off with a graceful Trinitarian blessing. Thus the closing words impart a sense of serenity, in contrast with the turbulent turn the letter takes at chapter 10.[1]

The lection begins with a formulaic "finally" (literally, "as for the remaining") signaling the epistle's conclusion. What remains, besides the exchange of greetings all around (v. 12) and Paul's closing prayer (v. 13), is a final hortatory moment, expressed in five second-person plural imperatives (v. 11a). Most commentators regard the NRSV translation of the first of these imperatives, "farewell," as erroneous. The same verb in 1 Thessalonians 5:16 clearly means "rejoice"—likewise probably here. Objections to translating it thus allege an incongruity of Paul's

Homiletical Perspective

At the end of 2 Corinthians' many ups and downs come these three sweet verses. After the storm of tears, rebukes, recriminations, and self-justifications this letter represents, they appear as something of a rainbow. Certainly the last verse, beloved for its liturgical use (in the worship of all of Judeo-Christian history, it is hard to imagine that there is a verse recited more often), seems to have the power in and of itself to set things straight. Straightness, tidiness, or Myers-Briggs J-ness is one of the aims of this short passage: "put things in order"; "agree"; "live in peace"; "kiss" (Paul doesn't say, "Kiss and make up," but presumably this is as close as a first-century theologian comes to that injunction. He is certainly concerned that the Corinthians be reconciled, with each other and with him).

The verses give off a whiff of desiderata. They sound like something an ecclesial Bobby McFerrin would have written: "Put things in order." "Don't worry." "Go placidly." "Agree." "Wear sunscreen." "Live in peace." The problem with the end of 2 Corinthians is like the problem with many desiderata. The advice seems a bit quick. Whether the last few verses of 2 Corinthians represent a rainbow or a makeup kiss, they seem a bit tacked on. Are they forced? Are they sincere? Do they represent something that Paul feels must be said but that he cannot

---

1. Most modern scholarship maintains that chapters 10–13 constituted the body of a separate letter (see 2:4) written before the events eliciting the sense of relief and consolation Paul expresses in chapter 7.

2 Corinthians 13:11-13

Theological Perspective

To say that God is triune is to mean that God is social in nature. It is also to say that those made in the image of God are likewise intrinsically social. There is one God, and the unity of this one God is absolute; yet this God is described in Scripture as three persons: Father, Son, and Holy Spirit. Scripture speaks primarily of the roles that each person plays *in relation to human salvation*: the Father sends the Son to redeem the God-created world, the Son lives and dies for the world, the Spirit draws people to salvation and into community. The Bible also gives glimpses into the extraordinarily mysterious and holy internal life of the Trinity.

The creeds affirm that the Son is "eternally begotten of the Father," of one being and one substance with the Father. The fully divine Son also became human through his incarnation, suffered, died, and was raised on our behalf, to win salvation. The Western church affirms that the Holy Spirit eternally proceeds from the Father and the Son, meaning that the Spirit always has been, always is, and always will be flowing out of the very existence of the Father and the Son—kind of like the good and vital "spirit" that flows out of a joyful relationship between a husband and wife over many years. The whole church affirms that the Spirit plays a leading role in sustaining God's people today.

It is easy to think of the solitary Father being first, choosing then to beget the Son, and then the Spirit proceeding from Father and Son together. But Scripture describes an *eternal* relationship between Father, Son, and Spirit. There never was a time when God was not three persons. Father, Son, and Spirit were present in creation (Gen. 1:26–28; Prov. 8; Col. 1:15); they have been in relationship since "before the foundation of the world" (John 17:24). Yet there have been historical stages in God's relationship with humanity, including the decisive stage in which God as the Son took on human nature in Jesus, and the succeeding stage in which the Spirit has been poured out upon the church. The interaction with humanity has affected God; for example, in the incarnation, God for the first time takes human nature into the divine nature through the experience of Jesus the Son. The three persons of the one God have related in dynamic and varying ways to the world at different stages, even while eternally coexisting as Father, Son, and Spirit.

At times in Scripture we are given glimpses into the quality of the relationship between Father, Son, and Spirit. This is perhaps nowhere depicted more sublimely than in Jesus' prayer in John 17, one of the most exalted and dazzling sections of the entire

Pastoral Perspective

fractured the congregation, and their conflict is real. Now Paul plans to return to Corinth, and he does so at the height of the conflict, when he is most vulnerable and when the congregation faces the real possibility of schism.

In this time of vulnerability, folks in the pews can relate to Paul's first two directives to the church of Corinth. His first directive, which speaks to people in conflict in every generation, invites them into a time of self-examination and self-improvement. It continues the theme of verse 5 requiring folks to "examine" and "test" themselves. His directive to "listen to me" (not those other "apostles") continues his efforts to restore his authority. The superapostles threaten Paul's authority and apostleship, and his reputation within the congregation begins to diminish. His response attempts to restore that authority, suggesting that the community may find their way out of this conflict and restore unity by finding the fault within.

People in our pews can relate to this response. When confronted with a situation of conflict, they understand the tendency to hurl accusations at the other and to assume the identity of the innocent victim. While a mature approach to conflict can lead to meaningful conversation and mutual understanding, respect, and growth, more often folks allow conflict to alienate the parties and to break relationship. Paul's relationships have become tenuous, and they could lead to brokenness.

While Paul's initial directives are not without a reasonable purpose, he does not limit his concluding words to his self-defense and authority restoration. In short form, he returns to the major theme of the brokenness of Christ's body within the Corinthian church. His next two directives, "be of one mind" (NRSV "agree with one another") and "live in peace," stress the centrality of unity and relationship within the body.

Like a good mother, Paul demonstrates a protective instinct to ensure the survival of that flawed community that he birthed. Beyond that personal motivation, Beverly Gaventa, New Testament professor at Princeton Theological Seminary, asserts that for Paul "the relationship among believers has a Christological warrant; it is based directly on God's action in Jesus Christ. Believers do not belong to themselves . . . believers belong to Christ, and the relationships among believers must reflect the One to whom they belong."[1]

---

1. Beverly Gaventa, *Texts for Preaching: A Lectionary Commentary Based on the NRSV—Year A* (Louisville, KY: Westminster John Knox Press, 1995), 343.

telling the Corinthians to rejoice after the verbal drubbing the last four chapters of the letter administered. However, an exhortation to "cheer up"—translating the imperative more colloquially—fits well in this context. The exasperation Paul expresses in chapters 10–13 is due largely to the Corinthians' fawning on competing evangelists critical of him. Paul would rather not play the disciplinarian when he next visits (see 12:20, 13:1–2) or use "the authority that the Lord has given [him] for building up and not for tearing down" (13:10).

The second imperative in verse 11 is translated variously, since the verb in Greek is ambiguous in voice. This form can bear both reflexive and passive meanings. "Put things in order" is how the NRSV renders *katartizesthe*, but "pull yourselves together" more nearly approximates the reflexive sense. It can also mean "be restored [by God]" when taken as passive voice.[2] Either coheres with Paul's prayer in 13:9 for their *katartisis*, their "restoration" to wholeness. Paul's audience could have felt both reflexive and passive meanings; modern readers need not limit the sense to either.

The third imperative (*parakaleisthe*) has the same ambiguity of verbal force and also a range of meanings from "exhort or encourage" to "console." This verb *parakaleō* and the cognate noun *paraklēsis* are extensively and markedly employed in the opening thanksgiving of the letter (1:3–7) with the sense of "console" and "consolation." The reflexive use of this verb in 13:11 as "exhort one another" makes sense as a closing exhortation to take responsibility for the state of the church. Various renderings of the passive work too: "be exhorted" (NRSV: "listen to my appeal"); alternatively, "be consoled," that is, in light of Paul's preceding rebuke. Following this latter, one of the earliest Latin commentators on the epistle urges that "before there will be any consolation, let them forsake their present predilection."[3]

The fourth and fifth imperatives entail no such lexical problems. The NRSV's "agree with one another" can be given more literally as "think the same thing" or "set your mind on the same thing." "Live in peace" (NRSV) admonishes the Corinthians with respect to relations within the church, not with outsiders as in Romans 12:18. We can read these final two imperatives in light of the factionalism previously marring the church (see 1 Cor. 3). More

say with feeling? After three chapters of ugly wrangling with Satan's ministers (11:14–15), it is difficult to see how Paul can move so swiftly to this pretty benediction.

There are plenty of pastors who can empathize with Paul, of course. Embroiled in conflict, exhausted with defending themselves, feeling not merely underappreciated but wrongly criticized, some pastors today know the lure of the easy benediction only too well. They live week by week with the temptation to paper over discord with a few liturgical syllables, a hasty wave, or an insincere smile. Most pastors also know the risk to credibility and integrity that those choices represent. How can a preacher pronounce the blessing on a congregation that is at odds with him or her? The question is a vexing one. If a "don't worry, be happy" attitude to church conflict is not an option, how does a pastor of a church in conflict end Sunday's service? More challenging still is the question, how does an embattled preacher find a word for his or her congregation in this text?

In the identification with the conflict between the apostle Paul and the Corinthians lies one homiletical approach to these verses. A clue to understanding Paul's ability to finish a fight on a note of harmony is suggested by the expanded benediction of verse 13. Apart from 2 Corinthians, each of Paul's undisputed letters concludes with a benediction that references Christ's grace—only Christ's grace. "The grace of the Lord Jesus be with you" appears at the end of the first letter to the Corinthians. "May the grace of our Lord Jesus Christ be with your spirit, brothers and sisters" is used at Galatians' conclusion. None of the other letters' sign-offs mentions the other members of the Trinity. However, at the end of 2 Corinthians Paul stretches his customary benediction to include such references. The question of why Paul makes this shift is an interesting one.

The change is too significant to be considered a rhetorical accident or fillip. Paul is making one last push to reach the Corinthians. Paul seems driven by the need to offer the Corinthians wider and deeper resources for this troubled chapter in their life. He expands his customary benediction in order to underscore the resources that lie behind the grace of Christ. He believes the Corinthians need to be reminded of the love of God available to them. Perhaps most of all, they need to be reminded of the Holy Spirit's power to create communion. A sermon that focuses on the power of the Holy Spirit to create and sustain the fellowship of the church through periods of division is one way to make appropriate use of this text.

2. Thus M. J. Harris, *The Second Epistle to the Corinthians* (Grand Rapids: Eerdmans, 2005), 930–42.

3. Thus the anonymous fourth-century Roman cleric known as Ambrosiaster (my trans.), who authored the first complete Latin commentary on Paul.

2 Corinthians 13:11-13

Theological Perspective

Bible. In this lengthy prayer, Jesus depicts the internal relational dynamic within the Trinity as involving endless mutual self-giving, a delighted deflection of attention to one another, and joyful love. The followers of Jesus are described as the blessed recipients of the overflow of this love; they are beginning to participate in this same quality of relationship that exists within the Father-Son bond.

In this prayer the boundaries between the divine Persons are extraordinarily permeable. They exist, literally, "in" each other. It is not even correct to say merely that the Son is in the Father; this would be logical to our minds, but it is not what Jesus says. The Son is in the Father, and the Father is in the Son, and the disciples are in both. There are no hard and fast boundary lines between Father, Son, and disciples; love appears to have dissolved them—*and this is precisely the goal.* Jürgen Moltmann refers to the "intimate indwelling and complete interpenetration of the persons [of the Trinity] in one another."[1] Jesus seems to be praying that this kind of love, *a love that can dissolve all kinds of boundaries and divisions,* will complete its work on those human beings in whom it has already begun—that is, in his disciples—and will eventually spread to others in the world who will be drawn into the community of faith.

In the end, the goal is a cosmic unity that emerges when love dissolves interpersonal boundaries so that all divine and human persons will spiritually be one.[2] This is the kind of oneness enjoyed by the triune God, and human beings are invited to participate in it through faith. It is the very goal of God in the world, and we know it by faith as the coming shape of the human future, when all the tragedy, difficulty, and limits of our relationships with each other will be overcome at last.[3]

DAVID P. GUSHEE

Pastoral Perspective

Paul reminds folks in our pews that our conflicts, whether situated around the pettiness of our insecurities or the significance of the honest interpretation of Scripture, reach far beyond broken human relationship. Our bickering and brokenness reach far beyond a door slammed in one's face or a friendship ended. As people allow the unity of Christ to become more and more fractured, they unwittingly and unfaithfully make the dangerous claim that we no longer belong to Christ. Now they give themselves over to that which is not Christ. They give themselves to inappropriate anger, or the destructiveness of hatred, or the poison of self-absorption.

Paul's call to unification may seem less than helpful to folks who know the overwhelming presence of hurt and brokenness. They know the experience of the loss of sacred friendship. They have seen the hope of reconciliation erode over years wasted in divisive animosity. They have heard the silence of adversaries talking around and over one another, rather than with and to one another. So, while they understand the call for the adversarial "superapostles" who threaten them to engage in a process of self-examination, they often perceive as impossible the directive to find community. "The time for discussion has passed," people easily say. "The animosity is too all-consuming," others add. "Our differences are irreconcilable," some offer. In many situations—ecclesial, political, military, interpersonal—the road to unity seems forever closed, and it seems beyond human ability to find that reconciliation.

Paul's final words give voice to the possibility of hope even in the despair of dark brokenness. He voices the assurance that people do not face this overwhelming challenge alone. As in all of Paul's undisputed letters, he acknowledges and claims the presence of the grace of God. As God has proven time and again, God can bring about resurrection, even when death is a certain reality. God can find reconciliation, even when that road seems forever closed.

In his benediction—which many people in church pews will recognize only as an indication that the service is concluded—Paul gives the greatest hope to the church of Corinth and the church of today. Far from offering a satisfactory treatise on the nature of the Holy Trinity, these verses point to the relational nature of God and remind us of the potential of relationship through God. As the Gospel writer of Mark says, "For mortals it is impossible, but not for God; for God all things are possible" (10:27).

DAVID M. BENDER

---

1. Jürgen Moltmann, *History and the Triune God* (New York: Crossroad, 1992), 86.
2. The language comes from John D. Zizioulas, *Being as Communion* (Crestwood, NY: St. Vladimir's Seminary Press, 1985).
3. This essay depends heavily on David P. Gushee, *Only Human* (San Francisco: Jossey-Bass, 2005).

Exegetical Perspective

recent events may have created new lines of division or exacerbated residual old ones. The entire church will hardly have embraced those other teachers, whom the apostle depicts in grim terms (see 10:12; 11:1–6, 12–15). While it is doubtless too simplistic to speak of pro-Paul and anti-Paul elements at Corinth, his correspondence shows the apostle did not have carte blanche with the whole church, but was often compelled to argue, explain, and defend his conduct as an apostle.

The relation between the string of imperatives and the following "peace benediction" (v. 11b) is unclear. Does the future tense—"and the God of love and peace will be with you"—signify that God's presence will ensure that the Corinthians fulfill the mandates of Paul's imperatives? Does the first "and" hint that, rather, God's continued favor depends on their hearkening to the admonition? The priority of grace in Paul's thought weighs in for the former interpretation; but as Paul employs a clearly conditional peace benediction elsewhere (Gal. 6:16), the latter reading cannot be fully excluded here, particularly in light of the stern tone taken in the latter part of this letter (e.g., 13:10).

The ritual exchange of a "holy kiss" Paul mentions (v. 12)—a predecessor of the later liturgical kiss of peace—would not have been an erotic kiss, but more like the greeting still practiced in Mediterranean and Middle Eastern cultures. The extension of this greeting from "all the saints" to the Corinthian Christians testifies to the sense of corporate, but not merely local, identity animating the church.

The final verse and closing benediction solemnly express the realities and persons constituting the world of faith of the author and his audience: the grace that comes from Christ, the "free gift" (Rom. 5:15); God's love which sent him; and the "fellowship [*koinōnia*; NRSV: "communion"] of the Holy Spirit" (13:13). Is the Holy Spirit that in which believers have "fellowship" or share in, or is the fellowship meant that which the Spirit itself grants? Despite linguistic arguments for the former, the latter interpretation is not implausible, as Paul elsewhere coordinates the work of the Spirit and Christ (see Gal. 4:6 and Rom. 1:4). While the apostle makes no attempt to sort out the relations between God's love, Christ's grace, and the Holy Spirit's fellowship, this verse found some application in the Trinitarian controversies of the fourth century.

STEPHEN A. COOPER

Homiletical Perspective

Another approach for dealing homiletically with this passage is suggested by the calendar. Though Trinity Sunday gives opportunity for the examination of the great mysteries of hypostatic union, perichoresis, and the *filioque*, some congregations will prefer more homely truths. The mystical realities associated with the doctrine of the Trinity are often too abstract for all but the most motivated listeners to consider for more than a few moments. An exploration of the liturgical practice of benediction might be used to engage the congregation in more concrete ways.

There are a number of interesting questions about the practice of benediction. Some have to do with the ritual's symbolic meanings. Why do some traditions make the sign of the cross during the benediction? Is it better symbolism to raise only the right hand or to raise both? Should only clergy be authorized to give the benediction? Why or why not? The history of the practice can also provoke interest. The practice of raising a hand in blessing the people at the end of the worship service did not become common until the late Middle Ages. The ways the ritual has changed since, its association with the Trinitarian formula, and its roots in Jewish worship may represent fruitful avenues of inquiry. Finally, the issue of power associated with the benediction may be of particular interest to some congregations. What kind of power or authority does the Trinitarian formula suggest? Are there options for wording the benediction that emphasize power? Are there gestures that might de-emphasize it? Which would be most appropriate to your understanding of the Trinity?

Finally, it might be possible to explore the Trinitarian elements of today's text in connection with the history of Trinity Sunday. Popularized in the West after the death of Thomas à Becket (he was consecrated as bishop on Trinity Sunday in 1162), it enjoys a peculiar association with his story. His story and the story of other lives propelled by the grace of the Lord Jesus Christ, the love of God, and the communion of the Holy Spirit make fitting use of this peculiar but sweet passage.

JANA CHILDERS

Matthew 28:16-20

¹⁶Now the eleven disciples went to Galilee, to the mountain to which Jesus had directed them. ¹⁷When they saw him, they worshiped him; but some doubted. ¹⁸And Jesus came and said to them, "All authority in heaven and on earth has been given to me. ¹⁹Go therefore and make disciples of all nations, baptizing them in the name of the Father and of the Son and of the Holy Spirit, ²⁰and teaching them to obey everything that I have commanded you. And remember, I am with you always, to the end of the age."

Theological Perspective

In the ultimate act of Matthew's drama, Jesus meets his disciples in Galilee—the land of the Gentiles (4:15)—gives them final instructions, and promises them the same empowering fellowship with the triune God that he has.

Earlier in his ministry, Jesus sent out the Twelve and gave them the authority, or power (10:1, *exousian*), to cast out unclean spirits, heal the sick, and proclaim the good news that the kingdom of heaven has come near (10:7). Jesus had been doing the same things preceding this commissioning of his closest followers. The only distinguishing mark of his ministry was teaching; Jesus did it, the disciples did not. In this final commissioning of the disciples, Jesus widens the audience—from Israel to all nations—and adds teaching to the charge of *all* of his followers.

These instructions reveal an assumption that, on the face of it, is pretty amazing. The disciples are to do what he had been doing and with more far-reaching effect.

How could they possibly do these things? They could only by the same power (28:18 *exousia*) available to Jesus. It was the power of Father, and of the Son, and of the Holy Spirit, in whose name they were to baptize disciples from all the peoples of God's creation. Jesus had been given that power, and he promised them that he would be with them to the

Pastoral Perspective

This is Trinity Sunday, but people who have cancer probably do not care. This is Trinity Sunday, but those young couples who cannot get pregnant probably do not care either. "But, this is Trinity Sunday," proclaims the worship committee. Even so, the family dealing with the wayward teenager, the couple headed for divorce, the person who has lost a job, they do not care. Does it really matter to them that God is Father, Son, and Holy Spirit? They just want to know that God is God and that God somehow knows who they are, where they are, what they are doing, and what they need.

It can be a heady discussion to talk about the Trinity. If you look up the history, it was not an easy doctrine to nail down. There is a ton of mystery that surrounds the person or persons of God. Some people seem entirely clear about it; others are confused, and still others could not care less. The truth is that preaching from a stance of trying to defend the Trinity will make for a tedious sermon and will be like firing a shot over the bow of your people's real lives.

Why do we even need a Trinity Sunday? It does not hold a candle to Christmas or Easter. It does not get a lot of press. Maybe that is because it is so confusing and we really do not know how to talk about it. The great Augustine had to reduce it to a very simple illustration. He used the example of a tree.

Exegetical Perspective

Matthew ends with words of Jesus. Not a report about the disciples or a comment by a narrator or even an expectation of the coming of the Spirit, but his voice, his commission, and his promise of his presence move the narrative into a future shaped by the good news of the kingdom—a future not only for the disciples in the text, but for all disciples always.

This resurrection appearance of Jesus to the disciples is preceded by alternating scenes of discipleship and conspiracy: the burial by Joseph of Arimathea, accompanied by Mary Magdalene and the other Mary (27:57–61); the securing of the tomb by the religious authorities and Pilate (27:62–66); the women's visit to the tomb, their conversation with the angel as the guards lie like dead men, and Jesus' appearance to them (28:1–10); and the plot of the authorities to conceal the resurrection (28:11–15). This plot is reminiscent of the intrusion of Herod's violence alongside the worshiping Gentile magi, which together shape the birth narrative (1:18–2:23). Matthew's story opens and closes with unlikely miracles, visits by angels, and trips to Galilee. Where the earlier account ends with a small child in a family of returning refugees fleeing in fear, this one features the same Immanuel in full resurrection glory with all authority over heaven and earth. The threat and promise of the birth narrative have come full circle.

Homiletical Perspective

Almost surely the reason this passage was selected as the lectionary Gospel reading for Trinity Sunday is because it includes the baptismal formula, which mentions all three persons of the Trinity. It would be a mistake, however, to imagine that we have in these verses anything like a fully developed doctrine of the Trinity. For one thing, it is simply too early in church history for that. Despite some popular misconceptions, Christian theologians do not sit around for fun in ivy-covered buildings weaving doctrines out of wisps, shadows, and thin air. Christian doctrines tend to originate like river bridges built by armies; that is, they are assembled on the fly in seasons of need and are crafted in the field to bear the weight of people marching on a mission.

The doctrine of the Trinity was not dreamed up in a theological think tank but was articulated by actual worshiping and serving Christians who, under stress and in the face of questions and challenges, were sweating it out to say with clarity just why they were willing to live a life that looked foolish to others, caring for widows and orphans, suffering persecution, and spilling their own blood—all of it for the wild notion that the Spirit had gathered them into the life of the God, the God who in Christ was making peace with the world. It was a couple of centuries after Matthew wrote his Gospel that the church

Matthew 28:16-20

Theological Perspective

end of the age (v. 20). It was in their relationship to him and his to the triune God that they would access the power to heal, proclaim, and teach.

We rarely see in the New Testament a Trinitarian formula. This passage (v. 19) may reflect one used during baptism in the Matthean community.[1] Though we should not read into this passage too much of the later developments of Trinitarian doctrine, later affirmations about the nature of God were derived from reflection on this passage, among others in the canon. Some of those later affirmations might, then, shine an interesting light on Matthew's thoughts about the nature and effects of the power that animated Jesus and was promised to those who trusted him.

Protestant theologian Arthur McGill observes that the ancient Arian controversy was not just a fourth-century-church political struggle in Alexandria or an esoteric clash of philosophical frameworks—though it certainly contained elements of both.[2] Rather, McGill argues that Arius and Athanasius—and their followers—disagreed about the very nature of God and God's power in the world and in human life. For McGill, what one believed about those issues—whether God was a singular, isolated, utterly transcendent reality or a plural, involved, immanently transcendent reality—made a profound difference in the way one lived one's life.

For Arius, the Son could not have been coeternal or coequal with the Father. Therefore, Arius argued that "there was when he was not"—implying that the Son was created by the Father, like everything else. Arius assumed that God was an utterly unique, self-contained, and self-sufficient reality. To say that there was, from eternity, a coequal partner with the Father implied, for Arius, a need or vulnerability in the Father. To say that there was need or vulnerability in the Father—in God—suggested that God could change; God could be affected by another. Given the changeableness and fragility of human life and the suffering it entails, to say that God changes was unthinkable for Arius. There must be an unchangeable reality that is unmoved by vicissitudes of mortal, finite life. God is that reality. There must be a force or power in the universe greater than that to which we must succumb. That force is God's irresistible power.

Athanasius believed that the incarnation of God in Christ revealed a different kind of God and a

Pastoral Perspective

The root is wood; the trunk is wood; the branches are wood: one wood, one substance but three different entities. Okay, so try preaching that! Short sermon. They will love it.

Perhaps we can come at it another way. What if there were no Trinity? Jesus told us to go and baptize people in the name of the Father and of the Son and of the Holy Spirit. What if we baptized people only in the name of the Father? Besides sounding awkward, it would deny the very work and person of Christ and the ongoing activity of the Spirit. It would not be a full picture of who God is. You would be immersed into the fullness of a very powerful, mysterious, but detached God. That could lead us to mere mysticism.

What if we just baptized people in the name of Jesus? "I baptize you in the name of Jesus. Amen." That would miss the person of "God the Father Almighty, the Maker of heaven and earth,"[1] that part of God that is larger than what we can see or understand and is beyond our logic and reason. It would also miss the Holy Spirit, the ongoing presence of God with us today.

What if we said only, "I baptize you in the name of the Holy Spirit"? What is missing there? Missing would be the awesomeness and creativity of God the Father and the redemptive work of Jesus Christ, who is God in human flesh. We would miss the part of God who rose from the dead to overcome our sinfulness. Please do not leave that out!

Shirley Guthrie writes, "The same God who is God over us as God the Father and Creator, and God with and for us as the incarnate Word and Son, is also God in and among us as God the Holy Spirit."[2]

You cannot go out into the world, according to Jesus, without all of that. We are immersed (or sprinkled) into the whole being of God, whether we understand it or not. We are not powerless in the world; we are not disconnected from the omnipotent God as Creator, or from the redeeming work of God in human flesh, or from the very presence of that same God in the Holy Spirit, who dwells within us and among us and sometimes outside of us. That is a tremendous gift to celebrate for people who are sitting in the pew feeling detached, isolated, alone, angry, deserted, depressed, grieving, hopeless, fearful, anxious, wounded, ashamed, and tired.

Jesus did not just send the church out to perform the ritual of baptism. The world will not be fixed by

1. *The New HarperCollins Study Bible*, rev. ed. (New York: HarperSanFrancisco, 2006), 1721, note on Matt. 28:19.
2. Arthur McGill, *Suffering: A Test of Theological Method* (Philadelphia, PA: Westminster Press, 1982).

1. The Apostles' Creed.
2. Shirley C. Guthrie, *Christian Doctrine*, rev. ed. (Louisville, KY: Westminster John Knox Press, 1994), 80.

Matthew's ending draws together many strands from the Gospel. As 28:16 sets the scene with a reference to the eleven remaining disciples, we are reminded of the betrayal and despair of Judas. The movement to Galilee, away from the center of the establishment in Jerusalem, evokes not only the birth narrative but also Jesus' move to Galilee after John's arrest (4:12–17). The mountaintop brings to mind the temptation with Satan's offer of all the splendid kingdoms of the world, which Jesus rejects in favor of the kingdom of heaven (4:8), the teachings of the Sermon on the Mount (5:1; 8:1), Jesus' retreat for prayer (14:23), his healing of the crowds (15:29), his transfiguration (17:1), and the Mount of Olives (21:1; 24:3; 26:30).

When the disciples see Jesus, they worship, but some doubt. The reference to worship points back to the magi of the birth narrative and to the women who have worshiped Jesus already in 28:9. This verb for *doubt* occurs elsewhere in the NT only in Matthew 14:31, where it again appears alongside *worship*. There Peter, after having stepped out in faith to walk on the water with Jesus, becomes frightened by the wind and begins to sink. When he is saved, the disciples worship Jesus. Matthew chooses to make room for doubt alongside worship in the wonder of the scene on the Sea of Galilee and in the glory of the resurrection. Like the presence of Thomas in John's resurrection account, this creates space for doubting worshipers now to find themselves in the resurrection story as well.

In contrast to the tentativeness of the disciples, the statement of Jesus in verses 18–20 is solid as a rock, with the fourfold repetition of the word "all" (*pas*) underscoring the complete fulfillment of God's plans for the crucified, resurrected Messiah: all authority, all nations, all that Jesus has commanded, all the days (translated "always").

Jesus' authority has been mentioned repeatedly throughout the Gospel (e.g., 7:29; 9:2–8; 21:23–27), by the crowds who acknowledge it after the Sermon on the Mount and elsewhere and by his opponents who question it. That Jesus' authority is in heaven and on earth points back to the Lord's Prayer (6:10) and to Jesus' own prayer in 11:25–27. What was already true in 11:27 is revealed in fullness in the light of the resurrection.

On the basis of that authority, Jesus commissions his disciples to go and make more disciples. Now the Gentiles, who have been regarded as the suspicious other in many parts of the narrative (e.g., 6:32; 10:5; 20:25), are included along with Israel in the sending

needed to lay down the planks in this particular Trinitarian bridge. Matthew has only a fragmentary doctrine of the Trinity. Probably about all Matthew knows at this point is that Christians must speak devoutly of Father, Son, and Holy Spirit, and that such talk did not violate the Jewish insistence upon belief in the one true God.[1]

Another reason Matthew's Gospel does not present a fully formed theology of the Trinity is because, in his particular patch of the swamp, Matthew was up to his neck in other sorts of alligators. His challenge was not, precisely how do the persons of the Godhead relate to each other?—as we said, that comes later—but, how can we get the provincial and timid followers of Jesus of Nazareth to venture out into the frightening world with the gospel?

That is the key to understanding this passage we sometimes call the Great Commission. The scene is one of near-comic irony. Jesus says, "All authority in heaven and on earth has been given to me," but nothing in the surroundings seems to support such a claim. If Jesus had been speaking to vast multitudes, rank upon rank stretching toward the horizon as far as the eye could see, with the Mormon Tabernacle Choir humming the "Hallelujah Chorus" in the background, perhaps it would seem plausible. However, Jesus is on an unnamed mountain in backwater Galilee with a congregation of eleven, down from twelve the week before, and even some of them are doubtful and not so sure why they have come to worship this day.

What Jesus tells them presses credulity even further: "Go therefore and make disciples of all nations." "Nations," by the way, does not mean "nations" in the modern sense of nation-states, but something more like "foreigners," "tribes of people who are not at all like you," or, to put it succinctly, "Gentiles." These disciples were Jews, and they knew the Scripture. God had promised Abraham that all the tribes of the earth would one day be brought into the family of God, that even the alien Gentiles would bow before Israel's God (Gen. 12:1–3); but like a lot of things in the Bible, this was a truth easier to swallow when it was a nice thought in the prayer book, rather than something you were expected to strap on your boots and get done. Telling this little band of confused and disoriented disciples that they were to herd all the peoples of the earth toward Mount Zion in the name of Jesus would be like standing in front of most congregations today—many of them small and all of them

1. See M. Eugene Boring, "Matthew," in *The New Interpreter's Bible* (Nashville: Abingdon Press, 1995), 8:504

Matthew 28:16-20

Theological Perspective

different kind of divine power. Rather than an isolated monad, God from eternity is relational; between the Father and Son, for example, there was, is, and always will be mutual self-giving. The unity within God is a "unity of love, a unity in which the identity of each party is not swallowed up and annihilated, but established." Whatever the Father does the Son does; the Father has given all things into the hand of the Son (John 5:29ff.; 3:35). God's power, then, is not self-possessive and self-preserving like that of the Gentiles, who "lord it over" others and tyrannize them (Mark 10:42). Quoting the *Epistle to Diognetus*, McGill observes that "force is no attribute of God." Rather, God's power, and that of Jesus, is self-giving.

God exercises powerfulness by giving; God nourishes the Son and creation by communicating God's own reality to them. In the strength of that sharing, when Jesus meets the coercive power that threatens to take his life, he does not protect his own identity by trying to hold on to it. He serves us by allowing it to make good on its threat, knowing that his life rests not in his power to preserve it, but in God's willingness to sustain it. In so doing, Jesus "exposes the pretense of satanic power"; that is, "dominative power is exposed as impotent, as unworthy of our awe and reverence."[3] When we understand that, we are freed from the fear that causes us to hold anxiously to our lives and our possessions and are freed to love others by sharing all that sustains us.

Jesus invites us into the mutuality and power of the divine life. He sends us to invite still others, from all nations. He does not leave us alone in that work, nor does he leave us powerless. He promises his presence and a power that does not coerce but serves and persuades.

STEPHEN B. BOYD

Pastoral Perspective

merely getting everyone wet. Saying the words "Father, Son, and Holy Spirit" is not magic. The more difficult task is that of making disciples.

Disciples are students. They are like interns. Interns are watching, practicing under supervision, asking questions, making mistakes, and learning from them. Jesus said very clearly, "'Go therefore and make disciples of all nations'" (v. 19a). Go make students of Christ. Put people in internships, into a lifelong learning process. That is a major paradigm shift from making church members or whatever else we substitute for discipleship.

Making students of Christ and immersion into the fullness of God go hand in hand. We cannot make ourselves or anyone else a student or intern of Christ without the work of the Holy Spirit. The work of the Holy Spirit is dependent upon what and who Jesus was and is. Christ keeps pointing to the Father. So therein lies the power. It is in the Trinity, the fullness of God, to which we are attached as students.

Maybe Trinity Sunday ought to be a bigger deal. It silently sits there on the liturgical calendar, offering us the entire being of God in a relationship that we do not deserve but can celebrate having. It is a day to celebrate the One to whom we belong, in life and in death, through the gift of our baptisms. It is a day the students pay tribute to the Teacher!

STEVEN P. EASON

---

3. Ibid., 76, 77, 82, 85, and 94 quoted in this paragraph and the paragraph preceding it.

Exegetical Perspective

to all nations. The hope for the Gentiles has already been expressed (4:14–16; 12:17–21), along with their exclusion (15:24), but now their inclusion is unqualified. The distinctions that marked Matthew's account of the ministry of Jesus are to be transcended in the resurrection life of the church.

The command to make disciples consists of two activities: baptizing and teaching. The baptismal formula points back to the baptism of Jesus himself in 3:13–17, in which the Spirit descends on him as the voice from heaven proclaims him the beloved Son. This is the point at which Trinity Sunday comes into view, as Jesus tells his followers to reenact his story in the baptism of new disciples, enfolding them in the life of the Trinitarian God, with the Son as their Immanuel, the Father loving them as his own, and the Spirit descending like a dove to lead them out.

The teaching is to include all that Jesus has commanded—a third evocation of the Sermon on the Mount with the other discourses surely intended here as well. Jesus' good news of the kingdom is not information to be rehearsed; rather, the commission is to teach new disciples to enact what Jesus has taught as a way of living in the world.

The teachings of Jesus are not the last word. The last word is that *there is never a last word*. The Greek does not literally say "Remember" at the opening of the last sentence, as the NRSV suggests. Jesus is not to be a memory only. "Behold!" Jesus says, "I am with you." The one who is named Immanuel, "God with us," before his birth will be with his followers all their days until the close of the age, when the kingdom, which has come near and is like a mustard seed taking root or a treasure buried in a field, will reach glorious fulfillment.

The passage offers a fitting denouement not only to the Gospel, but also to the church's celebrations of Easter and Pentecost. Although the drama and beauty of that season may be complete for the year, the postresurrection life with Jesus is always, every day, beginning anew.

Behold, Immanuel, always!

MEDA A. A. STAMPER

Homiletical Perspective

of mixed motives and uncertain convictions—and telling them, "Go into all the world and cure cancer, clean up the environment, evangelize the unbelieving, and, while you are at it, establish world peace."

That is the point, or close to it. The very fact that the task is utterly impossible throws the disciples completely onto the mercy and strength of God. The work of the church cannot be taken up unless it is true that "all authority" does not belong to the church or its resources but comes from God's wild investment of God in Jesus the Son and the willingness of the Son to be present always to the church in the Spirit.

Garret Keizer, a minister in Vermont, tells of conducting an Easter vigil in his little church. Only two people show up for the service, but Keizer nonetheless lights the paschal candle and says the prayer. "The candle sputters in the half darkness," he writes, "like a voice too embarrassed or overwhelmed to proclaim the news: 'Christ is risen.'" He goes on:

> But it catches fire, and there we are, three people and a flickering light in an old church on a Saturday evening in the spring, with the noise of the cars and their winter rusted mufflers outside. The moment is filled with ambiguities of all such quiet observances among few people, in the midst of an oblivious population in a radically secular age. The act is so ambiguous because its terms are so extreme: the Lord is with us, or we are pathetic fools.[2]

So it is always with the church. We take a fragmentary community, a fragmentary faith, a fragmentary understanding of the Trinitarian God, and we go into the world with everything Jesus has taught us. Either the Lord is with us and all authority has been given to Christ, or we are indeed pathetic fools.

THOMAS G. LONG

---

2. Garret Keizer, *A Dresser of Sycamore Trees: The Finding of a Ministry* (New York: Penguin, 1991), 73.

Isaiah 49:8-16a

8 Thus says the LORD:
In a time of favor I have answered you,
  on a day of salvation I have helped you;
I have kept you and given you
  as a covenant to the people,
to establish the land,
  to apportion the desolate heritages;
9saying to the prisoners, "Come out,"
  to those who are in darkness, "Show yourselves."
They shall feed along the ways,
  on all the bare heights shall be their pasture;
10they shall not hunger or thirst,
  neither scorching wind nor sun shall strike them down,
for he who has pity on them will lead them,
  and by springs of water will guide them.
11And I will turn all my mountains into a road,
  and my highways shall be raised up.

Theological Perspective

Even though we are reading this in Pentecost, in the ecumenical liturgical calendar, this text is also appointed for the Eighth Sunday after the Epiphany, Year A. As such, the promise of God's grace and release—following YHWH's judgment on Israel in Isaiah 1–39—ushers the church into Ash Wednesday and Lent. On this day, the church hears God's promise of continuous presence ("your walls are continually before me," v. 16) just a couple of weeks before the reality of death is spoken to begin the Lenten season ("Remember you are dust, and to dust you shall return"). God know the walls need restoration. The people stand poised to enter the time of prayer, fasting, and almsgiving with the assurance that despite death, desolation, and constant suffering, God is rebuilding.

Read in the time after Christ's Epiphany—when he is revealed as beloved of God, the one to whom humanity should listen—the church receives in this text another revelation, now spoken into our own time, whatever the age. Isaiah proclaims that the people themselves are inscribed into the palms of God's hands. See the image: when God raises a hand in gesture of blessing, we look into the divine palm as in a mirror. The gesture of blessing holds the people up to themselves as a sign of God's own compassion. One epiphany is laid upon another.

Pastoral Perspective

"All-ee, all-ee in free." The children's cry invites all who are in hiding, who have not been found or caught by the seeker, to come home. All come home free, without penalty, without cost. Calling all the children home.

The children's cry is echoed by parents in neighborhoods all over the world calling their children home: "Sally. Ishmael. Seong Im. Muhammad. Peter. Simeon. Nilanjana. Micah. Rajwant. Amrit." Come home for dinner. Home for schoolwork to be finished. Home for safety in the night.

Admittedly, home for some children is a terrifying place when parents are absent, or abusive, or addicted to various substances. For these children and for others, finding home may mean leaving home. Still, home is a place we yearn for and want with our child's yearning heart. Even those living in exile carry the seeds of this longing for generations.

That yearning is what God is touching in this passage from Isaiah. Those in exile are being called home, from the north and south, east and west, from all places far off. This vision is beyond belief to those who have been in exile for decades. Their days—no, years—have been dark with feelings of separation, loss, and abandonment. "The LORD has forsaken me, my Lord has forgotten me," they lament (v. 14).

>¹²Lo, these shall come from far away,
>   and lo, these from the north and from the west,
>   and these from the land of Syene.

>¹³Sing for joy, O heavens, and exult, O earth;
>   break forth, O mountains, into singing!
>For the L ORD has comforted his people,
>   and will have compassion on his suffering ones.

>¹⁴But Zion said, "The L ORD has forsaken me,
>   my Lord has forgotten me."
>¹⁵Can a woman forget her nursing child,
>   or show no compassion for the child of her womb?
>Even these may forget,
>   yet I will not forget you.
>¹⁶See, I have inscribed you on the palms of my hands;
>   your walls are continually before me.

Exegetical Perspective

In a basic sense, the biblical story is a narrative of a barren woman who has been given children, loses them, and then is given them back. From the barrenness of Sarai (Gen. 11:30) to the abandonment of Jerusalem/Zion ("How lonely sits the city that was once full of people!" Lam. 1:1), we arrive at Isaiah 49. There Zion is seen to be not only "unforgotten" but surrounded by children she did not even know she had. "Who has borne me these?" she asks (49:21). This is a story to give Mother Jerusalem, and Mother Church, hope.

First, Zion declares that she has been forgotten, not just by her children, but by her Lord. Here, as in Lamentations, her husband represents her Lord. "How like a widow she has become!" (Lam. 1:1) As Zion has chased after other partners (see Isa. 1:21), she fears she has been forgotten forever by the Lord: "The L ORD has forsaken me, my Lord has forgotten me" (Isa. 49:14). It is one thing to be abandoned. It is worse to be abandoned *and forgotten*.

So the Lord declares that such forgetting of Zion is impossible—as impossible indeed as a woman showing no compassion to the child of her womb (v. 15b) or forgetting her nursing child (v. 15a). This is a bond even stronger than that between husband and wife (at least in the contours of this argument). The Lord's commitment runs even deeper still: "Even

Homiletical Perspective

As a preacher reads the opening poems of Isaiah 40–55, she or he realizes the change in landscape from the previous chapters. Israel is in exile. The opening poem in chapter 40 affirms the Lord's promise to comfort Israel and to bring deliverance (40:1–3). In the context of the new day dawning for the people of God, God calls on Zion to herald the good news (40:9). However, when Zion finally does speak, she does not utter good news. Rather, it is a word of lament and rebuke against God, "The L ORD has forsaken me, my Lord has forgotten me" (49:14; cf. v. 24; cf. also Lam. 5:20). Such utterance is understandable in light of Israel's captivity in Babylon. The book of Lamentations illuminates the anguish and forsakenness Israel feels. In the opening poem of that book, five times the exiles exclaim that they have no one willing to comfort them (Lam. 1:2, 9, 16, 17, 21).

Their cry continues to echo through the ages. Many living in poverty feel alone and forgotten by God. Those in abusive relationships, those abandoned or neglected by parents and loved ones, cry out in anguish. Those battling the disease of cancer and those suffering economic hardships all feel a sense of abandonment. God has forgotten us! At one point even Jesus felt forsaken by God (Matt. 27:46).

God responds to Zion's despairing cry on this occasion with assurance that this is not so: "I can no

Isaiah 49:8-16a

Theological Perspective

This is liturgical theology. The gesture speaks. The relationship between God and God's people is established in the gathering itself. The high priest, the Lord of hosts, raises a hand, and by doing so, embodies a covenantal relationship that is as intimate as eating the body of Christ or drinking the blood or embracing the lover. To be inscribed (tattooed!) onto God's own flesh is the opposite of nailing hands to a torturous death. The inscription on God's palm proleptically reverses the sin of crucifixion by forgiving it before it even happens. With compassion, the Lord speaks as a mother assuring her infant.

Theologically, this Sunday in Lent serves as a fulcrum in the teetering shift between judgment and grace found everywhere in the Scriptures but in especially poignant measure in Isaiah owing to the majesty of the poetry. God's Word contains both judgment and grace, pain and healing, rod and staff. Isaiah 49 does not demolish the terror of Jerusalem's devastation (for in this world suffering is never done), but in its presence heaps upon the hearer images of good pastures, food and drink, shelter, paths that are not difficult to walk, joy, singing, comfort, compassion, and incredible intimacy.

Israel/Zion cries out its existential problem in the lament of verse 14: "The LORD has forsaken me, my Lord has forgotten me." Here we are, O Lord, bereft of clarity, sent into exile, shown no hope, unable to move, unbelieving. Utter loss articulates the distance between abandonment and fulfillment. On one theological level, the problem is the human need for belonging and protection. Zion is in terrible pain. The oppressor's power seems to be absolute. The cry of Isaiah 1–39 shows the people scattered, holy places destroyed, the future impossible. This text, in contrast, holds out the possibility of trust, calling the prisoners to come out of hiding. Isaiah speaks the Word of the Lord to the people's despair and sets forth for them the image of the relationship between mother and child.

Who is God here? Not just mother to a longed-for child. The people also know that God, who is steadfast and righteous, has left them defenseless in the face of the enemy. This is the theodicy problem: Is God not powerful over evil, or did God, in fact, create suffering? Why does evil exist? In this text we ask, did the Lord cause the oppressor's victory over Zion? Even if the Lord simply let the destruction take place, is such passivity more excusable or understandable than outright aggression? The language of Isaiah offers troubling words in many texts, among them: "Now the LORD is about to lay waste

Pastoral Perspective

This sense of being abandoned by God and disconsolate in faith can be felt by those who are considered saints of the church, as well as those who struggle with sins of their own making. Some might call this a dark night of the soul that can be experienced by both saint and sinner. It may appear in various ways throughout one's lifetime. In such times, the way home to God seems like a gulf that cannot be crossed.

Here God takes the initiative. Although the physical journey seems immensely difficult and challenging, for this homecoming God promises to be the guide. The passage will be smooth and the way easy, God assures. Even the land itself will participate in the joy of this homecoming and reconciliation. The desert will offer shady pathways and springs of water. The heavens will shout for joy. The earth will rejoice. The mountains will burst into song. God is the Lord of nature, and all of nature will join in the celebration, singing the pilgrims home.

There is more. An outer journey like this always involves an inner journey as well. In order to turn toward home and embark on the journey, those in exile must step out of the fears that imprison them, out of a sense of hopelessness and meaninglessness. To empower their trust, God addresses their feelings of abandonment: "Can a woman forget her nursing child, or show no compassion for the child of her womb? Even these may forget, yet I will not forget you. See, I have inscribed you on the palms of my hands" (vv. 15–16a).

These beautiful words sing of love, forgiveness, and acceptance by God, who knows our humanity as creator and has assumed our humanity as Jesus Christ our Lord. God's care and compassion continue through all human experience, the good and the bad, the dark and the light. We have never been forgotten or abandoned, even though it may feel that way.

A clergy friend was getting a pre-Easter haircut during Holy Week. He happened to be preparing for his Good Friday sermon and sharing some thoughts with his barber. He asked his barber what Good Friday meant to him, soliciting the man-on-the-street opinion. "Going home," his barber said. "Going home."

In his years of ministry, Jesus traveled the countryside with no home of his own. "Foxes have holes, and birds of the air have nests; but the Son of Man has nowhere to lay his head" (Matt. 8:20). In this, Jesus is telling us that home is not a physical space after all, but an inner sanctuary, a place we can always go to and return from. This is not a place of

these may forget, yet I will not forget you" (v. 15c). This point is driven home, paradoxically (cf. the Lord's use of a rainbow as a mnemonic device in Gen. 9:16), by the fact that Zion's name has been inscribed on the palm of the Lord's hand. So much for the laws regarding tattoos (Lev. 19:28)! Whenever the Lord stretches out a hand (one has to be willing to anthropomorphize to preach this passage!), the Lord will see the name of Zion and remember. As the tassels on the sleeves of faithful Jews remind them of covenant loyalty to God, so the name of Zion on the Lord's palm reminds God of covenant loyalty to Zion. This is a first, fundamental word of hope.

A second, more remarkable word of hope is that the Lord will make God's fidelity visible and tangible by bringing Zion's children back to her. As the servant has been given as a covenant to the people (though the referent for the second-person objects in verse 8 remains ambiguous), so the return of God's people to Zion makes tangible the Lord's covenant with her. A second exodus, wilderness parade, and conquest of the land (note the language of land and apportionment in verse 8) is now afoot—one that will change Zion's problem from abandonment to overcrowding: "Surely now you will be too crowded for your inhabitants" (v. 19); "The children born in the time of your bereavement will yet say in your hearing: 'The place is too crowded for me; make room for me to settle'" (v. 20). Prisoners will be set free (v. 9). The Lord will shepherd this flock "along the ways" (vv. 9–10). The highway announced in chapter 40 will now be complete, as mountains are brought low and valleys raised up (v. 11). All of this will not only turn Zion's weeping into joy (v. 13), but will be experienced by her as a sign and seal of her partner's fidelity to her: "You shall put all of them [her returned children] on like an ornament, and like a bride you shall bind them on" (v. 18). Here is a sign more tangible than a mark on the Lord's palm: Zion's children resurrected and returned into Zion's presence. This is a second, more embodied word of hope.

There is still more to come.

This would be an extravagant word of hope if it were just a private homecoming, a domestic scene between a husband and a wife and their children. This ingathering, however, takes on cosmic proportions. These children are going to come home not only from the north and west (in the direction of Babylon), but from Syene (in southern Egypt, almost to Ethiopia) (v. 12). This truly is a four-directional collection—from east and west, from north and south. This celebration not only inspires kings and

more forget you than a mother can forget her child" (49:15). On many occasions, Scripture describes God's love, compassion, and care for Israel in maternal terms (e.g., Exod. 19:4–6; Num. 11:12–13; Isa. 42:14; 66:13; Hos. 11:1–9; Matt. 23:37). Maternity is a powerful image of God's compassion for and commitment to Zion. It offers hope to the exiles.

We have experienced and witnessed the love a mother possesses for her offspring. We witness it in the animal world, from a robin shielding her babies in the nest to a bear defending her cub. We witness it in the human world: mothers willing to sacrifice their own lives to protect their children.

Recall the compelling story of Rizpah in 2 Samuel 21:1–14. Out of revenge for what Saul had done, her two sons were taken by the Gibeonites and impaled on a mountainside. For six months after, Rizpah stayed by the dead bodies of her sons as they hung on the tree to keep the birds and animals away. This story inspired the poem by Rudyard Kipling, "Mother o' Mine":

> If I were hanged on the highest hill,
> *Mother o' mine, O mother o' mine!*
> I know whose love would follow me still,
> *Mother o' mine, O mother o' mine!*[1]

A mother's love for her children is one of the most powerful expressions of love a person will ever witness or experience.

However, sometimes mothers do forget. A few are even abusive and negligent. Sometimes, though, a mother's neglect is completely unintentional; just a brief distraction, a split second of forgetfulness, and the child runs into the street in front of a car. In a moment of haste, the child is left in a van on a hot summer day. For just an instant a mother runs to answer the phone with the child in the bathtub.

When I was around thirteen years old, the child of a young mother in our church drowned in the bathtub. The mother was finally cleared of any intentional wrongdoing. However, during the course of the investigation a debate over her fitness as a mother raged on in the local media. Since our family knew her well and knew the kind of mother she was, my dad wrote a letter to the editor in the paper defending her. However, the mother was grief stricken and could not forgive herself for what happened. One day she went to a nearby reservoir and drowned herself. She took her life in the same way

---

1. See "Classic Literature" Web site: classiclit.about.com/library/bl-etexts/rkipling/bl-rkip-mother.htm

Isaiah 49:8-16a

Theological Perspective

the earth and make it desolate . . . and scatter its inhabitants" (24:1). The Lord as the actor, judging and destroying, is even affirmed when YHWH offers to Israel a compassionate word in 40:1–2 through the prophet Isaiah: "Comfort, O comfort my people, says your God. Speak tenderly to Jerusalem, and cry to her that she has served her term, that her penalty is paid, that she has received from the LORD's hand double for all her sins." The people have endured enough suffering to now be reprieved. Even beyond that, the Lord makes sure that the people have been adequately compensated in the way required by the law in Exodus 22:7–8, which says the thief must repay double. That the Lord has given double acknowledges that the Lord has stolen from them.

We see that God is simultaneously the judge who let the people be carried off by the oppressor and a mother who has only compassion for her infant. We are not allowed to settle on any one theological construct for God. This text invites our amazement at the inability of human beings to fathom a power that is both judgment and grace. Although we cannot easily see in the same person (or divine being) both an enemy and a companion who will not let us drop into the abyss, this is the image Isaiah over and over again paints for us of God's own self.

Nevertheless, the inscription on God's hand reigns over this text as a sign of the final notion we are to retain of our Lord. Just as the people are inscribed on God's palm, the liturgical year itself traces the inherent paradox of a complex God—judge and savior, destroyer and nursing mother—onto the body of Christ, the church, week after week by moving from one proclamation of truth to another. God's way with God's people is both a hard challenge and an enveloping cradle. One without the other is too shallow an understanding of God and of our relationship with God.

MELINDA A. QUIVIK

Pastoral Perspective

escape, but an opening to what is deepest and truest and most authentic in our lives.

This understanding is amplified in his last comments to his disciples before he is crucified. On the night he is betrayed, "knowing . . . that he had come from God and was going to God" (John 13:3b), Jesus takes a towel and washes his disciples' feet. They share a meal together. Afterwards, he assures them that he will never leave them orphaned (John 14:18). Instead, he promises that he and his Father will come to them and make their home with them (John 14:23). Furthermore, he tells his disciples that the Holy Spirit will come and remind them of this truth (John 14:26). In the spiritual sense, home is the center of the human soul. There we find our Lord himself.

Today, many have felt exiled from faith, and are seeking a way home. For them it is a distant "land." Seekers are finding many ancient yet new pathways through various spiritual practices. These practices draw on the tried and true ways of meditation, centering prayer, *lectio divina*/sacred reading, and silence. Today's pilgrims also seek God in nature and in the world's concerns. They seek God in service and travel, in prayer groups and worshiping communities, in the eyes of friends and strangers, in the ordinary routine of daily life and in set-aside times of retreat. In these ways, they both find and are being found by God.

A sixth-century iconographer captures this truth in his beautiful image of Jesus with his arm around a second-century monk named Abbot Mena. So too is Jesus' arm around each one of us. He has promised never to leave us. Coming home is a discovery that he is there and has always been there, ever ready to be our companion, whenever we are ready to be his. Even as we yearn for home, our Lord yearns for our opening the door and inviting him in. When we do, like the disciples on the road to Emmaus, we find that our eyes are opened to discover or rediscover his loving friendship.

CAROLE A. CRUMLEY

queens to release Zion's captive children (in contrast to the recalcitrance of Pharaoh in the book of Exodus); it leads these royal figures to journey with them, carrying them on their shoulders, converting them to the role of foster mothers and fathers: "Kings shall be your foster fathers, and their queens your nursing mothers" (v. 23). This reunion, like the giving of the servant (in v. 6), is truly too remarkable a thing to limit to Jacob and Israel alone. This homecoming, this act of God's fidelity, will shine like a light to the nations, "that my salvation may reach to the end of the earth" (v. 6). Before this parade is finished, not only the heavens and the earth, but the mountains will join in praise (v. 13).

The utter extravagance of this chapter, within which these selected verses are nestled, would seem to shout out for this passage's location on Easter Sunday or Pentecost Sunday or World Communion Sunday—any Sunday meant to stress God's ability to remember and gather up and convert the whole world into the stage of the Lord's salvation: "Then all flesh shall know that I am the LORD your Savior, and your Redeemer, the Mighty One of Jacob" (v. 26). Is this too much hope to handle—for both Mother Zion and Mother Church? Does this dream burst the bounds of the Lord's kingdom for both Christians and Jews? Let the preachers and the rabbis decide.

RICHARD BOYCE

her child died. That's the depth of a mother's grief and love.

Obviously a mother should not and must not go to that suicidal extreme to demonstrate her love; yet I cannot but think of the second stanza of Kipling's poem as he uses the language of hyperbole to express the intensity of a mother's love.

> If I were drowned in the deepest sea,
> *Mother o' mine, O mother o' mine!*
> I know whose tears would come down to me,
> *Mother o' mine, O mother o' mine!*

Even though a mother for a moment can unintentionally forget a child, God cannot; it is not even in God's nature (49:15b). The promise-making and promise-keeping God says to all disciples, "I will never leave you or forsake you" (Josh. 1:5; Heb. 13:5).

Because of God's love for Zion, God serves as a surrogate mother by birthing and nurturing other children belonging to Zion that she does not even know exist (49:20–23). God creates life where there is no life. God is able, if necessary, to raise up stones from the ground as offspring of Abraham (Matt. 3:9).

As proof of the maternal promise, God inscribes the name and the image of Israel on the palm of God's hand (49:16). God even marks Israel to assure her that she will never be forgotten (Deut. 6:6–9) and circumcises her heart as a covenant seal between God and Israel (Deut. 10:16; 30:6; Jer. 4:4; Rom. 2:29).

God will also place someone in the midst of Zion who will minister to her and represent to her God's compassion (49:5). This servant leader will willingly suffer for the sake of bringing Zion to YHWH. God appoints the Servant to comfort, lead, and inspire (49:1–6). The leader will serve as the shepherd to the people, calling them out of exile, and bringing them home (49:9–11).

A sermon on this text will reaffirm God's love and compassion for God's people. God's people must understand the intensity of God's devotion and the passion of God's love. This message parallels the message of the Gospel text for this Sunday, in which Jesus reassures the disciples that God cares more for people than for all of creation (Matt. 6:25–34).

DAVE BLAND

Psalm 131

¹O Lord, my heart is not lifted up,
 my eyes are not raised too high;
 I do not occupy myself with things
 too great and too marvelous for me.
²But I have calmed and quieted my soul,
 like a weaned child with its mother;
 my soul is like the weaned child that is with me.

³O Israel, hope in the Lord
 from this time on and forevermore.

Theological Perspective

The theme this week is quiet trust—in God and our own capacities to navigate life's turbulence. The experience to which the psalmist points touches the depths of human understanding and feeling. It addresses our basic orientation in the world: are we trustful or fearful? Each path has consequences, and the psalmist suggests one is better than the other.

Long ago, I served as a national park ranger in the high mountains of the western United States. One year, I had a housemate who previously had never left metro New York City. He found the quiet, the massive forests, the wildlife, and the relative lack of pavement quite unsettling. One evening when there were no clouds or a moon, I took him to a clearing where we could see the vast constellations of stars above our heads, including the northern lights. He was shaken, feeling small and insignificant and out of his frame of reference, while I found myself wonderfully at home in what seemed like a cosmic embrace. It is almost that kind of difference to which our psalmist points today; he asserts, calmly and straightforwardly, that our calling is to be at home, trustful of God's love and abiding presence with us. It is trust in that loving presence that gives a constructive direction to our lives.

What does it take to be effective? That is a huge question, so let me focus it: what does it take to

Pastoral Perspective

From the majestic heights of Psalm 104 to the stunning and perilous discovery of individual consciousness in Psalm 8 (the psalms for the two previous Sundays) this psalm now takes us to one of the necessities of human existence if we are to discover the meaning of our lives: the necessity of slowing down, of taking time to meditate, of finding a calm place in ourselves and in our lives to listen for God's voice. We spend most of our lives scrambling to find ourselves, trying to find our true home. In this short psalm we are reminded of that longing and its source, and we are also pointed toward finding our way home.

Like a child who has been lifted up into her mother's arms to find solace, here we see the psalmist contemplating her fate and her destiny. Her fate is that she is weaned—she has discovered her separation from her mother and from her source of life. It is part of God's created order that she will be weaned from her mother. She will discover and experience individuation, a glorious and frightening journey. That is her fate and, indeed, the fate of us all. Her destiny—her destination—is not yet determined. Her destiny will be shaped significantly by her reaction to her discovery that she is weaned, that she is a separate individual from her mother and from everyone else, including God.

Exegetical Perspective

Psalm 131 is twelfth in a group of fifteen psalms called Songs of Ascents (Pss. 120–134)—a designation that derives from the superscription (not printed above) that introduces each psalm. The plural noun *ma'alot* is related to the Hebrew verb that means "to go up," hence the translation "ascents." It is not precisely clear what the term means in these psalm titles, but many scholars take it as a reference to "going up" to Jerusalem and regard these as pilgrimage psalms.[1] The brevity of the songs, along with the frequent references to Jerusalem and Zion (see Pss. 122, 125, 126, 128, 129, 132, 133, and 134), would commend these psalms for use by pilgrims in the Diaspora en route to a festival in Jerusalem. Along with the other fourteen pilgrimage songs, Psalm 131 then is a song about life "on the way." The psalmist is in liminal space between home and the eventual destination and is therefore vulnerable to dangers along the way. Each of these psalms, in its own way, grapples with the life of faith throughout the journey.

As for literary type, Psalm 131 is perhaps best described as a psalm of confidence (cf. Ps. 23, which also speaks of journey). Its canonical placement beside Psalm 130, a lament, is likely intentional.

---

1. For other possibilities that have been suggested, see Hans-Joachim Kraus, *Psalms 1–59: A Commentary*, trans. Hilton C. Oswald (Minneapolis: Augsburg, 1988), 23–24.

Homiletical Perspective

We are offered here one of the Psalter's most beautiful psalms of humility and trust. Indeed, Psalm 131 can help us reflect upon the developing faith of the early Christian communities in this time after Pentecost. The psalm commences with a protestation of humility, as the psalmist speaks of his freedom from worldly ambitions: "O Lord, . . . I do not occupy myself with things too great and too marvelous for me" (v. 1). The preacher may choose to highlight the gentle tones of humble trust as if echoing from the chimes of a nearby steeple, or to emphasize the whispered words of a confession from an honest worshiper who lays his/her heart open to the eyes of God, exemplifying that only one thing is of value: being united with one's God in a relationship of sincere trust. In either case, the lesson in life is the same: humility is usually a prerequisite of genuine trust. The psalmist expresses the desire to refrain from being arrogant and to keep from boasting of virtuous deeds: "I have calmed and quieted my soul" (v. 2). Otherwise, one might fall prey to sin that is implied by a heart that is "lifted up," as in Proverbs 18:12 (NAB; NRSV "haughty"), and "haughty eyes," as found in Psalm 18:27, suggesting more than vanity. What one most wishes to avoid is an arrogant self-reliance that defies God (Ps. 73:6–9).

Psalm 131

Theological Perspective

handle change well? I have worked with organizations of different kinds over the course of my career, and each—whether a government agency, a retailer, an educational institution, or a community of faith in congregational or another form—has faced some kind of deep challenge. I have needed to learn how to function in that kind of environment, and after some time it has simply become more familiar.

Here is a metaphor for this kind of experience: navigating whitewater. Back in my ranger days, at one point I was assigned to be in charge of a raft on the Snake River. I learned that being in charge is very different from simply being part of the crew. What did I need to know and, based on that knowledge, then actually do, in order to be effective? First, I needed to know that I was *able* to command the vessel. That confidence came ultimately not from words, but from actual experience—from practice and from learning from some people who had been doing that kind of work for a long time. This confidence did not mean that I knew answers to all questions that might arise as you float downstream; but it did mean that I could make relevant connections between the experience our crew was having and the goal—successful completion of the journey.

Such confidence meant that I had to know how to read the circumstances around me—the river itself, the nearby environs ashore, the bigger environment (especially the skies, for we often talked of daily lightning storms), and also the people on the raft. People were the variable demanding most focused attention: Who is fearful? Who is likely to be filled with bravado at the outset and then wilt early into the river-running? Who is mentally fragile and shares unwarranted anxiety or irrelevant suggestions on how to act? Who cannot work well with others? Who *is* a team player, whether experienced in this task or not? Finally, how do I nurture all of them into a cohesive team for the downstream experience? Making such judgments about others, sometimes very quickly (and sometimes needing revision, as new experiences show I missed something), would not be possible if I did not have a basic inner confidence in my capacity to read people—an aspect of knowing myself.

It has sometimes been said that one of the tasks of growing up is to regain the innate wisdom of infancy. Pressures from families and peers, especially the incentives and rewards related to coming of age, have us neglect—perhaps even push to the margins of awareness—some basic insight we may have had all along. We of biblical faith would claim that this

Pastoral Perspective

Each of us must come to terms with this fate and this destiny. Many of us come to see our separation as terrible news, as evidenced by the number of babies crying in church nurseries when they are initially left there by their parents. As we grow, we often answer the anxiety created by this separation by allowing other gods to pacify our fear and our dread. Whether it is busyness or money or tribalism or nationalism—the answers offered to us are myriad—we often turn ourselves over to other gods, both as individuals and as communities. The church itself is not immune to this process.

Here the psalmist suggests a different path—a process of maturation in which we come to accept our fate, our individuation, and then move toward a stance of trust, of seeking to hear God's voice in this journey. Rather than fleeing from it or raging at it, we are asked to shape our destiny as weaned individuals with integrity. The psalmist suggests that, rather than clinging to our mother's leg (or finding another leg to which to cling), we seek to discern the possibilities and indeed the strengths that are at the heart of our sense of separation. We are not asked to become heroic individuals. Instead, we are asked to consider that there is a larger world out there, with God at its center. In this world we can find love and meaning in ways that we had not previously imagined prior to being weaned. While we are not able to crawl back into our mother's womb or even find the comfort of suckling, we may find that we can recover that powerful love, and because of our individuation, we can find ways to share that love with others.

In the great parable of the waiting father in Luke 15, we see Jesus' acknowledgment of this human dilemma—one child flees into hedonism, and the other into self-righteousness. Like the psalmist, Jesus suggests in this story that the goal of our lives is not to live out of flight or rage, as these two sons do, but rather to live out of love, as the waiting father does. It is a love strengthened and refined by having come through this process. It is a process that can enable us to move toward being more the loving parent and less the anxious and raging children.

The psalmist asks us to take a step back to recognize that separation and individuation can be a source of both blessing and curse. Our calling as children of God is to find space to allow God's Spirit to speak to us in our sadness and in our rage, to help us hear that there are possibilities of life—yes, even great possibilities of life—in this need and in this longing to be connected. Authentic communities are built upon it, and at its best the church builds this kind of

Exegetical Perspective

References to the "soul" that waits in Psalm 130:6 and the "soul" that is quieted in Psalm 131:2, along with the repeated line "O Israel, hope in the LORD!" (130:7; 131:3), tend to draw the two psalms together. The quiet calm of Psalm 131 is a fitting response to the anguished cry from "out of the depths" of Psalm 130.

Psalm 131 is among the briefest in the book of Psalms and yet is quite remarkable because of its gripping imagery and mood. It consists of two sections: verses 1–2, which address YHWH; and verse 3, which exhorts the human community, Israel.

The psalm boldly opens with utterance of the divine name, YHWH (v. 1). Then follow three negative expressions that describe the character of the psalmist (cf. Ps. 1:1). First, the poet's "heart (*leb*) is not lifted up." Unlike some modern popular notions, Israel associated the heart not especially with emotions but rather with thought and volition. The expression denies any trace of arrogance and haughtiness that would presume to know or be too much in the presence of God. The psalm next affirms that the poet's "eyes are not raised too high." Psalm 18:27 affirms that God brings down those with "raised [NRSV "haughty"] eyes" but saves those who are humble and lowly. Psalm 131:1 thus locates the poet among those who are meek. Further, the psalmist is not overly concerned with things that are too "great" or too "marvelous." As scholars have noted, this expression likely does not refer to people's efforts to achieve special status within the human community (e.g., power, prestige, knowledge). Rather, the Hebrew words used here for "great" and "marvelous" (*gedelot; nipla'ot*) most commonly refer to words and deeds of YHWH and not human accomplishments.[2]

The stance that the psalmist takes here is akin to the acknowledgment of Job at the end of his intense encounter with YHWH: there is always more to know about God than humans can possibly know. To be sure, Psalm 131:1 does not advocate complacency or a lack of rigorous inquiry on the part of the human community into matters of human life or God. However, the text does acknowledge that there are limits and that human pursuits are best carried out in full awareness of human limitations in the presence of God.

The similes of verse 2 are rich, as they draw upon the relationship between a mother and a weaned child in order to articulate a mode of existence. In fact, this language has led some scholars to suggest

2. See Patrick D. Miller, *They Cried to the Lord* (Minneapolis: Fortress Press, 1994), 240.

Homiletical Perspective

The preacher might also hear a song of thanksgiving as the psalmist, having let go of great aspirations and ambitions, finds a balance of mind and heart that enables satisfaction with what has been granted to him. We the hearers now define humility as the key to the life of one who is faithful and thus becomes faith-filled. This leads us to the threshold of a lifestyle that enables us to question how we come before our God.

What is their prayer like, the preacher may inquire, as they attempt to enter into the holiness of such a relationship with God? Indeed, the ultimate question to embrace is, can we come to our God as we are, trusting to be received and believed? If so, we can then travel with this ancient text into the twenty-first century holding a countercultural stance toward life and work. We may be able then to abandon the demands of a 24-7 work ethic and the pressures of climbing the social and economic ladders of success! Our prayer would imitate that of the psalmist, asking that we neither seek fame nor set our hearts on the riches of the world. Such prayerful satisfaction, we realize, does not come easily or without struggle. This is true for both the psalmist and the worshiper in the pew. The second verse says it clearly: "But I have calmed and quieted my soul, like a weaned child with its mother; my soul is like the weaned child that is with me."

Coming to such peace may be the journey of a lifetime. The task of the preacher is to raise the appropriate reflections. How much of our own arrogance and sinfulness—our striving for success, recognition, and wealth—must be relinquished? How does the soul journey from being like the infant who is crying loudly for its mother's breast to become the weaned child who quietly and contentedly rests on its mother's lap, happy just to be with her? The challenge for the preacher continues to provide guidance in appreciating the rest found by the psalmist and the safety discovered with God. In the midst of this comes the love and happiness experienced in intimate communion. The worshipers too, after a struggle, reach an awareness in which their desire for God is only for God and not a means of satisfaction or fulfillment.

In the Gospel text for this Sunday, from the Sermon on the Mount (Matt. 6:24–34), the message of the psalmist is reinforced as it offers various examples of the same kind of trust in the Lord, refusing to allow anxiety and unbelief to rule our lives. The passage makes clear that living for Christ is a very different reality from worldly living and suggests that

Psalm 131

Theological Perspective

natal knowledge is not the understanding of a content-specific type, but rather a deep and quiet confidence that we are all right, that we are loved, that we count for something. It is this to which our psalmist points us today: "I do not occupy myself with things too great and too marvelous for me. But I have calmed and quieted my soul, like a weaned child with its mother; my soul is like the weaned child that is with me" (vv. 1–2).

The apparently growing phenomenon of children who are actively abused or passively neglected makes it harder to maintain this assertion, but here we must make a basic theological claim: God calls all human beings into a loving relationship, despite what others of us might do to inhibit or prevent its actualization. That some of our brothers and sisters have never known anything other than slavery, prostitution, mental abuse, or debilitating disease and poverty, does not invalidate our conviction that God loves all of us and enjoins those of us who are more privileged than others to use that privilege to help transform circumstances for others so that they may live better. (One thing I have learned from people in other nations is that even those who currently see no hope for their lives actually do still often hope for something better . . . perhaps a faint glimmer of the loving presence of God within.)

To be known and loved by another, *and* to have a quiet confidence and trust in that love as abiding and deep—that is the insight of the weaned child, which we are called to know in our relationship with God. It is this foundation of quiet trust and confidence that serves as the basis of our effective functioning in the raging waters of life. Our psalmist enjoins us all to "hope in the LORD from this time on and forevermore" (v. 3); this is certainly not to be an ephemeral trust, but life-sustainingly permanent. That makes all the difference.

DAVID G. TRICKETT

Pastoral Perspective

community and thrives upon it, a community where we can celebrate our individuality and also acknowledge our need for God and for one another.

There are also great dangers in this longing. Inauthentic communities derive from this longing too—communities built on rage and sadness that express themselves in meanness and exclusivity and repression. The church has unfortunately nurtured these kinds of community as well. As a counter to this danger, the psalmist asks us to remember and to recover our true nature. We are children of God. The psalmist also points us back to Psalm 8: we are just a little less than God. We are creatures of our fate and creators of our destiny. Therein lie the great possibility and the great danger. Biblical, theological, and human history remind us of both; in light of this, we are asked to adopt a stance of humility and affirmation.

The psalmist suggests that one place to seek this humility and this affirmation is in meditation and in silence, in taking time to listen for our own voice and for God's voice. Some commentators hear the psalmist's words in verse 1 as passivity and submissiveness. In our age of relentless activity and distraction, perhaps we can hear these words as an invitation for thoughtfulness, for listening, and for reflecting upon our "caughtness" and upon building a life of loving engagement in the middle of it—not quite "consider the lilies of the field" (Matt. 6:28), but definitely "my soul waits for the Lord" (Ps. 130:6). The psalmist reminds us that these reflective moments of listening are not passivity but, rather, pregnant moments where the voice at the center of the mystery may speak to us in ways that we had not previously imagined.

NIBS STROUPE

that the psalmist may well have been a woman. Although it is impossible to be certain, the suggestion is certainly plausible. Elsewhere in the Bible women burst forth in song and thanksgiving (Exod. 15:21 [Miriam]; 1 Sam. 2 [Hannah]; Luke 1:46–55 [Mary]). To hear Psalm 131 as a woman's song of confidence would not be out of bounds. The verse begins with an emphatic affirmative expression that could be translated "Surely" ("but" in NRSV). While verse 1 affirms what the poet *has not* done, verse 2 boldly announces the stance the psalmist *has* taken. The psalmist has chosen to "smooth," or calm, and quiet the soul. The word "soul" (*nephesh*) is better understood as an "entire being" that consists of both the body and its animating life force, not simply as some spiritual entity distinct from the physical body. Here the totality of the poet's life has been calmed. This is graphically depicted through the image of a weaned child (not a nursing infant) that returns to the mother for ongoing comfort and nurture. The image of two categories of people (women and children) that were typically marginalized in the ancient world to portray a wholesome stance before YHWH is striking.

Verse 2 does not tell the reader precisely what has enabled the psalmist to feel calm and quieted. Perhaps, like the mystery of the bond between a mother and her child, the poet's manner cannot be fully explained. However, the bold exhortation for Israel to hope in YHWH that comes in verse 3 leads one to believe that the experience and presence of God somehow help account for the psalmist's attitude. In fact, the surrounding presence of YHWH in verses 1 and 3 encompasses all that the psalmist is not (v. 1) and is (v. 2). It is the inscrutable presence of YHWH that accompanies, nurtures, and calms the poet throughout the pilgrimage journey.

V. STEVEN PARRISH

we find the courage not to worry (Matt. 6:25, 27, 31), but rather to rest in the Lord.

So we return to the psalmist, and through the invitation of the preacher the eyes of our hearts gaze upon the image of a mother God whose very presence gives assurance and peace to the child who, fully satisfied and safe, snuggles into her arms. Sheltered in love, the child now has come to love her for her own sake, not for any need or want that she can satisfy.

The psalm concludes with the words of one convinced of the message, and the psalmist cries out to the whole community of Israel to hope confidently in God: "O Israel, hope in the Lord from this time on and forevermore" (v. 3). Yes, filled with a sense of security that comes with a learned trust in God, the psalmist can now exhort the people of Israel to await the promised coming of divine consolation and reassurance. Although verse 3 may be a liturgical form, it exemplifies that the individual experience and personal confessions of the believer who boasts of a relationship of trust with God can influence and encourage the whole community. This song of trust, in which the psalmist gives up self-reliance and becomes like a child enjoying its mother's comfort, having calmed and quieted one's soul, can provide a model for Israel's faith, the faith of the local community, the faith of the church. The preacher can help the congregation to "put on" such faith in the circumstances of their lives, which indeed become difficult and at times all-consuming. The call to "hope in the Lord" becomes ever more necessary. There is no limit to our hope, for we are "weaned" children of a God who has calmed and quieted our souls!

CONSTANCE M. KOCH, O.P.

1 Corinthians 4:1-5

¹Think of us in this way, as servants of Christ and stewards of God's mysteries. ²Moreover, it is required of stewards that they be found trustworthy. ³But with me it is a very small thing that I should be judged by you or by any human court. I do not even judge myself. ⁴I am not aware of anything against myself, but I am not thereby acquitted. It is the Lord who judges me. ⁵Therefore do not pronounce judgment before the time, before the Lord comes, who will bring to light the things now hidden in darkness and will disclose the purposes of the heart. Then each one will receive commendation from God.

Theological Perspective

The Christian church has wrestled throughout its history with questions of leadership. The Bible leaves traces of many different models of religious leadership, all of which have found adherents even to our own day. Is the Christian leader to be a priest, or prophet, or ruler, or rabbi, or presbyter, or pastor, or scribe, or (deputy) shepherd, or bishop? Is the Christian leader a friend, coach, mentor, CEO, or counselor? Here Paul labors to argue to the Christians in Corinth that Christian leaders are "servants" and "stewards of God's mysteries" (v. 1).

These are humble images. Both "servant" and "steward" suggest dependence and subordination rather than independent superiority. Both servants and stewards manage important matters entrusted to them by persons of far greater power, to whom they are strictly accountable. Paul seems to be saying that there is no meaningful status or power difference among fellow servants and stewards. Apollos, Cephas, and Paul are fellow servants and are therefore not to be understood hierarchically or made into competing power centers. This would be so much easier if the One before whom they actually stand in submission was physically present, as in a wealthy Greco-Roman household in which it is quite clear who owns the place, as opposed to who merely serves there. There are good reasons

Pastoral Perspective

The Christians in Corinth live in a place of questionable reputation, and they endeavor to grow their community in a society that is rich with religious plurality and rife with prurient distractions. In this environment, the task of claiming a unique, authentic Christian identity must offer a tremendous challenge.

In addressing this church, Paul's communication might seem as confusing as it is enlightening for their identity formation. Up to this point, at the conclusion of the first part of this letter, Paul adopts a handful of diverse images in referring to Corinthian Christians. He refers to them as those "sanctified" and "called to be saints" (1:2), babies (3:1), God's coworkers (3:9), the temple of God (3:16–17), unwise fools (3:18), and Christ's (people) (3:23). Now, after this colorful and confusing mixture of images, Paul assigns to the Christians in Corinth and those evangelists who have grown that community the imagery "servants of Christ" and "stewards of God's mysteries" (4:1).

So they are simultaneously the weakest and the most sanctified, the servants and the coworkers, the house of God and the fool, the rich and poor, the Greek and Jewish. They can easily find themselves lost in the deluge of conflicting labels and the expectations that may conceal their authentic selves.

Folks worshiping in church pews may relate to this ambiguity. They navigate the sometimes competing

Exegetical Perspective

Paul's discussion of the office of apostle follows his treatment of the weighty issue signaled in 1:10, the divisive tendency among the Corinthian Christians to exalt those who brought them into the faith and to form factions based upon these personal connections. In the face of such misunderstanding of the role of the apostle and of the nature of the relation of believers to them, Paul suggests a helpful rubric under which to consider the propagators and administrators of the faith: "servants of Christ and stewards of God's mysteries." This passage pauses for a moment from the fierce criticism the apostle levels against the Corinthian church in chapter 3, a tone that picks up later in the letter. A note of sober warning sounds in 4:3–5 when Paul uses questions about himself to remind the church of the coming judgment, part of the basic apocalyptic picture he assumes them to hold. The apostle's implicitly threatening language anticipates his open slap at the most virulently "arrogant" individuals whom he indicts in 4:18–21.

The thrust of Paul's argument regarding Corinthian factionalism connects the question of ministerial authority with the larger issue concerning the limitations of human self-evaluation. Paul's judgment about himself does not and cannot justify him (v. 4b); and the Corinthians should cease to pretend that their human judgments are more than that (3:18).

Homiletical Perspective

On its surface the text seems to reflect concerns not widely shared by twenty-first-century Christians. Paul defends his apostolic authority, holding himself up as an example of servanthood. He urges the Corinthians to suspend judgment and reminds them that God's tribunal is the only one that counts. None of these immediately suggests promising themes for a contemporary sermon. However, beneath the text's surface lurk a few interesting tensions. One or two of these may help the preacher and congregation find a way into the surprisingly relevant layers of this text.

The theme of "judging vs. not-judging"[1] makes a particularly promising entrée. It is what some scholars call an "aporetic tension." The Greek root of "aporetic" means "to be at a loss." It is the kind of thing that happens to a person torn between two poles of an issue *and* riddled with doubt.

In this text, Paul is at something of a loss. Despite his apparent confidence (Paul seldom sounds anything but sure of himself!), he seems to harbor second thoughts on the subject of judging. His torn-ness shows in the contrast between the strong statement he makes against pronouncing judgment (4:5) and the serious judgment he renders just a few verses later

---

1. Cornelia Cyss Crocker, *Reading 1 Corinthians in the Twenty-first Century* (New York: T. & T. Clark, 2004), 204.

1 Corinthians 4:1-5

Theological Perspective

why the church has so often stumbled over leadership problems.

Paul expresses vivid clarity about his accountability to Jesus Christ alone. Paul's accountability to his invisible but most real Judge appears to make him uninterested in the judgments of others upon him—whether in Christian community or beyond (v. 3a). At first this claim appears to be an appeal to individual conscience over against the judgment of the community. Paul then radicalizes the matter still further when he claims, "I do not even judge myself" (v. 3b). For the moment his conscience is clear, but this does not mean that he is innocent (v. 4). Only God will judge him, and God will do this judgment upon Christ's return, not before (v. 5).

At one level, these statements reflect a perennial tension between Christian community and the Christian individual in discerning the good, the true, and the right. Christian history is rife with instances in which the judgments of the Christian community, whether as a whole or through its designated leaders, have clashed with the conscientious convictions of a dissenting individual. Different Christian traditions have attempted to navigate these issues in different ways. Roman Catholicism has sought to preserve communal order and discipline through hierarchically determined and enforced theological and moral commitments, while working to preserve maneuvering room for reasonable individual differences. Baptists tend to share a common commitment to individual freedom in interpreting Scriptures and responding to the dictates of conscience; yet even Baptists gather in congregations that find they must settle upon shared understandings of at least core beliefs and practices in order to function together in community.

Paul's comments touch upon and helped to contribute to a stream of Christian theological-ethical thought that has puzzled over the existence and functioning of conscience in a good-yet-fallen world. Following Thomas Aquinas, Catholic thought has tended to have a relatively optimistic view of the capacity of the human being, even apart from saving grace in Jesus Christ, to discern basic moral principles and to be prompted internally to make moral judgments tending toward the right and good and away from the wrong and evil—and to feel pangs of guilt after the fact for having chosen wrongly. This mysterious rational (and emotive) capacity to discern the right and recoil from the wrong is basically what is meant by conscience in Christian tradition.

Classical Protestant moral thought has tended more than Catholic thought to emphasize the various

Pastoral Perspective

expectations of exhibiting strength while admitting weakness; of serving diverse roles as child, spouse, parent, volunteer, employer/ee, leader, and friend; of maintaining cultural and religious fidelity without building barriers or assuming a judgmental role. They know the burden of a world that imposes sometimes contradictory expectations, and they struggle to discover the people they are called to be.

Coupled with this notion of authenticity is the call to be "faithful" (v. 2, NIV; NRSV "trustworthy"). This call presents an enormous challenge to early-church Corinthians in a culture that supports the worship of many gods and adopts as a major business the artisanship of what the Hebrew Bible might refer to as "graven images." This seaport town hosts many lonely sailors who have long been at sea. It is renowned for superficial wealth and abuse of the poor. If faithfulness involves the choices of the elect, then the Corinthian community embodies many tempting choices and potential impediments to its fulfillment.

Folks worshiping in our twenty-first-century churches—and, even more importantly, those who are not—identify well with this challenge to act faithfully in a world of overwhelming choices. We face questions of how to choose Jesus in a world that offers to the nondestitute instant access and instant gratification. How do we choose Jesus in a world that is more than ever divided along economic and political lines? How do we choose Jesus in a postmodern world that emphasizes individuality and tends to question all authority? How do we choose Jesus in a world that offers so many other choices to worship—self, work, power, entertainment, consumerism, technology, divisiveness? Church members join their Corinthian spiritual ancestors in daily engagement with these questions.

Finally, in the world of the first and the twenty-first centuries, as we seek to claim our authentic selves and make choices that are faithful to our call in Jesus, how can we know whether we are progressing or regressing? This text dedicates three out of its five verses to answering that question.

As he is writing this letter, Paul listens to the beginnings of criticism from the Christian people in Corinth. These people are circling themselves around certain key leaders, including Paul, and alienating those outside of their circle (1:11–13). Paul attempts to address this criticism in these verses, but the criticism intensifies and becomes more divisive by the time he writes his next letter in 2 Corinthians. Paul concludes that too many folks

Exegetical Perspective

Written in late 53 or early 54 CE,[1] the letter addresses a church community without established clerical offices (note the inclusion of "bishops and deacons" in the greeting of the somewhat-later letter to the Philippians). The lack of local, stable leadership would have left the church particularly vulnerable to power struggles based on secular status and wealth (not that ecclesiastical offices eliminate that vulnerability). While Paul evinces a generous attitude toward other leading figures in the spread of the gospel, such as Cephas (Peter) and Apollos (3:22; 4:6), he feels a special relation to the Corinthian church as its founder, which makes him a "father" to its members (4:15). In this light are explicable the impatience, anger, and zeal to correct the church that Paul displays in various passages of the letter.

The apostle clarifies his role and, by association, that of other leading teachers/missionaries as well: he and they are "assistants of Christ and stewards of God's mysteries." The sense of the term "assistants" (*hypēretas*) is enlarged by the metaphorically richer "stewards." Stewards were in charge of the distribution and preservation of a household's goods; they were known for being under the scrutiny of—and hence particularly answerable to—their lord. In the Greco-Roman world, capable slaves were entrusted with such positions; their need to be "faithful" to their lord makes the simile (which follows after the one about the farmer at 3:6–9 and the builder at 3:10–15) quite apt to illustrate his point about himself, Apollos, Cephas, and others. Each is expected to be a faithful steward "of God's mysteries," clearly an awesome charge. God's stewards are what they are by belonging to Christ and by being responsible for the goods that belong to God.

Paul hopes that enlightening the Corinthians on this point will ameliorate their tendency toward faction. His elucidation of the role of apostle gives him an opening to address criticisms levied against him by some among the Corinthians. Verse 3 coolly expresses his lack of ultimate concern for their all-too-human judgments about himself; and he reminds the Corinthians of what they supposedly know and should acknowledge. The Lord is coming soon; one must avoid hasty judgment in that light (v. 4). Paul's conscience as to his own conduct in his office as apostle is clean, but he accepts that his own judgment as to his own state is limited and provisional in view of the judgment that will ensue when

Homiletical Perspective

(5:1–5). In the chapters following his prohibition of judging he exhorts the Corinthians, not just once but a number of times, to "decide rightly."

It is perplexing. How can Paul say, "Judge for yourselves," about food sacrificed to idols (10:15) to the same people to whom he has just said, "Do not pronounce judgment before the appointed time, before the Lord comes"(4:5)? How can he list the "discernment of spirits" as a gift of the Spirit (12:10) or urge believers to judge each other instead of letting lawsuits go to court (6:1–6), when he has already admonished the Corinthians against doing God's job? Paul is of at least two minds when it comes to the role of "judging" or discernment in the community of faith.

The problem of discernment and the perplexity associated with it are familiar to many contemporary congregations. For some in the community of faith, the question about the appropriate role of judging could hardly be more pressing. Over the last decade, congregations have faced greater temptation to be facile and dogmatic about their judging. Some have succumbed. As post-9/11 tensions have ebbed and flowed, so, it seems, has Christian forbearance.

Many Christians, especially North American Protestants, would agree with the statement "God alone is Lord of the conscience."[2] Yet since the ink dried on that line of the Westminster Confession of Faith, the church has hardly known a moment's peace. We are plagued by the kind of disrespectful disagreement that might be expected in a group that claimed a "my way or the highway" credo or a "my church right or wrong" motto. For a community that claims oneness in Christ, our divisiveness betrays a sad hypocrisy. At best it shows an astonishing capacity for cognitive dissonance. For a people who profess a certain tolerance on many doctrinal issues, we have become very good at hairsplitting. We drop our plumb lines with a frequency and ease that belie what we say we believe.

One group within the body of Christ judges gay and lesbian people to be worthy of membership but not ordination, another of ordination but not the episcopate; another refuses to have any association with any L, B, G, or T whatsoever. One group within the body of Christ judges the national flag appropriate to their decorating scheme; another bars it from the building. One group within the body of Christ judges that Paul means it literally when he says that women

---

1. C. K. Barrett, *The First Epistle to the Corinthians* (New York: Harper & Row, 1968), 5.

2. Westminster Confession of Faith, 6.109, in *The Book of Confessions* (Louisville, KY: Office of the General Assembly, 1999), 143.

1 Corinthians 4:1-5

Theological Perspective

ways that sin and ignorance distort the judgments of conscience. Our consciences can err due to over-scrupulousness or lack of scruples; due to self-interest or self-hatred; due to misunderstandings and mis-readings of the details of actual situations; due to problems in character development and various psychological or social maladies. It has been quite possible to despair of the prospects of living according to the hoary maxim "Let your conscience be your guide," in light of all that can go wrong with conscience.

For this reason it is most interesting that in this passage Paul does not really appeal to his conscience, nor does he claim any infallibility in his judgments. Paul appears to argue that he has sought to serve Christ faithfully in ministry but can only take an agnostic position concerning whether his behavior has met with Christ's approval. This is not a "let your conscience be your guide" position, nor is it some kind of appeal to broad moral, rational, or biblical principles. Instead, Paul offers a kind of naked vulnerability before God. He does not cover himself with any form of heteronomous security but simply waits for the judgment of Christ. This is reminiscent of the position Dietrich Bonhoeffer ended up articulating during his days of participation in the conspiracy against Hitler. He did not appeal to conscience or principles. His responsibility was to God alone, and God alone would make the judgment.

The theme of such a climactic Last Judgment of God on the life and deeds of every person resounds throughout the Bible. Paul is not original here in envisioning a reckoning in which Christ "will bring to light the things now hidden in darkness and will disclose the purposes of the heart" (v. 5b). The very idea of such a scene causes great consternation among many who do not like the image of God or Christ as judge or the very idea of some receiving a negative eternal judgment. Certainly many Christians have abandoned the concept. However, in the NT at least, this coming judgment is eagerly awaited. That great Day at last brings the kingdom of God in all of its fullness, an end to all injustice and victimization, and the vindication of those who have served Christ faithfully. The events of that Day can be trusted because Jesus Christ can be trusted. Precisely because Christ can be trusted to do the judging, we need not spend our time judging ourselves or others even now.

DAVID P. GUSHEE

Pastoral Perspective

are wasting too much time forming opinions (many negative) and casting judgments upon Paul and one another.

Twenty-first-century folks are more than prepared to enter the conversation at this point. Our society both thrives upon and is poisoned by our love for the judgmental. In the post-Watergate, post-Vietnam world of the West, society has come to value people who can uncover truths and reach logical conclusions and judgments. However, society tends to listen intently to judgments reached even without the benefit of facts uncovered or arguments well reasoned.

Our televisions are filled with "reality" competitions that celebrate their sharply opinionated judges and call upon the whole of society to participate electronically in the ranking of participants. Many people, from preachers to politicians to pundits, point to one segment of society or another and judge them responsible for all of the woes of the world. Political campaigns are often full of emotion and devoid of information. Politicians misrepresent their opponents and overpraise themselves. We voters often choose without much reflection. Internet news and story distributors encourage the inquisitive public to cast judgment by voting on the issue raised by the story. While our qualifications are lacking, we join our first-century brothers and sisters in our readiness to serve as judge and jury on the attributes and faults of others.

Unlike Paul (v. 4), we even demonstrate the occasional ability for honest self-reflection and self-judgment. Paul's words may bring relief to folks who weary of finding themselves as the brunt of society's judgment. They may give strength to folks who emotionally batter themselves because of their inadequacies. They may give warning to folks who too readily assume God's role as judge. They may give courage to folks whose faithful choices and authentic selves are met with skepticism and contempt. They may give hope to people who recognize the darkness in which we live and have little patience for the light to come. They may give insight to folks who do not recognize that we worship and work and serve for an audience of One.

DAVID M. BENDER

Exegetical Perspective

the Lord shall come (v. 5). That is the time of ultimate judgment and justification, even for those who found and build up the churches (3:5–15).

Paul's recourse to the return of Christ and Last Judgment in defense of his apostolate works primarily to put to rest the conflicting judgments about his own person. The apostle may have reckoned, however, with the possibility that the factionalism was too deeply entrenched to be altogether uprooted. Even then the Corinthians have grounds to defer their desire to see their favorite apostle receive due praise, to defer it until judgment day, when God will make clear the worth of each one (3:13–14). For the time being, the Corinthians need to regard their founding and supporting teachers under appropriate auspices, namely, as stewards of God, each of whom is distributing goods for which they are equally responsible to the ultimate distributor. While there is indeed a "glory" or a "boast" for Paul in his appointment as messenger of the gospel, it is the glory of a responsibility (9:15–16), not a done deal by which he can rest on his laurels. Human beings, including those invested with awesome responsibilities by God, are not proper objects of boasting (see 1:31), even for those who love them for all the right reasons.

By using the slight sketch of the coming judgment in verse 4, Paul probably intends to put on notice those disrupting the peace of the church at Corinth through their continuing to live in worldly ways by seeking to raise their status through their associations with respected figures. At the return of Christ, all hidden motivations will be made apparent: God "will shed light on what is hidden by darkness and will expose the secret thoughts [literally, "thoughts of the heart"] people have" (v. 5, my trans.). Romans 2:16 contains a similar note on how "God will judge the hidden things people have, according to my gospel, through Jesus Christ" (my trans.). Toward the end of 1 Corinthians (chap. 15) Paul provides an extended explanation of the ushering in of the kingdom; for now, the brief mention of judgment day is sufficient to emphasize the gravity of the church's problems with factionalism.

STEPHEN A. COOPER

Homiletical Perspective

should be silent and subordinate in church; another welcomes them into the pulpit. One group champions Palestinian causes; another sides with Israel. One speaks out about "choice," another about "life."

To all the groups and subgroups within the body of Christ, 1 Corinthians 4 offers a few important reminders. First, Paul says, it is important to remember that the purposes of the heart are largely hidden (v. 5). Until the heart and its intentions are brought out into the open, Christians should forebear to judge each other. Sermons that stress the long horizon of judgment by relating stories of martyrs or sharing "how my thinking has changed" testimonies are the kind of sermons that might deal faithfully with this aspect of the text.

Second, in this passage Paul's focus on his own relationship with the Corinthian church suggests that he is thinking about judging *people*—especially those who live within or who lead the community of faith. For Paul this may be quite a different matter than discerning the truth of issues. While we may disagree over ideas, Paul seems to say, ad hominem arguments have no place in the faith community's discourse. While we may speak heatedly or use vivid language, hate speech is entirely out of order among us. In contemporary culture's struggle with inflamed rhetoric (the abortion debate, talk radio, the Middle East conflict) the preacher will find many points of application for a sermon on this topic.

Finally, today's text suggests the possibility for a sermon that lifts up the notion of balance in the Christian life. This approach to the text sees judging in a larger perspective. It claims that even if some judging among believers is unavoidable, we may take a page from the apostle Paul's book. It may be far better for us, as for Paul, if we can arrange our lives so that judging operates as "a very small thing" (v. 3) and not as the be-all and end-all of our life together. Sermons that offer imagery that evokes the bigger picture of Christian spiritual life and speaks of the magnitude and majesty of God may capture some of the wisdom behind this passage.

JANA CHILDERS

Matthew 6:24-34

24"No one can serve two masters; for a slave will either hate the one and love the other, or be devoted to the one and despise the other. You cannot serve God and wealth.

25"Therefore I tell you, do not worry about your life, what you will eat or what you will drink, or about your body, what you will wear. Is not life more than food, and the body more than clothing? 26Look at the birds of the air; they neither sow nor reap nor gather into barns, and yet your heavenly Father feeds them. Are you not of more value than they? 27And can any of you by worrying add a single hour to your span of life? 28And why do you worry about clothing? Consider the lilies of the field, how they grow; they neither toil nor spin, 29yet I

Theological Perspective

As finite, physical creatures, we are dependent upon those around us—human and nonhuman—for our survival. If we go without water for more than three days or without food for more than three weeks, our vital organs and systems shut down, and we die. We cannot guarantee, on our own, that we will have a constant supply of water or a consistent source of food. In order to live, therefore, we are radically dependent on others—many of whom we do not even know; we are vulnerable, then, to strangers.

This morning I ate cereal for breakfast. I began to wonder about the chain of production that allowed me to go to the pantry, pour cereal into a bowl, add milk, and eat what I needed until around noon, when my hunger will lead me again to the pantry. I wondered, who was the cashier who checked my wife out when she bought the box of cereal at the grocery store? Who stocked it on the shelves? Who trucked it to the loading dock? Who processed the grain at the plant? Who transported the grain to the plant? Who planted and harvested the grain? What herbicides or pesticides did they put on the grain? Where did the water come from that irrigated the field?

What medieval theologian Catherine of Siena said back in the fourteenth century is no less true today. She believed that God could have created us in such a way that we had in ourselves everything we needed

Pastoral Perspective

When we read biblical texts outside of the church, the words sound extremely different from what they sound like on Sunday mornings in the comfort and protection of our sanctuaries. Imagine reading this text on the floor of the New York Stock Exchange: "No one can serve two masters; for a slave will either hate the one and love the other, or be devoted to the one and despise the other. You cannot serve God and wealth" (v. 24). The Word of the Lord. Thanks be to God? It sounds different in that context.

Read this passage to someone who is packing up the office after losing a job: "Therefore I tell you, do not worry about your life, what you will eat or what you will drink, or about your body, what you will wear" (v. 25). It just reads differently in that context.

Read this text to someone who has received a life-threatening diagnosis: "So do not worry about tomorrow, for tomorrow will bring worries of its own. Today's trouble is enough for today" (6:34). Amen to that!

These sayings of Jesus can sound glib, noncompassionate, overly simplified, and even naive. That would be the case if there were nothing to replace the anxiety or the worry about life as we experience it. Simply to tell someone not to worry does not give him or her much help. If you are going to take something away, you should have something to

tell you, even Solomon in all his glory was not clothed like one of these. ³⁰But if God so clothes the grass of the field, which is alive today and tomorrow is thrown into the oven, will he not much more clothe you—you of little faith? ³¹Therefore do not worry, saying, 'What will we eat?' or 'What will we drink?' or 'What will we wear?' ³²For it is the Gentiles who strive for all these things; and indeed your heavenly Father knows that you need all these things. ³³But strive first for the kingdom of God and his righteousness, and all these things will be given to you as well.

³⁴"So do not worry about tomorrow, for tomorrow will bring worries of its own. Today's trouble is enough for today."

Exegetical Perspective

Part of a larger section on possessions in the Sermon on the Mount (6:19–34), this passage begins with a choice reminiscent of Joshua's "Choose this day whom you will serve" (Josh. 24:15). This choice is between two lords (NRSV "masters"): God and Mammon (the Aramaic word translated "wealth" in v. 24).

The reference to loving one's lord links this teaching to the greatest commandment (22:37): "You shall love the Lord your God . . . with all your soul (*psychē*)." This connection is reinforced with references to your *psychē* (trans. "life") in verse 25. If you love God with your whole *psychē*, your loyalty cannot be divided.

God and Mammon offer opposing worldviews. One worldview maintains that your well-being, your very *psychē* (life, soul), is dependent on your ability to accumulate, by cleverness or hard work or the accident of birth, wealth and status, which are fundamental to your survival and in short supply. This is the worldview of those who call Mammon lord. The alternative worldview, taught in the Sermon on the Mount and embodied in Jesus, is that Mammon as lord is an illusion. Wealth is impermanent and vulnerable, and you will spend your energy protecting it rather than the reverse (6:19). All the treasure in the world cannot cause you to live and grow. By

Homiletical Perspective

The words of Jesus are beautiful, of course. "Look at the birds of the air. . . . Consider the lilies of the field. . . . Therefore do not worry." Taken as poetry, the cadence is lilting, the imagery evocative. Jesus, however, is not a dreamy poet; he is a prophet and more, and he is here preaching a sermon that he means to be taken seriously.

Taking these words seriously risks letting them die the death of a thousand qualifications. Yes, the birds of the air do not sow or reap or gather into barns. They do not pay mortgages or college tuitions, either. True, the lilies of the field neither toil nor spin, but they also do not need health insurance and have never had to apply for a job.

When Peter Gomes of Harvard preached on this passage at an exclusive girls' school in Manhattan, he thought Jesus' words about not worrying would calm the anxious overachievers who often populate such academies. Indeed, the sermon seemed to go well . . . with one exception:

[A]t the reception, the father of one of the girls came up to me with fire in his eyes and ice in his voice, and told me that what I had said was a lot of nonsense. I replied that I hadn't said it, that Jesus had. "It's still nonsense," he said, not easily dissuaded by an appeal to scripture. "It was anxiety that got my daughter into this school, it was

Matthew 6:24-34

Theological Perspective

to live complete and fulfilled lives. God, though, chose not to do that. Rather, speaking in God's voice about God's intentions, she writes,

> I could easily have created [humanity] possessed of all that they should need both for body and soul, but I wish that one should have need of the other, and that they should be my ministers to administer the graces and gifts that they have received from me. Whether [one] will or no, [one] cannot help making an act of love.[1]

Indeed, if we are to flourish or even survive, we must make an act of love. We must receive what we need from others, and we must share what they need from us. If we do not receive from others, we will die. If we do not share what we have, they are less likely to share what we need from them; we both will die. We simply cannot help making an act of love. It is love or destruction.

According to Howard Thurman, that great inspiration of the civil rights movement, "Human beings, all human beings belong to each other, and anyone who shuts himself away *diminishes* himself, and anyone who shuts another away from themselves *destroys* himself."[2]

Because of the way God created the world, our own truest self-interest is inextricably tied to that of others. So pursuing God's kingdom, or righteousness, is to participate in and contribute to the great exchange by which we all survive and flourish. It is to honor others by receiving their goods and virtues and then sharing our own goods and virtues vital to others.

To pull away from the interdependent network or web of creation, because we are anxious and afraid, is, then, both suicidal and homicidal. It is like holding one's breath, believing that if we only hold on to what we have, we will not die. All we accomplish is letting the carbon dioxide build up in our bodies, with the result that it begins to poison our system and we have no room to take in the oxygen we so desperately need to live. As Pilgram Marpeck, the sixteenth-century Anabaptist, observed,

> The health of the soul consists of the love of the neighbor. Whoever does not love him, does not love his own soul and seeks, with ignorance, his own advantage to his own greatest disadvantage.[3]

Pastoral Perspective

put in its place. Remove the anxiety and replace it with what?

During my residency to become a pastoral counselor, one of my supervisors taught a class on grief. He used the story of Moses's leading the children of Israel out of Egypt to the promised land. In Egypt, they were "Somebody." Your "Somebody" is the person who you are right now while you are reading this. It is your identity. Sometimes we have to leave our "Somebody" to become "Somebody else." Something happens. We lose our money. We lose our health. We lose a marriage. We lose a job. We have to leave our "Somebody" and become "Somebody else."

That is not always so neat and clean. In between somebody and somebody else is the wilderness of being "Nobody." In the "Nobody" state, I am neither who I was nor who I am going to be. I am lost. It is the wilderness.

You can feel that lostness in the pews of our churches today as people are moving from the "Somebodys" they were to the "Somebody elses" they have to become. It can be argued that sometimes we need to become "Somebody else," but moving through that transition does warrant some compassion. It warrants patience and kindness. It is too simple to just tell people, "Do not worry." It sounds Pollyannaish. They need something to fill the gap.

Would Jesus be so thoughtless as simply to tell folks who are in the "Nobody" state, "Do not worry"? Is Jesus glossing over our concerns? Does he expect us to act as though it does not matter? Do we just will ourselves not to worry, or is he offering an alternative?

He points us to nature. Look around and see how God operates in the natural world. Those principles also operate in the human world. Jesus points to birds and lilies! The Son of God uses birds and lilies to teach human beings about how God operates? Jesus' word is not overly complicated, but it is difficult to grasp. Trust.

Erik Erikson is known for his research in the area of human development. He identified several stages of development, each its particular task. The first and most basic task of human development, according to Erikson, is that of "basic trust."[1] We learn basic trust from our experiences as infants. The consistency with which our parents meet our needs communicates to us that we can trust the world and others to provide for us. If this does not happen, we

---

1. Catherine of Siena, *Treatise on Divine Providence*, in Ray C. Petry, ed., *Late Medieval Mysticism* (Philadelphia: Westminster Press, 1957), 282.

2. Howard Thurman, *The Search for Common Ground* (Richmond, IN: Friends United Press, 1986), 104.

3. See Stephen B. Boyd, *Pilgram Marpeck: His Life and Social Theology* (Durham, NC: Duke University Press, 1992), 69.

1. Erik Erikson, *Identity and the Life Cycle* (New York: W. W. Norton & Co., 1980), 57.

contrast, God can do those things for the world and for every living thing in it.

"Therefore" in verse 25 links verse 24 to what follows, and "I tell you" situates the passage in the history and eternal presence of Jesus. Then the central theme of the passage is introduced: "Do not worry." The verb "worry" appears six times in verses 25–34. Elsewhere in Matthew the verb appears only in 10:19–20, where again the basis for not worrying is the Father's care. The noun appears in 13:22 in the parable of the Sower, where the worries of the world and the lure of wealth choke the word and it yields nothing. There, as here, it is a question of the incompatibility of the two lords of verse 24.

The passage does not change from being about Mammon to being about feelings of anxiety generally. It is always about trusting in God's power and love, over against the power of wealth and privilege. From the perspective of the good news of the kingdom of heaven, it is precisely this teaching that is an antidote to anxiety, a comfort, and a joy: the joy of the person in 13:44 who finds the kingdom of heaven buried in a field and sells all he has to buy that field.

Jesus presents the implications of choosing God with three illustrations, punctuated with rhetorical questions to draw listeners in. The first illustration (v. 26) is the feeding of the birds by the Father, which is evocative of the request for daily bread in 6:11. References to God as Father occur seventeen times in the Sermon on the Mount. This relationship of care and trust, further developed in 7:7–11, is the basis on which the teachings are given.

The illustration does not suggest passivity. The very expression "birds of the *air*" (literally, "heaven") suggests flight, and the passage does not say that the birds need not build nests or find their food. Sowing and reaping and gathering into barns are absurd for birds, impossible and unnecessary activities for them. The suggestion is that the accumulation of wealth as a strategy for sustaining human life in the world is similarly absurd and counterproductive.

As if the listener had said, "But I am not a bird," the next illustration (v. 27) is about human beings, who cannot add a cubit to their height by worrying. This may be a metaphorical reference to adding hours to your life, as the NRSV translates it. Either way, the message is the same: You cannot by your own anxious efforts add anything fundamental to who you are.

In the final illustration (vv. 28–30) Jesus points to wildflowers growing in a field, uncultivated plants

anxiety that kept her here, it was anxiety that got her into Yale, it will be anxiety that will keep her there, and it will be anxiety that will get her a good job. You're selling nonsense."[1]

The notion that one ought to glide through life, thoughtless for the morrow, is certainly no way to cope in a complex, postindustrial society, and it is tempting to see Jesus' words as a lovely, but sentimental impracticality. That is, until we pull back the camera for a wide-angle view and note the context in which Jesus spoke them.

Context, as they say, is everything. The first key context is Jesus' own life. According to Matthew, Jesus did not waft blithely through life, like some flower child, humming "Don't Worry, Be Happy." Far from living a life where necessities grow freely on trees, Jesus told one of his would-be followers that the birds of the air may have nests, but he did not even have a place "to lay his head" (Matt. 8:20). Jesus may have said, "Do not worry about tomorrow," but the same Jesus later fell on his knees at Gethsemane because his own tomorrow had a cross in it, and he was "deeply grieved, even to death" (Matt. 26:38). Whatever Jesus' words about the birds and the lilies may mean, in the context of his own life and ministry they are in no way a provocation to view life as a free all-you-can-eat buffet or to believe that we are somehow immune from the deep concerns of mortality.

The second important context of Jesus' words is the Sermon on the Mount itself, which is, if nothing else, an invigoration of the faithful imagination, an invitation to see an alternative reality, a reality in which God is a loving parent instead of a distant tyrant, a reality in which the meek are the landowners, the merciful are the legislators, the peacemakers are the celebrities, and the people the Roman occupiers would consider to be participants in a bizarre religious sect at best and dispensable insurrectionists at worst turn out to be the salt of the earth and the light of the world.

When Jesus asks us to "look" at the birds of the air and to "consider" the lilies of the field, he is not asking us to imitate sparrows and flowers. He is rather asking us to peer more deeply into that alternative reality called the kingdom of heaven. New Testament scholar Robert Tannehill reminds us that the verbs here—"look" and "consider"—are exceptionally strong. Jesus wants us not merely to glance

---

1. Peter Gomes, *The Good Book: Reading the Bible with Mind and Heart* (New York: HarperOne, 2002), 179.

Matthew 6:24-34

Theological Perspective

We ourselves cannot transform the carbon dioxide into oxygen; only plants can do that. We can, though, honor them by doing what only we can do—protect them from unnatural harm. To hold our breath—to cut ourselves off from the resources we need for survival—not only destroys us, but, by extension, robs others of what they need from us.

The ordering of God in creation—the righteousness of God—and the provision of what we and others need for our flourishing are two sides of the same coin. Jesus tells his followers to "strive first for the kingdom of God and his righteousness, and all these things will be given to you as well" (v. 33). They will. That is simply the nature of the universe that God has created. To believe that our deepest interests conflict with those of others is to misunderstand the nature of reality and the generosity at the heart of it. It is a failure to grasp the way the universe works. Fear and the hoarding it produces stop the flow, or great exchange, by which the universe functions and they lead to death. Love and the self-giving it motivates contribute to the reciprocity by which life is sustained. The choice is simple—life or death.

The decision to follow the way of life, however, is frightening. We have all known those who seem motivated more by fear than by love, by hoarding than by generosity. We have known those whose reflex is to exploit our vulnerability and that of others, rather than respond to meet it with compassion and self-giving. In the face of such a one, or in the face of institutions that seem bent on exploitation, choosing life requires a courage born of faith, hope, and love.

STEPHEN B. BOYD

Pastoral Perspective

learn "basic mistrust." Erikson writes, "There are millions who profess faith, yet in practice mistrust both life and man [sic]."[2]

Religious practice, church membership, theological debates are one thing. Trust is something altogether different. Trust is based not upon what we can see but upon what we cannot see. It is based upon past experience. We look back for trust in moving ahead.

From a pastoral perspective, we can go deeper than simply telling people, "Do not worry." We have a biblical record of God providing in the midst of scarcity, crisis, failure, and despair. We also have our own stories of God's providence and grace. If that is not enough, then look at the birds and the lilies. We have evidence in nature that God will sustain us. We have the privilege of preaching hope based upon the activities and the person of God. Replace the worry with trust. There is evidence for it.

What do you gain by hanging onto the anxiety anyway? Jesus asked that question. What is so valuable about panicking? What do you have to lose if you let go of that anxiety and gain a deeper sense of composure based on trust in the providence of God? That is the tradeoff Jesus is asking us to consider.

It is callous to just tell someone who is in a dire situation not to worry. There is plenty to worry about; we are human beings, and worry comes all too easily. However, if we the church are going to ask for a nonanxious life, we have to offer something in its place. Abandon your anxiety, for a life that is surrendered to the loving providence of God. If there is no such providence, if you are just engaged in wishful thinking, then you die a fool who trusted in God. Consider the alternatives.

STEVEN P. EASON

---

2. Ibid., 66.

Exegetical Perspective

that the poor might burn for fuel but that exceed Solomon's splendor in glorious beauty. The verb "labor" (*kopiaō*) appears again in 11:28–30: "Come to me, all you that are weary (*kopiaō*, KJV "labor"). . . . Take my yoke upon you . . . and you will find rest for your souls (*psychē*)." This supremely comforting invitation echoes and undergirds the images and imperatives of comfort in 6:24–34.

Verse 31 is a restatement and development of the theme: "Do not worry." The Gentiles, who do not know God, seek after all these things, but, as in the introduction to the Lord's Prayer in 6:8, the Father knows your needs before you ask. On that basis, there is a return to the choice of verse 24. Instead of seeking unnecessary wealth, the one who chooses God as lord is free to seek (*zētein*) God's kingdom and the righteousness flowing from it like water; and 7:7 promises that everyone who searches (*zētein*) will find. While you could not *add* a cubit to your life (6:27), God will now *add* to you (the same verb, translated here "give") all that you need.

Kingdom references are laced throughout the Sermon from beginning to end and mark the Lord's Prayer at its center (6:10). Righteousness, which appears five times in the Sermon, characterizes the kingdom ethic, which is based on abundance, not scarcity, and on care for all people, not privilege for a few. Together they are Matthew's keys to understanding life with God.

The promise is not that there will be no trouble (v. 34); Scripture never makes that promise for the children of God. Still, Jesus urges the disciples and the crowd and his followers in every age to choose the one who loves them. Mammon does not work as a defense against future troubles; it depletes the *psychē* and creates needless burdens, like birds trying to plant food or lilies trying to labor and spin. By contrast, God's strange, countercultural kingdom promises the glorious beauty of the lilies and the soaring freedom of the birds to those who take upon themselves the yoke of the crucified, risen Jesus and find their treasure there.

MEDA A. A. STAMPER

Homiletical Perspective

at, mull over, or note quickly, but to *look* . . . really look.[2] If we look long enough and hard enough at the birds of the air and the lilies of the field, suddenly there will break into our imagination a slice of that alternative reality, a world not of tooth and claw but a world of providential care, a world in which the One who created it delights in tending the garden and nourishing the creature.

What if we live in that world? What if we live, not in a world where we have been abandoned to our own devices, but in a world of divine abundance, a world where "your heavenly Father knows that you need all these things" (v. 32), a world not ruled by acquisitiveness and insecurity, but a world in which God gives gift after gift after gift? How we view ourselves and our lives depends upon which reality we believe we are living in. Theologian Arthur C. McGill once said that it does no good to command people to be generous and unselfish, because "whether people serve themselves or serve others is not in their power to choose. This is decided," said McGill, "wholly in terms of the kind of world in which they think they live, in terms of the kind of power that they see ruling the roost. In New Testament terms they live or die according to the king that holds them and the kingdom to which they belong."[3]

So Jesus invites us, through the birds and the lilies, to see truly the world of loving providence in which we live. Once we have seen that, really seen it, then we can turn back to the world of mortgages and tuitions, even a world of crosses and tyranny, and go out in faith and confidence that ultimately, as Julian said, all manner of things shall be well.

THOMAS G. LONG

---

2. Robert C. Tannehill, *The Sword of His Mouth* (Philadelphia: Fortress Press, 1975), 62–63.
3. Arthur C. McGill, *Suffering: A Test of Theological Method* (Philadelphia: Westminster Press, 1982), 92.

Deuteronomy 11:18-21, 26-28

[18]You shall put these words of mine in your heart and soul, and you shall bind them as a sign on your hand, and fix them as an emblem on your forehead. [19]Teach them to your children, talking about them when you are at home and when you are away, when you lie down and when you rise. [20]Write them on the doorposts of your house and on your gates, [21]so that your days and the days of your children may be multiplied in the land that the LORD swore to your ancestors to give them, as long as the heavens are above the earth. . . .

[26]See, I am setting before you today a blessing and a curse: [27]the blessing, if you obey the commandments of the LORD your God that I am commanding you today; [28]and the curse, if you do not obey the commandments of the LORD your God, but turn from the way that I am commanding you today, to follow other gods that you have not known.

Theological Perspective

Throughout the book of Deuteronomy, as in this passage, the Lord, speaking through Moses, commands us to take the words of the Lord to heart and into our very souls. How do we accomplish this? Deuteronomy, which is not just a code of law but also a sermon that preaches it, demonstrates what it takes to gain profound knowledge of the will and ways of God. It shows us that religious education is not a matter of applying good teaching technique to the content of faith. The means of knowing God that form us for love and service are organically rooted in faith. Who God is and what God requires of us dictate the pedagogy by which God is best known.

This passage emphasizes three acts of teaching and learning that both stem from and lead to deep understanding of God and the things of God.

Remember. God opens our minds to instruction by reminding us what God has already done on our behalf. "These words" in today's passage and the almost identical section of Deuteronomy 6:6–9 refer to the Shema, the great instruction the Israelites have just been commanded to hear that the Lord is one and is to be loved with heart and soul and strength. They also refer to the longer history recalled throughout Deuteronomy, the story of "the LORD, who brought you out of the land of Egypt, out of the

Pastoral Perspective

At the heart of Deuteronomy is the concern that the people of Israel find a meaningful central identity. Deuteronomy is dedicated to the exploration of the questions: In relation to other peoples, who are we? In relation to other nations, who are we? In relation to worshipers of other gods, who are we? Deuteronomy calls the people to keep the God who led them out of Egypt at the center of their lives. It warns them that life without God at the center will be a very difficult life.

The central concern of Deuteronomy is nationalistic. It is also spiritual, moral, and pastoral. The questions Deuteronomy explores are questions the pastor explores as she leads her people. The questions Deuteronomy lifts up are the concerns the pastor addresses as he preaches God's word. Identity questions are ultimately questions of survival and purpose. Some of us are part of communities in which the question of survival is paramount. The central question our people ask is, "How am I going to make it through the day?" Some of us are part of communities in which survival concerns are less pronounced but meaning concerns are heightened. The central question becomes, "I am going to make it through the day, but so what?" In both questions identity provides a central point of reference. Remembering who we are helps us make it through

Exegetical Perspective

Deuteronomy is presented as the last words of Moses, spoken to those that had survived the postexodus journey of nearly forty years. Moses, about to depart from his people as they enter the land of promise, reviews all—or much—they have experienced. Since the stories are also offered in Exodus, Leviticus, and Numbers, the information is not new; but the retrospective angle and the distinctive perspective that the Moses of Deuteronomy offers for the consideration of all his hearers, ourselves included, is.

Suppose your family has just undergone a difficult and traumatic journey and arrived at a destination. You are then asked to write the story of a similar adventure of your great-grandparents as they led their kin on a similar trek, to arrive at some place they desired to be. As you research and write up the old story, it will be infiltrated—and richly enhanced—by experiences you have just had. Your journey will sensitize you more to what your relatives experienced than would be the case if you had never left your armchair. Your story thus will make good use of two perspectives: one quite recent and one much older.

It is similar with Deuteronomy. The setting is Moses's review of the postexodus journey, sometime in the second millennium BCE; those are the details provided. Scholars also sense strongly the more recent

Homiletical Perspective

The long season between Pentecost and Advent is perfect for focusing on ecclesial growth (the liturgical color is green, after all). This passage, encouraging us to choose to place divine teachings in our hearts and souls, to breathe them in, to live them with our community's children, to allow them to form our identity, invites the preaching of holy directives into the soul of our congregation. A significant portion of who we are as a faith community comes from preaching. God's words are to be as close as our own breath and as essential to our survival. Claremont theologian Marjorie Suchocki instructs us: "In the process of your regular preaching, you are giving your congregation the fundamental symbols that in the providence of God become the lens through which your parishioners organize and interpret the meaning of their experiences, and so direct their actions."[1] Our preaching assists what Deuteronomy 11 directs. The consciousness and conscience of congregations are being shaped in part through the cumulative effect of our preaching.

Notice that the passage does not report what "these words of mine" (v. 18) are, so sermons must reenvision what they mean for our congregation at

---

1. Marjorie Hewitt Suchocki, *The Whispered Word: A Theology of Preaching* (St. Louis: Chalice Press, 1999), 65.

Deuteronomy 11:18-21, 26-28

Theological Perspective

house of slavery" (Deut. 6:12). Remembering the words and the story they tell are important, because they warm the heart with gratitude. They foster a readiness to hear the commandments that are about to be handed down.

Under some circumstances remembering God's mighty acts and loving provisions for us is not too difficult. In services of covenant renewal, the Israelites regularly recalled what God had done for them, as do Jews today and Christians in their own liturgies. On a daily basis, however, all people of faith are easily distracted by competing demands for our attention and focus. To combat this tendency, Deuteronomy prescribes mnemonics, memory devices to prevent "these words" from being forgotten.

Commentators debate whether the order to bind the words "as a sign on your hand, and fix them as an emblem on your forehead" (11:18; 6:8) was intended to be taken literally, but since at least the time of Second Temple Judaism, many observant Jews have done so. They tie *tefellim*, leather boxes, on their foreheads and strap them to the backs of their hands. The boxes contain words on parchment, sometimes the words of passages like this one that describe this practice, or in some traditions the Ten Commandments or the Shema. Significantly, *tefellim* are worn only on weekdays. Such reminders are not needed on the Sabbath and on holy days. Pious Jews also put mezuzahs, parchments in cases, on the doorposts to their houses, and in ancient times "these words" were inscribed on the stone gates of their cities.

Christians have their versions of these practices: crosses worn as pendants, religious pictures and sayings on the walls. They all come to the same point: the first step toward a deeper understanding of God is to remember—every day, not just on special occasions—what one already knows of God's goodness and care.

Re-present. The Israelites are instructed not only to remember the words of the Lord, but also to teach them to their children "when you are at home and when you are away, when you lie down and when you rise" (v. 19). Constant personal instruction, in intimate residential settings and in public, is not a cost-effective method of education. Giving learners a workbook or, in a more contemporary mode, a computer program is far more efficient. These impersonal pedagogies may not, however, be effective ways to teach what God wants us to know. Truth about

Pastoral Perspective

the day. Recalling who we are helps us define our purpose in times of tension and times of calm.

While the survival of the people is a concern in Deuteronomy, it is a less pronounced concern than it was in Exodus. In Deuteronomy the people have survived the wilderness. They have made it to the boundary of the promised land. It appears that they will make it through the day. Thus the questions the people ask are changing. Their survival questions have not been eliminated, but they are also becoming identity questions. Deuteronomy recognizes this change of perspective and gives voice to the questions that come with it. Indeed, it is a pastoral book, a pastoral effort.

Today's text provides meaningful answers to the meaningful questions of identity. It teaches the people that they find identity as they take the living story of their covenant with God to heart, as they "put these words of mine in your heart and soul" (v. 18a). The people are then instructed to do something tangible with God's words, God's story, God's covenant. The verbs that follow are *bind, fix, teach, talk,* and *write.* Taking these actions will result in the ongoing gift of a land to call home, the lasting promise of a place in which they will dwell securely. In the final verses of this text, these actions are described as a choice. To take them is to choose a blessing. To refuse to take them is to choose a curse.

The pastor must allow room for cultural difference and historical distance in helping her community apply the teachings of this text to her community's search for identity. The pastor must help his community decide what in this text is timeless and what is time bound. The following questions are important in this ongoing work of sifting, sorting, discerning, and deciding:

1. How does God's ongoing story of liberation find tangible expression in the life of our community? Is it expressed in the ministry we undertake? Is it expressed in the words we speak? Is it expressed in the songs we sing? Is it expressed in the prayers we offer? Does this story shape our identity?
2. What symbols do we use to identify ourselves with and connect ourselves to God's ongoing story? Sometimes we convince ourselves that "mere symbols" and "physical things" do not matter. We argue that since they are not eternal they are not significant. In contrast to this line of thinking is a short dialogue between an Episcopalian priest and a grieving widow in Gail Godwin's novel *Evensong.* In reference to her recently

Exegetical Perspective

(perhaps sixth-century) experience of Israel, exiled in Babylon and now returning to attempt to live in the land of promise as their ancestors did, as God's people. The stories are those of the exodus, but the experience and ethos may be more plausibly those of the survivors of life in Babylon. We, reading in the twenty-first century, approach from our own experience as well. The layering intensifies the meaning.

In the section of the book concluding with today's portion, Moses retells the story of Mount Horeb (elsewhere called Sinai), where Israel is offered a covenant with God. Though the people seem to accept the terms, they struggle to do so, falling soon and often into situations our text calls "idolatry," worship of other gods. Though Moses urges obedience to the Ten Commandments, he inevitably returns to what he makes the cardinal or "hinge" sin, the worship of gods other than YHWH, who has covenanted with Israel.

In today's verses, Moses preaches commitment to the terms God has offered and that the people have, verbally at least, accepted. He begs the people to "keep" the law, in all the senses of that word in English (as well as in Hebrew). They are to place the word—which we may understand as enclosing the relationship with God, personal and communal—in their hearts, center for human thinking, feeling, and deciding.

Then he adds: Also place it everywhere your eye will fall upon as well. Wear it like a bracelet, bind it as a headband. We may think of the wristlets worn today to remember persons or causes, and we are surely familiar with signs worn on our clothing to recall to ourselves and others what we want to keep before our eyes, in our awareness. Traditional Jews wear such markers with their attire to this day. Moses continues to elaborate on the ways God's word is to be kept: Speak of it constantly, he urges, teaching it to your children, pondering it yourselves: when you travel, when you are at home; in the house, outside the house; working, walking, resting; dawn to dusk, and then at dawn again—in short, always. Write the words where you will see them, he admonishes. These words are for keeping.

Moses stresses what is at stake. These words are for life: Your life depends on remembering them, keeping them, loving them. This is where our dual perspective comes in. Moses, about to leave his people in the capable hands of Joshua, warns them that only by implementing all God has said can they expect to thrive, once they cross into the land. We can hear as well the leaders of the groups of people

Homiletical Perspective

this time. Just as there is appropriately a sense of urgency for people preparing to enter the promised land, so we should communicate the importance of these ideas for our people. The future is always at stake. The sermon should remind us that in each generation we are stepping into new arenas. All around are political, social, and cultural forces at work. We must continually decide whom we will follow. Moses's directions call us to live out of our commitment to YHWH, where godly virtues shape us into a compassionate community whose influence spreads grace abundantly throughout the world.

Of course the sermon needs caution in discussing the "cursing" parts. When God's directions are not followed, there are consequences, but not because God throws proverbial lightning bolts of punishment. Rather, bad things result from our disregarding divine ways. Since creation is interrelated, when we turn from holy ways, we experience our corporate life as "cursed."

Society is swollen with examples. When a local factory lets 200 workers go because of budget cuts, we are all affected. If the salaries of the executives are ten times the salary of an average worker, it does not take a mathematical genius to figure out that cutting the salaries of a dozen executives could have saved many of those workers' jobs.

When the weather was most bitter last winter, we heard reports of people dying from exposure. When someone is allowed to freeze to death, we are all affected. Our humanity is eroded. The gifts that that person brought to the community are lost. Even the gift of being a person who needs us was ignored. We are all lessened by such tragedies—and lessened even more when we ignore the deaths.

Alternately, anyone who has ever eaten at a soup kitchen knows that those around the table easily share information about where to get the next meal, what shelter might have room if a place to sleep is needed, or where clothes and other necessities are available. Often these quite vulnerable folks easily share what they have with people they met only in line or at the table. They seem to understand that the welfare of each influences our corporate welfare. Perhaps they just remember that not having a place to sleep is a terrible curse, and they do not want anyone else to have to experience it.

Hear the blessing part coming in? In various places in the Hebrew Bible, Moses is depicted as conveying divine directions that honoring God is reflected in our caring for those who are less able to care for themselves. Instructions to care for widows,

Deuteronomy 11:18-21, 26-28

Theological Perspective

God, wrote the Scottish theologian Thomas Torrance, is personal

> and must be communicated personally and historically. That is to say, the Truth must be communicated to us by other persons in time. It is not something that we can tell to ourselves, or to which we can relate ourselves timelessly. . . . In order to learn the Truth we must allow others to tell it to us and instruct us.[1]

For the knowledge of God to touch our hearts and shape our souls, we must learn from others whom it has touched and shaped, and then we must in turn impersonate the faith and teach it to the next generation.

Obey. Today's reading comes at the end of the prologue section of Deuteronomy, and it concludes with a traditional ancient Near Eastern form, the promise of blessing for keeping the commandments and of curse for disobedience. This may seem like an abrupt and threatening turn from the theme of knowing and loving God, but in Deuteronomy the whole-hearted, single-minded love of God and faithful obedience to God's commandments are inseparable. Christians sometimes dismiss this collation of love and action as outmoded, because the grace of God in Jesus Christ has displaced "works." Deuteronomy, however, has its own ways of describing the action of grace. God makes God's chosen people capable, "circumcising their hearts" (Deut. 30:6) so that they can love *and* obey: "Surely, this commandment that I am commanding you today is not too hard for you, nor is it too far away. . . . No, the word is very near to you; it is in your mouth and in your heart for you to observe" (Deut. 30:11, 14).

It is as true for us as it was for Moses's audience: the knowledge of God that flows from remembering God's graciousness to us and from learning God's love and God's law from exemplary teachers—this kind of learning gives us the motivation, clarity, and courage to enact the word ourselves. Thus, keeping the commandments (literally, in Hebrew, "the words") with all our heart and mind and strength is a means and an end of religious education, and the greatest benefit of the love of God.

BARBARA G. WHEELER

Pastoral Perspective

deceased husband, Paul, the widow Helen says, "Our living room at Christmas without any tree would be an insult to Paul. If I can't have his faith I can at least let myself be carried along by the forms, wouldn't you say." The priest, Margaret, replies, "Absolutely, on some days the forms completely carry me . . . On other days, enough glimpses of meaning break through to keep me from feeling like a fraud."[1] In what ways do the symbols of our place in God's story carry us?

3. What are we teaching our children? What do we intentionally communicate to them about their place in God's story? What do we unintentionally communicate to them? Do we understand that a child's world is alive with the potential to experience God?

4. Is there a connection between what we profess at church and what happens in our homes? What part of God's ongoing story of liberation do we take home with us? Grocery stores, restaurants, and other purveyors of food and meals have discovered that the "take home" market is a booming market. In the early days of television, the church at which I am the pastor produced a program entitled "The Church in Thy House." The program did not last, but the title is a reminder of the challenge of Deuteronomy to take God's story home with us.

5. How do we handle the blessing-and-curse portion of this passage? Many of us like to think that we are above serving God only because we think that our service will cause good things to come into our lives. Doubtless the limits to this line of thinking are well documented. However, is there not a certain level of safety, sanity, and serenity that comes from seeking to align our lives with God's story? Is there not a joyous identity in seeking to find identity in keeping the commands of our Creator?

The pastoral concerns of Deuteronomy lead us to consider the practices and professions of our community. They lead us to ask what kind of identity these are leading us to form and find. They connect us with a tradition that is both ancient and ever new.

H. JAMES HOPKINS

---

1. Thomas F. Torrance, *The School of Faith: The Catechisms of the Reformed Church* (New York: Harper & Bros., 1959), xxxiii.

1. Gail Godwin, *Evensong* (New York: Ballantine Books, 1999), 126.

Exegetical Perspective

returning from their own experience of Egypt-of-the East (Babylon), that they and their families will survive to the extent that they obey God's word, keep it prominent and fruitful in their lives. God has made the promise of life in the land to long-ago ancestors. The question is not whether *God* will come through but how *we*—all of us as God's people—will do.

Moses grows stern near the end of the passage, to conduce obedience. Every leader of God's people knows that the record is mixed at best, abysmal at worst. The Moses of the story's setting can well recall—and does—the trail of struggle across the wilderness for forty years. The leaders of later generations surely know that their people will not have done much better. The land is always in danger of being lost; exile has happened more than once. Moses uses strong language here, words bold and clear: A blessing and a curse. The blessing is life on the land; the curse is to be driven from it. How do we choose well, "keep" the law so that life on the land can be embraced? Moses has already given his best advice: Internalize it, externalize it, talk it, do it.

Deuteronomy is often accused of making these basic life-and-death, blessing-and-curse options simple and self-fulfilling. The word "retribution" is charged, suggesting that good deeds are rewarded and bad ones punished. The reality is much more complex and not so easy to discern. Moses in Deuteronomy makes it clear that human deeds have consequences and that one's actions affect others. However, the strength of the passage (exhortatory preaching at its best) is that it challenges hearers to make God's relational word so treasured—lovingly kept—that it is the deepest joy of God's people. Historical studies make abundantly clear that the reasons for exile from the land, whenever it happened, arose from complex political, social, and economic factors not easily reducible to disobedience. As we read the passage, we need to take care not to oversimplify the texture the book offers us.

BARBARA GREEN

Homiletical Perspective

immigrants, and orphans are explicit. Just distribution of land is required. In other words, the welfare of the whole depends on the well-being of each. Pastor, scholar, and civil rights leader Martin Luther King Jr. preached this idea, explaining: "We are all caught in an inescapable network of mutuality, tied into a single garment of destiny. Whatever affects one directly, affects all indirectly. We are made to live together because of the interrelated structure of reality."[2]

To care for those who are vulnerable reflects our commitment to the teachings of YHWH. The NT is not the only place we get the sense that God believes what we do for others we do for God. Anytime people share in the gift of caring for those in need, we are all enriched. We might say that in caring for others we are all "blessed." The Deuteronomist clarifies this by putting into Moses's mouth the invitation to receive blessings from following the ways of God, and the warning that dishonoring God's ways leads to sadness, impairment, and affliction.

Unfortunately, our preaching on this text requires the admission that sometimes the stinkers thrive. It is not self-evident that the faithful are blessed and the unfaithful cursed. Some executives cut jobs and redecorate their offices. Their only worries seem to be where to stockpile their wealth unobserved. The words of Moses are to those folks too. For their selfish hoarding and their disregard of vulnerable persons (recently unemployed, returning veterans, persons with disabilities who need a job), all of society suffers. They may have three homes and secret bank accounts, but they are also affected by a society where the future is uncertain, where people are disheartened or desperate.

Our actions, individually and corporately, matter; each makes society stronger and better, or weaker and crueler. We get to choose whether we will follow the words of YHWH. So the sermon needs to spell out ideas (even specific suggestions) for individuals and the congregation to breathe in divine directives and to live out of the words of God in their hearts and souls.

MARY ALICE MULLIGAN

---

2. Martin Luther King Jr., "A Christmas Sermon on Peace," in *A Testament of Hope: The Essential Writings and Speeches of Martin Luther King, Jr.*, ed. James Washington (San Francisco: HarperCollins, 1991), 254.

Psalm 31:1‑5, 19‑24

¹In you, O Lord, I seek refuge;
   do not let me ever be put to shame;
   in your righteousness deliver me.
²Incline your ear to me;
   rescue me speedily.
 Be a rock of refuge for me,
   a strong fortress to save me.

³You are indeed my rock and my fortress;
   for your name's sake lead me and guide me,
⁴take me out of the net that is hidden for me,
   for you are my refuge.
⁵Into your hand I commit my spirit;
   you have redeemed me, O Lord, faithful God.
. . . .
¹⁹O how abundant is your goodness
   that you have laid up for those who fear you,
 and accomplished for those who take refuge in you,
   in the sight of everyone!

Theological Perspective

Some of the most exemplary lives of faith and faith-fulness are lived by people at the margins of society. God is a source of solace and strength for the poor, the lame, and those who are frowned upon in polite company on account of how they look, or what they eat, or whom they love. Of course, some critics have suggested that this phenomenon may simply be an act of projection—an effort by the downtrodden to imagine a better life for themselves. An alternative explanation seems more persuasive; namely, that the comforts that mark most of our lives—health, wealth, and social acceptance—tend to make us forgetful of our utter dependence on God. Those who live on the margins have no such luxury; they are reminded of that dependence every day.

The German theologian Friedrich Schleiermacher famously described religion as "the feeling of absolute dependence." While such language now strikes us as too much a product of the romantic era's enthusiasm for the emotions, and as pointing toward too experiential an account of the Christian faith, the phrase still expresses something quite important. Those who are convinced that they do not need to depend on anything outside of themselves find it very difficult to have faith in anyone or anything. Only when we recognize the existence of something "ever greater" (and beyond our direct

Pastoral Perspective

The lectionary sometimes makes strange choices. The suggested verses from Psalm 31 seem to focus on the happy-speak side of faith. Although one may not choose to have an entire psalm read in every worship service, especially the longer ones (it takes a really accomplished reader to add to the worship experience rather than detract from it), it might be a soulful experience to hear and meditate upon this psalm, especially those verses which the lectionary has deselected. After all, how much of our pastoral lives are taken up by the misery of others (or our own misery)?

It really matters little who wrote this psalm or why. It speaks to our immediate lives. Any one person in the church could have written this from his or her own experience at some point in his/her life. Any pastor could have written it.

Unfortunately it is a cliché to say that life today is too fast, too expensive, too secular, too _____ (fill in the blank).

Sometimes life is too long. Modern medicine is bent on extending the years one lives regardless of the quality of one's life. How do we respond to those prayers that begin, "O Lord, please take me now . . ."? One feels great sorrow seeing one's parent or other loved one become too feeble to be independent. Imagine the misery the person feels who no longer has

²⁰In the shelter of your presence you hide them
     from human plots;
  you hold them safe under your shelter
     from contentious tongues.

²¹Blessed be the LORD,
     for he has wondrously shown his steadfast love to me
     when I was beset as a city under siege.
²²I had said in my alarm,
     "I am driven far from your sight."
  But you heard my supplications
     when I cried out to you for help.

²³Love the LORD, all you his saints.
     The LORD preserves the faithful,
     but abundantly repays the one who acts haughtily.
²⁴Be strong, and let your heart take courage,
     all you who wait for the LORD.

Exegetical Perspective

The psalm is an individual prayer of lament and a
plea for God's help. It closes with a word of praise
and thanksgiving for help received or anticipated.
The opening lines, verses 1–5, clearly indicate the
psalmist's sense of God's active presence, even in the
midst of the suffering and sense of loss expressed in
the body of the complaint or lament.

The religious setting of complaints and laments in
the book of Psalms includes a widespread belief that
suffering comes about as a consequence of human sin
and failing. Worshipers know that God sees all and is
well aware of human misdeeds, but the community
sees the suffering and infers misconduct on the worshiper's part and displeasure on God's part. Some
laments contain protests of innocence; others
acknowledge the worshiper's guilt. Still others cry out
for help quite apart from confession of sin or protestation of innocence. The situation is desperate, God
alone can help, and God may be persuaded to do so!

The first three verses are almost identical to the
words of Psalm 71:1–3. These verses and the two
that follow open the lectionary reading. They offer a
profound prayer to God for help, marked by a clear
sense of the intimacy between the Deity and the
worshiper. The psalmist has deep need but knows
without question that God can be depended upon to
come to the worshiper's aid. In fact, these opening

Homiletical Perspective

In the first verse of this psalm and two other times
within it, the reader encounters the word "shame."
The connotations of shame for the psalmist's community and our communities are rich. Inherent in
the concept of shame is *expectation*. The writer had
great expectations of God, and God had great expectations of God's people. Expectations that YHWH
had of the people and expectations that the people
had of YHWH are spelled out in the biblical
covenants such as the Mosaic covenant. The
covenants contain details of the conditions under
which the children of Israel would be blessed and
those conditions under which the people of Israel
would be cursed. The people fully expected that if
they were faithful to God and followed the law, they
would be blessed. That was the agreement.

The writer of this psalm was baffled. He expected
God to deliver him. He expected God to protect him
from his enemies. He expected God to shelter him
from the exigencies of life. He trusted in God. However, YHWH seemed to have abandoned him, and he
did not understand why. The psalmist did not provide any details about his circumstances or why
exactly he felt God abandoned him. However, even
without the particulars, the preacher can highlight
the fact that people in our faith communities also
have high expectations of YHWH. Some expect that

Psalm 31:1-5, 19-24

Theological Perspective

control) do we make space for God in our lives. This explains why those who live life close to the bone often find themselves focused on the transcendent, while those of us leading lives of quiet desperation often find it difficult to make room for faith.

The close connection between dependence on God and faith in God is a frequent theme in the Psalms. God is described as the only one in whom we rightly place our trust—the only one on whom we can reliably depend. The opening verses of Psalm 31 capture this notion beautifully; using metaphors of refuge and rock, of crag and tower, the psalmist praises God's solidity and protective care. We who live most of our lives indoors, sheltered from the weather and from predators, may not always appreciate the tremendous relief that a hiker experiences upon reaching a simple hut during a mountain snowstorm, or happening upon a rocky outcropping to use as a lookout. Those whose lives are less protected by human artifice may find themselves particularly grateful for the kind of refuge that only God can provide.

Of course, such reliance on God may strike us as naive. We're not likely to tear down our houses, give away our savings, or forgo the latest medical treatments as a way of reminding ourselves that "God will provide." At the same time, it would be unwise to imagine that we can depend entirely upon our own ingenuity. Do we really ensure our safety when we surround ourselves with more and more layers of protection—more walls and fences and security systems? Does not such behavior simply cut us off from the rest of the world, from the wonders of creation and from the joys of human community? Simon and Garfunkel once sang, with deep irony, of those for whom the word "rock" describes not God but themselves: "I am a rock; / I am an island."[1] This is, of course, one possible strategy of protection; after all, as the songwriter points out, such inanimate objects "feel no pain"; they never cry.

The alternative to such self-reliant isolation is an acceptance of our own dependence—on the world around us, on other people, and ultimately on God. This does not necessarily entail a belief that God will put a physical roof over our heads or round up our enemies in a giant net, but a willingness to rely on God for our ultimate protection makes many of these threats seem less threatening.[2] If we believe ourselves to be deeply loved by God, can we really be

Pastoral Perspective

control over her mind or body. When we feel weak, vulnerable, scared, we need refuge, we need a rock to which we can cling. Where will we find that strong fortress that can save us? In the gossiping community we call church? In the stressed pastor's office?

Sometimes life is too short. The drunk youthful driver takes out several innocent young lives. The pain is too much. Our eyes waste away from grief, our souls and bodies also. Upon whom do we call to find relief? Where will we find deliverance?

Life is just too hard for some persons. Even the most beautiful, most delightful, and most intelligent persons sometimes struggle to see the light at the end of the tunnel. Addictions are powerful demons and often appear to win the battle in this life. Depression can drain the lifeblood out of the strongest soul. Where is the speedy rescue?

A desperate mother calls the first church number she can put her finger on. She has three children, her husband has left her, and she is pregnant. Is abortion a sin? How does God feel about her? Will she be condemned for eternity? The pastor inserts words of comfort between the frantic questions, and then the phone is dead. There is no caller ID. Who was she? Where did she go? What will she do? Both the mother and the pastor feel alarm and cry for help.

Just now, as this author is working on this essay, a woman calls to say that one of her dogs suddenly has died. "When will it stop? First my mom, then my dad, and now Rex." She has just returned home from an extended visit to care for her parents, and stayed to care for the estate of her deceased parents. "You should read Psalm 31. It just really speaks to your situation." She immediately picks up her Bible and reads the psalm. Tears pour through the phone as she says "Yup," and then "Oh, that's beautiful. Thank you. While I was away, I searched for another church and finally found one that felt like home." Supplications were heard. Refuge was provided.

"My cancer has returned. I just don't know if I can fight it anymore. I don't know what I'm supposed to learn from this. What should I be doing? How should I pray? What should I read?"

Read the Psalms. Thank God for the Psalms. They reflect the height and depth of human experience. Feelings are not sanitized, but exposed in raw light.

Look at all the disheartening feelings listed in this psalm—shame, horror, terror, scorn, dread, contempt. The lectionary deselects some of the most depressing, but attention should be paid. Life is not always fun. Christians must deal with these very human emotions in life.

---

1. Paul Simon, "I Am a Rock."
2. On this point, the testimony of pacifist Christians is particularly moving. See, for example, John Howard Yoder, *What Would You Do? A Serious Answer to a Standard Question* (Scottdale, PA: Herald Press, 1992).

Exegetical Perspective

lines are less a prayer for help than an affirmation of trust and confidence in God. That is why the lines have such a large place in the hymnody and prayers of synagogue and church.

At the same time, the middle part of the psalm, verses 6–18, show how real is the suffering of the poet. Of course, one must allow for possible exaggeration, for descriptions of suffering and a sense of abandonment by God that are designed to move the Deity to pity and compassion, even as our prayers often dramatize our actual situations. In this middle section of the psalm we do not find much of the language of attack upon one's accusing enemies or upon God. The complaint is colorfully and powerfully presented, but the worshiper does not appear to believe that human enemies are all around, hoping for the worst to befall the worshiper.

The prayer of praise and thanksgiving that concludes the psalm, the remaining verses of the lectionary text, express heartfelt praise and thanks to God for deliverance. It is never possible to know what will have happened in the psalmist's experience to warrant such praise and thanksgiving. It may, of course, be anticipatory, born of the worshiper's confidence that help is ready at hand and can be counted on completely. It may be a sense of divine intervention, the proof of which lies in the heart of the worshiper. Since many complaints are voiced by those suffering illness or physical deprivation, healing and God's answer to prayer may be evident to all. We may be sure, even so, that the answers to the prayers of Israelite worshipers were similar to the experiences of worshipers in any time or setting.

Several texts in the book of Psalms depict the intimacy between God and the worshiper. That intimacy is memorably expressed in 31:1–5. The spiritual depth of the lines reminds one of Psalm 73, where the worshiper, after vividly portraying evildoers who seem oblivious of God's presence and justice, concludes with the worshiper's recognition that the holy and righteous God holds the worshiper by the hand and will never let go. Our psalmist knows this reality very well indeed. God can be trusted to provide the worshiper's needs; in the meantime, God sustains until the needs are met. Texts such as these, through the centuries, have comforted and consoled the devout who experience pain and loss and even a sense of abandonment by God. How can God, who has created human beings in the divine image and likeness, finally abandon those who share the divine image? These texts are a reminder that religious faith is a unique phenomenon. Its ground is mysterious,

Homiletical Perspective

if they are faithful to God and live lives with which God is pleased, they will be blessed. Some fully expect that God will meet all of their needs and the needs of their families. Some people expect to live happy, healthy lives.

However, when something goes awry, such as losing a job, an unexpected health crisis, or loss of a close friend or family member, they may become baffled. They may even experience a crisis of faith. They may be confused by the apparent contradiction between the image of God as faithful and image of God who allows tragedy to strike in their lives. Though Christians today do not live under the strict auspices of the Mosaic covenant, we still have expectations of God through our faith in Jesus Christ. Our people call on God in times of trouble, fully expecting God to help. The preacher should explore the people's expectations of God. Do people in the congregation understand their relationship with God in terms of a fixed-contract covenant? Do they feel that if they live good lives they should expect benefits in return? What are realistic expectations of God?

The preacher should also explore how the concept of shame is influenced by class. The psalmist expected God to bless him so that he could maintain a certain status or image in his community. The psalmist's use of the phrase "be put to shame" betrays a concern about what others thought of him. If he suffered in tangible ways, he would appear to be faithless in a community that believed one's behavior was tied to the favor of God in one's life. The psalmist writes of being the *scorn* of his adversaries, a *horror* to his neighbors, and an *object of dread* to his acquaintances. The writer was humiliated by the public nature of his suffering. He wanted God to answer his cries and respond to his need to be restored in good standing. He was tired of being an outsider because of his life circumstances.

The preacher can highlight the importance of image and status of many people in our faith communities. The economic crisis has provided fodder for exploration of pitfalls of the pursuit of image and status. Before the crisis, many people in the United States were living above their means. Many were so intent on creating and maintaining images of success that they purchased homes, clothes, and electronic gear they could not afford, to impress people they often did not really know. Some people lived their lives paycheck to paycheck with little or no savings because that was the best they could do. However, others lived above their means by spending all of their monthly income, plus money they did not have

Psalm 31:1-5, 19-24

Theological Perspective

so unsettled by those who seek to slander us? If God's care is apparent even to those trapped in a besieged city, might we (who typically face rather less danger) learn to recognize and appreciate it as well?

When the psalmist praises God for protecting us from our enemies and hearing the sound of our entreaties, this need not be taken as implying that we need never take action on our own behalf, or that belief in God will solve all our problems. It does suggest that recognizing ourselves to be *dependent* beings can make all the difference; when mindful of God's care, we are less distracted by our own forms of self-reliance.

For Christian readers of this psalm, there is a special poignancy in God's role as refuge and stronghold for who suffer this world's slings and arrows; in Christ, God encountered them quite directly, in the flesh. This too may help us to understand why those who live at the margins of society find themselves drawn so ineluctably back to God; God knows these margins well.[3] We are particularly reminded of this in verse 5 of Psalm 31, since it was used by Jesus himself to express utter dependence on God: "Into your hands I commend my spirit" (Luke 23:46).

DAVID S. CUNNINGHAM

Pastoral Perspective

Look also at all the words expressing positive feelings—love, trust, courage, safety. Who is this God that can hear all our worst fears and can still inspire trust and courage? Who is this God that can become a shelter in the storm? Where can one find this God? Is it really true that God takes care of all who are faithful? "The LORD preserves the faithful" (v. 23). Really? In what way? What happens to the unfaithful?

This psalm should not be used to create a safety net for Christian believers and a fence to keep out unbelievers. After all, the psalmist, writing hundreds of years before Christ, had no reason to expect a savior in the form of Jesus. However, Psalm 31 does have something to say about the power of trust to preserve one's sanity. There are those prayer warriors who maintain a trust in Love even when they feel the greatest scorn. There are those disciples who can smile even when they are dying painfully. There are those believers who have managed to carry their heavy weight of doubt for years, and still have a strong back of faith. Then there are the "outsiders" or the "de-churched" or the "believers in exile" or the "seekers" who are yearning for a refuge in a safe community where they are accepted as they are, doubts and blisters and all, and are loved into thinking of their new church as *home*—rock, refuge, rescue, deliverance, fortress, abundant shelter.

Throughout Psalm 31, the author bounces from highs to lows and back to highs. Our lives as Christians are fraught with daily challenges. We know in our heads that God is always with us, but it is in our lowest moments that our hearts truly turn to God. Perhaps, paradoxically, it is in those times of distress that we can return to happy-speak faith, praising God for life in the midst of death, for health in the midst of disease, for love in the midst of loneliness.

STEVEN D. MILLER

---

3. Liberation theology often emphasizes God's solidarity with the oppressed, but powerful testimony also comes from those who are marginalized in spite of their "mainstream" lives; see, for example, the work of James Allison, including *The Joy of Being Wrong* (New York: Crossroad, 1998) and *On Being Liked* (London: Darton, Longman & Todd, 2003).

its operations often unfathomable, but its reality for those who commit their spirits to God is undeniable.

These beautiful and poignant words of faith and trust serve as a counterpoint to Israel's realism in describing the world of pain and suffering, as clearly known and portrayed in the Bible. As we ponder the words of the text, we may well set them alongside other texts—for example, Job 7 and Jeremiah 20—where the individual does not find God the trustworthy partner. Rather, God appears as one to escape, malevolent, persecuting, torturing, and clearly the enemy. More ambiguous is the great Psalm 139, where God's presence is both the problem and the solution of the problem. God is inescapable, but does one really wish to escape? God knows every thought, so that one cannot even hide one's thoughts, but this very God formed the embryo itself.

Psalm 31 shows us a worshiper delighting in God's active presence and intimate companionship. It also shows, realistically, the plight of individuals trying to make their way in a difficult and often hostile world, and it closes with praise and thanksgiving for the God who delivers from trials and is pleased to live in companionship with those who will accept that companionship.

The psalm closes with the summons to the community to wait for the Lord. The psalmist uses the familiar wisdom motif: God rewards the righteous and gives evildoers their due. In the meantime, the psalmist invites all to do what the psalmist seeks to do: anticipate God's demonstrating that the worshiper's faith is well founded. This waiting for God is made possible, then and in any age, by actual experience of the divine presence, an actual demonstration of God's goodness in one's life. Strangely, this experience of God's goodness may be hidden from the eyes of everyone except the worshiper.

WALTER J. HARRELSON

(credit), to support habits of conspicuous consumption. So when some of these people lost their jobs, they not only lost their homes, but also lost their status and experienced great shame. The economic crisis has provided an opportunity for all people to reconsider the priorities of their lives. In our capitalistic society, material possessions such as houses, cars, clothing, and electronic toys and gadgets become the measures of success. If some people are not able to live according to a certain standard of living, they may believe that they are being put to shame.

Though the psalmist had misgivings and appeared to be having a crisis of faith, he ultimately retained his faith in God. God did hear his supplications and answer. The writer advised the people of God to love God and to wait for God. The psalmist, using his personal testimony, was able to assure people in his community that God was faithful. Since God had been faithful to him, God would certainly be faithful to them as well. There may be times in the lives of believers when they feel as if God has abandoned them. The testimony of other people who have suffered can be helpful as sermon illustrations. Perhaps the preacher can even share a personal testimony of a time when God brought her through a situation in which she initially felt abandoned by God. Personal testimony can be powerful, as long as the preacher does not make himself the hero. There may have been a time when the preacher felt embarrassed by his life circumstances because he did not seem to be as blessed as others. Perhaps this psalm can help the congregation to remember that God sometimes does not respond when we want or in the way we want. Even though God operates on a different timetable, God is faithful and will not abandon the people of God.

DEBRA J. MUMFORD

Romans 1:16-17; 3:22b-28 (29-31)

1:16For I am not ashamed of the gospel; it is the power of God for salvation to everyone who has faith, to the Jew first and also to the Greek. 17For in it the righteousness of God is revealed through faith for faith; as it is written, "The one who is righteous will live by faith." . . .

3:22bFor there is no distinction, 23since all have sinned and fall short of the glory of God; 24they are now justified by his grace as a gift, through the redemption that is in Christ Jesus, 25whom God put forward as a sacrifice of atonement by his blood, effective through faith. He did this to show his righteousness, because in his divine forbearance he had passed over the sins previously committed; 26it was to prove at the present time that he himself is righteous and that he justifies the one who has faith in Jesus.

27Then what becomes of boasting? It is excluded. By what law? By that of works? No, but by the law of faith. 28For we hold that a person is justified by faith apart from works prescribed by the law. 29Or is God the God of Jews only? Is he not the God of Gentiles also? Yes, of Gentiles also, 30since God is one; and he will justify the circumcised on the ground of faith and the uncircumcised through that same faith. 31Do we then overthrow the law by this faith? By no means! On the contrary, we uphold the law.

Theological Perspective

Our lesson from Paul's Letter to the Romans opens with verses that were the crucible of the Protestant Reformation; but, as we shall see, they encapsulate a central theological truth that all Christians today can affirm.

Late in life Martin Luther recalled his life-changing insight into the meaning of Paul's words, which came to him while he was still a conscience-stricken young Augustinian monk.[1] "I was absorbed by a passionate desire to understand Paul in his Epistle to the Romans. Nothing stood in my way but that one expression, 'The justice of God is revealed in the Gospel' (Rom. 1:17). For I hated those words, 'the justice of God,' because I had been taught to understand them in the scholastic sense as the formal or active justice whereby God, who is righteous, punishes unrighteous sinners." Luther, however, would not give up: "I kept hammering away at those words of Paul, wishing passionately to know what he meant."

The translator faces a dilemma in rendering the Greek *dikaiosynē* and its cognate terms. The most accurate modern English term for the noun is usually "righteousness" rather than "justice," but the verb is best translated "to justify" (though "to make

1. Preface to Luther's *Collected Works* (1545), as cited by E. Harris Harbison, *The Christian Scholar in the Age of the Reformation* (New York: Charles Scribner's Sons, 1956), 120.

Pastoral Perspective

Congregations are not immune from prejudice and discrimination against those within the church whom they feel are less fit for the kingdom. The task of creating unity among opposing groups within a church requires wisdom and patience, especially when the dispute is steeped in disagreement regarding the doctrines and practices of fellow believers. One need only check the records of mainline congregations to observe the length of time it took for the various denominations to disavow the practice of slavery and to ordain women as deacons, elders, and pastors. The recent debate over the ordination of openly gay and lesbian persons in the Presbyterian Church (U.S.A.) is another example of the arduous task of resolving church fights. Much is at stake. When Christians define themselves over and against those in the body who hold different beliefs, they create division in the church. This inner turmoil weakens the work and witness of the church. Focusing on what is common among opposing groups, rather than what is different, can be a helpful way for pastors to resolve differences in their congregations. It is this approach Paul uses when seeking to repair the rift between Jewish and Greek Christians in Rome.

Paul begins his discourse by declaring the power of the gospel to save those who believe. Having made this statement, he moves on to underscore in verse

Exegetical Perspective

Paul has just indicated to his letter's recipients that the gospel he proclaims is without geopolitical borders or social distinctions: God has entrusted him with good news for everybody (1:14). For this reason he sets out the précis of his letter (1:16–17) with the glad boast that he is "not ashamed of the gospel" (1:16). Why should he be if God purposes to save all people in the very same way (by "obedience of faith") by the very same instrument (through the gospel) and for the very same end (for righteousness)?

The repetition of the explanatory "for" (*gar*) orders the flowchart of this passage. Clearly not everyone is convinced by Paul's gospel, and therefore he must explain its theological grammar. In fact, we know from the letter's concluding admonition (16:17–20) that there are opponents afoot in Rome who apparently think he should be ashamed to preach his gospel! Paul's intended visit, now delayed because of his risky relief mission to Jerusalem (15:22–33), not only will fortify the congregation's faith against such internal threats (1:11) but will give him opportunity to respond directly to the charges leveled against him and his mission to the Gentiles.

The phrase "power [*dynamis*] of God" may carry an apologetic subtext: Paul has no reason to be ashamed of what he preaches, because it occasions a demonstrative revelation of God's righteousness

Homiletical Perspective

The apostle Paul begins our verses by staking a claim for the gospel, anxious to share it and proclaim it to others. As he describes it, the gospel is power, the power of God for salvation. Paul is speaking to a people who live in a culture in which military might is seen as a means of power; so he presents here a different kind of power—the power of God that opens the door to salvation (the divine, spiritual power that works to save humanity from the bondage of sin, death, and the evil one personified, Satan).

Paul contrasts the power of God to other kinds of power that gain a foothold in the world—power acquired through possessions and wealth, military might, political position, corporate leadership, and so on. This power is in contrast to the power with which Satan tries to tempt Jesus. In that situation, the devil takes Jesus to a high mountain and shows him all the kingdoms of the world, promising to give all to Jesus, if Jesus will just fall down and worship him. Jesus responds, "Away with you, Satan! for it is written, 'Worship the Lord your God, and serve only him'" (Matt. 4:10). The apostle Paul contrasts the power of God with all worldly power, no matter how great. Knowing this power for himself, Paul is not ashamed to proclaim its power of salvation.

In 1:16b–17 and later in 3:22b–31, Paul introduces major themes that he will unpack in much

Romans 1:16-17; 3:22b-28 (29-31)

Theological Perspective

righteous" is also possible). The important point for the modern reader is that Paul uses a single Greek concept for which no one English word will suffice. In order to grasp the significance of Luther's dilemma—as well as his eventual solution—it is important to see that God's *dikaiosynē* contains aspects of what we think of as both justice and righteousness. Here is how he describes that solution:

> After I had pondered the problem for days and nights, God took pity on me and I saw the inner connection between the two phrases, "The justice of God is revealed in the Gospel" and "The just shall live by faith." Then I began to understand that this "justice of God" is the righteousness by which the just man [sic] lives through the free gift of God, that is to say "by faith"; and that the justice "revealed in the Gospel" is the passive justice of God by which He takes pity on us and justifies us by our faith, as it is written, "The just shall live by faith."[2]

Luther sometimes expressed his spiritual crisis in the question "How can I find a gracious God?" One way to put the solution is to say that he found that God on the cross of Christ. The "connection" he says he found is the identity of the righteous God of the law with the derelict on the cross. The Christian becomes "just"—righteous in the eyes of God—not by fulfilling every jot and tittle of the law but by throwing himself or herself on the mercy of Christ, the Son of God who died for his or her sins, and the sins of the whole world.

The negative corollary of this justification by faith is the repudiation of what Luther calls works righteousness, the futile attempt to "get right with God" through some act or endeavor on the part of the sinner. At the time of the Reformation, the kind of works that the Protestants found so objectionable were typically religious acts, such as collecting relics of the saints, going on pilgrimages, endowing masses for the dead, and even the Eucharist itself, interpreted as a repetition of Christ's sacrifice for the benefit of sinners today.

For Christians in the global society of the twenty-first century, the temptation to substitute works for faith is more likely to take the form of moralistic striving (trying to be good enough to please God), whether through individual acts of piety or by means of political and social action. The point is not that such works are wrong in themselves, but that they must be, not a substitute for faith in Christ's sacrifice, but fruits of faith, performed out of gratitude rather

Pastoral Perspective

16 the far-reaching, inclusive, and impartial nature of the gospel and points to the plurality of persons who accept it. Because believers come from varied backgrounds and cultures, at times we are bound to disagree with each other. According to Leander Keck,[1] a primary disagreement that Paul is addressing in this epistle is the observance of Torah, particularly as it relates to dietary restrictions. Jewish Christians thought it was necessary to adhere to the law. Greek Christians did not; in fact, some wanted to dismiss altogether Jewish people and their role in salvation. When we dismiss—or worse, demonize—those with whom we disagree, we rob the gospel of its power to bring together all who have faith in it.

Thus Paul emphasizes the inclusive nature of the gospel when he says that salvation is available "to the Jew first and also to the Greek" (1:16b). His statement does not suggest that it is only these two groups who will receive salvation; rather, he illustrates by their distinct difference the all-encompassing reach of the gospel. Paul makes it clear that all are restored to a right relationship with God through the faithfulness of Jesus Christ (3:22). All believers, Jews and non-Jews, share this common faith in Christ and his faithfulness.

Our common faith draws attention to our common condition called sin. Sin is the failure to uphold God's law. Paul says that "all have sinned and fall short of the glory of God" (3:23). Sin puts all believers on the same page with God and reveals that our relationship with God is broken. This brokenness creates a crisis for humanity. Cut off from God we are destined to die, for Paul makes it clear later that "the wages of sin is death" (6:23). The good news of the gospel is that instead of death, God acts in Christ to justify and redeem believers. Paul tells us that our justification and redemption is a gift of grace, unearned and unmerited (3:24).

Redemption may be analogous to a bailout of an inmate held captive because of his misdeeds. When we think of redemption in this manner, we can conclude that God "put forward" (3:25) Christ Jesus to bail us out. Jesus pays the bail and frees us from death by his blood. God's sacrifice of atonement is effective for our redemption because of Jesus' faithfulness. God acts in Christ to show God's righteousness. God "passed over the sins previously committed" (v. 25b), knowing that God would in time reveal Christ and justify those who believe in him.

2. Ibid.

1. Leander E. Keck, *Romans*, Abingdon New Testament Commentaries (Nashville: Abingdon Press, 2005), 31.

Exegetical Perspective

among believers when he does so! Simply put, the full-bodied experience of God's righteousness within the community of believers, which Paul will delineate in chapters 5–8, supplies the content of salvation. This community who covenants with God by its "obedience of faith" (1:5; 16:26) consists of "the Jew first and also . . . the Greek" (1:16). While this prophetic formula maps the historic progress of the mission of the Messiah and of his disciples, which was to the "Jew first," Paul's keen emphasis throughout the letter is on the equality of "everyone who believes."

The meaning and syntax of the phrase, "righteousness of God," are contested, and the decisions the exegete makes are decisive for understanding Paul's argument. Paul's use of "righteousness" in Romans means more than God's rectitude, which is aptly demonstrated in saving both Jew and Greek without partiality (2:6–11); "righteousness" also characterizes God's saving activity that proves beyond doubt God's faithfulness to promises made to Israel according to Scripture (1:2), which make clear the universal reach of God's redemptive grace (cf. Isa. 40–55).

The "revelation" of God's righteousness is one effect of a preached gospel that testifies to and clarifies God's faithfulness and fairness. In fact, the absence of an announcement of God's faithfulness and fairness would gut a gospel of its power to save. The reception of this word about God's righteousness in faith has the second, more concrete effect of a converting *experience* of God's forgiveness and transforming grace: God "right-wises" the sinner into a saint (1:7), which then confirms the truth claims of Paul's gospel.

Paul's quotation in Romans 1:17b of Habakkuk 2:4b glosses the obscure phrase, "from faith to faith" (NRSV "through faith for faith"). While perhaps a reference to "everyone who believes" (v. 16)—that is, "from the first to the last believer"—it is more likely that "faith" means faithfulness, as it does for Habakkuk, which is the condition by which the righteous will experience future blessing of promised "life." Significantly, the prophet's linking of faithfulness to righteousness and righteousness to life supplies the essential theological grammar of Paul's gospel, which is more fully developed in 3:21–31. In this passage, which many think relates the epicenter of Paul's message, God's righteousness "has been disclosed . . . through the faithfulness of Jesus Christ for all who believe" (3:21–22, my wording). If the present text is read by this subsequent elaboration, "from faith to faith" (1:17) could be translated to mean that

Homiletical Perspective

greater detail later in this letter, that is, the "who, what, and how" of this salvation. Salvation is available to *everyone* who has *faith*, and in this salvation the *righteousness of God* is revealed.

Faith holds the key to salvation. It is not the law; it is not the works that people do. It is faith. This Romans passage serves as a great equalizer for those who think that they have greater access to God because of who they are, people who have the law and follow the commandments, or because of the works that they do. In the early verses of chapter 3 Paul argues, however, that there is not one single person who is righteous. All of humanity is accountable to God (3:19), whether under the law or not. While the law prescribes works of righteousness, the law serves to bring forth the knowledge of sin (3:20). With that is the recognition that no one is able perfectly to fulfill the works of the law. Paul makes the point that *all* Jews (those under the law) and Greeks/Gentiles (those not under the law) have sinned, and *all* fall short of the glory of God.

The "glory of God" is an interesting phrase. It is tempting to think of this glory as an aura that shines in, through, and around God, and is simply unreachable. Rather, consider that this glory is the likeness of God within each of us—the human's "original estate as created in the likeness of God."[1] If our true character is in the image and likeness of God and we have sinned, then we have fallen short of our true spiritual nature. We have, to date, missed the mark of our true selves, have yet to reach the fullness of who we are created to be and have veered away from our right relationship with our Creator. Sin holds us back from our true spiritual selves and from God. None is righteous, but faith opens the door to our salvation.

The faith of which Paul speaks is faith in God through Jesus Christ. God's work manifested in Jesus is redemptive, bringing back to God those who have veered off from God, who have fallen short. The work of Christ serves as a sacrifice of atonement, removing the deserved punishment due for the sins committed, and resulting in reconciliation with God. We are now justified, that is, brought back into a right relationship with God. While we as preachers may tend to shy away from the bloody gore that goes along with atonement sacrifices, we cannot neglect or forget the importance and efficacy of the acts done through Christ on the cross. Our redemption and justification become effective through our faith

---

1. Gerald R. Cragg, in *The Interpreter's Bible* (Nashville: Abingdon Press, 1954), 9:430.

Romans 1:16-17; 3:22b-28 (29-31)

Theological Perspective

than from fear or duty. To put the problem most pointedly: the person insistent on achieving righteousness though his or her own efforts is in effect refusing God's grace by behaving in a way that implies that Christ's sacrifice was in vain. Like an obstreperous toddler, the self-righteous moralist is saying, "I can do it *myself*!"

Today, as a result of the ecumenical discussions of the past half-century, this teaching no longer divides Christian from Christian. In the words of the "Joint Declaration on the Doctrine of Justification" by Lutherans and Roman Catholics, "Together we confess: By grace alone, in faith in Christ's saving work and not because of any merit on our part, we are accepted by God and receive the Holy Spirit, who renews our hearts while equipping and calling us to good works."[3]

Why does Paul open his exposition of this central Christian teaching by insisting that he is "not ashamed of the gospel" (1:16)? In the ancient world, the good news of the crucified God often evoked horror and outrage. Crucifixion was not only a gruesome and horrible way to die but was also intended to humiliate its victim, stripping him naked and holding him up (literally!) to the scorn and ridicule of the crowds. One need only read the reactions of the onlookers at Jesus' crucifixion to see how it worked (e.g., Mark 15:16–20, 29–32; Luke 23:35–37). To suggest that God would allow himself to be abused in this way was scandalous. The gospel can be scandalous to people today too, causing some Christians—and some Christian churches—to be ashamed of it and seek to minimize its offense to the modern world.

The verses with which our reading opens, Romans 1:16–17, express the gist of justification by faith, which Paul then elaborates in Romans 3:22b–28. In the final verses (3:29–31), which should not be omitted from the reading, Paul emphasizes that this gospel addresses all, Gentiles as well as Jews, and makes the important point that justification by faith, far from "overthrowing" God's law, in fact upholds it.

GARRETT GREEN

Pastoral Perspective

Having made his argument that we are redeemed through Christ Jesus and justified by him, Paul in verse 27 turns to the subject of boasting. Some Jewish Christians believed that because the law was given to them, they enjoyed status over Greek Christians. Paul puts an end to this by suggesting that all believers operate under the law of faith (3:27–28). He appeals to the notion of having one law in claiming that "God is one" (v. 30). Paul concludes by noting that the one God justifies all people, circumcised and uncircumcised, Jew and Gentile, by the law of faith, and that this action does not overthrow God's law, but upholds it (vv. 30–31).

As mentioned previously, pastors may use this passage to build unity among disaffected groups in the church. They can present sermons on the common condition of our humanity and the common cure in Christ. The text can also be used to remind parishioners that we are all made right with God by faith in Christ and that he is God's gift of grace for us. The stress of the homily can be that our righteousness is not a result of our adherence to the law or religious rituals and observances. Strength of character and courage of conviction do not justify our position with God, since all have sinned. Nor does being "right" on an issue rectify our status with God. We are made right by faith in Christ Jesus.

Additionally, sermons on how to live by faith, especially when there is conflict within the church, are appropriate for this passage. It is clear in the text that the faithfulness of Jesus is what makes his life effective for our salvation. Faith then implies action. Living by faith can mean acknowledging our unity in Christ, and stressing our unity in diversity when we disagree, trusting God to work through each of us to resolve our conflicts.

DIANE GIVENS MOFFETT

---

3. The Lutheran World Federation and the Roman Catholic Church, "Joint Declaration on the Doctrine of Justification" (Grand Rapids: Eerdmans, 2000).

God's righteousness is revealed "from (Christ's) faithfulness to (human) faith."

Indeed, Romans 3:21–31 grounds the revelation of God's righteousness and its continuing redemptive repercussion within history in the faithfulness or obedience of Jesus to God's purposes (cf. Phil. 2:5–8). Moreover, to believe in Jesus shares in his act of obedience to God—an "obedience of faith," as Paul puts it at the beginning and ending to frame his letter (1:5; 16:26). In particular, Jesus' faithfulness is publicly demonstrated in his death, and its salutary effect demonstrates God's faithfulness to everyone who believes.

Although Paul spills little ink in discussing Christ's atoning death, which undoubtedly was well known to his Roman readers/auditors, he does appropriate two OT typologies of salvation to secure its importance as the means by which every sinner in need of a savior (3:23) may be "justified by [God's] gift of grace" (3:24). Both these biblical typologies (Exodus and the Day of Atonement) envisage salvation as a gift of sheer grace—initiated by God, at God's expense, and brought to realization by God. There is no reason then for believers to "boast" in their salvation (3:27–28), since they are merely the beneficiaries of a redemptive transaction between a faithful God and God's faithful Christ (3:26).

The principal symbol of atonement is *hilastērion*, which recalls the ark's cover, or "mercy seat," where the blood of the offering was sprinkled during the Day of Atonement liturgy for the forgiveness of Israel's sin (Lev. 16:13–15). Among the various translations of this catchword, "mercy seat" is best, since Paul's intent is to locate the blood of the sin offering at a particular and public place—the cross—not only to "demonstrate" God's righteousness for all to witness, but to make its transforming effect accessible to everyone "through faith" (3:25).

This essential point is elaborated by images of a second typology. The combination of "the redemption" (3:24), freedom from slavery through a ransom paid, and "passed over the sins" (3:25) recalls the biblical story of Israel's exodus from Egypt for a new life in a promised land. In this sense, the blood of Christ is a Passover offering to God and a sign of a people's rescue from their slavery to sin (cf. Exod. 12:11–13).

ROBERT W. WALL

in God through this Christ who was slain and yet resurrected.

There is another crucial point that Paul wants to make perfectly clear. Everything that God has done for us in Christ is unearned and undeserved. Persons are now justified by God's grace. It is God's free gift to humanity—free for us, costly for God and Christ.

When one thinks of this in terms of Paul's statement that it was because of God's forbearance (God's willingness to refrain from giving human beings what they deserve as a sinful people) that God passed over sins previously committed, *all* could/should breathe a collective sigh of relief and lift up holy hands in thanksgivings and hallelujahs to the God of our salvation. "The wages of sin is death, but the free gift of God is eternal life in Christ Jesus our Lord" (Rom. 6:23).

There is one further aspect that Paul discusses: God's righteousness that is being disclosed through faith in Jesus Christ for all who believe. The curtain on God's righteousness is being pulled back, and God's righteousness is exposed, uncovered for all to see and experience. This is God's revealing, into the hearts, the lives, and the communities of those who believe.

In this set of verses, it is God who is righteous. It is God who has graciously acted on our behalf through Jesus Christ to give us an opening and access to God's own righteousness. It is God who moves beyond distinctions between Jews and Gentiles, to make plain that God is God of *all*. Our response is to have faith in God through Jesus Christ. With this, the door to salvation is graciously open.

DIANE TURNER-SHARAZZ

Matthew 7:21-29

²¹"Not everyone who says to me, 'Lord, Lord,' will enter the kingdom of heaven, but only the one who does the will of my Father in heaven. ²²On that day many will say to me, 'Lord, Lord, did we not prophesy in your name, and cast out demons in your name, and do many deeds of power in your name?' ²³Then I will declare to them, 'I never knew you; go away from me, you evildoers.'

²⁴"Everyone then who hears these words of mine and acts on them will be like a wise man who built his house on rock. ²⁵The rain fell, the floods came, and the winds blew and beat on that house, but it did not fall, because it had been founded on rock. ²⁶And everyone who hears these words of mine and does not act on them will be like a foolish man who built his house on sand. ²⁷The rain fell, and the floods came, and the winds blew and beat against that house, and it fell—and great was its fall!"

²⁸Now when Jesus had finished saying these things, the crowds were astounded at his teaching, ²⁹for he taught them as one having authority, and not as their scribes.

Theological Perspective

This passage invites us into a theological debate regarding the nature of Christian faith, a debate that began with the first followers of Christ and continues to our day. At hand are two important questions regarding faith: How does one know oneself to be a person of faith in a way that is not self-deceptive? What are the consequences of maintaining a faith that is not true? The passage comes at the end of a lengthy soliloquy by Jesus that begins with Matthew's account of the Beatitudes, and concludes with an important phrase, "he taught them as one having authority, and not as their scribes." While each of the five great discourses in Matthew has a similar concluding formula, reminiscent of Moses's words in Deuteronomy, this passage makes the strongest claim of all: Jesus is not speaking with the relatively meager authority of one just interpreting the Word of God, but with an authority proximate to that of the Word of God. This unique source signifies that the content of this teaching is not up for debate, but it is to be embraced by those who follow him. However, theology is faith seeking understanding; so there is a landscape of opinions on the nature of faith and the consequences of not having faith.

At the beginning of this passage, Jesus states that not all who call to him, "Lord, Lord," will enter the kingdom of heaven. The important appellation

Pastoral Perspective

The Sermon on the Mount concludes with a strong exhortation by Jesus to his listeners. Those who have heard what Jesus has said are to do God's will; that is, they are to be active rather than passive, and they are to adhere to Jesus' words rather than those of false prophets. Though not experiencing a firsthand account of Jesus' oration, those in the pews listening to this warning and to the parable of the wise and foolish builders may question whether they themselves are doing enough, and whether the commitments they have made are well placed. As anxieties rise and foundations are tested, however, an opportunity occurs to assess a community's strength so it can build more wisely for the future.

The preacher will most likely focus on the seven verses selected for this week, but the passage relates to the entire Sermon (Matt. 5:1–7:29). Even the first three verses of our text, which stand somewhat apart, are linked by the "then" of verse 24, giving the imagined dialogue between Jesus and those who say to him, "Lord, Lord," a more comprehensive understanding. Believers are called to do far more than acknowledge Jesus' lordship; they are to take on the challenge his entire address presents. It may therefore be helpful to include in the sermon or in the service's liturgy reminders of other passages from the Sermon on the Mount. There is, however, plenty

Exegetical Perspective

In 70 CE, the Jewish revolt against the Roman Empire ended with the destruction of the Jewish temple and the fall of Jerusalem. Most biblical scholars believe the Gospel of Matthew was written sometime after this devastating Jewish defeat. While Jewish law had always played an important role in the life of the people of Israel, with the loss of the temple and its leadership (the priest and Sadducees) as well as the loss of the highest authoritative body of Judaism (the Sanhedrin), the law became even more important within Judaism. Under the leadership of the Pharisees, strict observation of the law became the source of Jewish identity. According to Pharisaic interpretation of the law, to be Jewish meant to keep oneself separate (i.e., "holy") from those considered impure. As a result of the destruction of the temple and the fall of Jerusalem, the law and the Pharisees played a much more significant role during the time Matthew was written than they had during the ministry of Jesus.

In Matthew, the scribes and Pharisees are presented as Jesus' primary opponents (9:11, 34; 12:2; 27:62). The Sermon on the Mount (Matt. 5:1–7:27) is the first of five major discourses delivered by Jesus in the Gospel of Matthew.[1] The discourse does not

Homiletical Perspective

At the end of this first major discourse by Jesus, the crowds are "astounded" at Jesus' authoritative teaching (v. 28). Their astonishment could be due to what Jesus says about those who say, "Lord, Lord," to him. Those who call him "Lord" (*kyrios*) are "the disciples (8:25; 17:4; 14:28; 16:22; 18:21) and those coming to faith in Jesus (8:2, 6, 8; 9:27–31; 15:22, 25, 27; 17:15; 20:30)," because in Matthew's Gospel only outsiders call him "teacher" or *rabbi*.[1] Thus, these words target followers of Jesus, who themselves may be shocked by what he says. This word will be a challenging one for many congregations. It calls for integrity between internal adherence to God's will and external actions, because there are those who wear sheep's clothing on the outside, but are ravenous wolves on the inside (7:15). Through this passage, preachers have an opportunity to speak about the interaction of belief and practice, personal piety and social witness.

In the first segment, one learns that confessing "Lord" does not guarantee one's entrance into the kingdom of heaven, even if one says the right things (e.g., Lord) and does the right things in Christ's name, like prophesying, exorcizing demons, and other powerful deeds (v. 22). Even these can be told

---

1. The other four discourses are 10:5–42; 13:1–52; 18:1–35; 24:3–25:46.

1. Luke Timothy Johnson, *The Writings of the New Testament: An Interpretation* (Philadelphia: Fortress Press, 1986), 181.

Matthew 7:21-29

Theological Perspective

"Lord, Lord" is used only seven times in the entirety of the Bible: three times in the Hebrew Scriptures, three times in Matthew, and once in Luke, with this being the first time that the term is used in the New Testament. Its occurrences in the Hebrew Scriptures (Add. Esth. 13:9; 2 Macc. 1:24; and 3 Macc. 2:2) all refer exclusively to God in the context of creator and king, and so Jesus' use of this term to refer to himself, twice in quick succession within this passage, is a clear portent of the revelation of Jesus' divinity. In claiming for himself this radical use of a scriptural term for God, Jesus argues that it is appropriate and right for those who follow him to refer to Jesus in the same way that they would refer to God, "my Father in heaven." In the Matthean narrative, the understanding of faith is forever changed, for the direction and focus of faith are not only to God, but to Jesus as well, with little distinction for the believer made between faith in God and faith in Jesus.

If there is a differentiation for the believer regarding how faith in God and faith in Jesus are to be understood, it may come through the phrasing that only the one "who does the will of my Father in heaven" (v. 21) will enter the kingdom of heaven. That is to say, it is not the person who does whatever Jesus commands who will receive an eternal reward, but the one who follows the will of God. Therein lies an interesting theological shift, for while there may be a claim for Jesus' divinity presented here, Jesus does not equate his will and witness to the will of God. This may represent a theological understanding of the implicit human fallibility of Jesus on the part of the author of Matthew.

While this passage clearly presents Jesus as bearing an authority greater than that of those who interpret scripture, it does not go so far as to claim Jesus *is* the very same authority as God. There is a substantive judgment made on those who prophesy, cast out demons, and do "deeds of power" in Jesus' name, but who do not do the will of God. While we recognize that the listed actions typically would be thought as "good," Jesus makes the claim that such actions, even if they are done in Jesus' name, bear no merit unless they are done in obedience to God's will. In fact, Jesus goes so far as to name those who do what normally would be thought of as good works, but accomplished apart from the will of God, as "evildoers" (v. 23), literally "workers of lawlessness."

There is the sense that their actions done without the will of God are made all the more egregious by attempting to wear the mantle of Jesus' authority through claiming that they have done these deeds in

Pastoral Perspective

within this short selection to explore. Just as the Sermon contains words of warning as well as advice, so does this smaller passage. Just as the larger discourse must have left its ancient listeners unsettled, so do these concluding verses leave us.

In an age when many churches find it difficult to bring new people to a confession of faith, being told that some who cry, "Lord, Lord," will not enter the kingdom of heaven is particularly discouraging. Most if not all of those in the pews will be believers, but many will have lingering questions about their own fate. Moreover, they may worry about those in their family, in their community, and in the world who do not believe. The original audience must have also experienced a combination of wonder and dread when hearing Jesus' strange message. If Jesus' ministry marked a new and marvellous understanding of God's plan for God's people, perhaps the unsettling nature of this passage can provide a fresh outlook on the church's outreach as well as a better understanding of assurance.

Some lapsed members and those we call "unchurched" may not have lost their faith in God, but rather lost interest in an institution they deem inactive and unhelpful. While troubling in many ways, Jesus' words can nonetheless inspire those— both inside and outside of the church—who desire the Christian faith to be more than a declaration of belief. Being a Christian is more than calling yourself one, and a church that is actively living out God's message will be more attractive than one indifferent to Jesus' reign. For people seeking increased relevance from the church, Jesus' declaration that heaven is for those who *do* the will of God (as opposed to those who simply talk about it) may be highly intriguing. While Jesus' stern words may give pause to those who came into worship feeling comfortable with their faith, the exhortation may prove a helpful motivation to those same people who wish to have their spiritual lives reinvigorated.

More than awakening faith, however, Jesus is concerned with aligning one's faith properly. His demand is not to *do*, but to *obey*. Setting off with our own agenda under the banner of Christ gets us no closer to the heavenly realm. Indeed, verse 23 indicates it will distance us from the One who threatens to deny us and send us away. How troubling this message must have sounded to those who eagerly crowded around Jesus all those years ago! How disturbing it continues to be for congregants and church leaders who wish to be faithful but who recognize that personal desires and the discernment of God's will often

present Jesus as simply reinterpreting the old law and challenging the self-centered Pharisaic interpretation by offering his own more authoritative interpretation (5:21–48); it presents Jesus as also offering a new law. In the image of a Moses-like teacher, Jesus ascends a mountain and presents the law (i.e., the will of God) to the people of God. Throughout the sermon, as throughout most of Matthew, Jesus emphasizes the importance of true discipleship. True disciples are not simply those who claim to know the will of God; they are those who are willing to "follow" Jesus (4:19; 8:22; 9:9; 10:38; 16:24; 19:21) and to do the will of God (7:21; cf. 6:10; 12:50; 21:31).

It is Jesus, not the scribes and Pharisees, who is *the* authoritative teacher of God's will (7:29; cf. 28:18). The scribes and the Pharisees are presented as self-righteous hypocrites (23:1–36). According to Matthew, they know the will of God but they do not practice the will of God. They are "false prophets, who come to you in sheep's clothing but inwardly are ravenous wolves" (7:15). They represent a "tree that does not bear good fruit" (7:19; cf. 3:7–10). This is why Matthew's Jesus begins this sermon by informing the listeners that "unless your righteousness exceeds that of the scribes and Pharisees, you will never enter the kingdom of heaven" (5:20).

The conclusion to this sermon (7:13–27) presents a series of warnings that is meant to parallel the series of blessings that begin the sermon (5:3–12). The listener has to make a choice between two ways—one leading to life, the other leading to death (7:13–14; cf. Deut. 28). The choice that one makes is represented by the way one lives. Jesus tells his listeners, "You will know them by their fruits" (7:16, 20). "Fruits" represent the way that we live. "Good fruit" represents living an ethical life.

It appears that doing the will of God is about living an ethical life focused on the well-being of others. Those whom Jesus rejects appear to be those who have lived their lives focusing on themselves and taking pride in their own spiritual gifts and abilities. They emphasize their ability to prophesy and cast out demons and do deeds of power. Such acts, however, do not represent the law. That is why Jesus says, "Depart from me, you evildoers" (lit. "workers of lawlessness"; see 13:41; 23:28; 24:12). Immediately before this final section of the sermon, Jesus summarizes the law by saying, "In everything do to others as you would have them do to you; for this is the law and the prophets" (7:12; cf. 22:34–40). The fruits produced by a good life are not "deeds of power"; they are ethical acts focused on the well-being of others.

on the day of judgment, "I never knew you" (v. 23), because somehow these individuals did not do "the will of my Father in heaven" (v. 21). They are "evildoers" or "workers of lawlessness," because they do not follow the law of God, the Torah. The works done are generally acceptable (10:5–15), but the issue is obedience to God's will, God's law. What is implied is that one can say the right things and do the right things, but have a wrong relationship with Jesus and thus not be known by him. What does it mean to know Jesus? The lips of some people confess him, but their hearts are still far away from the Way.

Moreover, this situation raises such questions as, "What is the will of God? How does one come to know God's will?" Matthew emphasizes the will of God throughout his Gospel (6:10; 12:50; 18:14; 21:31; 26:42), and this takes precedence over any respectful address like "Lord." To make proper confessions does not necessarily lead to genuine practice, and religious practice does not necessarily suggest rightly obeying God's will. In this setting, appropriate action or practice must stem from listening to God's will. Right action is connected with hearing and following the words of Jesus, who fulfills the law (5:17–20).

Outward action is critical in doing the will of God, but it is intertwined with inward obedience to the law of Christ. The question becomes, in what is the church's action rooted? When Jesus tells the dichotomous story of the wise man's house foundation and the foolish man's house foundation, he suggests that doing God's will is everyone who "hears these words of mine and acts on them" (v. 24). They are on solid ground, a rock, because they listen to the words of Christ and then act on those words. If one only listens, without acting on them, they are on a slippery slope, sinking sand. It implies that disconnection from the Word or "these words of mine" is disastrous and leads to a "great" fall (v. 27). Whoever is left standing after life's stormy rains, floods, and winds will be a sign that the will of God has been done. Hearing and doing are linked in Christian discipleship, and both are necessary to do God's will. Acting without hearing will lead Jesus to say, "Go away from me" (v. 23), but hearing without acting is just as lethal. Thus the continuity between hearing and doing is vital for contemporary Christians.

At the end of both segments of the text (vv. 23, 27) there is a demise of sorts, a "descent into hell," for those who do not know Jesus but seemingly act in his name, and for those who know Jesus (or at least hear his words) but do not act upon them at all.

Matthew 7:21-29

Theological Perspective

his name. This is important source material from the Gospels for the theological position that claims we are justified by faith, not works. Paul takes up this matter in Galatians and Romans, and eventually the stance of "justification by faith, not works" becomes the center of the Protestant revolution in Christian theology. From the beginning of intra-Christian dialogue, however, is the argument made in James that "faith without works is dead" (Jas. 2:26), the powerful counter of Roman Catholic theology to Luther's theology.

How does one know whether or not one is acting in accordance with the will of God? While some theologians maintain that it is possible to do the will of God by following the Scriptures, John Calvin's position—that we cannot know whether we are justified or damned—stands as an unsettling argument against understandably desirable certainty. According to Calvin, while we cannot know whether we are predestined for heaven or for hell, if we find ourselves inclined to do the good through our faith, which is an unmerited gift from God, we may find comfort in that faith, which would seem to bring us in accordance with God's generous will.

Jesus maintains that there is a real penalty for those who hear but do not act on his words, a "great fall" (v. 27), reminiscent of Proverbs 14:11, "The house of the wicked is destroyed, but the tent of the upright flourishes." The essential theological message of this passage for Christian believers today is to live reflectively, representing the will of God and the advice of Jesus as best they may, so that they do not merely know the Gospels, but live the good news.

STEPHEN BUTLER MURRAY

Pastoral Perspective

get blurred! Do we *need* an air conditioning unit for the sanctuary, or just *want* one? Is that proposed mission trip down south appealing because of the work involved, or because it is down south?

The parable of the Wise and Foolish Builders is all the more evocative then, in that it imagines two similar but crucially different scenarios: a house built on rock and a house built on sand. In his commentary on this passage, New Testament scholar M. Eugene Boring notes that when built, the houses are equally sturdy. Dry sand feels secure, and a decision to build on it may seem sound at the time; but if one knows that a flood is coming, such action becomes foolish. The wise builder is wise, not because of greater intellect, but because of greater insight: he is able to see the danger that a future flood would bring and make a decision based on that vision. Likewise, those who listen to Jesus gain "an insight into the eschatological situation" and are wise to act on it.[1]

With such imagery congregants, budget planners, church leaders, and mission directors may feel increasingly unsteady, wondering if foundations laid for current programs were indeed built on solid ground. Instead of inspiring panic, the message of Jesus is received with astonishment, with acceptance, and—by the wise—with thanksgiving. Just as those who heard the Sermon noted that Jesus spoke with authority and with new and valuable insight, those who today have their assumptions questioned and their foundations tested can nevertheless accept Jesus' warning as a gift. After all, it is better to reassess our faith, our intentions, and the basis of our plans now than after the rain starts to fall, the waters rise, the wind blows, and the house shakes. Even when news is unsettling, it is better to be forewarned than surprised.

ALEXANDER WIMBERLY

1. M. Eugene Boring, "The Gospel of Matthew: Introduction, Commentary, and Reflections," *The New Interpreter's Bible* (Nashville: Abington Press, 1995), 8:218.

Exegetical Perspective

According to Matthew's Jesus, doing the will of God means practicing God's "perfect" compassionate ethical behavior toward others (5:48; cf. 19:21).

Matthew makes it clear that the way one lives today will have implications on what one experiences "on that day" when divine judgment is passed (7:22). The criterion for judgment will not be what one knows, what one believes, or what impressive spiritual gifts and abilities one possesses. The criterion will be the life one has lived and how well one has cared for others. The author explicitly illustrates this in the most powerful ethical statement of the Gospel and one found only in Matthew. In the final days before his crucifixion, Jesus makes it clear that only those who live a life committed to the care and well-being of others—especially the most vulnerable of society—will inherit the kingdom of God (25:31–46).

In Matthew, it is not simply those who have heard the words of Jesus and are familiar with his teachings who will enter the kingdom of God; instead it is those who act on Jesus' teachings, which focus on compassionate, ethical treatment of others. It is the compassionate, ethical treatment of others that represents the will of God and that provides the foundation for communities, societies, and nations to withstand the storms of life. Those who hear and act on Jesus' teachings are wise disciples, who build enduring ethical communities. In Matthew, a disciple (*mathēteusate*) is one who has been taught (*mathēteutheis*) and who practices what she or he has been taught. Matthew's Jesus is the ultimate teacher, and his followers are true disciples, who not only practice what they have been taught, but who are commissioned to "Go therefore and make disciples (*mathēteutheis*) of all nations . . . teaching them to obey everything that I have commanded you" (28:19–20).

GUY D. NAVE JR.

Homiletical Perspective

Both activity and inactivity can be detrimental. There is a holistic presentation of what determines faithful living: doing the will of God. Mere hearing or acting will not suffice; Matthew stresses hearing and doing, inward adherence to the Word and outward practice of the Word. One is not greater than the other. Congregations that lean toward social justice ministries without development of personal piety must hear this Matthean call. Likewise, churches that stress personal spirituality to the neglect of social ministry must also hear this challenge.

In light of this creative tension of the will of God, preachers would do best to proclaim a way of life that is both/and, not either/or, when it comes to personal piety and social action in the world. The blend of a vital inner and outer life is a challenge and necessity, because the neglect of either will cause a spiritual fall (vv. 23, 27). Sermons on this passage will do well to present a balanced portrait of the life of faith. Purely listening or purely acting is insufficient, but when the two are in relationship, one's life can be rock solid and reveal that one knows Jesus and "does the will of my Father in heaven" (v. 21).

This text moves us to investigate the spiritual foundations of our lives. Who or what is the source of our action? Is it the words of Jesus? On what is our religious house built? These questions must be posed, because spiritual activity in and of itself is not necessarily faithful discipleship. One can be active yet still not know Jesus (v. 23). As N. T. Wright notes, "Mighty deeds are not a final indication of whether someone really belongs to Jesus or not,"[2] nor, may I add, are faithful creeds. A sermon based on this portion of Scripture will be a sobering wake-up call to those of us who cry, "Lord, Lord."

LUKE A. POWERY

2. Tom Wright, *Matthew for Everyone* (London: SPCK, 2002), 77.

Hosea 5:15–6:6

> 5:15I will return again to my place
>   until they acknowledge their guilt and seek my face.
>   In their distress they will beg my favor:
> 6:1"Come, let us return to the LORD;
>   for it is he who has torn, and he will heal us;
>   he has struck down, and he will bind us up.
> 2After two days he will revive us;
>   on the third day he will raise us up,
>   that we may live before him.
> 3Let us know, let us press on to know the LORD;
>   his appearing is as sure as the dawn;

Theological Perspective

Confession of sin, the first step toward repentance of failures and offenses against God, is a feature of virtually every liturgy in Jewish and Christian tradition. It opens believers to all the other movements of worship: hearing God's word of judgment, mercy, and challenge; responding in gratitude and self-giving, thanksgiving and praise; drawing close to God and to each other in love and communion; and going out to show the world God's saving intentions for it. However, despite its pivotal importance in the process of worship, the confession ritual is often a hurried recitation, a barrier to clear on the way to the excitement of reading Scripture, hearing it preached, and responding to the word in dramatic ways.

What are we doing, and what is God doing, as we confess our sins and look to God for forgiveness? Hosea quotes the confession of his people, the Israelites, in response to his earlier oracle of indictment: "There is no faithfulness or loyalty, and no knowledge of God in the land. Swearing, lying, and murder, and stealing and adultery break out; bloodshed follows bloodshed" (Hos. 4:1b–2). He then delivers the Lord's agonized response. In the course of just a few lines, Hosea tells us the theological dynamics of confession, judgment, and pardon.

Pastoral Perspective

"Can the pastor in good conscience lift up the restoration promised by God without at least noting the devastation threatened by God?" After reading Hosea's words together, a clergy group of which I am a part framed this question. We found ourselves drawn to the promises of God's renewal while we found ourselves avoiding the threats of God's destruction. Certainly we are not alone in this conflicted response to Hosea's words. Certainly we are not the first to struggle with this tension in the text.

The study Bible I keep on my desk focuses its interpretive energy on the promise found in verse 1 of chapter 6 and on the insights found in verse 6 of the same chapter. In selecting "Come, let us return to the LORD" (v. 1) and "For I desire steadfast love and not sacrifice" (v. 6) for further explanation the editors of the commentary section of this Bible lift up essential teaching. They also play it pretty safe. They offer no further commentary on verses like "Therefore I have hewn them by the prophets" (6:5a). In this decision they represent a widespread inclination when it comes to dealing with this text. The question remains, what about the whole text?

Given the opportunity for acknowledgment, most congregations will grasp the tension between the desire to speak words of comfort and reticence to issue words of challenge. They will recognize that this

he will come to us like the showers,
   like the spring rains that water the earth."
⁴What shall I do with you, O Ephraim?
   What shall I do with you, O Judah?
Your love is like a morning cloud,
   like the dew that goes away early.
⁵Therefore I have hewn them by the prophets,
   I have killed them by the words of my mouth,
   and my judgment goes forth as the light.
⁶For I desire steadfast love and not sacrifice,
   the knowledge of God rather than burnt offerings.

Exegetical Perspective

Hosea's language is among the most difficult to interpret confidently, for several reasons, not least his tendency toward wordplay and the uncertainty of many features of the language. Translations used in liturgy need, sometimes, to sound clearer than is warranted, and Hosea's circumstances need sketching if we are to proceed responsibly.

Though virtually all the prophetic books were edited around the time of the exile to Babylon (sixth century BCE) and so bear traces of later events, Hosea seems to offer us access to his own time as well, which is the mid-to-late eighth century (roughly contemporary with Amos and overlapping with Isaiah and Micah). He ministered in the northern kingdom, Israel, which had been substantially independent of southern Judah for nearly two hundred years. By Hosea's time, the threat of extinction loomed. Israel would fall to Assyria in 721, with some of its people being exiled eastward and some fleeing southward. Hosea's language suggests he was struggling with the leaders of Israel over two main issues: social injustice and religious violations. Those sins seem commonplace in the prophets, but some nuance is called for here.

The leaders of Israel (kings and elites) were locked in a struggle not wholly of their own choosing over collaboration with the Assyrians, a powerful and

Homiletical Perspective

The leadership of ancient Israel hedges its bets during times of political unrest, making secular alliances with questionable neighbors, while neglecting its loyalty to YHWH. Preaching from Hosea's pointed response is appropriately pointed too, because as individuals, as congregations, as communities, as nations, and as a world, we have made secular alliances that we believe will keep us safe. In reality, such unions may be pulling us away from the One who is divinely committed to us. We can easily peal off a list of where we modern people put our trust: in long-term job contracts, in a built-up military, in security systems for our homes, in having enough in our 401(k) to retire comfortably. Our world pressures us to make sure we are protected, so any sermon on this passage should listen carefully to Hosea's warning that unholy alliances actually make us more vulnerable in this uncertain world.

Of course we must not preach against proper and significant international agreements, treaties, and pacts. It makes sense to join forces in our congregations, communities, and nations to increase stability, welfare, and safety. It is a righteous effort to make friends instead of enemies, to commit ourselves to working together toward a world fitting God's purposes. However, in our alliances we must guard

Hosea 5:15-6:6

Theological Perspective

God Makes Confession Possible. An often-practiced technique for motivating people to repent of their sins is to generate fear. The theory is that if they can be moved by terrifying images of eternal punishment, they will decide to admit fault and seek forgiveness. John Calvin, whose followers have sometimes employed such measures, insisted in his lecture on this passage that no human manipulation, including the preaching of fire and brimstone, can induce repentance. The only effective motivator is the *prior* knowledge of the love of God:

> The beginning of repentance is a sense of God's mercy; that is, when men [*sic*] are persuaded that God is ready to give pardon, they then begin to gather courage to repent. . . . For it cannot be, that men [*sic*] will obey God with a true and sincere heart, except a taste of his goodness allures them.[1]

The confessing Israelites quoted by Hosea bespeak this truth. Indeed, most of their confession is a demonstration that they already know the quality of God's mercy. After tearing them and striking them down for their transgressions, the Lord will, they say (or maybe sing—the confession is a poem), turn to them as surely as the sun will rise, reviving them as the spring rain does the parched winter earth.

God Has Not Yet Pardoned Us; God Has Already Pardoned Us. The Lord's response to the Israelites' confession is not, as they clearly hoped, an assurance of pardon. The Lord first expresses exasperation (What shall I do with you?), then delivers a sarcastic indictment of their inconstancy, and finally reminds them what God, with the help of prophets, does to the unfaithful and requires of the faithful. Commentators hear in this complex response mixed messages about the Lord's reception of the Israelites' confession. The Lord both doubts the Israelites' sincerity and affirms it. Their love will quickly evaporate "like the dew" (v. 4d); therefore their confession is a rote recital (as ours too often are), in the category of outward religious rituals like burnt offerings, which are not what God wants. At the same time, God affirms God's desire for "love and . . . the knowledge of God" (v. 6), which are precisely what the Israelites have offered by saying that they will "press on to know the Lord" (v. 3a) and to "live before him" (v. 2b). Together these statements of rejection and acceptance of the people's confession tell the beginning and the end of the full

Pastoral Perspective

tension is similar to the tension they experience in their own lives when, as parents, they have to confront the inappropriate behavior of a child. They want to promise the child that their love for them is unyielding. They need to make sure that the child understands that their actions have consequences and that they, the parent, might need to supply those consequences. They will recognize the dissonance in the text as similar to the dissonance they feel when, in standing for justice, they find themselves standing in opposition to members of their family, members of their community, members of their congregation. There are moments when, in order to be for the greatest good, people are forced to step outside their personal comfort zones and be against that which is less than the greatest good. It is often very hard for polite and pleasant people to do this, for we have been taught that it is undesirable to be thought of as divisive.

Further, given the opportunity for acknowledgment, most congregations will find it helpful to admit that the perceived tension between the building God and the breaking God is a call to reexamine the safe and manageable Gods that many of us have created for ourselves. Perhaps they overstate the case, but the words of theologian Belden Lane remind us that there is a tendency in many of us and in many of our congregations to make our peace with a very "safe" God. "I really don't want a God who is solicitous of my every need, fawning for my attention, eager for nothing in the world so much as the fulfillment of my self-potential. One of the scourges of our age is that all of our deities are housebroken and eminently companionable; far from demanding anything, they ask only how they can more meaningfully enhance the lives of those whom they serve."[1] If nothing else, paying attention to the words of Hosea gives us reason to reassess our tendency to create Gods in our own image.

Having been given the opportunity to acknowledge the questions that arise from Hosea's prophecy, most congregations will welcome the accompanying opportunity to reconsider the ways in which they experience God's healing and God's binding. They will appreciate the invitation to think about the way God's refreshment makes itself known in human history.

It is my experience that individuals, families, communities, and congregations do experience God's restoration. It is my hope that this restoration may be also experienced by nations and by the earth

1. John Calvin, "Commentaries on Hosea, Lecture Sixteenth," in *Calvin's Commentaries*, vol. 13, *Commentaries on the Twelve Minor Prophets*, trans. John Owen (Grand Rapids: Baker Book House, 1979), 216.

1. Belden C. Lane, "Fierce Landscapes and the Indifference of God," *Christian Century*, October 11, 1998, 907.

oppressive imperial neighbor to the east. Assyria was hungry for the bounty of Israel—grain, wine, and oil—and was determined to control access to Egypt and beyond via the roads that ran through Israel. The king and elites of small Israel were not in a position to refuse participation and hoped, no doubt, to make the relationship as nonharmful as possible. The Bible is generally critical of the kings of Judah and Israel for their relations with their neighbors, but to some considerable extent, they had very limited choice, options that were mostly poor. We may discern that some of the leadership chose their paths wrongly, but there was no avoiding the imperial Assyria (and later Babylon) when they came calling, demanding submission and tribute. Hosea critiques his leaders (king, nobles, priests, prophets) for violations of decency in the enthusiasm with which they abused the poor in order to meet their international obligations. The social justice violations were thus partly the result of being pressed by powers to the east but also because the leaders of Israel sought their own comfort at the expense of the land's poor.

The second general situation Hosea criticizes is false worship, and this needs explanation, if we are to understand another dilemma faced by all participants. The Bible, again generally, makes "strict Yahwism," sometimes called "YHWH alone" (one deity, no consort, no physical representation, no liturgy except as prescribed in Torah) the default situation for Israel's whole existence (from Abraham and Sarah ever afterwards). The reality was not so clear. Israel, along with everyone in the general neighborhood of the ancient Near East, had experience of a divine world that was richly plural and sensate. No deity was alone and unembodied. That Israel comes in time to a commitment to a monotheistic religion is an extraordinary achievement, one too complex to detail here.

In Hosea's time, monotheism was a novel idea that prophets like himself were struggling to teach and preach. We might liken it to the early days of the Reformation in Europe, where certain practices that were once normative became proscribed. Some people willingly abandoned old ways and embraced new ones; for others, it was more difficult—not simply because people were stubborn and disobedient, but because change in religious practice is hard. So Hosea preaches at a time of political, social, and economic crisis and decline and advocates as well a radical religious shift. His preaching is, at best, challenging!

In the passage for today, the prophet takes the voice of God, speaks for God in the first person. How he knows to do that we cannot tell, but so he

against relationships and behaviors requiring us to act as if we do not know God.

Think of churches cutting outreach and mission spending, cutting the custodian's hours, dreading additional cuts, yet believing that congregational difficulties could be solved if they just hire a pastor of family ministries to bring in new families. Think of communities that allow school funding to be cut and classroom sizes to increase, recycling services to be eliminated, then cheer when a casino is planned, because it will bring needed jobs, as if that will solve everything. Consider our refusals to limit carbon dioxide emissions, believing that trusting businesses to make wise decisions will make us more secure. Consider believing that if we can just keep Iran from developing a nuclear weapon, then we will be safe. In our homes, our communities, and our nations, we have made unholy partnerships trusting they will protect us. The preacher does well to consider what alliances have been made in the community, even within the congregation, that draw us away from relationship with God.

No wonder Hosea reports God's easy ability to imagine our panicked return, counting on divine constancy, when things get rough. God's words strip away human facades, recognizing our fickle commitments. Our love is fleeting, "like the dew" (v. 4d), yet YHWH desires constancy, our "steadfast love" (v. 6a). Hosea invites us to see that we cannot be tied to these other ideas and institutions if we are to be properly connected to YHWH, for God is not like an addle-brained Granny, ignoring whatever dalliances we get involved in. Rather, ours is the fiercely loving Parent who cares enough to correct and discipline. The Holy One desperately wants to maintain real relationship with us, yet we often think it is enough to lip certain words Sunday after Sunday. When we are reminded of our infidelity and neglect, we are quick to cry out, "You, God, are the One we love. It will not happen again! We promise." In reality our words sound more as if they come from the mouth of an abusive husband. We cry and bring flowers, return to religious rituals and perfect Sunday attendance, but these are not equal to an honest return to God.

In an interview on National Public Radio the author of a book on how to deal with personal disasters admitted that on the night when his own burglar alarm went off, he "managed to do everything wrong." Likewise we can be proficient in describing how we should be in relationship with God but fail miserably in living it out. So the sermon needs to

Hosea 5:15–6:6

Theological Perspective

story of repentance. God embraces a people who are certain to be fickle and inconstant, like the prostitute whom Hosea was ordered to marry. God will cast them out, as the adulteress (Hos. 3:3) was put away for a period. Then after a time, "on the third day" (v. 2b), the light of the love of the faithful God will shine on them again (some think that Hosea married the unfaithful woman a second time). Then God's people will rise, contrite, changed, and loved even in the likelihood they will stray again.

The Judging Word and the Saving Word Are the Same. Hosea's overarching theme is that God severely punishes infidelity—promiscuous political alliances and lust for the material benefits that the worship of other gods might bring—in order to restore God's unfaithful people. In this passage, both the people and the Lord are quoted as affirming that same fundamental truth: God punishes, not to destroy, but to heal and save. The affirmation corrects a common theological error, the tendency to portray God's judgment as something outmoded or superseded by grace. In fact, the wrath of God, though searing and painful, is gracious. Only by experiencing the separation from God that we have brought about by our selfishness and defiance are we prepared for the amazing experience of grace—the knowledge of God and *hesed,* the steadfast love of God, that are showered on us, no matter what, and that are then required of us. In our confession, we should pray for the punishment that accomplishes this, as G. K. Chesterton does in his poem:

> Bind all our lives together,
> Smite us and save us all.[2]

Confession Is the People's Work. Chesterton's words point up one more facet of confession emphasized in Hosea. It is an act that the people of God are called to perform together. "Come," say the Israelites, "let *us* return to the LORD; for . . . for he will heal *us* . . . and bind *us* up" (Hos. 6:1, emphasis added). God chooses, judges, forgives, and saves not only persons but also a people, whom God empowers to sustain each other's faith, teach each other the knowledge of God, show each other the loyal love God has shown them, move together as God's body in the world, and confess their sins and failures to God in one voice.

BARBARA G. WHEELER

Pastoral Perspective

itself. Individuals are likely to say that they experience God's restoration as forgiveness from sin, peace in the face of uncertainty, courage in the face of challenge, hope in the face of despair, recovery in the face of addiction, health in the face of illness. Families are likely to say that they experience God's restoration as joy in being together, in reconciliation after disagreement, as strength in the face of shared loss, as the ability to remember in the face of relentless change. Communities are likely to say that they experience God's restoration when they are able to replace injustice with justice, inequality with equality, division with unity, and discouragement with opportunity. Congregations are likely to say that they experience God's restoration when diversity replaces homogeneity, when vision replaces fear, when worship replaces worry, when ministry replaces murmuring.

It becomes more problematic to describe how nations experience renewal. The election of new leaders is sometimes the occasion for optimism. However, optimism is not the same as renewal. Further, the renewal of the nation is not the same as the nation gaining military might, economic power, or political advantage. Perhaps the answer is that nations experience renewal when the well-being of their most vulnerable citizens becomes their highest priority.

We live in a time when it is abundantly clear that the earth awaits God's renewal. It is not so clear who speaks for the earth. We are left to trust that renewal will come when, in the words of poet Wendell Berry, "We join our work to Heaven's gift, Our hope to what is left."[2]

Finally, congregations know that, like those to whom Hosea speaks, their commitment to knowing God easily wanes. It is the pastor's work to help the hard questions of the faith and the deep hope of renewal become more than the topics of discussion and the subjects of sermons. It is the pastor's work to offer these as consistent opportunities to experience God, as opportunities to "press on."

H. JAMES HOPKINS

---

2. G. K. Chesterton, "O God of Earth and Altar," in *English Hymnal* (London: Oxford University Press, 1909), #562.

2. Wendell Berry, "The Clearing Rests in Song and Shade," in *A Timbered Choir: The Sabbath Poems 1979–1997* (Washington, DC: Counterpoint, 1998).

Proper 5 (Sunday between June 5 and June 11 inclusive)

Exegetical Perspective

does. The divine persona the prophet offers is deeply emotional—angry and sad, determined and uncertain by turns. The language is painful to read and hear, since God seems petulant and ambivalent, even sometimes manipulative. The language is highly charged. Hosea offers us the Deity waiting for the elites to paint themselves into a corner and then emerge to beg God, whom they have neglected and offended, for help. The prophet allows us to hear God imagining the plan: "Let us return to the one who has power over us, our healer and wounder, the one who seems hidden but is bound to reappear" (6:1–2, paraphrased). It is difficult to discern tone here. Is this a sincere return to God, a faith-filled recital of God's qualities of vitality? Is it cynical and expedient, a sort of desperate last resort? A preacher needs to proceed carefully here, and there is no scholarly consensus on the matter.

When Hosea finishes God's rumination on what the people are saying, we hear God's response to their plan. And again, divine emotion is evident: "'What shall I do with you, Ephraim?'" (v. 4). God muses, calling Israel by a term of endearment and intimacy. God reviews that Israel—like the deity imaged here—is changeable in emotion and commitment. The metaphor of evanescent morning dew (v. 4d) suggests both consistency and brevity of Ephraim's attendance—leaving God uncertain of the way to proceed. Here God reviews divine punishment, while at the same time owning a need for a response from Ephraim and Judah that rises from love and not simply obligation or convenience. The divine soliloquy breaks off here (such speech threads the whole prophetic book) to conclude that what God desires is "steadfast love and not sacrifice" (v. 6a, a phrase repeated several times in the prophets)—meaning not one *or* the other but both; no cult except with compassion.

The information presented here should slow us down from overconfidence that we know what Hosea's hearers should have done, could have done. It reminds us that their options were difficult and uncertain, with much at stake for them as they chose. Hosea also portrays God in a very intimate and vulnerable way, reaching out as human beings often do when love seems abused and endangered. What comes through, however, is the love that God exhibits and hopes to have reciprocated.

BARBARA GREEN

Homiletical Perspective

show the congregation how they can strengthen their relationship with God and the world God loves.

We are called to reevaluate our "religious behaviors," our questionable alliances, and consider how we might return to God. Most sermonic time could be spent on describing what a relationship with God looks like, not just what vulnerability our unholy alliances allow. Sermons might make the connection between a relationship with God and proper relationships in the world. For many preachers this is no easy task, yet laity express a deep desire for sermons to communicate more about God.

Consider findings from a Lilly Endowment project: "When researchers asked each interviewee what they want or hope to hear about God in the sermon, one thing became clear immediately. People are not hearing all they want to know about God from the pulpit."[1] People want to hear what a proper faith community in divine relationship looks like. Sermons need to show people what it means to please God with steadfast love, not sacrifice, and to seek knowledge of God, not bargain with burnt offerings. Preaching might articulate what these directives look like in our settings. People are listening for the connection between spiritual fulfillment and righteous behavior. They want to know how to live faithfully in a world that sometimes seems to have gone crazy.

The season of Pentecost is upon us. If we believe the Holy Spirit moves on the earth and indwells the church, then we are confident that we have tremendous power available to us. It is the responsibility of clergy to teach the ways of God (torah), the tradition of faithful social responsibility. If we want to know God, Jeremiah 22:15–16 tells us, then we do justice and righteousness, taking up the cause of those on the margins. As Asian theologian C. S. Song clarifies: "Religion is no longer what we do in our spare time. It is not a pastime that does not have to be taken seriously. It has to do with the ultimate meaning of life."[2] Who we are in relation to God reveals who we are as a people. A sermon on this passage is a fine place to show people how to know God by assisting their understanding of our social responsibility in relation with God.

MARY ALICE MULLIGAN

---

1. Quoted in Mary Alice Mulligan and Ronald J. Allen, *Make the Word Come Alive: Lessons from Laity* (St. Louis: Chalice Press, 2005), 5.
2. C. S. Song, *Jesus, the Crucified People* (1990; Minneapolis: Augsburg Fortress, 1996), 25f.

Psalm 50:7-15

[7]"Hear, O my people, and I will speak,
 O Israel, I will testify against you.
 I am God, your God.
[8]Not for your sacrifices do I rebuke you;
 your burnt offerings are continually before me.
[9]I will not accept a bull from your house,
 or goats from your folds.
[10]For every wild animal of the forest is mine,
 the cattle on a thousand hills.
[11]I know all the birds of the air,
 and all that moves in the field is mine.

[12]"If I were hungry, I would not tell you,
 for the world and all that is in it is mine.
[13]Do I eat the flesh of bulls,
 or drink the blood of goats?
[14]Offer to God a sacrifice of thanksgiving,
 and pay your vows to the Most High.
[15]Call on me in the day of trouble;
 I will deliver you, and you shall glorify me."

Theological Perspective

Of all the issues that have caused theological conflict for Christianity (both internally and in its relationship to other faiths), few have been more neuralgic than that of *sacrifice*. Christians have been divided as to whether their faith requires ongoing acts of sacrifice and whether such sacrifice should be ritually encoded in worship. Some have argued that Jesus' death on the cross was a sacrifice made "once for all" (Rom. 6:10) that eliminates any further expectations in this regard. Others consider this too rigid an account of justification—one that tends to cause Christians to be allergic to any form of sacrifice and to label it "works righteousness." Is sacrifice a part of the Christian faith? Should it be embodied in our worship rituals? If so, what form should it take?

As if these questions were not enough, Christian attitudes toward sacrifice have affected Christianity's stance toward the ancient Judaism from which it sprang. This is particularly notable in the Epistle to the Hebrews, where the author offers a thoroughgoing allegory of the sacrifice of Christ as a direct (and superior) replacement of the sacrificial system of the temple. Certain interpretations of this account can easily strain Jewish-Christian relations; at their worst, they can imply a virulent supersessionism that degrades Judaism and, along with it, all forms of sacrifice.

Pastoral Perspective

Last Sunday's psalm offered hope to the battered and torn, a sturdy refuge for the lost and scared. Next Sunday's psalm is filled with praise and thanksgiving to God, the Creator, the Source of all goodness and love. This Sunday's psalm is the preacher's opportunity to finger-point and fist-pound. Psalm 50 reads like a stern sermon to a hypocritical congregation rather than a piece of worship liturgy. God is the preacher, and God is not very happy.

The congregation has not been fulfilling its end of the bargain with God. Apparently the people have lost their way. Instead of worshiping God out of their own need for God and thankfulness for God's steadfastness, they have decided that God should be grateful that they show up with a dead animal once in a while.

God apparently knows that the people are following the letter of the law (it reads as if there has been a satisfactory quantity of dead animals deposited in the church) but have totally disregarded the spirit of the law. Where is the gratefulness? Where is the joy? Where is the sincerity? Where is the offering of self in praise and thanksgiving as a holy and living sacrifice?

The community has been behaving badly. The people have become lazy and self-centered. They spend their time with thieves and adulterers. They gossip and lie about each other; they even slander their own brothers and sisters. They have forgotten

Exegetical Perspective

This psalm is surrounded by a powerful complaint of an individual that ends in an act of thanksgiving (Ps. 49) and the greatest of the confessional or penitential psalms (Ps. 51). The psalm reads like the denunciation of a prophet, with its fierce attack upon worshipers who suppose that God needs their sacrifices or can be moved to accept them and favor them, even when their conduct belies their professions of faith and commitment to God's ways.

This kind of prophetic diatribe has been called a "covenant lawsuit," a kind of charge at law by the Deity, akin to the initiation of a trial before the elders and judges in behalf of one who is aggrieved by the actions of another. See, for example, the large part of Deuteronomy 32 and the opening verses of Hosea 4 for instances of this "covenant lawsuit." One can see in our psalm the familiar prophetic charge against Israel that Israel's worship of God may seem like a transaction in which both the worshiper and the Deity benefit, with each having something to gain from the other. The Latin phrase often used to designate this understanding is *do ut des*, "I give in order that you may give."

The point, however, is a subtle one. Authentic worship does involve, in a sense, a transaction, a partnership, with both parties "gaining" from the transaction, for the Bible makes it clear that God delights in

Homiletical Perspective

In this psalm, God is speaking to two different groups of people—the faithful ones and the wicked. Though God is speaking to different groups of people, the message is the same: offer to God sacrifices of thanksgiving. The faithful do a good job making sacrifices to God according to the law. In fact, God even says that God has no issues with the sacrifices of the faithful. In the law, burnt offerings were made as acts of atonement for sins already committed, and they required adherence to strict guidelines. So the fact that the faithful continually brought burnt offerings before God and God had no issues with them speaks well of their commitment to atoning for past sins and adhering to the law.

In verses 7–14, God lets the faithful know that God does not need their sacrifices. The language used in these verses insinuates that some of the faithful may conceive of God as a human being rather than a divine being. What God wants is for the faithful to have an attitudinal shift.[1] Rather than having people conceive of God in anthropomorphic terms, God wants the people to realize that God needs nothing from humans. Humans do, however, need much from God. Humanity is dependent on

1. Artur Weiser, *The Psalms, a Commentary* (Philadelphia: Westminster Press, 1962).

Psalm 50:7-15

Theological Perspective

As any careful reader of the Old Testament is bound to observe, the supposedly intact "sacrificial system" of ancient Judaism was constantly evolving; moreover, Jews were divided about it (in ways that would be mirrored, centuries later, in various Christian controversies). This complexity is apparent in Psalm 50; God reminds the people that everything that they bring as a sacrifice is already God's own, "for the world and all that is in it is mine" (v. 12). Such texts give the lie to anti-Jewish claims that its sacrificial system had posited a bloodthirsty God who could be satisfied only when appeased with fresh meat.

While the internal complexities of Jewish attitudes toward sacrifice should be left to scholars of that faith, the question remains for Christians as well: what form of sacrifice, if any, does the Lord require? I clearly remember a conversation with a colleague of mine—a fellow parishioner who was also a New Testament scholar—in which he argued that Christians should abandon the language of sacrifice altogether, given how much mischief had been made with it through the centuries. He had a point; that language has been used by everyone from slaveholders seeking to justify slavery, to pastors offering the dubious comfort of "It's just the cross you will have to bear." My friend even suggested that the Epistle to the Hebrews should be voted out of the canon, given the anti-Jewish ways in which it is sometimes read.

I wonder, though, if the language of sacrifice might not be redeemed.[1] It should be noted that in Psalm 50 God does not actually condemn sacrifice; in fact, verses 8–15 are something of an aside. God is actually preparing to accuse the people of various forms of bad behavior (see vv. 16–20) and, along the way, pauses to emphasize that these accusations do not concern improper sacrifice (v. 8). In fact, since the entire created order is God's, the purpose of the sacrifice cannot be to fill some divine lack or need. (Later Christian theology would emphasize that God never lacks or needs anything; otherwise God would be dependent on something outside God.) Thus, sacrifice must have another purpose altogether.

That purpose is revealed in verse 14: "Offer to God a sacrifice of thanksgiving, and pay your vows to the Most High." Sacrifice should be offered in appreciation for what God has already done—not as

1. I am particularly persuaded by the work of René Girard and his collaborators on Christianity's unique power to redeem sacrifice—precisely because, in Christ, God is able both to offer and to absorb it. See René Girard, *Things Hidden since the Foundation of the World*, trans. Stephen Bann and Michael Metteer (Stanford, CA: Stanford University, 1987).

Pastoral Perspective

all about the God who brought them out of slavery and into the land of milk and honey, the God who fed them and traveled with them every step of the way through the wilderness. Now that they have settled in their new home, the people have become fat and self-satisfied. They think they have accomplished for themselves this life they now call their own. They think that God is no longer as important or as necessary as once YHWH might have been, oh so long ago. God is not much different from their neighbor. The congregation can fulfill its obligations with a cursory nod to tradition.

Most Americans now claim to be churched if they make it to church three times a year. Christmas, Easter, and Mother's Day should be enough. The average charitable gift of mainline Christians is about 2 percent of their income. That should be enough. Most Christians say they support torture, but only for terrorists. That should be enough.

Some of the best church attendees may make it to services 90 percent of the time (that should really satisfy God!), but service to God or the community does not quite fit into the schedule.

It is not enough. None of it is. God is different from their neighbor. God is their refuge in times of distress, their rock in times of faithlessness. God is still very much alive, still creating, still prodding, still leading, still surrounding the earth with divine presence, still greeting the sun in the morning and the moon at night, still setting a watch over the souls of the people. God is still calling the people home.

The pastor-preacher may not wish to pound the pulpit quite as vigorously as the prophet-preacher might. After all, providing nurture, safety, and healing is the main task of the shepherd, not finger-pointing. Nonetheless, once in a while even the best shepherd feels like throwing rocks at the whining, quarreling sheep. What part of the church membership vows do they not understand? Nearly all churches expect their professing Christians to make certain promises and live by them, including renouncing evil, being a disciple of Christ, following the way of Jesus, showing love and justice, witnessing to one's faith in Christ, growing in the faith, participating in church activities, worshiping regularly, being loyal to the local and denominational church, and supporting the ministry of the church with prayers, financial gifts, and gifts of time in service. The tired pastor may sigh and say to herself, "If only . . ."

There are always excuses, some of them valid—economic collapse, divorce, devastating illness, aging, on and on. Financial pledges are cut in half.

the gifts of love and praise by worshipers. Companionship with God, biblical writers clearly understand, pleases God, even as it blesses and enriches human life. The difference is, however, evident to see. Devotion to God includes devotion to God's ways. Sharing goods with God involves readiness to share life and goods with fellow human beings.

The psalmist does not despise sacrifices and offerings. How could a worshiper in ancient Israel do so? Sacrifice is a part of Israel's worship, despite sharp denunciations of such acts in several prophetic texts (Isa. 1; Hos. 6; Mic. 6; Amos 5; Jer. 7). The key is unmistakable in texts such as this one and in Psalm 51. God desires praise and thanksgiving, the authentic human motive behind the act of sacrifice. Sacrifices are not essential, but (as Ps. 50 declares), God does not reprove the community for bringing sacrifices. God does reject false notions of what such offerings to God mean and are intended to mean. This is one more example of many in the Bible that a so-called "Protestant principle" is at work in biblical religion. Radical monotheism implies that no object or place or rite or office is indispensable in God's dealing with Israel and the world of nations. Not even Zion is inviolable (see Jer. 7 and 26 and Mic. 3). Zion's most holy institution, the temple, is also not indispensable. Psalm 50, along with Psalms 40 and 51, builds this principle into the liturgical texts of the temple itself. What a testimony to Israel's understanding of God!

The verses preceding our lectionary text present a great theophany: God appears as Creator and Lord of the universe, but not in the customary mode. That customary mode is to call attention, largely, to the glory and splendor of God. The Creator describes in brief detail how the universe was formed and how God governs and sustains that universe. Here, however, the theophany presents God coming as judge to deal with earth's disorder and failings. To see the vast difference between this theophany and others, compare 50:1–6 with Psalm 104:1–9. For the author of Psalm 50, the Creator God is a dreadsome being. These verses very well prepare the way for the covenant lawsuit that follows.

In verses 16–23, which conclude our psalm, we have a prophetic denunciation as fierce and unrelenting as any words of Israel's prophets. They describe in greater detail the cause of God's complaint in verses 7–15. The words close with a liturgical reference that makes this prophetic denunciation a clear part of the regular worship of the community. As noted above, this sort of prophetic diatribe,

God. God seeks to raise the awareness of the people by requiring them to offer sacrifices of thanksgiving for what God has already done on their behalf. Questions that may prove fruitful for the preacher are, If the faithful were truly faithful, why did they need to hear a message from God about thanksgiving? Would offering thanks not come naturally to people who were attempting to live lives that were pleasing to God? Were the faithful ungrateful? Did they not understand why offering thanksgiving to God was important?

Perhaps the preacher can help the people to understand the importance of thanksgiving by encouraging them at least to begin to count the ways in which we are all blessed every day—blessed as individuals, blessed as families, blessed as communities. The preacher can share that, in addition to glorifying God, thanksgiving has the benefit of increasing awareness of what we already have and highlighting the value of blessings we often take for granted. One way to raise awareness of the need for thanksgiving is by stories or illustrations of people who took many of the blessings in their lives for granted until they were no longer experiencing certain blessings in their lives. For example, there are people who used to take their health for granted, until they became sick. There are people who used to take their jobs for granted, until they lost their jobs and suffered financial hardship. There are people who used to take their intimate friendships for granted, until they lost close friends or family members to tragedy or disagreement.

The preacher should also challenge the congregation to defy the cultural norms that compel us never to be satisfied with what we have or even who we are. Our culture often insists that we continually strive for more, while not informing us that more can be a never-ending abyss of discontentment and disillusionment. Being reminded of what God has already done in our lives can help congregants to realize that it is possible to reach a state of contentment—actually to be satisfied with what we have. Is being content with what we have a godly trait?

God also wants the wicked to bring thanksgiving as their sacrifice. The wicked in this text are people who know God but have forgotten God's ways and disdained discipline. God chastises the wicked for all of their ungodly behavior, such as talking about their relatives and keeping company with sinful people. God threatens to inflict physical punishment. Rather than allowing people in the congregation to find fault with the wicked in the text, perhaps the

Psalm 50:7-15

Theological Perspective

some form of appeasement or as a kind of bribery of God.[2] God's desire for sacrifice is due, not to the filling of a gap, but to its significance as a token of our gratitude. In asking for sacrifice, God asks only that we recall the "infinite qualitative difference" between ourselves and God—we are wholly dependent on God for our creation, preservation, and all the blessings of this life—and that we acknowledge this reality in our worship and our actions.

This notion, which found its way into the English-language liturgy as the "sacrifice of thanksgiving and praise" of the *Book of Common Prayer*, is not merely an attempt to differentiate Protestantism from the "sacrifice of the mass" in Roman Catholic theology (though it has often been understood in this way). More broadly, it represents an attempt to make an appropriate place for the language of sacrifice within the Christian tradition—one that interprets it along the lines of Psalm 50. This perspective pushes back against any effort to understand sacrifice as a form of appeasement or satisfaction, since everything already belongs to God; we really have, quite literally, nothing of our own to offer. By, instead, placing the accent on the elements of thanksgiving and praise, sacrifice comes to be seen as signifying our gratitude for God's goodness toward us, rather than something that will "move" God to act in our favor. God indeed promises to deliver us when we call (v. 15), but not because God's hand is somehow forced by our demands. Rather, God's grace precedes our actions; our needs are known before we ask (Matt. 6:8). God elected to love and care for us, not only before we made any sacrifice, but before the foundation of the world.

DAVID S. CUNNINGHAM

Pastoral Perspective

Leadership positions are resigned. Out of total exhaustion and not out of an evil heart, a slip of the tongue about the man who always seems to be sick (what is it with him, anyway?), or the pastor's naughty kid, or the liturgist's inability to read common words, or the soprano being off key causes hurt feelings.

Many excuses are just plain wicked. The smell of Richard who never changes clothes and sits on the front pew is overwhelming. Who can worship with him there? The preacher is anticountry and antitroops, and no, I'm not going to say anything to him, but we will find a way to get rid of him. There are too many strangers in this church. Somebody has been sitting in my grandmother's pew, and I just cannot take it anymore. Nobody talks to me in fellowship hall at the coffee table. I guess I am invisible.

Perhaps the church has decided that after all these years we finally have God figured out, tamed, leashed, and caged. Do we not have all the right answers and the right to impose those answers on others' questions? Do we not know what God needs better than God does? The rules say God needs a dead animal on a regular schedule. We can do that, and that should be enough.

No, there is more, isn't there? Perhaps it is time for a little confession and pardon.

This hungry God still issues the invitation (or is it a command?): "Call on me in the day of trouble; I will deliver you, and you shall glorify me" (v. 15).

STEVEN D. MILLER

---

2. For some helpful reflections on sacrifice, particularly with respect to various theories of atonement, see Mark A. McIntosh, *Divine Teaching: An Introduction to Christian Theology* (Malden, MA: Blackwell, 2008), chaps. 4–5.

built as it is into the worship of the community, serves a remarkable purpose in the liturgy of the community. The temptation of any worshiping community, it seems, is to value, rightly, the beauty and power of its rites and practices and words, but to do so too much. Form and content easily get out of balance. The power of ritual is also its danger. Perhaps it is a good thing that we have only three psalms in the psalter that raise so powerfully the danger of ritual let loose from moral foundations: Psalms 40, 50, and 51. It is, at the same time, a great thing that we *do* have these three critical evaluations of ritual.

Verses 7–15 contain just the right balance between ritual and moral commitment. Sacrifice in any society has many dimensions of meaning. The author of Psalm 50 delights in sacrifice when it is recognized to affirm the worshipers' praise and thanksgiving. The beauty of the sacrificial system for ancient Israel is made wonderfully clear in Sirach 50 of the Apocrypha. There the high priest is surrounded by a "garland" (Sir. 50:12) of fellow priests, all engaged in presenting to the community the holiness and glory of God viewed by those who gather around the great altar in the temple precinct.

Contemporary hearers of this text can hardly fail to feel the weight of such a picture of the worship of God and the perils of such worship. To approach God is to be exposed to One who knows the secrets of the heart, who discerns our thoughts from far away, and who, while welcoming worshipers, does not leave them as they came. What a blessing to have texts such as this one that help to keep clear and clean and morally significant our worship of God!

WALTER J. HARRELSON

preacher can point out that the wicked in this text are not people outside of the community of faith. They are insiders. By pointing out the fact that the wicked are insiders, the preachers can remind the congregation that we all have the potential to live as if we have forgotten God. Like the wicked in the text, we may talk negatively about people in general and our relatives in particular. We may hang around people who badly influence our behavior. We may know what is right in the eyes of God, but do what is wrong anyway.

God also reminds the wicked about the benefits of bringing sacrifices of thanksgiving. First, sacrifices of thanksgiving honor God. Thanksgiving is a way of publicly acknowledging what God has done in our lives. Second, those who bring sacrifices of thanksgiving receive salvation. As Christians, we believe that we are saved from sin by grace rather than works. The preacher can easily remind hearers of the grace that abounds in thanksgiving. Having blessings for which to be thankful is a result of God's grace. Being able to offer thanks to God verbally or physically is a result of grace. Having the ability to think through the many ways we have been blessed is a result of grace. The preacher should also explore the benefit of thanksgiving for the spiritual well-being of believers. When we as believers take the time and exert the effort to thank God for God's many blessings, we are also building our faith. Recounting what God has done reinforces our belief in what God can do.

When preaching the sermon, it is important for the preacher to end the message with the hope offered by the writer of the text. Though this passage chastises the people of God for not making sacrifices of thanksgiving to God, it does provide hope that God is willing to forgive the people for past oversights and give them a chance to start anew.

DEBRA J. MUMFORD

Romans 4:13-25

¹³For the promise that he would inherit the world did not come to Abraham or to his descendants through the law but through the righteousness of faith. ¹⁴If it is the adherents of the law who are to be the heirs, faith is null and the promise is void. ¹⁵For the law brings wrath; but where there is no law, neither is there violation.

¹⁶For this reason it depends on faith, in order that the promise may rest on grace and be guaranteed to all his descendants, not only to the adherents of the law but also to those who share the faith of Abraham (for he is the father of all of us, ¹⁷as it is written, "I have made you the father of many nations")—in the presence of the God in whom he believed, who gives life to the dead and calls into existence the things that do not exist. ¹⁸Hoping against hope, he believed

Theological Perspective

This week's lesson from Paul's Letter to the Romans continues the theme of justification by faith that was introduced last week, but here a new concept appears—the promise—and a new character in the drama of faith, Abraham. Even Christians who ought to know better sometimes find themselves assuming that faith is primarily a matter of believing things on the basis of little or no evidence. Now it is obvious that being a Christian involves believing that certain things are true: especially that God was incarnate in Jesus Christ, and that God raised him from the dead for our sake. Nevertheless, faith is something more than and quite different from mere belief: it is not just a matter of "*believing that . . .*" (holding certain things to be true), but rather a matter of "*believing in . . .*" (trusting the person who tells you these things). Early in the story that the Bible tells—in chapter 12 of Genesis, to be precise—God makes a promise to Abraham. It is not too much to say that the whole rest of the story, right down through the book of Revelation, is about the fate of that promise. Because some people (starting with Abraham) believed God's promise while others did not, the story becomes a struggle and a drama, in which God fulfills his promise in a way that no one could possibly have anticipated.

The opposition between faith and the law runs throughout our passage, and understanding how it

Pastoral Perspective

Paul begins this passage by indicating that the promise of God illustrated in Abraham rests on faith. This promise is apart from the law and demonstrates the grace of God guaranteed to all Abraham's descendants. By substituting "the world" as Abraham's inheritance (v. 13), rather than the "land" as indicated in the book of Genesis (Gen. 12:7), Paul makes the point that Abraham's descendants include Jews and Gentiles. This he expounds upon in verse 16, when he states that Abraham "is the father of all of us." The importance of the promise being based on faith rather than the law is underscored by the fact that the law is connected to God's wrath. Those who do not keep the law suffer the penalty of their misdeeds. Gentiles did not adhere to the law and Jews could not perfectly follow the law; so, if based upon the law, the promise would be empty and void. However, where there is no law, there is no wrath (v. 15b)—that is why the promise is based upon faith. Having successfully argued his point concerning the fulfillment of the promise based upon faith, Paul then expounds upon faith. His understanding is important for pastors helping parishioners to apply faith appropriately.

A young woman was so zealous for God that she enrolled in seminary to prepare for ministry. Among her classmates was a student suffering from a form

that he would become "the father of many nations," according to what was said, "So numerous shall your descendants be." [19]He did not weaken in faith when he considered his own body, which was already as good as dead (for he was about a hundred years old), or when he considered the barrenness of Sarah's womb. [20]No distrust made him waver concerning the promise of God, but he grew strong in his faith as he gave glory to God, [21]being fully convinced that God was able to do what he had promised. [22]Therefore his faith "was reckoned to him as righteousness." [23]Now the words, "it was reckoned to him," were written not for his sake alone, [24]but for ours also. It will be reckoned to us who believe in him who raised Jesus our Lord from the dead, [25]who was handed over to death for our trespasses and was raised for our justification.

Exegetical Perspective

Paul brackets his crucial exposition on the revelation of God's righteousness (3:21–31) with the claim that his gospel message "is attested by the law and the prophets" (3:21) and upheld by the law (3:31). Responding to the interlocutor's prompt in 4:1–2, he proceeds to provide a straightforward Torah commentary on Genesis 15 and drills down in particular on Abraham's "obedience of faith," which God credits with the gift of righteousness (4:3–8; cf. Gen. 15:6). Since Abraham is not yet circumcised (see Gen. 17), Paul contends from precedence that faith rather than circumcision must be God's preferred marker of covenant keeping (4:9–12). In this way, Abraham is typological of all believers, Jew and Gentile, for whom righteousness has been credited to their account because they place their trust in God, rather than in their Jewish birthright or in their circumcision as a prosletye Jew.

The present passage shifts Paul's concern away from "father Abraham" to his descendants and the promise God made to Abraham about them according to Genesis 15. The exegete should take note of the special vocabulary Paul introduces in verse 13 to develop this theme: God makes a "promise" (vv. 13, 14, 16, 20) to Abraham that his "descendants" (lit. "seed," vv. 13, 16, 18) would "inherit" (vv. 13, 14; "be the heirs," v. 14 NRSV) the world, which is realized

Homiletical Perspective

Paul continues in these texts to make his claims for faith over against law, and grace over works. Paul presents Abraham as the example. In the early part of chapter 4 (vv. 1–12), Paul raises the question whether Abraham is justified by his works under the law or by his faith. From what circumstance is righteousness reckoned to Abraham? Paul points out that scripture, specifically Genesis 15:6, speaks of Abraham, saying, "And he believed the LORD; and the LORD reckoned it to him as righteousness." It is the believing, the faith, that causes righteousness to be reckoned to him, and this reckoning occurs before he is circumcised under the law (Gen. 17:26). The circumcision is given as the seal of the righteousness he has previously received by faith.

All of this occurs, according to Paul, so that Abraham will be the ancestor of all who believe outside of the requirement of circumcision, as well as of the circumcised who follow Abraham's example of faith. As the result, all of these persons who believe can/will have righteousness reckoned to them. Paul wants to make sure that all understand that God's promise that Abraham would inherit the land, and that he would be the father of many nations, is not dependent upon the law, but upon faith. Thus the promise may rest on grace. It is God's unearned, unmerited gift to Abraham and,

Romans 4:13-25

Theological Perspective

works is essential to grasping Paul's theological point. The central claim is straightforward, however often it has been misunderstood or misinterpreted. If the promise to Abraham ("that he would inherit the world," v. 13) depended on the law, we would end up with a contradiction. Luther puts it this way: "For the Law, as long as it is without faith which fulfills it, makes all people sinners and establishes the fact that they are guilty and thus unworthy of the promise, indeed worthy of wrath and desolation, and in consequence it turns the promise into a threat."[1]

Jesus was making the same point when he told the Sadducees, who tried to justify themselves by claiming they were descendants of Abraham, "God is able from these stones to raise up children to Abraham" (Matt. 3:9; Luke 3:8). The promise cannot possibly be fulfilled by following the law, since, as Paul himself has said earlier in his letter, "all have sinned and fall short of the glory of God" (Rom. 3:23). In other words, if the promise to Abraham depended on his descendants obeying God's law, the situation would be hopeless, for the promise could not possibly be fulfilled, since "the law brings wrath" (v. 15). So the conclusion is unavoidable: "For this reason it depends on faith, in order that the promise may rest on grace and be guaranteed to all his descendants" (v. 16). Where the rubber hits the road for Christians is not how they behave (the law), but whether they believe God's promise (faith).

Abraham, in Paul's account, is the great exemplar of that faith because he did believe God's promise to him, in spite of its evident absurdity. After all, the man was *old* ("about a hundred years," Paul says, and thus "already as good as dead," v. 19). On top of that, his wife had never been able to bear children, even when she was young. *This* is the man who is supposed to be "the father of many nations"? Nevertheless, Paul insists, "No distrust made him waver concerning the promise of God, but he grew strong in his faith as he gave glory to God, being fully convinced that God was able to do what he had promised" (vv. 20–21). Here is the heart of the doctrine of justification: this faith, this utter trust in God's word despite all odds, "was reckoned to him as righteousness" (v. 22). In other words, his faith counted as fulfilling the whole law. Paul then turns to us and emphasizes that these words "were written not for his sake alone, but for ours also" (vv. 23–24). As Calvin comments here, "Let us also remember that

Pastoral Perspective

of muscular dystrophy that made it hard for him to walk. One morning after class she observed him having trouble walking down the long flight of stairs. In an effort to encourage her classmate she told him, "If you have faith, brother, God can heal you." Her humble, but wise peer, smiling, turned to her and said, "I do have faith. God already has." His response indicated a deeper understanding of faith. It is this understanding of faith that Paul seeks to illustrate in this passage of Scripture.

Contrary to what many believe, Abraham is not someone Paul suggests that we imitate. Rather, he is the example of the attributes of faith. In his life we see God's power operating—calling "into existence the things that do not exist" (v. 17). We learn from this passage that Abraham was "hoping against hope" (v. 18) he would become the father of many nations. The hoping against hope is important to understanding faith. Abraham did not hope in himself, because he considered his body dead; the subject of Abraham's faith was God. Abraham believed God could bring forth life from the dead and that God would fulfill God's promise to make him "the father of many nations" (v. 18). In sharing Abraham as the example of faith, Paul suggests God as the object of our faith.

At first glance, believers may find Paul's assertion in verse 19 difficult to understand. Those of us who know the biblical story are aware that Abraham struggled in faith, especially as the fulfillment of the promise was prolonged (see Gen. 17:15–17). However, in stating that "he did not weaken in faith" (v. 19), Paul implies that Abraham did indeed struggle with his faith as he acknowledged his age and Sarah's barrenness. In verse 20, Paul makes another difficult assertion, that "no distrust made him waver concerning the promise of God." The understanding of this statement becomes clear when we understand the meaning of verse 20b. Leander E. Keck and other New Testament scholars agree that the better translation is "Abraham was made strong in faith."[1] The one who made Abraham strong was God. Abraham gave glory to God because he was convinced in what "God was able to do" (v. 21). Therefore, Paul tells us Abraham's faith was reckoned as righteousness (v. 22). The righteousness is not something Abraham earned because he believed hard and did not struggle in his faith. It is not how hard we believe, but the One in whom we believe, that makes us right with God.

---

1. Martin Luther, *Lectures on Romans: Glosses and Scholia*, ed. Hilton C. Oswald, trans. Jacob A. O. Preus, *Luther's Works*, vol. 25, gen. eds. Jaroslav Pelikan and Helmut Lehmann (St. Louis: Concordia, 1972), 281.

1. Leander E. Keck, *Romans*, Abingdon New Testament Commentaries (Nashville: Abingdon Press, 2005), 129.

through the "righteousness of faith" (vv. 13, 22) rather than through "the law" (vv. 13, 14, 15[2x], 16). Paul's substitution of an inherited "world" (i.e., creation; cf. Rom. 8) for historic Israel's land promise (Gen. 15:18–21) may already hint at the direction of his following argument, which includes an international contingent of non-Jews among Abraham's heirs.

Neither can God's promise to Abraham be brokered by the Sinai covenant, because "the law brings wrath" (v. 15) rather than righteousness, without which the covenant promise of life is "nullified" (cf. 1:17). Paul has already established by scriptural appeal that righteousness is God's gift to those who believe (v. 16): adhering to the law in order to secure Abraham's inheritance only "empties" faith (v. 14; NRSV "is null") and so also the righteousness paired with it according to Paul's gospel. Paul argues that the "law," rather than righteousness, produces "transgression" in wakeful, willful violation of the covenant and therefore justifiably provokes the wrath of a covenant-keeping God (cf. 5:13).

Paul's most dramatic point is scored in verses 16–17a, which is sharply given without verbs, subjects, or objects to concentrate its plain meaning: Abraham establishes the single criterion for covenant keeping "for all his descendants," who are marked out by faith so that their inheritance "may rest on grace." What is not plain is the identity of the group Paul calls "adherents of the law." While they are Jewish in practice, it remains unclear whether they are also Christians in faith. If the referent is to all Torah-observant Jews, then this might sound a preliminary note to his controversial commentary in Romans 11 regarding the prospect of ethnic Israel's salvation at the coming apocalypse (see 11:25–27).

Paul is not interested in defending why a person's faith should attract God's attention. He is content to qualify a particular kind of faith as effective—Abraham's faith. A sketch of Abraham's faith is introduced ironically as "hoping against hope" (v. 18a). Even though childless and landless, Abraham came to trust God as the Creator who brings life from death/who calls nonexistent things into existence (v. 17b). If such a God is believed, then surely there is good reason to hope. The keen emphasis of Paul's commentary on Genesis 15 is not the theo-logic of Abraham's faith, however, but that he actually believed. The purpose of Paul's gospel is to evoke an "obedience of faith" (cf. 1:5; 16:26)—a concrete decision to trust God as reliable. The good news is that such a decision has a salutary effect: Abraham

consequently, to all who believe in this resurrecting, creating God.

In preaching on this text, one is dealing with an inherent question that hearers may ask themselves: Is God really able to do what God has promised? Is there a basis upon which we should stake our trust? Paul's implied response in using Abraham as the example is that God was able to take those who were "as good as dead" in their reproductive possibilities and to bring back life (resurrection) so that a son could be born from them and the promise could thus be fulfilled. In addition, from the beginning of this letter to the Romans, Paul has put forth the foundation that God has raised Jesus from the dead (resurrection). Abraham and Jesus are both examples of God's resurrecting, restorative, and creating power—a sure reason that we can trust in God's promises.

There are several emphases in this text that the preacher might build upon in the sermon. Paul's use of Abraham gives us a wonderful model for living in faith. For example, Abraham lives out his faith by placing his emphasis not upon who *he* is, but upon who *God* is. God is the one who gives life to the dead. God is the one who calls into existence the things that do not exist. The power and glory are in God who is able.

Abraham "hopes against hope." Regardless of what is seemingly evident in his circumstances, Abraham puts his trust not in the present circumstance but in the God of promise. This elderly Abraham, married to this elderly Sarah, both of whom are certainly beyond procreating age, is promised a son by God. How can this be—especially when our bodies are "good as dead"? Abraham's response to God's promise is to move beyond circumstantial impossibility to the surprising movement and power of God to bring forth from the impossible the possible—to resurrect that which has been dead and to bring forth the new where there was nothing before. Certainly Hebrews 11:1 fits here: "Now faith is the assurance of things hoped for, the conviction of things not seen." The preacher can help the congregation explore the way persons and congregations sometimes look at their seemingly evident and impossible circumstances and conclude that what God has promised is not feasible, because they cannot "see" it, reason it out, or fathom the how of it. What other obstacles render supposed believers faithless or doubters?

Emphasis can be placed upon the fact that the seemingly impossible circumstances served to strengthen Abraham's faith when he looked at the

Romans 4:13-25

Theological Perspective

we are all in the same condition as Abraham. Our circumstances are all in opposition to the promises of God."[2]

So it seems that Christian faith is, after all, about believing without evidence—even believing in the very face of the evidence! Many Christians seem to miss this point in their anxious quest for empirical "evidence" that the Bible speaks the truth. There *is* evidence, of course, but not of the kind that will satisfy blasé modern rationalists trying to mimic natural science. The greatest evidence that God is trustworthy is the resurrection of Jesus from the dead (vv. 24–25), a fact whose truth we can affirm only by the "demonstration of the Spirit and of power" (1 Cor. 2:4). Our faith is guaranteed by the God "who gives life to the dead and calls into existence the things that do not exist" (v. 17). For this reason, Paul writes that Abraham, the exemplar of faith, believed the promise "hoping against hope" (v. 18). Luther comments that this verse shows "the difference between the hope of people generally and the hope of Christians. For the hope of people in general is not contrary to hope but according to hope, that is, what can reasonably be expected to happen." Christian hope, on the other hand, is hope for what is naturally unreasonable; yet that hope is certain, because only God can do it, and God has promised to do so.[3] As the Letter to the Hebrews puts it, "Now faith is the assurance of things hoped for, the conviction of things not seen" (Heb. 11:1).

In our passage Paul is exhorting us, like Abraham, to trust in God's promise despite its commonsense implausibility, hoping against hope in the power of the Holy Spirit to justify our lives before the throne of God.

GARRETT GREEN

Pastoral Perspective

The importance, not of faith in our own will and volition, but of faith in God is further expressed in the concluding verses of this passage. Paul explains that the words "it was reckoned to him" were not written for Abraham's sake alone, but for ours also (vv. 23–24). Paul then restates what he says all along—that we who believe in God who raised Jesus from the dead will also be reckoned as righteous. He further elaborates on the events that led to our justification by reminding us that Jesus was "handed over to death for our trespasses and was raised for our justification" (v. 25).

We live in a world where people advocate the prosperity gospel and "name it, claim it" philosophies.[2] Such thinking places the believer's faith at the center of power. Some would even lead us to believe that if our faith is strong, we can have anything. When this is the case, how hard one believes is the determining factor for the fulfillment of God's promises. This reverses the intent of God's grace and places people in the position of power. It can produce a weight of guilt in Christians when the promise is not realized. On the other hand, if the promise is fulfilled, the emphasis can be on the believer's faith—"power" that steals God's glory. In both cases, faith is misappropriated as the object of the believer's will and volition.

Pastors may use this passage to help persons who mistakenly consider their faith as the object of faith. A sermon on the dangers of believing in faith would be appropriate, for Paul is not teaching belief in faith per se, but belief in God who is powerful. Faith is important because faith is the agency of righteousness. For Christians, Christ is the agent or content of our faith. It is in him that we believe.

DIANE GIVENS MOFFETT

---

2. John Calvin, *Romans and Thessalonians*, trans. Ross Mackenzie, *Calvin's New Testament Commentaries*, vol. 8, eds. David W. Torrance and T. F. Torrance (1960; Grand Rapids: Eerdmans, 1995), 99.
3. Luther, *Luther's Works*, 25:283.

2. Positive Confession, PMA, *Prosperity Gospel and the New Age*; http://www.rapidnet.com/~jbeard/bdm/Psychology/posit.htm.

"became the father of many nations" populated by "numerous . . . descendants" who will inherit the world (v. 18; cf. v. 13; Gen. 15:5).

The quality of Abraham's faith is persuasively described as lacking doubt—an important feature of ancient rhetoric. In fact, "faith" (*hē pistis*) is repeated in the dative case (vv. 19–20) to form the critical quality of his faith: "he did not weaken in [his] faith . . . but he grew strong in his faith." The passive voice, which the NRSV fails to pick up, makes clear that his exemplary faith does not grow on its own but has outside help—namely, the Creator God who brings life from death (v. 17b). This conception of Abraham's God recalls Paul's earlier portrait of the Creator who discloses the truth of God's "invisible nature . . . in the things that have been made" (1:20, my trans.). Unlike an ungodly and wicked humanity that rejects the truth about God (so 1:18–32), Abraham expresses the polar opposite response to God: he believed in God's promise and gave glory to God (5:20–21; cf. 1:21).

Finally, Paul returns to the interlocutor's initial question regarding the relevance of Abraham's biblical story for Christian faith (see 4:1–2). The salient issue for Paul is not that the Creator God has the power to bring life from death (so v. 17b); this is assumed by any Jew. Rather, he seeks to establish the Lord's resurrection as the public confirmation of God's faithfulness to the promise made to Abraham and his descendants (v. 13). For this reason, Paul returns to the cross and to a Jesus "who was handed over [*paredothē*] to death for our trespasses," whom God then makes alive "for our justification" (v. 25).

This concluding claim alludes to the Servant of Isaiah 53 for biblical support. The Servant's suffering is an expression of his covenant faithfulness (Isa. 53:11; cf. Rom. 3:22), and on this basis "the Lord has laid [*paredōken*] our sins" upon him (cf. Isa. 53:6, 12) for our justification. Against this prophetic backdrop, God's resurrection of Jesus not only vindicates his faithfulness but confirms that its effect for our sake is salutary for any who trust him.

ROBERT W. WALL

obstacles that God would have to overcome in order to fulfill God's promise to him. When God fulfills the promise, God will certainly receive the glory. The preacher has the opportunity to give examples of how God has shown resurrecting, restorative, and creative power within the community or individual lives.

The preaching of this text can seek to bring understanding of Abraham-like faith to the hearers. However, it should do more than that. One hopes that it will also seek to enable and empower the congregation to act upon their understanding. This faith is not passive; it requires a behavioral response. This text calls hearers to move from walking by sight to walking by faith. It requires not spiritual blindness but spiritual courage to move forward when all evidence tells you to stand still or turn away. It invites hearers to walk alongside or in the faith footsteps of Abraham by stepping out and acting upon what they believe.

In the movie *Indiana Jones: The Last Crusade*, Indiana has the opportunity to come into the presence of the Holy Grail, the cup used by Jesus at the Last Supper. The promise of the Holy Grail has been given, the steps have been laid out, but there are obstacles to overcome. The greatest obstacle calls Indiana to step out onto the "emptiness" of a deep and wide chasm, with no evidence of that which will uphold him. It is only in believing, in having a faith upon which he will step out, that he will receive the promise.

"Now the words, 'it [Abraham's faith] was reckoned to him' [as righteousness], were written not for his sake alone, but for ours also. It will be reckoned to us who believe in him who raised Jesus our Lord from the dead, who was handed over to death for our trespasses and was raised for our justification" (Rom. 4:23–25). It is only when we believe in God and step out on this faith that we will have our faith reckoned to us as righteousness.

DIANE TURNER-SHARAZZ

Matthew 9:9-13, 18-26

⁹As Jesus was walking along, he saw a man called Matthew sitting at the tax booth; and he said to him, "Follow me." And he got up and followed him. ¹⁰And as he sat at dinner in the house, many tax collectors and sinners came and were sitting with him and his disciples. ¹¹When the Pharisees saw this, they said to his disciples, "Why does your teacher eat with tax collectors and sinners?" ¹²But when he heard this, he said, "Those who are well have no need of a physician, but those who are sick. ¹³Go and learn what this means, 'I desire mercy, not sacrifice.' For I have come to call not the righteous but sinners." . . .

¹⁸While he was saying these things to them, suddenly a leader of the synagogue came in and knelt before him, saying, "My daughter has just died; but come and lay your hand on her, and she will live." ¹⁹And Jesus got up and

Theological Perspective

The two passages from Matthew that we are invited to consider are rich theological material. The first passage, Matthew 9:9–13, is representative of the calling narratives of the disciples, specifically that of the calling of the tax collector Matthew. The second passage, Matthew 9:18–26, in which a dead girl is raised and a woman is healed, is a careful and beautiful commentary on the vital power of faith.

In the calling of Matthew, Jesus is walking along and sees Matthew sitting at his tax booth. It is unclear whether Jesus speaks, "Follow me," as an invitation or a command, just as it is unclear whether Matthew finds his socially unsavory work to be personally satisfying or merely necessary for the maintenance of his family. In the brisk narrative, Matthew gets up and follows Jesus, seemingly leaving behind his everyday labor of tax collecting for his newfound vocation of discipleship. All that we know of Matthew are his name and his work, and as he moves from work to vocation, Matthew's identity changes fundamentally also.

Matthew's old life is not hours old when following Jesus lands him directly in the company that he had left, at dinner with tax collectors and sinners. The mantle of his new vocation is so fresh that he must have blended in unblinkingly as one of the social and moral outcasts at the table, most probably

Pastoral Perspective

Many encountering this text will be reminded of the saying "A church is a hospital for sinners, not a museum for saints." Though the preacher's use of this saying risks ignoring that people seeking Jesus in this passage have physical as well as spiritual needs, the adage reminds us that, like a hospital, a church is a place where many different people, with many different needs, come looking for help.

With a compelling but problematic analogy between sinfulness and sickness, Jesus presents himself not only as a healer who goes looking for sinners in spiritual need (Matthew in the toll booth) but also as the one to whom those with physical problems can turn (a leader of the synagogue whose daughter has died, a hemorrhaging woman). As a doctor would not hesitate to treat someone or refuse assistance to those in pain, Jesus' ministry is marked by both urgency and accessibility. Both those who are outcast and those who are part of the social establishment find in Jesus a compassionate heart. Both those with acute needs and those with chronic pain find healing power. Both those who reach out and those who need to be beckoned find attentive aid. The correlation to a Sunday service is easily made: no matter who is sitting in the pew, no matter what ordeals congregants are undergoing, this passage gives assurance

followed him, with his disciples. ²⁰Then suddenly a woman who had been suffering from hemorrhages for twelve years came up behind him and touched the fringe of his cloak, ²¹for she said to herself, "If I only touch his cloak, I will be made well." ²²Jesus turned, and seeing her he said, "Take heart, daughter; your faith has made you well." And instantly the woman was made well. ²³When Jesus came to the leader's house and saw the flute players and the crowd making a commotion, ²⁴he said, "Go away; for the girl is not dead but sleeping." And they laughed at him. ²⁵But when the crowd had been put outside, he went in and took her by the hand, and the girl got up. ²⁶And the report of this spread throughout that district.

Exegetical Perspective

Matthew 8:1–9:34 presents a collection of healing miracles. The healings are the first in Matthew. They occur immediately after Jesus' delivering of his Sermon on the Mount (5:1–7:29). The healings depict the compassion and mercy toward others demanded by Jesus in his sermon. The healings also represent a crossing of social boundaries firmly entrenched within both Roman society and Jewish law. Jesus both touches and is touched by those considered "unclean" according to Jewish law. He touches and heals a leper (8:1–3; cf. Lev. 13). He heals two demon-possessed men who live in a cemetery among the dead (8:28–34), and he touches the body of a dead girl (9:23–25; cf. Num. 5:2; 19:11–13). He is touched by a woman suffering with a continuous bodily discharge of blood (9:20–22; cf. Lev. 15:19–30). Not only does Jesus heal and advocate for Jews oppressed by the Roman Empire and those from the lowest strata of society; he completely disregards class and ethnic boundaries by healing the servant of a Roman centurion (8:5–13) and raising from the dead the daughter of a Jewish leader (9:18).

Seeing Matthew working at the tax booth, Jesus approaches him and says to him, "Follow me" (v. 9). It is the same thing he says to the fishermen, Peter, Andrew, James, and John, when he calls them (4:18–22). After being called, Peter, Andrew, James,

Homiletical Perspective

Why are the "sick" the focus of Jesus' ministry of mercy (v. 12)? What about healthy and wealthy Christians who benefit from the political empire? The heart of Jesus' ministry may make a well-off, latte-drinking, Christian-flag-toting suburban congregation uneasy. Righteous Christians are not the center of Jesus' ministry, but sinners are. A sermon on this text may move according to the passage, tracking the outsiders whom Jesus makes insiders, by calling them, sitting with them, and touching them. Each scene reveals Jesus becoming more intimate with the marginalized.

Calling. Jesus calls Matthew, a tax collector, and says, "Follow me" (v. 9). Matthew was socially despised and hated by the Roman subjects because tax collectors were known to be corrupt and committed to the imperial system. His tax collection helped sustain the empire's elite and unjust status quo. Jesus' call disrupts his commitment to earthly empire and calls this man to be part of another empire with different standards. As Warren Carter notes, "Following him means encountering God's empire."[1] This divine kingdom welcomes social outcasts like Matthew. The next scene of action only confirms this.

1. Warren Carter, *Matthew and the Margins: A Sociopolitical and Religious Reading* (Maryknoll, NY: Orbis Books, 2000), 217–18.

Matthew 9:9-13, 18-26

Theological Perspective

colleagues and familiar names. Looking upon this display, the Pharisees critically ask Jesus' disciples why Jesus would eat and socialize with such noxious people. Jesus responds by recalling Hosea 6:6, saying that God desires mercy, not sacrifice, for "I have come to call not the righteous but sinners." This is an interesting interplay, because the Pharisees, who often are portrayed as self-righteous, clearly are not the party with whom Jesus seeks discourse.

In qualifying his fellows at dinner as sinners, Jesus categorizes them as people in need of redemption, people who may acutely desire redemption but fear they could never attain it, due to their lifestyle and work. This preferential option for the sinner over the righteous person is reminiscent of Gustavo Guttiérez's claim of God's preferential option for the poor. Just as the poor are most in need of God's generosity and grace, so too are the social and moral outcasts among Jesus' dinner party. To take this one step further, if we interpret Jesus' response to the Pharisees as prioritizing his call to sinners over the righteous because the righteous do not understand themselves to be in need, we are left wondering if Jesus offers any call to those who deem themselves "righteous."

Might it be that sinners recognize their own need, while those who see themselves as righteous are too full of pride and hubris to comprehend their need for God's graceful mercy? Declaring oneself righteous before Jesus is to make a claim that no mortal could ever sustain. We all are sinners, but the sinner who understands her need is different from the sinner who claims to need no assistance; the former welcomes Jesus into her life, while the latter slams shut the doors of hospitality. Christ holds close those who are most in need of God's mercy and who recognize their need.

The second passage is important because it places an immediate reversal of fortune upon the powerful and the righteous. A leader of the synagogue, supposedly among the most righteous men of all, arrives, with both an insurmountable need and a startlingly clear faith in Jesus' capacity to overcome the insurmountable. The man's daughter has died, and he is certain that if Jesus will come and lay his hand on her, the girl will live. Without comment or question, Jesus gets up to follow him. As he does so, a woman who has been suffering from hemorrhages for twelve years also comes forward. With a clear faith in Jesus' ability to heal her, she reaches out to touch the fringe of his cloak. The text is unclear if this is menstrual hemorrhaging; if it is, the woman would be ritually unclean in the Jewish tradition,

Pastoral Perspective

to everyone that Jesus is available and eager to provide healing.

Indeed, perhaps the challenge for the preacher lies not in convincing the listener that our own needs are appropriate to bring before God, but rather in making sense of how our physical, emotional, and spiritual needs relate to the burden of sinfulness that Jesus also addresses. Jesus comes to heal wounds and to forgive sinners. The preacher should keep both in mind. Unintentionally, however, a sermon that equates a church with a hospital could make the implicit argument that ailments are directly connected to sin and that those with physical and emotional needs are in greater need of repentance.

Such discussion need not be emphasized in a sermon, but a connection between sin and disease or contamination does appear in this passage and may occur to some who hear this story. The aversion of the Pharisees to the tax collectors and sinners is echoed by the social stigma the woman with the hemorrhage would have encountered. Both the tax collector and the woman are considered outcasts because they are "impure," a view many in our churches and in our communities may assign to themselves. While desperation will inevitably lead people to request help, a perception of low self-worth can hamper a person's willingness to seek acceptance or pastoral attention. Some hearing this text may believe that they do not deserve help, either from the church or from God.

However, the question of how our status (our social position, our sense of worth, our physical health) intersects with our relationship with Christ makes this passage all the more powerful to hear and all the more useful for addressing pastoral concerns. Throughout the narrative, conventions are turned upside down, barriers are broken, and segregated peoples intermingle. The holy Jesus calls out to the sinful tax collector and sits at table with those whom the observing Pharisees consider undeserving. A leader of the synagogue throws protocol aside when he bows down before an unorthodox rabbi. A woman who would have attracted scorn in public nevertheless ventures out into a crowd to reach the one she knows can help. With the touch of his hand, Jesus brings a dead girl back among the living. If such lines as these can be crossed, then surely whatever issue is burdening a congregant, he or she can find encouragement in these verses.

For along with Jesus, this passage provides us with an unlikely hero and an unforgettable heroine: the synagogue leader who humbles himself and the

Exegetical Perspective

John, and Matthew immediately leave their vocations and their families in order to follow Jesus. In Matthew, true discipleship is demonstrated by a willingness fully to follow Jesus (see 8:22; 10:37–38; 16:24–25; 19:21, 27–29).

By calling Matthew into the community of disciples and by eating with him and other tax collectors, Jesus reorders social and communal relationships by including the excluded. Tax collectors were social outcasts among Jews because they were seen as collaborators with Roman imperial authorities. They were Jews who not only collected taxes for Rome, but also made their margin of profit by collecting more money than was legally due, increasing their own personal wealth. Considered disloyal and traitorous, they were despised and shunned by most other Jews (see 5:46; 18:17; 21:31–32). The Pharisees are presented as offended by Jesus' acceptance of and interaction with tax collectors. They criticize Jesus for violating social protocol by eating with "tax collectors and sinners" (9:11; 11:19).

Jesus responds to the Pharisees' criticism by saying it is the sick not the well that need a physician. Similar proverbs were common among Greek philosophers. Many Greek thinkers considered philosophers to be physicians of the soul. In addition to the proverb, Jesus quotes the prophet Hosea, "I desire mercy, not sacrifice" (v. 13; Hos. 6:6; repeated in Matt. 12:7). In Matthew, mercy takes precedence over ritualistic practices and religious traditions (5:22–24; 23:23). The quotation, which is not cited by Jesus in the other canonical Gospels, supports the emphasis in Matthew on the merciful compassionate treatment of others (see 5:38–48; 7:12; 25:31–46). It is mercy, not religious rituals (i.e., "sacrifices"), that the sick need, and it is mercy that Jesus brings (9:27; 15:22; 17:15; 20:30–31). Matthew's Jesus goes beyond the Pharisees' self-righteous interpretation of Jewish law so as to include mercy, which results in a reordering of social relationships to include the excluded. For Matthew's Jesus, mercy is at the heart of the social ethos he came to promote (5:7; 18:33; 23:23).

The mercy of Jesus is at the center of his healing of the dead girl and the hemorrhaging woman. While the Greek text simply identifies the father of the deceased girl as "a leader," rather than "a leader of the synagogue" (v. 18), nothing in the text suggests he is a Gentile rather than a Jew. As a Jewish leader, the father is most likely aware that for Jesus to lay his hand on a corpse would defile Jesus.[1] Likewise, the woman who

1. In Mark 5:22, the man is identified as a synagogue leader named Jairus, whose daughter is not yet dead when he comes to Jesus.

Homiletical Perspective

Sitting. Jesus calls not only social outcasts but moral outcasts too, even sitting with them for a dinner meal (v. 10). Whom do we welcome to our tables? With whom do we take time to sit? This text nudges preachers to explore whom we accept. We know Jesus eats with outcasts, but do we? Who are the sick in our day? Table fellowship says something about who is accepted in our social networks. Jesus assumes a more egalitarian social order than was the norm in his day. His inclusivity at the table is an indictment against the status quo. He eats and sits with the demonized, demonstrating that no one, even sinners, is beyond the reach of God's mercy.

Christians may feel excluded by Jesus' radical inclusion at the table, but the disciples are also sitting at the table with Jesus and the outcasts. A sermon on this text may be able to explore the ways Christians are sick and not well. One should not automatically assume that we are not tax collectors and sinners in some way and in need of mercy. However, one must also acknowledge the ways some believers exclude others because they are different. While Christians can be viewed as the "sick," the socially marginalized today are truly the prisoners, prostitutes, pimps, AIDS victims, dope dealers, and the like. These are the ones whom many drive by, rather than sit by, like Jesus. Those engaged in social ministry toward those mentioned may be affirmed in their ministry, whereas others may feel convicted by the mercy ministry of Jesus. This will depend on the congregational context. One thing is for sure: Jesus reaches out to the margins, calling us to follow him in this mercy mission. To whom do we minister? If we follow him, we will not only sit with outcasts, but touch them.

Touching. Jesus gets more intimately daring when he touches outcasts, despite all the social mores of the day. In verses 18–26 we have two examples of the sick to whom Jesus is called. They are both women. One is dead. The other is bleeding to death. Surprisingly, in the midst of these scenes where the emphasis is on Jesus' ministry to outcasts, he remains open to the powerful and privileged in society, indicating that no one is beyond his mercy. A "leader of the synagogue" (v. 18), most likely a civil administrator, pleads with Jesus to go and "lay your hand on" (i.e., touch) his dead daughter, and Jesus answers the prayer of this desperate dad. What father would not do everything in his power to help his little girl? (However, preachers should still be aware that there are fathers who abuse their children.)

Matthew 9:9-13, 18-26

Theological Perspective

and for her to touch Jesus himself would be to make him unclean as well. So it is a clever theological move by the author of Matthew that she reaches not for Jesus, but for his clothing.

Jesus' response to the woman is breathtaking and theologically meaningful; he tells her that what has made her well is her faith. Jesus does not claim to have done anything to have made her well, nor does he require anything of the woman; instead, he acknowledges that her faith is the agency of her healing. This is a powerful echo of what Jesus has said to the Pharisees in verses 12–13; the one who is healed is the one who recognizes her own need and has faith. Just so, the leader of the synagogue comes to Jesus in need, setting aside any vanity or self-righteousness in expressing his faith, and Jesus responds by restoring his daughter to life. It is noticeable that Jesus does not claim any great power in doing this, instead maintaining that the girl merely has been sleeping, and is not dead, which causes the professional mourners who are present to mock him. It seems as though it is the faith of the father, a leader of the synagogue, that is the agency that leads to his daughter's revivification.

In these passages, Jesus comes to those who are in need and recognize that they are in need. The righteous either are not in need or are too full of hubris to understand how deeply they are in need. Further, faith is a restorative agent unto itself, a graceful, unmerited gift from God that precedes the presence of Jesus, providing the rich and fertile soil from which the acts of Jesus may grow, may bloom.

STEPHEN BUTLER MURRAY

Pastoral Perspective

unwanted woman who has the moxie to grab hold of Jesus' cloak. They come from different places and for different reasons. One is at the top of the social ladder; the other has been left off entirely. One has an urgent and dire need; the other has a chronic and more complicated condition. Both have faith. Both, regardless of sinful status or personal circumstance, receive attention from Jesus and a miraculous result. Jesus reminds us of their equal value when he turns to the woman and calls her "daughter," the term the man uses when referring to his own little girl. All are children of God, and it is to those of us in need that Jesus has come.

The men and women listening to this passage who may be contemplating their own ailments or questioning their own worthiness should be encouraged by the universal accessibility this story ascribes to Jesus. Ministers and other leaders may find their lofty positions all the more precarious as they listen to the hypocritical denunciations of the scoffing Pharisees, yet they can find comfort in the attention Jesus pays to a synagogue leader who approaches him with a father's plea. Those in the congregation who are sitting with invisible pains or who do not feel comfortable with voicing their concerns can be reassured by the inclusive invitation Jesus extends to Matthew and inspired by the plucky faith of a long-suffering woman.

The passage naturally lends itself to an invitation to healing, and the sermon could easily lead to additional liturgy along these lines. The preacher may wish to include a litany for wholeness and healing within the service, offer a special prayer after the sermon, or simply extend a promise of availability to any who need special attention. Regardless of how this passage shapes the overall service, those hearing this story from Matthew can leave knowing that, no matter what their circumstance, the healing Jesus provides and the acceptance Jesus offers are available to all who believe.

ALEXANDER WIMBERLY

has been hemorrhaging for twelve years surely knows that Jewish law declares her unclean and that her touching Jesus will defile him. There are, however, no hesitations exhibited by either the Jewish leader or the hemorrhaging woman. Both apparently have faith not only in the healing power of Jesus but also in the mercy of Jesus.[2]

While the father of the deceased girl is an influential Jewish leader, he kneels before Jesus when asking him to lay his hand on his daughter. The act of kneeling is a gesture acknowledging social inferiority. The death of the leader's daughter is a tragedy that would be common at that time. Nearly half of all children during Jesus' day died before they reached the age of five.[3] Their familiarity with infant mortality is most likely one of the reasons the people laugh at Jesus when he says the girl is "not dead but sleeping." It is also probably one of the reasons the report of resurrecting the girl spread throughout the district.

Unlike Mark's account of the healing of the hemorrhaging woman (Mark 5:27–29), the healing in Matthew is not associated merely with her touching Jesus' garment. In Matthew, Jesus looks at the woman and greets her with the words, "Take heart, daughter; your faith has made you well" (v. 22). After this explicit act of mercy, the woman is instantly made well. Matthew identifies God's healing power as residing not in Jesus' clothing but, rather, in Jesus' mercy. In Matthew, God's power has always been associated with mercy. That is why Jesus says, "Go and learn what this means, 'I desire mercy, not sacrifice'" (v. 13).

GUY D. NAVE JR.

After the leader comes to Jesus, a woman comes to him. On his way to touch the hand of the girl, Jesus is touched at the fringe of his cloak by a woman on the fringes of society (v. 20). She is hemorrhaging, probably with a continuous menstrual flow, which according to Jewish law means that she is unclean and should not be touched (Lev. 15:19–30). Rather than Jesus touching her, she touches him, knowing that there can be healing just through a touch (v. 21). By touching Jesus, she is made "well" (v. 22) or, literally, "rescued." Jesus rescues her from dying a social and physical death. He risks contamination by touching her. Just as his body is touched by this woman, he touches another female body, the dead little girl.

The mourning music has already begun when he arrives, but this does not deter Jesus from touching the untouchable, death itself. To touch this dead girl on her hand meant being contaminated, but Jesus risks marginalization for resurrection. He "took her by the hand, and the girl got up" (v. 25). Touching this dead woman brings resurrection healing. In this instance, Jesus overcomes death, foreshadowing what he will do in the future, "getting up" just like the little girl. What is most striking is how Jesus risks his reputation by (1) reaching out to women and (2) offering healing to them through a touch. Our society may not be exactly like that of Jesus, but preachers can speak to how women are still ostracized and how their voices are muted in many church pulpits; Christians who oppose ordination of women may need to take another look at Jesus' relationships with women.

Moreover, the healing touch of Jesus raises questions about what healing is and how healing takes place. Can Jesus heal like this today? Can he raise the dead? Healing may be physical, but it is also relational and social, restoring the marginalized into community, where they can be lovingly touched again. Nothing can replace a restorative healing touch to those who need to know they are not alone, even in death. What kind of God will go all the way to touch death in order to destroy it for us? A God whose ministry is one of mercy.

LUKE A. POWERY

2. Cf. Matt. 14:34–36. Matthew omits the account of Jesus' asking who touched him and the woman approaching Jesus "in fear and trembling" (Mark 5:30–33).
3. See Roger Bagnall and Bruce Frier, *The Demography of Roman Egypt,* Cambridge Studies in Population, Economy and Society in Past Time 23 (Cambridge: Cambridge University Press, 1994), 87.

Exodus 19:2-8a

[2]They had journeyed from Rephidim, entered the wilderness of Sinai, and camped in the wilderness; Israel camped there in front of the mountain. [3]Then Moses went up to God; the Lord called to him from the mountain, saying, "Thus you shall say to the house of Jacob, and tell the Israelites: [4]You have seen what I did to the Egyptians, and how I bore you on eagles' wings and brought you to myself. [5]Now therefore, if you obey my voice and keep my covenant, you shall be my treasured possession out of all the peoples. Indeed, the whole earth is mine, [6]but you shall be for me a priestly kingdom and a holy nation. These are the words that you shall speak to the Israelites."

[7]So Moses came, summoned the elders of the people, and set before them all these words that the Lord had commanded him. [8a] The people all answered as one: "Everything that the Lord has spoken we will do."

Theological Perspective

No theological topic has fallen farther or faster in the popularity polls than the doctrine of election. Along with globalization has come increased religious pluralism almost everywhere. In settings newly aware of the challenges of religious diversity, the idea that God has chosen a particular group—and, reciprocally, may not have chosen others—meets with intense resistance. In its most explicit form, the doctrine of double predestination (God elects some for salvation and bars others from it) has always generated strenuous theological controversy.[1] Today, the suggestion that any group has a special designation from God unsettles those who are working to create tolerance and mutual understanding between religious traditions.

What, then, are we to make of these verses in Exodus that tell of the first election of a group by God? Moses and his followers have arrived at Sinai, where they will remain for the better part of two years (Num. 10:11), while the events transpire that are recounted in the rest of Exodus, all of Leviticus, and the first part of Numbers. Moses goes up to the

1. John Calvin, the best-known promoter of the doctrine, described the violent reaction it produces: "When the human understanding hears [this doctrine] . . . it breaks forth into random and immoderate tumult" (*Institutes of the Christian Religion* 3.23.1, ed. John T. McNeill, trans. Ford Lewis Battles, Library of Christian Classics [Philadelphia: Westminster Press, 1960]).

Pastoral Perspective

To read the story of arrival of the whole congregation of Israel at the foot of Mount Sinai is to encounter a story rich with points of interaction for pastor and people. In the story we encounter questions such as these:

1. What was the unique call of the congregation of Israel? What is the unique call of our congregation?
2. In what ways was the congregation of Israel uniquely blessed? In what ways is our congregation uniquely blessed?
3. For the congregation of Israel, what responsibilities came with their blessings? For our congregation, what responsibilities come with our blessings?

This text begins with the notation that the Israelites came to the foot of Mount Sinai from Rephidim. What was Rephidim? What does Rephidim represent for us in our journey as God's people? In the Exodus narrative, Rephidim was a place of both human need and God's provision. It was a place where humans questioned both God and Moses, and a place of divine response to those questions. At Rephidim the people wondered if God knew what God was doing and if they could trust

Exegetical Perspective

This crucial turning point in the long story of God's people occurs three months after the exodus from Egypt. That event of liberation has been celebrated with songs of joy (Exod. 15), but realities of life in the wilderness have set in soon enough. Before arriving at God's mountain (called Sinai here, Horeb elsewhere), the refugees from Pharaoh's land have experienced bitter water, sweetened for them; they have felt hunger and been told how to gather manna; and they have been attacked by Amalekites, but saved, thanks to God and Moses. Moses has begun to struggle with the challenges of leading such a large and conflicted group and has, on the advice of his father-in-law, secured helpers. It is fair to say that by the time the community camps at the foot of Mount Sinai, the difficulties of freedom are being experienced.

The form scholars discern biblical writers to be using when they discuss desert travails is called a "murmuring story." At the surface, deficient water, scarce food, and opponents are the problems encountered, and we no doubt can understand the temptation of people to complain; but the basic issue introduced, and highly relevant for the Sinai encounter, is more serious than even food and water. When the Israelites complain, their language inevitably resists the whole deed that God has done for them, and they call for a return to Egypt. What is

Homiletical Perspective

Preaching from the theophany on Sinai is no easy task. The exegesis recounting Israel's being taken into covenant relation with YHWH is historically intriguing, as well as theologically significant. However, this lengthy story of Moses's mediating a conversation between YHWH and the Israelites probably seems supernatural, archaic, and foreign to our twenty-first-century congregations. It is far fetched to imagine anyone hearing a message directly from God, then schlepping down and up a mountain to pass the message to one's community and returning to God with their response. People may enjoy hearing the religious importance of the story, but it seems mired in the past. What contemporary word can the preacher offer?

Obviously the sermon can open our understanding of the glorious good news of God's initiating relationship. YHWH's reception of the Israelites (imperceptive people that they appear to be in this text) indicates a willingness to covenant with faltering, imperfect humanity. If this is who YHWH is, then there is good news for subsequent generations and even Gentiles, for the history traced in the Hebrew Bible promises to open divine benefits to all the nations. Genesis 12:3 promises that through Abram all the families of the earth will be blessed, regardless of lineage. Of course the Exodus 19 passage does say,

Exodus 19:2-8a

Theological Perspective

mountain of God, who tells Moses to tell his followers that they have been chosen by God to be a kingdom and nation that keeps God's covenant and sets an example of holiness to the rest of the world. Duly elected, the people, in one voice, agree to serve.

The Lord's choice of the people at Sinai models three aspects of election that correct misconceptions about it and re-present it as a doctrine that still speaks to people of faith, perhaps *especially* to those faced with the promise and the challenges of religious pluralism.

Election Is a Process. The closely linked events of election, salvation, and call are often associated with single dramatic moments: Moses's call from the burning bush (Exod. 3:3–4) is a prime example. The invitation and challenge to Moses's followers to become God's people must also have been a galvanizing moment. Neither it nor the spectacular theophany that follows (Exod. 19:16–19), however, is a bolt from the blue. God's choosing and subsequent self-revealing has been going on for a long time, as the Lord reminds Moses: God dealt with the Egyptians, freed the Israelites, and now has carried them, on "eagles' wings . . . to myself" (v. 4). If election is understood as a slow, deliberate process—God prodding, directing, and enticing—it may also be evident that God's choosing goes constantly. It is threaded through the length of our lives and very likely through the lives of all creatures of God. In this view, election may be understood as an experience that people who approach God from different directions have in common, rather than as a status marker that elevates one group above the rest.

Election Entails Responsibility. Critics of the doctrine of election point out that, all too readily, "the elect" come to think of themselves as God's pets, singled out for special favors and exempt from the worst penalties for bad behavior. However, the election of the Israelites is anything but the granting of special privileges. Election is for a job, a mission: to be "a priestly kingdom and a holy nation" (v. 6). In the same way that one tribe, the Levites, to which Moses is said to have belonged (Exod. 2:1), functioned as priests for all of Israel, so all of Israel is to be the priest, the holy servant of all the nations of the world. To fulfill this role requires difficult disciplines: obeying the Lord and keeping the covenant, the details of which are about to be spelled out at very great length. Understood as a calling out for special responsibility, election can be seen not as special honors for a

Pastoral Perspective

the leadership of Moses. At Rephidim God provided water for the easily disgruntled congregation.

Rephidim was a place of both pain and provision. The people were called to move beyond both the memory of the pain and the security of the provision. They were to move on to new experiences, new challenges, and new revelation. They were to move on carrying with them the lessons of history, the lessons of Rephidim. In their life as the people of God, they would be asked to remember these lessons. There are contemporary questions that come to pastor and people. Is there a Rephidim in our story? What lessons did we learn from our Rephidim? Have we had the opportunity to apply these lessons to new situations?

As the narrative continues, Moses, as representative of the people, then went up to the mountain. On the mountain he heard God's voice and received God's instruction for the people. In the text there seems to be a clear and ordered line of communication. There seems to be a clear and ordered chain of command. God spoke to Moses. Moses spoke to the people. The people were expected to take Moses's words as God's words.

Our world may not mirror the world of the text. With good moral, theological, and experiential reasons, many would not want to be part of a hierarchical community, a community in which God spoke only to the pastor, in which the pastor was the sole voice of God for the people. The questions we are presented with are:

1. In our community, when, where, and how do we hear God's voice?
2. Are there times when the pastor is the voice of God for us?
3. Are there times when the people are the voice of God for the pastor?
4. Are there times when what the pastor hears God saying and what the people hear God saying are in conflict?
5. Are there times when the congregation is the voice of God to the larger community?
6. Does the community respect our voice?

Using the imagery of the eagle, God told Moses, "I bore you on eagles' wings and brought you to myself" (v. 4b). The imagery of God the eagle carrying us is stirring imagery. It suggests that God's initiative is all important, that God's choice of Israel fills Israel's life with meaning. Indeed, it was essential for Israel humbly to remember that its very being was an

Exegetical Perspective

at stake, then, even before we arrive at Sinai, is whether Israel is willing to be God's people or prefers Pharaoh.

Today's reading is *set* somewhere in the second millennium, long before any events that can be dated with certainty. The *production* of the story, undoubtedly later, is complex, plausibly a text woven by two or three distinct traditions (sometimes called Yahwist, Priestly, and Elohist). Scholars remain uncertain over how these ancient materials took shape, but we may not be far wrong to assume that, for a narrative as important as this one, all the traditions and voices wanted to participate. Such a view makes sense, since the story begun in today's reading is one of the stories of origins of the Hebrew people. We may be accustomed to think of that story as taking shape around Abraham and Sarah, or recommencing with the young Moses, or perhaps emerging as Saul and David contend over leadership. However, another birthday of God's people is at this event narrated at Mount Sinai.

What will unfold is a covenant or treaty agreement between God and people, enunciated in Exodus 19 and then specified in the blocks of legal material that follow in chapters 20–23 and in the latter chapters of Exodus (and continue into Leviticus, Numbers, and Deuteronomy as well). The covenant is ratified and celebrated (Exod. 24). We have in today's reading the very beginnings of the long event, enough to see the shape of it.

With the people gathered at the foot of the mountain, Moses ascends to hear God's initial words. The location of the mountain is uncertain, despite centuries of efforts to locate it. The story indicates it is somewhere in the Sinai Peninsula, east of Egypt and south of the land of promise. How can the location of so crucial a site be uncertain, many wonder, and with cause. Given the significance of this event of covenant between God and people, it seems the site should have been remembered. Scholars suggest that, so far as the Bible is concerned, the people must learn to seek God in Jerusalem; so the location of Sinai goes hazy. In any case, the event and its maintenance are more important than the geographical location. Moses, leaving the people below, ascends Sinai to learn from God what is on offer.

When God instructs a human being to speak, the instructions are often summarized, and we, reading, are informed as the characters in the story are addressed. Here, however, such is not the case. God's words are explicit and formal: "'Thus shall you say . . .'" God details (v. 3). What is articulated is the

Homiletical Perspective

"*You* shall be my treasured possession out of all the peoples" (so the tribes of Israel are uniquely chosen). However, Christians and all other peoples are included in the reminder that "the whole earth is mine." So one question the sermon could address is, what is *our* covenant relationship with God?

Answers to this question could come from the preacher's spending time with the mission or vision statement of the congregation or the creed we repeat weekly. What have we claimed as our identity? This Sunday's worship could be the highlight of a congregation's annual covenant renewal. The sermon could ask: Since we are not the priestly people or the holy nation referred to in the passage, who are we? We could then go on to explore the claims of allegiance the congregation has made in response to God's gracious initiation. What does it mean that as individuals and as a congregation we have pledged to live out our communal faith, recognizing the sovereignty of God and our responsibility as a community of faith in God's world? If God called the enslaved Hebrews into a covenant of liberation and righteousness, we who are called together in worship and faithfulness before this same God are called to righteousness and liberation too.

The preacher will need to assess what this means in light of the current congregational situation. How are we righteous in our worship and in our living out of the faith? How might we be stretched or challenged to further righteous faithfulness as we renew our congregational covenant? Part of the sermon could be well spent clarifying the connection between our faith claims (our theology) and our individual and corporate living out of the faith (our ethical reflection and decisions).

Regardless of whether the preaching is part of an annual service of covenant renewal or merely bringing a timely message for today, part of the sermon would need to address how easily we make promises corporately and individually. After prayer and study, a congregation may eagerly promise to raise its mission giving 5 percent in the next five years, only to be caught short when the challenge includes raising it 1 percent this year. Remember how many of us easily plan to exercise more over the summer, only to be embarrassed when someone asks if we have exercised additionally this week. So we want to be careful not merely to lift up the claims of our creed or mission statement, as if repeating something makes it so. Who we have pledged to be as a congregation involves our needing regularly to spend spiritual and physical energy imagining what that means in our concrete living.

Exodus 19:2-8a

Theological Perspective

favored few but rather as a mandate to all nations and to all religious communities as well.

Election Creates a People. Though Scripture speaks almost exclusively of the elect collectively, as a chosen people, much theological wrangling has focused on which persons have been picked by God and which rejected, and how to tell the difference. God does choose persons for special tasks. At the burning bush Moses is given a herculean one. Almost immediately, though, God forecasts the extension of that call to the whole people of Israel: Moses will lead them to the very mountain on which he received his instructions, and there they will receive theirs (Exod. 3:12). As they do, as they hear what the Lord has destined them for and expects of them, the motley crew of Israelites becomes the people Israel—a constituted nation with one identity and, at least for the moment, one purpose. Their first act as a holy nation is to speak together "as one: 'Everything that the LORD has spoken we will do'" (v. 8).

Theologian Christopher Morse mines the concept of election and its counterweight, damnation, as God's actions directed toward collectives rather than individuals who emerge labeled as "elect" or "reprobate." If all have fallen short of the glory of God and are in "solidarity in sin," Morse asks, what does God finally intend for all of us? Is it possible that God means eternally to condemn our offenses and the social practices and structures that institutionalize our evil deeds, rather than individual persons among us? And by the same principle, might not the entire motley human crew be called, in the end, to be God's holy people?[2] Perhaps so. Perhaps someday, in the fullness of time, all humanity, chosen by God, may answer God's call as one: "Everything that the LORD has spoken we will do."

BARBARA G. WHEELER

Pastoral Perspective

expression of God's will. It is important for our congregations humbly to remember the same. The congregation of Israel was asked to believe that it was chosen by God and carried toward its destiny by God. While there is the danger of arrogance in suggesting that our congregations also are chosen by God and carried toward our destinies by God, it will likely be a meaningful exercise for us to consider the ways we too have been borne on eagles' wings, to ponder the ways those wings continue to propel us forward.

The writer of Exodus does not want the congregation of Israel to think only of their election. The writer wants the congregation to give equal attention to the responsibilities that come with being carried by the eagle. The writer wants the congregation to see that it must choose to accept these responsibilities. The words of God to the people are, "If you obey my voice and keep my covenant, you shall be my treasured possession out of all the peoples" (v. 5). The emphasis in this verse falls on "If." The emphasis falls on the response of the congregation.

As pastor and people there are questions that confront us:

1. Do we talk as much about our responsibilities as about the blessings we are promised?
2. In inviting others to join our congregation, do we promise that their needs will be met, or do we focus on our mission of meeting the needs of the larger community?
3. If we wax eloquent about the ways we are carried by the wings of God, do we acknowledge that those wings carry us not only to vistas of splendor but also to points of great need?

This text closes with the people affirming that they would do absolutely everything that Moses had asked them to do. As the story moves forward, it becomes clear that this was a promise that was beyond their ability to keep. There is a temptation for our congregations to say, "Thank God, we are not like them." This, of course, would be overstatement on our part. Better to acknowledge that now, as then, there is a gap between what we are and what we aspire to. This gap, however, does not signal the end of the story, for the congregation of Israel or for the congregation we call ours.

H. JAMES HOPKINS

---

2. Christopher Morse, *Not Every Spirit: A Dogmatics of Christian Disbelief,* 2nd ed. (Edinburgh: T.&T. Clark; New York: Continuum, 2009), 335–43.

Exegetical Perspective

basis for all that follows. God's basis for offering—prescribing—this new covenantal relationship is the deed of liberation in Egypt. "You have seen what I did to the Egyptians," God reminds his hearers (v. 4), recalling the whole act of liberation and the resistance to it. We may already hear that the resistance has not been only that of the Egyptians. The Israelites themselves have contemplated—demanded—return to Egypt, where food and water were better.

God then characterizes, by contrast, his dealings with Israel: "I bore *you* on eagles' wings," God recalls (v. 4), prompting us, if not the original hearers, to review the three months of desert struggles. God continues instruction to Moses, words Moses is to repeat at the foot of the mountain: "If you obey my voice and keep my covenant . . ." There are specifics noted, the promised basis of the relationship between God and Israel. Israel is to become God's "treasured possession," a particular special choice of God's, promised to no other peoples. Israel is, distinctively again, named comprehensively as a kingdom of priests and a holy people. Solid gifts are extended by God, if Israel is able to receive them.

Moses descends (the first of several trips up and down as the passage continues), and sets before the elders of the people what he has been commanded. In an extraordinary action, the people respond as one: "Everything that the LORD has spoken, we will do."

That seems a wonderful reply. As the episode and the telling of it continue, it is not quite so simple. Thus far, in this reading, the people have done well to respond wholeheartedly to what God has said. Moses reports their words back to God, who has to have been pleased. Though we can read on in the story, this is a good place to pause. It is easy to concentrate generally on the failure of God's people to obey, to accept what God offers them, since the preponderance of narratives stress that failing. Here, however, they do well, indicating a wholehearted desire to move into relationship with God distinctively. That is well done.

BARBARA GREEN

Homiletical Perspective

The lines put into God's mouth are great poetry: "You shall be my treasured possession out of all the peoples. . . . you shall be for me a priestly kingdom and a holy nation" (vv. 5–6). What a glorious promise! Consider what it meant to live out a "priestly" responsibility. The Levitical and priestly families were separated out of "normal" life. Today those we know as pastors and priests are still expected to mediate rituals between God and humanity. They serve. So, even though most of our parishioners are Gentiles and laity (not children of Levi), we still appropriately invite them to consider their responsibilities, believing that Gentiles too are God's treasured possessions and fit for participation in a holy people. Preachers must help congregations figure out their covenant role with God as we participate in proper worship, keep spiritually fit, and join in service to humanity.

Remember that this passage begins the theophany on Sinai. Hindu saint and radical social organizer Mohandas Gandhi had thoughts on theophany too. He wrote: "To a people famishing and idle, the only acceptable form in which God can dare appear is work and promise of food as wages."[1] Our congregations must be encouraged to see the needs of the people around us and figure out how meeting some of those needs is required by our covenant relationship with God.

Our twenty-first-century world can certainly use whatever we have, and our faith is deepened by sharing. What does our congregation have to give to God and the world? Sermons can advise our congregations how to embrace our suffering sisters and brothers: for instance, the ones who sleep in vulnerable places each night, either outdoors because they have no home or locked into their home with someone who abuses them. Certainly our worship life needs not merely to mention the needs of the world, but to raise specific concerns and cast the light of the gospel on them. Sermons can offer helpful clarification of our covenant understanding of who we are, spelling out in concrete terms how we might faithfully relate to God, to people within our faith community, and to people beyond our walls.

MARY ALICE MULLIGAN

---

1. *The Collected Works of Mahatma Gandhi*, vol. 21, Aug.–Dec. 1921 (Ahmedabad: Navanjivan Press, 1966), 289.

Psalm 100

[1]Make a joyful noise to the LORD, all the earth.
[2] Worship the LORD with gladness;
   come into his presence with singing.

[3]Know that the LORD is God.
   It is he that made us, and we are his;
   we are his people, and the sheep of his pasture.

[4]Enter his gates with thanksgiving,
   and his courts with praise.
   Give thanks to him, bless his name.

[5]For the LORD is good;
   his steadfast love endures forever,
   and his faithfulness to all generations.

Theological Perspective

By its very nature, worship is directed toward someone or something else; nevertheless, it tends to reveal as much about the *worshiper* as it does about the object, person, or deity being worshiped. The features or characteristics that I choose to honor and praise in others may (or may not) accurately describe them; but the very fact that I choose to focus on *these particular* characteristics (and not on others) says a great deal about my own cares and desires. The fact that I choose something as the object of my worship would seem to indicate that, in my judgment, this "something" is worthy of honor and praise.

Theologians have often pointed out that human beings tend to engage in acts of worship, whether they believe in any god or gods.[1] We all have objects that we consider worthy of praise: a finely crafted musical instrument, say, or a particularly talented actor, or a beautiful panorama that appears after a bend in the road. "Magnificent!" we say, making it clear that we have encountered something genuinely praiseworthy. Whether such praise rises to the level of *worship* is, of course, another matter; such terminology usually indicates a form of praise that is particularly intense

---

1. See the thoughtful reflections in Philip D. Kenneson, "Gathering: Worship, Imagination, and Formation," in Stanley Hauerwas and Samuel Wells, eds., *The Blackwell Companion to Christian Ethics* (Oxford: Blackwell Publishers, 2004).

Pastoral Perspective

Enough lamenting (Ps. 31); enough finger-pointing (Ps. 50); now let us rejoice! Psalm 100 is a very familiar psalm, one that many of the older generation will have memorized. It may be time to let people remember it in the King James Version. A memorized psalm or an old gospel hymn can transport a person into at least the memory of an experience of God, or more likely, a direct experience of God.

This psalm begins by inviting all the earth to make a joyful noise to God. However, one may ask how that can be possible, given so much misery in life. It is almost a call to revolution. Let all the earth rejoice in God the Creator, in spite of murder, war, and frightening climate change. Let us be glad in the presence of the Divine, in spite of depression and debilitating illness. Let us sing thanksgiving, in spite of poverty, hunger, and AIDS. Look death in the eye and make a joyful noise. Grab evil by the neck and shout loud hosannas!

Why? Because God still is God. All the earth—animal, plant, mineral, men, women, and children—still belongs to God the Creator. God still longs for us to enter the Shepherd's fold and come into the Sovereign's gate with thanksgiving, because at its core, life is Love. The intention of the universe is toward harmony, peaceful coexistence, desiring the best for the other. Even though one culture or

Exegetical Perspective

This communal invitation to praise and thanksgiving is a beautiful invitation to the congregation to render praise to God as an act of worship is beginning. No doubt, this psalm soon became a much-used word of praise and thanksgiving, found suitable for many occasions, including family and individual acts of devotion, just as it continues to be today.

The only textual question appears in verse 3, where the Hebrew sound *lo* allows for two readings. Here, the more likely reading is the *lo* that means "to him" (NRSV "we are his"), rather than the KJV reading *lo'* that means "no" or "not" (KJV "and not we ourselves"). It seems unlikely that the psalmist would have entertained the idea that human beings created themselves.

One of the key terms in the psalm deserves special comment. The closing words of the psalm in the KJV speak of God's goodness, mercy, and truth (NRSV goodness steadfast love, and faithfulness). These terms help define the very character of God. More will be said about them below. Here it is important to note that God's goodness includes both esthetic and moral elements. The Hebrew term means "fair," "fitting," "appealing," and not only morally good and upright.

The term in verse 5 translated "truth" in the KJV also has a wider meaning than is normally associated

Homiletical Perspective

This is one of the most beloved psalms in the entire corpus. As a hymn, it is often employed to set the tone for engaging and celebrative worship because of its joyful and robust language. When read well, it can certainly gladden the heart and entice even the most reluctant of worshipers openly to worship God. It is important also to note that one of the reasons this psalm is so powerful is because it is in motion. Four of the five verses begin with an action verb ("make," "worship," "know," "enter") that compels the reader or hearer to do something. Perhaps the best way for the preacher to start thinking about how to approach this text is by asking, why? Why is the psalmist exhorting listeners to make a joyful noise to God? Why should the people worship God with joy and gladness? Why was the writer writing about thanksgiving? Why should members of the writer's community be thankful?

In the second stanza of the psalm (v. 3) the preacher encounters revealing phrases such as "we are his," "we are his people," "the sheep of his pasture." These phrases highlight a connection between the people and God that indicates *belonging*. These phrases remind us that the identity of the people of Israel was intricately woven to their relationship with God. For the Israelites, belonging to God came with the responsibility of living their lives in ways that

Psalm 100

Theological Perspective

and sustained over a period of time. We all have various forms of devotion, not all directed toward God. In fact, most of us tend to be rather generous with our praise, heaping it onto everything from consumer goods to works of art (and a wide assortment of human beings) with surprising regularity. One only need attend an occasional football game, rock concert, or political rally, in order to witness levels of adoration and praise that are difficult to distinguish from worship. In fact, if an outside observer were to try to determine what we worship (based on how we spend our time and energy), "God" would probably be fairly far down the list.

Thus, given that Christianity (like a number of other faiths) has traditionally claimed that God alone is worthy of worship and praise, something would appear to be seriously out of joint. We usually resolve this difficulty by using the word "worship" only when speaking of our devotion to God and using other terminology when speaking of rock stars and sports heroes (regardless of the depth and endurance of our devotion to them). I believe, though, that using the same language for the various objects of our affection and attention is a helpful reminder of the fact that we do sometimes find ourselves engaging in something very much like "worship" with things that are not God.

Regardless of what language we use to describe our various allegiances, the truth is that they are divided and that they sometimes come into conflict with one another. Augustine tells us that many human difficulties arise from our tendency to *love* the things that we ought to *use*, and to *use* the things that we ought to *love*.[2] We get so wrapped up in the materials and methods that we employ to live our lives that we start treating these objects as ends in themselves—enjoying the objects themselves rather than using them to pursue worthier goals. On the other hand, we sometimes endow the truly worthy objects of our affection—like other people and God—with a merely instrumental value, as though their primary purpose were to help us obtain lesser goods.

In the face of these difficulties, Scripture has an important word to offer. One of the purposes of the Psalms in general, and of Psalm 100 in particular, is to help us to clarify and reaffirm the true object of our worship: God alone. In just five verses, this psalm captures the essence and nature of the proper human disposition toward God. The first two verses

2. Augustine of Hippo, *De doctrina christiana* (variously translated *On Christian Doctrine* or *Teaching Christianity*), section 3.

Pastoral Perspective

another or all of them together may appear to be hurtling toward self-destruction, Love is steadfast and endures forever. Therefore, joyful noises are appropriate!

Perhaps it is helpful to look at the church's worship experience with a critical eye. Can pastoral concerns be addressed by worship? What on a Sunday morning provides encouragement and healing? How can worship be designed to create an experience of God's presence for inspiration, comfort, healing, and nurturing?

Come into God's presence with singing! Imagine Jesus singing the Psalms in the synagogue. Surely Jesus and his disciples worshiped together often. Did they sing in four-part harmony? Did they rediscover the presence of God as they joined their voices in praise?

God's gift of music is a magnificent healing agent, lifting hearts to commune with the angels. Nursing homes are eager to invite anyone to bring music to the residents. Eyes light up as the troubled mind drifts away to other, healthy, happy times. Even if a particular song is not familiar to a resident, the music itself has power to comfort.

Permit me to tell a personal story. The beginning days of vacation were comically disastrous. The first time the power steering pump in the truck went out, we were fortunate to be safe in a parking lot waiting for the tow truck. The second time it went, we felt lucky to be only twenty miles west of the same town, waiting by the side of the road, staring at the beautiful scenery, taking silly pictures of each other. We laughed as we bounced along the highway in our little pickup truck secured by heavy chains on top of the tow truck. The third time the steering went (it is now the third day in the same town), the joy disappeared. When the transmission of the loaner vehicle we used to retrieve our second car from home in order to continue our road trip refused to engage, it was time for simmering rage. My wife feared the worst—that I would not recover from this latest insult to my ego. Finally, we were on our way once again, traveling in her ever-trustworthy but too-small car.

A favorite CD was playing as we continued our journey—old gospel songs set to marvelous harmonies and stringed instruments. The scowl on my face softened as I recognized a song my parents used to sing—"I'd rather have Jesus than silver or gold." During the next song—"Never will give up, oh no . . ."—my toe began to tap. The next track—"Remember I'm a human, and humans forget, so remind me, remind me, dear Lord"—required my

with the English equivalent. In the present text, the central meaning is "trustworthiness." For the psalmist, God is good and also glorious, true, and utterly trustworthy.

Thanksgiving is an act that is marked by spiritual dangers. Self-satisfaction can lead one to thank God that one is not like other, flawed human beings, as in the Gospel reference (Luke 18:11). The opposite danger is that one devalues the human self, created in God's image and likeness, by self-debasement, picturing oneself as the worst of sinners, a great challenge to God's capacity for mercy and forgiveness. Perhaps the most dangerous spiritual temptation, however, is to be resentful toward the benevolent giver, as one offers thanks that can hardly be authentic and heartfelt. Our psalm avoids these dangers admirably.

The psalmist invites all to come with demonstrations of joy and gratitude, offering no formulas or rituals that must be observed. All that is required is sheer joy and thanksgiving, displayed with sound of voice and instruments.

The short poem is a whole, offering little need for a breakdown into its several divisions. One may, of course, recognize the summons to praise and thanksgiving in verses 1–2, followed by the call to recognize just who this One is who is being praised: God the Creator, to whom all belong, as those who owe their very existence to the Deity. Then verses 3–4 repeat in other terms the summons to praise, and the poem closes with the ground or basis for praise: God's goodness, and enduring mercy, and unending faithfulness. These text divisions, however, make a smooth and utterly pleasing whole—an act of praise and summons to praise that has found an enduring place in Jewish and Christian worship.

While the psalm no doubt arose in connection with the worship of God in the Jerusalem temple, serving as a hymn of praise used in entrance ceremonies on festive days, such a specific setting in life for the psalm must surely have quickly broadened to include general acts of communal praise and thanksgiving. Indeed, it seems likely that its use as a hymn for the community would have broadened to include acts of praise and prayer for family and individuals, as noted above.

The psalm has one other feature that should not be missed. While the summons to "all the earth" (v. 1) to praise God may be translated "all the land"—thus perhaps remaining a summons not to all nations but to all Israelites to render God due praise—the latter translation is not necessary.

were pleasing to God. Living godly lives was hard work that translated into the regulation of every aspect of life, including diet, dress, relationships (marriage, divorce, adultery, treatment of poor and widows), worship/priesthood, sacrifices and offerings. By following the law, the people of Israel lived very different lives from their neighbors.

It will be important for the preacher to explore whether belonging to God or being in relationship with God also influences our human relationships today. Should our relationship with God be evident in the ways we interact with all people? Does belonging to God influence with whom we choose to develop close friendships or ultimately choose to be our spouses or partners? Does belonging to God influence our business pursuits by informing with whom we choose to do business? Does belonging to God compel us to give to others more than we receive? Are there areas of our lives that should not be influenced by our relationship with God? Are some of us willing to compromise our godly principles out of a need to belong to certain groups?

In addition to pursuing the concept of belonging, the preacher can also pursue the concept of goodness. "For the LORD is good" (v. 5). What does this mean? What does the goodness of God look like? The psalmist suggests that the Israelites were recipients of God's goodness in the form of never-ending love and faithfulness. Throughout the Hebrew Bible, we find that when the people called upon God, even when they had been disobedient, God heard their cries and came to their rescue. God loved the people and continued to be faithful, even when the people turned their backs on God and worshiped other gods.

Have people in the congregation experienced the never-ending love and faithfulness of God as individuals? As families? As members of the worship community? Are there people in the congregation who acknowledge times in their lives when they have not lived godly lives, but experienced the love and faithfulness of God nevertheless? Are there people in the congregation who have called upon God for help in various situations and circumstances and have felt that God not only heard their cries, but helped them in times of trouble, even when the trouble was of their own making?

The preacher could also explore other images or embodiments of the goodness of God for the parishioners. Do the people perceive God as good when they have their basic needs met, such as food, shelter, clothing, health care? Does the goodness of God take the form of material goods, such as money, homes,

Psalm 100

counsel us to adopt an attitude of joy, service, and praise toward God. The third explains why: God is our maker and our master, like a shepherd caring for sheep. The fourth verse returns to the imperative mode of verses 1–2, encouraging us to offer praise to God in a venue expressly designed for this purpose (here signified as the temple, with its "gates" and "courts"). Finally, the fifth verse picks up the thread of verse 3, again providing a warrant for these acts of worship: God's goodness, mercy, and faithfulness are qualities that are truly worthy of praise.

Despite the conciseness and beauty of these five verses, they may strike us as somewhat reductive. Given the general theological principle that God alone is worthy of our worship, the psalm hardly tells us anything new. However, as creatures who tend to seek out some object of worship, we do need regular reminders of where that worship is most properly directed. By keeping this psalm ever before our eyes and allowing it to be written on our hearts, we find ourselves bidden to use what should be used, and to love what should be loved—rather than the other way around.

Given the pervasive presence of the Latin (Vulgate) Bible for a thousand years of Christian history, the Psalms often became known by their opening Latin words. Our English "Make a joyful noise" is rendered in a single Latin word—*jubilate*—that resonates with English words such as "jubilation" and "jubilee." Hence, this psalm also serves as a persistent reminder that our worship should always be marked by the deepest and most profound joy.[3]

DAVID S. CUNNINGHAM

bass harmony. My wife glanced in my direction. A smile was too much at this point, but I could feel the cloud lifting. I did not have the strength to resist the music. Joy would recapture me.

Psalm 100 calls the congregation to remember the ancient hymns, the good old gospel songs, the classical anthems that proclaim the faith of the church; however, not everyone can sing or play an instrument. Are there other ways to make a joyful noise in worship? What else provides food for the soul? The liturgy of worship often includes public prayers, litanies, calls to worship, Scripture reading, proclaiming the Word, passing the peace, and even a time for a lack of noise—blissful silence. The congregation praying together the Lord's Prayer in perfect cadence, as one voice, is a sound that sends chills up a pastor's spine. The call and response of the Great Thanksgiving is surely a divine conversation.

Is there a more pleasurable noise than babies yelling or crying in church, or children being shushed by their mothers? What about the elderly woman sitting next to her aging daughter and saying aloud, "What did he say? He sure is cute!" The joyful noise of chatter during the passing of the peace indicates a community delighting in each other's company. The lifting up of personal concerns during prayer provides a channel for hope and healing. Even the shifting and coughing during silence is a reminder of our humanity and of God's loving care for us all. Listen for the noise outside the church building—birds singing praise, dogs barking a welcome to their people, traffic conveying passengers to do whatever they will do.

Praise is thanksgiving. Worship is being truly present to God. As we bask in God's presence, let the glad noise begin.

STEVEN D. MILLER

---

3. Those wishing to explore this connection further should consult David Ford and Daniel Hardy's fine book on the theology of worship, aptly entitled *Jubilate* (London: Darton, Longman & Todd, 1984), recently reprinted as *Living in Praise* (Grand Rapids: Baker, 2005).

Exegetical Perspective

Israelite voices frequently call upon all peoples and lands to join in praise and thanksgiving. All peoples are God's people; God's blessing to Israel through Abraham (Gen. 12) is a blessing that has in view "all the families of the earth." Although many of Israel's psalms are of course expressive of Israel's own experience of the Deity's power and presence, others—like this one—are suitable, and may be designed, for the worship of all individuals and groups and religious communities.

Many of the biblical psalms devoted to the praise and thanksgiving of God express gratitude for benefits received by the individual or the community. (For example, Psalm 103 is in effect an almost lyrical commentary on Exodus 34:6–7.) This communal act of praise shows no such connection. It is a kind of confession or creed, presenting the community with a summary statement of who God is, what the very character of deity is experienced to be. Such documents in the Bible must have been of immense importance to Israel, for they sum up the community's best and most beautiful ways of speaking usefully and memorably about God. Many similar texts in the Hebrew Bible do the same, but no brief biblical text better than Psalm 100 portrays the very heart of God as loving and merciful, with mercy vastly outreaching God's just demands.

The only psalm that offers sheer praise to God, with no grounding in God's goodness or deeds of mercy, is Psalm 150. In that psalm, worshipers are called to praise God with voice and with many other aids to praise. Every living being is to join in the praise. Not a word is heard of benefits received. As other psalms point out, praise is due to God because of who God is perceived to be, in virtue of the Deity's own character. Psalm 100 almost joins in that affirmation, but in this instance we may be glad that the psalmist offered a motive. What better general motive for the worship of God is imaginable than the psalm's closing words: "For the LORD is good; his steadfast love endures forever, and his faithfulness to all generations"?

WALTER J. HARRELSON

Homiletical Perspective

cars, and clothes? Is the goodness of God embodied in good health? Is the goodness of God demonstrated in the blessings of power and influence conferred upon God's people? Are human conceptions of the goodness of God influenced by class and status? If so, how can parishioners discern which expectations of God are realistic and which are culturally conditioned? Why should congregants even care if their expectations of God are realistic or not?

Although *belonging* to God is an important theme of this psalm, it does not overshadow the dominant theme of joy. This psalm is not primarily about the responsibilities associated with belonging to God, but rather about the joy—joy in God that the psalmist believed should be expressed with great fervor, zeal. Words like "gladness," "singing," "thanksgiving," and "praise" indicate that the people of God should worship God with everything they have—their bodies, voices, spirits, and minds. Worship of God should be a celebration. The preacher can ask the congregation what they do to celebrate people and mark important events in their lives such as birthdays, anniversaries, graduations, weddings, and promotions. Do they make noise when they attend celebrative events? If they can celebrate people and events with great zeal, can they not celebrate God with the same zeal? How would approaching worship as celebration transform worship experiences?

The preacher can structure the sermon by introducing new thoughts with action verbs to match the structure of the psalm. For example, when speaking about joy and why the people of God should be filled with joy, the preacher can begin with the verb "rejoice." When inviting the people to worship God with their bodies, as well as spirits and minds, the preacher can begin with verbs such as "make," "clap," or "dance."

DEBRA J. MUMFORD

Romans 5:1-8

¹Therefore, since we are justified by faith, we have peace with God through our Lord Jesus Christ, ²through whom we have obtained access to this grace in which we stand; and we boast in our hope of sharing the glory of God. ³And not only that, but we also boast in our sufferings, knowing that suffering produces endurance, ⁴and endurance produces character, and character produces hope, ⁵and hope does not disappoint us, because God's love has been poured into our hearts through the Holy Spirit that has been given to us.

⁶For while we were still weak, at the right time Christ died for the ungodly. ⁷Indeed, rarely will anyone die for a righteous person—though perhaps for a good person someone might actually dare to die. ⁸But God proves his love for us in that while we still were sinners Christ died for us.

Theological Perspective

In our lessons from Romans over the past two weeks, Paul has been developing his theology of justification by faith. Today we reach the culmination, the fulfillment of God's promised righteousness, as Paul expounds the fruits of God's justification of sinners. He begins chapter 5 with the assumption that justification is already complete: "Therefore, since we have been justified by faith" (Rom. 5:1 ESV). What follows can be described as the consequences or fruits of justification. Paul names two of them: as a result of our justification through faith in Christ's righteousness, "we have peace with God through our Lord Jesus Christ" (v. 1), and we have the "hope of sharing the glory of God" (v. 2). In other words, we enjoy *peace* in the present and hope for *glory* in the future.

Christian theologians over the centuries have developed some language that can help us better to imagine the distinction Paul is making. The Protestant scholastic theologians of the sixteenth and seventeenth centuries liked to distinguish among various kingdoms or reigns within God's plan of salvation. Using the key terms from Romans 5:2, they distinguished the *regnum gratiae*, the kingdom or rule of grace under which we live now, from the *regnum gloriae* (or *regnum Christi*), the kingdom of glory under the future reign of Christ. Theological

Pastoral Perspective

In this opening verse of Scripture Paul shares peace with God as a benefit of the Christian's faith. This peace is caused by the resolution of hostility that exists between humanity and God because of sin. Paul reminds us that it is "through our Lord Jesus Christ" that animosity dissipates and the struggle of humanity against God resolves. As recipients of peace, believers gain access into a place of grace through Jesus Christ. John Newton spoke of such grace in his well-known hymn, "Amazing Grace":

> Amazing grace, how sweet the sound,
> that saved a wretch like me!
> I once was lost, but now am found,
> was blind but now I see.
> 'Twas grace that taught my heart to fear,
> and grace my fears relieved;
> How precious did that grace appear
> the hour I first believed![1]

In the words we learn that it is by faith Newton understood himself to be saved and ushered into a state of grace. Paul also makes it clear in Romans 5:2 that Christians stand in this grace. It is unearned and undeserved. This is why grace is so amazing.

1. John Newton, "Amazing Grace," in *The New Century Hymnal* (Cleveland: Pilgrim Press, 1995), #547.

Exegetical Perspective

Most interpreters recognize the opening sentence of this passage (5:1–2) as transitional, not only summarizing what has been said but marking out new territory to explore. Some plot the various themes gathered here as an overview of a Pauline salvation history, which climaxes in what God has already done "through our Lord Jesus Christ" and concludes with "the hope of God's [coming] glory." Paul's shift in style from a sustained argument from Scripture to a deeply personal description of a shared experience ("we," "us") indicates a concern to clarify the nature of the righteousness that God credits to the believer. This is hardly presented as a forensic repositioning of the believer's legal status before a righteous God; rather, it concerns the repair of a relationship between a loving God and a community with whom God now lives at peace.

The phrase, "through [*dia*] our Lord Jesus Christ," recalls 3:22, that it is "through [*dia*] the faithfulness of Jesus Christ" (my trans.) that God's salvation-creating righteousness is credited to those who trust him (cf. 1:16–17). To "have peace" is one real benefit of this purchase that shapes a full range of the community's spiritual (see 8:6; 14:17) and social (see 14:19) relationships. To obtain "access [*eschēkamen*] to this grace in which we stand [*hestēkamen*]" is yet another benefit. This theological

Homiletical Perspective

Paul begins with the premise that we are justified by faith, picking up where he left off in the previous chapter. He has argued that point and now moves forward to what that means for us. The result is that we have peace with God. This justification by faith opens the way to God's salvation, the new relationship with God. Those who believe have been brought into a right relationship with God, have fellowship with, and are in unity and harmony with the God of all creation. Now there is no more hostility toward God in one's spirit or in one's actions. Having peace with God is something Paul and other New Testament writers emphasize. Paul seeks it for his readers and hearers in his letter greetings ("grace and peace to you") and in what he desires and prays for his hearers. For example, "May the God of hope fill you with all joy and peace in believing, so that you may abound in hope by the power of the Holy Spirit" (Rom. 15:13). Peace in God opens up the possibility of rest in the God of our salvation.

This peace, this new relationship with God, has been brought through Jesus Christ, who is understood to be our Lord. Jesus gives us access, through our faith, to this grace, this unearned, unmerited gift of God, in which we now stand, in which we now have our solid footing and confidence.

Romans 5:1-8

Theological Perspective

concepts such as these enable us to orient ourselves in the life of faith. In our present life in the world, we live by faith under the rule of grace, enjoying our peace with God, while not yet experiencing the fullness of the glory that is our ultimate destiny in Christ. This peace that is the present fruit of reconciliation with God has both a subjective and an objective dimension. We experience it in our lives as inner peace, that sense of contentment that comes from having a clear conscience; but this subjective peace is grounded in objective reality, since the warfare of sin, the rebellion of the sinner against God's grace, has in fact come to an end in the sacrificial death of the Prince of Peace (see Isa. 40:1–2 and 9:6), who gave up his life that we might live.

For many people the most difficult part of this passage comes where Paul reminds us that we Christians not only rejoice in the hope of glory, "but we also boast in our sufferings" (v. 3). It may not be so hard to accept that we must suffer for our faith under the *regnum gratiae*, this provisional world in which sin and death have been dealt a mortal blow but still rage on until the end of the present age; but can we *rejoice* in our sufferings, or boast in them? As Karl Barth reminds us, the degradation, the contempt, and persecution that Christians inevitably suffer at the hands of the world are in fact their badge of *honor*.[1] This note is sounded repeatedly in the New Testament, beginning with Jesus himself: "*Blessed* are you when people revile you and persecute you. . . . *Rejoice* and be glad, for your reward is great in heaven" (Matt. 5:11–12). We rejoice because this suffering, which appears to ourselves and to the world as dishonorable, is in fact a form of human honor, to which Jesus called his disciples when he exhorted them to take up their cross and follow him. According to Paul, suffering produces endurance, which leads on to character and ultimately to hope, "because God's love has been poured into our hearts through the Holy Spirit that has been given to us" (v. 5).

Our lesson culminates in one of those magnificent passages where the entire gospel seems to be concentrated into a few words. Romans 5:6–8 encapsulates the whole sweep of God's grace in the justification of sinners. The first point to note is that God has acted "while we were still weak"—that is, at the point where we could do nothing to help ourselves. Christ's act on our behalf is not an event in which we cooperated. We did not do it with God; rather, God did it for us. That is Paul's point in verse 7,

Pastoral Perspective

Paul invites the subject of boasting back into his discussion in verse 3. Earlier, in 4:2, Paul speaks of boasting in a negative way, because the boasting is based upon being justified by works. The boasting that Paul now refers to is boasting in the hope of sharing God's glory in the future. This hope is sure and certain because of the experience of grace the believer has in the present. Furthermore, God is the subject of the boasting. Christians boast in the grace of God, which amplifies God's goodness toward those who do not deserve it. This boasting is appropriate in Paul's mind because it calls attention to what God has done. When boasting brings attention to the grace God lavishly gives to believers through Jesus Christ, it brings glory to God, for in Christ the favor of God toward us is demonstrated. This favor is granted, not because of our goodness, but because of God's goodness.

Pastors may use these verses from the passage to inspire celebration among congregants. These words remind us that we are indeed a blessed and highly favored people. This text would also be meaningful for those who have experienced public embarrassment because of misdeeds. Those who struggle with addictions and habits that haunt them can be reminded through this passage that we cannot win God's favor. We need only accept God's grace.

After speaking of the hope of sharing the future glory of God, Paul in verse 3 turns to the present sufferings and suggests the response of the believers should be to boast about our sufferings. Most of our people would not understand the notion of boasting in sufferings, so it is important to note that Paul understands suffering is not something we seek. What he is suggesting is that the only reason we can boast in our sufferings is because of what we know. He goes on to list what we know in verses 3 and 4— suffering produces endurance and character. Both of these attributes are needed, given the present struggle taking place between Jewish Christians and Greek Christians whom Paul is addressing. While endurance is self-explanatory, a better understanding of the term "character" is needed in order to understand Paul's point.

Many scholars agree the translation of the NJB, "tested character," depicts more accurately what Paul is seeking to illustrate.[2] Our tested character is what produces the hope that Paul speaks of in verses 4 and 5. It is a hope that we are sure of because "God's

---

1. Karl Barth, *Church Dogmatics*, III/4 (Edinburgh: T.&T. Clark, 1961), 675.

2. Leander E. Keck, *Romans*, Abingdon New Testament Commentaries (Nashville: Abingdon Press, 2005), 138.

word picture, created by wordplay, does not imply a legal standing but a sacred place where believers, cleansed of sin, can now approach a holy God in whose company they are now formed by the operations of divine grace. In subsequent chapters, Paul explores the effects of the grace that shapes Christian discipleship in partnership with Christ.

The ambivalence of the believer's present "boast" when paired with the hope of a future "sharing the glory of God" envisages an essential characteristic of Christian existence prior to the consummation of God's final victory over sin. On the one hand, the believer rejoices in the benefits of God's victory through Christ (see 5:11); on the other hand, there is a realistic awareness that creation still awaits its full redemption at the final revelation of God's glory (see 8:18–25). This hard tension always qualifies the believer's present experience of divine grace.

"We also boast in our sufferings" (v. 3) admits to present hardships facing all believers. While this is tempered somewhat by the finality of their prior "boast" in God's coming victory over those very forces that occasion "our sufferings," this ironical phrase expresses the expectation of a costly discipleship under the lordship of the Crucified One. Still, Paul supplies a flowchart of well-known Jewish virtues that envisages the gain of pain worked out during the believer's spiritual formation. The phrase "and hope does not disappoint us" (v. 5a) may underwrite the reasonableness of the expected product of this formative process, which is the outpouring of God's love "into our hearts through [dia] the Holy Spirit" (v. 5b).

The phrase "the love of God" can be interpreted either as a subjective genitive (i.e., "God's love for us"), which might expect either an experience of divine presence or confession of divine action (so v. 8), or as an objective genitive (i.e., "our love for God"), which might elicit the prior boasts in God's glory in the midst of human suffering. Either genitive is plausible in this context, and both may very well be intended; however, the destination of divine love ("heart") and its agent ("the Holy Spirit") may suggest the objective sense. When the Holy Spirit directs the community's formation, especially when its circumstance is hardship and heartbreak, then the endgame is a chastened love for God (see 8:22–27).

The stark description of humanity outside of Christ in verses 6–8 as "weak," "ungodly," "sinners," (culminating with "enemies" in v. 10) effectively stages Paul's summary of the abrupt turn in human history that has brought about the community's

"We have obtained access to this grace in which we stand" (v. 2). It has been said that the language used here is suggested by an Eastern court where only those entitled can enter the king's chamber. Others are excluded, unless someone will introduce them.[1] Our Lord Jesus Christ brings us before God, gives us access to the Almighty One. Paul speaks in terms that indicate it is already done. He is not speaking of some future occurrence, but names the present reality of those who are justified by faith.

The emphasis in this Scripture passage is upon what God has done, specifically, what God has done for us in Christ. This becomes the basis for all that is to follow. As hearers of Paul's words, we are struck by the contrast that is made between humanity and Christ. Humanity in its most sinful, weakened state is the least deserving of God's mercy and goodness. Then, at the right time, when humanity needs God the most, Christ dies for the ungodly. Humanity would rarely die for a good or righteous person, but Christ died for us while we were yet sinners. Paul reminds us that this is proof of God's magnanimous love. Over and over, we are told that "Christ died for us." Christ died for *us*—an undeserved, unmerited, loving act on our behalf by our Lord, who now gives us access to God. God in Christ has done so much for us.

When Paul brings up the possibility of having a reason to boast, it is surprising. In earlier chapters (e.g., 2:17, 23; 3:27; 4:2), boasting has been an issue, because it has been connected with the pride of what one has been able to do for oneself. Here Paul redeems the term and moves it from one's own works to the only place that one can really boast: proclaiming the goodness of God and what God has done for us in Christ. Boasting becomes more a matter of rejoicing or being triumphant because of God's goodness. Paul states that one can now boast in two things: the hope of sharing the glory of God, and our sufferings. *Hope* is the initial key word here. We are trusting in and have hope in the God who restores to us our true character and destiny and fellowship with God.[2]

Our second basis for boasting is in our sufferings. It does not seem like much to boast about, but Paul is assuring us that we can be triumphant in our sufferings. Rather than being destroyed or challenged by our sufferings, we can triumph through and over them. Paul's words are certainly not meant to celebrate our experiences of suffering. However, when

---

1. Gerald R. Cragg, in *The Interpreter's Bible* (Nashville: Abingdon Press, 1954), 9:453.
2. Ibid., 454.

Romans 5:1-8

Theological Perspective

where he emphasizes the utterly gratuitous nature of Christ's sacrifice. It is not as though we were basically good people who needed his help. If that were the case, Christ's willing death would surely be meritorious, in a way that is rare but not unique in human history: "perhaps for a good person someone might actually dare to die." The redemptive act of Jesus Christ was performed on behalf of those who were not only helpless but also undeserving of help. In his death Jesus is no mere "role model," as we like to say, showing us how to do what he did. No, he really died, and by so doing accomplished what we could never do for ourselves. By means of this unmerited and therefore wholly gracious act, "God proves his love for us."

Even though we do not share in Christ's sacrifice as coredeemers, however, we do participate in his death by grace, since he died for us, in our name, and as our representative. The fact that he died *for us* means that in actual fact we too have died, by virtue of *our* participation in *his* death. The New Testament witnesses speak quite graphically at this point: "For you have died, and your life is hidden with Christ in God" (Col. 3:3). "One has died for all; therefore all have died" (2 Cor. 5:14). "I have been crucified with Christ; and it is no longer I who live" (Gal. 2:19–20). A little later in Romans, Paul says that in baptism "we have died with Christ" (Rom. 6:8). The full statement in this verse tells us why it is so important, and why (even though it is death!) it is nevertheless gospel, good news: "But if we have died with Christ, we believe that we will also live with him. . . . So you also must consider yourselves dead to sin and alive to God in Christ Jesus" (Rom. 6:8, 11).

GARRETT GREEN

Pastoral Perspective

love has been poured into our hearts through the Holy Spirit" (v. 5). This love so saturates the being of the believer in his or her present predicament that he or she is certain of the hope, even though it is yet to come. It is this understanding of what is yet to come that led writers of the Negro spirituals to compose songs such as "Nobody Knows the Trouble I See." The opening lines of the melody tell of the trouble the African slave knows in America:

> Nobody knows the trouble I see.
> Nobody knows but Jesus.
> Nobody knows the trouble I see.
> Glory, Hallelujah![3]

The words speak of the present and that which is to come. Many African slaves endured the suffering of slavery because they knew the present power of God's love and the future glory that awaited them. What Christians know about the future inspires us to act appropriately in the present. The future glory is not to be used as an anesthesia or opiate to make us passively accept pain. Rather, the love of God is so powerful that it sustains us through suffering and empowers us to act according to our faith.

In verses 6 and 8 of this passage, Paul speaks of Christ's dying for the ungodly. This act proves God's love for us because it is done "while we were still weak" or "yet sinners." Therefore, Christ's death makes plain the unmerited favor of God toward sinful people. The parenthetical musings of verse 7 appear to be Paul's inner thoughts on the matter. He reasons that it is rare that a person would die for a good or righteous person. Truly, God's love is amazing.

Pastors may use this passage to speak of the paradox between what is now and that which is yet to come. Sermons on suffering and hope or the courage to act in light of what we know would also be appropriate for this sacred text. A liturgy that celebrates African American history and the struggles of African slaves in America would also be appropriate.

DIANE GIVENS MOFFETT

---

3. *Nobody Knows de Trouble I See,* http://www.negrospirituals.com/news-song/nobody_know_de_trouble_i_see.htm

experience of peace with God. The temporal placement of this turning point is called "the right time," not because of a right mix of geopolitical contingencies that literally made the Christ event possible, but because reconciliation was in God's plan all along.

The purpose of verse 7 is less clear. Based upon manuscript evidence, several interpreters have suggested that it was added later to Romans, doubtless as a parenthetical aside (perhaps with v. 6, whose transmission is also corrupted and uncertain). If so, one can easily imagine how a later scribe, stunned by Paul's singular portrait of a sinful humanity, may have inserted a straightforward contrast of worthies—"righteous" verses "good" persons—to extend the scope and necessity of Christ's atoning sacrifice to every person, a Pauline thematic.

Although tautological—since being sinners is a necessary precondition for needing atonement—Paul uses confessional formulae to cast a memorable pattern of salvation: "God proves [an ongoing action] God's love for us. . . . Christ died [past, completed action] for us" (v. 8). The ongoing preaching of the gospel assumes the availability of God's love for every sinner because of the continuing merit of Christ's prior death.

Paul brings this transitional text to conclusion in verses 9–11 by repeating core themes (e.g., justified, death, boast, reconciliation/peace) and placing them against the horizon of God's coming victory. "Much more surely then" introduces a pair of *minori ad maius* ("from lesser to greater") arguments in which he reasons that if we have already been justified by Christ's death, then surely we will escape the coming apocalypse of God's "wrath" (v. 9; cf. 2:5); and if as "enemies" we already are reconciled to God "through the death of [God's] Son," then surely we will "be saved by his life" (v. 10). The jarring juxtapositions—God's "love for us" (v. 8) and "the wrath of God" (v. 9), "enemies" and "reconciled" (v. 10)—shape the community's anticipation of its future with God and evokes one final "boast in God" that humbly acknowledges that its reconciliation with God is received "through our Lord Jesus Christ" (v. 11).

ROBERT W. WALL

we do suffer, we are not, nor do we need to be, defeated. He explains that the experience of suffering can bring persons through a series of results. As we stand in the grounding of our faith, and go through trials and tribulations, our suffering can produce endurance, the ability to be strengthened to keep going as we take each step forward. When we have endured with patience, the endurance produces a strengthened character, and this character can move us toward a stronger hope. Our hope is fruitful because it is hope in the God in whom we have faith.

Preachers can refer back to the experiences of Abraham and Sarah in Genesis as an example of persons who endured adversity, heartache, and difficulties before they received the result of God's promise to them. Examples of more contemporary situations in which groups, communities, or individuals have come through their sufferings would be helpful in making the point of the triumph that is possible, while the preacher will be careful not to trivialize the sufferings of anyone. Paul reminds us that "hope does not disappoint us, because God's love has been poured into our hearts through the Holy Spirit that has been given to us" (v. 5). God's love has already been given to us, as being poured into our hearts by the very Spirit of God that has already been given us.

Sermons on this text can serve as an encouragement to move persons not only to believe, but to find comfort and strength in the God in whom we have put our faith. This text serves as an assurance of the confidence that we can have in God, while helping us to maintain our humility and stance of thanksgiving to the God who loves us so much.

DIANE TURNER-SHARAZZ

Matthew 9:35-10:8 (9-23)

9:35Then Jesus went about all the cities and villages, teaching in their synagogues, and proclaiming the good news of the kingdom, and curing every disease and every sickness. 36When he saw the crowds, he had compassion for them, because they were harassed and helpless, like sheep without a shepherd. 37Then he said to his disciples, "The harvest is plentiful, but the laborers are few; 38therefore ask the Lord of the harvest to send out laborers into his harvest."

10:1Then Jesus summoned his twelve disciples and gave them authority over unclean spirits, to cast them out, and to cure every disease and every sickness. 2These are the names of the twelve apostles: first, Simon, also known as Peter, and his brother Andrew; James son of Zebedee, and his brother John; 3Philip and Bartholomew; Thomas and Matthew the tax collector; James son of Alphaeus, and Thaddaeus; 4Simon the Cananaean, and Judas Iscariot, the one who betrayed him.

5These twelve Jesus sent out with the following instructions: "Go nowhere among the Gentiles, and enter no town of the Samaritans, 6but go rather to the lost sheep of the house of Israel. 7As you go, proclaim the good news, 'The kingdom of heaven has come near.' 8Cure the sick, raise the dead, cleanse the lepers, cast out demons. You received without payment; give without payment.

Theological Perspective

This extended passage includes the "Missionary Discourse," the fourth of Jesus' five great discourses in Matthew. Opening with a narrative in which Jesus communicates that there is overwhelming need among the masses and crowds, Jesus commissions the twelve disciples as "laborers into his harvest" (9:38). What is theologically pertinent about this passage is that many Christians believe that this commissioning is relevant not only to the twelve apostles, but to the life of every Christian believer and seeker.

In Matthew 10:5–6, Jesus instructs the apostles specifically not to go among the Gentiles and Samaritans, but to proclaim the good news among the Jews only. This is the only use of the term "apostles" in the Gospel of Matthew. The fact that there are twelve apostles sent out intentionally symbolizes a new Israel and its twelve tribes. To equip them for their task, Jesus gives the apostles authority to carry out the same deeds that he performs, including authority over unclean spirits, casting them out, and curing disease and sickness. Noticeably absent is any stated authority to teach, an authority that seems to be reserved for Jesus alone. This does raise the question of whether the apostles were indeed preachers and evangelists, or if such teaching was Jesus' province alone. It seems strange that, in a Gospel wherein the authority of Jesus' teaching is given such importance

Pastoral Perspective

Jesus makes it look easy. He goes to all the cities, preaches in all the synagogues, and cures every single ailment. No distance is too great, no audience too skeptical, no disease too severe. Jesus gets it done. When he commissions his disciples to carry out his ministry, things get much more difficult. For anyone setting off on a new task—we can think especially of graduates leaving school or church members being commissioned for special service—these verses offer a sobering assessment of what lies ahead for those who follow in Jesus' footsteps.

The divine mission Christ gives is to be applied to this world, with its political reality, its social divisions, and its systemic disorder. Despite the challenges, despite the questionable likelihood of success, despite our inevitable difficulty in accomplishing what he could do far more easily than we, Christ confidently sends us out. This text forces us therefore to acknowledge the gap between the ideal and the real, and then to take a major leap of faith in our own discipleship.

The preacher needs to decide whether the parenthetical section of 10:9–23 is to be included. If the passage stops at verse 8, the disciples' commission seems relatively feasible; what they are to do is what Jesus has already shown to be possible. However, as the passage continues, we hear the requirement of

⁹Take no gold, or silver, or copper in your belts, ¹⁰no bag for your journey, or two tunics, or sandals, or a staff; for laborers deserve their food. ¹¹Whatever town or village you enter, find out who in it is worthy, and stay there until you leave. ¹²As you enter the house, greet it. ¹³If the house is worthy, let your peace come upon it; but if it is not worthy, let your peace return to you. ¹⁴If anyone will not welcome you or listen to your words, shake off the dust from your feet as you leave that house or town. ¹⁵Truly I tell you, it will be more tolerable for the land of Sodom and Gomorrah on the day of judgment than for that town.

¹⁶"See, I am sending you out like sheep into the midst of wolves; so be wise as serpents and innocent as doves. ¹⁷Beware of them, for they will hand you over to councils and flog you in their synagogues; ¹⁸and you will be dragged before governors and kings because of me, as a testimony to them and the Gentiles. ¹⁹When they hand you over, do not worry about how you are to speak or what you are to say; for what you are to say will be given to you at that time; ²⁰for it is not you who speak, but the Spirit of your Father speaking through you. ²¹Brother will betray brother to death, and a father his child, and children will rise against parents and have them put to death; ²²and you will be hated by all because of my name. But the one who endures to the end will be saved. ²³When they persecute you in one town, flee to the next; for truly I tell you, you will not have gone through all the towns of Israel before the Son of Man comes."

Exegetical Perspective

At the end of a collection of accounts of healing miracles by Jesus (8:1–9:34), the author provides a summary of Jesus' ministry (9:35–38). Harking back to 4:23, these four verses close the section highlighting Jesus' teachings (chaps. 5–7) and Jesus' actions (chaps. 8–9). The verses are transitional, moving from the introduction of Jesus as the ethical, merciful, Jewish Messiah to the commissioning of twelve disciples to follow in their teacher's footsteps. The verses suggest that Jesus' teaching, preaching, and healings are all motivated by compassion (9:35–36; see also 14:14; 15:32; 18:27; 20:34). Jesus sees the people as "harassed and helpless" (lit. "oppressed and thrown to the ground") sheep in need of a shepherd to defend and care for them. Matthew portrays Jesus as the compassionate shepherd caring for his sheep (see also 18:10–14; 26:31).

Shifting to an analogy of a harvest, Jesus' compassion for the people causes him to recognize how abundant the harvest is and to acknowledge how great the need is for laborers. Compassion transforms the problem of oppression into an opportunity for deliverance. Jesus' plea to his disciples to "ask the Lord of the harvest to send out laborers into his harvest" (9:38) foreshadows the summoning and commissioning of twelve disciples to go forth as "apostles" (lit. "those sent out").

Homiletical Perspective

The crowds that continue to be "amazed" by Jesus (9:33) are in fact the ones in most need in this scene. These crowds are everywhere (7:28; 12:23; 14:13; 21:46) but have really been getting nowhere in life because "they were harassed and helpless, like sheep without a shepherd" (9:36). Jesus sees that they are the tired, walking wounded. Furthermore, they have no shepherd and are "lost" (10:6) because there is no one to show them the way. To be a sheep without a shepherd in the Old Testament was a way of saying that Israel had no prophet or king to look after them or to lead them in the right way (Num. 27:16–17; Isa. 40:11; Ezek. 34:1–6). They have had no one to care for them until the real shepherd, Jesus (2:6), sees them in need. He is the one they have been looking for, and now he is looking at them. The needs of the people, the crowds, are emphasized right at the beginning. Their trouble is made explicit, and the reader waits to see what the shepherd's response will be to human need. What is the church's response to human need? Do we care, or could we not care less?

Jesus sees their plight and is not numb to their need. Rather, he has compassion for them (9:36). His compassion is deeply embodied, rising out of his "bowels" or "guts," which is where the word "compassion" in this context stems from. The same language is used in 14:14 and 15:32, for this shepherd is

Matthew 9:35-10:8 (9-23)

Theological Perspective

teaching is not among the listed authorities granted to the apostles.

Further, Jesus puts restrictions upon the twelve apostles, including the acceptance of voluntary poverty and their not wearing clothing that might confuse them with wandering Cynics or Essenes. They are to stay with other believers and converts to their missionary movement. Jesus assures them that, if they are not shown hospitality, such ill treatment will have extreme consequences. Nonetheless, Jesus warns them that they will encounter suffering and persecution, that they are sheep among wolves, and offers them counsel on how to survive and continue their mission.

In the midst of what seems like an early missionary's practical handbook, there is a sudden theological shift. When speaking about the possibility that the apostles will be betrayed and handed over to secular powers, Jesus advises them in Matthew 10:19–20, "When they hand you over, do not worry about how you are to speak or what you are to say; for what you are to say will be given to you at that time; for it is not you who speak, but the Spirit of your Father speaking through you." This is a powerful moment in what otherwise seems like a fairly pedestrian and banal list of instructions and restrictions. The apostles are given the assurance that when they find themselves in times of trouble and persecution, the very Spirit of God will speak through them.

This is not the gift of prophecy or preaching, nor is it the assurance that everything will be all right. However, Jesus offers the implicit promise that God will be with the apostles and act through them in their times of trial. After warning the apostles that they will find themselves in the midst of danger, Jesus then promises that they will be able to endure to the end, because the Spirit will be with them and acting through them. The context of this promise is important, because Jesus maintains that it is when they are persecuted, when courage fails, that the presence of the Spirit will be made apparent.

Theologically, this passage is important in several ways. First, we are assured that Jesus did not see the world as his alone to evangelize, but that he commissioned others to minister in his name and bearing his authority. In this sense, we are drawn back to the very founding of the Christian movement in claiming our authority today as ministers, priests, and lay leaders. Further, we understand to what extent Jesus grants his authority, and that the authority implied within ministry is neither infallible nor absolute, but given for certain purposes. The call to ministry and evangelism

Pastoral Perspective

poverty, the prediction of multiple confrontations, the probability of bodily harm, and a question about the success of the mission. The further we go on, the more unpleasant the undertaking sounds.

Listeners will not have to hear much of the passage, however, before wondering if anyone apart from Jesus is up to the job. Cure the sick? Cleanse the lepers? Maybe. Cast out demons? Raise the dead? Few will feel up to those assignments. When we juxtapose Jesus' accomplishments with the disciples' impending task, the followers of Jesus seem destined to fall short of his performance. While Jesus went to all the cities and villages, the disciples are to remain strictly among their own kind. Jesus preached in every synagogue, but the disciples will find some houses welcoming, others unfriendly. Jesus met throngs of people and cured all of their diseases; the disciples in turn will encounter hardship after hardship and suffer much themselves.

Those early followers, as firsthand witnesses of what was possible with Christ, could very well have gone off with confidence, determination, and nerves of steel. We, however, may feel more like sheep without a shepherd. Many modern Christians lack the confidence to talk about their faith even with those sitting next to them in church, let alone strangers in neighboring towns. The disciples may have been willing to shake the dust off their feet and try the gospel somewhere else, but in our multicultural world we grow hesitant to approach anyone, for fear of seeming too pushy with our faith. Perhaps the original followers of Jesus had success curing diseases and performing miracles, but many would consider our prospects of such achievements very slim indeed.

Nevertheless, just as the disciples were sent out to those towns in ancient Israel, the followers of Jesus continue to be challenged to take little more than faith out into this world and get Christ's work done. It is a world that requires much faith, and many congregants may wonder if we have enough to accomplish what is required. As Jesus makes the distinction between Gentiles and those in the house of Israel, we are reminded of the ongoing political divisions and cultural rifts in our world, in our nation, even within the church. As we hear of how the good news was spread effectively all those years ago, we struggle to think how we can broadcast that message in a world so overwhelmed by information, distraction, and competing ideas of truth. When the disciples are sent out and told to take nothing with them and to receive no payment, such resolve makes the modern church's relationship with wealth seem all the more

While Jesus' disciples form a group larger than the Twelve, Jesus selects a small group to send forth as apostles. The number twelve represents the tribes of Israel and is symbolic for the restoration of Israel to its former national glory (19:28). The Twelve whom Jesus commissions have most likely been recruited earlier and have spent significant time with Jesus (4:18–22; 9:9–13). After summoning the Twelve, Jesus gives them the power and "authority" he possesses, which enables them to do the things he has done (7:29; 9:6–8; 21:23–27; 28:18).

Jesus' instructions to the Twelve (10:5–42) comprise the second of his five great discourses.[1] Like the first discourse (the Sermon on the Mount), Jesus' instructions reveal what appears to have been an imminent eschatological expectation held by Jesus (10:16–23; cf. 7:21–23). As apostles, the Twelve are sent out as representatives of Jesus to continue his work (10:16–25, 40–42; 28:16–20). Jesus says to them, "See, I am sending you out like sheep into the midst of wolves" (10:16). This echoes the warning he gives his disciples in the Sermon on the Mount when he says to them, "Beware of false prophets, who come to you in sheep's clothing but inwardly are ravenous wolves" (7:15). The literary context of both warnings suggests that the "wolves" are Jewish religious leaders (5:20; 10:16–18, 23).

Picking up again on the shepherd motif, Jesus presents himself as a shepherd concerned exclusively for "the lost sheep of the house of Israel" (10:5–6; see 15:24). The idea of "lost sheep" builds on the earlier depiction of the people as "sheep without a shepherd" (9:36). The prophet Ezekiel condemned "the shepherds of Israel" who abused, oppressed, and scattered many of the Jewish people, creating sheep without a shepherd (Ezek. 34:2–10). Because the people have no shepherd, Jesus comes as a shepherd to rescue the lost and scattered sheep of Israel, restoring the nation of Israel.

Only Matthew presents Jesus as instructing the apostles to avoid Gentiles and Samaritans and to go only to the people of Israel. This restriction is lifted at the end of the Gospel (28:19) by the resurrected Jesus, who commands the disciples, "Go therefore and make disciples of all nations" (28:19a). While Jesus is presented in Matthew as fulfilling a ministry exclusively to Jews, Gentiles are frequently praised for their faith and presented as followers and future inheritors of God's kingdom (2:1; 8:10–12; 15:28; 21:43; 22:1–14). Matthew's genealogy of Jesus even

1. The other four discourses are 5:1–7:27; 13:1–52; 18:1–35; 24:3–25:46.

consistent in his ministry of mercy and compassion. He is moved by what he sees and moves toward concrete action as a response to the needs of the people. The compassionate response of Jesus is so critical because this is what leads him to action. Churches may see needs in front of them, but this does not guarantee a compassionate response or loving mission based on the needs of people. Churches may not even recognize the needs staring them in their face; thus, a preacher can also be helpful in showing congregations where and what the needs are.

The compassion of Jesus is what leads him to a call to mission. Seeing needs and a having a compassionate response to them call for faithful action. Ironically, when Jesus tells the disciples to pray that the Lord will send out laborers into the harvest (9:38), they become the answer to their own prayer. They are the ones they are praying for, reminding us that we may be the answer to our very own prayers. The disciples become the laborers in the harvest, but before they are called "apostles" (10:2), meaning "sent out," they are summoned by Jesus and given authority (10:1).

These apostles are imperfect, including betrayers and Zealots, yet they are called and commissioned by the Compassionate One to do service in the world. The Lord of the harvest empowers them and equips them for what is to be done. The authority the disciples have is the authority of Jesus; thus, Jesus is the one meeting the needs of the people through his disciples. We do not meet needs; God does. God does not leave the church alone in her mission but equips the saints for ministry in the world. What mission looks like will look different for every congregation, based on the needs of the surrounding community "crowds"; but it is clear that the church is to be "those sent out," apostolic in nature. Centripetal mission is not enough; God desires centrifugal mission. We do not send ourselves out; the Lord of the harvest sends us out on a mission. What is this overall mission?

The mission appears to be the proclamation that the kingdom of heaven is near in word and deed. This good news is wrapped up in that particular message (i.e., "The kingdom of heaven has come near," 10:7) and its manifestation through curing the sick, raising the dead, cleansing lepers, and casting out demons. This type of mission toward the sick, dead, leprous, and demon-possessed may be a distant cry from churches that reach out only to those who look like them and cannot harm them. Jesus calls the disciples to a risky mission because of his compassion on needy people. Words alone are insufficient; this

Matthew 9:35–10:8 (9–23)

Theological Perspective

is incapable of warding off criticism and persecution, and perhaps even welcomes such dangers as inevitable. The cost of discipleship here is high, and Jesus emphasizes the dangers of following him.

Second, this commission is to renew Israel, not to evangelize to the nations. Proclamation of the good news is meant first for the Jews only, with the commission changing to the broader scope of all nations only after Jesus' death and resurrection. Jesus seeks to bring the elect people of God together in faithful coherence, which is stated in the context of Jesus' portent at the end of the passage: "When they persecute you in one town, flee to the next; for truly I tell you, you will not have gone through all the towns of Israel before the Son of Man comes" (10:23). It is debatable whether Jesus refers to the persecution of the Jews of 70 CE, when Jerusalem and the temple are destroyed, but this use of "Son of Man" tends to be in the form of judgment.

Third, the threat to those who do not welcome the apostles and listen to their words is dire, as Jesus invokes divine wrath on the order of what occurred at Sodom and Gomorrah. Particularly interesting about this claim in Matthew is that Jesus does not say that God will punish those who act against God or contrary to the will of God, but that such radical punishment is appropriate simply for not welcoming and listening to the apostles. The healing of Israel, the primary mission of the apostles at this stage, is given such priority that one does not need to act against God in order to merit fiery wrath; one merely needs to encounter the good news with an unreceptive heart. There is a force behind this claim that demonstrates theologically how vitally important the rejuvenation of the covenant is between God and Israel. No power or principality has standing prior to the mutual claims that the covenant places both upon God and God's chosen people. The reinvigorating of that covenant is prior to any commissioning that Jesus makes to preach to the nations.

STEPHEN BUTLER MURRAY

Pastoral Perspective

disconnected from the needs of those continuing to live in poverty. We cannot but wonder what, if any, hardships we would personally be willing to undergo for our beliefs. If we view the twelve disciples as inferior substitutes for Jesus, the gap between the real and the ideal seems tremendously wide for those of us hearing this commission today.

However, we must acknowledge that throughout history, amazing things—seemingly impossible things—have been done and continue to be done through ordinary members of the church. Jesus' words have encouraged and motivated far more than the twelve disciples listed in these verses. Due in part to the efforts made by faithful Christians, diseases thought to be incurable have been eradicated, unjust laws have been overturned, and individuals who thought some doors would never open have seen them swing wide. Perhaps most humbling of all is the fact that in many parts of the world where Christians are persecuted today, Christianity not only survives but thrives.

When such accomplishments occur, they leave the faithful ascribing success to a higher power, and rightly so. It is Christ who enables us to do what we could not do on our own. This passage leaves as a mystery why Christ includes us in his mission and how exactly we meet success through him, but the faithful do achieve miraculous things. Perhaps it is because Jesus continues to have compassion on shepherdless sheep. Perhaps it is because prayers have been answered and enough laborers have been sent out into the bountiful harvest. Perhaps the words of the Father's Spirit have been spoken through the right people at the right time.

Perhaps the followers of Christ have found the faith to see that the gap between the real and the ideal can in fact be bridged. Jesus, at least, seems to think we can get the job done, even if it will not be easy.

ALEXANDER WIMBERLY

presents three (possibly four) Gentile women (Tamar, Rahab, Ruth, and possibly Bathsheba) as ancestors in Jesus' lineage (1:1–6).

This tension between Jewish exclusivity and Gentile inclusion most likely reflects the historical development of the Jesus movement. The Jesus movement began as an exclusively Jewish movement. By the time of the writing of Matthew, however, the author's community had abandoned Jewish exclusivity and was most likely composed of Gentiles as well as Jews. While the historical Jesus was apparently concerned with an exclusively Jewish mission, the resurrected Jesus prepared the way for Matthew's community by commanding his followers to make disciples of all nations.

The apostles' message is essentially the same as the message of John the Baptist and Jesus—that God's kingdom has arrived (10:7; 3:2; 4:17). While much of the emphasis in the Pauline epistles and within much of contemporary Western Christianity is on the preaching of Jesus as the saving act of God, it appears from the commissioning of the Twelve that Jesus instructed his disciples to preach the good news that God's kingdom (i.e., "the kingdom of heaven") has arrived. The arrival of God's kingdom is demonstrated by the deliverance of the oppressed—the sick being cured, the dead being raised, lepers being cleansed, and demons being cast out.

Jesus concludes the instructions to the apostles (10:8b–15) by addressing the issue of financial remuneration. Compassion for others, not financial gain, should always be the motivation for the work of the ministry. Jesus reminds the apostles that they freely received God's deliverance and that they should freely offer it to others (cf. 2 Cor. 11:7). While Jesus acknowledges an awareness of the apostle's need to be provided for (10:10b–11; cf. 1 Cor. 9:3–18), an apostle should never worry about material provisions (cf. 6:25–34), nor should personal financial gain ever be an objective. Through local hospitality the apostles are to share in the resources of those to whom they are sent (cf. Phil. 4:14–20). While Jesus assures the apostles of God's provision, he also warns them of the coming persecutions and that they will be treated as Jesus is treated (10:16–25).

GUY D. NAVE JR.

mission must have visible signs for "the message about the coming of God's rule must be rendered believable through concrete demonstrations of God's caring."[1]

Furthermore, this caring mission requires no paid salary: "you received without payment; give without payment" (10:8). Fundamentally, the gospel is free. Human needs have no price on them. They just need to be met, at least in the realm of the kingdom of God. Prosperity preachers who require a donation to their ministry in order for their congregants to receive a blessing should be indicted by these words of Jesus. A needy person does not have to "sow a seed" in order for Jesus to meet his or her need.

This is good news, because the movement of this passage reveals that when there is a need, Jesus shows compassion, and his compassion causes him to send out others on a mission to serve those in need. God provides avenues to meeting human needs, and this compassionate ministry is free for the "lost sheep." All Jesus desires is that the lost be found. A sermon based on this passage could begin with the trouble in the text, by talking about the need of the crowds due to their helplessness. It could then move toward aspects of grace evident in the text: Jesus' compassion and his sending out disciples to meet the needs of others. In this way, the movement of the text would shape the movement of the sermon. Lastly, the function of a sermon on this text should be to send the congregation out into the world with compassion. This sermon should have a strong call to mission, as the passage itself does. It is insufficient just to see human need but not be sent out to do something about it.

LUKE A. POWERY

1. Douglas R. A. Hare, *Matthew*, Interpretation series (Louisville. KY: John Knox Press, 1993), 111.

Jeremiah 20:7-13

> [7]O Lord, you have enticed me,
>   and I was enticed;
> you have overpowered me,
>   and you have prevailed.
> I have become a laughingstock all day long;
>   everyone mocks me.
> [8]For whenever I speak, I must cry out,
>   I must shout, "Violence and destruction!"
> For the word of the Lord has become for me
>   a reproach and derision all day long.
> [9]If I say, "I will not mention him,
>   or speak any more in his name,"
> then within me there is something like a burning fire
>   shut up in my bones;
> I am weary with holding it in,
>   and I cannot.
> [10]For I hear many whispering:
>   "Terror is all around!

Theological Perspective

Christians sometimes have a hard time dealing with other believers who are in pain and are angry at God. Admitting that they themselves have such feelings can be even harder. It is as if we are afraid that such anger is blasphemy. John Calvin, for example, seemed quite uncomfortable with the prophet Jeremiah's angry accusation that God had deceived him.[1] He therefore came to the conclusion that the prophet must have been ironic, seeking to show his critics that their rejection of his prophesies are actually a rejection of God's own words. The "useful doctrine" that Calvin took from this passage is that all who teach the Word must be sure of their calling, so that they can "appeal to God's tribunal" when any dispute happens.

A closer look at this passage, however, reveals a very different meaning. Jeremiah has the misfortune of living in a time of great social upheaval. It is his unpleasant task to warn the people of Jerusalem that their city will be destroyed, a message that does not make him popular. In this passage, as in the chapters that precede it, Jeremiah expresses his grief and anger at his task. He does so in the strongest language, accusing God of having deceived him by

Pastoral Perspective

I have never been able to trust a prophetic voice that seemed too eager. In matters of justice, especially divine justice, the words are always hard to speak, and they are even harder to hear. No one willingly rushes in to share such words unless they have ulterior motives, and such motives are rarely of God. Jeremiah, though, laments his call from God, because responding to it has made him a "laughingstock" (v. 7).

Responding to God's call sometimes leads to poor grammar. Like Jeremiah, we find ourselves using double negatives to get to the heart of the matter. We do not respond to God's call simply because it is exciting and intriguing and full of promise. We respond to God's call because we cannot *not* respond.

When Susan was an undergraduate, she ran in the "preprofessional" crowd. Her friends were premed, pre-law, pre–hedge fund manager; you know the crowd. Everyone assumed she was one of them. But Susan was also involved in campus ministry and in her local church. She loved mission trips and often volunteered to run the church nursery during committee meetings. She participated in worship leadership and loved simply being in church. She would invite her friends to join her, but she was often on her own.

---

1. John Calvin, *Commentaries on the Book of the Prophet Jeremiah and the Lamentations*, trans. and ed. John Owen (Grand Rapids: Eerdmans, 1950), 3:27.

Denounce him! Let us denounce him!"
  All my close friends
  are watching for me to stumble.
"Perhaps he can be enticed,
  and we can prevail against him,
  and take our revenge on him."
¹¹But the Lᴏʀᴅ is with me like a dread warrior;
  therefore my persecutors will stumble,
  and they will not prevail.
They will be greatly shamed,
  for they will not succeed.
Their eternal dishonor
  will never be forgotten.
¹²O Lᴏʀᴅ of hosts, you test the righteous,
  you see the heart and the mind;
  let me see your retribution upon them,
  for to you I have committed my cause.

¹³Sing to the Lᴏʀᴅ;
  praise the Lᴏʀᴅ!
For he has delivered the life of the needy
  from the hands of evildoers.

Exegetical Perspective

It has been said that the "confessions" of Jeremiah are the most characteristic feature of the traditions concerning his ministry. Other prophets were commissioned to bring words of judgment and hope, to challenge political and religious leaders, to carry out dramatic signs, and generally to stand in the breach between God and people. However, in the book of Jeremiah we have an account of the cost to the prophet, both in narratives portraying his suffering and in words that he directs back to the God who has commissioned him. This passage stands close to the end of the series of these confessions (11:18–23; 12:1–6; 15:10–21; 17:14–18; 18:18–23; 20:7–13; 20:14–18), offering both what is most representative of the genre and what is most expressive of the distinctive theological crisis it represents in Jeremiah's career.

The Confessions as Laments. Scholars have long recognized the affinities between Jeremiah's agonized cries and the laments of the Psalms. Like the laments, Jeremiah's words contain highly stylized language describing his rejection and shame, the threats of anonymous enemies, and, above all, strenuous, seemingly blasphemous accusations directed at God.

Jeremiah complains that he has become "a laughingstock" whom "everyone mocks," and that his prophetic speech brings upon him only "reproach and

Homiletical Perspective

An extraordinary and compelling crucifix hangs on the wall of the Cathedral College Chapel (formerly the College of Preachers, originally intended to have been called the College of Prophets) at the Washington National Cathedral. As steel filings are attracted to a magnet, even the most casual observer will be drawn to this curious piece of art. Sculpted from bronze on wood by the gifted artist Gurdon Brewster, it depicts another figure on that Celtic cross with Jesus. They hang together, facing one another. Their arms are lovingly wrapped around each other.

Who is this other figure? The observer will probably conclude that it is you, me, everyone in need of that embrace. Each of us is there on that cross, timelessly wrapped in the arms of the crucified Jesus the Christ. The title of this crucifix is "Welcome Home." Pastoral preaching, at its best, urges and invokes every participant (preacher first) into the embracing arms and heart of God. Pastoral preaching is always about "Welcome Home."

There is a terribly essential twin to "Welcome Home" preaching, however. It is prophetic preaching. At its best, prophetic preaching exhorts every participant (again, preacher first) to "Leave Home," to be driven by the Spirit into the wilderness of today's world, to wrestle with and defiantly to proclaim God's countercultural Voice amid the monumental injustices

Jeremiah 20:7-13

Theological Perspective

calling him to be a prophet. The Hebrew here might even, according to some commentators, evoke the imagery of seduction and violation, although other translators prefer a milder term such as "persuaded." The implication here is that Jeremiah has found himself helpless before God's powers of persuasion (or simply before God's power) and is now suffering the consequences. He has become an object of contempt and ridicule. Indeed, he is in a no-win situation. He is compelled to speak against Jerusalem and encounters hostility as a result. On the other hand, when he decides to stop speaking, the word of God burns inside of him, and he has no peace then either. To make matters worse, God seems absent, both when he speaks and when he remains silent.

In light of all this, Jeremiah's anger and anguish seem quite understandable. What does seem strange is that his anguish is then followed by an expression of confidence in God and even a call to praise God. Is Jeremiah expressing his own emotional roller-coaster ride here? Are we witnessing the psychological breakdown of the prophet? If that is the case, this passage contains little by way of a "useful doctrine" and merely evokes pity for the much-maligned prophet. The structure of Jeremiah's complaint, though, which echoes that of the psalms of lament, points to a richer meaning.

His confession starts with an invocation (in this case, one would almost say a "calling out" of God), followed by a description of the predicament of the prophet. This is followed by a confession of confidence, a petition, and a command to praise. While this confession therefore certainly comes from the heart, it is not merely a raw cry of jumbled emotions, but a lament rooted in an intimate relationship with God. Moreover, the cultic format indicates that this intimate relationship with God is not only that of the individual, but that of one of the people of God. Some commentators even suggest that Jeremiah is expressing the whole nation's complaints and petitions in an individual format. Either way, the fact that Jeremiah expresses himself in a format recognized for expressing spirituality in the Hebrew Bible indicates that this calls for a theological interpretation rather than a psychological one.

The accusation against God we encounter here is therefore an expression of faith! It is not the antithesis of spirituality; it is part of it. Lament, and even anger at God, is not the opposite of faith in God. Doubt and struggle in the face of vocation are not necessarily negations of that vocation. The prophet struggles with the realities of the life of faith, but this

Pastoral Perspective

Those experiences and feelings and urgings slowly began to be shaped into a sense of call to ministry. The burning began deep within Susan's bones until the call simply became irresistible. She received a fellowship from the Fund for Theological Education in 2000. It allowed her to meet others from across the nation who were also exploring ministry. She received a stipend to support her seminary education. She felt at home suddenly, and she felt her heart expand with hope at the promises that lay before her.

Sensing the call is one thing; telling others about it is another. Perhaps she expected folks to be excited for her, but that was rarely the response. As she shared with friends, they often thought she was joking. She was on the fast track and headed toward "the big bucks." Why would she throw it all away to become a pastor? Most of her friends thought it was just a phase and that she would eventually come to her senses. It was not until she entered seminary that they realized she was serious.

For some, Susan's sense of call changed their friendship dramatically, and not for the better. Perhaps most painful was the response from her parents. It was the summer before her senior year. Her parents began the "next steps" conversation with her, wondering where their amazing young daughter was headed in life. She had so many options, so many opportunities. They talked about the exciting things her friends were doing and wondered who might accompany her on her journey. It did not escape Susan's notice that seminary was not one of the options her parents listed. She took a deep breath and plunged in: "Mom. Dad. I plan to go to seminary in a year. I feel called to be a pastor." Silence. A couple of blinks. Still nothing. Finally, her father spoke. "Young lady, we have invested over $100,000 in one of the finest private colleges in the country. You are not going to waste it by going into the ministry!"

The Lord had enticed her, overpowered her, drawn her into the life and leadership of the church. It was not so much a choice as it was a fire in her bones, something she could not possibly hold in. However, all of her close friends, even her family, thought she had already stumbled, fallen short of her promise.

Susan has been ordained and served the church for almost five years now. Her story is not "happily ever after," for the work is hard. It is often lonely. She often finds herself making choices when bills come due at the end of the month, and in those moments she can all too easily hear her friends' voices again,

Exegetical Perspective

derision all day long" (vv. 7–8; cf. the concentration of these terms in Pss. 22:7–8; 44:13–14; 79:4). The prophet also characterizes his enemies vaguely as "all my close friends" (v. 10, lit. "the men of my peace"; cf. Ps. 41:9: "Even my bosom friend [literally, "the man of my peace"] in whom I trusted") and pictures them as conspiring against him (cf. v. 10 with Ps. 31:13).

Comparisons with the psalms of lament also reveal the integrity and logic of verses 7–13 as a unit. It is tempting to feel that verses 11–12 offer too abrupt a resolution of verses 7–10: How can the prophet accuse God vehemently of leaving him open to mockery and danger, and then declare in the next breath that God is with him "like a dread warrior" who will cause his enemies to fail? What are we to make of the joyous, plural imperatives of verse 13: "Sing . . . ; praise the LORD!"

However, the structure of verses 7–13 is fully characteristic of the lament genre: (i) a brief *opening address*, directed to God (v. 7, "O LORD"); followed by (ii) the *complaint* (vv. 7–10), in which the lamenter's affliction and isolation are vividly described and the enemies are portrayed and quoted; followed by the most characteristic feature, usually introduced by an adversative ("but" or "nevertheless"), in which the lamenter gives (iii) a strong *confession of trust* in God (v. 11) and directly (iv) *petitions* God (v. 12, "let me see your retribution upon them"). Finally, laments usually conclude with an element of praise, present or in prospect, directed to the larger community, to whom testimony of God's deliverance is directed (e.g., Ps. 22:22–31!).

The lesson is that Jeremiah is not completely on his own, empty hearted before God as he tries to articulate his distress. He is instructed by the community's language of worship, which gives both a rhetorical and a theological frame to his grief: he is compelled by his tradition to hold together his anger and his confidence in a way that gives holistic expression to what we might feel is conflicted.

The Particularities of Jeremiah's Lament: Two Thematic Verbs.

Being introduced to the conventions of Jeremiah's lament, we are still interested in what he says. The opening words, which set the tone, have generated much comment: "O LORD, you have enticed me, and I was enticed; you have overpowered me, and you have prevailed" (v. 7).[1] The verb *pathah*, translated here as "enticed," can carry sexual

Homiletical Perspective

of our contemporary culture. God's against-the-grain Voice yearns, even weeps, for a fervent partnership with twenty-first-century Jeremiah preachers.

Those of us who contend with this text will quickly note that we are encountering a deeply troubled prophet. If the truth is told, we will be excavating, most probably, the "lost prophet" within our own preaching ministry. To lose the prophet within us is to risk serious damage to our vocation, to say nothing of the authentic mission and ministry of our congregation.

Megan McKenna writes terrifying words for would-be prophetic preachers:

> Prophets are difficult to talk about because they are not like us. . . . They are intent on making us see the truth about ourselves, which can result in our feeling humiliated and shamed. . . . They never let up until we change, or until we make a choice, or until we attack back, or until what they say comes to pass, or until they disappear or die. . . . They go after everyone indiscriminately, but especially governments, the economy, the military, leaders, other prophets. . . . Then they turn on us as a people and on us as individuals. . . . They lay our lives bare, down to the bone, marrow, and soul. They break through our well-planned worlds to say that we are the problem.[1]

It would be helpful, I think, for every preacher to read this text from Jeremiah again and again, whether we preach it or not. Maybe it would be helpful to pour ourselves into this text in our own private places—in our studies late at night, in empty church buildings, on secluded hillsides. There we might embrace Jeremiah's aching resentment, his awful loneliness, and his burning anger. There we might honor this dark moment in his life.

In doing so, we might also bring some honor to those dark moments in our own lives when, seeking to be relentlessly faithful to God, we have tasted bitter rejection from our "Jerusalem" congregations, from our own "close friends" (v. 10). Go back and read Jeremiah's memoir of his call to prophetic ministry (1:4–10). In both of these texts he exposes his anger, because God has given him no alternative. Now, in Jeremiah 20, after some years in the prophetic pulpit, Jeremiah's feelings have become even more troubled, even more pronounced. There is bitter indignation within him at being consistently "overpowered" (v. 7) by God. Every time Jeremiah determines to silence his own prophetic voice, there

---

1. Cf. NJB: "You have seduced me, Yahweh, and I have let myself be seduced; you have overpowered me: you were the stronger."

1. Megan McKenna, *Prophets: Words of Fire* (Maryknoll, NY: Orbis, 2001), 1.

Jeremiah 20:7-13

Theological Perspective

is not, as Calvin feared, blasphemy. It seems that there is room for that struggle in the life of faith.

In short, Jeremiah is not just expressing conflicting emotions in a bizarre prophetic display. Rather, in expressing his own anguish, doubt, and, yes, anger, the prophet shows us something of the life of faith. The life of faith is not always serene. It is not simply quiet submission to God's will. It is, rather, a life of struggle with God and God's will. Indeed, one could argue that this is where we get reassurance that God's grace is, after all, sufficient. When Jeremiah is uttering his lament, God does not come to him in a thundercloud or burning bush, nor in the rich silence of a morning meditation. God does not seem to respond to Jeremiah at all. Nevertheless, Jeremiah's lament turns to praise. Even in the midst of his despair and anger, Jeremiah knows that the God who has overpowered him is the sovereign God whose grace is sufficient.

In his famous sermon "You Are Accepted," theologian Paul Tillich wrote that grace strikes us when we are in great pain and restlessness, when we walk though the "dark valley of a meaningless and empty life," when despair destroys all joy and courage.[2] This sermon, written by a man whose life was marked by personal and cultural turmoil, expresses something of the prophet Jeremiah's struggles. Jeremiah's prophetic task takes him to the edge of despair. He experiences the silence of God and the derision of his fellow Judahites, even to the point of feeling violated by that same prophetic calling; but when he expresses his pain, he does so in the faith language of his people. His response to pain reminds us that there is room for lament in faith, and indeed for public expression of pain in worship, for the grace of God is sufficient.

RACHEL SOPHIA BAARD

Pastoral Perspective

see her father's anger. Nevertheless, every Sunday she still stands before her congregation, her community, sharing the good news she knows in Jesus Christ, because she cannot help but speak it. Her bones would be incinerated if she did not speak. The life is not without its challenges, and yet she could not live without it.

Susan's ministry is not what some would describe as prophetic. It is profoundly pastoral. and yet her decision to follow her sense of call is in and of itself a prophetic act. Such acts are not limited to ordained ministry. There are others: the doctor who chooses to serve a rural or urban community; the lawyer who takes on the cases his partners will not touch because there are no billable hours in them; the banker who takes a risk on a family trying to turn their lives around, knowing she is assuming some of their risk; the teacher who, although he was trained as an accountant, falls in love with the four-year-old preschool class and simply cannot *not* respond; the PR executive who, after volunteering with the fifth-grade remedial reading class, finds that all she wants to do is be with those children, to experience the overwhelming sense of joy she experiences when one such child recognizes the words on a page for the very first time.

God is always and already enticing us. God can and will overwhelm us, sometimes for a moment, sometimes for a lifetime. In those moments, it is rare that those who know and love us will cheer us on, but the fire in our bones will find its way out, even if it must exhaust our defenses to get there. How many years did Mother Teresa serve in the most challenging of situations with no sense of God's presence, and yet the fire burned within her, and she could do no other? In the end, we too may find ourselves, weary and worn, singing praise to the Lord, feeling Jeremiah's knowing smile as the only blessing of a day well spent.

TRACE HAYTHORN

---

2. Paul Tillich, *The Shaking of the Foundations* (New York: Charles Scribner and Sons, 1948), 153–63, quote from 161.

overtones: it is used straightforwardly of sexual seduction in legal and ethical contexts (Exod. 22:16; Job 31:9), and of sexual "leverage" in the stories of Samson's downfall (Judg. 14:15; 16:5).

It is important to note, however, another range of the use of *pathah* particular to the prophetic literature. In Ezekiel 14:9 the word is used to describe God's judgment upon a prophet who dares to address God on behalf of an idolatrous people: "If a prophet is *deceived* [Heb. *pathah*] and speaks a word, I, the LORD, have *deceived* that prophet, and I will . . . destroy him from the midst of my people Israel." The same word is also used in 1 Kings 22:20–22 to describe God's determination to "entice" Ahab to his death by sending a lying spirit upon his prophets.

In these two cases we have an explanation of how prophets can be led to give false prophecy in order to accomplish God's judgment. Jeremiah has complained that God has given him a message that has not been fulfilled (15:6; 17:15)—he is subject to derision, like the sad man with sandwich boards at the bus station who announces day after day, "The end is near!" Even his erstwhile colleagues—now his prophetic rivals?—hope that he has been "enticed" (*pathah*) (v. 10), so that his words will be ineffective and they will be vindicated. Does Jeremiah fear that God has made him a false prophet, whose word will not come about and who will himself be destroyed?

Another repeated word in this confession takes us to a different conclusion, though. The word *yakal* ("be able, have power, prevail, endure") occurs four times in the passage, describing the interactions of the central characters of the lament: God, Jeremiah, and the enemies. It is used initially of God, who has "overpowered" and "prevailed" over his prophet (v. 7). Jeremiah has tried to withdraw from his commission, but he has not prevailed in this (v. 9, "I *cannot*"). Jeremiah's opponents, seeing his distress, hope that God is on their side and they can "prevail against" the prophet (v. 10). Jeremiah, now moving to his paradoxical confession of trust, knows that this overwhelming God is still with him, so that his "persecutors . . . will not prevail" (v. 11). Jeremiah's dismay, but also ultimately his hope, is that God alone "prevails."

JAMES T. BUTLER

is within him "something like a burning fire shut up in [his] bones" (v. 9). That fire will not be contained. He has grown "weary with holding it in" (v. 9). In spite of himself, Jeremiah can do nothing but climb, reluctantly, back into his prophetic pulpit, bearing (and making bare) God's message once again.

Maybe it is just as well that today's text is appointed to be read in churches on a summer Sunday. There will be fewer people worshiping in this Ordinary season when Jeremiah's extraordinary lament is proclaimed. Actually, today's NRSV translation is not quite as harsh as some of the other translations. Today's reading begins:

> O LORD, you have enticed me, and I was enticed;
> you have overpowered me, and you have prevailed.

Rabbi Abraham Joshua Heschel concludes that these words from Jeremiah "describe the impact of God upon his life [as being] identical with the terms for seduction and rape in the legal terminology in the Bible." He translates the verse to read, "O Lord, Thou hast seduced me, and I am seduced; Thou hast raped me, and I am overcome."[2] Whew! One wonders how that translation might play at coffee hour.

Ultimately this text affirms that the abiding foundation and strength for prophetic preaching resides in the conviction of "Presence preaching." God is unfailingly present for Jeremiah, "like a dread warrior" (v. 11)—and God's unceasing presence is sufficient!

On the wall in both of my offices (over my garage at home and at the Divinity School) hang identical plaques with a cardinal memo: "Bidden or not bidden, God is present." Eminent psychologist Carl Jung had those words chiseled, in Latin, in two places: over the entrance to his home in Zurich and on his tombstone.

Those words are etched deep in the soul of Jeremiah. They are also carved, as sacred reminder, within brave prophets of every age, including today's voices. Every honest preacher knows what it is to be God-haunted, God-disturbed, God-burdened, God-emboldened, God-blessed. Prophetic preaching is grounded and shaped on the anvil of God's presence and God's eternal blessing. "Bidden or not," God's presence is benediction enough for prophetic preaching.

Maybe Presence preaching is just another face and form of "Welcome Home."

DOUGLASS M. BAILEY

2. Abraham J. Heschel, *The Prophets* (1962; repr. New York: HarperCollins, 2001), 144.

Psalm 69:7-10 (11-15), 16-18

⁷It is for your sake that I have borne reproach,
  that shame has covered my face.
⁸I have become a stranger to my kindred,
  an alien to my mother's children.

⁹It is zeal for your house that has consumed me;
  the insults of those who insult you have fallen on me.
¹⁰When I humbled my soul with fasting,
  they insulted me for doing so.
¹¹When I made sackcloth my clothing,
  I became a byword to them.
¹²I am the subject of gossip for those who sit in the gate,
  and the drunkards make songs about me.

¹³But as for me, my prayer is to you, O LORD.
  At an acceptable time, O God,
  in the abundance of your steadfast love, answer me.

Theological Perspective

How should Christians read Psalm 69 today, recognizing it as Scripture for both Jews and for Christians? From the perspectives of our different communities, obviously we will not come to the same conclusions about its meaning and significance. Are there ways, though, that Christians should read the psalm, acknowledging that *two* covenant peoples turn to the Bible as Scripture, not only the church? Do Christians have any examples to follow in search of better models for reading that can help us struggle against anti-Jewish bias?

One example of a pioneering Christian reader in this regard was the Reformer John Calvin (1509–1564). Calvin was born into a world where Christians followed the lead of Augustine and read the Psalms as full of references to Christ on every page. By making a distinction between the literal and spiritual meaning of an Old Testament text, and then expanding the spiritual meaning through a quest for symbols, types, and allegories of Christ, this perspective led Christians to lose the message of the Bible for ancient Israel and for the Jewish people.

As a student of Renaissance scholarship and Hebrew language, Calvin returned his readers' attention to the historical and literal meaning of the psalms in their original contexts. He was informed about Jewish interpretation of the Bible. He found

Pastoral Perspective

We all have moments, days, or weeks when we simply want to ask God, "What are you thinking?" or "Where are you?" Those are usually the times when we are feeling particularly picked on, as if, no matter what we say, no one—not even God—is listening. We can feel as though we have done all we are supposed to do, and still we are disconnected from both God and our community. The good news is that we are not alone in that feeling, because people of faith have struggled through such times for millennia.

While Psalm 69 is one of many attributed to David (thus linking it to the kingship of David and connecting Jesus to that line), it is also possible that the psalm was written at the time of the exile. This gives us two options for interpretation: as an individual lament addressed to God, or as a collective cry for help. Either way, the psalm gives voice to the human who seeks God and rails at God's absence; it appeals to God for justice and requests that all who seek God's justice remember God's preferential option for the poor.

This portion of Psalm 69 comes from someone who is completely miserable. Not surprisingly, these verses have been connected to some of the "woe is me" passages that we find in Job (e.g., Job 3), as well as to the passion narratives at the end of Jesus' life and ministry. These narratives include the stories we

With your faithful help ¹⁴rescue me
   from sinking in the mire;
let me be delivered from my enemies
   and from the deep waters.
¹⁵Do not let the flood sweep over me,
   or the deep swallow me up,
   or the Pit close its mouth over me.

¹⁶Answer me, O Lᴏʀᴅ, for your steadfast love is good;
   according to your abundant mercy, turn to me.
¹⁷Do not hide your face from your servant,
   for I am in distress—make haste to answer me.
¹⁸Draw near to me, redeem me,
   set me free because of my enemies.

Exegetical Perspective

Psalm 69, located toward the end of Book II of Psalms (Pss. 42–72), is a lament in which the psalmist pleads for God's rescue. Six petitions to God (vv. 1a, 6, 13–18, 22–25, 27–28, 29b) alternate with five complaints to God (vv. 1b–5, 7–12, 19–21, 26, 29a). The remainder of the psalm emphasizes the psalmist's promise to praise God (vv. 30–33) and may also reflect a later addition that makes the psalm relevant to what the Israelites experienced after their exile in Babylon had ended and they had returned to Jerusalem (vv. 34–36).

The circumstances that led to the psalmist's complaints are not mentioned explicitly, although some interpreters infer from verse 4 that people have raised false accusations against the psalmist, or from verses 1–3 and verse 26 that the psalmist has some kind of serious illness. If an illness is the context of the psalm, then the author believes it has been precipitated by sin and so has led to his alienation from his own family (v. 8) and to persecution by his enemies (v. 26).

Verses 7–15 follow the psalmist's initial petition (v. 1a) and complaint (v. 1b–5) to God, and then a second petition (v. 6). The psalmist first begs God to "deliver" or "save" (*hoši'eni,* v. 1a) him or her, and then places before God the desire to avoid an imminent death. The psalmist's impending death is

Homiletical Perspective

According to Walter Brueggemann, Psalm 69 is characterized by the theme of "the innocent sufferer." "This psalm," he writes, "states with great rhetorical power and with no timidity the central incongruity of Israel's life with YHWH. The speaker is utterly devoted to YHWH."[1]

Like a typical lament, the psalm offers hope in the midst of suffering. Although there is no logical, empirical basis for such hope, the speaker expresses confidence in YHWH, anticipating divine deliverance from the troubles of life. It is also possible that Jesus' immortal words in the Sermon on the Mount, teaching love of enemies and asking for prayers for those who persecute us,[2] were a response to some of the angriest implications of Psalm 69.

The experience of the psalmist reflects the universality of unjust human suffering. In this instance, readers/hearers are encouraged to put our trust in God for deliverance from trouble. The examples of Jeremiah, Job, the Suffering Servant of Isaiah, and Jesus are all pertinent to this issue. For Christians, the ultimate example of unjust suffering is the cross of Jesus.

1. Walter Brueggemann, *Theology of the Old Testament: Testimony, Dispute, Advocacy* (Minneapolis: Fortress Press, 1997) 379.
2. Bernhard W. Anderson, *Out of the Depths: The Psalms Speak for Us Today,* rev. and expanded ed. (Philadelphia: Westminster Press, 1983), 87.

Psalm 69:7-10 (11-15), 16-18

Theological Perspective

that Christian allegorical readings of the Psalms failed to ask about the encounter between the psalmists and their God. One historian summarizes Calvin's approach: "To fail to take God's dealings with Israel seriously . . . is to do injustice not only to Israel, but much more so to God himself."[1]

Nevertheless, Calvin reads the Psalms as a Christian in the context of both testaments. He says of Psalm 69: "David wrote this inspired ode . . . in the name of the whole Church, of whose Head [i.e., Christ] he was an eminent type."[2] Calvin finds in this psalm a "representation . . . of the common condition of all the people of God," both in ancient Israel and the Reformation (46). The Psalms are given to the church to instruct us in salvific wisdom, as a "mirror" of God and our relationship with our Redeemer, and to provide us with an example in the figure of David. In sum, Calvin reads the Psalms with a double sensitivity to (a) their original context in the life of ancient Israel and (b) how they speak prophetically of Christ and his inclusion of the nations into God's covenant with Israel through the church.

In Calvin's reading of Psalm 69, David becomes a spokesperson for both Christ and "all true saints who are . . . members of Christ" (48). From the sufferings of the psalmist, Calvin builds an analogy between the situation in ancient Israel and his own audience. "The reading public in [Calvin's] day consisted mainly of refugees seeking protection from the religious persecution taking place in their home countries."[3] Calvin himself had fled Paris in 1533 as a refugee of the French Reformation. The psalm instructs us that "even in the most profound depths of adversity faith may hold us up, and . . . elevate us to God" (48). In fact, God allows his oppressed people "to deal familiarly with him at the throne of grace" (53).

Calvin notes that John 2:17 applies to Jesus the words of Psalm 69:9a: "Zeal for your house will consume me," and that Paul in Romans 15:3 applies to Christ Psalm 69:9b: "The insults of those who insult you have fallen on me." The examples of David and Christ are meant to encourage embattled believers: "Since Christ, in whom there shines forth all the majesty of Deity, did not hesitate to expose himself to every species of reproach for the maintenance of

---

1. Wulfert de Greef, "Calvin as Commentator on the Psalms," trans. Raymond Blacketer, in Donald K. McKim, ed., *Calvin and the Bible* (New York: Cambridge University Press, 2006), 89.
2. John Calvin, *Commentary on the Book of Psalms*, trans. James Anderson (Grand Rapids: Eerdmans, 1949), 3:45. Page sources of subsequent quotes are in parentheses.
3. Herman J. Selderhuis, *Calvin's Theology of the Psalms* (Grand Rapids: Baker Academic, 2007), 142.

Pastoral Perspective

hear during Holy Week of the betrayal and arrest of Jesus, his humiliation and subsequent crucifixion. In the later verses of the psalm text, there is an allusion to heaven and earth praising God and to God's saving the covenant people—verses that have been linked to the joy and new life of the resurrection.

Just as Psalm 22 speaks to Jesus' anguish on the cross, this psalm speaks to the alienation with which humankind struggles in our relationship with God. The psalmist, like Jesus, is rejected, persecuted, mocked, and insulted—not because he has forgotten God, but because of his deep faithfulness. In the early church, many would have been acutely familiar with this psalm; indeed, John 19:28–29 seems to allude to Psalm 69:21 when Jesus is given only sour wine or vinegar to drink. The psalm speaks to the particular connection of God with God's people, especially with those who live on the bottom social stratum.

Like Jesus and the psalmist, one can sometimes live as a stranger within one's own community. With that comes alienation from those we know and love, due not only to important issues but also to matters that sometimes seem pointless, as we seek to live an authentic life, true to ourselves and true to what God has called and created us to be. Psalm 69 is a prayer for help when one is rejected by one's own family and community, when one is feeling like the stranger or the alien, for doing nothing more than seeking to do what God has called us to do or to be, whether that is to preach the gospel, teach, serve, or carry out any other vocation that calls to us in our lives.

One phrase of note in this text is, "It is zeal for your house that has consumed me" (v. 9). This is very strong language. "Zeal" is another word for fanaticism, and as one looks over history both recent and ancient, fanaticism does not look like a particularly healthy way to live, nor does it generally result in the best outcome. In a time of great upheaval, it is tempting to become zealous and fanatical about that which is most important to us, often at the expense of what others hold dear. At the same time, it is zeal that has fed the lives of the mystics and many believers. What the psalmist evokes here is the need for connection and a balanced relationship, through which the believer can feel the presence of the Divine at work in community. Indeed, in John 2:17 Jesus' prophetic action in the temple reminds his disciples of Psalm 69:9.

The psalmist rails at God for God's neglect in the midst of stalwart belief and support. Then there is a moment of clarity. The psalmist is reminded that all will occur in "an acceptable time" (v. 13) or in the

Exegetical Perspective

described figuratively as the result of waters that have reached his or her "neck" (v. 1b) so that he or she is about to be overtaken by these waters. The Hebrew word *nephesh,* translated as "neck" (v. 1b), literally means "life" or "soul." The unspecified calamity that the psalmist experiences is symbolized as so overwhelming that submersion within its "deep waters" (*ma'amaqqe-mayim,* v. 2) and "miry depths" (*biyen me'ula,* v. 2), without any foothold to push back upward out of the muck, is quickly overtaking the psalmist and leaving the psalmist exhausted (v. 3).

Ironically, calling and waiting for God to bring assistance (v. 3) from many enemies (v. 4a) and false accusers (v. 4b) have left the psalmist's mouth dry, even though water is swirling all around. The emphatic "you" (*'atta*) that begins verse 5 accentuates the psalmist's awareness that God can see the "folly" and "guilty deeds" the psalmist has done, but which nonetheless do not include any deeds that his or her enemies have charged. The accusations of the psalmist's enemies recall the condemnation that Job's friends make against him (Job 4, 8, 11, 15).

In the midst of these accusations, the psalmist makes a second petition. In this petition, the psalmist asks that those who wait with hope for God not be ashamed "because of me" and that those who seek (*mebaqseyka,* v. 6b) God not be dishonored "because of me." The psalmist implies in the complaint (vv. 7–12), which begins the lectionary reading for this Sunday and follows the petition (v. 6), that they could experience "reproach" (*herpa,* v. 7) undeservedly. The word "reproach" in nominal and verbal forms appears five more times in the psalm (vv. 9 [2x], 10, 19, 20), each time referring to the psalmist's being insulted by others because he or she has expressed faithfulness to God.

In verse 10, the psalmist is "reproached" (NRSV "insulted") because of fasting, but in the rest of the psalm for no specific reason. Verse 8 indicates that the psalmist has experienced perhaps the worst possible type of shame, that of alienation from family members ("kindred," *e'hay*; "my mother's children," *bene 'immi*), a situation which then, of course, grossly worsens the psalmist's ordeal and recalls similar situations of alienation in Job 19:13–14 and Jeremiah 12:6. The psalmist voices the unfairness of the circumstances in verses 9–12: in spite of being faithful, he or she is insulted (vv. 9–10), belittled (v. 11), and taunted (v. 12).

Even so, despite the circumstances, the psalmist, as indicated in verse 13a, remains faithful and turns to God in prayer, trusting that "at an acceptable

Homiletical Perspective

It is thus not surprising that Psalm 69 was used by many of those who first told and interpreted the story of Jesus' life, death, and resurrection. The experience of the psalmist is not unlike that of Jesus. According to J. Clinton McCann, "Jesus was persecuted not for being faithless but for being faithful." Like other prayers for help, "Psalm 69 finally communicates God's intimate, incarnational involvement with the lowly and the oppressed."[3] The experience of the psalmist reminds us that life is a mixture of both good and bad, happiness and sorrow, but above all, that we need to place our trust and hope for deliverance in God.

The text, rooted in metaphorical language, does not make clear the context for the lament. It is hard to determine whether the writer is actually sinking or his expressions are emblematic of one of life's existential predicaments. The language vividly evokes a near-death experience through the imagery of drowning. At the height of this experience, the psalmist's "throat is parched" (v. 3), which is an expression of how desperate his cry has become. The writer is running out of time, and the passage is an agonizing petition for help from God.

The language of this psalm, like the rhetoric of black religion, is born out of a hope that God will hear the cries and pleas expressed in the prayers and songs of the oppressed, that God's righteous redemption will be manifested "right now."

Exploring the theme of "life on the brink" might provide a good homiletical approach to this text. When we think about the cyclical state of the economy—the loss of jobs, the loss of income, the loss of retirement, the loss of investments; Detroit and Pontiac, Michigan, where old GM plants and Ford plants that once ran twenty-four hours a day and employed thousands of people are now closed—it is clear that a lot of folk are suffering. Plenty of folk are scared and worried.

We have been bamboozled and hoodwinked by human greed and the callous disregard of the little people by the bankers and finance gurus all across the nation and world. Minorities and poor people—working people who are struggling to survive—have been dealt a disproportionately hard blow. We feel as if we have been in the boxing ring with Muhammad Ali or some other knockout champion. We have had the breath knocked out of us by a right jab and a left hook that we did not see coming. Now we are on our

---

3. J. Clinton McCann Jr., "The Book of Psalms: Introduction, Commentary, and Reflections," in *The New Interpreter's Bible* (Nashville: Abingdon Press, 1994), 4:954.

Psalm 69:7-10 (11-15), 16-18

Theological Perspective

his Father's glory, how base and shameful will it be for us to shrink from a similar lot" (56).

This psalm speaks to those who have true enemies in established religion and society. Ironically, those who follow the example of David and Christ are opposed by those in positions of authority: "the very persons who presided in the cause of justice, and the dignitaries of the Church, were . . . ringleaders to others. *As the same thing happens in our own day*, it is not without cause that the Holy Spirit has set this example before our eyes" (59, emphasis added).

God has not left God's people defenseless before our opponents. In the community of the covenant, the partners, God and beloved people, communicate through prayer. Thus David, Jesus, and the very words of the psalm itself become an example for us to pour out our overwhelmed hearts in prayer to the majestic Sovereign who made heaven and earth, the only one who can redeem us from the pit of chaos. In this fellowship of prayer that ultimately includes David *and* Jesus, Israelites *and* disciples, Jews *and* Christians, "God's mercy is proved by indubitable effect when he succors his servants who are reduced to the very depths of despair" (61).

Like the psalmist, Calvin was a realist about the spiritual life. He knew that to be called among God's elect people provided no exemption from suffering. His first note on Psalm 69 is its similarity to Psalm 22: "My God, my God, why have you forsaken me?" Although God's "steadfast love" (vv. 13, 16) is affirmed, Calvin writes, "It is a very difficult matter to believe that God is merciful to us when he is angry with us, and that he is near to us when he has withdrawn himself from us" (62).

There is much that we can learn from those called into God's covenant who read the Psalms under conditions of persecution: "For God will save Zion and rebuild the cities of Judah" (Ps. 69:35).

ROBERT A. CATHEY

Pastoral Perspective

fullness of time. Just when we feel the most underwater, we are reminded that God works in God's own time. In those moments when we want a sign from God but we do not get what we expect, we often assume that God has left us.

Like the psalmist, we operate a bit like the farmer in the flood who ignored two boats and a helicopter as he waited for God to lift him off his roof. We pray for God to act or speak to us, sometimes not noticing the ways God is already acting and speaking. Sometimes those revelations or epiphanies of God come in ways that we do not expect, and we are blessed when we pay attention to them. Even Job, who like the psalmist was persecuted for his faith, rails at God about all he has done in God's name. God responds to him by saying, "Where were you when I laid the foundation of the earth?" (Job 38:4). Where were you when all this came into being? Where were you when I created all that is?

The psalmist reminds us that on those days when life has hit us hard, we are not alone, because people have been railing and angry at God throughout history, and God can take our anger. On those days when we feel far away from God, we are reminded that we are not alone, and God can take our distance. When we feel that all around us have turned their backs, the psalmist reminds us that God calls us to live into what is right in front of us. This is all God asks.

KATE COLUSSY-ESTES

Exegetical Perspective

time" (NRSV) or "in the time of your favor" (NIV) God will indeed "answer" and will respond out of "steadfast love" (*hesed*). This third petition (vv. 13–18) returns to voice the initial request in verse 1a, but in more detail: that God provide the psalmist rescue from sinking into "the mire" (v. 14) and "the deep waters" (v. 14) and from being overtaken by "the flood (v. 15)," "the deep" (v.15), and "the Pit" (v. 15), all of which represent death and separation from God and family.

In addition, the psalmist specifically requests, "Let me be delivered from my enemies" (*'innasela missone'ay*, v. 14), a group left unnamed (vv. 18 and 19), but for whom the psalmist minces no words in the remaining petitions and complaints in vv. 19–29, describing their cruelty and asking God to punish them. This plea for punishment of enemies stems not from vengeance but from a desire that God display love, compassion, faithfulness, justice, and righteousness for the poor and the oppressed, including the psalmist, activity that is central to God's very identity.

In verses 16–18 the psalmist again asks God to answer (*'aneni*), once more acknowledging God's "steadfast love" (*hesed*) but also mentioning God's "mercy" (*rahamim*), and then repeats the request with urgency by requesting that God "answer quickly" (*'aneni maher*). The psalmist even wants to see God's face and acknowledges that God's nearness is needed, in order that one be redeemed (*ga'al*) and set free (*pada*) from the enemies who are troubling him.

Rather than depending upon family members or next of kin to act in the role of redeemer (*go'el*), the psalmist refers to God in this role, not only since the psalmist has no family members to fulfill this role, but also because the psalmist views God as the one on whom and through whom life depends. This closeness to God is accentuated by the psalmist's referring to himself or herself as God's servant (*'ebed*).

EMILY R. CHENEY

Homiletical Perspective

knees trying to get up, trying to catch our breath, trying to get reoriented, but our heads are still swirling around like spinning wheels.

We are experiencing life on the brink, on the edge. We are standing on the edge of a disaster, the edge of destruction, the edge of despair. The brink means that the edge is unsafe; it is the danger zone. We are living a life on the brink, not just economically, but spiritually as well. We are losing our grip, losing our ability to stand steady and stare at the devil with determination and hope. Life on the brink is life on the verge of falling off the wagon, on the verge of throwing in the towel, on the verge of throwing up our hands, on the verge of losing our minds.

Life on the brink means standing at the threshold of danger—at the place where danger begins, at the place where danger is imminent. Life on the threshold of danger means that the door, the gate to danger, is right in front of us. One step forward could lead to destruction. Life on the threshold of danger is how we feel sometimes in our relationships, in our families, in our churches, on our jobs, and in this economy.

In this text the psalmist is lamenting, crying out, wailing, complaining. This psalmist says, "I have become a stranger to my kindred, an alien. . . . I am the subject of gossip, . . . the drunkards make songs about me" (vv. 8, 12). He goes on and on about his sorrows and pains. He has been alienated in spite of his devotion and service. The preacher can develop a theme around the reality of alienation in spite of devotion, or assert that alienation and devotion are not mutually exclusive.

The final words of today's passage reiterate the psalmist's confidence that YHWH is able and willing to help (vv. 16–18). The preacher should express this confidence too, for no alienation is so great that God cannot overcome it.

JAMES HENRY HARRIS

Romans 6:1b-11

¹ᵇShould we continue in sin in order that grace may abound? ²By no means! How can we who died to sin go on living in it? ³Do you not know that all of us who have been baptized into Christ Jesus were baptized into his death? ⁴Therefore we have been buried with him by baptism into death, so that, just as Christ was raised from the dead by the glory of the Father, so we too might walk in newness of life.

⁵For if we have been united with him in a death like his, we will certainly be united with him in a resurrection like his. ⁶We know that our old self was crucified with him so that the body of sin might be destroyed, and we might no longer be enslaved to sin. ⁷For whoever has died is freed from sin. ⁸But if we have died with Christ, we believe that we will also live with him. ⁹We know that Christ, being raised from the dead, will never die again; death no longer has dominion over him. ¹⁰The death he died, he died to sin, once for all; but the life he lives, he lives to God. ¹¹So you also must consider yourselves dead to sin and alive to God in Christ Jesus.

Theological Perspective

Romans 5 culminates in an overwhelming crescendo of grace. Paul tells the history of creation from the perspective of its eschatological end. One man's trespass led to condemnation for all. God gave the law, but the powers of sin and death turned this good gift to their own ends. Then, Paul writes, "where sin increased, grace abounded all the more" (5:20). Now one man's act of righteousness leads to justification and life for all (5:18). In chapter 5 Paul tells the story of a relentless, resourceful God who is determined to speak the last word. That last word is "eternal life through Jesus Christ our Lord" (5:21).

Then, after that last word comes a next word, a question whose very utterance reveals the ways in which the fullness of redemption is not yet realized: if an increase in sin sparks an even greater abundance of grace, why not remain in sin? "What then are we to say?" Paul asks. "Should we continue in sin in order that grace may abound?" (6:1)

It is tempting to brush the question aside as a rhetorical foil, but the question flows directly out of Paul's train of thought. It is akin to the questions people pressed on Jesus. It is the kind of question put to Augustine of Hippo, Marguerite Porete, Martin Luther, and Martin Luther King Jr. One of the best measures of Christian preaching is to ask if it invites this kind of question. Do we preach a grace

Pastoral Perspective

Paul's Letter to the Romans is like a theological symphony. In order to appreciate a particular passage, it is essential first to listen to the entire masterpiece, lest the preacher miss any of the leitmotifs on sin, grace, and law that carry over from one movement to the next. Since this passage appears in the lectionary during the leisurely days of Ordinary Time, there may even be an opportunity for the preacher to offer a sustained series of sermons on Romans. Yet whether this is one sermon in a series or just one sermon, it is important to set this passage in the broader context of Paul's sustained discourse on grace and sin.

Preaching from Romans is no easy task. To modern ears, Paul's theology of sin and grace sounds discordant and out of tune with modern life. If my church is any indicator of the state of mainline congregations, much of Paul's lyrical theology falls on deaf ears. First of all, while we are still into sinning, we are not into "sin" language. The sin sickness for which grace is the cure is no longer a recognized disease in the American church.

Secondly, there is a widespread post-Enlightenment discomfort with the (il)logic of the resurrection. Thus the theological hinge of this passage, not to mention much of Paul's theology, requires some careful explanation. Finally, in its present form, the

Exegetical Perspective

Introduction. The well-known dichotomies throughout Romans are particularly striking in the central sixth and seventh chapters, making preaching from these verses particularly challenging. The seemingly contrasting elements include death vs. life; sin vs. righteousness; slavery vs. freedom; law vs. grace; passions vs. sanctification; time vs. eternity; opportunistic law vs. spiritual and good law; doing evil vs. being good.

Interpretative Possibilities. How these chapters are finally interpreted usually depends on the preacher's understanding of the purpose and outline of Romans as a whole. The listing of a few of the possibilities demonstrates the choices faced. What is the main goal of Paul's letter? To contrast the Old Testament law with the gospel of Jesus Christ and demonstrate how Israel and the Gentiles can make one church? To explore the individual or corporate schizophrenia that is experienced by believers when they cannot do the good they want to do? To oppose the military might of world imperialism by exposing the conflict between Roman political and religious propaganda and the overwhelming power of the gospel of Jesus Christ? To develop a carefully written rhetorical treatise that convinces readers to support the mission work of the church (the anticipated Spanish

Homiletical Perspective

Romans 6 opens with a question Paul anticipates from his correspondents: does liberation from Torah (the Law) fling open the gates to anything-goes sin (license)? Modern congregations may respond to Paul's vocabulary with a yawn. They are as unlikely to recognize themselves as burdened by law as they are to glance around for gateways to unbridled behavior. Thus the preacher's first task may be to help them recognize that both sides of Paul's conundrum (law or license?) are alive and well in their lived experience.

Actually, most parishioners know all about chafing under the constraints of external demands. They may not identify cultural expectations as law, but they know the weariness of trying to make themselves acceptable to their God, their neighbors, and themselves. They labor not only to constrain the compulsions, bad habits, and destructive behaviors that undermine human flourishing; they also labor to pick up the markers society lays down for success: markers like swell families, enviable jobs, and youthful physiques.

Most parishioners also have known the intoxication and costs of rebellion when rationalization overruns a behavioral checkpoint. For some, it may only be a distant memory of dissolute behavior when exams gave way to spring break; for some, the

Romans 6:1b-11

Theological Perspective

so persistent and powerful that it makes sense to ask if people should continue in sin so that grace might abound?

The call for "relevant" preaching can tempt us away from the fullness of this gospel. A sermon on four biblical rules for raising children, for instance, will not inspire anyone to ask if we should flout those rules so that God's grace might increase. A call to do simple things to save the earth will not invite questions about creating more pollution so that God's redeeming power might be more visible. The absurdity of those questions marks the distance of much of our proclamation from Paul's.

The details of the question matter. Not just any question about the power of grace will do. No one would ask the question of verse 1 after hearing a gospel of breezy acceptance. H. Richard Niebuhr caricatured liberal preachers in the Progressive Era as teaching that "a God without wrath brought men without sin into a kingdom without judgment through the ministrations of a Christ without a cross."[1] Such proclamation might lead someone to ask, "What then are we to say? Is there no such thing as sin?" It would not, however, lead to a question about the desirability of remaining in sin for the sake of expanding the glorious, costly abundance of grace given through the death and resurrection of Jesus.

Romans 6 demands preaching that provokes the question of verse 1, with all its potency and particularity: "Should we continue in sin in order that grace may abound?" Preachers should be stalked by questions like this after preaching from Romans.

We should also have good answers. Paul's answer is first sharp—"By no means!" (v. 2)—then expansive. He reminds Christians in Rome of their baptism. Baptism unites Christians to Christ so completely that we share in his death and resurrection. Our old self is crucified with Christ on the cross, and that death breaks the power of sin over our lives. We die with Christ, we are buried with Christ, and, Paul writes, we will surely rise with Christ to "walk in newness of life" (v. 4).

Paul understands baptism as a type of exodus. As Israel once labored under Pharaoh, so humanity labored in bondage to sin. As Pharaoh's power was broken once when Israel passed through the waters of the Red Sea, so sin's power over us was broken when we passed through the waters of baptism. Israel came through the water into the wilderness—a

---

1. H. Richard Niebuhr, *The Kingdom of God in America* (Chicago: Willett, Clark & Co., 1937), 193.

Pastoral Perspective

mainline Christian faith is distinctly noneschatological, without any pressing sense of God's culminating work. Given these challenges, the key to preaching this passage is to find a creative way to clarify Paul's theological message by connecting it with contemporary experience and Christian practices.

The main thrust of chapter 6 is to head off any misunderstandings about the relationship between sin and grace. Three verses previously, Paul describes the boundless power of grace in these terms: "where sin increased, grace abounded all the more" (5:20b). Clearly, he worries that Christians might take this as encouragement to sin. "By no means!" Paul states emphatically (6:2). Just because the power of grace outstrips the power of sin is no reason to sin.

When my son was in preschool, he accidentally spilled an entire carton of milk on the floor. He was devastated by his mistake. So as I mopped the floor, I reassured him that everything was going to be just fine. I said, "Look! Now the whole floor is nice and clean!" He turned to me and said brightly, "Hey! Maybe I should spill on the floor more often!" By no means! Just because God in Christ Jesus has the power to make things right is not an invitation to do wrong.

Another approach to the sermon is through the sacrament of baptism. In our baptismal liturgy, the charge to the parents concludes with the words, "This is a day to remember and to be kept sacred." To be honest, I do not think anyone really does this. In the mainline liberal tradition, baptism has become a somewhat toothless sacrament, a life event not unlike graduation or the prom. Baptism is a gift we give to our children, but not the focus of our attention or a wellspring of theological meaning making. When I first arrived at my present church, there was not even a baptismal font in the sanctuary.

Paul's remarks to the church in Rome in chapter 6 remind us that baptism is more than simply a rite of passage. It is a radical change in identity, one that opens up new possibilities. There is a "before" and an "after." Before, we were slaves to sin, without even the hope that we could do what is right. After, we have the opportunity truly to live and be "alive to God in Christ Jesus" (v. 11). A preacher could explore Paul's theology of sin and grace by examining the community's attitudes, rites, rituals, and implicit or explicit theologies of baptism.

Another key element of Paul's message is the matter of identity. Through baptism, we are given a new identity in Christ Jesus. Our day-to-day lives will not change, though, unless we embrace this new identity. Paul believes right identity precedes right actions.

Exegetical Perspective

mission in particular)?[1] To engage the church in the cosmic battle being waged by God through Christ against universal spiritual terrorism brought into the world through sin?[2]

Baptism as an Example. In Paul's discussion of baptism, for example, preachers are often pressed to choose between a physical and a metaphorical understanding or between an individualistic and a universalistic application. The baptism of Jesus recorded in the Gospels is assumed here but a direct connection with John the Baptist and the incident in the Jordan are not mentioned. It is also striking that, although the baptism of an individual person through immersion (or sprinkling) and the powerful change that comes about through that event and/or conversion may be in Paul's mind in the first part of chapter 6, it is not possible to rule out the cosmic element of cleansing and redemption.

Baptism for Paul goes beyond a literal interaction with water and moves immediately to a symbolic understanding of death and life (vv. 3–4). The death he is writing about is the death of Jesus on the cross and the physical death of individual believers when their physical lives come to an end and they are buried. Death is also seen, though, as a metaphor for baptism. If a person stayed under water indefinitely, he or she would surely drown (as in the Red Sea, 1 Cor. 10:1–5). Death also takes on a symbolic force similar to that elaborated in 1 Corinthians 15, where the very concept of death as a universal constant is completely eliminated through Christ (1 Cor. 15:24–26, 54–57); death itself is dead and buried with him (Rom. 6:9).

Perhaps it is not possible to give the preacher exegetical certainty about which of these aspects of baptism should center the sermon. The focus will need to be determined by what is going on in the hearts of the members of the congregation to whom the sermon is being preached, what is happening in the world at the time, and the conflicting demands within the preacher.

Sin and Righteousness. Verse 1 begins by referring back to chapter 5. Here Paul sets up a question asked, either by himself or by a fictional narrative interlocutor,

---

1. For this perspective and an exhaustive review of possible interpretations of Romans, see the analysis in Robert Jewett, *Romans*, Hermeneia (Minneapolis: Fortress Press, 2007).
2. See Beverly R. Gaventa, "The Cosmic Power of Sin in Paul's Letter to the Romans," *Interpretation* 58 (2004): 229–40. Other articles in the same issue discuss recent paradigm shifts in the interpretation of Romans that must be considered.

Homiletical Perspective

occasion is as fresh as an affair, addiction, or abuse set in motion by sudden good fortune or reversal, hubris or self-doubt, too much work or too little.

What then are preachers to say? Does Paul's message still bear good news to our people? As he begins to sketch out an ethical framework in verses 1–11, Paul's argument moves through themes of impossibility, possibility, and responsibility. Each theme offers rich opportunities to help our parishioners appropriate the good news.

Impossibility. Paul argues throughout Romans that it is impossible for us to escape the dominion of sin by our own efforts, but if preachers use this as a warrant to flog our parishioners as "totally depraved," they will have missed his point and his good news. Paul seeks to inspire not enervating despair but rather energizing gratitude and love.

Paul has peered down into the deepest springs of human conduct. There he finds that humanity's universal turn from God-centeredness to self-centeredness, the capital-S sin, has resulted in a universal distortion of the self's very being, of the self's very means of navigation (1:21–23), unleashing a cascading catastrophe of small-s sins (1:26–32). Since "being" precedes "doing," better "being" must precede better "doing." Yet, as the self is now "futile" in its thinking, it can neither heal its distorted being, nor change its sinful doing. The self is enslaved to sin (v. 6).

Most modern parishioners so prize their presumed autonomy that they may recoil at claims of enslavement; but connect the dots to Paul's succinct summary of the human predicament at 7:15, and recognition should flicker across their faces. The stories change from pew to pew, but regret and estrangement are common enough: because we cannot conquer old compulsions and addictions, because we have betrayed someone we love, or because we are just plain tired of falling short of the marks we set for ourselves.

Like so many AA members, we have all confronted behavioral flaws over which we are powerless. We have all found it impossible fully to live up to the ideals we associate with human flourishing. These are grim shackles indeed, until we realize that God has already acted to free us. God has already intervened to break the dynamic of self-centeredness and recenter the self back to God-centeredness.

Possibility. Impossibility is enervating, a prescription for "weak resignation"; so the main thrust of Paul's

Romans 6:1b-11

Theological Perspective

place where Pharaoh no longer held power over them and where God traveled with them, but still not the promised land. Even so, we move through the waters of baptism into a place where sin no longer has dominion, where God is with us, and where the fullness of resurrection life is still to come.

Romans 6 offers few resources for thinking about questions that often come up in contemporary debates about baptism. Paul does not directly address the question of infant baptism. He does not tell us whether we should baptize by immersion, sprinkling, or pouring. However, his image of baptism as exodus offers an important correction and supplement to the lived sacramental theology of our congregations. Paul makes clear that baptism is not only an event between the individual and God, but also a union with Christ that connects the baptized one with all the faithful in every time and place.

So, too, baptism is not a family celebration; it is incorporation into the body of Christ, and thus into a set of commitments that may call family ties into question (see Matt. 10:34–38; Luke 14:26). Baptism is not a magic spell that protects a person from peril in this world and the next. On the contrary, in binding us to Christ, baptism places us on the way of the cross. Baptism is not a celebration of the waters of life, at least not in any simple sense; it is a drowning, an act that renders us "dead to sin and alive to God in Christ Jesus" (v. 11).

Dead to sin and alive to God, the baptized one *cannot* remain in sin without betraying who she has become. So baptism grounds Paul's answer to the question in verse 1. It is not that acts of sin have become impossible for baptized Christians—our own lives make that clear enough. Even after the exodus, the children of Israel can long for the fleshpots of Egypt. Nevertheless, something has happened. A page has turned, not only in individual lives, but also in the eschatological history of the world; and, by the grace of God, there is no going back.

TED A. SMITH

Pastoral Perspective

When my cousin entered medical school, students were instructed to call each other "doctor" from day one. They were not really doctors, but people who were living, learning, and growing into this new identity as doctors. Using the title was a way to remind them of the goal toward which they were striving.

In the same way, I once knew a minister who always addressed his congregation as the "saints of God." While I am relatively certain few of these people considered themselves saints in the popular sense of that word, just hearing themselves called saints made them feel ennobled and reminded them of who they were. Like those medical students, they were living, learning, and growing into a new identity. There is a "fake it 'til you make it" element in both cases, but it underscores the role self-understanding plays in shaping human behavior. Through baptism, we have been given a new identity; embracing that new identity has the power to shape our behavior and move us to action.

This leads to a final theological element in Romans 6: the necessity of connecting faith with action. Modern Christians are masters of compartmentalization. What we believe does not always shape how we live. David Bartlett says it well: "We think that because our hearts belong to Jesus, our bodies, our checkbooks, our votes, and our property values belong to us."[1] From Paul's point of view, this is impossible and the logic is simple: "we have been buried with him by baptism into death, so that, just as Christ was raised from the dead by the glory of the Father, so we too might walk in newness of life" (v. 4). Notice Paul says "walk," not "think" or "believe." Baptism brings about a radical change in our identity, a change that has implications for every aspect of our lives. It is not a demand, but a glorious possibility—to be alive to God. That good news should be music to our ears.

SHAWNTHEA MONROE

---

1. David L. Bartlett, *Romans*; Westminster Bible Companion (Louisville, KY: Westminster John Knox Press, 1995) 61.

Exegetical Perspective

about the nature of sin. Perhaps it is one that actually arose in the Roman church or was posed sarcastically by Paul's opponents: if so much good comes through God's forgiveness of sin, why not sin all the more and increase the presence of grace?

To this possibility Paul replies with his curt "No way!" (NRSV "By no means!" Gk. *mē genoito*; also in 6:15). The believer cannot deliberately rebel more against God or purposely miss the mark, since he or she is already dead to these possibilities. In the previous chapters Paul has discussed righteousness and justification by faith alone exhaustively, as the way in which God gives forgiveness and love (1:17; 2:13; 3:4–5, 21–26; 4:2–25; 5:1–21), and they cannot be cast aside in a dismissive intellectual flourish.

Compound Community Concepts. Throughout this pericope Paul uses a number of compound words and expressions (in Gk. the verbs start with *syn*, "with"). In most cases they provide an intimate concept of how close the believer can be to the Lord Jesus. One who has faith is "baptized *into* Christ," "baptized *into* his death," "buried *with* him," "united *with* him" in resurrection, "crucified *with* him," has "died *with* Christ," is "alive to God in Christ Jesus." More is involved than personal salvation. The fellowship one has with Jesus is also corporate. In this post-Pentecost period, preachers have to be aware of how the Spirit, as the concluding remarks in Romans 8:1–17 indicate, binds all believers together in the plural, as "children of God" (8:14–17).

Paul likes to force his readers and hearers to decide how to be with Christ personally while struggling with the necessity of being one who is also fully engaged in the world. For him ironies prevail: having been apart from Christ under the law, we now live with him in the church's gospel; although we were dead when we thought we were alive, we are fully living only when we die and are raised up by God with all the saints.

EARL S. JOHNSON, JR.

Homiletical Perspective

argument is that what was impossible in the old age, under the domain of sin and death, is now possible in the new age, under the domain of grace and life. Continuing a theme he lays out in Galatians 2:19–20, Paul here argues that the Christ event is actualized in each Christian life through baptism. As baptismal candidates are lowered into the water, they are baptized into Christ's death (v. 3), personally undergoing the crucifixion of their old self (v. 6). As they rise from the water, they emerge engrafted, in solidarity with the risen Christ. As they appropriate the gifts of Christ's death and resurrection (vv. 4, 5, 8), they are newly liberated to "walk in newness of life" (vv. 4, 11).

Preachers may thus emphasize the new, empowering possibility by extolling the baptized Christian's new "participation," "union," or "identity," with the risen Lord. Some parishioners may squirm at suggestions that the rite is anything more than an expression of faith or historic reenactment, but there can be little question that Paul anchors life's new possibilities in the real spiritual effects of baptism. "For Paul, baptism 'into Christ' makes one a participant in an *event*, not an ideal or a myth. Basic for this understanding is the conviction, widely held at the time, that a religious ritual *does* what it symbolizes."[1]

Responsibility. Paul posits an "already but not yet" eschatology, so he is under no illusion that temptation and sin no longer beckon. However, as it is now possible to walk with Christ in the "newness of life," it seems only natural to Paul that we should do so: "So you must consider yourselves dead to sin and alive to God in Christ Jesus" (v. 11). Given our new identity, status, and solidarity with Christ, to do otherwise is a contradiction in terms.

Perhaps the key phrase for preaching the turn from possibility to responsibility is "you must consider." Paul's exhortation rests on a presumption that it is still left to Christians to exercise their newfound freedom by consciously appropriating and enacting their new identity. Reflection, discipleship, and congregational celebration all integrate the gift of the new identity and the behavior. Since being precedes doing, better being may now naturally issue forth in better doing. As David Bartlett teaches, "The old saw is not a bad one when understanding Paul's moral exhortations: 'Be who you are.'"[2]

HAROLD E. MASBACK III

---

1. Leander E. Keck, *Romans*, Abingdon New Testament Commentaries (Nashville: Abingdon Press, 2005), 159.
2. David L. Bartlett, *What's Good about This News?* (Louisville, KY: Westminster John Knox Press, 2003), 19.

Matthew 10:24-39

²⁴"A disciple is not above the teacher, nor a slave above the master; ²⁵it is enough for the disciple to be like the teacher, and the slave like the master. If they have called the master of the house Beelzebul, how much more will they malign those of his household!

²⁶"So have no fear of them; for nothing is covered up that will not be uncovered, and nothing secret that will not become known. ²⁷What I say to you in the dark, tell in the light; and what you hear whispered, proclaim from the housetops. ²⁸Do not fear those who kill the body but cannot kill the soul; rather fear him who can destroy both soul and body in hell. ²⁹Are not two sparrows sold for a penny? Yet not one of them will fall to the ground apart from your Father. ³⁰And even the hairs of your head are all counted. ³¹So do not be afraid; you are of more value than many sparrows.

Theological Perspective

This week and for the next two weeks, the important theological theme of discipleship emerges in Matthew. As you prepare this week's sermon, therefore, it is wise to pause and think through (as well as feel through) your own understanding of discipleship—the ways in which you seek to live out your sense of discipleship in your life and witness—as well as what you observe the congregation, or those beyond it, working through as they seek to be faithful to God's call in their lives. In doing so, you may find aspects of discipleship other than those discussed here, and in the weeks to follow, it may be good to explore them with your congregation.

Keep in mind that "disciple" means "learner." What are the important aspects of learning the faith that you wish to highlight? What are some ways you see others and yourself seeking to learn about the faith that you can use as examples to help listeners look inward and outward as disciples? What are the special qualities of learning that have private and public expressions in our daily living?

The questions are many and rich. The famous lines in verses 34–39 of this passage ("Do not think that I have come to bring peace to the earth; I have not come to bring peace, but a sword") can open up volumes for listeners of the Word and the preacher of the Word, if the focus of the passage is on

Pastoral Perspective

My mother-in-law Connie, a faithful Christian woman who in retirement has become a daily attender of Catholic mass, needs no lectionary commentary to know that she does not like this passage. She refuses to listen to my argument that this is but a collection of sayings given by Jesus to the disciples as they set out on a mission of healing and preaching good news. She knows already that the life of faith will include times of struggle and even opposition— she is a faithful Catholic laywoman, after all. Every Christian disciple knows that along the way of faith, some disciples will suffer as Christ suffered, and that the community of the faithful must seek to persevere even in times of fear.

But in this passage, she insists, Jesus goes too far. The Jesus that she knows comes to bring peace, not a sword. While she has spent enough time around the church to recognize that discord happens within the community of the faithful, her Jesus would never have encouraged such division in the midst of family.

Here is Jesus promising to set a son against his father and a daughter against her mother. "Whoever loves son or daughter more than me is not worthy of me" (v. 37), my mother-in-law reads, shaking her head. "How," she wonders, "did this ever get into the Bible?"

We can weave a fanciful cloth of critical explanation, but if in the preaching of this text we fail to

³²"Everyone therefore who acknowledges me before others, I also will acknowledge before my Father in heaven; ³³but whoever denies me before others, I also will deny before my Father in heaven.

³⁴"Do not think that I have come to bring peace to the earth; I have not come to bring peace, but a sword.

³⁵For I have come to set a man against his father,
and a daughter against her mother,
and a daughter-in-law against her mother-in-law;
³⁶and one's foes will be members of one's own household.

³⁷Whoever loves father or mother more than me is not worthy of me; and whoever loves son or daughter more than me is not worthy of me; ³⁸and whoever does not take up the cross and follow me is not worthy of me. ³⁹Those who find their life will lose it, and those who lose their life for my sake will find it."

Exegetical Perspective

The present passage is part of the so-called "Missionary Discourse," which is the second of the five major discourses in Matthew. Matthew seems to have conflated two different mission traditions (Mark 6:6b–13 and Q 10:1–20) and added still other sayings from Q. The present pericope, located in the latter part of the discourse, addresses the issue of the responses the disciples might encounter as they carry out their mission (10:16–33) and the principle of discipleship (10:34–39).

The Missionary Discourse is presented in the narrative world of Matthew as instructions that Jesus gives his disciples as he sends them out in mission at one particular moment during his Galilean ministry. However, it seems to contain some sayings, including the present pericope, which would certainly have better applied to a later period than the time of the historical Jesus. This phenomenon, called "transparency" and quite common in Matthew, often reveals the life situation of the Matthean community, either at the time of composition of the Gospel or some time prior to it. In the present context, it seems to reflect the difficulties experienced by the followers of the Jesus movement, mostly because of unfavorable reactions to their ministry by the Jewish authorities.

This pericope is immediately preceded by a controversial saying of Jesus that predicts the coming of

Homiletical Perspective

With Matthew's first readers, we overhear Jesus' instructions to the Twelve before sending them out and so find ourselves challenged to consider our own role in spreading his kingdom message in word and deed (10:7–8). Not surprisingly (for an activity that intends radical transformations of the social order), this kingdom mission leads to conflict. The difficulty in preaching today's text is not the complexity of its concepts, but the seeming disconnect between the palpable threats of the world it displays and the "safe" world most of us inhabit.

What compromises have been made to secure such "safety"? Contemporary opposition to following Jesus is usually more subtle, but no less real, than that faced by Matthew's first readers. It is the preacher's task both to make these challenges explicit and to give voice to the courageous response made available through an encounter with this text. In negotiating this text's claim upon the present, the preacher will wrestle with several issues.

What Does It Mean to Be Like Jesus? The section begins with the truism that the disciple should be like the teacher (v. 25); but what is the teacher like? The answers given in this context can be unsettling. Jesus turns down the role of predictable, innocuous do-gooder: "Do not think that I have come to bring

Matthew 10:24-39

Theological Perspective

discipleship—the process of learning what it means to follow the ways of Jesus.

It is important to note that discipleship is a journey that includes learning, which is distinct from being an apostle or a messenger, who is sent to declare a message. The focus for us now is to try to understand what Jesus is seeking to teach us and what we are to learn from it. In this passage, our task is not to be the ones who deliver the teachings. Rather, we are to pause and learn from Jesus who we are to be, what we are to say, and how we are to communicate this with others. This pause is crucial as we consider one aspect of discipleship that is found in today's passage from Matthew: obedience.

One framework from which to explore the nature of obedience is that of power. We tend to think of power as control, rule, or domination. This understanding often flows from a more authoritarian model of obedience based on submission, in which the world is separated into entities with little or no interrelationship. Power becomes the property of these separated entities and is identified with domination or power over others. This concept of power involves the notion of invulnerability.

You may be tempted to follow this common perception of power based on Jesus' words in verses 34–36. Resist! Instead of assuming that power means invulnerability, consider the surrounding verses, in order to proclaim with clarity and precision the mystery of the realm of God. Here we are encouraged not to hold our knowledge of God working in and through Jesus in the small preserve of our hearts and souls, as though it were a possession. Instead, we are to use light and bold proclamation as disciples to share what we have experienced and come to know.

This fearless witness is not based on an authoritarian model of discipleship—one that depicts obedience as an exclusive self/other relationship based on an imbalance of power, so that the person asserting superiority is feared. Jesus is the strong mediator in verse 32, and God is the one who is judging and caring in verses 28–30. We are not to fear each other, but God, who gives Jesus the bold authority proclaimed beginning with verse 34. We are not to mistake God's great care for us as license for an anything-goes discipleship or one in which we are unthinking automatons. The latter is a behavioral technique rather than a standard of faithful witness.

The worldview of authoritarian obedience stresses order and does not tolerate continual change. However, the biblical worldview is one of movement toward a goal. The authoritarian model

Pastoral Perspective

consider Connie's concern—a concern that is surely shared by many sitting in our Sunday morning pews—then we will have failed to offer pastoral sensitivity at the point of profound human need, and will have missed the opportunity to speak to the power of the gospel at its most challenging. We live in a society that is well acquainted with familial discord. We must be careful indeed, lest this Scripture be read as some odd invitation to family dysfunction and disunity.

This text is a fine example of the biblical word's not saying what, at first glance, it seems to be saying. While an energetic proof-texter might turn to these verses to justify a religious cult's determination to split families apart, this Scripture does not so advocate. Jesus is actually addressing the faithful who seek to live into their Christian faith while facing conflict and discouragement, and even the threat to their physical well-being, because of the gospel's calling.

Sent on a mission of preaching and healing, the disciples have quickly learned what it means to face opposition and struggle. The cozy days of breaking bread with Jesus seem far distant when in response to the good news of the gospel they are rewarded with persecution. This will be a part of the Christian story in every generation to follow. "What are we to do when we realize that we are not strong enough to prevail?" Christians will ask.

The church will persevere, Matthew declares, in spite of all of the trials of this life. Even in times of fear, the gospel will be true. What of the individual disciple? The individual—and even the family, for that matter—must be of less concern than the overarching importance of proclaiming God's word. For individual lives, family structures, and the whole of society will thrive when the gospel's good news is heard and embraced. Until that time, we need not fear those who will destroy the body, for they cannot harm the soul. No death, not the death of a person or even of a sparrow, occurs but for God's will. Jesus is asking the faithful to keep on because of our love for him and because, in the end, it will be real and everlasting life that we find.

In the face of the conflict that disciples and Christian missionaries can expect, in the face even of personal and familial turmoil, Tom Long writes that four things will be seen. First, the Holy Spirit will surely be present and will never abandon us. Second, we will come to recognize that our suffering is not wasted, but is a testimony to faith. Third, even in the midst of our hardships, we will know that nothing can eradicate the gospel or destroy God's loving and

the Son of Man even before the disciples finish preaching in all the villages of Israel (10:23). This saying has no parallel in the New Testament, and the questions of its source and its authenticity remain unresolved. What Matthew must have taken this saying to mean is also very difficult to determine. The history of interpretation of this saying ranges widely. At one extreme, some scholars believe that this saying comes from the historical Jesus and that Matthew shares with him an apocalyptic eschatology, an expectation of the imminent Parousia of the Son of Man, whether he is identical with Jesus or not.

At the opposite end of the spectrum are scholars who lean heavily toward transparency, so that this saying is not so much a reference to the imminent Parousia as an indication that the redactor of Matthew insists on the continuing validity of the mission to the Jews, despite the failure Matthew's community has experienced with the synagogues at the end of the first century, when the Parousia of Jesus seems very distant. Whatever interpretive option one takes, it will inevitably affect the way our present pericope is interpreted, because 10:23 functions as if it were a preface to our pericope.

Taken together with the specific instructions in the earlier part of the discourse for the disciples as traveling preachers and healers, the present passage shows how vulnerable and without means of protection they are as followers of Jesus. If the master was slandered as Beelzebul and eventually executed, his followers should also expect to suffer as much, if not more (v. 25). In that sense, verse 24 is not just a general maxim but specific ethical exhortation for those who are suffering on account of the mission they are carrying out.

This may reflect not necessarily the sociocultural realities of the Matthean church as a residential community at the end of the first century in an urban setting, but an earlier period of the Jesus movement in rural Palestine, which was characterized by itinerant charismatic missionaries who had voluntarily left home and family (vv. 35–37), primarily but not exclusively because of their eschatological sense of urgency. From the perspective of tradition history, it may ultimately go back to a pre-Matthean source, and therefore the particular form of mission reflected in this layer of tradition may not apply to the Matthean community. However, by incorporating it into this discourse, Matthew preserves its ethos of radical abdication of one's possessions and family ties for the sake of Jesus.

The main exhortatory section (vv. 26–31) is wrapped in a ring composition with the same

peace . . . but a sword" (v. 34). Evidently there is peace, and then there is *peace*. The demands of the prince of true peace may very well feel like a sword cutting through lesser loyalties and making quick work of our flabby, commonsense morality.

If Jesus were really the enlightened and affirming nice guy we often insist on imagining, should he not have been able to stay out of trouble? What incited people to call him such appalling names (prince, not of peace, but of demons! v. 25)? Why would following him wreck families (vv. 35–36)? How did he end up on a cross (v. 38)?

The answer is not that his opponents had strange and unsettling ideas, but that he did. Contrary to popular opinion and bestselling books, not everything the follower of Jesus needs to know can be learned in kindergarten. Kingdom work, it turns out, is more controversial and subversive than conventional kindness. If the teacher gives offense, how much more the student (v. 25)?

Of course, giving offense is no great trick, and no sure sign of faithfulness. True discipleship is the art of seeking the kingdom with single-minded determination (6:33) and letting the chips fall where they may. The church that always manages to glide through life without ever rubbing anyone the wrong way may have reason to question whether it is truly *this* Jesus it honors as master and Lord.

To Be Afraid, or Not to Be Afraid? The text is of two minds on this point. The dominant theme is the fearlessness so often enjoined in Scripture (v. 26, 28a, 31). This is not the carefree bliss of the naive, but the tough-minded courage of those who have taken their stand with a full understanding of the risks. Given the certainty of opposition to those schooled in the ways of the "sword bringer" (v. 34), the community of disciples has an interest in forming people who are, frankly, difficult to intimidate (vv. 17–18).

On the other hand, this text assumes that fear does have a legitimate role to play in such formation. It presupposes a robust eschatology that includes the possibility of both vindication (vv. 26–27) and catastrophe (v. 28). The preacher must know her context well in order to judge the matter rightly, but it may be that the time has come for some mainline congregations to explore—rather than nervously to explain away—the proper fear of God. Matthew asks us to live in an odd theological tension: the God who attends to the fate of the sparrow and numbers the hairs of our heads (vv. 29–31) is nevertheless no pushover. God's intimate concern for our lives is

Matthew 10:24-39

Theological Perspective

of obedience cannot adequately express faithful discipleship, because this model is interested in the preservation of order and ultimately views the future with suspicion or fear.

Obedience concentrated *completely* on a higher and guiding authority other than God becomes blind to the world and only follows directions. It can tempt us to believe that if we follow the instruction of our teacher precisely, *we* will become the teacher. On the other end of the spectrum, it can persuade us to divest ourselves of all authority.

In short, this world-blindness can lead to discipleship and witnessing as ends in themselves, rather than as guides we need in our journey to greater faithfulness. This can lead to easy manipulation by authority figures for their own purposes. Here it may be good to pause and think through examples of how we fall victim to this temptation where the Bible, tradition, and experience are used as tools of repression rather than of growth and guidance.

Throughout this passage, obedience implies responsibility. A disciple of Jesus is one who first listens closely to the teachings of Jesus and then decides on the appropriate response. This response is found in a discipleship that summons us to develop our capacity for learning and growing in faith. Here, predetermined or routine preconceptions of the situation or the will of God are not appropriate and can often leave us shifting at shadows in the dark. Jesus requires a discerning obedience that has its eyes wide open, as we accept responsibility for the order of the world and engage in transforming it. This is the order of the world Jesus proclaims in verses 34–39.

EMILIE M. TOWNES

Pastoral Perspective

watchful care over the faithful. Finally, while family disruption will surely take place, Jesus is not against the family. Rather, there will be times when allegiance to Jesus causes a crisis of loyalty and forces a decision. The gospel shakes up values, rearranges priorities, and reorients goals. Writes Long, "To give one's life away in the name of Christ is to be given all that makes life free, holy and good."[1]

My mother-in-law is right when she challenges those who read this text as an invitation to family disunity, in the name of faith. Jesus invites us, instead, to recognize a faith that is able to overcome fear during persecution. Believers who know that their fate is in the hands of a loving God will understand that in this life there is nothing to fear.

Further, it is in the life of Christian discipleship that the providence of God can be known. No power is greater, no assurance more sound. What a remarkable offering of peace, for the sake of love.

Armed with such an assurance, believers are empowered to approach the cross in a new way. No more does the cross mean a passive acceptance of the injustice and misery of this creation. Instead, the cross is a sign of the realm of God that is to come, a strength that can be known by those who are obedient to the call of Jesus Christ in their lives. Those who live by the light of faith challenge the evil powers of this world with the certainty of believers, knowing that the way of God will prevail against every hurt and every challenge.

WILLIAM GOETTLER

---

1. Thomas G. Long, *Matthew*, Westminster Bible Companion (Louisville, KY: Westminster John Knox Press, 1997), 120–22.

phrase, "Do not be afraid (*mē phobēthēte/phobeisthe*)," put in *inclusio* (vv. 26, 31). Then right at the center is located the ultimate exhortation not to fear (*mē phobeisthe*) human opponents, but to fear (*phobeisthe*) God, who will mete out eschatological judgments for all (v. 28). This rhetoric of eschatological threat is balanced by language of God's care for even the smallest living things such as sparrows (vv. 29, 31). With the same pattern of presenting two opposite human fates, verse 32 provides an imagery of Jesus having a dual function, both advocate and prosecutor before God at the eschatological judgment.

The last part of the present passage begins with a declaration that Jesus came not to bring peace but a sword (v. 34). This saying is taken from Q (cf. Luke 12:51) and has a close parallel in *Gospel of Thomas* 16. The phrase "Do not think that I came" has a direct parallel in Matthew 5:17 and suggests that it comes from the evangelist himself. The topos of the eschatological war is typical apocalyptic imagery attested in various Jewish and Christian texts. Its adoption by Matthew in this discourse may caution the interpreter not to read realized eschatology into the Matthean text too easily. Yes, the kingdom is at hand, but as far as Matthew is concerned, the ultimate fulfillment of the eschatological peace is yet to come.

The final verse in this passage (v. 39) is the culmination of the ethical exhortation to endure persecution and to embrace costly discipleship. In the current context, it is taken from Q (Luke 17:33); but since it also has a parallel in Mark 8:35, it could be one of the instances in which Mark and Q overlap. In view of the existence of yet another similar saying in John 12:25, this saying falls in the category of multiple attestation, but the case for authenticity should not be pushed too far. The saying is based on the principle of *imitatio Christi*, and as such it may reflect a retrospective interpretation of the life and death of Jesus from the post-Easter experiences of the early Christian communities.

EUGENE EUNG-CHUN PARK

both a comfort and a claim. Indeed, God's all-encompassing claim upon our lives becomes our comfort: the very real dangers faced in the course of the kingdom mission are not avoided but, rather, utterly eclipsed by our ultimate concern.

The disciple knows on a visceral level that there are parts of the self more real than the physical that are at stake in this contest of loyalties (v. 28), and is motivated in part by the realization that to equivocate or renege in allegiance to Jesus and his kingdom message is to forfeit his advocacy before the Father (v. 33). Proper fear of God, however, always manifests itself in the world of human affairs as fearlessness.

What Does Jesus Have Against Families? Given the beating that the contemporary family takes from economic forces that systematically uproot and scatter extended families, and the dominant popular psychological narrative that demonizes families of origin, it feels a bit unfair to have Jesus pile on with words against familial ties (vv. 35–37). The first readers of this text faced family pressures to reject Jesus and his claims that are scarcely imaginable for many of us. It is even possible to construe this quotation from Micah 7:6 in verse 35 as a kind of comfort in the ashes of family bridges already burned.

Still, any way you slice it, Jesus is no champion of family values. He has kingdom values, and these are often not the same thing. It is remarkable how many stories depict Jesus in conflict with his own family or as the source of conflict in families. He insists that his followers prioritize the kingdom of God and God's righteousness. It should be no surprise that such a complete transformation of human loyalty would have serious repercussions for the many institutions that are displaced in the process.

This entire lection is finally about the radical choices that constitute the life of discipleship. To forsake lesser loyalties is to risk social death in hope of a new kind of life. The image most adequate to this wager is the cross and the life it promises beyond, not instead of, such dying (vv. 38–39).

LANCE PAPE

Jeremiah 28:5-9

⁵Then the prophet Jeremiah spoke to the prophet Hananiah in the presence of the priests and all the people who were standing in the house of the LORD; ⁶and the prophet Jeremiah said, "Amen! May the LORD do so; may the LORD fulfill the words that you have prophesied, and bring back to this place from Babylon the vessels of the house of the LORD, and all the exiles. ⁷But listen now to this word that I speak in your hearing and in the hearing of all the people. ⁸The prophets who preceded you and me from ancient times prophesied war, famine, and pestilence against many countries and great kingdoms. ⁹As for the prophet who prophesies peace, when the word of that prophet comes true, then it will be known that the LORD has truly sent the prophet."

Theological Perspective

This passage describes a "prophetic showdown" between the prophets Hananiah and Jeremiah. At stake was nothing less than the future of Judah: should they revolt against the Babylonians, as Hananiah proposes, or submit to their yoke, as Jeremiah urges?

The historical moment in which these events take place can be described as a *kairos* moment in history, a time of crisis in which God's people are called to discern the truth and act accordingly. The preceding decades have seen great social and political upheavals. At this point King Zedekiah is contemplating revolt against the mighty Babylonians. Later readers of this scene will know that the actors in this scene are standing on the edge of a cliff, as the decisions being debated that day will eventually lead to the destruction of Jerusalem and the devastating Babylonian exile.

The prophet Hananiah is convinced that the time of the Babylonians is almost over, that their yoke will soon be broken. This is a welcome and popular message, which everyone wants to believe. Even Jeremiah says, perhaps sarcastically, that he hopes Hananiah is right. Who would not want to see the exiles return and the temple vessels restored? Who would not want to get out from under foreign rule? However, as is so often the case with Jeremiah, he is called by God to

Pastoral Perspective

How does one know what to believe? When two very different messages sound equally true, when they have all of the marks and credentials that would lead one to believe that they are trustworthy, how does one know which one is true? What is more, when such messages are uttered in the name of God, how does one discern what is truly of God? Surely God would not utter blatant contradictions as God's will.

A church I know found itself in the kind of liminal space that pushed deep questions about its identity and direction. The church council gathered to pray together, to listen for where God was leading their community. After weeks of deliberation, two distinct paths seem to take shape. One was the "conservative" position, a decision to invest what resources the church had and focus on the ministries that they offered very well: Christian education, local outreach, and community fellowship. Let us call this the Jeremiah perspective. The other position became known as the "faith-filled" perspective, a decision to begin a capital campaign to renovate their tired, old facility, add more staff, and grow their church by as many as five hundred members over the next ten years. We could call this the hopeful voice of Hananiah.

Hananiah's voice won out. The capital campaign began, the construction began, and the church built a beautiful state-of-the-art worship center. Then a

Exegetical Perspective

Zedekiah and the "Yoke" of Nebuchadnezzar. The events of Jeremiah 28 occur within a three-month period in the reign of Judah's last king. Zedekiah, the third son of Josiah to sit upon the throne, had been installed as king in a caretaker role by Nebuchadnezzar after the Babylonian armies took Jerusalem in 597 (2 Kgs. 24:10–18). He had officially replaced his deposed nephew, Jehoiachin (= Jeconiah, v. 4), who was deported to Babylon along with other officials, warriors, and artisans. Zedekiah's role was a precarious one: only twenty-one at his accession, he owed his position and even his throne name to Nebuchadnezzar, and he would be responsible for maintaining order and collecting annual tribute for his Babylonian overlords. We know, moreover, both from biblical references and from Babylonian records, that Jehoiachin still was regarded popularly as "king in exile," so that nationalist hopes for the revival of Judah and the throwing off of Babylonian rule naturally involved speculation about Jehoiachin's return and restoration (28:4).

The "fifth month of the fourth year" (v. 1) of Zedekiah's reign would be July/August of 594. Chapter 27 presents us with the "prequel" of our story, in which Jeremiah is first commanded to dramatize his message by wearing a yoke. A group of envoys has come to Jerusalem from the neighboring monarchies

Homiletical Perspective

Gifted writer, biblical scholar, and African Methodist Episcopal Church elder Renita J. Weems offers words about the sometimes agonizing task of writing (and sermon preparation?):

> Every time I sit down to write I feel as though I have to poke around to find a new vein to slice in order to get the words to come. The most that a writer can hope for is to be surrounded by people who love her and care enough about her finished work to stand by with gauze and help bind her wounds when she has bled enough.[1]

Every preacher who labors to give birth to sermons will quickly agree with Dr. Weems. There are those times (more acute than some of us can hardly endure) when the Spirit is a long time arriving. Then there are those "dry vein" moments when nothing flows at all. The WordPerfect is pathetically imperfect. There is no need for gauze. The vein is barren.

Today's text from Jeremiah is dense and enigmatic enough to dry up the most passionate preacher's blood flow. For this reason, the wise among us learn to get started earlier than Saturday evening. (A friend and former parish pastor often remarked to me that he would still be in congregational ministry

---

1. Renita J. Weems, *Listening for God: A Minister's Journey through Silence and Doubt* (New York: Simon & Schuster, 1999), 103.

Jeremiah 28:5-9

Theological Perspective

be the bearer of bad news. Wearing a yoke around his neck to symbolize the rule of the Babylonians, he warns the people of Jerusalem to submit to the Babylonians if they want to live. He adds that history will show which one of them is the true prophet.

Since history did, tragically, show Jeremiah to be the true prophet, later readers may be tempted to dismiss Hananiah as a mere charlatan. After all, he is a bit of a showman, and he is also clearly the proponent of popular theology. However, while it is true that Hananiah gives the king advice that supports what he already wants, it may not be fair to characterize him as merely an opportunist who seeks to flatter the king. As Walter Brueggemann points out, it may be more correct to see the conflicting political advice given by the two prophets as rooted in conflicting visions of God and God's plans.[1]

Hananiah's trust in God's commitment to Jerusalem and the temple is not only a theologically respectable position to take, but is indeed rooted in the normative theological tradition of Jerusalem. Moreover, his words ring true in light of the fact that a similarly positive message from the prophet Isaiah comes true when Jerusalem is delivered from the Assyrian threat less than a century earlier. Indeed, at the time, it might have been perfectly respectable theologically to argue that Jeremiah's message of submission to Babylonian rule is rooted in a lack of trust in God.

Both prophecies offered to the king are rooted in the religious tradition of Judah, but they are not equally attuned to the complexities of that tradition. Hananiah believes that God's covenantal faithfulness means that God will now release his people from a yoke that they despise. Hananiah forgets, though, that God's faithfulness does not mean easy grace. He forgets that God's people cannot simply rest on God's past actions and expect deliverance as a matter of course. Jeremiah may wish that he too can be the bringer of glad tidings like Isaiah before him. Even if not all prophecies are of doom and judgment, though, he knows that the overwhelming message of the prophets has been of judgment.

In light of that history, it would be foolish to trust a feel-good prophecy unless there really is good ground to do so. Jeremiah knows all too well that the God who has called him to prophesy, despite his own protests, is a sovereign God. The God of the covenant is faithful, but this covenantal faithfulness

Pastoral Perspective

local plant closed, the economy turned south, and the capital campaign was suddenly in trouble. Staff positions were cut, new loans and lines of credit negotiated, and current programs reduced. To the credit of this community, those who spoke with Jeremiah's voice did not leave in righteous anger. Instead, they clung to their neighbors and wept as the forces of Babylon trampled their hopes.

Jeremiah proclaimed that the way to test the veracity of a prophecy was only through the lens of hindsight: if it came true, it must have been of God: "As for the prophet who prophesies peace, when the word of that prophet comes true, then it will be known that the LORD has truly sent the prophet" (v. 9). Of course, hindsight does little to help those facing difficult decisions in the moment.

As I write this, the United States (and the entire globe) is facing the worst economic downturn in the last eighty years. Within Congress, two loud and confident voices have emerged along party lines about how we can best address the situation. Which one is right? Perhaps more pointedly, which one seems to be more in line with the will of God?

In a similar way, many denominations and churches face deeper divisions than they have ever known. Issues of biblical authority, human sexuality, and common faith commitments have carved deep wounds into the body of Christ. Which side is right? Which side has aligned itself with the will of God? Like Jeremiah and Hananiah, both sides are using the language and symbols of prophetic utterance to advance their arguments. The question is not, whom shall we send; the question is, whom shall we follow?

In Jeanne DuPrau's *The Prophet of Yonwood*, Mrs. Beason seems uniquely gifted to discern the strange utterances of Althea Turner, a local woman who is in a sort of prolonged shock from visions she has while tending her garden. Mrs. Beason's confidence grows as she listens to Althea mumble in her stupor, offering the little town of Yonwood, North Carolina, her interpretation of the latest message of their prophet. As time passes, the messages grow in their severity, even as Mrs. Beason grows in power and community esteem. When the prophet awakens from her stupor, she learns how Mrs. Beason has interpreted her visions, and she offers corrections. It is hindsight (accompanied by insight) that makes all the difference.[1]

Hindsight brings little relief to such deep divisions. Surely, we will know something more of the

---

1. Walter Brueggemann, *A Commentary on Jeremiah: Exile and Homecoming* (Grand Rapids: Eerdmans, 1998), 250.

1. Jeanne DuPrau, *The Prophet of Yonwood: The Third Book of Ember* (New York: Random House, 2006).

Exegetical Perspective

of Edom, Moab, Ammon, Tyre, and Sidon—all vassals of Nebuchadnezzar (27:3)—to confer about throwing off Babylonian rule. The likely instigation for this rebellious talk, mentioned in the Babylonian Chronicle, is a revolt of Nebuchadnezzar's army in December 595/January 594. News of this insurrection may have emboldened Judah and its neighbors in the west to contemplate their own rebellion in the months that followed. However, Jeremiah's message to Zedekiah and the visiting envoys, dramatized by the heavy yoke across his neck, is that God has given these countries into the service of "King Nebuchadnezzar of Babylon, my servant" (27:6) and that three generations will submit to his yoke (27:7).

The Prophet Hananiah and the Prophet Jeremiah. In chapter 28 we are introduced to "Hananiah the prophet," who takes a public stand in the temple to rebut Jeremiah's prophecies. Within this short chapter each man will be called "the prophet" six times, dramatizing their confrontation and suggesting the difficulty in distinguishing their credentials.[1]

Hananiah, whose very name means "the LORD has been gracious," proclaims that "the LORD of hosts, the God of Israel" has already broken the yoke of Nebuchadnezzar, and that the pillaged temple vessels, King Jehoiachin, and all of the exiles will be returned to Judah within two years (vv. 2–4). Jeremiah's response is surprising: "Amen! May the LORD do so; may the LORD fulfill the words that you have prophesied" (v. 6).

Hananiah has delivered exactly the kind of message of nationalist hope against which Jeremiah has been warning (27:9–10, 14–15, 16–18), and Jeremiah has never hesitated to condemn prophetic opponents for giving false comfort to the people (23:16–17, 25–32). So it is hard to read this reply to Hananiah as a political maneuver or as resigned sarcasm. Is it possible that there is now a new word, that Judah has paid enough and the national agony is about to be lifted?

Jeremiah cannot respond to Hananiah's words, though, merely out of his hopes or his fears. His prophetic career, like that of Hananiah, stands in a tradition that stretches far back, and that tradition offers caveats: "But listen now . . ." (v. 7). There is a special burden of proof for those who prophesy peace. We are told nothing about Hananiah's motives, but the tradition knows of false prophets who eat at royal tables (1 Kgs. 18:19; 22:5–8) or who

---

1. The Septuagint lacks this tension, simply calling Hananiah "the false prophet" (*ho pseudoprophētēs*) in v. 1.

Homiletical Perspective

today, were it not for "the relentless return of Sundays.") In my own "relentless return" to this text, I have also learned to allow the text to read me.

More than any other voice in the Hebrew Bible, Jeremiah possesses six fundamental *P*'s for authentic ministry in every age, namely, that of Preacher, Priest, Pastor, Prophet, Post, and Price, the latter being the countless tariff one pays for being a prophet. It is Jeremiah the prophet who casts the largest shadow over the contemporary church. He is God's fierce and faithful messenger who tenaciously calls us to be centered in God alone. However, for all of his loyal efforts, Jeremiah finds himself broken in spirit and drenched in pain. Such is life for true prophets. Then we wonder why God has so few?

Now let us go to church in the Temple of the Two Prophets. The year is 594 BCE. The Babylonian armies have brutally conquered the Holy City. Many of Jerusalem's leaders have been captured and taken into exile. A congregation of remaining Jerusalemites gathers regularly in the temple. Jeremiah, weird and eccentric as always, is there wearing his ridiculous, self-imposed "yoke of straps and bars" (27:2) around his neck.

Symbolically Jeremiah is declaring that he is yoked to YHWH's servant (27:6)—Nebuchadnezzar, king of Babylon, of all people. The "good news according to Jeremiah" is that God is using Nebuchadnezzar and the powerful Babylonian army to change the hearts and wills of God's defeated people. Daily, hourly, regularly, Jeremiah urges them to repent and return to YHWH. He passionately prays for a transformation within God's people, some of whom are standing there in his presence, while others are in captivity "by the rivers of Babylon" (Ps. 137:1).

On this day another prophet, Hananiah, is in the "house of the LORD" (28:1). What a scene! Hananiah gathers Jeremiah, the temple priests, and all of the congregants together. He announces that YHWH has broken the "yoke" of the king of Babylon, that the "vessels of the LORD's house" will be returned "within two years" (v. 3), and that the captive exiles will soon return to Judah (v. 4).

All eyes turn to Jeremiah as he responds (in today's text) something like this: "Amen! Let it be so. We have a long heritage of prophets who have addressed the terrifying realities of war. Unfailingly, they have prayed for the peace of Jerusalem. If a prophet of peace proclaims God's bona fide truth, then you will see it come to pass. However, if it is not God's truth, then beware of comforting words from

Jeremiah 28:5-9

Theological Perspective

is not an insurance policy that kicks in automatically when you think you need deliverance from hardship. No, this is a faithfulness rooted in an ongoing, living relationship that requires asking, what is God's will today? God's will cannot therefore be discerned by looking at the past in a simplistic way. God's faithfulness remains the same, but the manifestation of that faithfulness may look very different today from the way it looked yesterday.

The difference between the messages of Hananiah and Jeremiah is thus far more than the difference between a message of prosperity and a message of doom. They operate with fundamentally different understandings of God and God's covenantal faithfulness. It may have been possible for the king to choose rightly—he did not have to wait for history to be the final arbiter of truth. Careful consideration of history and the way in which God acts might have steered the king away from a prosperity theology that promised good news rooted in a simplistic understanding of God's grace.

Like the people of Jeremiah's time, we too are often faced with the question, how do we choose between conflicting truth claims? This question becomes especially important in times of historical crisis. For believers, this question takes on a special urgency as they struggle to discern the will of God for their own lives, as well as for the church, their nation, and indeed the world. Jeremiah does not offer us a recipe for avoiding disaster and ultimately leaves it to history to decide. He does, however, help us to understand that the quick and easy answer, the popular position, the position held by the charming prophet, is not necessarily the true one. His message still rings true: beware of easy answers and simple solutions; and beware of resting on God's grace as if we own it.

Discerning the truth is not an easy matter, especially since we are so prone to be influenced by what we already want or what we think will serve our interests. What is necessary is a careful analysis of the tradition in which we stand and of the signs of the times that we can discern around us.

RACHEL SOPHIA BAARD

Pastoral Perspective

truth of these things as time passes, but that does not help us manage these days in which we live. Further, we know that historians will interpret the past in ways that may or may not shed light on truth. In fact, their interpretation may simply fan the flames of the old battles by interpreting the past through the lenses of the past. How then shall we live?

Whenever we are faced with such either/or decisions, real discernment begins not with more debate or panel discussions, not with another book read or another task force established. Discernment begins on our knees, perhaps even prostrate on the floor. Discernment begins in the posture of humility, because it is all too easy for us to assume that our certainty is born of God and that those who disagree are most certainly not of God.

It is not without irony that Hananiah uses the same kind of speech and prophetic actions that Jeremiah uses to make his case. It is no wonder that those who hear both men prophesy find themselves betwixt and between. In such a moment, it is not wise simply to choose a side. Instead, such moments compel us to invite God into our discernment, to listen more deeply than we have ever listened before, to pray that we may get far enough out of the way that God's will may find its way in.

While it almost always feels good to be on the side of those who are correct, of those who are part of the righteous cause, at times we are called to stand in what Parker Palmer calls "the tragic gap . . . the gap between what is and what could and should be."[2] Rather than moving too quickly to resolve the tension between the two perspectives, we are called to dwell in the covenantal love that brings God's will to life. Such gaps are not comfortable or easy, nor do they lead to quick resolution. They are, though, the means by which our broken and messy communities find their way closer to the realm God has longed for from the very beginning.

TRACE HAYTHORN

2. Parker Palmer, "The Broken-Open Heart," *Weavings* 24, no. 2 (March/April 2009): 7.

Exegetical Perspective

"cry 'Peace' when they have something to eat, but declare war against those who put nothing into their mouths" (Mic. 3:5). Even if Hananiah's motives are pure, his message stands against the preponderance of valid prophetic witness from the past that has announced "war, famine, and pestilence" in so many settings to so many audiences.

Jeremiah's appeal to the tradition goes beyond his general reference to previous prophets, moreover, to what the Torah presents as the Mosaic paradigm of prophecy. In Deuteronomy 18:20–22, Moses relates God's instruction for discerning false prophecy: if "the thing does not take place or prove true [lit. "come" (to pass)], it is a word that the LORD has not spoken." This is the criterion to which Jeremiah makes appeal: "when the word of that prophet comes true" [lit. "in the coming of the word (to pass)"] (v. 9). Fateful choices will be made in the interval—whether to serve Nebuchadnezzar quietly, in compliance with Jeremiah's words, or to find opportunities for resistance, following Hananiah—but the truth of the message will be demonstrated only by events.

In the sequel to this dramatic encounter (vv. 12–16), God confirms Jeremiah's doubts in an oracle. Hananiah has broken a wooden yoke only to forge an iron one (cf. Deut. 28:48), not only for Judah but for all of the nations who have been conspiring against Babylon. Hananiah, in fact, has not been *sent* by the LORD; but now, with an ironic use of the same Hebrew word, Jeremiah proclaims that Hananiah will be *sent off* the face of the earth (28:16). Two months later, Hananiah is dead. No explanation is given, but the words of Moses are fulfilled (Deut. 18:20: "that prophet shall die"), and Jeremiah is vindicated.

Why does Jeremiah waver in the midst of this contest, leaving the field to his adversary? Perhaps Reinhold Niebuhr is right to suggest that all true prophets stand ready to hear a new word from the Lord: "All of us will always have something of the false prophet in us, wherefore we ought to speak humbly. . . . Thus the Church can disturb the security of sinners only if it is not itself too secure in its belief that it has the word of God. The prophet himself stands under the judgment which he preaches. If he does not know that, he is a false prophet."[2]

JAMES T. BUTLER

Homiletical Perspective

a prophet who announces popular news which the crowds love to hear" (vv. 6–8).

Maybe it is Jeremiah's hard words that infuriate Hananiah. Maybe it is his body language, standing there in his crazy yoke. Whatever it is, Hananiah grabs the yoke from the neck of Jeremiah and physically smashes it to the floor of the temple. He then declares that, in this way, YHWH "will break the yoke of King Nebuchadnezzar from the neck of all the nations within two years" (28:11).

In a gesture of steeled nonviolence, Jeremiah walks silently out of the temple. However, one cannot but hear the immutable message ringing beneath his hushed steps: "Beware of any voice who will sell the soul in order to announce good news that makes for a popular pastor and prophet. There is a critical cost for peace. Peace requires soul justice and social justice!"

Several years ago, in a national urban ministry conference, one of the keynote speakers made this unforgettable statement, which seemed almost like a sidebar: "There are two great pathologies in our culture today. One of them is denial. The only antidote for denial is radical truth-telling. The other great pathology is despair. The only antidote for despair is radical hope, grounded in community."[2] I have never recovered from those breath-giving words. I hope I never do!

Is this Jeremiah text not a critical voice for every preacher and congregation, particularly those of us who would seek to announce comfort at the expense of announcing the cost of peace and justice? It invites us to become bold instruments of "radical truth-telling" and "radical hope," both of which are at the heart of God's radical dream for all of humanity.

DOUGLASS M. BAILEY

---

2. Reinhold Niebuhr, "The Test of True Prophecy," in *Beyond Tragedy: Essays on the Christian Interpretation of History* (New York: Charles Scribner's Sons, 1937), 110.

2. Walter Brueggemann, at "The City of God for American Cities: Reinventing the Urban Church,' June 2005, convened and led by the Center for Urban Ministry, Inc.

Psalm 89:1-4, 15-18

¹I will sing of your steadfast love, O LORD, forever;
  with my mouth I will proclaim your faithfulness to all generations.
²I declare that your steadfast love is established forever;
  your faithfulness is as firm as the heavens.

³You said, "I have made a covenant with my chosen one,
  I have sworn to my servant David:
⁴'I will establish your descendants forever,
  and build your throne for all generations.'"   *Selah*
. . . .
¹⁵Happy are the people who know the festal shout,
  who walk, O LORD, in the light of your countenance;
¹⁶they exult in your name all day long,
  and extol your righteousness.
¹⁷For you are the glory of their strength;
  by your favor our horn is exalted.
¹⁸For our shield belongs to the LORD,
  our king to the Holy One of Israel.

Theological Perspective

How should we read Psalm 89, recognizing it as Scripture for both Jews and Christians? In the theological perspective on Psalm 69 (pp. 152–56), I have offered John Calvin's reading of the Psalms as a model. Here I join Calvin's reading with a theological-critical reading by J. Clinton McCann Jr.[1]

The psalm can be divided into three sections: verses 1–18 are a hymn of praise to YHWH, verses 19–37 an oracle from God, and verses 38–51 a shocking lament. The three sections are held together by the repetition of two crucial characteristics: *hesed*, the "steadfast love" of YHWH (vv. 1–2, 14, 24, 28, 33, 49) and God's "faithfulness" (vv. 1–2, 5, 8, 14, 24, 28, 33, 37, 49). In the first two sections, the sovereignty of God (vv. 5–18) is placed in parallel with the Davidic monarchy (vv. 19–37), reminding us of the covenant with David and his household in 2 Samuel 7.

Then, in verses 38–51, God's love and faithfulness are called into grave doubt by the crisis of Jerusalem's destruction in 587 BCE and the apparent end of the Davidic monarchy. How could God's

1. John Calvin, *Commentary on the Book of Psalms*, trans. James Anderson (Grand Rapids: Eerdmans, 1949), 3:417–59; J. Clinton McCann Jr., "The Book of Psalms: Introduction, Commentary, and Reflections," in *The New Interpreter's Bible* (Nashville: Abingdon Press, 1994), 4:641–82. Page citations of Calvin are in parentheses.

Pastoral Perspective

"God's steadfast love endures forever," begins Psalm 118, a phrase used in many liturgies throughout the Christian church, particularly as part of Lent and Holy Week. The sentiment, however, is not expressed only in that psalm. The concept of steadfast love or loving-kindness (*hesed*) is present in much of the Hebrew Scriptures, and in particular this portion of Psalm 89. Almost exclusively a characteristic of God— the word is rarely used to describe humanity—*hesed* is found more than four hundred times in the Hebrew Scriptures. It is translated in a variety of ways including "mercy," "great kindness," and "faithfulness," but in general, these definitions fail to reach the depth of the real meaning of *hesed*. The word signifies deep loyalty or devotion, care and concern for all people, and might be best expressed as loving-kindness, a phrase that attempts to get at the breadth of meaning.

In Psalm 89, *hesed* is the bedrock on which the entire psalm stands, especially the verses to be considered here. This psalm reflects the steadfastness of *hesed* not only in the actual use of the word in verses 1 and 2, but also in the covenantal language surrounding David's reign as king of Israel. God's loyal support for David is made clear in verses 3 and 4, particularly in the language of "all generations."

Often connected to 2 Samuel 7 and to David's desire to build a house for the ark of the covenant,

Exegetical Perspective

Psalm 89, located at the end of Book III of Psalms (Pss. 73–89), has often been classified as a royal psalm, even though it includes hymnic material (vv. 1–2, 5–18, in which this Sunday's lection is found), an oracle (vv. 3–4, 19–37), a lament (vv. 38–51), and a doxology (v. 52). Unifying the diverse genres of material are repeated themes such as "steadfast love" (*hesed*, vv. 1, 2, 14, 24, 28, 33, 49) and "faithfulness" (*'amuna*, vv. 1, 2, 5, 8, 14, 24, 33, 49), conveying the idea that God's governance is similar to that of the monarchy by paralleling the reign of the Davidic king (or lack thereof) with that of God. This paralleling also prepares readers for the extent of the crisis depicted in verses 38–51, a crisis that indicates that Psalm 89 was not recited as part of the coronations of the kings or their annual celebrations. Instead, the description of this crisis suggests the end of the Judean monarchy that came about with the destruction of Jerusalem in 587 BCE, or perhaps the defeat of an unidentified Judean king before 587 BCE, voicing his defeat in verses 47–51. Either of these circumstances could have provoked the writing of this psalm.

Along with Psalms 2 and 72, also classified as royal psalms, Psalm 89 contributes an understanding of the issues and concerns that the exile broached and that receive a response in the remainder of the

Homiletical Perspective

Like other royal psalms, Psalm 89 may have been used at the coronation of a king or possibly at annual celebrations of the king's reign. This psalm in particular may have been shaped by Israel's experience of exile and its aftermath. It was both read and heard as an articulation of the theological crisis posed by the exile (vv. 5–18). As in other texts in the historical books, the Davidic kingship represents the ideal kingship for readers/hearers and eventually points to the Messiah. The Davidic throne will last "for all generations" (vv. 1, 4).

While Psalm 89 implies the existence of the divine council, as does Psalm 82, it is indisputable that YHWH is the only real and effective God. Even the gods are to praise God for God's faithfulness (vv. 5, 8; Ps. 82). The rhetorical questions in verses 6–8 emphasize God's sovereignty in all the earth. Verses 9–14 respond to those questions by offering "a rousing affirmation of God's cosmic rule."[1]

The use of the pronoun "you" focuses attention on God (vv. 9a, 9b, 10a, 11b, 12a) and God's activities. God's rule in history is evidence of God's cosmic power. For the psalmist, "the whole world

---

1. J. Clinton McCann Jr., "The Book of Psalms: Introduction, Commentary, and Reflections," in *The New Interpreter's Bible* (Nashville: Abingdon Press, 1994), 4:1035.

Psalm 89:1-4, 15-18

Theological Perspective

covenant with David continue when the people have lost their God-given land, king, and temple in the exile? How could the people Israel endure when it appeared in the course of history that God himself had broken the very terms of the covenant?

The triple tragedy of destruction, dynastic fall, and exile called into question the very foundation of Israel's being. The late twentieth and early twenty-first centuries are such a time for the historic Protestant denominations. Our church-related institutions have been displaced from the centers of cultural and social influence. Established Protestants have become disestablished demographically, intellectually, and financially. Most of our congregations are small, and clergy are slipping into the lower middle class. A process of downsizing and reengineering our organizational structures that began in the 1970s continues with no positive end in sight. Many church-related colleges, universities, and seminaries have traded their historic identities for more marketable personas. Church executives speak of a postdenominational era, and a spiritual malaise characterizes our solemn assemblies.

During the same period, religious right-wing movements have risen to international prominence. More shallow forms of individualistic piety and consumer-driven church affiliation are celebrated as the future of the faith. Parents wonder, will our children and grandchildren share the faith of their mothers and fathers? The global economic recession leaves us wondering whether God has a recovery plan for our denominations, congregations, and church-related institutions of education. Is God perhaps covering us with shame like the monarchy of Judah (v. 45)?

The reformer John Calvin (1509–1564) also lived in an age when the future of Christianity was in peril. In Psalm 89 he found both the encouragement to pray in light of God's providence in history and the psalmist's complaint that "God, as if he had forgotten the covenant, abandoned his Church to the will of her enemies, and, in the midst of strange disaster and mournful desolation, withheld all succor and consolation" (3:417).

Calvin was a realist about the spiritual life. To be numbered among the people of God's covenant was no guarantee of material or spiritual abundance. He notes that Psalm 89 begins not with the lament but praising the mercies of YHWH. "If when we set about the duty of prayer some despairing thought, at the very outset, presents itself to us, we must forcibly and resolutely break through it, lest our hearts faint and

Pastoral Perspective

this psalm can be heard as a companion to David's prayer. It may also bring to mind David's dancing before the ark in triumph as he brings it into the city (2 Sam. 6:12–16). The connection between Psalm 89 and 2 Samuel 7 reminds us of the importance of the psalms in the kingship of David, whether or not he is their author.

This psalm, particularly this portion of it, was likely used as part of special festivals. As one of the royal psalms, it would have been used for particularly important state events such as a coronation.[1] It also points specifically to the closeness of the relationship between David and God, where God is lifted up and praised, so that listeners are reminded of the covenant that is meant to last for "all generations."

While this language links David's kingship to the reign of God, much of the remainder of the psalm is filled with lament at God's perceived distance from the chosen people. Because of this disparity, there may be some question as to the unity of the psalm; it contains both hymnic and oracular components and so may be a composite of multiple writings.

Is that disparity actually a problem? Certainly for biblical scholars questions about authorship are important, but most people live a life filled with disparate elements. For each of us, there is excitement at some aspect of life, disappointment or even lament at another. In the portion to be considered here, we as believers are reminded of the constancy of God's love and our call to worship God.

For us the idea of *hesed* is overwhelming. We cannot fathom such loving-kindness as coming from God. We liken it to the love of a parent for a child, but human parents struggle, not necessarily with loving their children, but certainly with the constancy and faithfulness that is often tested. Especially now, in a world that seemingly changes moment by moment, the idea of the steadfastness, the deep commitment of this love is nearly inconceivable. Another aspect of *hesed*, that of faithfulness, is also brought to bear here. The praise of God's faithfulness to God's chosen people is shared from generation to generation, and the culture of worship by God's people is even more firmly established.

In these latter verses, we are encouraged to yield to God's sovereignty and to rejoice in the loving-kindness found there. Even in the midst of lifting up David and his kingship, we are reminded that David is not king without God, and that those who

---

1. James L. Crenshaw, *The Psalms: An Introduction* (Grand Rapids: Eerdmans, 2001), 6.

Exegetical Perspective

Psalms (Pss. 90–150) about God's continuing sovereign reign, despite circumstances that suggest otherwise. Verses 5–18 also begin to provide such a response by connecting God's sovereignty to the monarchy's sovereignty, with verses 5–13 evoking praise for God's faithfulness and unsurpassable sovereignty, verse 14 providing the climax, and verses 15–18 providing the people's suitable response to God's sovereign governance.

Throughout verses 9–13, the pronoun "you" (vv. 9a, 9b, 10a, 11b, 12a) and the pronominal suffix "your" (vv. 10b, 11a, 12b, 13a, 14a, 15b) emphasize how God acts by ruling, stilling, crushing, scattering, founding, and creating. God's reign is also stressed by referring to God's triumph (1) over the Egyptians during the exodus through God's "mighty arm" (*bizroa' 'uzzeka*, v. 10b; *zeroa' im-gebura*, v. 13) and "right hand" (*yemineka*, v. 13), also mentioned in Exodus 15; and (2) over the forces of chaos depicted as "Rahab" (*rahab*, vv. 9–10a), who represents an ancient mythological monster or sea dragon that God slew in the cosmological battle prior to creation (Job 9:13; 26:12–13; Ps. 87:4; Isa. 30:7; 51:9–10).

Rahab may also be a poetic name for Egypt here, but it is nonetheless meant to evoke praise for God's triumph over the primeval dragon as well as God's victory over Egypt on behalf of the Israelites. In both cases, the psalmist accentuates God's majesty and strength despite the current historical circumstances.

Verse 14 provides the climax of the psalmist's praise to God. Praise to God has begun with the psalmist's singing and speaking about God's steadfast love and faithfulness (vv. 1–2) and then continued by evoking the heavens to praise God as greater than all heavenly and earthly beings (vv. 5–7). The mountains, Tabor and Hermon, where people worship other gods,[1] have also offered praise to God (v. 12b). Verse 14 praises God by again extolling God's faithfulness and steadfast love (as in vv. 1, 2, 5, 8), but especially by mentioning righteousness and justice as forming the basis of God's governing. In Psalm 33:5 and Psalm 97:2b (see also Pss. 96:13 and 98:9), righteousness and justice are similarly associated with God's sovereign reign.

In this psalm in particular, however, "righteousness" (*sedeq*) and "justice" (*mispat*) are described as forming the "foundation of your [God's] throne" (*mecon kis'eka*, v. 14a). The lasting of David's throne "for all generations" (*ledor-wador*, v. 4), "as long as

Homiletical Perspective

belongs to God and God's creation will join in recognizing God's sovereignty."[2] Verses 15–18 describes the appropriate response to God's sovereignty in the form of celebration. This is a perfect homiletical point of entry to this psalm. The preacher can use a theme such as "something to shout about" and develop it accordingly. The focus verse is "Happy are the people who know the festal shout" (v. 15).

"Somber and sad" may be a better way to describe the national disposition as I write. In the year that United States President Barack Obama was inaugurated, the bottom fell out of the world economy, and persons in Europe, Asia, and Africa scrambled to prevent a total economic meltdown. People lost jobs that they never imagined would collapse or disintegrate. Factories, corporations, and small businesses were all affected by the near collapse of capital markets. Poor people got poorer, and even the rich felt the pinch. The soup lines at church were getting longer and longer, and the number of persons gathered around the door to ask for food more than doubled in the year following the collapse.

The faces of the people in line were devoid of life's luscious and fragrant smiles. Their expressions seemed to me like the personification of lament and defeat. So when I read the mixed messages inherent in this psalm, I understand the complexity and the dialectic of the human spirit. Lament and praise, sadness and celebration, joy and sorrow are part and parcel of being human.

The focus of verses 1–18 is the praise part of the psalm, as the antithesis to the lamentable woes of our human situation.

> I will sing of your steadfast love, O LORD, forever;
> with my mouth I will proclaim your faithfulness to
>   all generations. (v. 1)

An economic crisis, no more than a serious illness or a natural disaster, does not cancel out the sovereignty of God. Yes, we have suffered and we have been oppressed. The historical fact of nearly three hundred years of chattel slavery of African Americans, followed by systemic acts of injustice embedded in law and custom, cannot be denied. However, black people in the United States and many other oppressed people are not bitter and foaming at the mouth in anger and propagating violence and war.

---

1. See Artur Weiser, *The Psalms*, Old Testament Library (Philadelphia: Westminster Press, 1962), 592.

2. Ibid.

Psalm 89:1-4, 15-18

Theological Perspective

utterly fail" (3:419). Psalm 69 grew out of a struggle within the psalmist, who sought to encourage God's people: "it was not without a painful and arduous conflict that he succeeded in embracing by faith the goodness of God, which *at that time had entirely vanished out of sight*" (4:420, emphasis added).

The reformer applies the encouragement of Psalm 89 to the church in his own violent age, for he believed in the unity of God's covenant for both the children of David and Jesus' disciples. He signifies this by referring to both peoples of the covenant as "the Church." For "God did not enter into [the covenant] with David individually, but had an eye to the whole body of the Church, which would exist from age to age" (3:421). As a Christian reader of the psalm, Calvin does not conclude that the covenant with David ended with the destruction of the monarchy. For a future son of David would vindicate God's promise to the king and his household.

The anchor of Calvin's confidence in the covenant is the providence of God that he finds celebrated in verse 11: "the same God who had been the deliverer of the chosen people exercises supreme dominion over the whole world. From the fact that God created all things, [the psalmist] concludes, that it is He who actually presides over, and controls whatever takes place in heaven and in earth" (3:427). In our post-Holocaust world, some Jews and Christians wonder if "control" is the best metaphor for how God governs the process of world events. These psalm readers come closer to Calvin when he uses other metaphors for divine power: "faith ought to depend on the Divine promise . . . by which God is represented as coming forward and *alluring us to himself* by his own voice" (3:421, emphasis added). If God acts to lure the world and his people into covenant rather than impersonally control us, then history is a time of both tragic failure and future hope in divine-human relations.

ROBERT A. CATHEY

Pastoral Perspective

recognize the sovereignty of God are rewarded. For Christians, this understanding brings to mind the life and teachings of Jesus, as well as the call to live a life in accordance with God's will. Just as the life, lineage, and kingship of David point us to the sovereignty of Jesus as the Christ, so Psalm 89 supports the Messiah in the same way.

For many, the idea of the sovereignty of God is a simple matter; others reject the language of kingship as too hierarchical. The kingship of God, however, seems to set most human hierarchy on its head. In the example of God's selection of David as king, God has chosen the least likely candidate. David, either as shepherd or as king, is not the kind of leader who looks good on camera or speaks like the greatest of orators. Instead, he is simply God's chosen one—the one who seems the most unlikely at the time, yet who plays an integral role in the larger story.

That larger story subverts the human idea of what kingship is and reminds us that it is God's infinite generosity and loving-kindness, *hesed*, that allows us to live and move and have our being. The vision of that larger story supersedes time and removes believers from the needs and constraints of time. The psalmist begins by saying, "I will sing of your steadfast love, O Lord, forever; with my mouth I will proclaim your faithfulness to all generations."

These words were not only written for those who may have sung the liturgy in the temple, but also remind us that God's great loving-kindness, *hesed*, will continue toward all those who will walk in the light for ages to come.

KATE COLUSSY-ESTES

Exegetical Perspective

the heavens endure" (*kimey samayim*, v. 29), continuing forever "like the sun" (*kassemes negeddiy*, v. 36)—the fulfillment of this promise in the covenant with King David (v. 3) is rooted in the righteousness and justice that undergird God's throne.

In verses 15–18, the psalmist turns to provoke the people to praise God, mentioning that their continual ("all day long," *kol-hayyon*, v. 16a) adoration means that they are "blessed" (NIV; NRSV "happy," *'asrey*, v. 15a). They are blessed as they join in the festal activities (v. 15a) celebrating God's enthronement (Ps. 47:5; see also Ps. 33:3), and as they seek to obey God by walking in God's "presence" (NIV; NRSV countenance, lit. "face," *panim*, v. 15b). In addition, they are blessed as they praise God's essence (lit. "name," *sem*, v. 16a).

The psalmist parallels the people's praise of God's name (v. 16a) with their praise of God's righteousness (v. 16b) to express again how integral "righteousness" (*sedeq*) is in God's reign. The psalmist elaborates on God's presence among the people by attributing their "glory" (*tip'eret*) and "strength" (*'uzzamo*) to God (v. 17). More importantly, the favorable status of their king, mentioned here in the imagery of a "horn" (*qarnenu*, v. 17b; see also Pss. 75:10, 92:10), emphasizes that their leader's strength depends on God.

Verse 18 accentuates the way in which the king's leadership depends on God by stating that the king "belongs" to God (literally, "is of YHWH"), but also stresses that the king provides the people protection by referring to him as "our shield" (*maginnenu*, v. 18). This shift prepares readers for the extensive discussion of the Davidic Messiah in verses 19–37, which elaborate on the promises and the covenant that God made with David, especially the continuance of the Davidic line.

Unfortunately, the lectionary reading does not include verses 38–51. The psalmist does not at all prepare readers for the turnabout of events in verses 38–51, in which the psalmist laments that God has rejected the Davidic king, renounced the covenant made with him, and withheld support during battle with enemies.

EMILY R. CHENEY

Homiletical Perspective

O Lord God of hosts,
> who is as mighty as you, O Lord?
> Your faithfulness surrounds you.
You rule the raging of the sea; when its waves rise,
> you still them. (vv. 8–9)

Instead, black people are singing praise to God and proclaiming God's faithfulness and God's sovereign power. This is almost unbelievable—inexplicable on one level and fully understandable on another. It is an "in spite of" theology that understands God as a God who, in the language of the black church tradition, "may not come when you want Him, but is always on time." God is an on-time God, even if it takes hundreds of years for the shackles of slavery to be loosed and unjust laws overturned.

You crushed Rahab like a carcass;
> you scattered your enemies with your mighty arm.
The heavens are yours, the earth also is yours;
> the world and all that is in it—you have founded
> them. (vv. 10–11)

As Christians who live in hope that justice and righteousness will ultimately prevail, we also believe that in spite of the condition of the economy, in spite of joblessness, in spite of the stress and distress that engulf us, in spite of the dark pall of clouds that like smoke have obstructed our view of the sun's bright rays of a new day on the horizon, we still have something to shout about.

Righteousness and justice are the foundation of your
> throne;
> steadfast love and faithfulness go before you.
Happy are the people who know the festal shout,
> who walk, O Lord, in the light of your countenance. (vv. 14–15)

Yes, we can celebrate and shout, not because of what we have endured, but because of who God is. We have something to shout about today, and it does not have much to do with us or what we have done. It has nothing to do with our achievements, nothing to do with our accomplishments, nothing to do with our righteousness, nothing to do with us at all. It has everything to do with the sovereignty of God. Because God is God, we can shout. God's sovereignty alone gives us hope, and that hope alone is reason to shout and celebrate.

JAMES HENRY HARRIS

Romans 6:12-23

¹²Therefore, do not let sin exercise dominion in your mortal bodies, to make you obey their passions. ¹³No longer present your members to sin as instruments of wickedness, but present yourselves to God as those who have been brought from death to life, and present your members to God as instruments of righteousness. ¹⁴For sin will have no dominion over you, since you are not under law but under grace.

¹⁵What then? Should we sin because we are not under law but under grace? By no means! ¹⁶Do you not know that if you present yourselves to anyone as obedient slaves, you are slaves of the one whom you obey, either of sin, which leads to death, or of obedience, which leads to righteousness? ¹⁷But thanks be to God that you, having once been slaves of sin, have become obedient from the

Theological Perspective

The lectionary breaks the sixth chapter of Romans into two sections, verses 1b–11 and verses 12–23. These two parts have sometimes been mapped onto doctrines of justification and sanctification. The text seems to invite this mapping: in most English translations, the words "justification" and "sanctification" show up throughout the chapter. It seems reasonable to associate verses 1–11 with justification, as it is full of indicative statements about God's work of reconciliation. Classic Protestant accounts of justification have defined it as God's declaration that a sinner is righteous—not because of anything the sinner has done, but because of God's gracious decision to count the righteousness of Jesus Christ as belonging to the sinner. This imputed righteousness puts the accent on God's initiative in the work of justification, and it fits with the emphasis on God's action in the first part of chapter 6.

The second half of chapter 6—full of imperative exhortations to righteousness—seems to fit with sanctification, the process of regeneration by which a sinner becomes not just counted as righteous, but actually transformed for holy living. The associations of the two parts of the chapter with justification and sanctification also have fit with Protestant tendencies to speak of the two doctrines in sequence, as if justification somehow precedes sanctification.

Pastoral Perspective

The great idol of the modern age is personal independence. In the United States, we want health care without restrictions, wages without taxes, cell-phone plans without limits. We are heavily invested in the illusion that we think for ourselves, choose for ourselves, and do for ourselves. This makes today's passage from Paul's Letter to the Romans both offensive and essential. It is a word we and our people need to hear.

There is one serious obstacle in this passage that the preacher must negotiate: the word "slavery." Paul lived in an age where the relationship between slave and master needed no explanation; it was understood and accepted by all. In our day and age, the word "slavery" calls to mind 300 years of social sin and evil, and we want nothing to do with it. What does Paul mean when he says we are slaves? He is really driving toward the idea of ultimate allegiance, loyalty, obedience, and service. To be a slave, as Paul understands it, is to surrender your life to the control of another. When slavery is defined in this way, it turns out we are all slaves of one sort or another.

A friend of mine is a slave to fashion, and fashion is a fickle master indeed. Every season brings a new set of requirements, new clothing and accessories to be purchased, new trends to be adopted. Sometimes she looks fabulous; other times she looks ridiculous;

heart to the form of teaching to which you were entrusted, [18]and that you, having been set free from sin, have become slaves of righteousness. [19]I am speaking in human terms because of your natural limitations. For just as you once presented your members as slaves to impurity and to greater and greater iniquity, so now present your members as slaves to righteousness for sanctification.

[20]When you were slaves of sin, you were free in regard to righteousness. [21]So what advantage did you then get from the things of which you now are ashamed? The end of those things is death. [22]But now that you have been freed from sin and enslaved to God, the advantage you get is sanctification. The end is eternal life. [23]For the wages of sin is death, but the free gift of God is eternal life in Christ Jesus our Lord.

Exegetical Perspective

In a passage central to an understanding of Paul's overarching concerns in Romans, two cultural constants in the lives of the church members in Rome—the institution of slavery and the presence of the military—serve as vivid metaphors to help describe the true nature of belief and action. Since members of the church probably saw slaves and soldiers every day (and some members were slaves), these illustrations must have been very meaningful.

In regard to slavery, for example, Paul argues that all people, whether they are Christians or not, are dominated by someone or something other than themselves. For him, the twenty-first-century concept of self-control and personal determination is out of the question. His understanding of human nature is that men and women cannot help but be enslaved to someone or something—to a slave owner, to a theological or philosophical concept, to cosmic forces of evil (see Rom. 8:38–39; Eph. 3:10; 6:12; Col.1:16; 2:15), to powerful passions and desires (Rom. 6:11–14, 19), or, in a positive sense, to righteousness and the service of the living God (6:6, 14, 18–22). Today pastors might refer to this concept in terms of obsession, compulsion, or addiction. Until people exchange negative addictions for positive ones, they cannot truly live.

Throughout the Roman Empire, where slaves may have made up as much as one-third of the

Homiletical Perspective

The day's reading brings us into Paul's discussion as he is laying out an ethical framework for Christian communities liberated from the power of sin and death. Having argued in 6:1b–11 that baptized Christians have appropriated a new "identity" with the crucified and risen Lord, Paul moves in verse 12 from the indicative to the imperative, introducing an argument that the Christian's new identity now enables and therefore requires a new, liberating obedience to God.

Paul's transition must have been difficult enough for ancient readers, just warming up to his message of God's unconditional love. Our parishioners, shaped by the Enlightenment's exalted notions of the individual's capacity for unfettered reason and liberty, will be all the more likely to recoil when Paul frames his exhortation in terms of slavery. The appeal will be particularly difficult for those parishioners reading our civic creed of "life, liberty, and the pursuit of happiness" as establishing unchecked personal freedom as the prerequisite for the happiness they pursue. As the lectionary nestles our reading after Memorial Day and Flag Day and just before the Fourth of July, lectionary preachers may use Paul's argument in sermons helping parishioners to rethink the consequences of arbitrary freedom and to reexamine just what values we are lifting up on our national holidays.

Romans 6:12-23

Theological Perspective

Sequential accounts of the doctrines have had great pedagogical and polemical importance through the centuries. They make clear that we do not "earn" our justification. Righteous living is not the condition of reconciliation with God, but the content and consequence of that reconciliation. Sequential accounts also manage to hold together a gospel declaration of God's initiative in salvation with a gospel imperative for holy living. Sequential accounts locate sanctification as a free, joyful response to God's prior gift of justification. Because God has reconciled us to Godself and all creation, we can and do pour out lives of praise, service, and witness. God justifies, and we come to sanctified life in response.

Although the sequential account can lead us deep into bottomless truths, the idea that justification precedes sanctification should be held loosely and used always with pastoral wisdom. John Calvin, often cited as a source for a sequential account, stresses in his commentary on Romans 6 that "both parts of redemption"—justification and sanctification—should be understood "under the name of *grace*."[1] If justification and sanctification are useful tools for understanding the work of God, a unifying grace offers a more basic category. So a sequential account of grace should not be allowed to harden into an order of salvation that gives stages of reconciliation experienced by every believer and found in every chapter of Scripture. In particular, the sequential account should not determine our reading of Romans 6:12–23 such that we read these verses as relating *only* to sanctification.

Reading verses 1–11 as about justification and verses 12–23 as about sanctification misses the details of both passages. It misses Paul's discussion of walking "in newness of life" in verse 4 and the account of mortification and regeneration—classic themes of sanctification—in verses 5–8. It also misses Paul's announcement of the baptized one's transfer from the dominion of sin to the dominion of grace—a good statement of justification—in verse 14. Talk of sanctification appears in the early part of the chapter, and talk of justification in the latter. A strictly sequential reading of the chapter will miss these rich details.

A hardened sequential proclamation of justification and sanctification can also miss the complex realities of human lives. Serene Jones asks what happens when the story of justification followed by

Pastoral Perspective

sometimes she looks uncomfortable. Nevertheless, she has pledged her allegiance to *Vogue* and takes her orders from its editor.

Some people are slaves to physical fitness, arranging their lives and relationships around trips to the gym and rigorous workouts. Some people have pledged their allegiance to personal wealth and are guided by the whims of Wall Street. If you want to know who your master is, pay attention to what occupies your thoughts and how you spend your time and money. We are all serving something or someone. This passage invites us to ask the question, whom do you serve?

Paul sees only two possible masters: righteousness (God) or sin (everything else). He sees nothing wrong with having a master—everyone has one. It is *whom* you serve that makes the difference. New Testament scholar David Bartlett describes it this way: "There are loyalties that liberate."[1] The only way to win is to surrender to God. As an old hymn says, "Make me a captive, Lord, and then I shall be free."[2]

When I was a teenager, I had a creative way to keep myself out of trouble. When friends would call and ask me to do something I knew was questionable, I found a way to say no without losing face or popularity. I would ask my mother's permission, but add, "I need you to tell me no." She would say no, so I could say to my friends, "My mom won't let me go." As a teenager, surrendering control to my mother allowed me to do the right thing without a struggle. This is the strange yet wonderful logic of Paul's theology of salvation. God is on our side and has our best interests at heart. If we devote ourselves to God's will, God will lead us to abundant life.

There is another message implicit in this Romans passage that Christians need to hear: we are not equal to God. For decades, mainline Christianity has been chipping away at divine transcendence. These days, many thinking people view Jesus less as Lord and Savior and more as wise sage and role model. I think this post-Enlightenment correction was a natural and necessary response to some versions of the Christian faith that depicted Jesus as an arbitrary judge for an angry Father God, but the pendulum has swung too far, in my opinion. My denomination's most recent hymnal has a clear theological preference for nontranscendence, which means that Jesus (read: God) does not stand over us but is,

---

1. John Calvin, *Commentary upon the Epistle of Saint Paul to the Romans*, trans. Christopher Rosedell, ed. Henry Beveridge (Edinburgh: Calvin Translation Society, 1844), 159, emphasis original.

1. David L. Bartlett, *Romans*, Westminster Bible Companion (Louisville, KY: Westminster John Knox Press, 1995), 65.
2. George Matheson, "Make Me a Captive, Lord," 1890.

population, slavery was a constant pernicious force. Some people were born as slaves, some were sent into slavery through military conquest, and some even sold themselves to pay off debts. Paul understands it as given and does not question its justness or morality (in Philemon, for example). In various New Testament passages he and other writers acknowledge that some church members are actually enslaved. Although they are encouraged to be content with their lot, their owners are ordered to treat them with Christian charity as brothers and sisters (Eph. 6:5–9; Col. 3:22–24; 1 Tim. 6:1–2; Phlm. 16).[1]

In Romans, the inevitability of slavery is discussed in terms of *dominion*, a word that denotes ownership, mastery, sovereign rule, lordship, or government control. In 5:14, for example, sin is described as a power that dominated human spiritual life during the long period between Adam and Moses. Because of the one man, Adam, sin enslaved all of humanity in its negative grip, and it will not be completely divested of power until death itself is destroyed (5:18–21; see also 1 Cor. 15:25, 28).

In Romans 6:12–13, Paul is especially concerned with the control that sin has over the ethical behavior of believers: "Do not let sin exercise dominion in your mortal bodies, to make you obey their passions." Here the "mortal body" (Gk. *thnētos*) refers to human nature and human anatomy, both of which are perishable. Because the mortal body is especially vulnerable to temptations and immoral behavior, this corruptible nature that dies must be infused by God's Spirit so it can live (Rom 8:11).

As Paul puts it elsewhere, the perishable body must put on imperishability, the mortal, immortality (1 Cor. 15:53). Our sinful nature must die "so that the life of Jesus may be made visible in our mortal flesh" (2 Cor. 4:11). When human beings are slaves to sin, they are captured by forces that cause them be controlled by "passions" (v. 12) and the weakness of the flesh (5:6; 8:3, 26; 1 Cor. 15:13). These behaviors are contrary to God's will, activities like undisciplined partying, drunkenness, sexual promiscuity, lewdness (Rom. 13:13–14; Gal 5:16–20; Col. 3:5–10; 1 Thess. 4:3–5). They do not simply need to be controlled or curbed to make things better; they must be eliminated, crucified, put to death.

For Paul, the change from sinful behavior to Christian discipleship is more than attitude adjustment or

Freedom from or Freedom For? Most of our parishioners probably think of freedom in terms of "freedom from": freedom from the tyranny of a distant crown; freedom from governmental meddling in how we speak, associate, and worship; or even freedom from meaningless jobs, middling marriages, or conventional mores. Their measure of freedom is the degree to which they are free from constraints.

Plainly, Paul would not agree. For Paul, "I want what I want when I want it" thinking would have been anathema, a certain prescription for falling back under the dominion of sin, subjected to the tyranny of our passions (v. 12). As theologian Rudolph Bultmann writes, the illusory freedom to do whatever we want merely "delivers us up to our drives, to do in any moment what lust and passion dictate. . . . Genuine freedom is freedom . . . which withstands the clamor and pressure of momentary motivations."[1] This genuine freedom is possible only when conduct is determined by a motive that transcends the present moment, which is obedient to a higher call: a call from God.

Paul understands well the appeal of freedom, but he also understands that mere "freedom from" this law or that obligation never leads to flourishing life unless it is linked with "freedom for" a higher, heartfelt commitment. As Paul emphasizes in verse 17, the very reason God liberates us from sin is so that we may "become obedient from the heart to the form of teaching to which [we are] entrusted."

Paul's view is entirely consistent with, rather than contrary to, our nation's earliest conceptions of freedom. As Alexis de Tocqueville writes, "I think I see the whole destiny of America embodied in the first Puritan who landed on these shores."[2] In that first Puritan, de Tocqueville sees "freedom from" popes, archbishops, and kings exercised as "freedom for" covenantal love of God and neighbor. A careful reading of our national hymns reveals the same dynamic: "Confirm thy soul in self-control, thy liberty in law. . . . who more than self their country loved, and mercy more than life! America!"[3]

Present Arms! From the very first chapter of Romans, Paul describes behavior as binary. The human is either God-centered or self-centered (1:21–25). God and perdition are linked by a one-lane road: we are

---

1. See the studies by James S. Jeffers, *The Greco-Roman World of the New Testament Era* (Downers Grove, IL: InterVarsity, 1999), 220–36, and Robert Jewett, *Romans: A Commentary*, Hermeneia (Minneapolis: Fortress Press, 2007), 51–53.

1. Rudolph Bultmann, *Jesus Christ and Mythology* (New York: Charles Scribner's Sons, 1958), 41.
2. Alexis De Tocqueville, *Democracy in America*, trans. George Lawrence, ed. Francis Bowen (original 1835; New York: Doubleday Anchor Books, 1969), 290.
3. Katherine Lee Bates, "O Beautiful for Spacious Skies," written 1893, in *Selected Poems* (Boston: Houghton Mifflin, 1930).

Romans 6:12-23

Theological Perspective

sanctification comes to a woman whose life is marked not by pride—by too much self-assertion—but, rather, by a tendency to give herself to the definition of the powers and people around her. She might find herself unable to identify with the story, and therefore think herself left outside the gospel.

She might also identify with the story, embrace the shattering effect of justification, and hear encouragement to further dissolve herself in relations and institutions around her. The sermon would then call her to deepen the patterns that keep her from walking in newness of life. However, Jones argues, "with sanctification at the beginning, the first word to meet the woman who enters the doctrine of the Christian life is one that constructs her, giving her the center and substance she needs to become the subject then judged and graciously forgiven."[2] Sometimes the wise pastor will proclaim a grace that begins with sanctification.

Overidentifying verses 12–13 with sanctification can also miss the work of God in regeneration. The imperatives there stress human action, but sanctification—like justification—never happens without the power of God. There is a human role in justification, a place for faith, for assent, and there is a divine role in sanctification. The branches come to new life only through their connection with the vine.

Finally, overidentifying the imperatives of verses 12–23 with sanctification can suggest that sanctification is something we must be commanded to do, as if justification had been bought on credit, and now must be paid off with the hard work of holy living. The sanctified life is not an obligation placed on us because we have received the gospel. It is itself part of the gift of the gospel. Holiness is what we are made for. It is our deepest need and our highest joy. The best preaching will not impose sanctification as a grim set of imperatives to be pursued with gritted teeth. It will sing of the sweetness of sanctification, cultivating a taste for life abundant.

Freed from a smothering overassociation with sanctification, Romans 6:12–23 can sing songs of life in many different keys. The wise pastor will not miss the imperatives of this passage, but will let them speak of both justification and sanctification, always held together under the sign of grace.

TED A. SMITH

Pastoral Perspective

instead, our companion or our equal, someone who is there to help us make our independent decisions.

From Paul's point of view, this is nonsense. We are not independent players in this game; we have all declared for a team: "But now that you have been freed from sin and enslaved to God, the advantage you get is sanctification. The end is eternal life" (v. 22). Through baptism, we have become one with Christ. Our allegiance is to God, who stands with us precisely because God stands over us.

There is one more theme in this passage that has great preaching potential, the theme of living faith. Many young people have become disillusioned with organized religion because the church seems hypocritical—we say one thing and do another. It is a fair criticism. There is no lack of examples of good Christians who profess a faith that does not influence their lives. As a confirmation student told me, "They talk the talk but don't walk the walk."

Throughout chapter 6, Paul is encouraging Christians to walk the walk, to live for Christ, since they are now dead to sin. This is not something that happens automatically. It is a choice people have to make day by day: "No longer present your members to sin as instruments of wickedness, but present . . . your members to God as instruments of righteousness" (v. 13). Through baptism into Christ, God has created the possibility of our doing the right thing, but every Christian must choose whether or not he or she will do it. Our actions reveal our true allegiance and character. Paul puts it this way: "you are slaves of the one whom you obey" (v. 16); but I prefer the words of humorist Dave Barry, who once said, "A person who is nice to you, but rude to the waiter, is not a nice person."[3]

That is a message the church needs to hear.

SHAWNTHEA MONROE

---

2. Serene Jones, *Feminist Theory and Christian Theology: Cartographies of Grace* (Minneapolis: Fortress Press, 2000), 63.

3. Dave Barry, *Dave Barry Turns 50* (New York: Random House, 1998), 181.

behavior modification; it is a sign of the validity of the resurrection. Possibly rejecting the Platonic idea that the physical person with habits, desires, and passions is separated from the soul (the more spiritual part of human nature) at the time of death, Paul maintains that the mortal and immortal retain their unity as long as they are given eternal life through the power and resurrection of Christ. The end is not the separation of the essential parts of humanity. The end is continuity in the Spirit, the end is eternal life (v. 23).

The way in which this radical change is made possible is described in Paul's use of the second cultural metaphor, the military image of a soldier dressing for battle. "No longer present your members to sin as instruments of wickedness" but "present your members to God as instruments of righteousness" (v. 13, see v. 19). The NRSV misses the martial implications here since "instruments" in verse 13 does not convey an accurate sense of the Greek (*hopla*), "weapons, armor, shield, battle dress." This equipment is needed to protect "the members," that is, the vulnerable parts, the arms, legs, eyes, chest, sexual organs, and so forth.

When Paul says that the believer must not put on "instruments of wickedness" (v. 13) he means that in personal and cosmic battles against sin and death Christians cannot expect to win if they are dressed in destructive passions that weaken them. Instead, they should put on body armor described elsewhere in the New Testament: Christian soldiers dressed head to toe (Eph. 6:11–17), fighters putting on instruments of light (Rom. 13:12), believers with a two-fisted faith (2 Cor. 6:7), those possessing "power to destroy strongholds" (2 Cor. 10:4).

Paul's closing words carry this martial image to its conclusion. Just as soldiers know that they are risking their lives when they serve in the military, Christians need to face the fact that the payoff for serving sin is always death. If they prepare for battle with the protection and weapons of righteousness, however, nothing can prevent them from receiving their true compensation, eternal life in Christ Jesus the Lord.

EARL S. JOHNSON, JR.

heading toward God and life, or we are heading toward sin and death.

Here in chapter 6, Paul focuses first on getting us turned around and heading back toward God (justification, vv. 1b–11), and then on keeping us moving in the right direction (sanctification, vv. 12–23). In Paul's "already but not yet" eschatology, our inmost self may now be able to will the right (vv. 14, 17; 7:22), but it still must struggle against the temptations of our passions (v. 12).

Paul's central metaphor is enslavement. Like slaves in the ancient world, we have been transferred from our old master, sin, to our new master, God (vv. 17, 18, 22); and so our obedience must now turn from our old master to our new one (vv. 13, 14, 17, 19). Our parishioners may resist Paul's metaphor, but they will surely recognize his description of the human predicament, particularly when he pictures the humans as choosing either to present their members as "weapons" (an alternative translation of "instruments") of wickedness, sin, and impurity or to present their members as "weapons" of righteousness (vv. 13, 19).

Paul's argument is as grounded as the case against half-broken habits, as familiar as an alcoholic preserving abstinence to gain a five-year AA pin. While our parishioners will most easily recognize his argument as pertaining to our sexual organs, the dynamic works even if Paul means all the elements of the self that engage the world. When we present our sexual organs to promiscuity, our minds to vapid entertainment, our eyeballs to pornography, and our mouths to addictive substances, our own members become weapons against our better intentions. The wages we earn for this "presentation" are death (v. 23).

Of course, the same dynamic works in reverse. When we present these same members to self-control, they become weapons of righteousness, as resisting the temptation (suffering) "produces endurance, and endurance produces character, and character produces hope, and hope does not disappoint us, because God's love has been poured into our hearts through the Holy Spirit" (5:3–5). As that love pours into our hearts, our selves return to God-centered lives, an experience Paul understands as God's free gift of eternal life now, even as our hope points us to reunion with God at the end of the age (6:23).

HAROLD E. MASBACK III

Matthew 10:40-42

[40]"Whoever welcomes you welcomes me, and whoever welcomes me welcomes the one who sent me. [41]Whoever welcomes a prophet in the name of a prophet will receive a prophet's reward; and whoever welcomes a righteous person in the name of a righteous person will receive the reward of the righteous; [42]and whoever gives even a cup of cold water to one of these little ones in the name of a disciple—truly I tell you, none of these will lose their reward."

Theological Perspective

In just a few short sentences of power and compassion, we are challenged to think more deeply about what is meant by welcoming one another. It is only after doing so that we discover the reward that comes from the deep hospitality found in God's welcome of us. In today's reading, our theological focus is on compassionate welcome or hospitality as a form of service to Christ. Reviewing the list from verses 40–42, we realize that this welcome can and should be performed by us at any time and is not confined to large heroic acts by those eligible for sainthood. The simple, basic acts of kindness we perform in genuine welcome of one another are all that God asks of us. We must look around us to see who is in need and then do something about it.

Christian faith advocates compassionate welcome that encourages us to trust, to be open, to share, to eschew manipulating others, and to live a way of life that is beyond personal gain. We are also to be realistic about those things that distort and prevent us from the compassion described in last week's reading from Matthew. Indeed, the elements of our compassionate welcome are found in the paradox of our lives when human relationships of closeness, warmth, depth, and durability are also tinged with our alienation from each other.

Pastoral Perspective

My colleague at Yale Divinity School, the Irish liturgical theologian Siobhán Garrigan, tells a story from her travels around Ireland researching her book *The Real Peace Process*.[1] Arriving at a Presbyterian church in Northern Ireland, Siobhán was pleased to be greeted at the door by two women, church members, who seemed to invite her into conversation. Siobhán realized that these women were ushers of some sort, whose job it was to stand at the door of the church and interview newcomers as they arrived. They quietly asked her name and the first names of any other approaching strangers who wished to join in the morning worship.

Then Siobhán figured out what was happening. Hearing those names, the ushers would draw conclusions about the cultural and religious identity of each. Those with Protestant names were welcomed warmly and shown their seats. Those with apparently Catholic names, the Marias and the Catherines and the Patricks, were told that they were surely in the wrong church and sent on their way. I assumed that Siobhán must be referring to research done decades ago; surely no church would act in this way

1. Siobhán Garrigan, *The Real Peace Process* (London: Equinox Publishing, forthcoming).

Exegetical Perspective

This pericope is the concluding part of the Missionary Discourse in the Gospel of Matthew. It has a parallel at the end of the Q mission discourse (Luke 10:1–16), but not in the Markan mission discourse (Mark 6:7–13). After giving out various instructions to his disciples for their mission, including warnings of the dangers of persecution and suffering, the Matthean Jesus offers them final words of compensation and reward (*misthos*, v. 41). Matthew 10:40 has a close parallel in Luke 10:16, which means that the Q mission tradition already had the words of reward as its conclusion in its pre-Synoptic phase.

Matthew 18:5, which is taken from Mark 9:37, shows linguistic similarities to Matthew 10:40, but it probably came from a different source, since its reference is small children, not itinerant disciples. On the other hand, it is possible that Mark 9:37 is itself a modification of an earlier saying that originally had the disciples as its primary reference, like Matthew 10:40, but was later adapted to apply to small children.

The theme of the disciples' being received or rejected for their mission refers back to the main part of the Missionary Discourse (10:11–15) and is also related indirectly with the principle of *imitatio Christi*, one of the underlying principles of the theology of mission in Matthew's Gospel (cf. 10:24–25).

Homiletical Perspective

These verses conclude an extended discourse on discipleship and mission. The emphasis shifts from the trials of those sent out (10:16–39) to the responsibilities of those who host them (vv. 40–42). Within the logic of the narrative, these words are directed to the Twelve before they go out: Jesus and God stand in solidarity with them and the reception they will receive (v. 40). As readers we "overhear" this disclosure as exhortation and promise. If we "welcome" (show hospitality to) emissaries of Jesus in their great vulnerability, we can expect to share in their rewards. The description of these itinerants as "prophet," "righteous person," and "little ones" (vv. 41–42) may be stylistic emphasis, or they may designate different types of Christian missionaries known to the first readers of the Gospel.

The lection, repetitive despite its brevity, is transparently anchored in circumstances that offer no obvious analogical purchase for the contemporary congregation—a challenge for preaching. One strategy is to use the lection as an opportunity to preach a thematic sermon on hospitality. This injunction to host itinerant missionaries can be located within a larger biblical pattern of welcome to the vulnerable stranger (see, among others, Gen. 18:1–8; Lev. 19:33–34; Luke 24:29; Rom. 12:13; Heb. 13:2).

Matthew 10:40-42

Theological Perspective

Our will to achieve caring relationships is within our grasp, yet all too often, if left to our devices, we fall short of creating and nurturing the genuine relationships in which we develop into the people God calls us to be. Pride, ego, self-doubt, and their kin keep us from connecting with each other except in self-interested ways. Therefore we need God's embrace in our lives to live in this paradox and fulfill our faith, living in compassionate welcome with one another and extending genuine hospitality. In these four short verses, Jesus helps us steer away from distorting others and ourselves through false dependencies, unreasonable expectations, and unjustified hopes.

Compassionate welcome means approaching each other through God. This is how we recognize that genuine human relationships emerge from putting the grace-filled hospitality of God's love at the center of our lives and at the center of all our relationships. God's hospitality teaches us that close, loving, enduring relationships are to be valued along with distant, occasional, and abrasive ones—as difficult as the latter ones may be. This lively, and sometimes maddening, dynamic is the welcome Jesus speaks of in today's passage. Further, if we live into this welcome with each other, we will find the rich rewards of discipleship found in God.

As the preacher ponders how to connect the passage to today's hearers and doers, it may be wise to use part of the sermon preparation time to think through the ways in which compassionate welcome through hospitality works in a world that is shaped, in part, by varying oppressions and inequalities. How might we transcend orientations that make us participants in oppression? How might we become more sympathetic to and supportive of the efforts of oppressed people to accomplish social reforms—so that even an usher's greeting or a pastoral handshake becomes the *beginning* of radically changing our worlds to be more in line with God's realm?

It is important to acknowledge that in oppressive conditions, superficial hospitality alone is an insufficient response. The one who welcomes often continues to be at home and retains a good measure of control; this causes us to welcome those who are dispossessed, the little ones, into our own worlds on terms we ourselves have crafted. It is impossible to develop the reciprocal relationships expressed in this passage, for the host has near absolute control. Note that there is a difference between condescension and paternalism, and help people understand this crucial difference in thinking through the practice of genuine hospitality.

Pastoral Perspective

any longer. My hope was quickly dashed. This remains the current practice, Siobhán writes.

This is a story foreign to North Americans like me, I reasoned, because it is about a faraway congregation of Irish Presbyterians, who are nothing like us at all, still fighting their Protestant-Catholic battles. Luckily we have no such issues. Our society has moved past such discriminatory behavior. We have elected an African American president, after all, and knocked down all of the walls and boundaries. In our worshiping communities, everyone is welcome.

Confronted with the unsettling image of that Protestant church on an Irish hillside, we want immediately to dismiss such boundary keeping as abhorrent to the gospel. Perhaps, however, it is more familiar than we want to admit; a barring of the door may not be as unknown to us as we like to pretend. The churches that we know would never ask the name of a stranger in some covert attempt to find them out and send them off to where they belong.

Nevertheless, if we are to be honest about the church that we know, we would have to confess that, though we define our borders differently, we define them still—and more subtly.

We are curious about education and profession. In a church community like the one I know best, the higher the level of education, the warmer the community will be. While none will be turned away, we will tell ourselves that we simply have more in common with those who are like us. The implications of such questions are quite clear to all. Not so far, really, from deciding if the visitor's name is Protestant or Catholic in origin.

In other communities, the query will vary, from questions about neighborhood lived in to club memberships to schools that the children attend. All of this is considered within the realm of polite conversation. After all, will the uneducated truly feel uncomfortable in our parish? Will the less wealthy feel uncomfortable in another? Is there a dominant social or political perspective that one really needs to subscribe to, and that will prompt the community to be more open to the newcomer? Is there clarity about the norm for sexual identity or family model that really must be established before the doors of the church are flung wide open in welcome?

The Gospel lesson invites us to ask all of these questions about the quality of the welcome that we offer to one another within the body of Christ, the church. It goes on to suggest that while we might find a reward in gathering only with those whose names sound like our names, or whose education or

Unlike the immediately preceding passage, the promise of reward in this pericope is not phrased in eschatological language. Nevertheless, precisely because of this direct literary context, the present pericope may very well be interpreted in the eschatological sense by the intended audience. In 10:40 Jesus speaks only about the one who receives (*ho dechomenos*) the disciples, but what is not explicitly stated is just as clear. That is, the one who rejects the disciples of Jesus rejects Jesus, which amounts to rejecting God who sent Jesus. This point is made explicit in the Q mission discourse in Luke 10:16.

Verse 40 lays out the theme of the whole passage: the one who is sent represents the full presence of the one who sends. It corresponds to the Jewish principle of *shaliah* (the Hebrew equivalent of the Greek *apostolos*) attested later in *m. Ber.* 5:5, which says, "The emissary sent by a man [lit. belonging to a man] is like the man himself" (my trans.). The same principle is also cited in *b. Qidd.* 41b and *b. Sanh.* 110a. Both *m. Ber.* 5:5 and *b. Qidd.* 41b cite the *shaliah* principle in the context of discussing a *shaliah* who is sent by a congregation (*qahal*), not by an individual.

The cited principle itself refers to a person sent by another person. Since it is in the form of a maxim, the precise meaning of the Hebrew expression *kemoto* (like himself) in the cited *shaliah* principle cannot be determined. In that context, verse 40 is an application of such a principle to a concrete case of reward for receiving—and by implication, punishment for rejecting—the disciples of Jesus as his emissaries in this mission.

Verse 41 has no parallel in the Synoptic corpus and its origin is unknown. Whom the prophets (*prophētai*) and the just (*dikaioi*) refer to is also not clear. In the *Didache,* apostles (*apostoloi*) and prophets (*prophētai*) are used interchangeably as a reference to itinerant missionaries (11:4–6). Even though no direct literary dependency between the two documents can be established, one could say that in the Jewish Christian milieu, which Matthew and the *Didache* seem to share, prophets and the apostles were probably not sharply distinguished, especially when they were on their itinerant missions. On the other hand, we do not know whether the title *dikaios*, "just," in this verse is yet another designation for the missionaries.

Verse 42 is based on Mark 9:41, which is not part of the Markan mission discourse. Matthew changes the second-person-plural pronoun (*hymas*) of Mark 9:41 into "one of these little [*mikrōn*] ones." Matthew

This Jewish and Christian practice is in stark contrast to our own ideas about hospitality, which usually have nothing to do with strangers. We live in a culture that places great emphasis on making our houses comfortable and inviting, but the surge in "home improvement" has done more for the bottom line of Lowe's and Home Depot than it has for the actual practice of hospitality—even hospitality narrowly construed as gracious reception of those just like us. In the case of hospitality understood Christianly as welcoming the needy for the sake of their need, the situation is even more troubling. In the midst of a housing crisis, millions of carefully furnished guest bedrooms sit mostly forgotten until it comes time to dust. No wonder then that the fear of the stranger, the immigrant, the homeless is palpable in so much of our public discourse and policy.

Another and perhaps more adventurous approach is to stay closer to this text and see what happens. To begin, we can note that the hospitality the lection encourages is to be extended to missionaries—to those who come to us bearing the message of Christ. At first this seems like a nonstarter in the contemporary context. It was far easier for preachers before textual scholars convinced us that Matthew's "little ones" were not the needy in general, but traveling evangelists. The predicted "next Christendom" notwithstanding, how often does a congregation find itself in the position of hosting a travel-weary missionary come from distant lands to share the faith? If a guest speaker does come to town now and again, hospitality usually amounts to the arrangement of a suitable room in a convenient hotel.

What about the many "itinerants" that a congregation may encounter in the course of its various benevolence ministries? Perhaps the choice, between understanding the "little ones" as the poor and marginalized on the one hand, and kingdom missionaries on the other, is a false one after all. Is it possible to imagine the homeless or the chronically hungry as bearers of the Christian message who are in desperate need of our hospitality? Our immediate reaction is to insist on a clear distinction between those we understand as the objects of our charity and those who have something to share for the sake of our faith. How can someone be a missionary when they are not sponsored for such purposes by any institution? How can they be vulnerable traveling preachers when they almost certainly do not understand themselves in this way?

However, many of the people who hold no status in consumer society and come to us in need are, in

Matthew 10:40-42

Theological Perspective

One response from this heightened awareness is to realize that we must practice not only hospitality but also repentance. Turning from familiar behavior patterns that do not welcome others, we turn toward acts that signal our willingness to embrace and live the new ways of being found in God. In repentance, our positions of privilege are debunked, and these old ways of being "at home" are acknowledged as being morally bankrupt.

Although Jesus speaks of rewards in this passage, we should not offer compassionate welcome with the expectation that something will be returned to us. Love is not always met with love. Jesus is clear with his disciples that being his followers will be difficult at times and that they will suffer persecution. Sometimes love is met with crucifixion; yet we are called to love in the midst of hate—even in those times where it appears that hatred has won.

Compassion, then, grounds itself in a double paradox of love where love can lead to tribulation, which then leads us to greater love. With this in mind, we must remember that God's grace continues to act in and through the most hateful situations and that crucifixion is followed by resurrection. With compassionate welcome, Jesus calls us to put our love in jeopardy so that its blessings are made manifest in our lives and in the lives of others. We become the embodiment of Christian compassionate welcome that leads to hospitality in God's spirit of mercy.

The hospitality rooted in compassionate welcome is both a practice and a spiritual discipline in which we discover that by offering hospitality we may be welcoming something or someone new, unfamiliar, and unknown into our lives. This requires us to recognize another's gifts and vulnerabilities, the need for shelter and sustenance, and encourages us to open up our worldviews and perspectives as well as our hearts and souls.

As we extend hospitality to others, we may well find that we experience new insights and hear new stories of faith that redirect our perceptions. Such witness can stimulate our theological and spiritual imaginations so that we become new beings. This is the reward we will not lose.

EMILIE M. TOWNES

Pastoral Perspective

bank accounts resemble our education or our bank accounts, there is a cost to the kinds of exclusive behavior that too much of the church has tolerated for too long.

Jesus addresses the issue in the most personal of terms. He describes the love that families hold for one another, the tenderness with which we care for parents and for children. That tenderness and compassion must be our model for loving all who come into our lives, in Christ's name. When we welcome the stranger, we welcome none other than the Christ.

This may sound at first like terribly unsettling news. The ushers at the door of that Irish Presbyterian church behave as they do because they have been informed by a culture of distrust. Their desire to bar the door is born of the hope for security in their lives and in their tiny parish. We are more like them than we care to admit.

Now Jesus arrives and says, "Take that love for family, that love for your closest community, and extend it, extend it further and further still. Welcome in the stranger. Welcome in the one whose life you hardly understand. Not to change them, but simply because they too are God's."

Dare we preach that this is good news? We can imagine that it is good news to those who have been previously shut out, those who in the past have been made to feel unwelcome—if, that is, they are somehow willing still to join in our song of faith. Of course it will take more than a bit of grace for the stranger to be willing to risk approaching the church doors that have previously been closed.

No, the real good news is for those who have in the past guarded the door. Jesus insists that although we might pretend otherwise, we are not the gatekeepers of the community of God. We can bear that job no longer. Our work is to welcome, to offer an embrace when embrace is invited, and to give a cup of cool water for a hot summer day. Our reward, Jesus says, will be full indeed.

WILLIAM GOETTLER

picks up this phrase from Mark 9:42, which he preserves in Matthew 18:6, and uses it in this passage as a description of the disciples of Jesus as itinerant missionaries. This redactional work of Matthew seems to reflect a rather hostile environment, in which early Christian itinerant missionaries have to endure various kinds of hardship, including hunger and thirst. In that context, the Matthean Jesus says that whoever gives even a cup of cold water to one of these little ones will not lose their reward.

It has often been pointed out that Matthew uses a similar, if not the same, phrase, "one of the least [elachistōn] of these" in the parable of sheep and goats (Matt. 25:40, 45). Sometimes this association is used to qualify the meaning of the phrase "one of the least [elachistōn] of these" in the parable of sheep and goats as disciples of Jesus, which is a reasonable inference. Such a linguistic affinity, however, should not be used as a semantically limiting factor for the interpretation of the parable of sheep and goats. It should rather lead to a recognition that members of early Christian communities in general were indeed "little ones" and that wherever they came from, the disciples of Jesus were encouraged to identify themselves with the little ones in the world, who are also called to serve other such little ones in the world.

The present passage is primarily a promise of reward for those who receive the itinerant missionaries sent by Jesus. By implication, it is also an exhortation for the itinerant missionaries who are sent by early Christian communities in the name of Jesus not to despair, in spite of the opposition, persecutions, and sufferings that they might face, because their eschatological reward will be great. If the reward for those who receive the itinerant missionaries is great, how much greater will be the reward for the missionaries themselves in the eschatological kingdom of God!

EUGENE EUNG-CHUN PARK

fact, people of deep and abiding—or perhaps naive and childlike—faith. From medical missions in Central America to ministries of food and shelter in this country, I have often been struck by the vibrant faith of those who are served. By necessity more grounded in the finitude and fragility of the human situation, they seem more intuitive in their grasp of the gospel that we labor to believe. How confident and persuasive they can be as they bring their faith to speech! Articulate in praise, confession, and lament, they joyfully transgress the secular etiquette that has so completely silenced our testimony with scarcely a whimper of protest.

In the role of host we find ourselves strengthened in our own faith by these "little ones" who carry no money in their belt (10:9), no health insurance card in their purse. They cast themselves upon us in trust, and so create a cherished opportunity for the settled church to offer a simple cup of water to its Christ (8:20; 10:40–42; 25:40). Could it be that the Father knows that our hard-won second naiveté will never sustain us unless it is continually leavened with the more straightforward faith of these unlikely missionaries? If so, in practicing hospitality we also may find that we will not lose our reward (v. 42).

This approach to the text is perhaps best handled with a light touch. It probably will not hold up well under the determined scrutiny of hearers threatened by an overly strident presentation. If this way of seeing can be offered winsomely, though, even playfully, it may create space for the church to entertain an alternative construal of its benevolence activities. The goal is not to convince people that this is what the text is *really* about, but to show what it can mean if we let it—to stretch the limits of the church's imagination, and so to make available fresh and faithful ways of seeing and being.

LANCE PAPE

Zechariah 9:9-12

⁹Rejoice greatly, O daughter Zion!
  Shout aloud, O daughter Jerusalem!
Lo, your king comes to you;
  triumphant and victorious is he,
humble and riding on a donkey,
  on a colt, the foal of a donkey.
¹⁰He will cut off the chariot from Ephraim
  and the war-horse from Jerusalem;
and the battle bow shall be cut off,
  and he shall command peace to the nations;
his dominion shall be from sea to sea,
  and from the River to the ends of the earth.

¹¹As for you also, because of the blood of my covenant with you,
  I will set your prisoners free from the waterless pit.
¹²Return to your stronghold, O prisoners of hope;
  today I declare that I will restore to you double.

Theological Perspective

Zechariah's announcement of the coming Davidic king who rides into Jerusalem on a colt is part of the gradual development of a messianic expectation in Judaism. This passage also plays an important role in the Christian understanding of Jesus as the Messiah. By riding into Jerusalem on a colt just before his crucifixion, Jesus not only announces himself as Messiah, but also invites us to look into a rich prophetic tradition that can help us understand what it is that the Messiah does.

In this passage, Zion is called to rejoice in the knowledge that her king is on his way. This king is described as having three important characteristics that distinguish him from other rulers. First, he is one who rules in righteousness and justice; as such, the messianic king holds within him the hope of an oppressed people. Second, he is saved by God; in other words, he rules with God's help and does not rely only on his own strength.[1] Third, he is gentle (or humble), not proud and boastful.

The latter characteristic of the messianic king seems to be underlined by the fact that he is riding on a colt, the foal of a donkey. The donkey is indeed a humble animal, but its real significance lies in the fact that it is associated with the business of life rather

1. Ralph L. Smith, *Micah–Malachi* (Waco, TX: Word, 1984), 256.

Pastoral Perspective

The final scene in *The Spitfire Grill*[1] is filled with the sunshine of spring. People are picnicking. There are balloons wafting in the breeze. Laughter can be heard as children run about the meadow. It is the kind of scene that is best captured by the poems of Ann Weems, like "Balloons Belong in Church" or "Reaching for Rainbows."[2] This final scene is the first time in this powerful film that the clouds seem to have departed, that life has come to the tired old town of Gilead. It is not the kind of cheesy, emptily affected ending that neatly wraps up a story. It feels much more real, and it feels good. At any moment, it would not surprise me in the least to see a royal figure ride into the meadow on the foal of a donkey.

It is the new Gilead, the new Jerusalem. Of course, it has come at great cost. There has been no war, no battle, but there has been great loss in the death of Percy, the mysterious young woman who loved the town and its outcasts unto death. Now everything seems different, better, brighter, more hope filled than just hoping.

So many people know such hope and are, as Zechariah puts it, imprisoned by it. Every Mardi

1. *The Spitfire Grill*, directed by Lee David Zlotoff (Hollywood, CA: Castlerock Entertainment, 1996).
2. Ann Weems, *Reaching for Rainbows: Resources for Creative Worship* (Philadelphia: Westminster Press, 1980), 15–16, 20–23.

Exegetical Perspective

This passage announces the coming of a king as the occasion of joyful expectation for the people of Jerusalem. As Christians read this text, we experience a flash of recognition regarding the identity of this "king" and the setting of his momentous "coming," from the citation of this text in the Gospel narratives about Palm Sunday (Matt. 21:2–7; Mark 11:2–7; Luke 19:30–35; John 12:14–15). How would the first audience of the prophecy have understood this announcement? From the fresh vantage point of midsummer, what might we learn from hearing these words again?

The Setting and Character of Zechariah 9. The prophet Zechariah, who with his contemporary Haggai is one of the last prophets mentioned by name in the Old Testament, played an important role after the exile in encouraging the returned community during the critical period between the foundation of the Second Temple in 520 and its completion and dedication in 515 (Ezra 5:1; 6:14). Zechariah 9–11, Zechariah 12–14, and Malachi are widely regarded as anonymous collections of oracles that were drawn into the Minor Prophets at some later date, completing what would be "the Book of the Twelve."[1] So our

1. These three sections all begin with the same heading, *massa'* ("burden, oracle"), and are of similar length. The title associated with the third section, "Malachi" (1:1; 3:1), means "my messenger" and perhaps is not the personal name of a prophet.

Homiletical Perspective

When this Hebrew Scripture is read today, even those persons who occupy the farthest edges of congregational life will resonate with its familiar images:

> Rejoice greatly, O daughter Zion!
>> Shout aloud, O daughter Jerusalem!
> Lo, your king comes to you;
>> triumphant and victorious is he,
> humble and riding on a donkey. (v. 9)

As soon as this is proclaimed, many in the congregation will go immediately to Palm Sunday when "King Jesus" makes his triumphant and victorious yet humble donkey ride into Jerusalem.

Today's text is center stage for every Palm Sunday service. Second Zechariah (chaps. 9–14) receives major attention in the church year as Holy Week unfolds. This passage serves either as the Old Testament foundation for the Gospel lessons read in the Liturgy of the Palms, or as one of the appointed readings. This makes a good case for preaching Zechariah 9:9–12 on a summer Sunday, far from Palm/Passion Sunday.

The text affords the preacher a superb opportunity to unpack one of several compelling themes, such as (1) "a king who comes to you" (v. 9), inviting you into a movement; (2) a movement that includes "command[ing] peace to the nations" (v. 10); and

Zechariah 9:9-12

Theological Perspective

than the business of death. It is the animal used on the farm to help in the production of food and in the town to carry people and goods. It is the very antithesis of the horse, at that time largely an animal used for war. The colt therefore symbolizes the very acts that the messianic king is to perform, according to Zechariah: taking away the chariots and warhorses and breaking the battle bows (v. 10). His arrival and the mode of his arrival announce the end of war and the beginning of a universal peace under his rule.

This vision of the messianic king is rooted in the history of God's people. The king that is to come is to be a restoration of the house of David, and his kingdom will reach as far as that of Solomon. But the history that feeds this vision is more than a political history. It is first of all a theological history, the history of God's dealings with Zion. The messianic king takes this history to its logical conclusion by ruling in dependence on God. He brings God's peace instead of war. He is therefore as much unlike the kings of the past as he is like them. Indeed, he is God's "own man," and as such God is the true ruler of the messianic kingdom.

It is in light of this that the hope expressed in the second half of this passage might be best understood. Here God is speaking, announcing the deliverance of Zion's prisoners. Like their ancestor's son, Joseph, on his way to be sold as a slave by his brothers, Zion's lost children find themselves in a waterless pit, and are seemingly without hope. But they are prisoners of hope, for they are to be freed and restored to Zion. The messianic kingdom is not complete without the healing of God's people.

Has the Christian tradition been wrong to appropriate this passage for its understanding of who Jesus is? If the passage is taken out of the context of God's history with the Jewish people and seen to refer only to an otherworldly reality, then the answer to that question will have to be "yes." This passage, however, tells us a lot about God's message of hope and restoration, as proclaimed and indeed embodied by Jesus, and for that reason the final answer has to be that it is entirely appropriate to use this passage in order to understand who Jesus is. The theological question that is raised by this passage is what it means for the Man from Nazareth to ride into Jerusalem on a colt before being crucified by the powers of war and oppression. More particularly, we should ask how this passage helps us understand what Jesus' enacting of Zechariah's vision says about God, the God whom he knows intimately as his Father, and whose imminent kingdom forms the central focus of his ministry.

Pastoral Perspective

Gras, National Public Radio returns to New Orleans to visit a couple in the Lower Ninth Ward whose home was destroyed when the levees broke after Hurrican Katrina in 2005. What began as a battle with the forces of nature became a battle with the bureaucracies that were supposed to help. The people have come a long way since August 2005, but they certainly have not come to know the new New Orleans for which they long. Every year, the revelers come back, a few more each year, a little louder, a little more exuberant. Every year there is a glimpse of freedom from it all, albeit in a festival more suited for Bacchus perhaps than for YHWH. Even in such moments, the joy of what is possible overcomes the waterless pit of despair.

For some, the militaristic language of Zechariah presents a struggle; for others, it embodies their experience of triumph. A careful read, however, will note the reversals of power presented in the passage. It is not the powerful might of the chariot and the warhorse that prevails, but the humble one on not just a donkey but the foal of a donkey. Triumph and victory are not glorifications of the battle bow, but are instead the context for peace to reign. Such a peace will not reign simply over humanity; it will reign over the entire created order.

Shortly after the destruction on 9/11 of the Twin Towers in New York City, a friend of mine who is an AP photographer shared his story. He was working the scene and trying to capture images for the nation. He tried his best to stay objective, but it was still a tragedy painfully fresh, and objectivity was simply not possible. Throughout that first week, everyone at Ground Zero was a prisoner to hope, praying that someone might be found alive. As the days passed and that hope faded, the photographer found it harder and harder to capture images of the rescue workers.

One afternoon of another cloudless day, as he walked down the sidewalk in what had once been the shadows of the towers, he glanced down. There, in the crack of the sidewalk, a dandelion poked its way into the new light. It was not anything spectacular. In fact, the image itself was quite humble. With the roar of the machines and the shouts of the rescuers only a few feet away, the photographer fell to his knees and burst into tears at the realization that life, even in such a place as this, will persist. Amid the emerging nationalistic fervor that swept the United States into war, one man found a glimpse of eschatological hope in a weed on the sidewalk. I almost wish it had been a mustard plant.

passage comes from the very latest elements in Judah's prophetic canon.

An important feature of these later prophecies is their inspired appeal to earlier traditions. If Amos and Jeremiah threaten officials by proclaiming public oracles in royal sanctuaries, the prophets of these later times deliver highly coded reports of revelatory experiences framed by learned reinterpretations of earlier authoritative texts. This character of late prophecies, as inspired exegesis rather than proclamation, often makes it difficult to discern their historical context, but it calls us to pay close attention to their allusive appeals to earlier texts and themes.

The King Who Brings Peace. What may we say about this expected king in Zechariah 9? Although the geographical references in 9:1–8 offer tantalizing suggestions for the itineraries of various historical figures, they are far from conclusive. Should we think of Darius I (522–486), the Persian king who authorized the rebuilding of the temple in Jerusalem, and who passed through Judah early in his reign to deal with a revolt in Egypt? Do the allusions to Greece (v. 13) and the defeat of Tyre (v. 4) point to the much later arrival of Alexander the Great (333 BCE), who was remembered in legends as receiving a wonderful reception in Jerusalem? Does the passage present a purely ideal figure, portrayed in imagery that revives ancient motifs from Zion theology about Judah's royal line? Whether this is a purely ideal figure or an idealistic portrayal of some individual who is now difficult to identify, we come to the same expectation: a king who will be different from the general experience of kings, both in Israel and among the empires of the world.

The allusions of our passage emphasize the association of this king and his victorious appearance with the work of God. The herald's cry in verse 9, "Rejoice greatly, O daughter Zion! . . . Lo, your king comes to you," recalls earlier proclamations of the advent of YHWH:

"Sing and rejoice, O daughter Zion! For lo, I will come and dwell in your midst, says YHWH" (Zech. 2:10).

> Sing aloud, O daughter Zion;
>   shout, O Israel!
> Rejoice and exult with all your heart,
>   O daughter Jerusalem!
> . . . .
> The king of Israel, YHWH, is in your midst. . . .
>   a warrior who gives victory. (Zeph. 3:14, 15a, 17b)

(3) a movement that seeks to enlist all "prisoners of hope" (v. 12).

An Invitation into a Movement. Here is a fascinating paradigm for the Christian experience. An unnamed Hebrew king and the later Jesus of the Gospels (who embraces his forerunner's street theater) invite us to become active participants in a wild, upside-down, transforming movement. The leadership qualities of both biblical figures seem to be oxymoronic: paradoxically "triumphant and victorious" (v. 9) *and* a model of humility, representing a very different face and form of power. All of this gives opportunity to proclaim how when we, the church, are at our biblical best, we are such a bizarre, against-the-grain, mutually inclusive resistance and renewal movement.

Candidly, the very metaphor of the church as a movement is counter to what most of us imagine. We tend to perceive that the primary work of the church is framed in the form of an institution; yet one of the earliest images of the church is that of a cadre of followers of the risen Christ, who are referred to as "belong[ing] to the Way" (Acts 9:2).

Albert Nolan, a South African Benedictine, writes that "Jesus did not found an organization; he inspired a movement. It was inevitable that the movement would quite soon become an organization but in the beginning there were simply people, scattered individuals and groups"[1] who were known as the Way. How can we capture the excitement and the enthusiasm of the headline news that we "belong to the Way," that we are a people of a kingdom movement?

Let us be honest. Are we not changed much more by a movement than by an organization? Organizations and institutions conjure up perceptions that are fixed in form, devoid of urgency, lacking in a "Way" that invites us to become engaged, and, more often than not, imagined as structures rather than as souls. On the other hand, movements lend themselves to being oriented to people; they are energetic, fluid, and visionary; they connect us to a cause on which our very life may well depend.

A friend of mine often remarked, "People do not engage themselves in causes that are feasible; we commit ourselves to movements that are irresistible." Show us a congregation that understands its ministry in terms of a movement, and we will show you a congregation that is making an irresistible presence and witness in its neighborhood and its world.

---

1. Albert Nolan, *Jesus Before Christianity* (Maryknoll, NY: Orbis, 2004), 163.

Zechariah 9:9-12

Theological Perspective

The God whose rule is established by the messianic king, Zechariah tells us, is a God not of war and destruction, but of peace and restoration. This is the God who is announced by Jesus' action. Such is the kingdom of God. The Gospel writers do not misinterpret Zechariah's text when they appropriate it for their understanding of the historical significance of Jesus of Nazareth. The only misinterpretation has been the later vision of Jesus' God as a God of war. The temptation is still with us to turn Jesus' colt into a warhorse and make him serve an agenda of war and oppression. When we do that, we in fact deny any messianic identity for Jesus, for the Messiah is not a conquering hero, but a humble ruler who, fully dependent on God, brings peace to the nations and hope to the prisoners.

This vision of "what the Messiah does" contains a certain imperative for the believer who claims to believe in Jesus as Messiah. Our priorities are wrong if the focus of our inquiry is whether Jesus is indeed the long-expected king of the Jews, whether therefore Christians are right and Jews are wrong. Such an inquiry is itself all too often an act of violence. Our priority should rather be to ask ourselves whether our lives of faith are true to the messianic vision we see enacted by Jesus. When he rides into Jerusalem on a colt, he implicitly provides his followers with a code to live by: a code of peace rather than war, of restoration rather than destruction, of hope rather than the despair of the pit (v. 11).

RACHEL SOPHIA BAARD

Pastoral Perspective

Of course, Christian eyes cannot but see Jesus on that foal, riding into Jerusalem. All four Gospels remember Zechariah's prophecy as Jesus enters the holy city, as he begins his final journey to the cross. In reflecting on Zechariah's final promise—a restoration of double what was lost (v. 12)—I feel drawn to the promise of life in Jesus Christ. It is in Jesus that we too are restored doubly: we are restored in life, and we are restored in death. In Christ Jesus the promise of victory and triumph is not only about the wars we face with the powers of this world; we are promised victory over the ultimate enemy, death itself. Such a victory and such a promise are not a denial of death's reality; if it were, there would be no need for hope.

There are far too many among us who feel trapped in their "waterless pits" (v. 11). For years, someone very dear to me has wrestled with a drug addiction. When he is at his worst, he is at the very bottom of that pit. Slowly but surely, he begins to claw his way back out, but he knows the slightest slip can send him sprawling back to the bottom again. It is a chorus bracketed by merciless repeat bars, one which he sings over and over and over again. In the worst moments, the promise of new life seems too distant. He feels too guilty, too unworthy to claim the covenant.

Zechariah's promise is in the plural: it is for those who are imprisoned and those who long for the prisoners' release. It is a promise of restoration, of wholeness. As children of the covenant, we yoke our hearts to the promise of such new life, and we live for its realization: the new Jerusalem, the new Gilead, indeed, even the new (insert the name of your town here).

TRACE HAYTHORN

Exegetical Perspective

So also in Isaiah 40:9–12, Zion/Jerusalem is a "herald of good tidings" announcing the coming of God as a good shepherd. This is consistent with other late Old Testament witnesses that reinterpret royal symbols and apply them either to the community (Isa. 55:1–5) or to God's direct sovereignty. In Zechariah 9, however, these heraldic announcements are for a human ruler whose victorious appearance will signal God's renewed reign.

Verse 9 offers a series of descriptors for this king that bear close attention. The NRSV rendering of the first pair of these as "triumphant and victorious" is easily misunderstood as applied to a king's military prowess; the Hebrew words are more literally rendered "righteous and saved," that is, rescued by God. The second pair of descriptors, describing the king as "humble and riding on a donkey," portrays a monarch not bent on destruction but coming to make peace. The allusion to the "colt, the foal of a donkey" almost certainly invokes Jacob's blessing on the descendants of his son Judah, from whom the "scepter shall not depart" (Gen. 49:10–11). Here this common beast of burden not only expresses the continuity of a royal line, but is contrasted with the "chariot" and "war-horse" (v. 10) that have been the false trust of Israel's rulers (1 Sam. 8:11; 2 Sam. 15:1; 1 Kgs. 1:5; 10:26; cf. Ps. 20:7) and that the new king will "cut off" as he "commands peace to the nations" (v. 10d). The resultant domain runs far beyond tiny Persian Yehud: "from sea to sea, and from the River to the ends of the earth" (v. 10), a verbatim quotation from the description of the realm of the ideal king in Psalm 72:8.

Who are the prisoners in verses 11–12? Are they people who have remained in Babylon? Are they former inhabitants of "Ephraim" (v. 10), representing the northern kingdom, who have been promised a "hope" in earlier prophecies (Jer. 31:15–22; Ezek. 37:15–28)? Perhaps these prisoners are Judeans who are still oppressed, despite their return from exile (Neh. 9:36–37). The phrase "restore double" intimates a reversal of an earlier "double judgment" for sin (Isa. 61:7: "Because their shame was double, and dishonor was proclaimed as their lot, therefore they shall possess a double portion; everlasting joy shall be theirs"; similarly Isa. 40:2; Jer. 16:18; 17:18).

The anonymous prophet of Zechariah 9 calls people who are suffering to trust that God will supply good government and restore peace and prosperity, not by appeal to chariot or battle bow, but in continuity with trusted promises of old.

JAMES T. BUTLER

Homiletical Perspective

A Movement that "Commands Peace to the Nations." Zechariah seems bent on giving us a vital component for our congregational mission statements. We are always to be in the process of commanding gracefully and modeling boldly for peace, healing, and wholeness for all of God's global children. Many of us are not supporters of bumper-sticker religion, but this one works: "If you want peace, work for justice."

Franciscan spirituality teaches us that we cannot be *of* the poor and the oppressed, because many of us are not poor or oppressed. We cannot be *for* the poor and the oppressed, because that is just another form of control. Nevertheless, we must stand *with* the poor and the oppressed. Our salvation, our wholeness, and our peace are found finally in the authentic justice and wholeness of all others. Show us a peace-giving and foot-washing congregation, and we will show you a changing neighborhood around it. Show us a justice-driven congregation, and we will show you a changing city.

A Movement that Engages "Prisoners of Hope." Yet again, Zechariah gives us a powerful paradigm. To be engaged in the contemporary Jesus movement is always to be in the process of becoming "prisoners [and proponents] of hope." In this lifelong faith journey, we will discover that there is no such thing as a completed "prisoner of hope," no such thing as a truly faith-full Christian human being. There are only hope-full, faith-full Christian human "becomings." Prisoners of hope are always in process, on a winding pilgrimage, a sacred journey, a hope-full following of "the Way."

Sister Joan Chittister, in one of the deepest faith-forming and hope-imprisoning books in my library, writes:

> Hope is not a matter of waiting for things outside us to get better. It is about getting better inside. . . . it is about allowing ourselves to believe in the future we cannot see . . . about trusting in God. . . . then we can hope because we have no reason to hope. Hope is what sits by a window and waits for one more dawn, despite the fact that there isn't an ounce of proof in tonight's black, black sky that it can possibly come. . . . Hope is the last great gift to rise out of the grave of despair.[2]

Now there is a portrait of a "prisoner of hope." There is a movement worth one's life.

DOUGLASS M. BAILEY

2. Joan D. Chittister, *Scarred by Struggle, Transformed by Hope* (Grand Rapids: Eerdmans, 2003), 110–11.

Psalm 145:8-14

[8]The LORD is gracious and merciful,
  slow to anger and abounding in steadfast love.
[9]The LORD is good to all,
  and his compassion is over all that he has made.

[10]All your works shall give thanks to you, O LORD,
  and all your faithful shall bless you.
[11]They shall speak of the glory of your kingdom,
  and tell of your power,
[12]to make known to all people your mighty deeds,
  and the glorious splendor of your kingdom.
[13]Your kingdom is an everlasting kingdom,
  and your dominion endures throughout all generations.

The LORD is faithful in all his words,
  and gracious in all his deeds.
[14]The LORD upholds all who are falling,
  and raises up all who are bowed down.

Theological Perspective

How should we read Psalm 145 recognizing it as Scripture for both Jews and Christians? In the theological perspectives on Psalm 69 (pp. 152–56) and Psalm 89 (pp. 176–80), I offered John Calvin's reading of the Psalms as a model. Here I join Calvin's reading and other Christians' readings with comments by a contemporary rabbi, to encourage Christians to read the Psalms comparatively with our Jewish neighbors.[1] Rabbi Yehiel Poupko is Judaic Scholar for the Jewish Federation of Metropolitan Chicago. In a recent conversation, Rabbi Poupko shared with me his reflections on Psalm 145.

Rabbi Poupko describes Psalm 145 as the "prayer of all prayers" and the "entry way to the Psalms," to be prayed three times each day by the devout. According to the Talmud, "'Everyone who repeats the *Tehillah* of David thrice a day may be sure that he is a child of the world to come' (*Berakot*, 4b)."[2] Its purpose is the praise of God (vv. 1–7). Prayer should be offered to God, who is compassionate, majestic, and sovereign (vv. 8–13). The final section (vv. 14–20) answers the question of the very purpose of

1. John Calvin, *Commentary on the Book of Psalms*, trans. James Anderson (Grand Rapids: Eerdmans, 1949), 5: 271–84. Pages of citations are in parentheses.
2. James L. Mays, *Psalms*, Interpretation series (Louisville, KY: John Knox Press, 1994) 437.

Pastoral Perspective

Psalm 145, found at the end of the Davidic collection, is the only one of the psalms given the clear title of "Praise." It also appears in the Jewish prayer book more than any other psalm; it is and has been a vitally important liturgical piece for much of the history of God's people. The psalm also moves freely from language about God to addressing God directly. The portion of the psalm featured here contains its central core. Likely written in response to the exile and its aftereffects, its focus on the sovereignty of God is significant. It is a reminder that God once again hears the voice of God's people and frees them from an oppression that in some ways is of their own making.

Psalm 145 is filled with praise to God. Its acrostic structure (each verse begins with a successive letter of the Hebrew alphabet) allows it easily to alternate between praise and descriptions of God's generosity and numerous gifts, praising God from A to Z, as it were. Reading in a language other than Hebrew, we miss out on some of the subtleties and original depth of thought and artistry, but the content is the same.

Possibly used during major festivals, Psalm 145 (and this portion in particular) highlights God's compassion and mercy, which are always at the heart of God's kingdom and God's sovereignty. The psalm is very much a doxology—a hymn that expresses the

Exegetical Perspective

Psalm 145, located at the end of the fifth section of Psalms (Pss. 107–145), provides the climax for this section, focusing on the crisis of the Babylonian exile and the circumstances following it. Despite the disappearance of the monarchy, whose establishment and continuance have depended upon God's covenant with the Israelites (see Ps. 89:19–37), the psalmist affirms and praises God's sovereignty. The fullness or completeness of God's sovereignty is reinforced by the use of the word "all" (*kol*) seventeen times, with nine of these occurrences of "all" included in this Sunday's lectionary reading (vv. 9 [2x], 10 [2x], 12, 13 [2x], 14 [2x]), and by its acrostic pattern, with each verse beginning with a successive letter of the entire Hebrew alphabet, as in the acrostic pattern found in Psalms 25, 34, 37, 111, 112, and 119.

A chiastic structure is detected in Psalm 145. Verses 8–14 include the innermost section (vv. 10–13) and portions of its two side sections (vv. 7–9 and 14–16), each with three lines. Verses 3–6 and 17–20, which each have four lines, and verses 1–2 and v. 21, which have similar themes ("bless," "forever and ever"), comprise the rest of the chiastic structure.

In verses 7–9 and 14–16, moreover, the psalmist focuses on God's goodness ("your goodness," *tobeka*, v. 7a; "is good," *tob*, v. 9), mercy ("merciful" or "compassionate," *rahum*, v. 8a), love ("steadfast love,"

Homiletical Perspective

This psalm celebrates not only the kingship of YHWH, but also the glory, splendor, and majesty of the Divine. The psalmist brings into sharp focus the ineffable power of YHWH, which calls for celebration and praise. The praise that the psalmist affirms and alludes to speaks emphatically of God's character. God's activity reveals God's character, which is defined by grace, mercy or compassion, steadfast love, and righteousness.

The Psalms are a repository for the various ills and misfortunes that the human condition has to grapple with. They are a vital source of teaching and preaching today, because the banality of evil and the suffering of the innocent often characterize our world. Despite this reality, the Psalms encourage us to put our trust, not in kings and princes or other societal structures, but in God and God alone.

The text says, "The Lord upholds all who are falling, and raises up all who are bowed down" (v. 14). We fall down by ourselves, but we get up with the help of God. In the novel of the Nigerian writer Chinua Achebe, *Things Fall Apart*, the main character, Okonkwo, is a strong man who falls from greatness. Africans in the Ibo villages are the main characters. Okonkwo's life is dominated by a fear that lies deep within him. He fears himself and the

Psalm 145:8-14

Theological Perspective

prayer. Prayer should be made based on who God is: "the sheer gloriousness of God as sovereign and creator serves only one purpose, and that is to take care of the fallen, the bent over, etc."

Augustine selected Psalm 145:3 as the opening words of his *Confessions*: "You are great, Lord, and highly to be praised." In the opening paragraph to his spiritual autobiography, commenting on this and other psalms, Augustine addresses one of his greatest insights about God: "You stir [us] to take pleasure in praising you, because you have made us for yourself, and our heart is restless until it rests in you."[3]

This insight from Augustine inspired one of Calvin's own great insights: knowledge of God and knowledge of ourselves are woven together into one true quest. If we would come to know the truth about ourselves, we must come to a true knowledge of God our Creator and Redeemer. The right use of the Psalms and the other Scripture will bring us to this true, salvific knowledge.

Calvin finds Psalm 145 moves from a celebration of the power of God's general providence in all nature to God's special providence for Israel and the church. In verse 4 he locates the purpose of humanity: "all [people] were made and preserved in life for this end, that they may devote themselves to the praise of God" (5:273). From the language of the opening words of praise, Calvin infers that "the greatness of God is not that which lies concealed in his mysterious essence, and in subtle disputation upon which, to the neglect of his works, many have been chargeable for mere trifling." This brings him to an important theme of his theology: "true religion demands practical not speculative knowledge" (5:273). The works of God in nature and God's mighty acts in the history of his people are the subject matter of God's self-revelation, not secrets of esoteric wisdom reserved for spiritual elites. The knowledge of this Sovereign should lead us to the practical work of prayer and praise in the company of God's people.

What kind of deity is revealed? Calvin calls attention to how the psalmist in verse 8 quotes from the confession of faith in Exodus 34:6. Contrary to the papal authorities of his day, who, he says, proclaim "a dreadful God, from whose presence all must fly," the reformer finds in this psalm the God who is "inclined to mercy . . . and . . . helps us willingly, as one sympathizing with our miseries" (5:275).

3. Augustine, *Confessions*, trans. Henry Chadwick (New York: Oxford University Press, 1992), 3.

Pastoral Perspective

beliefs of the worshiping community—and as is often the case, it sings of the goodness and glory of God and God's generosity. More than simply enumerating the attributes of God, this portion of Psalm 145 reminds believers of the depth of God's kindness and faithfulness to God's people throughout history. It makes the work of God real and concrete, inviting humans to praise. God has cared and does and will care for God's people, and the people are reminded of God's power and glory in this hymn of praise.

In many corners of this world, the language of this psalm may seem very foreign. As people ask questions of God and struggle to find their path, their desire to praise and thank God may have to be prompted or cajoled. This can be true even in the midst of great privilege. Those who possess many gifts may no longer recognize them as gifts. For many, the language of praise and adoration may seem to have been co-opted by a segment of Christianity with which they do not identify. While such language is readily accepted within less liturgical circles, those in mainline churches may feel as if the language of praise is sometimes contrived.

Psalms of praise such as Psalm 145 give words and voice to those for whom language of praise is unavailable. When we live in a society of lament, all things become lamentable. For Israel during the exile, life was filled with grief. Texts such as Psalm 145 give the people of God something to live up to, a way of envisioning what life before God might be.

As a regular part of the liturgy, Psalm 145 can function like the Shema from Deuteronomy 6, reminding God's people who they are and whose they are. In being reminded of that deep connection to God, God's people are also reminded of the sovereignty of God. On the one hand, this text can suggest to a modern reader a vision of the faithful who regularly rejoice at the generosity of God, who see God's glory and sovereignty. On the other hand, one can look at these words and see the faithful who must be reminded of all that God has done. The history and the story of God's continuity of providential care are easily lost when things are going well; so texts like Psalm 145 remind the faithful to be thankful and act upon that gratitude.

When considering how the psalm might inform Christian practice, it is clear that the text was written with liturgy in mind. Used historically and contemporarily within Jewish tradition, set to music in multiple ways in the early Presbyterian Psalter, Psalm 145 has been central to the language of worship for centuries. Worship takes many forms and styles, with no

Exegetical Perspective

hesed, v. 8b; "compassion," *rahamayw,* v. 9b), kindness by upholding (*somek,* v. 14) and by raising (*zoqep,* v. 14), and generosity ("give them their food in due season," *noten-lahem ʿet-ʾoklam,* v. 15; "You open your hand," *poteha ʾet yadeka,* v. 16) in order to emphasize both the created world ("your works," *maʿaseyka,* v. 10) and faithful humanity ("your faithful," *hasideyka,* v. 10). Mentioned in the innermost section, humanity is portrayed as voicing gratitude to God for having all these attributes and for displaying them in "your mighty deeds" (*geburoteyw,* v. 12; see also v. 13b) as well as through "an everlasting kingdom" (*malkut kol-ʿolamim,* v. 13a). God's kingdom, mentioned four times (vv. 11a, 12, 13a [2x]), also has "glory" (*kabod,* v. 11) and "glorious splendor" (*kabod hador,* v. 12b).

The alternating of the psalmist's declaration of praise in verses 1–2, 4–7, and 10–12 and the psalmist's depictions of God's attributes in verses 3, 8–9, and 13a—with verses 13b–20 continuing with another description of God and verse 21 giving another declaration of praise—provides an additional approach for studying the emphases in Psalm 145. This approach allows readers to focus on the theme of praise and its expression as first voiced individually by the psalmist ("I will extol . . . and bless," v. 1, "I will bless . . . and praise," v. 2); then by both the psalmist and God's people ("I will meditate," v. 5b; "I will declare," v. 6b; "one generation shall laud . . . and shall declare," v. 4; "they shall celebrate . . . and sing," v. 7); then by all creation and faithful humanity ("shall give thanks," "shall bless," "shall speak . . . and tell," vv. 10–12); and last by the psalmist and all creatures ("will speak," "will bless," v. 21).

Praise for God by God's people and the psalmist in verses 4–7 follows with a description of God's attributes in order to explain why God should be praised. God must be praised because of caring for "all" (*kol,* v. 9) creation with "graciousness" (*hanun,* v. 8a), "mercy" (*rahum,* v. 8a), patience (lit., "slow to anger," *ʾerek ʾappayim,* v. 8b), "steadfast love" (*hesed,* v. 8b), "goodness" (*tob,* v. 9a), and "compassion" (*rahum,* v. 9a). The references to God as "merciful" (*rahum,* v. 8a) and as having an overarching "compassion" (*rahemayw,* v. 9b) include connotations of a motherly love, especially since both words belong to the same word family as the Hebrew noun *rehem,* which means "womb."

Praise for God by "all" (*kol*) creation and "all" (*kol*) faithful humanity resumes in verses 10–12; where they speak of the "glory" (*kabod,* v. 11) of God's kingdom and power so that all people may

Homiletical Perspective

white missionaries and colonizers who come to the village to evangelize.[1]

The gospel singer Donnie McClurkin's song, "We fall down, but we get up—for a saint is just a sinner who fell down and got up,"[2] also speaks of the frailty and strength of the human mind and body.

Things do fall apart, and people do fall down every day and in every imaginable circumstance. Life is filled with ups and downs. Our lives include highs and lows, good and bad, joys and sorrows—and not just these pairs of opposites, but also everything in between. Not just cursing and blessing God with the same tongue, not only praying and swearing, not just lying and truth telling or pious praise, but also pompous pouting as well. Life is not just filled with smiles and frowns—not just hopes and dreams but hopelessness and despair also occupy the same mind, the same body, the same person; that person is you. That person is me.

When we wake up each morning to the chirping sounds of the blue jay or the hummingbird or the cardinal whistling in perfect pitch an original tune, we can often thank God for these simple pleasures of life. Every day is filled not only with either/or, but both/and—both joy and sorrow, both good and bad, both right and wrong, both love and hate. Falling is an action that implies downwardness. We fall to the ground; we fall to the floor; we fall on our knees. Our bodies fall quite literally. This is a physical act of losing control, losing our balance.

This psalm of praise begins, "I will *extol* you, my God and King, and bless your name forever and ever." To extol is highly to praise, to lift up. To extol the name of God is to glorify God. The psalmist says:

> The LORD is gracious and merciful,
>   slow to anger and abounding in steadfast love.
> The LORD is good to all,
>   and his compassion is over all that he has made.
>   (vv. 8–9)

God sustains those who are downtrodden, dejected, and on the verge of despair. The Lord upholds all who are falling and raises up all who are bowed down. The preacher can build on this theme.

Take, for instance, "fear"—a ubiquitous opponent that constantly seeks to cripple us. Fear is a powerful opponent. There is another opponent, "doubt," whose job is to make you think you cannot accomplish that

---

1. Chinua Achebe, *Things Fall Apart* (New York: Anchor, 1994).
2. "We fall down, but we get up," words and music by Kyle Matthews, Above the Rim Music; BMG Songs, Inc.

Psalm 145:8-14

Theological Perspective

In the quoted words from Exodus, "as clear and satisfactory a description of the nature of God is given us as can anywhere be found" (Calvin), the divine character is *not* portrayed as brute power that pulverizes the human will into terror and submission. "Indeed no small part of the grace of God is to be seen in his *alluring us to himself* by such attractive titles" (5:275, emphasis added). God is the Sovereign who "invites us to seek after him," who draws us to himself, befriends us, who is "touched with sympathy for our miseries."

After such an inviting and inclusive portrayal of God's grace, however, Calvin sounds notes of exclusion: "As regards the ungodly, although God shows them his long-suffering patience, they are incapable of perceiving pardon, so that the doctrine on which we insist has a special application *to believers only*, who apprehend God's goodness by a living faith" (5:276, emphasis added). Calvin would call our attention to verse 20: "The LORD watches over all who love him, but all the wicked he will destroy."

Does this not call attention to a paradox within the psalm itself? In verse 9 we are told, "The LORD is good to all, and his compassion is over all that he has made." If we apply only an exclusive schema of reward and punishment, we miss the point of the psalm. The righteous spoken of in verses 14–20 are blessed, for they are connected with the abundant source of the very life of creation. They live in radical dependence on their created origins, and they flourish. The wicked, on the other hand, are those whose lives are grounded in their individual selves, cut off from their Creator. Ironically we live in a culture that values individual autonomy as the very hallmark of our human being. The psalmist values instead our corporate reliance on God alone.

ROBERT A. CATHEY

Pastoral Perspective

one way being correct for all, but with similarity across boundaries. Liturgical resources such as Psalm 145 can be used in a variety of ways to inform how we seek to share our gratitude and praise, whether as a responsorial psalm or a sung Psalter or a text for preaching. God calls to us, and we see God calling to us throughout the text. Our worship is in response to God's call, to God's reaching out to us and into our lives. God's loving-kindness and steadfast love are central to this portion of Psalm 145, and that same steadfast love reminds us of God's reaching out to us and of God's activity in our lives.

This portion of Psalm 145 ends with the affirmation that God "raises up all who are bowed down." This is a reminder that praise comes from people in all social locations, some of them more drastic than others. In recognizing the sovereignty of God, we as believers are called to act as God's representative and to be part of lifting up those who are bowed down. As people of faith who live in the reign of God and its many blessings, we are reminded that those blessings are for the least among us. In this life we cannot sing praise to our God unless we also recognize all the gifts we have been given and raise up all who are bowed down.

KATE COLUSSY-ESTES

Exegetical Perspective

know about God's powerful deeds and glorious kingdom. Why must all creation and faithful humanity praise God in this way? They are compelled to "give thanks to" (*yoduka,* v. 10) and "bless" (*barakuka,* v. 10) God and to "speak" (*yo'meru,* v. 11) and "tell" (*yedabbaru,* v. 11) about God's glory and power to people because God is a God whose kingdom endures (v. 13a), even though each generation must give way to the next generation.

The psalmist continues to describe God's attributes, but this time refers to God as "faithful" (*ne'eman,* v. 13b) as well as "gracious" (*hasid,* v. 13b). Verse 13b is missing in the major Hebrew textual tradition, but other manuscript evidence does provide a strong argument for both the NRSV's and the NIV's including it, even though it can be argued that a scribe added verse 13b in order to supply a line beginning with the letter *nun* to complete the acrostic pattern, as in the other psalms with this pattern (see first paragraph above). The line is found in one manuscript of the Masoretic Text and also in the Dead Sea Scrolls, the Syriac text, and the Septuagint. This line can also be accepted by arguing that we do not have sufficient evidence that scribes accidentally added it by repeating it or purposely included it to correct the meaning.

The phrase *becol-ma'asayw* ("in all his deeds") at the end of verse 13b is similar to *kol-ma'asayw* ("all that he has made") at the end of verse 9, but this similarity can indicate the integral connection of the verse rather than its later addition. Verse 14 then continues with explaining why creation and faithful humanity must praise God. God is portrayed as one who "upholds" those "falling" and "raises up" those "bowed down," references made to encourage the Israelites in the trying years during and after the Babylonian exile.

EMILY R. CHENEY

Homiletical Perspective

goal. Self-doubt has kept many from reaching their goals or achieving their dreams.

We are not alone in our falling, and falling is not an act of complete disintegration. We recognize that we fall in many ways. Some "fall on their face"; others "fall between the cracks"; still others "fall down"; and others "fall behind in something." It can be as concrete as your mortgage or your child support. Black people and the poor know what it means to fall behind in something. Sometimes we even slip and fall. Something catches us "off our watch," off guard, and we find ourselves falling, stumbling, going astray, or dropping to a lower position.

Falling can be a loss of greatness, like many who have fallen from the pinnacle of power and prestige. It can be a collapse like that of the Roman Empire or the United States stock market. However, the text says the Lord *upholds* all who are *falling,* which suggests that falling is a process—an incomplete act. Falling is a stumbling that ends in a non-fall. Have you not been walking on the sidewalk or in the hall of your building or running, trying to get somewhere, and suddenly you stumble, but something catches you—gravity, or the God who creates the gravity—does not allow you to fall? You straighten yourself up and keep on going.

That is what this text suggests when it says that "the LORD upholds all who are falling." To uphold is to support against an opponent. In the language of the masses, the Lord "ain't gonna" let us totally fall. No one knows what opponents you face today or the desires that engulf you; but the psalmist reminds us that there is a God whose greatness is unsearchable, whose power is infinite, who can calm our fears and release our burdens. The preacher can develop any number of sermons on this theme.

JAMES HENRY HARRIS

Romans 7:15-25a

¹⁵I do not understand my own actions. For I do not do what I want, but I do the very thing I hate. ¹⁶Now if I do what I do not want, I agree that the law is good. ¹⁷But in fact it is no longer I that do it, but sin that dwells within me. ¹⁸For I know that nothing good dwells within me, that is, in my flesh. I can will what is right, but I cannot do it. ¹⁹For I do not do the good I want, but the evil I do not want is what I do. ²⁰Now if I do what I do not want, it is no longer I that do it, but sin that dwells within me.

²¹So I find it to be a law that when I want to do what is good, evil lies close at hand. ²²For I delight in the law of God in my inmost self, ²³but I see in my members another law at war with the law of my mind, making me captive to the law of sin that dwells in my members. ²⁴Wretched man that I am! Who will rescue me from this body of death? ²⁵Thanks be to God through Jesus Christ our Lord!

Theological Perspective

Romans 7:15–25a is often read as Paul's anguished wrestling with his inability to keep the law. The lectionary nudges preachers toward these well-worn grooves. Today's text begins with 7:15—"I do not understand my own actions"—and so suggests that Paul's inner state is the subject of the argument that follows. Read this way, the passage describes a law that imposes impossible burdens. Paul longs to keep the law, but its demands exceed what he can do. The law measures his sin. More: the law incites sin by putting ideas into his head. In this interpretation, Paul cannot achieve righteousness by meeting the standard of the law; but God delivers him from those standards and from his guilty conscience, provoking the celebratory shout of verse 25a.

This line of interpretation has resonated strongly with a certain sort of introspective individualism that has flourished in the West. It has also resonated with Christian anti-Judaism. However, it fits poorly with the wider context of Paul's letters. In passages like Philippians 3:4–6 and Galatians 1:14, Paul does not seem troubled by an inability to keep the law. He describes himself as "blameless" with reference to "righteousness under the law" (Phil. 3:6). Such confidence grates against understanding Romans 7 as a story about individual guilt before an impossible standard.

Pastoral Perspective

There is something about this passage from Romans that sounds like an Alcoholics Anonymous meeting. "Hi, my name is Paul, and I'm a sinner."

"Hi, Paul!"

"I do not understand my own actions. For I do not do what I want, but I do the very thing I hate" (v. 15). After six chapters of complex theological teaching, suddenly Paul speaks in the first person and describes the inner struggle of every heart. "For I do not do the good I want, but the evil I do not want is what I do" (v. 19). We are shocked and relieved by this risky bit of self-disclosure. Paul can seem so perfect, so demanding, so holier-than-thou. Finally he has put all his cards on the table; he is a flawed and failed person, just like the rest of us.

If this approach to the text excites you, perhaps it is best not to mention that some scholars believe Paul is not speaking for himself here.[1] The "I" is the voice of Adam, the voice of all fallen humanity before experiencing God's grace. Certainly Paul has no illusions about his own moral perfection, and he is a Pharisee when it comes to knowing the law (Phil. 3:6). So whether he is speaking as Paul or as Adam, he lays bare the state of the human soul when

1. See David L. Bartlett, *Romans*, Westminster Bible Companion (Louisville, KY: Westminster John Knox Press, 1995), 69–70, and Paul J. Achtemeier, *Romans*, Interpretation series (Louisville, KY: John Knox Press, 1985), 119–20.

Exegetical Perspective

Complex Questions. In these verses the preacher is dealing with another complex passage, and we should not assume that it can be understood intuitively without careful exegetical study. Sermons could easily be based on Christian psychological experience but have little to do with what Paul is struggling to say.[1]

At least since the groundbreaking work by Karl Barth (1918), through Robert Jewett's massive commentary (2007), countless questions have been raised about Paul's vacillation about what he can and cannot do. A few of them indicate the hard work that awaits the careful sermon writer. Are these verses autobiographical or rhetorical? Are they ones raised by a zealous Jewish believer before conversion to the Christian faith, or reflections by a follower of Christ about what he used to think and do? Are the concepts of being free from sin until the law came in those of a child before his bar mitzvah, or the struggles of the Christian conscience after conversion? Are the questions about misplaced confidence in the law and constant onslaughts of sin limited only to Judaism and the Christian faith, or are they encountered by all religious people, once

---

1. See the warning of Thomas G. Long, "Preaching Romans Today," *Interpretation* 58: 265–74.

Homiletical Perspective

The preacher turning to this week's passage will have much reason to wince. Paul's portrayal of a self enslaved by an indwelling power is an equal-opportunity provocateur. Paul's enslavement language will jar parishioners accustomed to celebrating their freedom; his premise of an evil power abroad in creation will offend scientific notions of a rational universe; his portrayal of a divided self incapable of executing its own good intentions will ask children of the Enlightenment to forsake their inherited optimism about human capacities for self-determination.

In return, however, Paul offers his most penetrating insight into the human predicament, punctuated by three of the most resonant cries of the heart in all of Scripture. The preacher whose sermons help his or her congregation navigate the shoals of their resistance from "I do not understand my own actions" (v. 15) to "Wretched man that I am!" (v. 24) will find plenty of opportunities to share Paul's good news, "Thanks be to God through Jesus Christ our Lord!" (v. 25).

I Do Not Understand My Own Actions. Paul's first cri de coeur holds up a mirror, inviting every parishioner to contemplate their own life experience. Who among them will not recognize a reflection of their own inability to live up to their own ideals? Who

Romans 7:15-25a

Theological Perspective

A second look at Romans 7 begins to open up another line of interpretation. The shape of Paul's rhetoric suggests that this train of thought begins not at 7:15, where the lectionary begins, but at 7:13, with a rhetorical question and emphatic answer: "Did what is good [the law], then, bring death to me? By no means!" Paul has used the question-and-answer device throughout chapters 6 and 7 to introduce new topics, and it marks 7:13 as the beginning of a new argument. If Paul's argument begins here, though, the main topic is not his own righteousness, but the goodness of the law. This reading has the advantage of seeing 7:13–25 as a clear extension of the line of argument developed in the immediately preceding section (7:7–12), which opens by asking if the law is sin and concludes by affirming that the law is holy. The focus of Romans 7 is not the Pauline "I," but the law itself.

Paul insists that the law is "holy, and the commandment is holy and just and good" (7:12). The law is holy, but sin "worked death" in Paul "through what is good" (7:13). Sin is not just a series of personal peccadilloes, particular instances of failing to live up to some standard. It is not even the sum total of all those failings. Sin is an active, aggressive power that seizes hold of God's good gifts—like the law—and bends them toward death. Death came not because Paul could not keep the law, but because he could, and did. Sin has shaped the world in such a way that *keeping* a good, holy law extends the power of sin and death.

Paul is describing the way in which we do what we mean to do, on one level, but then discover that on a deeper, defining level, we are doing exactly the opposite of what we would hope to do (7:15). Paul is speaking from experience. What he counts as the greatest demonstration of the power of sin over his own life—his persecution of the body of Christ—came not because he failed to keep the law, but because he kept a law that sin had hijacked for its own purposes.[1]

Sin is so powerful that it can wrench God's gifts into serving its own ends. Nevertheless, Paul is clear that sin is not an independent rival to God. Sin remains entirely within the scope of God's saving work. Even sin's seizure of the law plays a role in redemption. It happens "in order that sin might be shown to be sin, and through the commandment become evil beyond all measure" (7:13d–e, my trans.).

---

1. Here and throughout this essay I have drawn especially from Robert Jewett, assisted by Roy D. Kotansky, *Romans: A Commentary*, Hermeneia (Minneapolis: Fortress Press, 2007).

Pastoral Perspective

it comes to sin: try as we might, we cannot help ourselves. Unlike small children, who cannot be held responsible for their actions due to ignorance, we are fully capable of distinguishing between right and wrong. We know what to do; we just cannot seem to do it.

What is worse is that the closer we get to choosing the right, the greater seems the temptation to sin. Paul says, "So I find it to be a law that when I want to do what is good, evil lies close at hand" (v. 21). These days, the landscape is littered with public figures who have feet of clay. We even take perverse pleasure in watching the righteous get their comeuppance. It cheers us to see the proud publicly humbled.

Maybe that is why this passage reminds me of an AA meeting—the humility. My church has a number of AA groups that meet in our building throughout the week, and quite a few church members who are "in the program." From what I have seen, there is nothing magical about the AA model; it is really quite simple. You admit you are powerless in the face of your addiction. You surrender yourself to a higher power. You confess your mistakes and find welcome and support in the company of others. Small victories are celebrated, and life is lived one day at a time. As a dear friend, now twenty-five years sober, puts it, "I'm not going to drink today. Tomorrow, I might, but not today."

In some ways, AA does church better than the church does, especially when it comes to Christian humility. In my affluent suburban congregation, we are heavily invested in perfection—or at least the illusion of perfection. We invest wisely, dress appropriately, and worship discreetly. Our children, like our homes, are well maintained and do us credit. Illness, failure, and loss are sources of shame and are therefore private experiences. Looking out at my congregation on a Sunday morning, I see people who embody the motto "Never let 'em see you sweat"; but God knows the truth and so does Paul: we are all sweating.

That is the power of this passage. In eleven short verses, first Paul assures us that doing the right thing apart from God's grace is a losing battle. It is not that we are simply weak or lazy or not trying hard enough. There are forces at work in us with which we cannot contend. The will may be strong, but the flesh rules the day.

The second thing Paul assures us is that we are not alone in this struggle; everyone is engaged in the same hopeless battle. I am convinced that one of the

they abandon previous practices and become disciples of Christ?

A Little History. After carefully examining the long history of interpretation regarding Paul's intentions in these verses, Robert Jewett concludes that they cannot be understood without a proper appreciation of the use of Greek rhetoric. Here, Jewett argues, Paul is employing *prosopopoeia* or "speech-in-character," that is, letting an imaginary person or character speak in the first person in order to make an emotionally effective argument. Paul's eightfold use of "I" (Gk. *egō*) in chapter 7 is an example of a kind of theatrical presentation verbalizing an author's viewpoint. Since it is possible to use this style of writing and still refer to a personal event, Jewett contends that these verses reflect a zealous Judaism that failed to bring about the good that Paul thought he could achieve by persecuting Christians (Acts 9; Gal. 1:13–17).[2]

Many years ago, however, C. H. Dodd demonstrated convincingly that the "I" passages in these verses not only reflect Paul's Damascus road experience but also express the intense spiritual turmoil and struggles he underwent even before that. It is hard to avoid the conclusion, moreover, that the battle between sin and righteousness continued in Paul's life even after his conversion, as it does for most Christians today. As Dodd put it, how his rescue came (or kept on coming) is not entirely clear, but this great personal confession "finds its fitting climax in a simple outburst of praise to God. One thing is clear: when Paul could do nothing, God did everything for him, and all that was left for him to do was to give thanks" (vv. 24–25).[3]

The Inward Struggle. A brief examination of Paul's continuing use of expressions that describe the Christian's inner spiritual state may help the preacher develop a sermon on these verses. Already, as has been pointed out in reference to 6:1b–11 (treated on pp. 159–63), Paul has drawn attention to what it means to be "baptized *into* Christ," "buried *with* him," "crucified *with* him," and "alive to God *in* Christ Jesus." In chapter 7 he expands this concept by referring to the way sin was "working death *in* me" (v. 13), "sin that dwells *within* me" (v. 17, 20),

would not lean forward to listen to someone promising a solution for this frustration at the center of human existence? With this one statement, Paul has gained a hearing for a sermon probing the deeper dynamics of sin.

Our parishioners may view Paul's concern for torah as "not their issue," since they feel they have little in common with first-century Pharisaic Jews. Still, they too have cobbled together a law of their own lives from their understanding of Christian virtues, family values, or any number of definitions of the good person. They too share a confidence in human potential to do the good, once it has been recognized; they understand sin to be acts of commission or omission by which they fall short of their own ideals; they believe that resolving the conflict between their good intentions and their actual deeds is a matter of trying harder. To holders of this perspective, Paul's language—"It is no longer I that do it, but sin that dwells within me" (v. 17)—will be a mystifying cop-out on a par with Geraldine's "the Devil made me do it" on the old *Flip Wilson Show.*

For parishioners to grasp the depth of Paul's argument, they must first understand that Paul views sin not as the breaking of a rule but, rather, as the distortion of a relationship. As Paul Minear says, Paul's understanding of sin can be traced back to Romans 1:21:

> What does the apostle see as the deepest, most stubborn root of sin, the root from which all sinning springs? What leaves [people] without excuse? How do we all become fools with darkened minds? What is it which brings God's wrath against all the ungodliness of [people]? Why does God give them over to the lusts of their hearts? How do [people] suppress the truth? The answer to all these questions is the same.... "They did not honor him as God or give thanks to him."[1]

This idolatrous distortion of our proper relationship with God, this turning from God-centeredness to self-centeredness, introduces a darkening of mind into the very center of our being (Rom. 1:21–25). The very turn to self-assertion unleashes a "fleshliness," the self's insatiable desire to secure its own acceptability through acquisition and possession rather than through trust in God's love. As Gregory of Nyssa writes, the self's trying to affirm itself is like those who scale a sandy slope. Even if they look as if they are traversing great tracts of ground on foot,

2. Robert Jewett, *Romans: A Commentary*, Hermeneia (Minneapolis: Fortress Press, 2007).

3. C. H. Dodd, *The Epistle of Paul to the Romans* (1932; London: Fontana Books, 1963), 133.

1. Paul Minear, *The Obedience of Faith; The Purposes of Paul in the Epistle to the Romans* (London: SCM, 1971), 106–7.

Romans 7:15-25a

Theological Perspective

When sin seizes the law, it shows itself for what it is. It becomes "evil beyond all measure." So it loses the attractiveness on which its (temporary and limited) power depends. Paul is not describing an internal struggle of individual will, but a cosmic drama in which sin overplays its hand, reveals itself as sin, and collapses under the weight of that revelation.

We can begin to understand that cosmic drama by recalling the confrontation between nonviolent civil rights marchers and law-enforcement officials on the Edmund Pettus Bridge in Selma, Alabama, on Sunday, March 7, 1965. When state and local lawmen clubbed peaceful marchers, a sinful power showed itself for what it was. While sin seized the bridge on that day, it lost the luster and legitimacy it needed to survive as a social order.

Reading Romans 7 in this way opens up a rich set of theological interpretations. It pushes us to tell the truth about the ways that sin flourishes, not only in our failings, but even in our best actions—our work for goods like peace, justice, equality, hospitality, the welfare of vulnerable people, the health of the planet, the proclamation of the gospel, and the sanctity of life. Sin deforms this world in ways that bend even ethical actions to death-dealing ends.

This reading of Romans 7 also points to a fuller account of God's work of reconciliation. If the problem were weakness of human will, then reconciliation would require nothing more than a little extra willpower. Jesus would be something like a really good life coach, someone who could help us keep our resolutions. If the problem, however, is the power of sin to twist the good gifts of God, even the law, to evil ends, then deliverance requires a defeat of that power. That is the gospel Paul proclaims. God does not just give individual humans the willpower to live our best lives now, or say that it does not matter if we do not. In Jesus Christ, God sets the cosmos free from bondage, redeeming the law and opening the way to life, and life abundant.

TED A. SMITH

Pastoral Perspective

reasons my parishioners are so reluctant to confess their failures and face their sins is that each person believes he or she is the worst offender. Then along comes Paul, like some sort of psychic, who accurately diagnoses the state of every soul. Yes, we are a mess, but so is everyone else. Hallelujah!

It is a rich passage for a sermon, but I offer a word of caution to the preacher. Paul's words invite a spirit of confession, and it is appropriate for the preacher to lay down a few of her own cards, showing that she too knows what it is to struggle against temptation and fail. After all, what do we model in the pulpit but a way to make theological sense of our own lives? We have all cheated our brothers, envied our sisters, or eaten with the pigs. We cannot expect our people to confess their struggles if we cling to the idol of our own perfection.

However, preachers have to be careful that our moments of confession neither reveal too much nor make us appear to be saints. So do not tell any stories that would make your mother wince, and never cast yourself as a hero, a prophet, or Jesus in any of your own stories.

Finally, so much of this passage focuses on the universal human failure to resist temptation and the power of sin that it is easy to get carried away. Certainly there are enough examples in our own lives and in the surrounding culture to create an unending litany of failure, some of it tragic and some of it hilarious. So it is essential not to lose track of the last two verses: "Wretched man that I am! Who will rescue me from this body of death? Thanks be to God through Jesus Christ our Lord!" (vv. 24–25).

Paul does not simply diagnose the sin-sick state of our souls; he names the cure. While it is liberating to confess our sins, true liberation comes from embracing the Savior.

SHAWNTHEA MONROE

"nothing good dwells *within* me" (v. 18), "I delight in the law of God *in my inmost self*" (v. 22).

To use a modern medical metaphor, it is almost as if Paul is comparing sin to a shingles virus that resides in the spinal column until it is activated by the stress of the law or to a cancer that is not known to have metastasized until it is revealed by a CAT scan. Sin is not just a behavioral aberration or something Paul does or does not do. It actually resides in him, it is housed in him (the verb *oikeō* comes from the word for "house"), it is domiciled in him like a parasite living off its host. It will not stop being destructive, it will not cease killing the person it is in until it is removed and replaced by something stronger—in Paul's view, by the Spirit of Christ. As he puts it in Romans 8:11, "If the Spirit of him who raised Jesus from the dead dwells in you, he who raised Christ from the dead will give life to your mortal bodies also through his Spirit that dwells in you" (cf. 1 Cor. 3:16).

As is pointed out in the study of Romans 6, Paul's concern is more than personal; it is communal and cosmological. The indwelling of the Spirit is also more than physical; it is existential and ontological. It becomes part of one's being. When Paul writes that he delights in the law "in my inmost self" (v. 22, *kata ton esō anthrōpon*), he admits that the law has a spiritual basis because it is recognized in his spiritual center, the place where God primarily speaks to the believer through the Spirit (see Eph. 3:16). When sin infects this center (after its true nature is identified by the law, 7:7–12), it has to be removed surgically (put to death) through Christ and have a transplant of the Spirit.

Although this medical comparison cannot be stretched too far, it does illuminate the kind of necessary and continuing healing process that Paul appears to describe for himself, for others, and for all creation. As he puts it in 2 Corinthians 4:16, even though our outer nature is wasting away, our inner nature (*ho esō hēmōn*) is being renewed every day.

EARL S. JOHNSON, JR.

they tire themselves to no avail. Each time the sand slides to the bottom, in such a way that there is a great effort of movement but not progress.[2]

As a consequence, we can no longer understand our own actions. Our inmost self can still intend the good (vv. 18, 19, 20, 21), but it cannot execute its good intentions, because it is overpowered by an insatiable power of self-assertion dwelling within (v. 17).

Wretched Man that I Am! Paul's second cry offers the preacher an opportunity to explore why the self cannot rescue itself from sin. It follows from Paul's argument that the self cannot heal the distorted relationship, cannot cure its self-centeredness by yet more self-assertion. The self's very apparatus for converting its good intentions into good deeds is infected by the futility of self-centeredness, and, in a curious way, straining at the levers of willpower just draws the self further away from God.

In the film *A Beautiful Mind*, the brilliant but psychotic mathematician John Nash assures his psychiatrist that he will deploy his analytic skills to cure his own illness. "You can't reason your way out of this," his doctor replies, "because your mind is where the problem is in the first place!"[3] Just so, Paul says, the self by itself can neither enact its good intentions nor heal its relationship with God. It can be rescued only from without.

Thanks Be to God through Jesus Christ our Lord! Paul's third cry points the preacher back to a sermon on grace. If Paul's bad news is that the self is trapped and cannot rescue itself, Paul's good news is that God intervenes to rescue the self through Jesus. The trajectory of Paul's argument can be seen as analogous to the twelve steps of Alcoholics Anonymous. The human's cry of dereliction (v. 24) is the cry of "bottoming out," of "step 1," admitting that he or she is powerless over sin. The human's cry of exultation (v. 25) is the cry of "step 2," coming to believe that "a greater power than ourselves could restore us to sanity." God's grace "restores us to sanity," drawing the self back to God-centered salvation.

HAROLD E. MASBACK III

---

2. *Gregory of Nyssa: Life of Moses*, Classics of Western Spirituality (Mahwah, NJ: Paulist, 1978), 117.
3. *A Beautiful Mind*, dir. Ron Howard (Universal Pictures, 2002).

Matthew 11:16‑19, 25‑30

16"But to what will I compare this generation? It is like children sitting in the marketplaces and calling to one another,

17'We played the flute for you, and you did not dance;
  we wailed, and you did not mourn.'

18For John came neither eating nor drinking, and they say, 'He has a demon'; 19the Son of Man came eating and drinking, and they say, 'Look, a glutton and a drunkard, a friend of tax collectors and sinners!' Yet wisdom is vindicated by her deeds." . . .

25At that time Jesus said, "I thank you, Father, Lord of heaven and earth, because you have hidden these things from the wise and the intelligent and have revealed them to infants; 26yes, Father, for such was your gracious will. 27All things have been handed over to me by my Father; and no one knows the Son except the Father, and no one knows the Father except the Son and anyone to whom the Son chooses to reveal him.

28"Come to me, all you that are weary and are carrying heavy burdens, and I will give you rest. 29Take my yoke upon you, and learn from me; for I am gentle and humble in heart, and you will find rest for your souls. 30For my yoke is easy, and my burden is light."

Theological Perspective

One of my favorite hymns from childhood is Judson W. Van DeVenter's "I Surrender All," written in 1896. Actually, as a child I was drawn more to the refrains of hymns than to the stanzas. The hymn's refrain is apt for today's passage from Matthew:

> I surrender all,
> I surrender all;
> All to Thee, my blessed Savior,
> I surrender all.[1]

This is the response I imagine Jesus hopes to hear from us following his invitation to discipleship in Matthew 11:28–30.

In the verses before this, Jesus has been clear that divine wisdom is proved right by its results (v. 19) and that he has a special relationship with God that he can choose to share with others. It is in this spirit that his powerful invitation to discipleship is issued at the close of today's passage from Matthew.

One of the many marks of this call to discipleship is that we understand the deeply theological nature of our quest, found in the context of our ministries— lay and ordained—and in the concrete ways we live out our faith. We find discipleship's moorings in the

1. Judson W. Van DeVenter, "I Surrender All," *African American Heritage Hymnal* (Chicago: GIA Publications, Inc., 2001), #396.

Pastoral Perspective

This curious Gospel text appears in the lectionary during the week of the Fourth of July national holiday in the United States. A pastor preaching in the United States cannot help but read the Scripture within that context, although doing so presents us with a bit of a pastoral puzzle, because the people, the nations, the whole generation, Jesus claims, have come up short. These are not exactly words of celebration for a faithful nation. While we might try to distance ourselves from those ways that Jesus describes, too much sounds familiar for us to discount this teaching entirely. Too much rings true.

The passage begins with the children of the land whose song is never quite understood. When they played a glad song, no one danced; when the song became a dirge, no one was moved to tears. They were no better understood than John the Baptist, no better understood than Jesus.

Jesus is not addressing the failure of individuals to respond, but of the society as a whole, indeed of the entire generation, a people who somehow fail to respond as they might to a song that is utterly clear. During a week of patriotic celebration, how can we fail to reflect on the ways in which our own generation understands—and fails to understand—the reasons for dancing and the reasons for weeping. We are so often and so easily lulled by the other songs and

Exegetical Perspective

The major building blocks of the literary design of Matthew are the five great discourses, each followed by a narrative unit. The current passage is part of the narrative section following the second great discourse, on the commissioning of the disciples by Jesus (9:35–11:1). This implies that a motif of Jesus' sending out his disciples for mission and the response, or the lack thereof, by the "towns of Israel" (10:23) is still in the background of our passage at the macroliterary level.

As for sources, Matthew 11:16–30 as a whole seems to come from Q, but each of its three subsections parallels a different part of the corresponding Q passages in Luke, that is, Matthew 11:16–19 with Luke 7:31–35, Matthew 11:20–24 with Luke 10:12–15, and Matthew 11:25–27 with Luke 10:21–22. This leaves Matthew 11:28–30 with no Synoptic parallel. It could either be from the Special Matthean tradition or from Matthew's own composition.

Less likely, but not impossible, is a conjecture that Matthew took the invitation, "Come to me," from Q, and Luke omitted it. These observations immediately raise source-critical questions about the original scope and sequence of the sayings contained in our passage in their pre-Synoptic stage in Q. Such questions are usually insoluble, but in this particular case scholarly opinions generally lean toward

Homiletical Perspective

Matthew 11 explores various responses to Jesus and his kingdom message and concludes with a renewed invitation to accept him and find rest. This lection can be divided into three distinct, homiletically rich sections.

John and Jesus. They could scarcely be more different, these two: John, the bug-eating wilderness prophet, and Jesus, who is known to love a good meal with all kinds of company; John, who wears scratchy shirts on purpose, and Jesus, who can occasionally be persuaded to invoke the power of YHWH to keep the wine flowing at a wedding reception; John, who addresses his hearers as a "brood of vipers," and Jesus, who in Matthew opens his signature sermon with congratulations (5:1–11). They turn out to be so different that John's once-booming "voice in the wilderness" is reduced to tentative questioning from the darkness of a prison cell (11:2–6).

Jesus explains that this is all part of God's plan (11:7–15). Then he tells a parable about the difference between himself and John and the rejection they have in common. He compares the people to fickle children who keep changing the rules of the game. John came "neither eating nor drinking" (v. 18), and they did not care for his style at all. He was too old school for their taste—too stern and

Theological Perspective

context of struggling for faith, love, hope, and justice as we accept the challenges and rewards of the double paradox of love we noted last week (pp. 188–92). In this ripening and ripening once again we discover God's wholeness as we seek to integrate our faith into our daily lives. This transformative discipleship is hard, necessary, and sometimes very lonely work.

As we live into it, we must remember that we are made in God's image. It is God who weaves the very fabric of our existence through yet another paradox of unconditional love, demanding that we share the rich rewards of God's grace and mercy with others. In doing so, we are called to live out of our possibilities and not our shortcomings by answering, "Yes!" to God's "What if?" As we do so, the love of God revealed in Jesus' witness moves us to grow in compassion, understanding, and acceptance of each other.

We must remain mindful that discipleship involves living our lives with integrity and faithfulness to God. As we come to a greater sense of self, finding our identity in God, we realize that we are developing the markers of our faith as we deepen our theological understanding of discipleship in ways great and small in our daily living. The discipleship to which Jesus calls us not only offers us rest but also guarantees us persecution. So we must live with the conviction that we are being called to live into a new vision of who we are to be and what we are to proclaim from what we have learned from Jesus' teachings.

A faith-filled theology of discipleship includes unpacking the gospel *into* living so that our theology of discipleship is not built on a partial gospel, producing ministries that are dying if not already dead. The vital discipleship to which Jesus calls us in this passage means that we must not place ourselves in the role of host or hostess in churches whose ministries are concerned only with when to do the next maintenance task, rather than how to construct places of welcome and sustenance. The discipleship to which Jesus invites us in this passage requires that we stretch into our ministries by focusing on his message and realizing that we will find rest for carrying the burden of the gospel by living out the unique mission to which Jesus calls each of us.

Another avenue that a theology of discipleship can open up for the preacher to explore is, what does it take for us to dream a world that is more powerful, more real, and more concretely and materially just? This line of exploration into the nature of the new heaven and new earth can come from persistently opening up verse 29 in relation to verses 16–19.

Pastoral Perspective

voices of our culture. Not only do we miss the moments that matter; we regularly dance when we ought to mourn for a world whose burden is heavy and for a people who need rest.

When Jesus turns away from the people gathered and lifts a prayer to God, we begin to realize just how clearly his focus is centered, not on the powerful, wise, and intelligent ones who so often attract our attention, but on the "infants" (v. 25), on those who are far from the places of influence that we so yearn for. We spend our lives seeking wisdom and intelligence, and now it seems that those are the very attributes that Jesus dismisses. In God's realm, it seems, the things that attract our very human attention are barely noticed. Worse yet, the blessings of God are intentionally hidden from those who are filled with the wisdom and wiles of this world. Instead, it is the infants of this world, the innocent and naive, who somehow understand best the ways of God.

This is a hard word to preach to a congregation full of successful people, or at least full of people who long for success in familiar, earthly terms. It is harder still to preach on the weekend of a national holiday that more commonly celebrates the strength and determination of a people and seldom even considers the virtue of humility.

Still, ours would not be the first voices raised on behalf of the oppressed of the earth. Karl Barth insisted that righteousness always requires favoring the "threatened innocent, the oppressed poor, widow, orphans and aliens. . . . God always stands unconditionally and passionately on this side and on this side alone: against the lofty and on behalf of the lowly; against those who already enjoy right and privilege and on behalf of those who are denied and deprived of it."[1] Several decades of liberation theology expanded on that biblical imperative, identifying Christ's radical word with the freedom struggles of many peoples, continually insisting that the saving word of the gospel is understood best when it is located in the midst of the experience of the powerless and the disenfranchised. A number of emergent church models are now being attempted that reject the old ways of doing worship and building community and seek instead to live the faith at the margins, without the encumbrances of physical property or established power.

Jesus is inviting a significant engagement and social analysis before he offers the frequently quoted words

1. Karl Barth, *Church Dogmatics*, II/1 (Edinburgh: T. & T. Clark, 1955), 386.

acknowledging a heavier redactional hand from Matthew than from Luke.

The first unit, verses 16–19, is preceded by a brief episode about an inquiry John the Baptist sends from prison through his disciples, asking whether Jesus is the "one to come" (11:2–3). Jesus gives them an answer and, as they are going away, then addresses the crowd with a short speech about John the Baptist, of which our passage (vv. 16–19) is the concluding part. The postpositive particle *de* at the beginning of verse 16, which is adversative rather than copulative in meaning in this sentence, refers right back to the declaration "Let anyone with ears listen!" in the preceding verse.

This linguistic connection sheds light on the ultimate meaning of the parabolic sayings in our passage. That is, there seems to be no one in "this generation" (v. 16) who really has the ears to listen. The original reference of "this generation" is that of Jesus, but through the redactional motif of transparency, it could also apply to Matthew's generation—or ours.

The parable itself (vv. 16b–17) has been a subject of much debate concerning which characters in the parable correspond to whom in reality, which should not concern us here. More important is the function this parable serves in the current pericope, which is to demonstrate the complete lack of proper response on the part of the people in general and especially the opponents of John the Baptist and Jesus. The interpretation part (vv. 18–19) sarcastically contrasts John and Jesus, in terms of both their lifestyles and the accusations they receive, but the point is the common absurdity of the slanders directed against each of them, not the contrast.

The whole section ends with a maxim, "The wisdom was justified by her works" (my trans.). The theologically loaded word *erga* ("works") used in the genitive plural in verse 19 harks back to the same word used in the accusative plural in the phrase *ta erga tou Christou* ("the works of Christ") in 11:2. Also, by inference, it refers to the series of deeds of Jesus in 11:5, which demonstrates the core of the gospel Jesus proclaims and enacts (cf. *euangelizontai* in v. 5).

In the intervening passage (vv. 20–24) the audience remains the same, but the subject changes. Now Jesus pronounces a prophetic judgment against the unrepentant cities of Israel, which represent the vast majority of "this generation" mentioned in verse 16, who do not respond properly to what Jesus says and does. Thus, the theme of the lack of understanding

demanding. So they played the flute, and said, "Come on, John, lighten up. Lay off the hellfire and dance to our tune." Then Jesus came and he was ready to dance—dance as they had never dreamed! Every meal was a party, as long as everyone was invited. Then they wailed about the company Jesus kept and called him "glutton" and "drunkard" (v. 19).

God's ways can be both too little and too much for us—God's agenda somehow simultaneously too "conservative" and too "liberal." We chafe under John's unapologetic insistence that a moment of decision is at hand for each of us—that we must examine our hearts, let the chaff burn away, and embrace God's future with our whole lives. However, Jesus can also rub us the wrong way. In his irrational exuberance he just does not seem to grasp that some people are beyond hope—that we must keep select company in order to keep our lives on an even keel.

Both of these messages are a threat to our hard-won autonomy. We long to maintain a happy medium between John's stifling demands and Jesus' frightening inclusiveness. So we keep changing our tune, insisting on the moderation (or is it the mediocrity?) that we can secure for ourselves, not the extraordinary future that God dreams for us and the world.

Knowing Jesus, Knowing God. So much of what is best in our world comes through focused effort. From brilliant theoretical breakthroughs to life-saving medical techniques to virtuosic musical performances, human excellence is an achievement. Such knowledge and mastery must be pursued with diligence. If you want to excel at something, get up early; concentrate hard; stay up late; and repeat; and repeat again; and again.

There are some things—including the most important thing—that do not work that way. Knowledge of God, it turns out, cannot be achieved. God is not just another thing in the world that we can reach out and take hold of by our own power. The more we grasp after knowledge of God by our own wits, the less we attain. At least, this seems to be Jesus' understanding of the matter. It is as if God is in hiding from those who are good at finding things in the normal way, even as those who show no prowess when it comes to understanding all kinds of other things seem to be adept at receiving the gift of God's gracious self-disclosure (vv. 25–26).

Of course no one understands this about God better than Jesus (v. 27). Perhaps that is why he can offer up a prayer of thanks (v. 25) at precisely the

Matthew 11:16-19, 25-30

Theological Perspective

In the latter four verses, the preacher has the opportunity to think through such themes as fear of the unusual or love of the outcast. Exploring how this relates to verse 29's call to take upon us Jesus' yoke and learn—one of the key tasks of the disciple—may bear rich fruit for reflection, as one thinks of the variety of illustrations one can draw from people going about their daily lives.

As important as learning is for discipleship, however, a theology of discipleship pushes us to think more deeply about how we express the lessons we have learned and continue to learn. We do this best in a community of discipleship that challenges us as it tells us the plain truth of our acts and how they affect those around us like ripples on a pond—or sometimes like tidal waves after an earthquake.

Finally, the preacher may wish to consult Dietrich Bonhoeffer's timeless book *The Cost of Discipleship*[2] to clarify how a theology of discipleship might be shared with one's community. Here the relationship between the teacher and student of discipleship must mature into helping the student understand how to apply her or his learning by sharing the good news of the demands and comforts of the gospel.

As Bonhoeffer leads readers through the dangers of cheap grace and reflection on the cross, he focuses on our formation as individuals, the power of the Beatitudes, and righteousness. One can imagine the different people who will hear this message and begin to craft concrete images for hearers to "see," "hear," and "feel" for themselves when Jesus says, "Come to me, all you that are weary and are carrying heavy burdens, and I will give you rest."

It is then that we can sing with relief and profound gratitude, "I surrender all."

EMILIE M. TOWNES

Pastoral Perspective

of comfort to those who are weary and carrying heavy burdens. That may well be the pastoral key to our reading this text: How does it speak to the hurting who are close by in our lives, and to the hurting who are far away? How are we engaged with those whose struggles are profound and whose needs are overwhelming? If Jesus is in fact insisting that his blessing is known, not by the mighty and the powerful, but by the infants and the lowly, then this is a time for us too to identify with the plight of those who live on the fringes of our society and the fringes of our lives.

We dare not move too quickly to those words of pastoral assurance, surely not before reminding ourselves and our congregation that Jesus is present more in times of need than in times of plenty, more in times of desperation than in times of certainty.

Rest is not offered to the strongest and the most powerful. Rest is offered to those who have been made weary by a world that fails to comprehend the burden of injustice. The yoke is made easy by the heavenly powers coming to the aid of those whose ways this world fails to understand.

In short, any who believe that they are responsible for their own salvation, through military might or political power, through intellectual prowess or personal magnetism, have no need of the comforting arms of Jesus. Jesus will not trouble them with heaven's gifts. To those who recognize their need for a savior, however, Jesus comes with comfort enough, lifting life's burdens and offering rest even for the lonely soul.

WILLIAM GOETTLER

2. Dietrich Bonhoeffer, *The Cost of Discipleship* (1937; repr., New York: Macmillan, 1966).

and proper response runs throughout the entire section, verses 2–24.

The second unit of our passage, verses 25–30, shows a shift in the texture of discourse from negative to positive. In terms of the literary type, it consists of a prayer (vv. 25–26), a statement (v. 27), and paraenesis (vv. 28–30). In contrast to what precedes, the prayer of Jesus brings to the surface of the text a previously unmentioned group, a small minority of people who listen, understand, and follow Jesus. By characterizing those who do not respond properly as the wise (*sophoi*) and the intelligent (*synetoi*), this saying of Jesus narrows down the scope of his opponents primarily to the educated leaders of Israel. Then, the target recipients of the divine revelation are identified as infants (*nēpioi*). This metaphor signifies the lowly in general, but it also refers to those who follow Jesus in particular, either as called disciples or as part of the crowd.

The form of invocation in the prayer of Jesus in verse 25 resembles that of the Lord's Prayer, but it should not be taken as a sign of Jesus' uniqueness. Invoking God as Father is a typical Jewish way of beginning a prayer. The claim that Jesus is unique is rather found in the content of the prayer, the language of the exclusive nature of the mutual understanding between the "Father" and the "Son," and also the designation of the "Son" as the sole medium of revelation (v. 27). This prayer has an almost verbatim parallel in Luke 10:22.

Such a claim to exclusive revelation is often identified as a marker of a sectarian, usually nascent, community at the margin, one that strives for legitimacy vis-à-vis the mainstream of the larger society to which it belongs. This aspect may very well illumine the nature of the Matthean community as well as the community behind Q, even though its applicability to the Lukan community may be debated. Therefore, the concluding paraenesis in vv. 28–30 should be interpreted against this background of the Matthean community's predicament as a minority movement in post-70 Judaism.

EUGENE EUNG-CHUN PARK

moment when things do not seem to be going well for him and his mission. When you are in tune with God's ways, persecution (chap. 10) and rejection (chap. 11) by the acknowledged experts is no great surprise. To the one who knows God best, it is perfectly clear that everything is going according to plan. It is the spiritual "infants" (v. 25), the least theologically sophisticated people, those with the fewest illusions about their own powers of understanding, who know how to receive Jesus in humility and so gain access to the one he came to reveal (v. 27).

The Yoke of Jesus. The final verses of the lection (vv. 28–30) are the most obvious choice for preaching. This familiar saying is widely understood to mean that following Jesus is easy, because, unlike the Pharisees, he is not too particular about how we live. This antinomian take on Jesus does not stand up to a close reading of the Sermon on the Mount, which expounds a more, not less, rigorous theological ethic (5:17–20). The "easy yoke" (v. 30) Jesus promises is all the more perplexing in light of the strenuous demands placed upon disciples in chapter 10, and the rejection depicted in chapter 11. How can Jesus offer rest when he asks so much?

What Jesus offers is not freedom from work, but freedom from onerous labor. Soul-sick weariness is not the inevitable consequence of all work, but rather of work to which we are ill suited, of work extracted under compulsion and motivated by fear, or of work performed in the face of futility. There is also the weariness that comes from having nothing at all to do that truly matters. The easy yoke means having something to do: a purpose that demands your all and summons forth your best. It means work that is motivated by a passionate desire to see God's kingdom realized. It means work toward a certain future in which all of God's dreams will finally come true. To accept the yoke of the gentle and humble Lord is to embrace the worthy task that puts the soul at ease.

LANCE PAPE

Isaiah 55:10-13

¹⁰For as the rain and the snow come down from heaven,
   and do not return there until they have watered the earth,
   making it bring forth and sprout,
      giving seed to the sower and bread to the eater,
¹¹so shall my word be that goes out from my mouth;
   it shall not return to me empty,
   but it shall accomplish that which I purpose,
      and succeed in the thing for which I sent it.

¹²For you shall go out in joy,
   and be led back in peace;
   the mountains and the hills before you
      shall burst into song,
   and all the trees of the field shall clap their hands.
¹³Instead of the thorn shall come up the cypress;
   instead of the brier shall come up the myrtle;
   and it shall be to the Lord for a memorial,
      for an everlasting sign that shall not be cut off.

Theological Perspective

Any clear vision of the future starts with hope. Pentecost is a story about hope. Now some weeks after Pentecost, to think and imagine new possibilities beyond our present circumstances remains a challenge to most mainline churches in the United States. Often the excitement of Pentecost is defused when we are faced with the complexity of life circumstances. Hope must be more than a mountaintop experience with the Spirit. It must be grounded in the concrete realities of both heaven and earth. This passage in Second Isaiah reflects an understanding of hope inspired by moments of transcendence in the context of everyday struggles of human existence.

The chapter starts with a hopeful invitation. YHWH's claim that "my ways are higher than your ways" (v. 9) is not a put-down to humans, but a challenge to look up. Hope not rooted in the concrete realities of the moment often leads to even deeper despair. However, the invitation in this text bases hope on a theological reality that is grounded in creation itself.

Although Hebrews 11:1 defines faith as "the assurance of things hoped for, the conviction of things not seen," Isaiah sees the evidence of God's faithfulness in the rhythmic nature of creation. Although YHWH's ways and thoughts are higher than the earth, things high will come down, just as

Pastoral Perspective

According to the prophet Isaiah, God's word is never shared without a good purpose; good is designed into everything. Events come together to bring completion and wholeness to our story of life, to attach meaning and lasting significance to it, even when we cannot see them coming. Recognizing the varied ways that life comes full circle—that the purpose for which we have been designed is accomplished—is a real gift to be cherished.

I am often struck by stories of faith I hear in my follow-up contacts with those who come to visit our church. I enjoy these follow-ups, which sometimes happen on the phone and sometimes over coffee. A comment shared by a recent visitor was noteworthy on its own, but has even more impact when viewed from Isaiah's perspective.

When I had lunch with the chief of heart failure and transplantation at a local major medical center, who with his family had made a first-time visit to our church, we dove conversationally into the meat of the matter. He shared his conviction that there is more than just a natural rhythm built into life, more than just karma, more than "what goes around, comes around." Through years of hands-on experience in dozens of life-and-death situations, he affirmed the good and redemptive purpose at work in life, even in the loss of life.

Exegetical Perspective

The invitation that opens chapter 55 of Isaiah continues in verse 10. The first words of the chapter call the thirsty and hungry to find water and food in abundant supply. The language of verse 10 identifies the word of God as a source of abundant water and food for the entire earth. The images of fertility, abundance, and prosperity accompany a note of exuberance to make this passage characteristic of the tone of Second Isaiah. Rain and snow water the earth in excess, generating a chain of production that ends in the doubled elements of seed and bread. A notable number of paired elements—rain and snow, bring forth and sprout, seed and bread, the sower and the eater—populates verse 10. This number heightens the sense of abundance that marks the opening and close of the chapter.

The passage (vv. 10–13) provides descriptions, convictions, and appeals about the word of God that tie it intricately into creation, nature, and human livelihood. The processes of the water cycle, of agricultural life, and of daily living find their referent in the word of God. While the author builds comparisons based upon these elements, the word of God also transcends the limitations of these elements.

We find a preliminary understanding of the water cycle here that sees precipitation returning from the earth to the skies. However, not all precipitation is

Homiletical Perspective

Must we mean what we say? Must we say what we mean? Is there a connection between saying and doing so essential that if this link is broken, a community will not survive? If this bond that binds human language and action together is destroyed, integrity and authentic relationship disappear. Our failure to trust God as Word is directly connected to our failure to stand by our own words. Truly prophetic speech is marked by this distinction: the Word "shall accomplish that which I purpose, and succeed in the thing for which I sent it" (v. 11).

Wendell Berry reminds us of the life-giving links between our life and our language in his book *Standing by Words*. Words lose their meaning when they are reduced to utilitarian ends, and promises made to be broken cannot serve as a means of grace.[1] If baptismal vows are pro forma, the prayers seem empty, the sermons contrived. If religious expression becomes indentured to institutional control, truth is eviscerated. Experience has a structure that is prior to language. but a dysfunctional relationship between language and action infects individual and communal integrity. When holy human dialogue is reduced to a means of crowd control,

---

1. Wendell Berry, *Standing by Words: Essays* (1983; repr., Berkeley, CA: Shoemaker & Hoard, 2005).

Isaiah 55:10-13

Theological Perspective

rain and snow come down upon the earth to nourish it back to health.

The natural cycle of creation is not a simple mechanical process that occurs automatically. The God pictured here is not a deist's distant watchmaker who simply winds the clock and allows it to run independently. Nor is this a God who can only respond out of the natural design of the created order. Isaiah's portrait is of a God who loves and cares about the people and is passionately involved with creation. The sources of hope are extensions of the Divine's personal involvement. God's word is not some benign cerebral exercise. The correlation to the metaphor is the promise that creative acts by "my word" will continue to "accomplish that which I purpose" (v. 11). YHWH's word is faithful, purposeful, and personal. A relationship of trust is established based on the trustworthiness of God's word, the same word present in the very act of creation.

Speaking to an exile people does present its own set of unique challenges. How do you inspire hope in a people who have been living under the governmental controls of a foreign nation? This is particularly problematic when living in exile becomes the new social and political norm. I often experience this problem when preaching in post–civil rights middle-class African American congregations. Although many will admit that there is still a problem in our communities, defining it has become increasingly elusive.

Once proclamation of hope can be nuanced by the context, celebrations occur as a natural response to the new life with God. Not only is there an up-and-down dimension to God's activity, but also a back-and-forth movement. The move back to the homeland out of exile will involve "going out" of captivity in order to be "be led back" to the land of promise.

Walter Brueggemann comments, "This is a homecoming, but not to the old city, to a home, an urban home, a city as a true home."[1] However, the celebrative activity of creation starts with this movement toward hope, demonstrated in Isaiah with the singing and clapping of hands by the mountains and the trees (v. 12). This is like the dynamics of many African American worship experiences, where celebration of the activity of God among the people is essential and there is no celebration of the heart alone; worship must also include a physical demonstration of the human involvement in God's

Pastoral Perspective

Quickly switching metaphors, he used a sports analogy from the baseball diamond to share another way of looking at this point of view with the indisputable statement that "God always bats last." The good doctor had just emerged from a session with a family who had lost a loved one but who were nonetheless immensely grateful for the caring and attentiveness provided by all the hospital staff.

For this man, it was clear that the loved one had lived a good life, had "fought the good fight" (2 Tim. 4:7), and had been given the gift of willingness during his wait for a heart transplant to return to the One who made him. This was not the first time the physician had encountered a family with this experience, nor did he expect it to be the last. So he observed that life does not return empty to those left in loss, but becomes deeper and richer through the prism of memory blessed with mercy.

At a church I served in the mountains of North Carolina, there was a columbarium up a hill behind the sanctuary. The congregation consisted predominantly of retirees, and funerals occured with some regularity. It was our practice to perform the inurnment with a small group of family and friends thirty minutes before the larger Celebration of the Resurrection held in the sanctuary. The columbarium was a well-designed structure providing a striking view of the Blue Ridge just above the walls, with the mountains silently affirming the human life being celebrated, the mountain laurel and dogwood trees bowing approval at the passing of one worldly life on its way nearer to heaven.

Some of the most memorable moments I shared in memorial services took place under the open sky at that columbarium. With plenty of branches hanging overhead, a service in the autumn would bring a small harvest of acorns to be used as illustrations for the grandchildren. I would find the nearly perfect acorn, partially buried in the dirt underneath the laurel, with a small bud beginning to burst from its shell. As I held it up for a grandchild to see and later to take home, it was easy to illustrate that God never leaves life empty, that God's purposes are always fulfilled, even through dying. All it takes is a seed for God to use to create a new and better form of life.

In the ancient Celtic mission, from the fourth through the seventh centuries, the pattern for worship was to gather around high-standing crosses underneath the open sky. The earth itself was the sanctuary of God, which included all things.[1] I have

---

1. Walter Brueggemann, "The City in Biblical Perspective: Failed and Possible," *Word and World* 14, no. 3 (1999): 248.

1. J. Philip Newell, *Christ of the Celts: The Healing of Creation* (San Francisco: Jossey-Bass, 2008). 110.

sufficient to generate productive growth. Similarly, variable occurrences of precipitation can place harvests and human survival in jeopardy. The comparisons serve on one level as a contrast between the variable productivity of natural processes and the dependability of the word of God. On another level, the comparisons call attention to the current time as a season of abundance. In a context of limited precipitation, occurrences of rain and snow feel like a time of surplus.

Second Isaiah declares confidently that God's word will never experience drought or scarcity (cf. Amos 8:11). In fact, in this passage the word of God appears to undo drought conditions that yield only scrublike vegetation (v. 13). Equally, the declaration that God's word never fails (40:8) is revisited here. This adds to the growing descriptions of the word of God throughout Second Isaiah: creative (51:16), prophetic (44:26, cf. 46:10–11; 48:15), bringing justice (45:13), teaching (50:4, cf. 42:16), revealing God's voice (52:6), public (45:19; 48:16).[1]

The vivid descriptions add to the appeal of the invitation in verse 1. God's word not only provides abundance and fertility; it makes things happen. In the same way that precipitation sets off a chain of events, when God's word goes forth, it produces God's intended effect. Three clear statements in verse 11 describe both the relationship between the word and God, called here *devari* ("my word"), and the effects of the word. The word goes out from God's mouth, returns to God, and accomplishes God's purpose and intent. Each phrase of the verse builds from the previous one, culminating in "success" in God's sending. The concerns here appear to be with more than just speech or the content of speech. The word of God consists not merely in speech, but in results, impacts, outcomes, and transformations. Claus Westermann offers, "God's word is a word that does things. When God speaks, something comes about."[2]

The descriptions of the nature of God's word in verses 10–11 provide the framework for the proof of these assertions, as well as a further invitation to live in the abundance of the word of God. The audience for the passage appears to be both specific and general. The unidentified hearers in the chapter can belong to the audience to whom Second Isaiah offers the promise of restoration and return after their deportation to Babylon. Consequently, the action of

the beloved community suffers from a drought of revelation.

Fragmentation of community follows a collapse of the understanding of covenant. Even the natural order fails to thrive if there is a radical disconnection between a promise made and a promise kept. It is precisely here in the wasteland that the prophet/poet of exile plants a vision of paradise. The cosmic, organic, and historic converge in the closing verses of the revelation, convicted of the potency of the Word that calls all of creation into completion. Paradise is summoned, called into being by the Word that creates, redeems, and sustains creation. Zion is now a witness to peace, not a prisoner of war. God's beloved community is surrounded by a land that will receive healing as well. The cypress replaces thorns, and myrtle takes the place of briers.

This closing vision is central to the Servant's experience of divine presence. Here the Word is working just as the One who is the First and the Last intends. Organic and seasonal images are linked to generative human cycles, and all are held in holy relationship. The parabolic and prophetic nature of this Word spans the limits of human time and culture. Ordinary words and actions take on a sense of mystery in the presence of the Word. This affirmation of eternity is rooted in the earth; there is an attachment to the particularity of a place known as "the promised land." This communal hunger for a place, this inherited homesickness is rarely generated by generalized space, but is evoked by memories for a specific landscape known by heart.

Is this place, this homeland, this notion of a space preserved by the promise of God, essential to the nature of that God? Must God have a holy land in order to be a Holy God? Those who believed that Judah could not be defeated had fused the identities of nation and God. The Babylonian shattering of national identity raised traumatic questions about the promised return. While the social and political implications of the fall of Babylon and the coming of Cyrus are configured in this prophecy, the songs of the singer reveal a God who will transfigure the broken dreams of a nation into the healing of all nations.

Such a longing will outlast any one life span, and the prophet of exile summons that memory in an effort to turn the hearts of the exiles back to the God who will not abandon them. It requires patience, discipline, hope, and a willingness to forgive those who refuse to listen. Such a lonely work can be fueled only by love, a love for a particular

---

1. Klaus Blatzer, *Deutero Isaiah: A Commentary on Isaiah 40–55* (Minneapolis: Fortress Press, 2001), 483.
2. Claus Westermann, *Isaiah 40–66* (Philadelphia: Westminster Press, 1969), 289.

Isaiah 55:10-13

Theological Perspective

liberation. As Paul Hanson notes, "ultimately salvation is God's accomplishment, to which humans beings need only open their hearts with rejoicing and their voices with songs."[2]

We in the black church are not celebrating just for celebration's sake. Nor is our worship merely a moment of emotional catharsis. As indicated in the prophetic claims of Isaiah, our hope is grounded in real observable change. Just as seasons are recognized by the changing colors of the leaves, the people of God will know that their lives have been restored when thorns have been replaced by the cypress, the brier by the myrtle. Liberation means change that is concrete and discernible. As in the parable in Luke 5:37–38, where Jesus says that "new wine" put in "old wineskins" will spill to the ground, likewise, the hopes and dreams of a better way often can be realized only through such physical and visible transformation.

Change serves another purpose besides cosmetic or structural transformation. It serves as a reminder of where we came from, in hopes that we never make the same mistakes again. So Isaiah offers an interesting theological perspective when he writes, "it shall be to the LORD for a memorial" (v. 13). Does God have trouble remembering? Is the need for a memorial (such as the rainbow in Gen. 9:13) an indication that God may not remember the promise?

This is the difficulty with metaphors and personifications of natural objects. Do we push their symbolism too far in the direction of realism? I say no. In this instance, the memorial functions as more than a marker for accountability. It is not only a sign to assure humanity that their exile will not happen again; it is also a commitment by God to the people, whether they are in exile or at home, to be an abiding presence among them. That is real hope.

JOHN L. THOMAS JR.

Pastoral Perspective

often thought how different it can be when worship is outdoors. God and God's creation are bound together in an inextricable, delicate way. It is the deepest promise from which good news is possible.

In the realm of human relationships, the need for a sense of purpose is nowhere made plainer than in the writings of Victor Frankl, whose essays on WWII concentration-camp survivors speak to the power of trusting in the purpose for which we were made. Quoting Friedrich Nietzsche, Frankl writes, "He [sic] who has a *why* to live for can bear with almost any *how*." Then he goes on to say, "Woe to him who saw no more sense in his life, no aim, no purpose, and therefore no more point in carrying on. He was soon lost."[2]

It is true consolation that we are made by a loving and compassionate God, and thus in our very being have a purpose for living—to reflect God's love and care in every breath we share. Although we live on this side of the veil of heaven and can often see only pain and loss, we do not see all that there is in creation. God has a purpose and an end for us greater and more glorious than we can begin to imagine.

Spring does not just arrive because the earth's axis tilts toward the sun. The warmth of God's presence arrives because God turns toward us in love. Forgiveness arrives because of the wideness of God's mercy. Joy arrives because we see a glimmer of our new life in God in our own. As Isaiah proclaimed so long ago, the word that goes out from the mouth of the Lord will not return empty, but shall accomplish its purpose and succeed in just the thing for which it was sent.

THOMAS W. BLAIR

2. Victor F. Frankl, *Man's Search for Meaning* (New York: Washington Square, 1963), 97. Nietzsche's words can be found in *The Twilight of the Idols and the Anti-Christ: or How to Philosophize with a Hammer* (New York: Penguin Classics, 1990), 12.

2. Paul D. Hanson, *Isaiah 40–66*, Interpretation series (Louisville, KY: John Knox Press, 1995), 182.

Exegetical Perspective

going out in joy (v. 12) reflects the image of the second exodus prevalent in Second Isaiah. In journeying back to their homeland, they will experience full proof of the efficacy of God's word.

In fact, their movement will embody the power of the word of God. The comparisons with precipitation from verse 10 continue in verse 12. This time the movement of people sets off a chain reaction that animates nature into singing and clapping, in the same way that precipitation leads to the activity of sowing and eating. Precipitation causes actions of the hands and the mouths of the sower and the eater; the movement of the people generates singing and clapping.

Precipitation causes vegetation to sprout; so too, the movement of the people leads to more lush vegetation (v. 13). As precipitation serves as a point of comparison for the word of God, the return of the deportees illustrates the efficacy of the word of God. In this way the assertions of verses 10–11 function doubly as evidence and invitation to live in the word of God.

The unidentified hearers can also be the general audience called upon to witness the efficacy of the word of God, experiencing it and functioning like it. Just as the word of God "goes out" (v. 11), so too the hearers "go out" (v. 12). As God anticipates the word to "return" successfully, so too the hearers are "led back" in *shalom* ("peace, success, prosperity," v. 12). As God's word produces its desired effect, so too the exit of the hearers results in the determined impact. The hearers do not effect the monumental and long-lasting transformations in nature (vv. 12–13); these occur as decreed.

The unidentified audience serves as a divine instrument in the same way the word functions as a divine instrument. These hearers embody the word of God in the world, and through them God speaks transformation to the world. They in turn witness to the power of God. Their presence speaks of a God whose word brings creation into being, sustains it, and transforms it. Their presence also speaks to a God who intervenes in history. A real, live audience testifies that they have seen the effect the word of God has in the world.

STEED VERNYL DAVIDSON

Homiletical Perspective

people who are in danger of forgetting who and whose they are. The clearest sense of identity we have of this late-sixth-century prophet, Isaiah of Babylon, can be found in the Latin phrase *anima quaerens verbum*, a soul in search of the Word. He— or perhaps she (there is little textual evidence to establish the personal identity of this prophet)— dedicates his or her life in service to the Word, the Holy One. A community in captivity to a dominant culture suffers from the erosion of their social purposes and carries the burden of religious desire that is alien to the empire.

As the focus of the Servant's revelation shifts from survival to preparation for homecoming, the everyday language of daily and domestic things gives way to a lyric vision that resonates beyond time and beyond human understanding. A dream of ordinary speech communicates a revelation that surpasses ordinary life through extraordinary experience. The Servant's first question, "What shall I cry?"(40:6), is answered in the closing. In the end is the beginning: "The word of our God will stand forever" (40:8).

Which word is that? What of the promise to David? What good is the covenant of peace to those struggling to survive the wars of Rome, or the Inquisition, or the Third Reich, or the current struggles of the West Bank and Gaza? Has the promise of homecoming and healing been sealed inside one nation, one border, one people? Where can we find the evidence for the Word that stands forever in this time and place?

Could it be we find it in these songs of an unknown Servant that preserve holy visions in the midst of human failure? These promises are remembered for generations after the community of this Servant returns from Babylon. How else can we explain how the songs of an unnamed singer from a marginal community survive the terrors of history and cultural amnesia of the world's great civilizations? Is the text sacred only because it survived, or is its survival actually the everlasting sign? God means what God says. The Word engages the world through the language and life of the prophets and the people of God again and again. Then the Word becomes flesh and dwells among us.

HEATHER MURRAY ELKINS

Psalm 65:(1-8) 9-13

[1]Praise is due to you,
  O God, in Zion;
 and to you shall vows be performed,
[2] O you who answer prayer!
 To you all flesh shall come.
[3]When deeds of iniquity overwhelm us,
  you forgive our transgressions.
[4]Happy are those whom you choose and bring near
  to live in your courts.
 We shall be satisfied with the goodness of your house,
  your holy temple.

[5]By awesome deeds you answer us with deliverance,
  O God of our salvation;
 you are the hope of all the ends of the earth
  and of the farthest seas.
[6]By your strength you established the mountains;
  you are girded with might.

Theological Perspective

This psalm of praise focuses on God's sustaining involvement in the world. That is to say, the psalm assumes from the outset that the Judeo-Christian God is not a distant creator who made the world, set it spinning, and then departed, like the deist notion of a watchmaker who winds up the watch and continues to exist only at far remove. Rather, God is an intimate creator who continues to live in close relationship to that which God has created. God is transcendent—beyond creation, not of creation—yet God is immanent, immersed in the nitty-gritty, everyday ups and downs of life.

Such ups and downs range from the vicissitudes of human experience to the contours of the landscape that surrounds us. Whereas the first half of the psalm focuses on God's sustaining involvement with people—their needs and their deeds—the second half focuses on God's sustaining involvement with the environment. God is in the city, and God is in the country. The muddle of politics and the grandeur of nature are both the realm of God.

Here we focus on the second half of the psalm, an awe-inspiring picture of bucolic beauty and fecundity. We find "lingering, intense, sensuous portraits"[1] of rain and of grain. Both are the gift of God, even

1. John Goldingay, *Psalms* (Grand Rapids: Baker Academic, 2007), 2:280.

Pastoral Perspective

Whenever I wonder *whether or not God understands* the human struggle, I read a psalm. The description of the human condition in the psalms is astonishingly honest and accurate. If we think we need to keep secrets from God to be loved, the psalms remind us that God knows us better than we know ourselves and still loves us. The psalmist assures us that "when deeds of iniquity overwhelm us, [God] forgives our transgressions" (v. 3).

Whenever I wonder *what God is doing* in the world or even if God is active in the world, I read a psalm. In particular, the psalms of lament presume that if we can get God's attention to our suffering and pain, God will act and things will be better. "By awesome deeds you answer us with deliverance, O God of our salvation" (v. 5a). At the heart of Israel's faith is the conviction that all life is sustained by God's breathing.

Whenever I wonder *how God is active in the world*, I read a psalm. In Psalm 65, we are given vivid pictures of God's creative care as the one who silences the seas (v. 7), waters the earth (v. 9), softens it with rain (v. 10), and provides (lit. "makes arrangements for") grain (v. 9) for the people. According to the psalmist, God has "made arrangements" so that all creation has what it needs to continue.

⁷You silence the roaring of the seas,
   the roaring of their waves,
   the tumult of the peoples.
⁸Those who live at earth's farthest bounds are awed by your signs;
   you make the gateways of the morning and the evening shout for joy.

⁹You visit the earth and water it,
   you greatly enrich it;
   the river of God is full of water;
   you provide the people with grain,
   for so you have prepared it.
¹⁰You water its furrows abundantly,
   settling its ridges,
   softening it with showers,
   and blessing its growth.
¹¹You crown the year with your bounty;
   your wagon tracks overflow with richness.
¹²The pastures of the wilderness overflow,
   the hills gird themselves with joy,
¹³the meadows clothe themselves with flocks,
   the valleys deck themselves with grain,
   they shout and sing together for joy.

Exegetical Perspective

This psalm is composed of three units, which are occupied with communal "praise that is due God" (v. 1). God is praised, first, for activity in the temple, particularly answering prayers and accepting vows (vv. 1–4 or 5). God is praised, second, for activity in creation, particularly for establishing mountains and quieting seas (vv. 4 or 5–8). God is praised, third, for the activity of giving the land of Israel torrents of rain (vv. 9–13).

Although the psalm can be divided neatly into three sections, what the psalmist does so well is to eschew tidy partitions of thought. Through lovely and imaginative poetry, the psalmist tends rather to bridge worlds that might otherwise remain separate. In our time, when efficiency demands compartmentalization, when science is set over against religion, when spirituality is contrasted with materialism, the psalmist offers a fresh perspective by embracing instead a holistic vision: (1) of God, (2) of humankind, and (3) of reality as a whole.

God. This psalm begins with an approachable God who forgives sins—even the overwhelming sorts of transgression that beset the community (v. 3)—and accepts their vows. God, however, is no pushover, a spineless dispenser of forgiveness in response to prayer and vows. The God who forgives (vv. 1–4) is

Homiletical Perspective

Preaching Psalm 65 is no easy task, because the psalm is messy. As the opening line makes clear, it is a psalm of praise, but the praise is offered for a number of reasons, not all of which are clearly related (for instance, forgiveness of sins, creation, and harvest). Many commentators argue that the psalm has three movements, delineated by the three appearances of the name of God in verses 1, 5, and 9—the first focusing on the temple, the second on the world, and the third on the fields. In truth, language and imagery overlap these divisions in ways that do not work together in some obvious strategy. It is a messy psalm, but then again praise is not always orderly, rational, and rhetorically well-structured. Just think of the flow of joys and concerns in many worship services.

Noting this messiness is not to imply that the psalm cannot be preached well. It simply means that the preacher must find a way into the text, a way to offer the text to the congregation that differs from an expository, line-by-line approach. To preach the messy flow of the text will lead to a messy sermon. The inroad will likely be one of two approaches: the preacher can either focus the sermon on the *experience* of praise represented in the psalm, or choose an *image* in the psalm as the anchor for the sermon.

Before we consider these two options, it is important to note that the psalm ends with, climaxes with,

Psalm 65:(1-8) 9-13

Theological Perspective

though it is the first portrait (vv. 9–10) that stresses God's vital role as the continuous actor and agent. God is the subject of nine consecutive verbs. It is God who visits, waters, enriches, provides, prepares, waters, settles, softens, and blesses.

In the second portrait (vv. 12–13), God is assumed as the creator, but it is the elements of that creation—the pastures, the hills, the meadows and the valleys—that are the subjects. They overflow, gird themselves, clothe themselves, and deck themselves so as to shout and sing together for joy. To whom do they do this? To God, their creator, of course.

Like the preface of a book that describes the one "without whom" the book could not be, so here the green fertile fields of God's creation attribute their harvest not to their good soil or their own fruitfulness, but to God's generosity. Here is vivid fulfillment of what Isaiah predicts: "the mountains and the hills before you shall burst into song, and all the trees of the field shall clap their hands" (Isa. 55:12). Their song is a psalm of praise to their creator.

The theological claim is simple and staggering. It is God's unprompted generosity and power that has caused creation to be and that continues to bring forth fruit. Here is creation theology at its best. The reality, however, is that the contemporary appropriation of creation has too often focused on the created rather than the creator—not least in debate about the means of creation.

Western theology owes much to the Celts for an appreciation of creation, especially in the context of worship; yet the West has been resistant to Celtic spiritual influence and creation theology more generally. It has been wary of pantheism, whereby God and nature are reduced to one another, as if creator and creation are equivalent (thus "Mother Nature"). Verses 12–13 stand counter to any pantheistic assumptions: meadows, hills, and valleys are glad to acknowledge their maker.

In one sense, the psalm's conclusion suggests that nature sets an example for humanity. Just as Isaiah's prophetic use of creation imagery serves to remind the exiles of God's ex nihilo capacity for newness (Isa. 40–55), so here, as elsewhere in the Psalms, creation imagery is invoked to guarantee the social order (e.g., Pss. 74, 77, 89). If God can bring the cosmic order into being, God can certainly restore human beings who stumble. In the second half of this psalm, the cycle of renewal in creation—from drought to rain, from winter to summer, from seed to harvest—provides the inspiration for

Pastoral Perspective

Whenever I wonder *why I should be grateful,* I read a psalm. Psalms that give thanks and praise for the abundance of God's gifts through creation remind us again and again that God's care is not limited by human need or even determined by what we request. As creator, God established the order in the universe, setting up the mountains and triumphing over chaotic cosmic waters. However, God is not only the creator of the world. God is the one who sustains the life brought forth.

Psalm 65 is a communal prayer of thanksgiving for God's awesome deeds of creation and salvation. God is pictured as one who acts as both creator and savior. As portrayed in this psalm, these two roles are not distinct from one another. Just as God stills the roaring of unruly waters, so God quells the tumult of warring peoples. Thus it is the creator God who has acted as savior. These marvels are acclaimed from east to west, from horizon to horizon—in other words, throughout the entire world.

The psalmist speaks in the name of the entire community and proclaims its gratitude to God for the abundance of creation. Chief among these blessings are the magnificent order and splendor of the universe, social harmony, and the fertility of the land. The water that was originally destructive is now manageable and life giving. This is the water that makes the land abundantly fertile. The psalmist uses vivid metaphors to represent this fertility. It is a vision of such abundance that even the "wagon tracks overflow with richness" (v. 11) because of what falls from the wagons. God's creation is full of bounty.

The psalmist's praise of God's activity in arranging the bounty of creation does not, however, fit the experience of everyone. Those who are without food in drought-stricken parts of the earth have difficulty acknowledging that God sustains the earth from rivers full of water. People whose lives were forever altered by the tsumani or rising tides from Hurricane Katrina are not likely to believe readily that God has tamed the roaring waters. Some people have seen only dry wagon tracks that resemble rocky gullies. As rivers flood and meadows burn, it would seem that God's arrangements of nature have failed. God seems absent. The sustaining, creative activity of God in the world is so hidden and so mysterious that it can be described only indirectly.

Even when the psalmist complains fiercely about God's neglect, the promise remains that God's absence is never permanent. The theological tenet of omnipresence is intended to declare that God is never absent—even though God may seem to be

an awesome God. The phrase "awesome deeds" (v. 5), which marks the transition between the forgiving God of the temple (vv. 1–4) and the powerful God who creates mountains and stills seas (vv. 6–8), is a dramatic term that evokes extraordinary actions. It conveys the "dread deeds" of God, who defends the right of the oppressed and sends arrows into the enemy of Israel's king (Ps. 45:4–5); God's liberating acts at the Red Sea (Ps. 106:22); the knitting of a child in its mother's womb (Ps. 139:13); and actions so awesome and unexpected that "the mountains quaked at your presence" (Isa. 64:3). The God who hears prayer and forgives sin and accepts vows in Psalm 65 is no wimpy God, but a God whose deeds could be turned to war, to the drama of liberation, to the miracle of birth, to actions that cause mountains to quake in awe.

Then there is something more in this psalm: this God cares about simple needs; this God sends rain. This is, in short, a practical God who responds to basic human need. Forgiving, accepting vows, and answering prayer—this is important. Creating the mountains and stilling the seas—awesome activities—these are important. So are the simple matters of grain in the pastures and flocks in the meadows. These need their rain, and this awesome and forgiving God gives it, and profusely so.

Humankind. The psalmist also refuses to divide humankind into insiders and outsiders, faithful and reprobate. This refusal is noteworthy because this psalm locates God in the temple: "We shall be satisfied with the goodness of your house, your holy temple" (v. 4). The psalmist even underscores this belief with a proverb containing two key verbs that depict election: "Blessed [NRSV "Happy"] are those whom you *choose* and *bring near* to live in your courts" (65:4).

Rather than allowing this conviction to lead to a condemnation of outlying nations that threaten the well-being of this house, the psalmist welcomes those from earth's farthest coasts to the temple. To the God who answers prayer "all flesh shall come" (v. 2). The God who delivers with awesome deed is "the hope of all the ends of the earth and of the farthest seas" (v. 5). Even the rain is not limited to Israel but is a sign that God visits "the earth" (v. 9). Therefore, despite a deep conviction that God dwells in the temple, that God has chosen Israel and brought it near, the psalmist refuses to exclude others, to mark them as outsiders. The psalmist joins at the hip a profound conviction that God dwells at the center of

praise for a bountiful harvest. In today's urbanized world, many of us are distant from plowing, planting, and reaping. We give thanks before a meal for food we have touched only at the very end of the production process. This is simply to acknowledge that whatever approaches preachers follow, urban and suburban congregations will have more steps to take to identify with the language and imagery of Psalm 65 than will rural ones.

First, the experience of praise in Psalm 65 is less one of "counting our many blessings" and more one of giving thanks for the one who blesses us in myriad ways. God is the one who answers prayers (v. 2), who forgives us (v. 3), who calls us into communion in worship (v. 4), who delivers us and is the hope of all (v. 5), who created the world and provides for its continued orderliness (vv. 6–8), who waters the earth that it might produce flocks and grain (vv. 9–13). In other words, Psalm 65 invites preachers and congregations to reflect on the character of God—known through God's creative, providential, and salvific interaction with the world—and invites this reflection to lead to a posture and life of praise and thanksgiving.

Second, the final movement of Psalm 65 (vv. 9–13, on which the lectionary focuses our attention) is dominated by water imagery. Indeed the lectionary chose this psalm because this imagery echoes the references to rain and snow watering the earth in the Isaiah reading for the day (55:10). However, the imagery functions differently in Isaiah 55 and Psalm 65. In Isaiah the image of rain and snow not returning to heaven until they have watered the earth and brought forth produce is a metaphor for the claim that God's word will not return empty, will not return until it has fulfilled God's purpose. In Psalm 65:9–13, by contrast, the water imagery is about water—literally. The psalmist praises God for the way God provides hydration for the earth and thus provides sustenance for God's people.

This literal reference to water in the psalm invites preachers in our day to engage their congregations in an eco-theological conversation. Does the way we care for stream and rivers, lakes and oceans, look as if we are praising God for the gift of water? How about the fact that our air pollution creates acid rain and snow? What about the way our poor care for the earth is changing climatic patterns and damaging the water cycle? Preachers who follow this line of thought must take care not simply to name the ways we have failed to praise God in our relationship to the waters of the earth, but must offer a constructive

Psalm 65:(1-8) 9-13

Theological Perspective

understanding God's ongoing work of restoration and re-creation in the first half of the psalm.

The psalm is certainly designed to inspire and to bring us, like the meadows and valleys, to shout and sing, to pause and wonder—not just at the marvel of creation, but at the first cause behind creation: God, the creator. This rhetoric is a challenge to our modern sensibilities. On the one hand, science is assumed to explain nature; thus secondary causes have apparently replaced the need for primary causality. On the other hand, humans have achieved such a level of autonomy that they tend to believe in no cause beyond the self. Walter Brueggemann asks, "Have we come to such a profane understanding of reality, such a reduction of creation to commodity, that we are incapable of speaking in this way?"[2]

The issue may best be conceived in economic terms. God is a God of abundance. As illustrated in the parables of the Sower or the Prodigal in the Gospels, there is no shortage of resources with God, whether those consist of the seed of God's word or the grace of God's forgiveness. By contrast, in a world that is largely economically driven, the resources are (by definition) limited. Without realizing it, scarcity becomes the lens through which we view all things, even in the church—except perhaps our capacity for iniquity (v. 3)!

Psalm 65 invites us to be newly overwhelmed— no longer by transgression and failure, but by the limitless resources of grace, flowing in a never-ending, ever-rejoicing cycle of abundance. "The river of God is full of water" (v. 9). It does not run dry.

JO BAILEY WELLS

Pastoral Perspective

absent. Because presence and absence are so connected in human life, the experience of God's absence is an unavoidable consequence of the experience of divine presence. Our dependence on God's presence makes the experience of God's absence all the more poignant. When we have known the life-sustaining nearness of God, the experience of God's absence is particularly painful. One of the consequences of experiencing the absence of God is that it creates a wintry sort of spirituality that is in solidarity with those whose horizon excludes God.

The psalmist uses vivid metaphors to point to the power and generosity of God in the wonders of creation. All of creation cries out to God in praise. This includes both the crops of the land meant for human consumption and the pastures intended for the animals. Hills and valleys and rivers and meadows bear witness to God. Sun and moon and stars praise God (Ps. 148:3–4). Israel testifies to the generosity of the creator God, and so does creation itself. Despite the incongruity between the claims of that testimony and what we see in daily life, the psalmist still declares gratitude and praise of God for the bounty of creation. Israel's belief in the faithfulness of God remains even when sovereignty of God is hidden.

When God seems hidden, creation cries out to God in praise and thanksgiving. The images of continuing creative activity in Psalm 65 bring us back to the one who has chosen us and saved through awesome deeds. The earth is blanketed with life. When we hear a valley "sing" or when we see meadow "decked out" splendidly (v. 13) or when hills are "girded" with joy (v. 12), we know that God is near. Creation sings before we do. It is creation's song we sing, in gratitude for the bounty we may not see. It is creation's splendor we celebrate in joy as the work of God, whose sovereign faithfulness is often hidden from view.

HERBERT ANDERSON

---

2. Walter Brueggemann, *The Message of the Psalms: A Theological Commentary* (Minneapolis: Augsburg, 1984), 136.

Exegetical Perspective

a national institution, the temple, with a belief that those on the outside also have their prayers answered, experience God's awesome deeds, and enjoy the fruits and fruitfulness of God's gift of rain.

Reality and Fantasy. The psalmist resists as well the tendency to opt for reality and to deride fantasy, to distinguish between history and myth. This refusal is evident in two respects. First, the psalmist traces the rich flow of water to "the river of God," which is "full of water" (v. 9), that is, to the Temple Mount. Psalm 46 imagines "a river whose streams make glad the city of God, the holy habitation of the Most High" (Ps. 46:4–5).

Ezekiel imagines an ankle-deep stream that becomes deeper as it flows from the temple to the Dead Sea, where it sweetens and enlivens the mineral waters (Ezek. 47:1–12; see also Isa. 33:21; Joel 3:18; Zech. 14:8). This belief, however, did not rest in reality but in the conviction that the temple was the epicenter of paradise, the source of the great world river (Gen. 2:10–14). We know that, in reality, there were small canals that transported small amounts of water to the temple and that the tunnel Hezekiah constructed was small enough to be vulnerable to enemy ambushes. In brief, reality and fantasy lay far apart, but this does not stop the psalmist from praising God for the waters that come from the temple to sustain fruitful harvests and healthy flocks.

The line between reality and fantasy is breached again when the psalmist describes the delight of the creation at the welcome presence of rain. Although the psalm contains tame descriptions—furrows are abundantly watered, ridges softened—it is replete with fantastic images: the year is crowned like royalty; God's wagon tracks drip fat and richness; the hills are clothed in joy, the meadows with flocks; the valleys are decked with grain and shout and sing with joy.

There is something delightful about the conclusion to this psalm, which makes much of rain, plain and simple. For the psalmist, there are not enough ways in everyday language to express delight, so the psalmist breaches the gossamer curtain that typically divides harsh reality from vivid fantasy. The basics of life, the fundamentals of food—which lie just within or, in drought, outside human reach—become the stuff of fantasy.

JOHN R. LEVISON

Homiletical Perspective

vision for how we can do better. In other words, the preacher needs to offer an ecological ethic that is presented as offering God due praise.

Another homiletical entry point into this psalm could lie in the fact that while in verses 9–13 the psalmist speaks literally of the water that providentially nourishes the earth, in verse 7 God is mentioned as silencing the roaring of the seas and waves. Following verse 6, which speaks of God establishing the mountains, this is clearly a reference to the image of God bringing forth creation from the formless void in Genesis 1. God places earth, with its orderliness, in between the waters above and the waters below. Even though water remains formless and disorderly and dangerous (which is mentioned a multitude of times in the Bible), God has nevertheless subdued the waters. This seems to be the psalmist's main point; but then, for just a second, the psalmist breaks out of referring to water literally and uses it as a metaphor for God's ordering of us:

> You silence the roaring of the seas,
> the roaring of their waves,
> *the tumult of the peoples.* (v. 7, emphasis added)

Having earlier named God as the one who forgives our transgressions, invites us into the temple, and is our hope of deliverance, the psalmist cannot help connecting the destructive force of water with the turmoil of humanity. Preachers would do well to note this parallel in the first half of the sermon. Then in the second half they could raise the question of what parallel is implied in the last part of the psalm. If God silences the waters and then uses them to nourish the earth, in what way is God redeeming us for usefulness?

O. WESLEY ALLEN JR.

Romans 8:1-11

¹There is therefore now no condemnation for those who are in Christ Jesus. ²For the law of the Spirit of life in Christ Jesus has set you free from the law of sin and of death. ³For God has done what the law, weakened by the flesh, could not do: by sending his own Son in the likeness of sinful flesh, and to deal with sin, he condemned sin in the flesh, ⁴so that the just requirement of the law might be fulfilled in us, who walk not according to the flesh but according to the Spirit. ⁵For those who live according to the flesh set their minds on the things of the flesh, but those who live according to the Spirit set their minds on the things of the Spirit. ⁶To set the mind on the flesh is death, but to set the mind on the Spirit is life and peace. ⁷For this reason the mind that is set on the flesh is hostile to God; it does not submit to God's law—indeed it cannot, ⁸and those who are in the flesh cannot please God.

⁹But you are not in the flesh; you are in the Spirit, since the Spirit of God dwells in you. Anyone who does not have the Spirit of Christ does not belong to him. ¹⁰But if Christ is in you, though the body is dead because of sin, the Spirit is life because of righteousness. ¹¹If the Spirit of him who raised Jesus from the dead dwells in you, he who raised Christ from the dead will give life to your mortal bodies also through his Spirit that dwells in you.

Theological Perspective

The majestic eighth chapter of the letter of Paul to the Romans begins with the gospel's astonishing conclusion: "There is therefore now no condemnation." The death sentence hanging over all humanity has been removed for those who are in Jesus Christ. This is a sudden reversal of death's judgment, announced in open court for all to hear. The gavel has come down and found you guilty, thus giving God his due. There is no loophole, no higher court to which one might appeal; the verdict is final. The law is God's terrible and inescapable judgment of the death sentence.

No one believes this, of course. When people receive the death sentence, they are forced by instinct to seek a gracious God apart from the law. Then Paul brings the new word that ends this old life: "But now, apart from law, the righteousness of God has been disclosed . . . through faith in Jesus Christ" (3:21). Paul preaches to those who are dead so that they stop contemplating their sorry state and behold their Lord Jesus Christ, for whose sake God raises the dead to a new life and declares, "There is therefore now no death sentence."

All stand condemned before God, but to whom belongs this gospel? Paul says it is "for those who are *in Christ Jesus*" (v. 1b). Who is in Christ, and how do they get that way? Likewise, who remains "in the

Pastoral Perspective

The brief opening line of this eighth chapter of Romans is nearly unbelievable: "There is therefore now no condemnation for those who are in Christ Jesus" (v. 1). Anyone who has lived has done things for which they deserve condemnation. Maybe "condemnation" is not a word we use, but surely "blame" and "guilt" are words we use. We receive word that a member of the church, a friend, is sick, and we promise to hold him or her in our thoughts and prayers. Life gets hectic and days go by without our uttering a single prayer or even having a sympathetic thought of our sick friend. The next week in church, we learn during announcements that our friend's health has worsened, and we wince at our own unfeeling, our failure to have allowed our friend's illness even to pierce our consciousness. Now we pray, "O God, help me remember to prepare a casserole or at the very least to send a card." If you are not guilty of a shortcoming like this one, there are undoubtedly other actions for which you feel guilt. All of us are deserving of some condemnation.

The phrase by which we confess sin "by what we have done, and by what we have left undone" covers just about all the things for which we are deserving of condemnation. If there is a boatload of guilt for the things we have done, there is surely an ocean full of guilt for the things we have left undone.

Exegetical Perspective

Paul has just concluded his poignant description of the human condition in Romans 7. Who will save us from our wretched captivity to the power of sin? Romans 8:1–11 provides both a logical answer and a powerful witness to life lived in freedom, a freedom that we cannot achieve but that is given by the Spirit through Christ's saving work. Paul's theology of grace is summed up in verses 3–4: sin's power, however great, cannot match the power of the Spirit. The Spirit frees us to live as God intends.

Perhaps because these verses provide such a distillation of Paul's theology, their translation and meaning are vigorously debated. The NIV reads that God sent his Son "to be a sin offering"—implying substitutionary atonement. The NRSV reads that Christ was sent by God "to deal with sin"—implying that Christ is victor. The Greek supports either translation. Regardless, Paul is clear that God accomplished for us through Christ what was impossible for us to do on our own. The One who frees us is the Son whom God sent, whether he was sent to bear the condemnation of God, the righteous judge, or sent to enter the battlefield for us and with us.[1] Christ

---

1. For the former, see N. T. Wright, "Romans," in *The New Interpreter's Bible* (Nashville: Abingdon Press, 2002), 10:575–76; for the latter, see Brendan Byrne, *Romans* (Collegeville, MN: Liturgical Press, 1996), 236.

Homiletical Perspective

Romans 8 is the crescendo of a powerful and difficult extended argument about faith and salvation. The first eleven verses make clear that the way of God and the way of the world, characterized here as "the flesh," are divergent ways of living and seeing. The way of God is life, and the way of the world is death. For many Western Christians today, who often view Jesus as a spiritual "booster," a moral teacher who will add value to their lives and help them do better, Romans 8 provides a challenging corrective.

Jesus and his teachings are not a helpful additive, like the protein powder in a fruit smoothie at Jamba Juice. Rather, through Jesus the Messiah, God decisively breaks through everything that separates us from God and makes it possible to live the life God intends for us. It is a life lived in right relationship with God, others, and the whole of creation. Through Jesus' resurrection, God is able to triumph over sin and death and provide a cosmic solution to the central problem of the human condition, separation from God and others, or sin.

When focusing on these first eleven verses of chapter 8, the preacher must be careful to define her terms in the vernacular of the congregation. Paul's language can sound strange and archaic. What does "flesh" mean? How about "sin," "law," and the "Spirit"? It is important for the preacher to distinguish *sarx*, the

Romans 8:1-11

Theological Perspective

flesh" (v. 9a), and what does it means to be "in the Spirit" (v. 9b)? What does it all mean? The theological issue has come to be called *union with Christ*. How are we united with Christ? What happens when such unity occurs? There is a long theological discussion that divides Paul into two parts on this issue; one part is a Protestant *actus forensis* (judicial declaration of guilt or innocence in the divine court), and the other part appears as a Catholic participation of the lower being in the higher that was considered to be a "mystical Paul." This has tended to force a false distinction into Paul's letters.

On the one hand, Paul is depicted as teaching an external, imputed righteousness that does not change the person but represents the new judgment made by God wherever faith is found. On the other hand, Paul is taken to imply that a mystical, ontological change occurs when Christ indwells a person by means of love; thus love perfects or completes faith. Briefly put, is one "in Christ" because of an external declaration that does not count the sin, or is one in Christ because of a metaphysical alteration or participation of the lower being in the higher?

There are three ways that the preposition "in" can be taken: locally (in us), instrumentally (through us), or modally (with or to us). Mystical versions have preferred the local "in" and so have thought of union with Christ as metaphysical elevation of the mortal into the immortal, so that the human becomes divine and avoids death. Time and place have had to be abstracted from this world. Interestingly, modern exegetical versions have preferred this, because it can be tied to enthusiasm among pagans or Jewish mysticism and so fit the thesis of the evolutionary development of the history of religions.

The Roman version has preferred the instrumental, in which the church serves as the ongoing incarnation of Christ. Christ the Lord, as the invisible head of the church, imparts his life to a particular ecclesial body. The Holy Spirit operates through church teachers who provide authoritative interpretations of Scripture that lead obedient disciples to their destinies in Christ. In the end, ecclesiology trumps Christology. The modal "in," implying a human possibility, also fails to describe what Paul means by "in Christ," as if Christ were present only when certain religious sorts really want to go looking for him, actualizing their potential.

Indeed, Christ is too active, too alive, too verbal, too present, and too much the actual Lord for any of these to work. What is missing from these interpretations of Paul's prepositional phrase is the truly

Pastoral Perspective

So how are we to believe this nearly unbelievable thing—that there is therefore now no condemnation for those in Christ? The key is perhaps found in the tiniest phrase: "in Christ." To be "in Christ" is categorically different from not to be "in Christ." It is not simply a difference of degree, but a genuine difference of kind.

To be "in Christ" is to be a part of something far larger than oneself. It is to encounter a power astronomically greater than the sum of all the willpower you have ever mustered, added to all the physical power you have ever exerted, added to all the clout you have ever had. Add all those up, and it is infinitesimal, compared to the power of God in Christ. There is a severe power shortage on our side. It is not that we are powerless, for surely we have the power to hurt others and ourselves, as well as to help others and ourselves. It is just that our power is so bound by our capacities, so limited by our perspectives, so tied to our locale. This may be what Paul means by the phrase "in the flesh."

To be "in Christ" is to be swept up in the power of the Spirit and be free from what has bound us, limited us, tied us. To be "in Christ" is not the result of something we do; it is something God does for us. Paul does not exhort the reader to get his or her act together and get "in Christ." Instead, he announces, he boldly proclaims: "But you are not in the flesh; you are in the Spirit, since the Spirit of God dwells in you" (v. 9). This proclamation is the good news.

It is difficult to believe this good news, but it is not impossible to believe it. To believe it is to reorient one's life toward a power greater than oneself. Even more, it is to have one's life reoriented by a power greater than any power we know in this world. Perhaps the greatest power we know in this world is the power of death, which ultimately conquers all of us and everyone we know. Death's power is not simply at the moment of our dying; it is a power that creeps into our lives, our communities, and our bodies long before the moment we breathe our last.

Ask any alcoholic about the power of death, and if he or she can speak truth, the words will be about the living death they know. Ask any parent of a child who is dying from a devastating disease, and you will hear of the power of death to break a heart even before the child's body gives up. However, even this power is not enough when compared to the power of "the Spirit of him who raised Jesus from the dead" (v. 11).

In the concluding lines of this portion of Romans, Paul proclaims that this Spirit "will give life

does for us what even God's law could not accomplish because of sin.

There is likewise debate about what Paul means when he uses the term *nomos* ("law"). Is Paul referring to Mosaic law, or does he mean natural law that governs all of human life? N. T. Wright argues that the definite article requires us to read "the law" as in "Torah." In this reading, the law caused sin to be gathered up in one place: on Israel, and then on Israel's Messiah, where it was defeated on the cross.[2]

Others read "law" more generically, insisting that Paul uses the word in a wide variety of ways, so that its meaning must be determined by context. The preacher must not resolve this tension by simplistically contrasting "law" and "grace." Earlier in Romans Paul argued at great length the inherent goodness of the law of God (7:1–13); to ignore this defense of the law is to misread Paul. The rightful contrast is, rather, between Adam and Christ, between life in the flesh and life in the Spirit.

Again, one must be careful. When Paul contrasts "life in the flesh" *(sarx)* and "life in the Spirit" *(pneuma)* he is not dissecting humans into two distinct parts, as if our bodies are inherently evil. This heretical dualism has caused enormous harm. Such a reading negates the scriptural affirmation that the substance of human beings is made in God's own image and given the breath of life. (In the LXX of Genesis 1, the word for "breath" is *pneuma*.) Moreover, it negates the very argument Paul makes in this passage: that Christ took on the likeness of the flesh *(sarx)* to condemn the sin of the flesh *(sarx)*, granting us life in our mortal bodies *(sōma)*. As descendants of Adam, we were condemned *to* sin; and *because of* our sin, we were condemned. Then, when God's own Son took the form of sinful flesh and did not succumb to sin, sin itself became condemned.

Indeed, what God has accomplished through Christ is the freedom truly to *live*. Because the Spirit of God dwells in us, we have the possibility of life and peace. An analogy I heard is this: Imagine you wish to paint, not in a beginner's sort of way, but beautifully, like Michelangelo. No matter how many lessons you take, how much you practice, how hard you try, you simply cannot do it. Even if you are very gifted, you will create only a facsimile of his masterful art. The only possible way to paint like Michelangelo is to *be* Michelangelo. Of course you cannot do that either—unless the spirit of Michelangelo is to live within you. Then, and only then, could you create such beauty.

2. Wright, "Romans," 578–79.

Greek word for "flesh," from *sōma*, translated "body," so as not to set up a gnostic mind-body dualism. Paul contrasts flesh and Spirit, not body and spirit. It is not our bodies that are the problem, but whom or what our bodies serve.

"Flesh" could be described as the fallen human condition, our focus on the self rather than on God. It is rebellion against God, idolatry or worship of things that are not God. "Flesh" also includes what Paul describes in Romans 7, our inability to "do the right thing" or what we want to do. As Paul puts it, "I do not understand my own actions. For I do not do what I want, but I do the very thing I hate" (7:15). Money, financial security, youth, health, work, good looks, busyness, and technology are just a few of the things we worship instead of God.

The preacher also needs to help the congregation understand that by "sin" Paul does not mean individual moral failings, but something larger and more pervasive. According to his argument up to this point, sin is a power that resides in the world and in us. This power or force makes it impossible to follow God or the law. It brings estrangement from God, from others, and from God's creation.

Additionally, Paul believes that all of us are obedient to something. If we are not obedient or "slaves" to God and God's ways, we are "slaves" to sin or whatever is not of God. This will be a hard sell in a culture that prizes autonomy and independence, and in which people understand themselves to be largely self-made. By contrast, Paul argues, I think rightly, that we give our allegiance to and are thus formed by God or what is not of God. If we are not obedient to God we are living in the realm of "death," even in this life. Through Jesus' resurrection we all have the possibility of moving from death, or life without God, to eternal life—life with God forever. Paul, like Deuteronomy 30:19, exhorts us to "choose life."

Law, although here it refers to Torah or the Jewish law, intended to give God's people life and keep them in right relationship with God, could be explained to an audience of Christians or seekers as our attempts to earn our way to God. They include all of the items listed under "idolatry," anything we do, say, or try to be to make ourselves acceptable to God and win God's favor. For overachieving Christians, this might be understood as our efforts to win an A+ from God. Paul's argument condemns this wrong thinking. We cannot do anything to earn God's favor or blessing. There is no way to earn our salvation. Rather, salvation and true life—both now and in the life to come—are a gift. As Paul writes in

Romans 8:1-11

Theological Perspective

eschatological. There is an end to the old creation and the beginning of a new in Christ: "For the law of the Spirit of life in Christ Jesus has set you free from the law of sin and of death" (v. 2). This is not a new metaphysical law; it is the Hebrew way of putting something to an end by applying the verb against the verb. Death is put to death. Law is "lawed" against, and this is the true work of the Holy Spirit. The letter killed—it ended in a death sentence. The Spirit is life. The law showed itself to be sick on account of the flesh (v. 3). Righteousness was always impossible for law; indeed, the law was never meant to make anyone righteous.

Instead, God sent his own Son—incarnate—who took the death sentence of sin in his flesh and pronounced a death sentence upon it. Not law, but Christ. You stood under the death sentence, and then Christ stepped in with a new declaration. Death does not bind him any longer. The goal of flesh is law that seeks to be righteous in one's own self, but ends in death. Eschatology turns this around. The Spirit's goal is to bring Christ to you while you are ungodly.

So the dramatic conclusion: "If the Spirit of him who raised Jesus from the dead dwells in you, he who raised Christ from the dead will give life to your mortal bodies also through his Spirit that dwells in you" (v. 11). This is not merely mystical union or instrumental ecclesiology; it is death to the old sinner and a new creation by the Creator Spirit, who places Christ's death sentence upon your death sentence, in order to create anew out of nothing.

STEVEN D. PAULSON

Pastoral Perspective

to your mortal bodies" (v. 11). By this Paul could mean that our bodies can get the air they need, the coursing blood required to keep them going, even the food and water to nourish them. Undoubtedly Paul means at least this; but there is most likely something more expressed here. Giving life to our mortal bodies is not simply giving them the essentials of bodily functions. It is to bring to our bodies, bound as they are to time and space, a power that is able to connect them to a movement of God's Spirit greater than ourselves.

This Spirit that we have "in Christ" is able to do so much more than we are able to do. On our own, we are not able to get it all done; so much is left undone. By this tiny phrase, "in Christ," Paul has said that we are not constrained by our limitations, shortcomings, failings; we are not even condemned by our cruelties, hurtful ways, hateful actions. Instead, we are free. *Free.*

"There is therefore now no condemnation for those who are in Christ Jesus" (v. 1). This freedom is nearly unbelievable, but not completely unbelievable. It is the freedom given to us to go beyond our limitations. It is the freedom of being part of God's movement with the world that transcends our locale and our lifetime. This freedom does not transport us out of our bodies into a netherworld beyond the pearly gates. Instead it frees us to live fully in this world, in this mortal body we have. This freedom is ours in Christ. It is the result of the power of God, a power greater than the sum of all the powers.

DAVID M. GREENHAW

Exegetical Perspective

So it is with Christ's Spirit dwelling in us. We are—thanks be to God—able to live life in the Spirit of God. It is not our own accomplishment, but Christ's Spirit dwelling in us, empowering us to live in God's righteousness. This is the "impossible possibility" of which the theologian Karl Barth writes in his commentary *Epistle to the Romans*.[3] By our own power and volition it is impossible; the history of humanity, and of God's people, is all the proof one needs. By the power of God, though, our minds can be set on what the Spirit desires.

A vivid contemporary example of this possibility comes from the 12-step tradition of Alcoholics Anonymous. For an alcoholic, there are two choices: the way of death and the way of life. The first step is to admit that we are powerless over alcohol and that our lives have become unmanageable. The second is to believe that a Power greater than ourselves can restore us to sanity. The third is to turn our will and our lives over to the care of God.

So it is for the Christian. Substitute the word "sin" for "alcohol," and you have the crux of this passage. We are powerless over sin, which will inevitably lead us to death; but in the Spirit we have the possibility of life. Sin is still a daily possibility; God has not eliminated it from this world once and for all—not yet. However, a life of righteousness is *also* a possibility now, because of the Spirit's power. As long as our minds are "on the flesh," sin will drive us; but if our minds are set on the Spirit—our will and our lives are in God—then life is not only a possibility, but a promise. This is the hope in which we live: that God who raised Christ from the dead will give life to us—body, mind, and spirit—through the power of the Spirit dwelling in us.

KAREN CHAKOIAN

Homiletical Perspective

Romans 3, "all have sinned and fall short of the glory of God; they are now justified by his grace as a gift, through the redemption that is in Christ Jesus" (3:23–24). It is only through God's grace, embodied in Jesus the Messiah, that we are saved. Further, we are saved through faith in God's promises, and this faith is not something we can or must conjure up, but something God gives us. Everything comes from God. All the initiative begins and rests with God.

"Spirit" is arguably the most important word in these verses; it appears eleven times. "Spirit" is not an impersonal force or a characteristic of human beings, but God's Holy Spirit, given to Jesus' followers after his resurrection to guide and comfort them. It is what Jesus' followers receive when they are baptized into Jesus' death and resurrected through the waters of baptism. The Spirit dwells in those baptized in Jesus' name and keeps their minds on the things of God and life, rather than the ways of death. The Spirit is their assurance of God's promises, the person of the Trinity who will guide them as they navigate the challenges of this life. The Spirit will give Jesus' followers peace, come what may.

All of this means, as is proclaimed in the first verse of Romans 8, that "there is therefore now no condemnation for those who are in Christ Jesus." This is good news indeed, for both the Jew and the Gentile who—in faith—live and proclaim the new creation inaugurated by Jesus' resurrection.

BLAIR ALISON POGUE

---

3. Karl Barth, *Epistle to the Romans*, trans. E. C. Hoskyns (1922; New York: Oxford University Press, 1968), 282.

Matthew 13:1-9, 18-23

¹That same day Jesus went out of the house and sat beside the sea. ²Such great crowds gathered around him that he got into a boat and sat there, while the whole crowd stood on the beach. ³And he told them many things in parables, saying: "Listen! A sower went out to sow. ⁴And as he sowed, some seeds fell on the path, and the birds came and ate them up. ⁵Other seeds fell on rocky ground, where they did not have much soil, and they sprang up quickly, since they had no depth of soil. ⁶But when the sun rose, they were scorched; and since they had no root, they withered away. ⁷Other seeds fell among thorns, and the thorns grew up and choked them. ⁸Other seeds fell on good soil and brought forth grain, some a hundredfold, some sixty, some thirty. ⁹Let anyone with ears listen! . . .

Theological Perspective

This parable and its interpretation are sandwiched between stories of opposition to the gospel. Chapters 11–12 contain multiple stories of opposition and misunderstanding of Jesus' ministry. Chapter 13 concludes with Jesus' hometown rejecting him. The parable in between these rejection/opposition narratives may be an answer to the question, why does the gospel find hospitable space to grow among some people but not among others? The flip side of this question is, what are the necessary conditions for fruitful discipleship? In answering these questions, Matthew gives us a practical theological explanation of why so many more hear than understand, why more disciples are planted than bear fruit, and which elements are necessary for fruitful discipleship.

Matthew gives his readers/hearers at least three points of view to consider. The preacher could harvest a rich theological field if she approached the facets with "and" rather than "or": this parable is the parable of the Sower, the parable of the Four Soils, *and* the parable of the Miraculous Yields. The resulting topics of this approach include the extravagant evangelism of God; the importance of understanding, perseverance, and attentiveness; and the miracle of faith.

The Sower. Whether one pictures the sower as preacher, teacher, evangelist, or missionary, as Jesus, or

Pastoral Perspective

This passage is often called the parable of the Sower, sometimes the parable of the Soils. Maybe it should be called the Hundredfold Harvest. Even if the harvest were only thirtyfold, this story would end with a miracle. Sevenfold meant a good year for a farmer, and tenfold meant true abundance. Thirtyfold would feed a village for a year and a hundredfold would let the farmer retire to a villa by the Sea of Galilee.

Bushels of abundance are where this parable leads. To be sure, Jesus starts with a good dose of realism. Everyone in the crowd nods his or her head as Jesus describes the trials of traditional first-century farming. Unlike a modern American farmer, who carefully prepares the soil with just the right pH balance and then injects the seed into the ground, farmers in Jesus' time cast the seed and *then* plow the land. With this scattershot approach, it is no surprise that some seed falls on hard soil, other seed on ground too rocky for good roots, and still other seed among thorns and weeds. Those are the facts of life, and everyone knows it, including Jesus.

Both Jesus and those who follow him also know such facts apply not only to farming, but also to his own ministry at that time. The seed of his teaching has fallen on rock-laden, thorn-strewn ground. In preceding chapters, the disciples lose faith during a storm at sea. The Pharisees want to choke out his

[18]"Hear then the parable of the sower. [19]When anyone hears the word of the kingdom and does not understand it, the evil one comes and snatches away what is sown in the heart; this is what was sown on the path. [20]As for what was sown on rocky ground, this is the one who hears the word and immediately receives it with joy; [21]yet such a person has no root, but endures only for a while, and when trouble or persecution arises on account of the word, that person immediately falls away. [22]As for what was sown among thorns, this is the one who hears the word, but the cares of the world and the lure of wealth choke the word, and it yields nothing. [23]But as for what was sown on good soil, this is the one who hears the word and understands it, who indeed bears fruit and yields, in one case a hundredfold, in another sixty, and in another thirty."

Exegetical Perspective

Matthew 13 falls in the midsection of each of the three major literary frameworks for this Gospel that receive support in today's academic circles. The most widely embraced is the traditional fivefold structural pattern, based on the belief that Matthew stylistically modeled his material after the five books of Moses. J. D. Kingsbury has argued for a simpler threefold pattern, consisting of the material leading up to Jesus' public ministry, the ministry itself, and the movement to Jerusalem with the passion and the ministry of the resurrected Christ.[1]

More recently Ben Witherington III has presented a sixfold structural pattern.[2] Within this structural formula, Matthew presents Jesus as a sage within the wisdom tradition. Whatever pattern Matthew followed, this chapter contains Jesus' personal assessment of the public response to his ministry. Through the ages these parables have served as aids to the church's assessment of public response to its ministries.

Through the eight parables collected in chapter 13, Matthew presents Jesus as understanding that within his life and ministry the kingdom of God has

1. J. D. Kingsbury, *The Parables of Jesus in Matthew 13* (London: SPCK, 1969), 130–31.
2. Ben Witherington III, *Matthew* (Macon, GA: Smyth & Helwys, 2006), 14–21.

Homiletical Perspective

"A sower went out to sow."

What do we make of a sower who throws seeds everywhere, even in such unlikely, seemingly unproductive places? Quite apart from best agricultural practices, what sort of worldview is suggested by someone who throws seeds on a well-worn path where birds can eat them, or on rocky ground where it is unlikely that they will grow, or among thorns that will choke them?

We scratch our heads and wonder at such a foolish waste of seed and other precious resources on the part of this sower. The logical place to sow seed, of course, is on good soil, and we readily take this message to heart. Even if we are not farmers, the lesson here is easily applied to our situation. If you ever set about to plant a new church, plant it in a carefully scrutinized, sure-to-grow neighborhood. If you ever decide to develop a new missionary opportunity, choose one where the odds are good and the possibilities are promising. If you ever decide to double your church's membership, then craft your message for a promising demographic and reach out to people who are motivated and purposeful and driven enough to receive and do something with it. Be strategic about location—like any self-respecting hamburger or gas station or grocery chain—and maximize your effort toward the arena of greatest

Matthew 13:1-9, 18-23

Theological Perspective

as God, the sower is one who spreads the good news; and we have a much more interesting story because the soil is not cultivated prior to seeding. Present-day evangelism techniques often emphasize plowing first: do your demographic work, determine your target audience, develop your communication strategies to fit your target. Do any of these strategies truly reveal the nature of the soil in which one is trying to seed the word? No. The sower does not know in advance what is beneath the soil's surface, where the ground is hard, where the soil is shallow, or where weeds will choke. Neither the church nor a preacher knows the quality of the soil before sowing. It is the purpose of the sower—the preacher, teacher, apostle, missionary, evangelist, and the church per se—to sow.

Four Soils. Sowing results in *some* disciples. In Matthew's interpretation of this parable, he once refers to the seed as the good news (v. 19) but otherwise uses "seed" to speak of "germinated disciples" who have begun to grow. The parable of the Four Soils—hardened, shallow, thorny, and good—serves to remind the church of the necessary conditions for fruitful discipleship. In order for disciples to grow, they must understand, attend properly, and persevere.

It would be hard to overstate the importance of understanding for Matthew. Without understanding, the word finds no place to implant, and the ever-near evil one, like the hovering bird, snatches away the potential of faith. Understanding opens the ground, but it is important to note that understanding does not mean mere acknowledgment. Rather, understanding is insight tied to urgency to act. Understanding is life-attuning knowledge.

Imagine finding yourself on a train track and coming to understand that a locomotive will run you over in ten seconds. That understanding leads to action! In Matthew's story, Jesus the teacher tries to impart to his hearers the fundamental *sine qua non* of discipleship: understanding that enables discipleship to begin. Through his Gospel, Matthew seeks the same end. Through its ministries, the church is called to do likewise.

Understanding, however, is a necessary, but not sufficient element for fruitful discipleship. Also necessary are attentiveness and perseverance. Matthew reminds us repeatedly (including in the lections for this Sunday and for the next two) that disciples must endure the evil one's powerful opposition. One form this opposition takes is persecution. Joy in response to receiving the gospel is wonderful, but "trouble or persecution . . . on account of the word" (v. 21) will arise.

Pastoral Perspective

message. Jesus is soon to experience the hard soil of his hometown as Nazarenes reject him. Jesus does not just tell this parable. He lives it.

So does the community for whom Matthew's Gospel is written. First-century Palestine is a hard time and place to be a Christian. Due to both poverty and persecution, massive numbers of people are migrating out of the region. Within the church itself there are dissenters and false prophets. With this parable, Jesus reminds his followers—and Matthew reminds his community—that rejection of Jesus' message does not mean the message is wrong or their efforts are folly. It is simply a fact of life, whether in farming or in faith.

Like Jesus, preachers cast the gospel as broadly as the sower in the parable does, with no guarantee where it will land. On Sunday mornings, we look out on congregations of people who are here for all kinds of reasons. There is the newcomer who is "church shopping" or "trying out" Christianity. There is the person in crisis who will vanish when things get better. There is the family who comes "for the kids" but quits once the kids' soccer season starts.

Standing in front of them all is the preacher, who has poured heart and soul into the sermon, in hope it will take root, but who also knows her odds are not any better than the sower's. Have you ever preached what you thought was a powerful message, only to have someone say, "Sorry, it didn't connect for me today," or offer the ubiquitous, "I like your new haircut"? Did you climb back into the pulpit the next Sunday and preach your next sermon?

That is our job, our calling. To sow the seed and to bear the heartache when it falls on rocky, arid, or weed-infested ground. In accepting that calling, we stand in solidarity with the people in our congregations who also know the hard truth of this parable. The parent whose words of guidance and compassion fall on their teenager's deaf ears knows hard-packed ground. The businessman who produces a quality product and pays employees a living wage, only to see his clients go where things are cheaper, is well acquainted with shallow roots. This parable reminds us all that we are not alone in such times, even as it reminded the first crowd who heard it.

The parable also reminds us where to keep our focus. In my own ministry I am often tempted to spend my resources—time, energy, hope—trying to coax, cajole, and beg for growth from inhospitable places and people. I can also spend much time despairing when the seed does not take root. The sower does not do that. He accepts the reality that

broken into this age and will continue to grow until such time as God determines appropriate for the consummation. The first of these parables and its explanation comprise the Gospel lectionary selection for this week. Noticeably missing from the lectionary are those verses (vv. 10–17) in which Jesus explains his rationale for teaching in parables: the secrets of the kingdom can be known only by those who are his disciples. Others may see and hear, but they are incapable of comprehending.

As a form of metaphorical speech, a parable can be anything from a one-liner to a longer narrative. Known usually as the parable of the Sower, our text follows the narrative pattern. Although Matthew says Jesus utilizes parables earlier in his ministry (5:14–16; 7:24–27; and perhaps 9:15–17; 11:16–17; 12:43–45), the block of teaching collected in this discourse consists entirely of parables, linked by verses devoted to the reason for teaching in parables; private explanations of two of the parables to the disciples; and general admonitions to listen.

The predominant theme addressed by the parables of Jesus is the kingdom of God. If the observation of C. H. Dodd that the purpose of a parable is to "tease the mind into active thought" is correct, then what better way to describe the indescribable kingdom of God than to tease the minds of those who would hear?

The discourse of chapter 13 further illuminates Jesus' answer to the kinship question with which chapter 12 ends. Assuming the sitting position preferred by wisdom rabbis/sages for teaching (v. 1), and echoing the setting for the "discourse (sermon) on the mount" during which the blessings and "laws" of the kingdom are presented, Jesus begins to share fresh lessons about the kingdom. These lessons focus on those who are his kin not by blood but by hearing and understanding what he says.

The parable of the Sower or Soils, one of six parables found in all of the Synoptic Gospels (Mark 4:3–9; Luke 8:5–8), begins and ends with the admonition to "listen." The accompanying interpretation moves "listening" to "hearing." Although the authenticity of the interpretation continues to be debated, the authenticity of the parable itself as coming from Jesus remains widely accepted. While it has been argued that the explanations found both in Mark and here are redactions of either the Gospel writer or a later church leader, the given explanation remains true to the parable itself. It addresses an issue that could well have been true to Jesus' own self-understanding and fits the pattern

result. Find the good soil and throw seed on *it!* It's just good business!

It seems obvious that the sower in this text is anything but a good businessperson. He seems willing to just fling that seed anywhere. Why does he do this? Maybe he does so in order to remind us that the gospel might be bigger than good business principles, bigger than just good soil. Since this is a parable, we may want to entertain the possibility that this sower throws seed just anywhere in order to suggest that "anywhere" is, in the final analysis, the arena of God's care and redemptive activity. This sower throws seed not only on good soil, but also amid the rocky, barren, broken places, in order to suggest that God's vision for the world is itself often apprehended in strange and broken places.

I once caught a glimpse of God and God's mercy in such a place. I was with a group of civic leaders— lawyers, politicians, foundation representatives, journalists—touring various outposts of our city's criminal justice system. It was near the end of the day, and we were visiting the juvenile court and detention center. That place was so depressing, its landscape marked by wire-mesh gates with large padlocks and razor wire wrapped around electrified fences. When the doors clanged shut behind us, I imagined how final they must always sound when adolescents—children!—are escorted there. We were led, floor by floor, through this facility by an amazing young judge who worked there. She showed us the holding cells where the new inmates are processed. She showed us the classrooms where an ongoing education is at least attempted. She showed us the courtrooms where cases are prosecuted.

Near the end of our tour, she led us down one bleak hall to give us a sense of the cells where young offenders lived. Each cell had a steel door with narrow slots about two-thirds of the way up, through which various pairs of eyes were watching us as we walked down the hall. Some of these children were accused of major crimes; some of them were repeat offenders. Most of them, we learned, had had little or no nurture across their brief lives—not from a primary adult who cared about them, not from family, not from neighborhood, not from church. It was hard to notice those eyes staring through narrow slots without doing something. So I lingered at one door and whispered to one pair of eyes: "God loves you." The eyes did not appear to register much, and sometimes I wonder what, if anything, happened next. Did that news fall on the path to get eaten by birds? Did it fall among thorns to get choked out? I will never know.

Matthew 13:1-9, 18-23

Theological Perspective

Disciples need to be prepared not only for persecution (troubles without), but also temptation (troubles within), especially in the form of anxious cares (see Matt. 6:25–32) and "the lure of wealth" (v. 22). Elsewhere (see Matt. 19:16–22), Matthew provides examples of disciples lured away by attention to their worldly anxieties or their attachment to wealth. In Matthew 6:33, Jesus' counter exhortation is to attend first to the "empire of the heavens."[1]

Miraculous Yields. Can we shift the interpretation of this text, however, from the descriptive to the hortatory? Jesus' community is populated not with passive seeds, who have no control over the soil in which they are planted, but with *agents*, who can shift themselves from rocky or thorny ground to good soil. The factor that disciples are not able to control, however, is whether or not the path is hard, whether or not there is understanding. Understanding, like faith, is a gift.

Considering the powerful opposition to the gospel—the evil one, hardened hearts, persecution, the anxiety-driven lure of wealth—it is a miracle that there are disciples and that the empire of the heavens grows. The yields are miraculous because, ultimately, all growth comes from God. Opposition may eliminate three-fourths of the seed, but the remaining seeds yield abundant fruit. Faith that initiates discipleship is a gift. Fruitful yield as the outcome of discipleship is a gift. While theologians have debated the contribution, if any, of human agency to the process of being saved, from the apostle Paul through the Reformation and into contemporary times, this claim is nearly constant: faith is a gift from God, and fruitful discipleship is the work of God in us. We might try to predict why some people receive faith and become fruitful disciples but, really, we do not know why some people receive faith and some do not, and whether those who first receive will be fruitful disciples.

The "therefore" to all this is the call to spread seed extravagantly, to school disciples in strategies to deal with opposition and temptation, and to give thanks to God for fruitful growth. Matthew's perspective is far away from belt- and gun-handle-notching evangelism. Perhaps this text should always be paired with Acts 2, in hopes of keeping the church both hopeful and humble in regard to evangelism.

GARY PELUSO-VERDEND

Pastoral Perspective

some seed, a goodly portion of it, will fall on bad soil, and he keeps sowing. As the next fifteen chapters of Matthew demonstrate, Jesus keeps spreading the word, no matter how dry, rocky, or weed-infested the ground. His followers are called to do so the same.

But like Jesus, we have yet another calling, also found in this parable. The story does not end with the inhospitable soils—though many sermons do. It does not even end with a normal harvest from the good soil. It ends with a miracle, a hundredfold harvest. It is our job to trust—and preach—that possibility as well.

The parable's ending is its greatest challenge. Jesus goes beyond simply encouraging his listeners to "keep on keeping on" in the face of rejection. Instead, his parable challenges them—and us—to believe in God's abundance.

If the parable ended with the sevenfold harvest from good soil, then *dayenu*, as our Jewish brothers and sisters might say. That would be sufficient, a good story of encouragement and hope.

However, this parable is not simply pragmatic. It is also filled with promise. We are called to proclaim that promise, even in the face of rejection and the reality of this world. Novelist Bebe Moore Campbell writes, "Some of us have that empty-barrel faith. Walking around expecting things to run out. Expecting that there isn't enough air, enough water. Expecting that someone is going to do you wrong. The God I serve told me to expect the best, that there is enough for everybody."[1]

That is the God this parable calls us to trust. Jesus knows the hard ways of this world. He also knows the abundant ways of God. May we as pastors have faith in God's abundance too.

TALITHA J. ARNOLD

---

1. Here and in the reflections on the next two Sundays, I use this translation from Warren Carter, *Matthew and the Margins: A Sociopolitical and Religious Reading* (Maryknoll, NY: Orbis, 2000).

1. Bebe Moore Campbell, *Singing in the Comeback Choir* (New York: Putnam, 1998), 131.

Exegetical Perspective

of the disciples' learning curve as presented by the parable.

Joachim Jeremias has made a strong case that the activity of the sower described within the parable was familiar in the context of the time.[3] It should be quickly obvious that the sower's intent is not to waste seed on poor soil but rather to cast seed onto whatever ground might produce the desired crop. Regardless of how good the seed is or how caring the sower is, some seed sown in such a fashion will land on soil under less than favorable conditions and result in no growth, poor growth, or truncated growth. There has been some academic discussion as to whether the resulting harvest should be regarded as bountiful or simply at the higher end of an average yield. Regardless, the portion of seed that does fall on good soil results in a hearty harvest.

That both the sower and the seed are constant, while the results across the four types of soil change, implies that the purpose of the parable is to assist the disciples, and perhaps Jesus himself, in understanding why the response to the gospel message shared so consistently varies so greatly. The sower and soil are understood as good. That some soils are labeled "bad" is not because of any choice of their own, nor is the good soil "good" because of what it does or does not do to make it more productive.

In understanding the soils, one must resist pushing the metaphor too far or reading into it more than the context warrants. The good soil is good simply because its nature provides an environment in which the seed can be nurtured to full maturity. Thus, the kingdom of heaven is like a bountiful crop produced in spite of what seem to be overwhelming setbacks.

The lectionary reading omits verses 10–17, which contain the disciples' request to Jesus to explain why he has chosen to teach in parables. Jesus responds that it "has been given [to them] to know the secrets of the kingdom of heaven" (v. 11). This gift is a new blessing or beatitude (vv. 16, 17). They have been given understanding. With that said, the focus of a disciple of any era should not be on good efforts that fail, but on celebrating the abundant harvest that is produced.

J. DAVID WAUGH

Homiletical Perspective

As the tour went on, the cumulative effect of all this brokenness got to one member of our group, who finally just stopped in the hallway and began to cry. When the judge noticed this, she paused in her narration, walked back and put her arms around that person, and, with tears in her own eyes, said, "I know. I understand."

I thought to myself, "If I am ever to be judged, I want a judge like that." Then it dawned on me—like a seed thrown onto my path—that indeed I do have a judge like that!

Our blessed judge—the holy One toward whose ultimate judgment we now make our way—is like the sower in this text. The parable, true to its form, is more like a riddle, hiding as much as it reveals about God. It must have been confusing to its original readers and hearers too, because an allegorical interpretation (vv. 18–23) was finally added to clean things up and drive home a good point about good soil.

Ultimately, though, with all due respect to the well-meaning allegorist, this parable is not so much about good *soil* as it is about a good *sower*. This sower is not so cautious and strategic as to throw the seed in only those places where the chances for growth are best. No, this sower is a high-risk sower, relentless in indiscriminately throwing seed on all soil—as if it were *all* potentially good soil. On the rocks, amid the thorns, on the well-worn path, maybe even in a jail!

Which leaves us to wonder if there is any place or circumstance in which God's seed cannot sprout and take root.

THEODORE J. WARDLAW

---

3. Joachim Jeremias, *The Parables of Jesus* (New York: Charles Scribner's Sons, 1963), 151.

Isaiah 44:6-8

[6]Thus says the LORD, the King of Israel,
  and his Redeemer, the LORD of hosts:
 I am the first and I am the last;
  besides me there is no god.
[7]Who is like me? Let them proclaim it,
  let them declare and set it forth before me.
 Who has announced from of old the things to come?
  Let them tell us what is yet to be.
[8]Do not fear, or be afraid;
  have I not told you from of old and declared it?
  You are my witnesses!
 Is there any god besides me?
  There is no other rock; I know not one.

Theological Perspective

Self-sufficiency is something highly valued for many in the United States of America, as well as a pervasive expectation throughout U.S. social, political, and religious life. It is also what we look for in leaders, even if we are sometimes disappointed with the results. Perhaps this is why the passage in Isaiah 44 is so appealing. Theologically, it is the perfect portrait of a self-sufficient God and representative of Israel's development as a religiously monotheistic nation.[1] From the very beginnings of the covenant with Moses in Exodus 20:2 and Deuteronomy 6:1–6 comes the insistence, "I, the LORD God, am One, and the only one whom you will serve." The consequences of failing to live into this covenant have always been devastating.

No one knows this better than the prophet Isaiah, who witnesses the fall of a nation because of its refusal to trust YHWH. For thirty-five years Isaiah proclaims the righteousness of God, as he sees his people carried away into Babylonian captivity. The tribe of Judah is now exiled along the banks of the Euphrates, surrounded by worshipers of foreign gods such as Marduk and Nebo. Chapter 44 reflects the period between 550 and 515 BCE, which brings most

1. Paul D. Hanson, *Isaiah 40–66*, Interpretation series (Louisville. KY: John Knox Press, 1995), 87.

Pastoral Perspective

God's mercy is as steady as a heartbeat; God's faithfulness is solid as a rock. Just as grace is a sheer gift of God, so also is the gift of being open to the possibilities of an unexpected future, trusting that all will be well when events are out of our control.

Sometimes God demands to be heard, but that does not always mean enveloping the hearer with bright lights and thunder. Sometimes God speaks words that are uninvited, unanticipated, and unexpected. Sometimes God puts us on edge or—better said—our anticipation of what God's message to us might be brings us to the edge.

The psalmist calls God a rock (Ps. 18:2), an image that can be taken many ways. Is God impenetrable and unfeeling, offering a place of safety and refuge, or is God secure enough for us to hold on to in a storm? When God demands to be heard, people are looking for a safe harbor. "I am the first and I am the last; besides me there is no god. . . . Let them proclaim it" (vv. 6, 7). This is what we want to hear clearly, distinctly, indisputably, with no misunderstanding or interference. When we are ready to hear God's word and are ready to be convinced of it beyond a shadow of a doubt, we are also ready to receive it as marching orders for the next steps of our lives.

In other words, when we are really prepared to hear God, there is no need for fear or anxiety, for the

Exegetical Perspective

Isaiah 44:6–8 stands among several other passages focused upon idol critique in Second Isaiah (41:21–29; 44:9–20; 45:20–25; 46:1–13). These critiques aim to displace the view of YHWH as a defeated deity, in the wake of the Babylonian attack on Jerusalem and the deportation of its leading citizens. The theological push-back takes the form of a court case with YHWH leading the prosecution against all other deities, which are regarded as ineffective idols. The outcome of the trial reassures the devotees of YHWH that they do not misplace their faith in their god.

The passage divides into four parts, each consisting of a different movement in the trial scene. First, YHWH comes on the scene with forceful self-descriptions (v. 6). Then comes a series of questions challenging the other deities to dispute the earlier claims (v. 7). Then a word of assurance conscripts the listening audience as witnesses on YHWH's behalf in the case (v. 8abc). The final verdict closes the passage (v. 8de), taking the form of a rhetorical question and a clear reply.

Divine Self-Description (v. 6). The extended messenger formula prepares the way for the divine self-identification that follows. Beyond the usual identification of the speaker, this formula adds three

Homiletical Perspective

Listen and live! It is a command; it is a plea. It is the heart of the revelation of the holy God to a people who have closed their ears and barricaded their hearts against the One who created, redeems, and sustains them. This is the voice of the Servant of the word, whose real name we have forgotten even though we know the words to all his songs. The potency and poignancy of this passage resonate across the centuries.

This is not just a random slice of human history; this is holy story told by one of the world's great oracles. What makes this singer want to sing? What does the Holy One want us to hear? That a nation broken beyond recognition will be born again? The anonymous singer knows how to get people's attention. He weaves memory and imagination together to create the dramatic encounter between a speaking God, *Deus loquens,* and a community that does not want to listen.

Why bother listening to an oracle of a deity who deserted the nation when the horrors of war destroyed everything? Why trust in a God who either would not or could not help when all hell broke loose? If faith still persists in the face of unspeakable loss, what good news comes from a jealous God angry with human sin and failure? Did not the prophets promise that judgment would come with

Isaiah 44:6-8

Theological Perspective

to doubt that chapters 40–55 represent the words of the original eighth-century prophet. Some refer to this section as Second Isaiah, or Deutero-Isaiah, the Prophet of the Exile or Consolation.

Regardless of whether we can identify the specific prophet in these times, it is clear that the spirit of the prophet who "in the year that King Uzziah died . . . saw the Lord . . . high and lofty" (6:1) needs now more than ever before, in the face of competing Babylonian traditions and religions, to affirm the self-sufficiency of YHWH above all other gods and kings. Thus, descriptions used only for a king are invoked in the pronouncement of Isaiah 44:6. It is the true "King of Israel" who now speaks. A personal claim is made on Israel by its "Redeemer," who challenges any other claimant in the matter.

The "I am" references are consistent throughout Scripture, denoting a theological explanation of the supremacy of YHWH's existence in the universe, as in Revelation 22:13. Simply speaking, the self-sufficiency of YHWH is not just a descriptive term, but an essential characteristic of God's nature. Thus in these verses an exclusive identity is clearly established before presenting the challenge.

Interpreting divine self-sufficiency from the words, "besides me there is no god" (v. 6d), applies only when comparing YHWH with other gods. The description does not seem to apply to YHWH's relationship with human beings, where there is an apparent role for human agency. Humans are called on to "proclaim" without "fear" against opposing forces. "You are my witnesses" (v. 8c) is a clear indication of divine dependency on the voices and actions of the people. Just as a judge depends on the testimony of eyewitnesses in deciding a courtroom case, so the self-sufficient God relies on the witness of the people in order to prove a case against competing claims.[2]

In the ancient world the reputation of one god among others usually rests on the successful lives of the people who serve the god. The witness is not only their material success, but their courageous faith when confronted by death and destruction. To "strive first for the kingdom of God and its righteousness" (Matt. 6:33) has discernible benefits. The story of Job is significant because of its radical claim against the myth that material wealth represents God's favor. Job's circumstances are not a result of anything he has done wrong, but make a theological claim against God's righteousness and just treatment of human beings.

2. Ibid.

Pastoral Perspective

God who made us all is the good shepherd of all things, and we can be at peace with God's sovereign reign. There is no other who can or will interfere with the good path set forth by God in the direction and purpose of our lives. (Yet, our *trust* in God should not slip into *chumminess* with God.[1])

So, how do we really hear a word from the ground of our being, from the eternal source of all creation? As a pastor I have found myself at times both a vessel and a mouthpiece, living through moments in which I have felt filled and used by God to help those whom I am called upon to serve. As with all of God's workings, this connection takes place in everyday ways. It does not happen often, but when it does, it is unforgettable.

I cannot produce a checklist of ways to prepare for hearing God in life, but I can point to a memorable example of how this took place for one person, at a time when God's presence was made plain and clear.

Before the first Gulf War in early 1990, a member of the church I served phoned me and asked that I come to his home on a Saturday morning to share a prayer. I said I would be honored to do so. He was being called up as a member of the National Guard to serve as medical staff on a ship in the Persian Gulf. We chatted a bit about what the upcoming months would bring: time away from his family, coupled with uncertainty, longing, tension, and high stress, perhaps even life-threatening danger.

As we began to sum up the situation, taking stock of the gravity of the moment, I offered a brief prayer. I asked God's blessing for the husband, along with his wife and two small children. I prayed for the father who would be separated from his family, for his wife who would be a functional single parent, and for their two little girls. I prayed for their safety, bravery, and trust in God's goodness. I promised to stay in touch with all of them though visits, phone calls, and e-mails for the duration of his tour of duty. It was a brief but deeply touching encounter.

Just before I left, I had a question. "What led you to call me to come over?" I asked him. "This is the first time I have been called to share a prayer with a family like this." The answer I received pointed far beyond me to the source of life itself. "It is something we felt very important to do for the two of us," the husband told me. "It is also a message we want our girls to learn early on in life. We have nothing if we have no faith."

1. For wonderful insight into this sensitive pastoral dynamic, see Susan R. Garrett, *No Ordinary Angel: Celestial Spirits and Christian Claims about Jesus* (New Haven, CT: Yale University Press, 2008), 60 ff.

attributes to YHWH. The messenger formula, "Thus says the LORD," already sets us up for the title "king," but the fuller claim, "King of Israel," appears surprising. In a period following the collapse of the monarchy, presumably during a time when notions of its revival may exist, this designation effectively rules out a human king. In fact, the three titles attribute to YHWH the survival and presence of what could be called Israel. As king, redeemer, and head of the army ("LORD of hosts"), YHWH engages in successful military battles and economic transactions to ensure that "Israel" survives.

When YHWH self-identifies in the single statement, "I am the first and I am the last," this rehearses the full sweep of biblical history. Hence, the title "King of Israel" forces the hearers beyond more recent history, when "Israel" as a national title no longer holds currency, back to the origins of the nation. In those origins, the stories of redemption from Egypt and settling in the land speak to YHWH's power. The back move situates YHWH at the head of all time and consequently of all history. This enables the claim to primacy in the two statements in the verse. As first and last, YHWH predates any other deity and will outlast all of them. The declaration "besides me there is no god" follows as the obvious conclusion.

Such a self-designation does not constitute monotheism as later theologians understand the idea. Rather, this boldly contradicts the current claims put forward on behalf of the Babylonian deities. The descriptions in the verse perform the work of delegitimizing other deities as of no effect and commending YHWH to the hearers as their God, who has been personally involved with them from the start.

The Cross-Examination (v. 7). The case for YHWH then advances to the questions put to other deities. A challenge to speak and provide contradictory evidence follows each question. This differs from the earlier ploy (41:21) of challenging opponents to appear and prove their power. The challenge consists of three actions that require the opponents to speak and act: "proclaim it," "declare it," and "set it forth." These verbs get to the power of a deity to create by speaking and ordering. The second part of the verse reduces the challenge posed to the opponents to a single action: "tell us." This action, though, rests upon the ability to reach back into the distant past and speak from there to the present. Both parts of the verse pose questions to the deities' power to transcend time and to effectively create a new reality.

invasion—destruction of everything treasured, and then exile? How long, how long, how long, O Lord, will it last?

Survivors who endure the loss of everything but life itself learn to harden themselves against the dangerous sound of hope. This is not a hearing loss; the people of the Holy One have stopped listening, even to themselves. Who wants to remember the terrorizing sounds of a community having its heart torn out? Their cries of grief, denial, and anger have gone unheard. They learn not to trust in the words of false prophets who promise that their God will keep them safe forever.

Post-traumatic stress syndrome is the twenty-first century's name for a condition that the people called Israel understand very well. Survivors of the nation called "chosen" have had to learn to speak softly, move quickly, and keep quiet as their enforced captivity in Babylon stretches into one generation and then two. They are strangers in a strange land, seemingly abandoned by their God. To try to hear hope would take away their last defense.

What kind of fool would break the nerve-wracking silence of despair? Somewhere in the back streets of Babylon an unnamed prophet of a marginalized community begins to sing a song. Somewhere in a ghetto some mother's child begins to sing songs that tell the truth, the whole truth, and nothing but the truth, so help us God. A slave in the great empire known as Babylon begins to brag about God who sets the captives free. A person of no consequence predicts that the time is coming when tyrants are reduced to the status of grasshoppers. Enemy rulers will be uprooted like weeds. Babylon's great horses of war and chariots of fire will be blown away, reduced to dust by the mere breath of the Holy One of Israel.

When the divine Voice calls to the imprisoned children of Jacob and Leah and Rachel, the tone turns gentle: "Do not fear, or be afraid" (v. 8). The Servant of the speaking God uses the language of the priestly salvation oracle, designed to comfort those who have suffered. What should be said to a people who are finding it hard to listen for the sounds of glory of the coming of the Lord?

Start a new song. Use the first-person address. Pick a fight. Insult the power brokers. Be as forceful as a defense attorney on behalf of the speaking God. Create some courtroom drama. Talk directly to those who know they have been weighed in the scales of justice and found wanting. Round up the usual suspects and treat them as if they are the jury. Use humor, use force. Tell them a story that they have

Isaiah 44:6-8

Theological Perspective

Thus, those who think that material wealth and prosperity are the only signs of God's presence will have little appreciation for the faithfulness born out of postexilic existence. The true witness of one's faith comes alive in the dark moments when it is difficult to see the blessings of God. The witnesses that YHWH seeks are those who are faithful regardless of their economic and political situations.

It is important to understand that the witness required by human agency involves both memory and experience, for YHWH understands that the preliminary counsel provided to the witnesses is derived from what was "told you from of old" (v. 8b). The telling is not simply a verbal instruction, although Isaiah places high value on the "word of the LORD." The word comes as YHWH's active participation in human history and experience. As Hanson states, "This historical focus is entirely consistent with all that we know of Yahwism from the biblical period."[3] The witness is to YHWH's liberating acts in the life of the people, both preexilic and during their exile.

The response to what might be a rhetorical question, "Is there a god besides me?" may also be an invitation to remember the events in one's own life narrative, in which case the only reasonable response is, "There is no other rock; I know not one" (v. 8e). Remembering is not merely a psychological exercise in recalling past events. To remember requires the collective consciousness of the community as practiced in its religious observances and celebrative acts of worship.

The context for remembering is captivity in Babylon. How then can YHWH expect such affirming conclusions? How can we "sing the LORD's song in a foreign land" (Ps. 137:4)? Slave songs and spirituals emerged out of the harsh realities of the antebellum South, as much of present African American theology is born out of suffering and displacement. Even in the midst of suffering and pain, a witness that affirms God's self-sufficiency is still possible.

The rock is a symbol of stability and protection. It provides the reader an insight into the relationship between YHWH and the people. In addition, the rock image is reminiscent of moments of testing and challenge. The inference here is that after the trial has been conducted and a case is made, the truth comes forth that no other god compares to YHWH.

JOHN L. THOMAS JR.

Pastoral Perspective

As I reflected on the event afterwards, I realized that it was one thing for this couple and their children to be faithful church members, and quite another for them to respond to the special urge they felt to receive a blessing on the eve of the soldier's departure for duty. The husband and wife could have turned to each other for support, but they wanted to be intentional in their turning to God, and I served as the messenger. What was most critical for this family was to be intentionally grounded upon the rock of their salvation. "There is no other rock; I know not one" (v. 8).

When I recounted this visit to a colleague in ministry, his reply was that I should treasure the moment I spent with the family, for times like those are rare indeed and very, very special. Over the course of another eighteen years in ministry, I have found that to be true.

Sometimes life's twists and turns are unpredictable. Looking life straight in the eye is not easy. The lesson in all of this may well be that we ourselves are not the rocks upon which everyone else needs to lean. Rather, it is for us to lean just as hard as we can on the rock of our own salvation, the Lord, the King of Israel. Then we will have no need to fear.

THOMAS W. BLAIR

---

3. Ibid.

Exegetical Perspective

That the verbs emphasize divine speech gets to the ancient understanding that words shape reality. As in earlier passages, the other deities fail to respond to the challenges (43:8–13).

The Witnesses (v. 8abc). Despite the failure of the opponents to make their case through their nonappearance, the trial continues with the calling of the witnesses. Words of assurance precede the question posed to the witnesses. The necessity of reassuring words reveals the relationship between YHWH and the witnesses. This relationship appears as old as YHWH. From "of old," YHWH, "the first," speaks to the witnesses. "Do not fear, or be afraid" stands not simply as the words of an attorney to ensure the witness's comfort. These words come from the context of a relationship that sees YHWH as constantly on their side.

For as long as time, history, and divinity exist, YHWH speaks on behalf of these people. The question to the witnesses contains, therefore, the answer to the questions posed to the opponents. In response to the question, "who has announced from of old?" comes the follow-up question or assertion: "Have I not told you from of old?" In response to the challenge to "declare it" and "tell it" (in both cases the Hebrew verb *ngd* "to tell or declare" is used), comes YHWH's assertion: I have "declared it." This may seem to be putting words into the mouth of the witnesses. The statement "You are my witnesses" calls for more than verbal assent to the assertions in this passage. The witnesses by their presence declare the truth of the divine claims.

The Verdict (v. 8de). The trial ends with a restatement of the essential question of the enquiry. The assertion in verse 6 is upheld in verse 8. The reframed assertion from "me" to "rock" hints at the relationship between YHWH and the people. The trial dismantles not only rival claims to divine supremacy but also competing interests in the relationship between YHWH and the people. Only YHWH deserves the name "rock" (Deut. 32:4, Ps. 18:31). This special name more than describes YHWH's nature. It marks the bond between the two parties, a bond that cannot admit rival claimants. While the verdict results in dismissing these claimants, the final statement, "I know not one," calls upon the people to issue a similar verdict about their relationship with YHWH.

STEED VERNYL DAVIDSON

Homiletical Perspective

half forgotten, a story about runaway slaves and freedom. Remind them of Moses and the Ten Words of life. Remind them of Miriam's song. The second exodus is coming. Tell them to listen and live. The Holy One who created the heavens can revise any human regime. The One who can summon the stars by name and order the sea to be still can bring homesick people home.

Remind them who they are, then remind them whose they are. Once they were nobody, no people. Now they are some people. God's got people! This revelation of God's presence will be seen not only by those held in exile, but by all people, everywhere, for all time. God will provide the evidence. God will make a way where there is no way. From the north and from the south they will be gathered. From the east and the west, from places well known and places unknown, the Rock and no other will create a way in the wilderness. The Redeemer and no other will lead them home. There was, and is, and will be no other.

Why would the Holy One go to such lengths to win this argument? Is it an act of ancient rhetoric or an irresistible sound of liberation? Who can predict the things to come? Only the One who is the First. Only the One who is the Last. Are there heartbroken exiles who need to be reminded that what happened once in Egypt, and Babylon, and Memphis will happen again? If you have been lost and now you are found, you are a witness. Are there any no-people who long to be now-people of the holy, living God? If you were nobody and now you are somebody, you are a witness. If you think God is not listening; if you have given up your dreams of finding a home. If you need shelter in the wilderness, trust your life to the Rock. Listen and live, as God is your witness.

HEATHER MURRAY ELKINS

Psalm 86:11-17

¹¹Teach me your way, O Lord,
    that I may walk in your truth;
    give me an undivided heart to revere your name.
¹²I give thanks to you, O Lord my God, with my whole heart,
    and I will glorify your name forever.
¹³For great is your steadfast love toward me;
    you have delivered my soul from the depths of Sheol.

¹⁴O God, the insolent rise up against me;
    a band of ruffians seeks my life,
    and they do not set you before them.
¹⁵But you, O Lord, are a God merciful and gracious,
    slow to anger and abounding in steadfast love and faithfulness.
¹⁶Turn to me and be gracious to me;
    give your strength to your servant;
    save the child of your serving girl.
¹⁷Show me a sign of your favor,
    so that those who hate me may see it and be put to shame,
    because you, Lord, have helped me and comforted me.

Theological Perspective

This psalm of personal lament, as it is classically categorized, offers very little detail concerning the supplicant's predicament. What is the lament? Verse 14 is tantalizingly terse: it describes a situation where life is threatened owing to some willful, powerful opposition.

The problem is named (rather than denied) but not explored. The lament is not private complaint or therapeutic self-narration, but an assertion of faith. Theologically, we are given an inspiring model for prayer in hard times: prayer need not center on the detailed circumstances of the pray-er. In the end, it is not about the sufferer, but about the One to whom the prayer is directed.

Perhaps most significant is the fact *that* God is addressed. Turning to God is itself an act of faith, quite apart from the assertions about God that follow. As in the classical Collect prayers of the Christian church, these serve to remind the psalmist of who God is and to heighten confidence that God indeed hears and answers. This is the appropriate context for making any request.

This kind of prayer both affirms and illustrates the logic of Hebrew monotheism. The psalm states, "There is none like you among the gods" (v. 8) and "You alone are God" (v. 10). In other words, in times of trouble, God is the *only* place to turn. There is no

Pastoral Perspective

The timid of heart, or people taught to be deferential to authority, or independent stoics are not likely to ask God for much. If we were told as children to fight our own battles or were scolded for whining or ridiculed for being needy, we are likely to hold back our tears, bury our fears, and tough it out. A politician got in trouble recently for saying publicly that American society has become a "culture of complainers." The negative response was not surprising from a society that prizes self-sufficiency and promotes autonomy. As a friend of mine would say, "Every tub must stand on its own bottom." Self-sufficiency is the American way.

The writer of Psalm 86 has no difficulty acknowledging neediness and asking YHWH to take very specific action against very specific people—"a band of ruffians" (v. 14)—who seek his life. Nor does the psalmist have any difficulty complaining about how "the insolent rise up against me" (v. 14). I am not sure it has ever occurred to me to ask God to do something to people who insulted me, even if they were mean and contemptuous about it. I will admit, however, that I have often hoped that God would show favors to me so that "those who hate me may see it and be put to shame" (v. 17a). Nevertheless, when we are to pray for others, we pray for their healing and their well-being, not their punishment or shaming.

Exegetical Perspective

The psalmist has a problem—actually a problem with many faces. A hateful group has struck terror in his heart. Words such as "insolent" and "band of ruffians" in the NRSV (v. 14) hardly capture the singeing fires of their hateful anger. There is more at stake here. Insolence entails rejecting God, plain and simple, refusing to live by God's commands. In Psalm 119:21, for example, God "rebukes the insolent, accursed ones, who wander from your commandments." These lawless thugs, in our psalmist's words, "do not set you [God] before them" (v. 14).

More horrifying still is that this vicious gang has set its sights on our psalmist and "terrified" (NRSV, "seeks my life," v. 14) him to the point of making him shake with fear, the way humans tremble in God's presence (Isa. 2:19, 21). This is no mere band of insolent ruffians but a gang of arrogant terrorists, unfettered by the constraints of Torah or the scantiest respect for God, and dead set upon destroying our psalmist out of sheer hatred.

Their terrifying tactics are working. The psalmist cowers and begs for release from their terrifying grip. This psalm, therefore, is a model of how to confront horrible, hateful human beings. The surprising lesson we learn, however, is that the battle is waged and won *within*, and within *the hated* rather than the hateful.

Homiletical Perspective

One of the difficulties in preaching the Psalter readings from the Revised Common Lectionary is that the boundaries of the readings are often set more because of the relationship between the psalm and the reading from the Hebrew Bible, or the liturgical preference for shorter readings, than on an exegetical understanding of the content and structure of the psalm itself. To preach on the Psalter lection, one will often have to expand the reading to include the whole psalm, or at least a larger portion of it. One would do well to do this with Psalm 86, but because of the psalmist's borrowing of language from other psalms and use of repetition of themes within the psalm, the preacher can speak from the ending to this prayer without cheating the fuller context.

Psalm 86 is an individual psalm of lament. The psalmist speaks of being under attack by enemies, but it is unclear what the nature of the attack is, or even if the language of such oppression is to be understood literally or metaphorically. To preach this psalm, however, this question need not be answered. It is important to convey in the pulpit the depth of suffering, not the specific details of it.

As a lament, the psalm raises questions concerning the purpose of prayer (and thus theodicy and the character of God's providence) that people in the pew need to hear and think about before a crisis

Psalm 86:11-17

Theological Perspective

one else committed to the people or with power to rescue them (v. 13). So we find the psalmist turning to God, in the hardest of times as well as the best. We find a demonstration of human loyalty and commitment that focuses on divine loyalty and commitment.

That aspect of steadfast love—of God's covenant commitment to the people summed up by the single-but-pregnant Hebrew word *hesed* (vv. 5, 15)—is the central theme throughout. Whatever the predicament, God is present and God cares. More than that, caring is so foundational to God's character and being in the world that God cannot *not* care. Throughout the psalm, this truth is celebrated through the use of conventional expressions and quotations borrowed from elsewhere in the tradition.

As with Mary in the Magnificat (Luke 1:46–55) and Jesus in the Lord's Prayer (Matt. 6:9–13; Luke 11:2–4), classical phrases of Jewish piety are recycled. On one level, the psalmist is saying nothing new; crudely, this might be described as quoting clichés. Looked at another way, the psalmist draws from the tradition in which he or she is steeped, yet applies it to a new circumstance in a new way. Contemporary culture is complimentary about such adaptation, calling it "thinking outside the box," "traditioned innovation," or "radical faithfulness."

The psalmist is drawing upon traditions from the book of Exodus in particular. The two statements about God's uniqueness in verses 8 and 10 link with affirmations of God's covenant character in verses 5, 10, and 15, all of which are associated with a pertinent moment in Israel's corporate disorientation. They stem from the narrative of the golden calf at Mount Sinai (Exod. 32–34) which follows immediately after the chapters detailing the making and sealing of the covenant and receiving of the law (Exod. 19–24 and 25–31).

One moment Israel enthusiastically enters into covenant with God, willing to "obey my voice and keep my covenant" (Exod. 19:5). The next moment, while Moses's back is turned (awaiting God's graciously giving a second round of stone tablets), the newly founded people of Israel blatantly violate the commandments just given by making and worshiping a golden calf. It is only Moses's intercession that averts God's anger, after which Moses boldly asks to see God's face. Although the request is denied, there follows the fullest self-revelation of God anywhere in the Old Testament, thirteen attributes of YHWH delivered on the lips of God himself.

In a context where Israel is far from deserving, Exodus 34:6–7 centers around the two basic aspects

Pastoral Perspective

As in many lament psalms, the purpose of the complaint in Psalm 86 is to motivate God to pay attention to our plight. The appeal of the psalmist is that YHWH will return to YHWH's true self in order to rescue the supplicant from serious danger: "For you, O Lord, are a God merciful and gracious, slow to anger and abounding in steadfast love" (v. 15). The irony in this psalm is that the "true" YHWH is not likely to do what the psalmist wants, because it would be counter to God's nature. Because YHWH is merciful and gracious and slow to anger, YHWH is not likely to shame my enemies or punish those who insult me.

The prayer of lament keeps prayer anchored in real-life experience and prevents it from drifting off into make-believe and empty phrases. Israel's faith and hope are all the more remarkable for refusing to stifle the voice of anger, pain, and despair. The psalms of lament are filled with terror and hurt and confusion and anguish and bewilderment because life is not going well. We lament when the one we love or the place where we live or the work we do or the financial security we had has been taken away and we feel empty and forsaken. Beneath the complaint against God is the belief that life is not going well because God is not paying attention. Strategies of denial and suppression are likely to lead to more despair and hopelessness rather than the renewal of hope. Telling the truth in the midst of suffering is the beginning of hope.

The practice of lament and arguing with God is an unsettling tradition of prayer because it includes the expression of complaint, anger, grief, despair, and protest to God. What makes lament such a bold practice of faith is that arguing with God is predicated on the belief that my protest or argument will change God or at least get God's attention. We are free to lament because we believe it is not God's intent to be absent permanently. We can protest against God and trust God at the same time. Although both appear sequentially in lament psalms, we see the possibility of simultaneously protesting and trusting.

My mother-in-law died recently at the age of ninety-three. She had lived a full and independent life until just before she died. In the end, however, she very much wanted to die. When her prayers to God to die went unheard, she became angry at God. She was a proper lady who never complained and never wanted to be any trouble. The lament psalms were comforting at the end, because they gave her freedom to voice her complaints to God.

Exegetical Perspective

A clue to this lesson lies in a shift between verses 1–4 and verses 5–17. The first four verses are rife with rationales that are grounded in the psalmist's character and actions. God is asked to respond because *I* am poor and needy, because *I* am devoted to you, because to you do *I* cry all day, because to you *I* lift up my soul. Then in verse 5 a change occurs, as the psalmist realizes that help lies in the character and actions of God. The word "for," or "because," now introduces the character of God: because "*you*, O Lord, are good and forgiving" (v. 5). From here on out, the psalmist grounds prayer in who God is and what God does: because "*you* are great and do wondrous things" (v. 10). There is something significant in this shift; it marks an inner transformation, a maturing, a recognition that God will act, not because of our virtues and virtuous actions, but because it is God's nature to liberate, to forgive, to demonstrate trustworthy mercy.

How will God accomplish this? Not with a sympathetic shoulder to lean on, nor with emotional support. God is not asked to erase fear or to wipe away tears. God is asked instead to direct the psalmist through teaching: "Teach me your way," the psalmist prays, so that he may "walk in [God's] truth" (v. 11; see Ps. 143:8–10). He understands that his ability to escape the claws of hateful people requires an intensity of focus and clarity of concentration that goes far beyond emotional impulses. Therefore, he prays for an "undivided heart" (v. 11), for the ability to follow God with his "whole heart" (v. 12). The psalmist prays to live without the paltry commitment of divided loyalties, to be wholehearted in his thanks and his ability to give God the glory that is God's due. There can be no such thing as half-praise, part-thanks, semi-truth. The psalmist needs to know God's commands, with his head fully engaged, *by heart*.

Why, however, is the psalmist desperate for teaching? The psalm itself is a pastiche of Israelite traditions. The primary depiction of God in this psalm, as abounding in steadfast love and slow to anger, lies at the heart of God's character in Torah (Exod. 34:6; Num. 14:18) and fans out into the Writings (Neh. 9:17) and the prophetic traditions (Joel 2:13; Jonah 4:2). Further, the prayer for "an undivided heart to revere your name" (v. 11) expresses the heart and soul of the wisdom tradition (Prov. 1:7). Even the verb that is translated "teach" shares its root with the word "Torah."

The psalmist, then, knows Scripture. That much is clear. Why then pray for learning? The reason

Homiletical Perspective

forces the question upon them. "Does God answer prayer?" "*How* does God answer prayer?" "Just the other day, I heard a television preacher tell the story of his mother praying for a swimming pool, and lo and behold, a man showed up at church saying that God had told him to give her a free swimming pool. If God answered her prayer for a swimming pool, why did God not answer my prayer when I prayed that my child's leukemia disappear?" Even without turning to the crass proclamation of a gospel of success, God can appear capricious when we are suffering. "Why does God seem to offer grace one moment and withhold it the next?"

Too often we think of prayer as if it were writing a letter to Santa Claus to get him to fulfill our wish list or making an appointment with our doctor to get her to write a prescription for what ails us. It is better to think of prayer as taking *everything* that concerns us at all levels of our life (celebrations, suffering, challenges) and laying them before the One who concerns us and is concerned for us ultimately.

Psalm 86:11–17 provides an interesting case study for reflecting on such an approach to God. The best sermon for reflecting on the text might be one that starts with the second half of the passage and works backward. Looked at in reverse, the lection has elements of a Lowry narrative loop: upsetting the equilibrium (oops), analyzing the discrepancy (ugh), disclosing the clue to resolution (aha), experiencing the gospel (whee), and anticipating consequences (yeah).[1]

The preacher can begin with the second half of the passage, which names the immediate concerns of the one praying. In verse 14, the psalmist names the suffering being experienced and then in verses 15–17 expresses confidence and hope that God will hear and answer the prayer. This seems straightforward enough. The preacher can easily draw analogies to the concerns we hold today and from which we desire relief. These range from individual illness to international violence (oops). The preacher can name the dynamics we discussed above—the experience of God's seeming to be silent in answer to some prayers (ugh).

In the next movement of the sermon, the preacher would back up to verses 12–13, where the psalmist intriguingly claims to have *already* been rescued by God—not just from suffering but from death itself! In other words, before naming the pain

---

1. Eugene L. Lowry, *The Homiletical Plot: The Sermon as Narrative Art Form*, expanded ed. (Louisville, KY: Westminster John Knox Press, 2001).

Psalm 86:11-17

Theological Perspective

of mercy and judgment, underlining how God's overwhelming mercy strongly predominates. Rather like the Apostles' or the Nicene Creed, these thirteen descriptors come to take on formulaic convention. They are widely quoted elsewhere in the Old Testament—often in situations of disorientation and darkness—and probably served a catechetical function for understanding the nature of God. On what basis may the psalmist presume upon God's graciousness? How might anyone be so sure of deserving that grace, while one's enemies are not?

This psalm explores the discipline of God's mercy. Unlike Jonah—who quotes (or rather subtly *mis*quotes) from the same Exodus formula in his lament concerning God's excessive mercy toward the Ninevites (Jonah 4:2)—the psalmist here understands God's ultimate claim upon and concern for the whole universe (v. 8) as well as God's freedom (v. 10; cf. Exod. 33:19, "I will show mercy on whom I will show mercy"). The psalmist affirms and delights in the greatness of God—whereas Jonah resents it—and responds with longing to learn God's ways and walk in them (v. 11), a precise articulation of the covenant ethic of *imitatio Dei*.

God's sole claim to be worshiped—another aspect developed from the Sinai texts—is understood and celebrated. God's "jealousy," as Exodus 34:14 puts it, evokes the same level of single-minded loyalty in return from this believer. "I give thanks to you, O Lord my God, with my whole heart" (v. 12). God's steadfast love is not taken for granted: for "you have delivered my soul from the depths of Sheol" (v. 13). In fact, the clearest criticism of the "insolent . . . ruffians" relates not so much to any injury they have caused the psalmist, but their lack of devotion to God (v. 14).

It is clear that the psalmist does not quote formulas from the tradition blithely, but with a depth of significance and devotion. Thus the lament is not about persuading God to show mercy in one place and to deny it in another. The blessings of God are far from a zero-sum game; indeed, they are ultimately intended and sufficient for all. Verse 17 is not so much a longing for revenge (as, for example, the ending of Ps. 137) as for transformation, whereby the insolent may be brought to long for God's favor as much as the psalmist does.

When Jesus says, "Love your enemies," perhaps this is what he means.

JO BAILEY WELLS

Pastoral Perspective

The presence of lament keeps ritual honest and allows grief to be real. When our prayers do not include protest, it is too easy to overlook the deeper pain and hidden ambiguities of private grief and public tragedy. It is the wisdom of both the biblical witness and the modern helping sciences that there can be no lasting recovery from serious trauma unless the pain is named and lived through. When individuals lament, they keep faith with God, who suffers with us. When the community laments, it demonstrates with its tears that suffering is not without meaning and that suffering is worth weeping over. In a time when violence and fear of violence are everywhere, the psalms of lament are a resource for healing and the restoration of hope. We are not powerless in the midst of suffering: we can lament.

The prayer of lament is still an uncomfortable practice for many people of faith. Even though there is strong biblical encouragement to "pray without ceasing" or "ask anything in the name of God," we are reluctant to presume on the Lord. There are four requests of God in this psalm that model what we might ask of God for ourselves. (1) "Teach me your way, O Lord" (v. 11a). The request for instruction fosters a humble spirit. The prayer is answered in the asking. (2) "Give me an undivided heart" (v. 11b). Asking for an "undivided heart" invites us to tend toward God with a prayer that deepens our single-minded devotion. (3) "Be gracious to me" (v. 16a). The prayer is for us. In the plea, we acknowledge that we are in need of God's charity and grace. (4) "Give [me] your strength" (v. 16b).

There is no hint of self-sufficiency here. The life of faith is constant receiving and letting go, never holding or possessing. We look to God for strength and not to ourselves. The request for strength is a countercultural word, because it acknowledges our neediness before God, who is "merciful and gracious . . . abounding in steadfast love and faithfulness" (v. 15).

HERBERT ANDERSON

Exegetical Perspective

peeks out of the very tradition he cites: God abounds in steadfast love and in patience—slowness to anger. This conviction first appears smack in the middle of the Ten Words (Exod. 20:6). It recurs, along with God's slowness to anger, when Moses, a second time, receives the Ten Words, which he shattered shortly after Israel constructed golden calves (Exod. 34:6). It occurs, coupled again with God's patience, when Moses stands in the gap between God and a rebellious people (Num. 14:18). Through a recurrent appeal to God's steadfast love and patience, the psalmist signals that he—not those who hate him—is the rebellious one, the one who needs forgiveness and patience.

Why must God exercise patience toward the psalmist? Presumably because the psalmist is in danger of violating God's clear and uncompromising Ten Words, in which God's steadfast love—which he cherishes—is mentioned first (Exod. 20:6) and second (Exod. 34:6). His enemies' hatred may be pressing him toward disregard of God's Torah. Has their hatred infected him, bending his divided heart toward the possibility of murder (Exod. 20:13)? Have their terrorist tactics twisted his devotion into a half-hearted commitment that allows him to consider destroying them with false accusations (Exod. 20:16)? Has their freewheeling belligerence, free from divine punishment, prompted him to covet this hostile mob for getting away with terrifying him (Exod. 20:17)? Is it possible that their hatred has distracted him from something as simple as the Ten Words and unfocused his loyalty and prompted him to consider becoming just like them: murderous, accusatory, jealous?

Why should he not covet? Unlike his hostile tormentors, he is poor and needy (v. 1), the mere son of a slave woman (v. 16; see Exod. 23:12; Ps. 116:16). Still, ultimately he prays not for the demise of his enemies, but, with grace born of prayer, merely for divine favor toward him that will shame them (v. 17). For what he has learned is this: *he*—not they—needs the patience and steadfast love of God; *he*—not they—needs to be forgiven; *he*—not they—needs renewed concentration to resist sin; *he*—not they—needs to focus upon Torah afresh, in order to resist the allure of hatred.

JOHN R. LEVISON

Homiletical Perspective

being experienced (present tense) and asking for help (future tense), the psalmist claims to have already received God's salvation (past tense).

The prayer for help is in *response* to God's help (aha)! We do not want to be dismissive of the very real hurt we experience in life or to offer a theological cliché, but in a sense the psalm seems to model an approach to prayer that affirms we can take whatever ails us to God, because God has already answered our concern—and that answer is the gift of God's steadfast love (v. 13). We must be careful not simply to turn this into another cliché: God is with us in our suffering. God as unaffected, ineffective observer of our suffering offers no good news. The preacher must unpack and show how God's immanence in the midst of human brokenness is healing, even if it is not literal cure (whee).

Finally, if we back up yet one more verse, we find something even more unexpected: before the psalmist praises God for the gift of salvation already received and then asks for salvation, the psalmist asks to be taught God's way (v. 11). Such a petition could be viewed as an attempt to butter God up before asking for what we want. If we connect the dots theologically, however, we find that the salvation that God has given and that we really seek in every situation is to be formed by God's steadfast, saving love, instead of by the circumstances of temporal, mortal existence. In other words, God's providential care is less about changing our circumstances and more about changing us. What a strange and wondrous claim to find at the end of a sermon on lament (yeah)!

A closing note: One might want to think of preaching on Psalm 86 this week and on Psalm 128 from the non-semicontinuous series next week. Both raise questions of God's providence, but they have very different tones. While this one is a lament, Psalm 128 is a Psalm of Ascent with tones of blessing.

O. WESLEY ALLEN JR.

Romans 8:12-25

¹²So then, brothers and sisters, we are debtors, not to the flesh, to live according to the flesh— ¹³for if you live according to the flesh, you will die; but if by the Spirit you put to death the deeds of the body, you will live. ¹⁴For all who are led by the Spirit of God are children of God. ¹⁵For you did not receive a spirit of slavery to fall back into fear, but you have received a spirit of adoption. When we cry, "Abba! Father!" ¹⁶it is that very Spirit bearing witness with our spirit that we are children of God, ¹⁷and if children, then heirs, heirs of God and joint heirs with Christ—if, in fact, we suffer with him so that we may also be glorified with him.

¹⁸I consider that the sufferings of this present time are not worth comparing with the glory about to be revealed to us. ¹⁹For the creation waits with eager

Theological Perspective

"If the Spirit of him who raised Jesus from the dead dwells in you, he who raised Christ from the dead will give life to your mortal bodies also through his Spirit that dwells in you" (v. 11). Spirituality unleashed from Christ is merely mysticism that seeks unity with God by transcending death, like the ill-fated flight of Icarus. Paul corrects this hyperreligious impulse by fixing the Spirit, as is the Spirit's wont, to Christ crucified. Which spirit is the Holy Spirit? The one "who raised Jesus from the dead." Now what can we say about the Christian life?

"We are debtors" (v. 12). Unlikely promise! We are debtors, that is true, but much of Paul's preaching comes in the form of "antithetical parallelisms." Here he makes a distinction between kinds of debtors: debtors *not* to the flesh (which debt is paid only by your death), but debtors to the Spirit.

Historically this has been confusing to Christians, since they have become accustomed to think of atonement as Christ's cross paying the debt owed to the law or the devil (or even to God). That would mean that sinners have a debt measured by the law, and Christians are debt free, due to Christ's merit or payment in the crucifixion. This would mean that once you were in debt; now with Christ you owe the law nothing. However, here Paul claims that Christians are *now* debtors, but that everything depends

Pastoral Perspective

A popular aphorism says, "What you see is what you get." One of those wise sayings that occupy the space we call common sense, it is usually uttered as a way to ensure that expectations do not get out of hand. It is often a helpful vaccine against disappointment, the counsel of realism against the foolishness of fantasy.

Oddly enough, such out-of-hand expectations, disappointment with the way things are, and fantastic foolishness are appropriate to the life of faith Paul describes in chapter 8 of Romans. The children of God are heirs to a future beyond their sight. What we will get is *not* what we now see.

To look at what we see might be worthwhile before taking up what it is that we get. For Paul, what we see includes the "sufferings of this present time" (v. 18). The sufferings of Paul's day could be enumerated best by a historian, but if what Paul proclaims has any relevance to us, it is good to attend to the "sufferings of *this* present time"—right now, right here. Where do we begin? With the travail of the creation, whose ice caps are melting due to the overheated consumption of self-centered and selfish human beings? With the last cries of species as they become extinct and disappear from the planet? By current estimates, up to one-fifth of all current living species will be extinct in thirty years.

longing for the revealing of the children of God; [20]for the creation was subjected to futility, not of its own will but by the will of the one who subjected it, in hope [21]that the creation itself will be set free from its bondage to decay and will obtain the freedom of the glory of the children of God. [22]We know that the whole creation has been groaning in labor pains until now; [23]and not only the creation, but we ourselves, who have the first fruits of the Spirit, groan inwardly while we wait for adoption, the redemption of our bodies. [24]For in hope we were saved. Now hope that is seen is not hope. For who hopes for what is seen? [25]But if we hope for what we do not see, we wait for it with patience.

Exegetical Perspective

Romans 8:12–25 continues Paul's exploration of God's gift of freedom through Jesus Christ: freedom from condemnation, from sin, from death. We are debtors to God for this gift, which is our only possibility of life, but only if we live in the Spirit and not in the flesh (*sarx*). As in the verse preceding, it is important to note that Paul is not condemning the human, embodied life; far from it! Indeed, it is God's gift that we live as God's own children, even in our bodies (*sōma*).

Both the analogy of freedom from slavery and the metaphor of adoption spoke vividly to the church in Rome. Made up of Jews, proselytes, and other non-Jews, many of whom were not native to Rome, the church was mixed across social strata, drawing largely from lower classes, including slaves and freed persons.[1] For Jews, slavery brought to mind the exodus, when God led God's people to freedom. Not only are Christians to understand themselves as "free" from their former slavery; they are made part of a new family by adoption, so much so that they may call God "Abba! Father!" (v. 15) in the very words of Christ's own prayer.

N. T. Wright describes this Spirit-inspired prayer as "the beating heart of [Paul's] whole sequence of

1. Brendan Byrne, *Romans* (Collegeville, MN: Liturgical Press, 1996), 10–11.

Homiletical Perspective

One of the major themes of Romans 8:12–25 is that of identity. Who are we, now that we have accepted God's gracious gift of Jesus the Messiah, and what will our life look like? Further, what are the tensions inherent in living in a period between the already of his death and resurrection and the not-yet of his coming in glory to complete God's redemption of the creation? God has raised Jesus from the dead, demonstrating definitively that nothing can separate us from God's love, companionship, and community. We have experienced the inbreaking of God's kingdom or reign, the inauguration of a new era of hope and possibility in which we, Jesus' followers, are to be a sign, witness, and foretaste of what is to come.

At the same time, we live in the "not yet." While God has broken into our lives and creation and bridged the gulf of estrangement between us, God's reign is not fully manifest. Sin or separation from God is evident in our world in so many ways, and it is often easier to focus on the disturbing events in the daily paper than on the ways God is working, through the Spirit, in our lives and world. It is easy to become discouraged. The preacher must help her flock understand the importance of living faithfully in the present while, like Abraham and Sarah, waiting in the hope of God's promises.

Romans 8:12-25

Theological Perspective

upon to whom the debt is owed. Debt owed the Spirit gives life; it does not take life away. Strange debt! According to the law, debt is not an asset; but debt to the Spirit does not function according to law. Debt to the Spirit increases your coffers; it does not empty them. Spirit debt is not what must be repaid, but what is paid to you. Christ said it this way: "To all those who have, more will be given" (Luke 19:26).

Debt is not your basic problem; it is to whom you owe debt that matters. When a beloved child needs help with college expense, long before she goes to college a parent is already there saving for an education. When the day comes to pay tuition, the parents gladly do it, and in fact make the child more indebted to themselves than ever before. Parents do not lend to their children as a bank does, because it is love, not law, that does it. Parents lend to open the debtor to the future, not to bind him or her to the past.

"If you live according to flesh, you will die; but if by the Spirit you put to death the deeds of the body, you will live" (v. 13). Why is it that the debt to the Spirit is life, and debt to the flesh is death? The Spirit is not law, but a person. The law cannot do what the Spirit does. The Spirit makes you indebted by making you a child and so an heir.

Unlike the Spirit, the functions of the body are to decay and die. This is not because the body is ontologically evil; it is because it stands under the curse. It has a bad lord in this old world, who is death magnified by the law, but an amazing thing happens when you become debtors to the Spirit. You cease being passive before death, and instead put the functions of the body to death. The Spirit gives you the power to put your own death to death. This is not a demand of Moses to overcome bodily functions, but the freedom of Christ to defy death.

On what grounds can you defy death, even the death of your body? On the ground of being a child of God, and so driven by the Spirit, not the flesh (v. 14). Children of God are driven by the Spirit of God, not a spirit of slavery—lest you think that being led by anyone other than yourself is always slavery. Christian freedom is having the name of God to call upon in time of trouble, and so we cry, "Abba! Father!" (v. 15). It is not we who must bear witness to ourselves; the Spirit bears witness to our spirit (v. 16), and this through the preaching of the word. What does that word say? If we are children, then we are heirs, "joint heirs with Christ" (v. 17). Before we run off with the family farm, joint heir means you will suffer like him, going through death, not around it. Suffering is not paying a mortgage in

Pastoral Perspective

We could begin with the whole creation, but what of the human race? The number of children dying of malnutrition is staggering. The imagination reels at the picture of mothers and fathers unable to provide enough food to keep their children from withering away before their eyes. It is more than we can stand to see; when the images appear on our television screen, we reach for the remote to make them go away.

We do not need to leave our own houses to see the suffering of the present time. Ralph Waldo Emerson said it well: "Every roof is agreeable to the eye until it is lifted; then we find tragedy and moaning women and hard-eyed husbands."[1] Things that appear to be well so often have troubling currents underneath. Simply look out over one's congregation and recall the stories of abuse, chronic illness, loneliness, and despair, frequently spoken of only in hushed tones, if at all.

What we see, while surely not all bad, is bad enough. "The way things are" contains enough pain and suffering to make one "groan inwardly" (v. 23). Even if one is optimistic and sees the glass as half full, it is still a long way from a cup running over.

Paul speaks here of hope. Hope is rooted in an ability to see what one does not yet see. Hope is anticipating an inheritance that has not yet been received. As Paul puts it: "we are children of God, and if children, then heirs" (vv. 16–17). Hope for a "glory about to be revealed to us" (v. 18) does two important things.

First, it creates the sense of contrast between what is hoped for and the present state of affairs—what we get. This contrast causes disquietude. Disquietude expresses itself in groaning: expressing the pain of experiencing the negative, the way things are not supposed to be, but the way things in fact are. The one who hopes hurts. The one who hopes has a restless heart. The one who hopes sees what we get, what is in front of us, and is disappointed.

Karl Marx warns that religion with its fantasies drugs those who suffer and perpetuates their plight.[2] Marx, though, is only partially right. One who hopes does not necessarily escape the suffering of the present time. In fact, in some instances the one who hopes may be the only one with the courage to endure the suffering of the present. This may be what Paul means when he says, "We wait for it with patience" (v. 25). Patience is not the same thing as

---

1. Ralph Waldo Emerson, "Experience," in *Selections from Ralph Waldo Emerson*, ed. Stephen E. Whicher (Boston: Houghton Mifflin, 1957), 255.
2. Karl Marx, *Critique of Hegel's Philosophy of Right* (1843; Cambridge: Cambridge University Press, 1977).

thought."[2] The presence of the Aramaic "Abba" implies a strong connection to Jesus' words in the Lord's Prayer, as far away as Greek-speaking Rome. It invites the image of a relationship with God that is not only familial, but intimate and familiar: led by the Spirit of God, we are children of God.

This image of God as Father did not originate with Christians. Paul taps into layers of historical meaning from both Greco-Roman and Jewish worldviews, then reinterprets them to point to Christ and our relationship to God. In the Roman Empire, Augustus declared himself a god, and later his son Julius claimed to be son of (a) god. For ordinary people to see themselves as "children of God" alongside the "son of god" was audacious and preposterous, yet this is precisely what Paul proposes. For Jews, Israel is God's son, his "firstborn son," who is freed in the exodus from Egypt (Exod. 4:22) and enjoys a unique relationship with God. The eschatological hopes of God's people rest on this identity and promise.

Now the exodus, the essential story of the salvation of God's people, is opened to become the covenant story for everyone led by the Spirit of God to call God "Abba, Father." Just as God led God's people through the wilderness to freedom, so the Spirit leads all of God's children to a life of freedom. All who are in Christ are children of God.

The logical sequence Paul employs is strikingly effective. For Paul to say, "*When* we cry, 'Abba! Father!'" (v. 15), implies that this is already a common way for Christians to pray. Calling God "Abba, Father," is evidence of the Spirit's actively moving in their lives, evidence that they are in fact God's children. If they are God's children, they are to think of themselves as in the same family as Christ, set to inherit all that Christ inherits. What Christ receives at his death is both suffering and glory.

Now Paul moves to the closing passage in this major section of Romans (5:1–8:39). As he began with suffering, patience, hope, and love, so he ends. In 5:3–5 he writes, "We boast in our sufferings, knowing that suffering produces endurance, and endurance produces character, and character produces hope, and hope does not disappoint us, because God's love has been poured into our hearts through the Holy Spirit that has been given to us." The suffering of "this present time" (8:18) must have created profound distress for the early Roman

Beginning with verse 14, Paul tells us that if we are led by the Spirit of God we are children of God. We are part of God's family. Further, we have "received a spirit of adoption" (v. 15). Adoption is a powerful metaphor, especially in a country where many families struggle with infertility and couples open their homes and hearts to children from all over the world. Adoption is an act of grace. The child who does not biologically belong to a family is embraced by that family and becomes a rightful heir to the family's riches. The fact that God has chosen us and incorporated us into a Christ-shaped family composed of men, women, and children from every country, race, and class is powerful indeed. Our adoption creates an intimacy that enables us, like Jesus, to call God "Abba" or Father.

As God's adopted children, we inherit a new identity. This identity, although the gift that brings life, also entails suffering. About this, Paul is clear: "I consider that the sufferings of this present time are not worth comparing with the glory about to be revealed to us" (v. 18). The list of daunting challenges that cannot separate us from God's love, provided at the end of the chapter, gives us a sense of the suffering Paul experienced as a result of his adoption as God's son.

Living as God's children demands our complete allegiance, our whole selves. We are, as Paul instructs us in Romans 12:1, to present our "bodies as a living sacrifice, holy and acceptable to God, which is [our] spiritual worship." We are not to be "conformed to this world," but "transformed by the renewing of [our] minds" (v. 2) so that we can discern God's will and leading. In Romans 12 Paul lays out in detail what life in the Spirit looks like. It is not just about being nice on Sunday, but about obedience in the whole of our lives. We are to love what is genuine and hate what is evil, be patient in suffering, persevere in prayer, offer hospitality to strangers, bless those who persecute us, and, perhaps hardest of all, "live peaceably with all" (vv. 9. 12, 13, 14, 18).

Here it is important for the preacher to explore the meaning of Paul's words in an increasingly post-Christian society. Twenty-first-century America is coming to resemble the era of Jesus' first followers in provocative ways. The church is no longer at the center of Western society. Attendance in the mainline churches continues to decrease. Religious options abound in the spiritual marketplace, and there are more "spiritual tourists" than ever before. Christians are increasingly on the margins of our society, freed more than ever before to become the countersociety

---

2. N. T. Wright, "Romans," in *The New Interpreter's Bible* (Nashville: Abingdon, 2002), 10:591.

Romans 8:12-25

Theological Perspective

order to get the property. Christian suffering is "not worth comparing with the glory about to be revealed to us" (v. 18).

We have this inheritance by faith, not by sight. Indeed, the whole creation is "waits with eager longing for the apocalypse" (NRSV "revealing," v. 19). The apocalypse is a strange thing for creation to await, since it is its own destruction, but the creation was subject to futility not as an expression of its own will, but "by the will of the one who subjected it" (v. 20). God did this "in hope." The whole of creation has been groaning as if it were in childbirth up to now, but it could never give birth. It does not have life in itself, there is no child within it. That was the old pagan belief, that somehow mother earth could produce life from itself; but it is creature, not the Creator.

Like the children who have become heirs, the creation itself waits for its new birth, since heirs have the promise of their inheritance, but have not received it yet. It groans in the meantime. Not only creation waits, but we ourselves wait (v. 23). For in hope we were saved. Hope means our lives lean forward to what is coming to pass, but we do not yet see it. "We wait for it with patience" (v. 25), not because the inheritance comes from us, but because it comes from the God who did not spare his only begotten Son.

STEVEN D. PAULSON

Pastoral Perspective

acquiescence. Patience in this sense is not satisfied with the present, but lives toward a future promised by God.

Second, hope fuels an imagination for the way things ought to be. Hope—hope for things that are not yet but are promised to us—empowers the one who hopes to confront the evils of this age, knowing their way is not the final way. The one who hopes is inspired to work in the present for things to get better in the present. In fact, the word "inspired" literally means "to have the Spirit."

Although Paul indicates that "hope that is seen is not hope" (v. 24), he also indicates that we "have the first fruits of the Spirit" (v. 23). It is important to hold these two together. If hope is only for something beyond our imagination, beyond our seeing, then it can easily become a flight of fantasy. In this sense it is "pie in the sky, by and by," and feeds the sort of escapism of which Marx speaks and against which the aphorism "What you see is what you get" warns.

Christian hope is not pie in the sky; it is hope rooted in what Paul calls "the first fruits of the Spirit" (v. 23). This metaphor of the first fruits means that in Christ we already have come to know the power of life over death. We already know freedom. We already know love. We have tasted the first fruits, and they have whetted our appetite for the final banquet. We do have out-of-hand expectations. Because we know the first fruits, we rejoice at the loving, the living, and the freedom. We hunger for more, and we cry out wherever love is absent, life is shortened, and freedom is taken away. The church of Jesus Christ is the community of sisters and brothers who live in anticipation of a new birth of freedom, a new day of loving, and an inheritance of life abundant.

DAVID M. GREENHAW

church, not just physical but spiritual distress. How are they to understand it?

Not—as one might think—as punishment from God, as the absence of God, or as proof that the Messiah had not yet come. Suffering in no way negates the glory, truth, and promise of the resurrection. Rather, suffering offers evidence that these Christians are in fact already united with Christ. Just as they pray the prayer of Christ, so they suffer the suffering of Christ. As part of God's family, they are subject to the same rejection of the world. As N. T. Wright proclaims, "The road to the inheritance, the path to glory (the two are now, at last, seen to be more or less synonymous) lies along the road of suffering."[3]

The road ultimately, however, leads to glory; of this, Paul implores, we must not lose sight. Indeed, the whole creation waits with eager longing for this glory to be revealed. It is like a woman in labor, who cannot wait for the pain to be over but, even more, cannot wait to meet the long-awaited child about to be born. Here, in this most human experience, suffering and hope are not contradictory, but inseparably interwoven. Paul's claims are expansive: everything will be redeemed—all of creation, our bodies, the substance of this earth. Everything that fell with Adam's fall will be set free by Christ's redeeming work.

In the meantime, while we wait, we live in the already-and not-yet, where here-and-now and there-and-then overlap and intersect. Christians fall far from God's intention when they hold one without the other. We have the first fruits of the Spirit—here, already—and we groan for redemption, which is not yet complete. If we fail to see the redemption that is already here, we will lose heart. If we fail to understand that there is more glory to be revealed to us, we will have lost hope. If we hope, however, for what we do not yet see, we will wait with the tension of eager patience. Suffering and hope hold no contradiction, for they are deeply connected in Christ, the One whose glory we have seen, the One who gives this creation life.

KAREN CHAKOIAN

Paul calls us to be. Although the shift of power away from the Christian mainline denominations can be painful, it can also be empowering, and the preacher can bring this fact home. This is an era in which Christians, more than at any other time in decades, can understand ourselves to be an alternative community to the destructive ways of life embraced by the larger culture.

Beginning with verse 19, Paul commences a powerful meditation on how the destiny of creation and the children of God are bound up together. Both suffer and are subject to decay and death. Both groan inwardly, like pregnant women in labor, eager for the new reality God has promised will be completely birthed into the world and made manifest.

Our reading concludes with a beautiful meditation on hope. Here the preacher might explore the fact that most Americans are optimistic, but not hopeful. We still cling to the myth of progress, despite unceasing wars and violence. Here we have assurance of God's promise. God is acting in our midst and will act in the future. The Spirit gives us assurance; the Spirit's presence is a pledge of what is to come; yet we are impatient.

Impatience is something that defines our current era. We want everything now, faster, and better. I am reminded of the *Book of Common Prayer*'s Ash Wednesday litany, in which worshipers acknowledge and confess the "impatience of our lives."[1] Times of economic distress invite us to reevaluate our priorities. The preacher has an opening to explore the spiritual gift and importance of patience. Patience is a fruit of the Spirit (Gal. 5:22) and something Paul calls us to, as we wait in hope.

BLAIR ALISON POGUE

3. Ibid., 594.

1. *Book of Common Prayer* (New York: Church Publishing, 1979), 268.

Matthew 13:24-30, 36-43

[24]He put before them another parable: "The kingdom of heaven may be compared to someone who sowed good seed in his field; [25]but while everybody was asleep, an enemy came and sowed weeds among the wheat, and then went away. [26]So when the plants came up and bore grain, then the weeds appeared as well. [27]And the slaves of the householder came and said to him, 'Master, did you not sow good seed in your field? Where, then, did these weeds come from?' [28]He answered, 'An enemy has done this.' The slaves said to him, 'Then do you want us to go and gather them?' [29]But he replied, 'No; for in gathering the weeds you would uproot the wheat along with them. [30]Let both of them grow together until the harvest; and at harvest time I will tell the reapers, Collect the weeds first and bind them in bundles to be burned, but gather the wheat into my barn.'" . . .

Theological Perspective

This parable appears only in Matthew. As was the case in the previous week's lection, Matthew 13:1–9, 18–23, seed is a key metaphor. Whereas in the previous parable all the seed was good seed, sown by a good sower, here we encounter two kinds of seeds sown by polar-opposite sowers. Furthermore, seeds in this lection do not represent faith *and* disciples but only disciples—disciples of God and of the evil one. Challenges for planting and spreading the gospel are not limited to issues of reception and persecution. There is also the issue that the enemy has sown disciples of evil in the community of faith. In dealing with this text, we will have to address the intertwined theological topics of ecclesiology and anthropology. We will also need to inquire into the appropriateness of the ecclesiology and anthropology Matthew offers.

This text expresses at least two ecclesiological claims regarding the nature of the church on earth: (1) it is a mixed body of two kinds of disciples; (2) the ultimate nature and destiny of every disciple will not be revealed until the judgment at the end of the age. The parable offers a descriptive and normative framework in which to understand a fundamental dilemma the church faces in every age this side of the triumph of the "empire of the heavens." The community of Jesus is called to imitate Jesus, to follow

Pastoral Perspective

The bearded darnel is a devil of a weed. It defies Emerson's claim that a weed is "a plant whose virtues have yet to be discovered."[1] Known in biblical terms as "tares," bearded darnel has no virtues. Its roots surround the roots of good plants, sucking up precious nutrients and scarce water, making it impossible to root it out without damaging the good crop. Above ground, darnel looks identical to wheat, until it bears seed. Those seeds can cause everything from hallucinations to death.

No wonder Jesus uses this noxious "cheat weed" to illustrate evil incarnate. Bearded darnel, also known as false wheat, is the botanical equivalent of the "ravenous wolves . . . in sheep's clothing" of which he has already warned (Matt. 7:15). Moreover, Jesus says, this evil is intentional. Unlike the preceding story about a sower, this is not a parable of happenstance, good seed falling onto infertile soil. Here the enemy deliberately sows cheat weed in a field of good wheat.

Paradoxically, this unflinching focus on evil gives the parable its pastoral power. Jesus clearly acknowledges the reality of evil. His parable illustrates evil's pernicious nature, underscoring both the necessity of eradicating it and the difficulty of doing so.

1. Ralph Waldo Emerson, "The Fortune of the Republic" (1878), reprinted in Ralph Waldo Emerson, *Miscellanies* (London: Adamant Media Corp., 2006), 396.

³⁶Then he left the crowds and went into the house. And his disciples approached him, saying, "Explain to us the parable of the weeds of the field." ³⁷He answered, "The one who sows the good seed is the Son of Man; ³⁸the field is the world, and the good seed are the children of the kingdom; the weeds are the children of the evil one, ³⁹and the enemy who sowed them is the devil; the harvest is the end of the age, and the reapers are angels. ⁴⁰Just as the weeds are collected and burned up with fire, so will it be at the end of the age. ⁴¹The Son of Man will send his angels, and they will collect out of his kingdom all causes of sin and all evildoers, ⁴²and they will throw them into the furnace of fire, where there will be weeping and gnashing of teeth. ⁴³Then the righteous will shine like the sun in the kingdom of their Father. Let anyone with ears listen!"

Exegetical Perspective

Addressing a growing concern within the young Christian community following the fall of Jerusalem, Matthew pairs the parable of the Sower with the parable of the Weeds. In the parable of the Sower, Jesus addresses the question of why responses to the gospel vary so greatly and so often seem unproductive. In the parable of the Weeds, attention shifts from an external focus to an internal focus. From the Christian community's formative days as a small band gathered around their sage to the present era, it has wrestled with the paradoxical nature of the church and the contradictory forces at work within it.

Thus, while the parable of the Weeds (vv. 24–30) is unique to the Matthean tradition, the situation addressed by the parable is not. If we accept the recognized view that Matthew was written not by an eyewitness of Jesus, but rather by someone writing within the church community of Antioch toward the end of the first century (80–90 CE), then the rationale for including this parable at this point becomes more evident.[1] The church at Antioch began as a church of Diaspora Jewish Christians following the initial Jerusalem persecution. As an urban church, it reflected the ethnic diversity common to large cities.

Homiletical Perspective

This parable shines a bright light on our inevitable human preoccupation with drawing lines between who is "in" and who is "out." An agricultural tale, it applies, as Thomas G. Long has said, "to the ministry of Jesus himself, to the life of the church, and to the future judgment at the end of the world."[1]

No doubt it was first a word of comfort to the disciples and followers of Jesus, aware of those weed-like opponents of Jesus. Their persistent criticisms, challenges, and hostility in the midst of his ministry were not due to flaws or deficits in his message, but rather to the work of his enemy, the devil. "An enemy has done this" (v. 28), the householder says, noting the presence of weeds in the field.

In our time, though, we hear this parable as an amazing insight into the life of the church. Like that field in which there grow both healthy wheat and destructive weeds, the church is a mixed-bag reality. Like the householder's servants who want to weed out the field's dangerous elements, we too either embody or suspect their surrogates in every age. Matters of behavior or theological and biblical orientation become the fodder for litmus tests of all varieties. Elements within each of our different

1. David Garland, *Reading Matthew* (Macon, GA: Smyth & Helwys, 2001), 3–4.

1. Thomas G. Long, *Matthew* (Louisville, KY: Westminster John Knox Press, 1997), 151.

Matthew 13:24-30, 36-43

Theological Perspective

Jesus, to present the face of Jesus to the world, and to act in his name according to his command to love.

The church, however, is never purely that community. In fact, the church is never pure, period. Without necessarily invoking the distinction between a "visible" and an "invisible" church, one has to conclude that the empirical church is not solely holy! Corporately, ecclesial entities sometimes act in a manner contrary to "what Jesus would do"; and in any given moment there are members of the church who are acting, publicly or privately, in un-Christian ways. The church is always expressing itself as a mixed body.

All this is the descriptive ecclesiology. The normative dimension addresses the question of what church leaders should do about presence of the other disciples. The answer here: leave the sorting to God for the day of judgment. For Matthew's community, leaving the wheat and weeds for God to sort does not preclude discipline exercised by church leaders (see Matt. 18:15–17), but exercising temporal judgments is distinguished from the eschatological judgment.

Augustine of Hippo gives us the classic understanding of the church as a mixed body, a *corpus permixtum*. Recall that Augustine was involved in controversies with Manicheans (the nature of good and evil), Pelagians (agency and grace in relation to salvation), and Donatists (the relationship between the purity of priests and bishops and the efficacy of their ministries, particularly sacraments administered by a "traitor's" hands). Augustine certainly does not argue that, in the face of manifest sin by "weedy" disciples, church leaders should do nothing and leave all the sorting to God.

On the contrary, church leaders are charged with discipline, from mild to severe (excommunication). Nevertheless, with his leadership experience and personal struggles as a Christian undoubtedly on his mind, Augustine concludes that it is impossible to maintain absolute outward holiness in the visible church and that an unholy action by a member does not disable the possibility of future holiness.[1]

Minimally, the parable of the Wheat and the Weeds serves as a caution against any ecclesiology that is tempted to collapse ecclesiology and eschatology, to identify the church on earth with the empire of the heavens. The church is not the fulfillment of

Pastoral Perspective

There is not a person in our congregations who does not know what Jesus is talking about. Sometimes our own lives resemble the farmer's infested field, with weeds and wheat intertwined in our souls, hearts, and minds. The apostle Paul certainly knows it: "I do not do what I want, but I do the very thing I hate" (Rom. 7:15). Members of AA or Alanon do too. The First Step confesses, "We are powerless over alcohol and our lives have become unmanageable." The Fourth Step is to do a "fearless moral inventory," sorting out the wheat from the weeds within.

Our personal experience of the enemy's sowing may be more subtle, as in the countless distractions we let derail us. E-mails, phone calls, and endless meetings can make it look as if we are working on the realm of God, but they may simply be symptoms of our own divided souls.

Sometimes our jobs can feel weed infested and under assault by the evil one. Like the servants of the parable, many in our congregations face the challenge of separating the weeds from the wheat in their workplaces. Maybe it is the middle manager who is glad for her company's big profits, but is not sure about the bookkeeping behind them. Maybe it is the teacher facing a clique of parents whose well-meaning criticism chokes out his creativity and care for his students. Perhaps it is the lawyer who is asked to look the other way for the "good of the firm."

These people may not be first-century Galilean farmers, but they confront evil every day. Jesus does too. Just before he tells this parable, the Pharisees—leaders of his own faith—try to trick him and begin their plot to destroy him. They look like true leaders, but they are as false and deadly as any bearded darnel where he is concerned.

Jesus and the author of Matthew also know that evil can infest the community itself. Elsewhere in the Gospel, Jesus warns against "false messiahs and false prophets," those who cry, "Lord, Lord," and seem faithful and caring, but who lead people astray and harm the community (24:24; 7:22). In contemporary terms, Kenneth Haugk, founder of Stephen Ministry, describes such people as "antagonists in the church."[2] By any name—antagonists, weeds, wolves, false prophets, false wheat—they are a reality in the community of faith. Jesus' parable acknowledges that hard truth.

At the same time, his parable clearly cautions against a rush to judgment. We cannot always tell initially what is a good plant and what is not. My

1. See Augustine, "Baptism, Against the Donatists (*De Baptismo Contra Donatistas*)," trans. J. R. King, esp. chaps. 4 and 5, in *A Select Library of the Nicene and Post-Nicene Fathers of the Christian Church*, ed. Philip Schaff (Grand Rapids: Eerdmans, 1956), 4:447–78.

2. Kenneth Haugk, *Antagonists in the Church* (Minneapolis: Augsburg, 1988).

Exegetical Perspective

With the population shift, especially following the destruction of Jerusalem, the shifting cultural settings of urban centers intensified the faith community's struggle with religious diversity.

With their base shifting and with growth such as that anticipated by the ending of the parable of the Sower, the question for the emerging church became, "How are we to deal with those who initially seem identical to us but over time are revealed as different from us in their expression of faith and/or their actions?" To put it more bluntly, "It seems to us that some of our number are as worthless as weeds, so how and when are we to rid ourselves of them?"

What church leader has not sought to decipher whether those who are obviously of a different seed are true reflections of the nature of the gospel or are detracting from its strength and witness by remaining in the faith community? As Matthew relates it, the parable presents one more question and answer about the kind of faith community the church must be, both to survive and to produce the desired kingdom.

If the parable is originally told by Jesus in the context described by Matthew—during a time when Jesus is moving toward his own time of trial and death in the company of disciples who reflect characteristics of both wheat and weeds—then its application by those same disciples in the years following the resurrection pops to the front. In their concern to sort out the evil from the good, they have only to be reminded of their own fickleness and betrayal to be aware of how easy it is to rush to judgment before the story is complete.

Ultimately this parable is eschatological, addressing themes of waiting and judgment, gathering and separation, preservation and destruction. The parable does not focus on the identity of the outside enemy. Rather the focus is on two potential responses to evil mixed with good. First comes the response of the slaves (not identified in the allegorical explanation that follows), who want to know if the householder has inadvertently sowed bad seed and—if so—whether they should rid the field of weeds. The other response is that of the householder: wait and live with the paradox until God's resolution at the consummation.

Questions arise as to the setting and the identity of the characters. Although addressed by the explanation given in verses 36–43, the questions are not completely resolved. What or who is the field of wheat into which the weeds are sown? Unlike the parable of the Sower, in which the good seed falls

Homiletical Perspective

churchly communions are forever troubled by how broadly or narrowly we should draw the boundaries of the contemporary church. Whom can we afford to let in, and who must remain out? Who is accepted by God, and why? Who is not accepted by God, and why not? In the very act of asking such questions, we so often assume that it is our job to draw up the specifications regarding the wideness of the church's welcome. How wide, really, can it be, and still be the church?

Maybe it is understandable that the servants push for clarity regarding the wheat *versus* the weeds. They are confident that, without any further delay, they can bring in the harvest, burn the weeds, and settle forever the problem of who is in and who is out. However, as Matthew tells the story, the master in this parable has greater wisdom. "No"; he says, "for in gathering the weeds you would uproot the wheat along with them. Let both of them grow together until the harvest" (vv. 28–29). Let both grow together until the harvest, he says, because one cannot always tell about these plants.

There is a strategy in these words of restraint that pushes away from premature clarity regarding such matters of discernment and makes room instead for a holy and purposeful ambiguity. This is not a vague and ungrounded "whatever" kind of ambiguity, but an ambiguity that is both wise and intentional. In our impatience with others, we often want to bring matters to a head and so determine whether others are in or out; but the God who is glimpsed in this parable models for us an infinite patience that frees us to get on with the crucial business of loving, or at least living with, each other. Often, in the space created by such patience, it is not just others, but we ourselves, who are welcomed into a larger reality. This is the sense in which we are "reborn" not just once, but over and over and over again.

This picture of a blessed mixture of weeds and wheat growing together until harvest is not just a glimpse of the faithful church in our own time, but is finally a glimpse of the future judgment at the end of time as we know it. At this level, the text points us to a God who does not merely tolerate endlessly a world that is a mixture of good and evil, faith and faithlessness, triumph and tragedy, but who finally, in God's own good time, acts both to judge and to redeem the world. Christians believe that, for the sake of this hurting and impatient world, and through Jesus Christ our Lord, God's realm will at last be completed and revealed in all its fullness. Meanwhile, this realm is thriving in us, around us,

Matthew 13:24-30, 36-43

Theological Perspective

God's promised reign. Consequently, it would seem the visible church as a mixed body could reflect profitably on all the following doctrines, metaphors, and depictions—each of which expresses one or more facets of the church's mixed nature:

—A hospital for the sick
—Noah's ark (one can stand the stench on the inside only because of the storm on the outside[2])
—The community of saints, militant and triumphant
—The being-saved community
—A *corpus permixtum*
—Sign and instrument, sacrament and foretaste of the empire of the heavens
—In need of discipline and compassion
—One, holy, catholic, and apostolic
—Reformed and reforming
—Conveyer of the means of grace, both to its members and to the world

The other theological topic to be noted here is anthropology. Theological anthropology is implied in every doctrine of the church, in any understanding of the nature of true community. Matthew's theological anthropology, as seen in this parable, and akin to the parable of the Sheep-Goats-Final Judgment in chapter 25, shares an anthropological assumption common in the ancient world: persons are of one type or another. A community or collection of persons may be a *corpus permixtum*, but each person is fundamentally of one type: a child of God or a child of Satan, a disciple of Christ or a disciple of the evil one.

Those who live in a post-Freudian world tend not to divide persons so neatly. We see mixed motivations, the noble and the base in each person. Recent brain research reveals evolutionary levels of the human brain, from the reptilian "fight or flight" instinct, to the amygdala where the shape of trauma is preserved, to the "God center" in the cerebral cortex. It may be fruitful for us to think about each Christian individual as a *corpus permixtum*. Each of us is some mixture of wheat and weed, of holy and unholy, of potentially fruitful and potentially destructive. This kind of anthropology would turn the normative conclusion regarding what is a fitting action away from waiting for God to sort at the final judgment and toward attending as a community and as individuals to that which increases the potential for holiness.

GARY PELUSO-VERDEND

Pastoral Perspective

grandmother, a master gardener, once transplanted some flowers from her garden into our front yard. Two days later, she was back, frantically digging up the same plants. "I made a mistake," she said, sweat dripping from her eighty-year-old face. "These are weeds, not the flowers I had intended! Quick, give me a hand before your mother gets home!" Although my beloved grandmother is scarcely the evil one of Jesus' parable, her story underscores the challenge of distinguishing good from bad, wheat from weeds, loyal opposition from heresy, healthy conflict from destructive antagonism.

Thus the landowner tells his servants to be patient and wait until the harvest, when they can see the difference by the fruit that is borne. Such patience is not an excuse for inaction or conflict avoidance. Later in Matthew, Jesus outlines how to deal with poisonous behavior within the community (18:15–17). If the behavior does not change, the person is to be considered a "Gentile or tax collector," separated from the community as the reapers separate weeds from wheat at the harvest.

That separation may seem harsh and unchristian, but Jesus knows only too well the wiles of the evil one. He knows that failure to deal with evil allows it to spread, just as seeds of the noxious darnel multiply and infest other fields. In his interpretation of the parable, Jesus identifies the reapers as angels who come at the "end of the age." This eschatological twist offers a final pastoral truth. The fact is, the weeds often win out in this life. Jesus knows that. So do the people we serve.

The parable's ending affirms that there is One who is stronger and smarter than the weed-sowing enemy. God will sort out the good from the bad. Again, that may sound harsh to our tolerant, enlightened ears, but this harvesttime judgment is the ultimate good news, be it for the person facing corruption in their workplace or those living in times and places of oppression. In a world where seeds of hatred and injustice are daily sown, the parable affirms unequivocally that God is still in charge. As an old hymn proclaims, "Though the wrong seems oft so strong, God is the Ruler yet."[3]

TALITHA J. ARNOLD

2. Robert MacAfee Brown, *The Significance of the Church* (Philadelphia: Westminster Press, 1956), 17.

3. Maltbie D. Babcock, "This Is My Father's World" (1901), *The Worshipbook* (Philadelphia: Westminster Press, 1970), #602.

Exegetical Perspective

among the weeds, here we begin with a field of good seed. Could the field be the faith community itself?

With the eye of imagination lit by this parable, the field depicts the community of faith, the newly sprouting kingdom. If the householder does not sow bad seed, then who does? The enemy, defined in the explanation as "the evil one" or "the devil," has gained access to and directly attacked the faith community. Thus the particular problem addressed is not the presence of evil in the world but, rather, the very real presence of the "not good," or outright evil, within the community of faith.[2]

As for the explanation of the parable of the Weeds, some scholars argue that the explanation attributed to Jesus in verses 36–43 is the creation of either the Gospel writer or perhaps a redaction added later by a church leader or scribe. While that is possible, the argument has not been strong enough to negate the likelihood that the explanation is authentically Jesus', at least in principle, as it fits the pattern of teaching employed by wisdom teachers.

The lectionary reading omits verses 34–35, in which Matthew identifies Jesus' methodology of teaching in parables as a fulfillment of prophecy. Although some ancient manuscripts identify the quotation referred to in verse 35 with Isaiah, the most likely source is Psalm 78:2. Following stronger manuscript evidence, the NRSV omits the attribution to Isaiah. With these two verses Matthew again asserts the distinction between the public proclamation of parables of the kingdom and the private teaching about the secret of the kingdom. The secret, or "that which has been hidden," has been hidden in plain sight since the beginning of the world.

As outlined in verses 14–16, what has been and continues to be required for understanding the secret of the kingdom is hearts that have not grown dull, eyes that see, and ears that hear. With verse 36 Jesus turns from the crowd and moves back inside the house once again with the admonition, "Let anyone with ears listen!"—at once a charge, a challenge, and an offer.

J. DAVID WAUGH

Homiletical Perspective

and even, miraculously, sometimes through us; and God is pleased to let all of it "grow together until the harvest" (v. 30).

Patrick J. Willson, a superb preacher and pastoral theologian, has said that

> Jesus did not say that the kingdom was like a rock, fixed and solid and firm and unchanging. Jesus did not say that the kingdom was like a giant machine, that you put some things in and you get some things out and that what you get out depends upon what you put in. He said it was like an enormous tree that grows out of a tiny seed. A tree that grows so enormous that all the birds of the air can come and find shelter in its branches, even strange little ducks like you and me. He said that God was like a housewife who puts a smidgen of yeast in the three measures of flour and that yeast yields its life into the whole batch of dough. That is the way that the kingdom is, growing from the very beginning into all that God has intended. . . . From the foundation of the world, the very first moment of creation, it is the kingdom that has been on God's mind, and God is infinitely patient as it grows.[2]

It is toward this very God that we are forever moving—individually, collectively, and as a cosmos. On such a journey as this, it is not our job to determine who is within and who is beyond this God's attention. It is rather our job to imagine everyone as belonging to this God, and therefore, with all that we can muster, to endeavor to embrace, through Jesus Christ our Lord, God's holy and purposeful ambiguity.

THEODORE J. WARDLAW

---

2. For another understanding, see David Garland, who argues that the "field" is to be identified with the "world" (*Reading Matthew*, 149–50).

2. Patrick J. Willson, "God Is Not Finished," a sermon preached at Grace Presbyterian Church of Midland, Texas, on August 9, 1981.

1 Kings 3:5-12

⁵At Gibeon the LORD appeared to Solomon in a dream by night; and God said, "Ask what I should give you." ⁶And Solomon said, "You have shown great and steadfast love to your servant my father David, because he walked before you in faithfulness, in righteousness, and in uprightness of heart toward you; and you have kept for him this great and steadfast love, and have given him a son to sit on his throne today. ⁷And now, O LORD my God, you have made your servant king in place of my father David, although I am only a little child; I do not know how to go out or come in. ⁸And your servant is in the midst of the people whom you have chosen, a great people, so numerous they cannot be numbered or counted. ⁹Give your servant therefore an understanding mind to govern your people, able to discern between good and evil; for who can govern this your great people?"

¹⁰It pleased the Lord that Solomon had asked this. ¹¹God said to him, "Because you have asked this, and have not asked for yourself long life or riches, or for the life of your enemies, but have asked for yourself understanding to discern what is right, ¹²I now do according to your word. Indeed I give you a wise and discerning mind; no one like you has been before you and no one like you shall arise after you."

Theological Perspective

Maintaining family traditions is important for social cohesiveness. There comes a time, however, when social conditions change, making it difficult to keep up some traditions. For instance, younger people are more mobile now than in previous generations. Therefore, family traditions like holiday gatherings are less frequent.

The appearance of the Lord at Gibeon signals Solomon's distinctive path away from the traditions and legacy of his father David. It represents a clear break from tradition. He builds his own house before attempting to build a house for the Lord. In this text, Solomon chooses to worship on the high plain of Gibeon instead of the traditional place of worship in Jerusalem, despite the return of the ark. For all intents and purposes, the Solomon administration will set a new direction for the nation.

Many scholars agree that the description of this event mirrors many local Near Eastern and Egyptian mythologies about the ascendancies of new dynasties. The narration of the inauguration of Solomon also serves as a literary device for the "political propaganda" common to many Near Eastern sources. Leong Seow argues, however, for the likelihood of Syro-Palestinian influences, including several

Pastoral Perspective

If you had one wish, what would it be? If you had one mulligan, one chance to take back one boneheaded thing you have done, what would it be? If a fairy godmother appeared at the foot of your bed before you went to sleep, what would you ask for? If you had a chance to sleep on it, what would you decide?

When God asks Solomon what he wants, the king asks for wisdom. Wisdom can be measured in many ways. Perhaps one measure of wisdom is not needing to make a wish to get what you most want. Wisdom is more than knowledge; it is also more than getting all you want out of life. Wisdom has to do with "alignment." The intent of the exercise of biblical wisdom is to bring the soul into alignment with God's ways, because the human soul has a propensity to become out of alignment with God's ways.

You might think of it like this: when your car's steering system is out of alignment, if you do not keep the steering wheel turned a little bit against the pull, then sooner or later you are going to head off the road right into a tree. With everything else being equal, this is certainly going to happen. Your car will veer off dangerously, unless you are consciously aware of the misalignment of your steering system.

The marks of true wisdom have to do with the acknowledgment of our need, our want, and our

Exegetical Perspective

The image of a pious Solomon disappears once this passage is read within the context of the whole chapter and the entire book of 1 Kings. The lectionary effectively cuts off the critique of Solomon's practice of worshiping at high places (3:3–4), a practice frowned upon in the Bible (e.g., 15:14). The text explains his presence at Gibeon, a principal high place, as being due to the lack of a temple in Jerusalem (3:2) while maintaining Solomon's love for YHWH (3:3).

The contradictions in the statements pile up in the declaration of Solomon's habitual presence at Gibeon (3:4). His sudden presence in Jerusalem, where he stands before the ark of the covenant at the end of the dream (3:15), also confirms the condemnation of his presence at Gibeon. The notice of his marriage to the Egyptian princess (3:1), as well as his presence at Gibeon, sets the stage for a reign ruined by idolatry and indulgence. The narrative of the pious king (3:4–14), heavily redacted to suit Deuteronomistic purposes,[1] proves ironic when read in the context of Solomon's accession to the throne and the details of his reign.

---

1. David McLain Carr, *From D to Q: A Study of Early Jewish Interpretation of Solomon's Dream at Gibeon* (Atlanta: Scholars Press, 1991), 32.

Homiletical Perspective

Imagine a community on the edge of survival. Its religious, economic, and cultural centers are in ruins. Its leaders have been ripped from their homeland. Now in exile, the community of YHWH faces the humiliation of being erased by the cultural power of an empire with powerful and alien gods. What can assist their survival when political, religious, and economic freedom is denied? When the last king of Judah dies, what can those who remember Zion do? Sing songs. Tell stories. Compose a history of kings.

A story is a temporary structure of human consciousness, but a story can also shape human perception, which will in turn alter history. The books known as First and Second Kings were once a single structure, the last book in a saga that included Deuteronomy, Joshua, Judges, and Samuel. It received its final shape in the early period of the Babylonian exile. Its intended audience would have included the leaders who were deported to Babylon, the poor who were left behind in Jerusalem, and the Jews who had taken refuge in Egypt.

So why this story in particular? What does the story provide? It provides identity. It provides a meaning to life to replace what has been lost in defeat and exile. In this story a young king comes to Gibeon to sacrifice on one of the high places where

1 Kings 3:5-12

Theological Perspective

parallels from Ugaritic literature.[1] Reference to Solomon's youthfulness should not be understood as simply chronological, but should be "understood as formulaic assertion of divine election" against the normal practices of the period, or opposing ideological forces.[2] It is an effective mythology often used in modern-day presidential elections, as was the case in 2008 of the election of President Barack Obama.

The divine approval of Solomon's kingship is made evident in YHWH's appearance in a "dream by night" in which the king is granted a wish: "ask what I should give you" (v. 5). The question appears to be not only a gesture of affirmation, but also a test of the king's true character, which has been questionable up to this moment. Solomon appeals to his father's legacy, but also wants to be anointed on his own merits. To be known as king based only on genealogical succession is inadequate. To do so would diminish the mythical potency of the king's rule. Although he acknowledges, "O LORD my God, you have made your servant king in place of my father David" (v. 7), Solomon longs for a unique quality to legitimize his kingship.

Solomon's request for wisdom appears to be the right question for the right time. It serves not only as an appeal to God, but as a practical request appropriate to changing times and contexts. Solomon does not need a rod and staff like Moses, because the Jews are not in captivity. Nor does he need military resources like his father David. The challenges before Solomon will be mostly administrative as he attempts to bring together tribes from the north and south under one united governing establishment. The request for wisdom and an "understanding mind to govern your people" (v. 9) is a practical and humble choice. One has to admire the wisdom in Solomon's request for wisdom.

Being able to "discern between good and evil" (v. 9) lies at the heart of many Old Testament narratives, particularly in Genesis 2–3. Adam and Eve's failure to "discern" the difference between good and evil becomes the bedrock of all human sin. According to the story, in the midst of the garden are two trees, the tree of life and the tree of knowledge. On the tree of knowledge there are two types of fruit, good and evil. Because they are on the same tree, it may be difficult for the first humans to distinguish one from the other.

---

1. C. L. Seow, "The Syro-Palestinian Context of Solomon's Dream," *Harvard Theological Review* 77, no. 2 (1984): 142.
2. C. L. Seow, "The First and Second Books of Kings," in *The New Interpreter's Bible*, ed. Leander E. Keck et al. (Nashville: Abingdon Press, 1999), 3:39.

Pastoral Perspective

emptiness. This is not an exercise in selfishness, seeking a quick fix for a newly found need, but an open, honest, and long-term quest to be other serving and not self serving. It all goes back to our "alignment" with God—that is, how our souls are aligned with what God wants and intends for us.

There is an old saying, "Be careful what you wish for . . . for you just might get it." In Solomon's case, he asks for what is most appropriate and right for the moment. Neither longevity, nor wealth, nor vengeance is on his wish list. We should all be so discerning and fortunate. Whether or not Solomon truly profits from the wisdom conferred on him is the subject of another Bible study.

It is said that people bring their own orienting systems into each new situation they encounter, especially those that demand creative responses. An orienting system is made of our habits, beliefs, relationships, and previous experiences; some are positive resources, while others can be burdens. We access them in different ways. They are like deposits in a bank waiting to be withdrawn. When key events arise in our lives, both the resources and burdens of our orienting systems may be called into action.

Orienting ourselves according to our *burdens* makes responding to situations more difficult. Orienting ourselves according to our *resources* helps us take on situations creatively and positively. Of course, in order to bring out our best resources, we need to know both what they are and how to appropriate them for use in any given situation.

I remember a fellow pastor telling me some years ago about a man in his congregation who had good, constructive, and viable resources, but he did not know it. The resources of his wisdom were buried under his burdens.

This individual was a self-described "wimp." A midlevel bank manager, he felt pushed around, bullied, manipulated, and generally ineffectual in his job. When he talked about his work, this fellow became sort of glassy eyed. His voice turned monotone and his shoulders slouched. My friend said he became tired himself just listening to this man. There was no energy in him, no focus, no dream.

In an effort to find some sort of spark in the life of this man, who was so in search of some sort of spark in his life, my friend tried to shift the focus of the conversation to earlier years. He found that the man had not only put himself through college by working two jobs but had also spent some time in the boxing ring and had flown airplanes on weekends. This was not the behavior of a wimp.

Exegetical Perspective

The passage resembles other theophanies where YHWH directs a message to someone (Gen. 12:7; 17:1; 35:9). Theophanies either take place at well-known sites or raise the importance of these sites (Gen. 12:6–9; 18:1–16; 26:24–25; 28:10–22). The passage speaks of the reputation of Gibeon as a "principal high place" frequented by Solomon (he "used to offer a thousand burnt offerings on that altar," v. 4), indicating its function as a cultic site. Although the site appears not to be associated with the worship of YHWH, a problem for the Deuteronomistic editors, YHWH appears to Solomon at this site.

The structure of the passage reflects the form of the theophany report. It first deals with the circumstances (vv. 4–5a), followed by the details of the epiphany (vv. 5b–14) and Solomon's response (v. 15). Apart from detailing the prestige of Gibeon as a cultic site where one expects a theophany, the introduction to the report offers the circumstances under which Solomon experiences the epiphany, "a dream by night." Both the form (dream) and the time ("at night") of the epiphany speak to the belief that deities use these extraordinary means to encounter humans. The contrast between Solomon's active presence in verse 4 and his passive reception of YHWH's appearance in the dream in verse 5 stresses the shift to YHWH in the passage at this point.

The details of the epiphany come in three parts. First, YHWH invites Solomon to make a request (v. 5b). In response, Solomon summarizes David's reign (v. 6) as the background for his petitions (v. 9). This forms the second part of the epiphany. The response to the invitation of verse 5 eventually comes in verse 9. In between these two statements, Solomon offers a self-deprecating assessment that fills out the picture of his piety.

The delay enables the multiplication of the pronouns that call attention to YHWH rather than Solomon. Even the petition is framed in YHWH's favor rather than as a request from Solomon. The language imitates the deference associated with the royal court where one petitions the king. The overused phrase "your servant" (vv. 6, 7, 8, 9) captures the excessive modesty that characterizes the passage. YHWH's reply to Solomon's petition forms the third part of the epiphany (vv. 10–13). This reply crescendoes to the ultimate gift of the promise of long life. It gets there by way of telling what Solomon does not request (v. 11), what he asks for (v. 12), and what he receives (vv. 13–14). The passage offers no obvious explanation for the divine excesses in verses 13–14.

Homiletical Perspective

the barrier between heaven and earth is thin. A new king comes on a dream quest, seeking for wisdom and a sense of self that only revelation can provide. God, not Solomon, is the central figure in this theological narrative, but the intention of God is to make Solomon great. Still, this is a story of a promise made to a people, not just to a king. The writer is calling a community to return to the God of their youth just like the young Solomon: "To walk before you in faithfulness, in righteousness, and in uprightness of heart toward you" (v. 6).

Solomon comes in search of self-knowledge. The story of his dream is a narrative quest for transformation. Solomon (and Judah) is seeking a transformation of self and relief from profound tension. "Although I am only a little child; I do not know how to go out or come in" (v. 7). This story may be a conscious attempt to remember what is lost and in the telling regain it. A dream quest by a king implies that the deepest wisdom is not reason, but revelation. Despite all the evidence of the exile to the contrary, this story seeks to return a people to a trust in YHWH, God of creation and liberation. The outcome is determined by the memory of what was known to be true at the beginning and what is hoped for at the end of the struggle as well as the right ending to the story.

This story of a dream begins as a response to a crisis. "What does it take to govern a great people?" The gifts Solomon asks for are the core of the Deuteronomic teachings: an understanding mind to govern, in essence, a "listening heart"; the ability to discern between good and evil (a reminder of Gen. 2:9); the understanding to discern what is right (to hear judgment, as in Deut. 11:18–21); lastly, a wise and discerning mind.

Biblical stories engage our community stories, and the interaction shapes identity on an individual and communal level. When an individual or a community perceives its structural integrity to be collapsing under the weight of external threat or inner disintegration, an urgent search for a sustainable narrative begins. The bits and pieces of experience, the core memories of existential wisdom that have been previously assimilated, now begin to fire up new connections like neural pathways. The traditions and truths that we have inherited begin to lay out the landscape through which we will have to travel. It seems as if the story tells us, rather than the other way around, and even when our final destination, the altered self, results in the rejection of these earlier pathways, they form the initial map for our journey.

1 Kings 3:5-12

Theological Perspective

Therefore, Adam and Eve are forbidden to take fruit from the tree of knowledge. The serpent tricks Adam and Eve into believing that jealousy is the reason for prohibiting them from eating from the tree of knowledge. Their transgression sentences humanity to a life where discerning the difference between good and evil is often an ambiguous choice, one that brings a series of catastrophic consequences.

The theological and contextual rationale for Solomon's request seems to meet with God's approval. The alternatives are selfish indulgence: a "long life and riches" or "the life of your enemies" (v. 11). Instead, Solomon asks for wisdom to "discern what is right," appropriating to himself an unprecedented legacy in Israel's history. It is also important to note that God's choice to grant Solomon's demands is not to be interpreted simply as an act of divine acquiescence. For YHWH to "do according to your word" (v. 12) is not about Solomon's wisdom, but is mostly descriptive of what God expects from the people in light of their changing circumstances.

The biblical record concerning the success of Solomon's kingship is indisputable in terms of his contributions to wisdom writings and the development of Israel's social structure. Of course, the pronouncement, "no one like you has been before you and no one like you shall arise after you" (v. 12), can be interpreted both negatively and positively. More important is how the reign of Solomon gives us insight into the character of a God who values social equality and justice in human relationships.

Consequently, the contextual issues in this text lend themselves to more fundamental ethical questions about leadership and the appropriate use of power within the community of the faithful. Is Solomon to be understood as a model for leadership in the church? Perhaps there are some lessons to be gleaned here. The larger sequence of events that unfold during the reign of Solomon point to more important theological insights than examples of church leadership.

JOHN L. THOMAS JR.

Pastoral Perspective

When the man talked about flying, he almost sparkled with energy. He seemed surprised when my friend made a comment about the difference between his style at work and his style behind the controls of an airplane. The key moment in the conversation came when this fellow himself recognized that his problem was not a "chronically wimpy personality," but a simple lack of identifying and tapping into his own resources. He pinpointed the solution for himself when he said, "I guess what I need to do is fly at work, huh?" People cannot cope using tools they do not believe they have.

The Hebrew word for "soul," *nephesh*, carries an anatomical and biological meaning. According to David Hansen, it implies neediness, vulnerability, and emptiness at the physical center of what it means to be human. The soul is empty. It is a bucket, not a geyser. The soul is made to want.[1]

This is not due to sin; it is just how we are made, but it is aggravated by our misalignment. Our spiritual vulnerability, our spiritual neediness, and our spiritual emptiness are all built in; this is our hardwired, standard circuitry. The essence of sin is the desire to fill up our buckets without God, to be self-sufficient and invulnerable.

Wisdom has to do with whom we entrust ourselves to; who we know can fill our empty buckets; whom we most believe, trust, and confide in. If we do not know what resources we have, we cannot use them to make happen what we want to happen. If we do not know what we want to happen, then we will not even know what to wish for in the first place. Wisdom arrives when the soul discerns its destiny, when life aligns in sync with the soul. Wisdom pleases the Lord when it is not self serving, but other serving.

THOMAS W. BLAIR

---

1. David Hansen, *A Little Handbook on Having a Soul* (Downers Grove, IL: InterVarsity Press, 1997), 13.

Exegetical Perspective

Solomon essentially requests a "listening heart" (Heb. *lev shome'a*). He asks this in order to rule competently as king. In his speech he recognizes his immaturity ("I am only a little child," v. 7) as well as his lack of military ability ("I do not know how to go out or come in," v. 7). His request suggests someone overwhelmed by the enormity of the leadership challenge and his inability to meet the challenge. Thus he asks for a "listening heart" ("understanding mind," v. 9 NRSV) as the means through which to govern rightly. At this point Solomon's humility may well reflect reality, as he asks not merely for guidance but also for openness to accept divine instruction.

Importantly, Solomon does not ask for wisdom, as other readings of this passage suggest (2 Chr. 1:10). Despite the indication that YHWH follows "according to your word," the gift of the "wise and understanding [NRSV "discerning"] heart" (Heb. *lev hakam venavon*) in verse 12 alters the request in verse 9 for a "listening heart." While the passage offers little to explain the discrepancies between the petition and its fulfillment, it seems to make sense of the excess gifts. In using the terms "wise" and "discerning," normally associated with wisdom, the passage implies Solomon's choice of wisdom and therefore his receipt of the benefits associated with wisdom: riches, and honor, and long life (Prov. 3:16; 8:18). The additional gifts, therefore, guarantee the young king the competence he needs to rule and the opportunity to rule for a long time.

The theophany ends as Solomon awakes from the dream (v. 15). Only then does the passage indicate that Solomon realizes his dream. In response to the theophany, he sacrifices and offers a banquet for his servants. While most of the report avoids the uncomfortable character of Solomon's cultic activity, this closing verse revisits his practices. His double sacrifice of "burnt offerings" and "offerings of well-being" is in keeping with the elaborate practice indicated in verse 4.

The feast for his servants fills out the picture of a person of excess in several parts of his life. By leaving open the time sequence at the end of dream—is it morning or still night?—the Deuteronomistic insertion of the offering of the sacrifice in Jerusalem jars the reader back to the critiques in the early section of the chapter. It also calls attention to the early chapters and disturbs the pious image of the king, offering instead someone who ascends the throne through deception.

STEED VERNYL DAVIDSON

Homiletical Perspective

All new perspectives will be measured against this primary orientation, even when it is understood to be severely limited or flawed. An unknown scribe in the early part of the Babylonian exile composes a narrative of the time before the temple is constructed. The wisdom that the young king requests from YHWH—a listening heart, the ability to discern good from evil—will sustain a post-temple generation in exile. They need to remember before as well as after.

What happens when stories collide or when life discrepancies threaten foundational meaning? A spatio-temporal dislocation is experienced, and a search for the lost sense of integrity begins. Competing narratives can sometimes be resolved by integration. One story may widen to accommodate an alternative narrative within itself. Two worldviews form an organic partnership. The covenant theology of David's eternal kingdom is juxtaposed with the requirement of obedience as the necessity for the community's survival: "If you will walk in my ways" (v. 14). What is the nature of a leader of a nation? He is wise enough to ask for wisdom, yet embedded in the narrative are the bitter seeds of failure. Solomon the wise will become Solomon the foolish; yet the nature of a God who promises to honor those who honor God remains at the heart of the story.

How do we inhabit such a story? By telling the story of one's own time with insight and in accord with the lines of interpretation laid out in the biblical tradition of narration. Telling this story suggests narrative preaching as the best form, since God's revelation through Scripture is primarily narrative in form. To be human is above all to have a story. To be holy is to be part of God's story. Our sense of self and community and world is relational and storied. This story of a dreaming king gathers up the history of a people of God past and present. It is a way for them and for us to remember into the future.

HEATHER MURRAY ELKINS

Psalm 119:129-136

¹²⁹Your decrees are wonderful;
     therefore my soul keeps them.
¹³⁰The unfolding of your words gives light;
     it imparts understanding to the simple.
¹³¹With open mouth I pant,
     because I long for your commandments.
¹³²Turn to me and be gracious to me,
     as is your custom toward those who love your name.
¹³³Keep my steps steady according to your promise,
     and never let iniquity have dominion over me.
¹³⁴Redeem me from human oppression,
     that I may keep your precepts.
¹³⁵Make your face shine upon your servant,
     and teach me your statutes.
¹³⁶My eyes shed streams of tears
     because your law is not kept.

Theological Perspective

In all of its twenty-two parts Psalm 119 is about devotion to Torah. Thus in verses 129–136 we see that devotion expressed: in terms of the blessings that flow from the decrees and words of YHWH (vv. 129–130); with reference to the passion that accompanies the psalmist's yearning for God's commandments and law (vv. 131, 136); and through petitions for favor, support, safety, and benediction that are entailed in commitment to God's name, promise, precepts, and statutes (vv. 132–135). Thus Torah "is valued beyond all else because in all its form Torah is the medium of the LORD."[1] In this valuing, ethical obedience and spiritual relationship become one in the psalm.

This melding of the ethics and spirituality constitutes a significant theological achievement not always well embodied in American church life. Some forms of American Protestantism have managed precisely to drive a wedge between ethics and spirituality. Most notably in their sometimes sub-Christian response to the issue of human slavery, churches were known to embrace a "spirituality" that overlooked the bearing of Torah on the issue. Concrete expressions of love of God and neighbor entailed in the struggle against the practice of slavery were set

1. James Luther Mays, *Psalms*, Interpretation series (Louisville, KY: John Knox Press, 1994), 383.

Pastoral Perspective

Psalm 119 is an ode to Torah—discordant music to most modern "liberated" ears. Aside from the common Christian afflictions of dismissing the authority of Hebrew Scripture, or thinking it has been trumped by the New Testament, many Christians consider Torah a burdensome word, if they consider it at all. Torah, for too many believers, is synonymous with the most obscure and onerous laws of the Holiness Code. If then the Torah were to be set to music, it should be in the form of a dirge, not an ode to joy. The psalmist knows better and so composes in Psalm 119:129–136 a song that any Jew or Christian can sing with joyful abandon.

In twenty-two sections, via a progression through the Hebrew alphabet, the psalmist lines out this ode to joy. Psalm 119:129–136 is the *Pe* section of the psalm (visually captured in the NIV). There is an unmistakable delight that runs through this section of Psalm 119, rejoicing that the Torah, the instruction, the teaching, the word of God is a divine gift to be cherished, not a heavy burden that oppresses us and that we disobey at our own peril. In this *Pe* section, the Torah of God gives us light whenever our path is cast in darkness. Human enlightenment, then, is a divine gift to those who attend to Torah. Therefore, it is no surprise that Torah leaves us panting in desire to fulfill the will of God (v. 131).

Exegetical Perspective

Whether one prepares to preach or writes academic essays, using the lectionary can lead to the joy of discovering a rarely touched passage that turns out to deserve attention. These few verses from a long and often neglected psalm constitute a treasure for the pulpit or lectern. Without the lectionary assignment, one could easily miss these trees in the forest of Psalm 119. Out of necessity, even the commentaries give scant attention to these verses, because space does not permit much reflection on them. Enough overlooking! These verses contain both passion and insight.

In Psalm 119, the poet starts each line of successive stanzas with a successive letter of the Hebrew alphabet. This pericope is the *Pe* stanza, so that each line begins with that letter. In English translation, the reader loses the skill of the poet, who works within the constraints of the acrostic structure to wrestle with obedience to the Torah (law, teaching, instruction). In this stanza, he recounts both the things that support his attempts at obedience and the things that interfere, as he covers a number of relationships. The stanza moves from the psalmist's own internal response to Torah to his relationship to the Deity, and then to his place within the human community. All of Psalm 119 is a Torah psalm, as are Psalm 1 and Psalm 19. The poem is addressed directly to the Deity, and so is in the form of a prayer. This section

Homiletical Perspective

At the start it is clear that this text does not lend itself to a sermon contrasting law with gospel. For the psalmist, the law *is* gospel. Surely we should begin thinking about our sermon by giving the psalmist his due. For him, and for his audience, what is good about this Torah? There are at least four possible strategies for a sermon.

First, note that the Torah is not simply "the law." One might risk a sermon that noted how many words the psalmist uses to talk about the wondrous gift that God has given Israel. In the NRSV translation the psalm rejoices in God's "decrees," "words," "commandments," "promise," "precepts," "statutes," and "Law/Torah." The translations represent different Hebrew terms for the gift that God has given Israel.

A careful reading of the psalm will steer us away from any sense that God's covenant with Israel was a matter of "legalism." The psalmist rejoices in the fact that God actually chooses to communicate with God's people. There would be no Torah if God did not care. Even before people knew that God loved them by giving them a Son, many knew that God loved them by giving them "decrees," "words," "commandments."

It is a cliché of the popular press (and not just among Christian writers) that the Old Testament God is demanding and the New Testament God is accepting. The preacher might want to compare the

Psalm 119:129-136

Theological Perspective

aside in the name of a supposedly authentic spirituality. "Genuine" spirituality was said properly to focus, not on matters of political or economic consequence, but only on things Scripture directly warranted as matters of Christian concern. This unhappy legacy did not disappear in the ensuing century but, rather, became a millstone around the necks of some denominational traditions, requiring great effort and much time for something more like the vision of Psalm 119 to hold sway in their teaching and practice.

Rather than driving a wedge between spirituality and ethics, Psalm 119 forges a bond between them. It unites a life of "keeping" God's teachings with a life lived in sustaining and nourishing relationship to God. It is in keeping the decrees that the psalmist experiences the wonder of being in community with God (v. 129). As the words of YHWH "unfold" in the experience of God's people, even the simple come to understanding (v. 130), illustrating the life-enhancing power of God's statutes. Indeed, these opening verses represent a virtually perfect echo of the well-known expression of the power of the law to sustain, "The law of the Lord is perfect, reviving the soul; the decrees of the Lord are sure, making wise the simple" (Ps. 19:7–8).

What is stressed in Psalm 119 is the "keeping" and "unfolding" of the decrees in the practice of a person. The precepts of God are not mere objects of contemplation. They are obligations to love God and neighbor that are enacted in the daily engagements of human community. Ethical action is the heart of the matter for one who understands the wonder and enlightening power of God's commandments. Still, since Torah is a primary form of God's presence, it is also embraced with a spiritual passion and intensity, with the same longing with which a thirsty animal pants "with open mouth" for water (v. 131). Moreover, when the law is not embraced in action, it issues in deep anguish, as the psalmist's "eyes shed streams of tears" (v. 136). Ethical obedience to God and spiritual relationship to God have become one in the psalm.

This inextricable relationship of ethics and spirituality is further manifest in the series of petitions that comprise the central section of this part of the psalm (vv. 132–135). One recalls God's habitual readiness, indeed God's "custom," to turn with graciousness toward those who seek to love God (v. 132). Thus obedient ethical action is accompanied by God's gracious embrace of the actor. Another acknowledges that obedience to God's decrees is forever dependent upon God's abiding

Pastoral Perspective

There is a longstanding tradition in many Christian churches of reading part of the Torah, the Ten Commandments, within Christian worship. This Torah reading serves as a regular reminder that the intent of God is gracious, and keeping the law not only makes glad the heart of God; it "imparts understanding to the simple" (v. 130). Popular forms of antinomian Christianity equate Christian freedom with being set free from the shackles of the law, but Matthew is quick to remind us that Jesus did not share such a negative view of the law. In fact, Jesus spoke to his disciples, "Do not think that I have come to abolish the law or the prophets; I have come not to abolish but to fulfill" (Matt. 5:17).

A popular piece of music sung in the congregation I serve understands that law and liberation are not opposites, but that liberation flows from embracing God's Torah, God's word. In this song, which has its roots in oppressed communities of faith, the people pray to God:

Order my steps in Your word.
Order my tongue in Your word.
Guide my feet in Your word.
Wash my heart in Your word.[1]

Notice that this modern song, like Psalm 119, prays with a repetitious cadence and celebrates the *Pe* section of the psalm in which the psalmist prays, "Direct my footsteps according to your word" (v. 133 NIV). In a society that bows to the idol of radical independence, the text from Psalm 119 invites us to bow instead in radical dependence before God, whose "decrees are wonderful" (v. 129).

Michael Morgan, organist at Central Presbyterian Church in Atlanta and author of *The Psalter for Christian Worship*, has set Psalm 119:129–136 to the tune *O Waly, Waly*. With the keen ear of a poet setting another poet's words to music, Morgan invites the people to sing:

Thy Word, O Lord, a lamp shall be
To guide my feet, to light my way;
The darkest path unto my prize
By Thy rich grace is bright as day.[2]

Like the ancient psalmist, Morgan teaches the community of faith to trust in a God who will not leave us wandering out in the dark, but whose grace "orders our steps" and "guides my feet."

---

1. Glenn Edward Burleigh, "Order My Steps," *Praises with the Orchestra*, Glenn Burleigh Music Workshop.
2. Michael Morgan, *The Psalter for Christian Worship* (Louisville, KY: Witherspoon Press, 1999), 160. Used with permission.

Exegetical Perspective

defies precise labeling, but it reverses the usual flow of a song of lament. Laments usually begin with complaint, but end in affirmation. This stanza begins with affirmation and ends in lament. The emotional effect of that flow is quite touching.

For his own part, the psalmist takes delight in the divine teachings. He does not think of Torah as rigid law, but as the gift of divine instruction. As is typical of the whole psalm, he uses a number of terms to flesh out the understanding of Torah: decrees, words, commandments, promise, precepts, and statutes. The list covers much of the concept of revelation in Hebrew thought, from giving of law to wisdom to prophecy. He wants fully to obey and follow. Contemporary English readers cannot silence the Platonic echo when they hear the term "soul." The psalmist does not think of a disembodied, inner self, but wants all of himself—body, soul, and spirit—to conform to the divine instruction. The rest of the psalm recounts his struggle to achieve that end.

In verse 130, he expresses the desire to plunge deeply into an understanding of the divine will and way. The Hebrew word can mean either "unfolding" or a "doorway," but both suggest deeper understanding and engagement. His desire to conform to the divine will involves more than intellect. His yearning leads him to use an ingenious metaphor of panting after this full engagement. Whatever specific image may lie behind the verse (a panting dog, a hungry person?), the verse speaks of a physical craving for a full appreciation and deep probing of Torah.

Verses 132 and 135 recognize the divine initiative in an understanding of Torah. The psalmist's own study and reflection, even his own yearning, will not suffice for the deepest penetration. Divine grace and favor make Torah available. Let the church put aside the outdated and inaccurate notion that Israel practiced a "legalistic" religion, seeking to earn the divine favor. The psalmist fully understands the unmerited turning toward and shining face of the Deity. Favor establishes the relationship and facilitates comprehension and practice of Torah.

In verses 133–134, conflict arises in this glowing tribute to divine Torah and the psalmist's eager desire to understand and follow. Within himself, he recognizes temptation to stumble and vulnerability to the power of iniquity. These verses refute any suggestion that the psalmist is self-righteous when he declares in verse 129 that all of who he is keeps the divine decrees. That verse represents as much hope as accomplishment. The psalmist considers iniquity

Homiletical Perspective

richness and diversity of Torah in Psalm 119 with the richness and diversity of the best-known Christian "torah," the Sermon on the Mount.

What we find in the Sermon on the Mount—blessing, teaching, instruction, commandment, exhortation, and encouragement—are all there in Israel's law as well. Torah not only foreshadows Christian obedience; it can shape Christian obedience.

Try preaching a sermon that enriches and expands our too easy Christian narrowing of what Torah means. Try it so that we may have a truer relationship with our Jewish neighbors. Try it so that we may have a truer relationship with a huge chunk of the book(s) we call our Scripture.

Second, in a different sermon the preacher might note that law can be its own kind of gospel. In his lectures in classes at Yale Divinity School, William Muehl often reminded us that the fact that God demands obedience is in itself good news. God gives us Torah (and the Sermon on the Mount, and the Great Commandment, and the parable of the Good Samaritan) because our activity, our obedience, counts deeply with God. Torah matters because we matter.

Parents and child-development experts alike remind us that setting limits is an essential part of love. Children left without guidelines are victims of neglect, however sugarcoated with affectionate excuses.

Our psalmist does not grudgingly accept the strictures of the law. He rejoices in law as an inestimable gift. "With open mouth I pant, because I long for your commandments" (v. 131).

Third, a sermon could attend to the complex interplay between God's demands and God's promises found in verses 133–134: "Keep my steps steady according to your promise, and never let iniquity have dominion over me. Redeem me from human oppression, that I may keep your precepts." Apparently the editors of the *New Oxford Annotated Bible* saw these verses as central to our section, because they described the section thus: "Praise of the law and prayer for deliverance from enemies."[1] How does the psalmist's joy in the law relate to his prayer to be spared the dominion of iniquity and redeemed from oppression? In verse 133 of the psalm, it almost looks as though the psalmist thinks that faithful obedience to the law might spare him from iniquity. In verse 134 it looks as though he is praying for freedom from oppression as a precondition for his own obedience.

---

1. *New Oxford Annotated Bible*, ed. Bruce M. Metzger and Roland E. Murphy (New York: Oxford University Press, 1991), 782–83.

Psalm 119:129-136

Theological Perspective

presence, keeping one's "steps steady according to your promise" (v. 133). Whatever impulses one has that contend against ethical obedience are mitigated not by human effort but by God's own help. A third petition remarkably combines redemption "from human oppression" with the purpose of "keeping" God's precepts (v. 134). One's spiritual quest for safety is thus tied to the ethical end of practicing Torah. Finally, the plea for God's blessing and peace, "[making] your face shine upon your servant," is paired with the petition "and teach me your statutes" (v. 135). In the psalmist's vision, the blessedness of abiding in the presence of God is never separated from living the gift of God's law.

In *After Heaven: Spirituality in America since the 1950s*, Robert Wuthnow describes profound changes that have taken place in the spiritual practices of Americans over the second half of the twentieth century. The shift has been from "a spirituality of dwelling that emphasizes *habitation*: God occupies a definite place in the universe and creates a sacred space in which humans too can dwell," to "a spirituality of seeking [that] emphasizes *negotiation*: individuals search for sacred moments that reinforce their conviction that the divine exists."[2] Though sympathetic with some of the reasons for the shift from dwelling to seeking, Wuthnow regards both as inadequate and argues for a practice-oriented spirituality.

Of most interest in relation to Psalm 119 is Wuthnow's research regarding those who have undertaken such a practice-oriented spirituality by undertaking "a cluster of intentional activities concerned with relating to the sacred."[3] Rather than occasional or random engagement with the activities, such spiritual practices require a significant amount of time and effort. The result is not a narrow interiority. Instead, both moral commitments and service activities emerge from spirituality conceived as practice.

Long before the discoveries of Wuthnow's research into late-twentieth-century American approaches to spirituality, the writer of Psalm 119 knew about practice-oriented spirituality. Such a spirituality concentrates time and effort on the statutes of the Lord, knowing that in learning them, the believer comes to know the brightness of God's face, and in keeping them, a life of ethical obedience flowers as the fruit of spiritual practice.

D. CAMERON MURCHISON

Pastoral Perspective

In the Gospel of Matthew, the disciples ask Jesus to teach them to pray, and he does. To teach them, Jesus borrows language from such psalms as Psalm 119. Among the petitions in his prayer, Jesus teaches his disciples to pray, "Do not bring us to the time of trial, but rescue us from the evil one" (Matt. 6:13). Not just at this point in the Gospel, but throughout his ministry, Jesus stands in the tradition of the psalmist, who is not naive about the power of cosmic and human evil, but is more confident in the ultimate power of God. In Psalm 119:129–136, the psalmist focuses on the evil that is often exacted in human affairs, praying to God, "Redeem me from human oppression" (v. 134).

For people of faith living on the other side of a century of war, death camps, apartheid, sexism, heterosexism, the social devastation of economic greed, and the lingering terror of 9/11, the psalmist echoes the ongoing desire of any believer and any community of faith, imploring God to "turn to me and be gracious to me" (v. 132). This petition is not an appeal for special privilege, but an expression of profound trust in God, who is more worthy of trust than any person, institution, organization, or government.

The God of Psalm 119:129–136 is a much larger God than the more diminutive God found in too many churches today. The God to whom too many pray today is more like a personal assistant than the great God Almighty, Creator of heaven and earth. This God to whom too many pray is one whom we dare not ask too much of, because this God is either too tired, too busy, or too impotent to attend to our prayers. Maybe the church could deepen its faith, expand its theology, and enrich its worship by spending a season listening to the entirety of Psalm 119, learning anew to pray with the sheer confidence of the psalmist, "Make your face shine upon your servant, and teach me your statutes" (v. 135).

GARY W. CHARLES

---

2. Robert Wuthnow, *After Heaven: Spirituality in America since the 1950s* (Berkeley: University of California Press, 1998), 3–4.
3. Ibid., 170.

Exegetical Perspective

to be an external force that exerts influence on him. He needs divine assistance to counteract its effect.

The danger lies not just in his own weakness. The disobedience of others threatens his obedience and delight in Torah. His quest for conforming to the divine will becomes more difficult. The term for "oppression" in verse 134 connotes injustice and corruption (Eccl. 5:8; Jer. 6:6). Is the psalmist himself a victim of oppression, or does he lament the oppression of others? In either case, the lack of justice grieves the psalmist and interferes with his ability to immerse himself in Torah and his relationship with the Deity.

The stanza closes with his lament over disobedience and oppression. Even drawing upon the divine resources to bolster his own obedience, he does not find solitary obedience to bring full joy. Only when all people obey can he find full joy. He weeps profusely for the disobedience of others.

The contemporary preacher finds much material for reflection and proclamation in this stanza. The poet shows clearly that faith is not a personal, private matter. The poet wants to relish a deep relationship with the Deity, but injustice and oppression block his path. The poet weeps that an indefinite "they" do not keep the law (translated by the passive in NRSV in v. 136). His tearful longing for full obedience to Torah resonates with the church praying that God's dominion come and God's will be done on earth, as it is in heaven. The preacher faces the challenge of communicating the passion of this poem. How does the preacher move the congregation from "How much can I get away with?" toward panting for deeper understanding and obedience? The imprecise, but moving, language of poetry may leave the reader not knowing whose oppression motivates the psalmist's tears, but the contemporary preacher can speak of the suffering caused by callous disregard of the divine teachings. Perhaps if the community of faith could understand the joy of deeper engagement and obedience to the divine teaching, and could share the psalmist's sorrow over the pain caused by the violence, hatred, oppression, lust, and greed of humanity, it could begin to long for divine grace and the unfolding of a deeper immersion in Torah.

CHARLES L. AARON JR.

Homiletical Perspective

One could also read these verses differently. The *Tanakh* translates verse 133: "Make my feet firm through your promise. Do not let iniquity dominate me."[2] Is it possible that here the psalmist prays, not to be spared another's iniquity, but to be preserved from his own iniquitous desires?

Verse 134 might not mean "If you free me from oppression, I promise to keep your precepts." It might rather be an honest acknowledgment that when I am burdened by oppression, I have a harder time following God's precepts, a harder time even thinking about God's precepts. If so, then the petition of the psalm is something like this: By your law preserve me from being oppressive and from being oppressed.

Fourth, a sermon could focus on what seems to be the anticlimax of verse 136. "My eyes shed streams of tears because your law is not kept." The addition of this verse to the reading is not simply an idiosyncratic decision by those who compile the lectionary. This verse brings to a close a discrete section of Psalm 119 and clearly is designed to bring our reading to a conclusion.

In this verse the psalmist makes the remarkable move from attention to his own piety to attention to the impiety around him. However, the observation that sin abounds is neither the occasion to congratulate himself nor the opportunity to berate others. The sinfulness he sees is an occasion for grief, for sympathy.

The psalmist foreshadows Jesus weeping over Jerusalem: "If you, even you, had only recognized on this day the things that make for peace! But now they are hidden from your eyes" (Luke 19:42). The psalm calls us from the temptation of the pious: to find hidden pleasure in the iniquities of our opponents. The psalm calls us from the temptation of those who seek to love the law: to judge others harshly and excuse ourselves easily. The psalmist foreshadows what Jesus says in his own interpretation of Torah: "You have heard that it was said, 'You shall love your neighbor and hate your enemy.' But I say to you, Love your enemies and pray for those who persecute you, so that you may be children of your Father in heaven" (Matt. 5:43–45).

DAVID L. BARTLETT

2. *Tanakh: The Holy Scriptures* (Philadelphia and Jerusalem: The Jewish Publication Society, 1985), 1258.

Romans 8:26-39

²⁶Likewise the Spirit helps us in our weakness; for we do not know how to pray as we ought, but that very Spirit intercedes with sighs too deep for words. ²⁷And God, who searches the heart, knows what is the mind of the Spirit, because the Spirit intercedes for the saints according to the will of God.

²⁸We know that all things work together for good for those who love God, who are called according to his purpose. ²⁹For those whom he foreknew he also predestined to be conformed to the image of his Son, in order that he might be the firstborn within a large family. ³⁰And those whom he predestined he also called; and those whom he called he also justified; and those whom he justified he also glorified.

³¹What then are we to say about these things? If God is for us, who is against us? ³²He who did not withhold his own Son, but gave him up for all of us, will he not with him also give us everything else? ³³Who will bring any charge

Theological Perspective

You were made debtors by the Holy Spirit, not to the law, but to the Father on account of the crucifixion of his Son. Your lives are now all hope, and hope is in things not seen. With the combination of the *certainty* of hope and hope's *hiddenness* comes the teaching of predestination.

Religion is supposed to relieve suffering, but the Christian life is always a life of struggle to "wait for it with patience" (v. 25). If you are justified by faith alone, then why do you not see it now? The weight of suffering has spawned a series of theories about how God elects, and impatience forces theologians to infer a *process* of election that considers suffering as progressive. Thus, Romans 8:29–30 is commonly set out as a series of steps leading to salvation or damnation: (1) foreknowledge, (2) predestination, (3) calling, (4) justification, (5) glorification.

Yet it is precisely against this that Paul speaks; suffering does not lead you somewhere; instead you are being brought to an end, so only Christ and his new creation remains. Instead of offering you the comfort of knowing the ordering of salvation, Paul provides the true comfort to a suffering Christian: no charge can be brought against God's elect, because "it is God who justifies" (v. 33), and this was done by "Christ Jesus, who died, yes, who was raised, who is at the right hand of God, and *who intercedes for us*" (v. 34).

Pastoral Perspective

This text is one of the favorites of many in the church. If 1 Corinthians 13 has become the obligatory reading at a wedding, Romans 8:26–39 has become *the* text for funerals. When Paul expresses his personal conviction—that he is convinced that nothing can separate us from the love of God in Christ Jesus—his statement is itself persuasive. It is one of the most important pastoral privileges to stand with those who have been weighed down by the power of death and proclaim with Paul, "No, these things cannot prevail." It is a testimony to the strength of Christian faith to witness what happens to those gathered at a funeral. Where the power of death is palpable, one can see how moved those gathered can be by the pastor's using Paul's words to express his or her own conviction that even death cannot separate one from the love of God.

Beyond the liturgical setting of a funeral, however, this text has much to offer. It speaks not solely of death, but of many matters that threaten separation. Separation is a genuine issue in our lives. In a splendid essay, the French philosopher Paul Ricoeur writes, "Ah! If only I could grasp and embrace everything!—and how cruel it is to choose and exclude."[1]

1. Paul Ricoeur, *Freedom and Nature: The Voluntary and the Involuntary,* trans. Erazim v. Kohak (Evanston, IL: Northwestern University Press, 1966), 445.

against God's elect? It is God who justifies. ³⁴Who is to condemn? It is Christ Jesus, who died, yes, who was raised, who is at the right hand of God, who indeed intercedes for us. ³⁵Who will separate us from the love of Christ? Will hardship, or distress, or persecution, or famine, or nakedness, or peril, or sword? ³⁶As it is written,

> "For your sake we are being killed all day long;
>   we are accounted as sheep to be slaughtered."

³⁷No, in all these things we are more than conquerors through him who loved us. ³⁸For I am convinced that neither death, nor life, nor angels, nor rulers, nor things present, nor things to come, nor powers, ³⁹nor height, nor depth, nor anything else in all creation, will be able to separate us from the love of God in Christ Jesus our Lord.

Exegetical Perspective

This text is the culmination of Paul's argument begun in 5:1, echoing and elaborating his words on suffering and hope. These verses provide a brilliant, moving closing statement that rests on the power of God's love (5:5; 8:35, 37, 39). Paul's concern is not existential, psychological, or individual, but eschatological: the completion of creation, already begun by God through Christ, intended from the beginning of the world (8:18–21).

The problem Paul must address is suffering, which he traces to sin. Through Adam sin was brought into the world (5:12–21). Christ, in the likeness of sinful flesh, destroyed the power of sin, which the law could not accomplish (8:3–4). With the Spirit of Christ in us, we are free from sin's power (vv. 9–11). What we long for (vv. 21–22), the glory to be revealed (v. 18), is already glimpsed in us, who have the first fruits of the Spirit (v. 23), the Spirit of him who raised Jesus from the dead and dwells in us (v. 11). We are heirs of that glory because we have been adopted as God's own children (vv. 15–16). Suffering too is part of our joining with Christ and must be understood in light of eschatological hope (v. 17).

The pericope begins rather awkwardly in verse 26, "Likewise." The subject is the Spirit of God. Romans 8 is infused with the Spirit: the Spirit's presence

Homiletical Perspective

In the final section of Romans 8 Paul cheers on the Christians at Rome, reminding them that "if God is for us, who is against us?" (v. 31). In this same spirit the preacher may choose to encourage her embattled, wavering, or discouraged congregation, reminding them that "we know that all things work together for good for those who love God, who are called according to his purpose" (v. 28). The tone is emotional and celebratory. The marathon runners are at the halfway mark, and Paul reminds them and us that God has already made it to the end of the race, and God has won. With God's help, we too can make it to the finish line and participate in God's victory.

Here Paul establishes the firm foundation that will empower and strengthen Jesus' followers during the hard work ahead of them, when the crowds are gone and the decorations removed. This is a helpful passage to read during periods of significant challenge and loss. In my tradition, the final part of Romans 8 is most often heard in the context of the burial office. There it is comforting and rousing to family and friends who grieve the loss of loved ones. Death is not the end, but the beginning of a new phase of life in God. Funerals, however, are not the only places we mark grief and loss, as pastors know all too well.

When reflecting on these verses, the preacher, like Paul, has the opportunity to proclaim defiantly that

Romans 8:26-39

Theological Perspective

Apart from a preacher, predestination is indeed frightening; but retrospectively, with a promise in the ear, predestination is assurance itself: "Who will separate us from the love of Christ? Will hardship, or distress, or persecution, or famine, or nakedness, or peril, or sword? . . . No!" (vv. 35, 37) Predestination without a promise is an awful fate. Predestination with a promise is the ability to pray with assurance against our own feeling.

Unfortunately even the greatest of our theologians have stumbled at this point. Augustine taught us to think of predestination as the distinction between *in spe* (in hope) and *in re* (in reality), so that we are not to think we possess a present salvation, but always await salvation in the future. God graciously keeps us from knowing our final state of salvation, lest our own work of preserving faith replace faith in God's predestination. Accordingly, God keeps the faithful in a moderate form of doubt, so that security does not become pride. The pilgrim way demands faith mixed with doubt, so that the predestination that starts Christian life meets the predestination that brings it to its completion.

Augustine's most faithful disciple, Calvin, recognized the problem with this, since it forces pastoral care into infusions of doubt rather than assurance; but Calvin's remedy also increased fear. He took Paul to be laying out a movement from a general to a specific communication. Thus Paul's "For those whom [God] foreknew, he also predestined" (v. 29) became an abstract, general instance of the unspoken mind of God. Then, "those whom he predestined he also called" became the matter of a personal, individual assurance in the form of an *inner* call. The die was cast for establishing an inner experience as the form of certain faith—reversing Augustine by making *in re* the basis for *in spe*. The reality of a present moment of faith is certainty of my predestined, eternal salvation.

Paul is laying out the teaching of Spirit and predestination in just the opposite direction. "The Spirit helps us in our weakness," not by turning us inward in self-reflection, but outward: "that very Spirit intercedes with sighs too deep for words" (v. 26). In suffering, a person who turns inward "does not know how to pray." Such a person does not know what God is up to. What is needed for faith to persevere is someone outside you, your own personal groaner, who gives the lament of your heart to the One who made the promise, not to the one who trusts it.

There is surely a call, but not an inner call; it is decidedly outside, since the person of faith is

Pastoral Perspective

Every choice we make along the way necessarily separates us from some other option. We cannot do everything, and so, when we do anything, we must exclude something. Such exclusion, such "leaving behind," is a source of great pain in human living. Even the most natural thing, like growing up, involves leaving something behind. One cannot become an adult without leaving childhood behind. One does not stay young forever, and so we leave behind our young adulthood with all its brimming potential. Nearly everyone understands that, in the usual course of things, one's parents will die before he or she does. We raise our own children with a full expectation that they will go away from us, step out on their own.

At the very heart of what it means to be human is separation from those things and those people we love. Several years ago, Kenneth Mitchell and Herbert Anderson published a book with the title *All Our Losses, All Our Griefs*.[2] The title itself speaks volumes. To be human is to have loss and grief. No one is able to escape loss and grief. Anyone who has remotely loved anyone or anything will suffer the grief of loss and will know the painful power of separation.

Portrayal of the powers that cause separation is part of the genius of the eighth chapter of Romans. Paul understands the conflict of cosmic forces that cause separation. He lists many of the forces. One of the first he mentions is hardship (v. 35). Because it is included in a long list, it is easy enough to pass over lightly; but hardship should not be passed over lightly.

Several years ago I heard a preacher who enthralled a congregation by repeating the simplest observation: "life is hard." She said it again and again, and with each repetition you could feel the visceral acknowledgment of those in the room. Life *is* hard. The hardness of life, the struggle it presents us nearly every day, is easy to pass over, but difficult ultimately to ignore. The best pastoral care is surely provided by those who know how hard life is and help us find ways to say it out loud.

Paul's list of those things that separate continues. It includes distress. Distress is a frequent force in our lives. When we cannot complete what we so want to finish, we are in distress. When we have done all that we can do, and it is still not enough, we are in distress. Like the waters flowing over a sinking ship, distress overwhelms us.

2. Kenneth Mitchell and Herbert Anderson, *All Our Losses, All Our Griefs: Resources for Pastoral Care* (Philadelphia: Westminster Press, 1983).

provides evidence that we are children of God and united with Christ (vv. 14, 17); the Spirit of God bears witness in our words when we pray, "Abba, Father" (v. 15). So the Spirit intercedes for us with "groans too deep for utterance,"[1] deeper than our ignorant words of prayer. This groaning of the Spirit joins the groaning of creation and our groaning (vv. 22, 23), but translates our longing into the very language of God. Even if our prayer and longing have little form and substance—we barely know what to hope for—the Searcher (v. 27) knows the Spirit's thoughts, which is the heart of God. Note the plural of the pronouns: the focus is not an individual's walk of faith or struggles in prayer, but God's redemption of God's people, and all of creation with them.

Verse 28 is rife with difficulties. The NRSV reads, "All things work together for good for those who love God," with footnotes: "God makes all things work together for good," or "in all things God works for good." The NIV reads, "In all things God works for the good of those who love him," with footnotes: "all things work together for good to those who love God," or "God works together with those who love him to bring about what is good." Is the subject "God" (ho theos, missing from some manuscripts), or "all things" (panta)? Is the verb (synergei) transitive ("works") or intransitive ("cooperates")? Is God working "with" those who love him or "for" those who love him, or simply "for good"?

Based on the context, I prefer: "God makes all things work together for good with those who love him." In Romans 8, God is the subject. God actively accomplishes the redemption of all things in creation. God works with us, who are the first fruits of God's redemption, and joined with God's Spirit for God's good work. This reading steers us away from the terrible misuse of this verse, which whitewashes human suffering as somehow "good," or implies that "good" is our reward for loving God.

Paul's focus is on the work of God. Verbs progress like steps along a path, leading to their inexorable goal. God foreknew/chose beforehand (proegnō), preordained/predestined (proōrisen), called (ekalesen), justified (edikaiōsen), and glorified (edoxasen) us to be conformed to the image of his Son, the first-born of a large family (8:29). Glorification is the end, shared life with Christ is the path, and God's family is our adopted community.

suffering in the name of Christ is not meaningless. As Jesus' followers we are called not only to be glorified with Christ, but also to suffer with Christ (v. 17). Living as Christians in a world that largely denies the reality and power of God will bring suffering to believers. On the cross Jesus showed us that suffering is no longer meaningless but can serve God's purposes. In Jesus' case, his suffering brought victory over death as well as new life, hope, and possibility.

Christians understandably struggle with the amount of suffering and pain in the world. They are acutely aware of and sensitive to it. They experience it in their lives and communities, and in the people they are called to walk alongside. They read about violence, brutality, and famine in the daily paper. It is easy to feel overwhelmed by all this suffering. Our understandable response is to ask, "Where is God?" It is hard to understand why God allows suffering and easy to believe that suffering indicates God's absence rather than presence. Does the pain in our world mean that God is somehow absent or uninvolved?

In the spirit of Romans 8, Paul would answer this stream of thought, "By no means!" The suffering we and our world experience is caused in part by sin, the pervasive power that works to destroy and undermine the things and creatures of God. God is stronger than sin, but sin is still an active reality in our lives and in the cosmos. Through Christ's death and resurrection suffering is no longer passed on, bringing endless cycles of destruction and pain. Rather, Christ absorbs and transforms our suffering. Through him the struggles we face can be transformed into endurance, character, and hope. God uses our struggles to bring us to spiritual maturity.

Rhetorically Paul uses a question-and-answer format to make his point here. The answers to his questions are short and obvious, creating the feeling of growing confidence and energy. By verse 35 Paul asks, "Who will separate us from the love of Christ?" While the answer is clearly "no one," Paul seizes the opportunity to lay out a laundry list of challenging conditions—all of them but "sword" faced by Paul in his own life: hardship, distress, persecution, famine, nakedness, peril, and sword. The conjunction "or" that introduces each challenge makes the list seem longer and more daunting than it might otherwise, and Paul's quotation of Psalm 44:22 make the challenges inevitable rather than chance. Paul then continues, "In all these things we are more than conquerors through him who loved us" (v. 37).

He then provides another list, this one even more daunting than the first, of things that cannot

---

1. Brendan Byrne's translation in *Romans* (Collegeville, MN: Liturgical Press, 1996), 266–67.

Romans 8:26-39

Theological Perspective

conformed to the image of God's Son in death. The sacrifice of the old life for "the other" does not appear as glory, but all things work together for good for these sorts. Predestination is not a neutral speculation about what is in the mind of an unpreached God. "Those whom he predestined he also called; and those whom he called he also justified; and those whom he justified he also glorified" (v. 30). These are not steps toward salvation; they are one and the same thing.

"What then are we to say about these things?" (v. 31) We turn away from fear about an unpreached God and listen to the God who is preached in the promise of Christ. It is one thing to take up predestination as a philosophical curiosity; it is quite another to hear God at the cemetery when you are burying your beloved. Psalm 44 belongs to you at that moment: "For your sake we are being killed all day long; we are accounted as sheep to be slaughtered" (v. 36).

People who do not have the Spirit as their personal groaner always run from God's first work of death. People who have the Spirit are patient in suffering. They do not despair but remain certain in their suffering. God's work must be hidden, so that you do not stop listening to Christ and depend upon your inner feeling. Instead, all depends upon the faithfulness of God to God's promise. Is our death evidence of God's inability to keep a promise? "No, in all these things we are more than conquerors through him who loved us" (v. 37). So this is how predestination sounds to a Christian: nothing "in all creation will be able to separate us from the love of God in Christ Jesus our Lord." Nothing? *Nothing.*

STEVEN D. PAULSON

Pastoral Perspective

Next in Paul's list is persecution. The prevalence of persecution makes this force especially significant. The violence done to women and men because of their inclusion in one group or another—be that grouping on biological, social, or convictional grounds—remains a force with devastating capacity to separate. Paul goes on, naming "famine, or nakedness, or peril, or sword." The forces that cause separation are many.

The weight of all the forces that bring separation into our lives would appear to tip a scale completely over. Few, if any, do not know the weight of these powers; so it is most remarkable when Paul proclaims to these powers loudly and firmly: "No." Shall these things prevail? Shall these things have the capacity to undo us, to undo the most central element of our lives—God's love? No, no, no! Paul makes a confession. He is convinced, he says, that nothing will prevail against God's love. The conflict of the powers is engaged head-on, and the victor is God's love.

Finally, however, the text also stands as judgment against our own complicity with the forces that separate. The church itself has far too often been a purveyor of persecution. Those who profess conviction of the power of God's love have fostered hardship, distress, and famine, or at the least have allowed them to fester undisturbed. Even those who have felt the judgment of their own complicity with the principalities and powers can be transformed by the power of God, who over and over again searches "the heart" and helps us in our weakness (vv. 26–27). Even when we do not know how to pray, the "Spirit intercedes with sighs too deep for words" (v. 26).

The firm no to the powers proclaimed in this text can form a rallying cry for those who resist the powers of evil. It is a biblical version of the song "We Shall Overcome." Proclaiming this jewel of the Christian canon at key moments when the church gathers is well worthwhile.

DAVID M. GREENHAW

Exegetical Perspective

Neither preoccupation with individual salvation nor nuanced argument on the nature of predestination is inherent in this text. God's plan is and has always been the redemption of creation; we will be restored into the image of God in which we were called into being and meant to live. These verbs emphasize what God has already accomplished. If we cannot see its completion yet, we can trust in God's sovereign rule, which we have already seen begun.

The passage continues to build, now with a series of rhetorical questions. The scene is a courtroom, a familiar eschatological image in Jewish apocalyptic tradition. In this strange court, our judge is also our advocate. Paul echoes the Servant Song of Isaiah 50:8–9: "He who vindicates me is near. Who will contend with me? . . . It is the LORD God who helps me; who will declare me guilty?" What kind of judge is this, whose love is so great it would not spare even his own Son—what even father Abraham was not required to do? Indeed, God gives (*charisetai*, the unusual verb form of *charis,* "grace") us all things *(ta panta)* with him (v. 32). Far from being our accuser, Christ died for us to condemn sin, was raised for us, and now intercedes for us (vv. 3, 16, 26, 34).

The list of threats to the Christian is long, and the threat to life is real, but suffering is a sign of neither futility nor separation from God. N. T. Wright frames it this way: "[T]he suffering of Christians was to be taken up into the ongoing purposes of God, not to add to the unique achievement of Jesus the Messiah but to embody it in the world."[2]

Ultimately, in all things *(ta panta)* we are more than conquerors through him who loved us. God's love for us in Christ Jesus triumphs over every power of this earth and beyond this earth (vv. 35, 38–39). If we have hope in the midst of our suffering, it rests in this love: God's love that makes us God's own beloved children, one with Christ, to share his glory. This hope nothing can ever take away.

KAREN CHAKOIAN

Homiletical Perspective

separate us from God's love. It includes "death," "rulers," "things to come," "powers," and "anything else in all creation." This is a list of all the things we humans fear the most. Poetically, triumphantly, Paul asserts confidence. Knowledge and experience of God's love should bring Jesus' followers peace. "What would it mean," the preacher may ask, "to live without fear?" If God's promises are true, if Paul is correct, we will never be separated from God's companionship and community. God will always have the last word.

It may be helpful here to explore the meaning of the phrase "the love of God." What does Paul mean by this? Perhaps "the love of God" is best described in verse 32: "he who did not withhold his own Son, but gave him up for all of us, will he not with him also give us everything else?" Our God's love is self-sacrificial. The fact that God gave his Son as a love offering on our behalf means that he will do anything, give anything, to ensure our spiritual flourishing.

Jesus' followers are called to participate in God's work of companioning others, walking alongside them as equals. We are to reach out to the world God so loved, the world far outside our church doors, the world that may not know the story of Jesus and of God's unconditional love for humanity. We are also to tell the world of God's power over death and all that separates us from the life abundant God offers. There is no reason to fear, and every reason to rejoice.

BLAIR ALISON POGUE

2. N. T. Wright, "Romans," in *The New Interpreter's Bible* (Nashville: Abingdon Press, 2002), 10:614.

Matthew 13:31-33, 44-52

³¹He put before them another parable: "The kingdom of heaven is like a mustard seed that someone took and sowed in his field; ³²it is the smallest of all the seeds, but when it has grown it is the greatest of shrubs and becomes a tree, so that the birds of the air come and make nests in its branches."

³³He told them another parable: "The kingdom of heaven is like yeast that a woman took and mixed in with three measures of flour until all of it was leavened. . . .

⁴⁴"The kingdom of heaven is like treasure hidden in a field, which someone found and hid; then in his joy he goes and sells all that he has and buys that field.

⁴⁵"Again, the kingdom of heaven is like a merchant in search of fine pearls; ⁴⁶on finding one pearl of great value, he went and sold all that he had and bought it.

Theological Perspective

This lection contains three sections: four parables of subversion (vv. 31–33, 44–46); a parable of sorting and final judgment (vv. 47–50); Matthew's self-understanding of his work (vv. 51–52). Because of similarities between the parable of the Wheat and Weeds, discussed in last Sunday's Gospel text (13:24–30, 36–43, pp. 260–64), and the parable here of Sorting a Catch of Fish, the following discussion addresses the first and third sections.

Mustard and yeast, a thief and a merchant. One is struck by the shady, subversive, corrupted presenting character of these parables, especially in contrast to the portrayal, in the other parts of chapter 13, of fruitfulness, separating weeds from wheat, and judgment that sorts the true disciples from the others. Mustard (v. 31) is a weed a farmer would pull from a field, but here God's empire is compared to the mustard seed, starting very small but growing into a shrub. Yeast (or leaven, v. 33), the agent that bloats and rots corpses and what a woman would clean from her house in preparation for Passover, is here a positive: God is fermenting the empire of the heavens within the world, like the woman who mixes—or spoils—flour with yeast.

Finding the empire of the heavens is compared to a man who finds a treasure (v. 44) in someone else's field and then liquidates all his assets to buy the field

Pastoral Perspective

I wonder if the crowds were disappointed—perhaps some of the disciples too? Jesus tells one more parable about seeds and plants, followed by stories of baking bread, plowing a field, and fishing. Yes, he throws in one story about a wealthy merchant, but all the rest are as ordinary as a mustard bush. No kings, or even princes, populate these parables of the kingdom. No military generals or revolutionary leaders to please Simon the Zealot or his colleague Judas. They must have felt let down.

I wonder if our congregations might be disappointed too. I doubt their visions of heaven include mustard bushes and housework. God is more often seen as "Lord" or "King" than farmer or baker woman. Likewise, most contemporary Christian music sings about "enthroning" Jesus, raising him up and exalting him in the highest heaven.

However, the stories Jesus tells of his kingdom and of that heaven are down to earth, literally. They are common stories about ordinary people—a tenant farmer, a housewife, fishermen—doing everyday things. This is hardly an exalted vision of God's realm.

Of course, that is the whole point. As Christians, we are called to believe in the incarnation, the mystery of the meeting of the divine and human in the person of Jesus Christ. In his parables, Jesus puts

⁴⁷"Again, the kingdom of heaven is like a net that was thrown into the sea and caught fish of every kind; ⁴⁸when it was full, they drew it ashore, sat down, and put the good into baskets but threw out the bad. ⁴⁹So it will be at the end of the age. The angels will come out and separate the evil from the righteous ⁵⁰and throw them into the furnace of fire, where there will be weeping and gnashing of teeth.

⁵¹"Have you understood all this?" They answered, "Yes." ⁵²And he said to them, "Therefore every scribe who has been trained for the kingdom of heaven is like the master of a household who brings out of his treasure what is new and what is old."

Exegetical Perspective

In *A Critical and Exegetical Commentary on the Gospel according to Saint Matthew,* Davies and Allison propose a simple three-part structure for this, the third of Jesus' discourses (13:1–53). The first part (vv. 1–23) offers an understanding of the mixed response to the ministry of Jesus. The middle section (vv. 24–43) describes the malicious work of the evil one as a second reason for the lack of favorable response (vv. 24–30, 36–43). The final section (vv. 44–53) discusses appropriate response to the discovery of the kingdom.[1] Each of the sections ends with a request for a further word concerning the content of the parables of that section.

Following that pattern, the six short parables of today's lesson fall within two of the three sections. We can see, however, four topical sections within this discourse. The parables of the Mustard Seed and Leaven (vv. 31–33) comprise a distinct section sandwiched between the parable of the Weeds and its explanation. These two parables focus on the contrast between the apparently questionable purity of the gospel proclamation and the amazing end result of the kingdom's virtue.

Of six parables contained within this lectionary passage, five follow a similar pattern. Five parables

1. See W. D. Davies and D. C. Allison Jr., *A Critical and Exegetical Commentary on the Gospel according to Saint Matthew,* International Critical Commentary, vol. 2 (Edinburgh: T. & T. Clark, 1991), 371.

Homiletical Perspective

A popular approach to this text is to focus upon the dramatic growth of the mustard seed—a tiny and unremarkable seed from which can grow, in practically no time at all, a fifteen-foot tree big and leafy enough to provide shade and habitat for birds in a hot Middle Eastern climate. This theme—of phenomenal growth from something small—offers great encouragement for the church in every age, and can be appropriately gleaned from this text.

This text offers another approach as well. Since it includes a string of parables referring evocatively to things that are hidden—the treasure hidden in a field; the one fine pearl hidden amid shovelfuls of ordinary pearls; the net full of fish in which the good fish are hidden amid the rest of the catch—the preacher may be invited to examine the text from another angle.

Mustard seeds too are hidden. Almost weightless and growing into weeds that sprout up wild, they would not often have been deliberately sown in the neat rows of a farmer's field. The preacher may thus wonder: is the primary emphasis of this parable on growth, or does the parable of the Mustard Seed, along with the parables that follow it in this text, point to something invasive and unpredictable about the kingdom of God?

Matthew 13:31-33, 44-52

Theological Perspective

without telling the owner about the treasure. What was the man doing digging around in someone else's field in the first place? His action is a theft. Merchants (v. 45) were held in the public esteem about as highly as our culture values used-car salespersons. Their motives and scruples were suspect. This merchant, however, in effect puts himself out of business by selling everything to make an ultimate purchase. Once one has sacrificed everything to make the ultimate purchase, there is nothing left to buy and sell.

These parables elevate convention-subverting persons and items to describe discipleship in the empire of the heavens. Whatever else they mean, these parables hint that God's empire—and therefore good citizenship in God's realm—is fundamentally different from Rome's.

These parables present a radical challenge to Christianity in the United States, where the Christian faith is predominantly a middle-class, convention-supporting religion. Once again, in this text Matthew presses us to consider the nature of discipleship. Ask most people which institution in society gives primary support to middle-class morality, good citizenship (think sanctuary, Christian flag positioned stage right), and personal responsibility; most people would say, "The church."

True, mainline churches no longer occupy the social position they once did; they are no longer "the mainline" in the way they were from the early 1900s through the late 1950s. However, the mentality of mainline lingers, along with the powerful affinity between "mainline" and "conventional." These parables challenge the mainline mentality by asking what it means to prepare to be a disciple fit for the empire of the heavens. If a society is basically healthy (in the sense of *shalom*, health flowing from the springs of peace and justice), one can imagine the church working in sync with society. The church should help people to be well adjusted and balanced.

What if a society resembles the empire of Rome much more closely than it does the empire of heaven, expressing in its policies and budget the values of social inequality and redemptive violence? Helping persons to *adjust* or *be balanced* to fit into a sick society is not the work of the gospel. As Warren Carter writes in commenting on the parable of the woman who leavens the flour, "if a person is well adjusted in a sick society, corrupting is the only path to wholeness."[1] The church's work in every age, more

1. Warren Carter, *Matthew and the Margins: A Sociopolitical and Religious Reading* (Maryknoll, NY: Orbis, 2000), 291.

Pastoral Perspective

that incarnational focus not on himself but on the world around him. "The kingdom of God is like" (vv. 31, 33, 44, 45, 47) the most common things in human life. Like Jesus himself, this everyday world embodies the sacred meeting of divine and human, if only we have the eyes to see and the ears to hear.

In that embodiment, his parables differ significantly from Greek or Roman myths or Aesop's fables. Jesus' stories have no gods in human disguise or talking animals, just real-life women and men going about their everyday work.

According to Matthew, the first thing Jesus does when he comes out of the wilderness is to proclaim, "The kingdom of heaven has come near" (3:2). He demonstrates that nearness every time he heals someone, reaches out to outcasts, respects women, or cares for the poor. He also demonstrates that nearness through these kingdom parables.

For Jesus, God's realm is not some esoteric kingdom in the sweet by and by, but as close as the next mustard bush or loaf of bread. That nearness, far more than the threat of eternal agony, is the basis for his call to belief. Of these five parables, only the last includes apocalyptic judgment and gnashing of teeth. The rest envision God in every nook and cranny of daily life, from kneading dough to plowing fields. Jesus transforms human life not by scaring the hell out of people, but by helping them see the heaven close at hand.

Offering such images of God's realm, Jesus echoes his ancestor Moses's farewell address to his people. At the edge of the promised land, Moses reminds the Israelites that "the word is very near" them, in their hearts and close at hand (Deut. 30:14). In his earthy kingdom parables, Jesus reaffirms that truth.

Moreover, Jesus does not use the seven wonders of the world to envision God's kingdom. He does not even use a stately cedar of Lebanon, but a lowly mustard plant. Its seed is a symbol of the tiniest thing, and the plant it produces is a trash tree—or more accurately, a trash bush, no matter how tall it gets. Mustards are the kudzu and salt cedars of their day. How is that for an image of God's realm?

Then there is the leaven for 100 loaves of bread, in a tradition where yeast is a symbol of corruption and impurity. In Jesus' parable, though, yeast becomes the agent of the miraculous growth of God's kingdom. If God can use mustard seed and corrupt leaven to grow the kingdom, imagine what God can do with you.

Abundance from the smallest of things, miraculous transformations from trash bush to tree of life, from

begin "the kingdom of heaven is like," followed by a short, pithy word picture. This formula, according to Witherington, follows the format of a wisdom teacher and strengthens his argument that Matthew's structural formula presents Jesus not as new Moses but rather as *the* Wisdom Teacher.[2] The exception is the final parable (v. 52), which could be considered simply a metaphorical description of a wisdom teacher.

The mustard seed and leaven parables utilize elements that either are not favored or are regarded as unclean to present lessons about transformation. Matthew's account of the mustard seed is shared with the Q tradition and with the noncanonical *Gospel of Thomas* (although in a slightly different form). Contrary to the often idealized image of the mustard seed today, the mustard shrub was not a highly regarded addition to one's garden in antiquity. It was a weed, a shrub brush that consumed valuable garden space. Like the weeds of the previous parable, mustard is a plant that one is sorely tempted to weed out and burn.

However, here Jesus emphasizes the surprising growth of something small and worthless into something that provides a place of shelter and nurture; he likens this to God's activity. The lesson of the prior parable is strengthened by pointing to what is ultimately of value to God's kingdom, when others would have deemed it junk.

Following the pattern of pairing parables to complement the image being drawn in the hearer's active imagination, the parable of the Leaven underscores the transforming power of the kingdom. The leaven in the parable is not the same as the yeast used in modern kitchens. In the culture of Scripture, leaven is almost universally understood as something evil or unclean.

The leavening agent of the time was created by setting aside a portion of leftover bread to spoil, in order to create leaven used in future baking. Not spoiled enough, it is worthless and cannot cause the new batter to rise. Allowed to spoil too long, it not only ruins the bread but can result in food poisoning. Leaven can be fatal. Only a small portion—like a mustard seed—is needed to leaven flour. The "three measures of meal" with which the woman mixes the leaven would produce enough bread for a wedding feast. Of additional interest in this parable (as in the parable of the Lost Coin found in Luke's Gospel) is that Jesus' role is likened to that of a woman.

Mustard seeds—lying undetected in a big sack of some other kind of seed—are finally thrown onto the waiting soil in the same handful as that other, more dominant seed; no one suspects for an instant that any plant other than the one that is planned will sprout and grow up. A mustard tree is not what is expected, but no one notices the seed. It is hard to see, hard to keep an eye on, but it has a way of mixing with what is more noticeable. At the end of the day, as it germinates and sprouts and grows, its final result radically reorients what is expected.

Maybe those disciples were shocked to hear Jesus say, "The kingdom of heaven is like a mustard seed," because maybe they would assume that the planting and cultivation of such a kingdom is more orderly and predictable, laid out in neat rows. The kingdom of heaven is like soybeans, or like beautiful rows of lavender or cotton or grapes. What goes in is what is planned, and is altogether similar to what grows up.

However, when the kingdom of heaven is like a mustard seed, maybe that suggests that nicely bounded rows of expected crops are forever being invaded and overturned by an inbreaking that is finally unexpected. Mustard seeds just hide there in the sack of other seeds or in the hand of an unsuspecting sower. In the same way, maybe a deeper meaning is hiding within this homely little parable.

More often than not, we want to draw clear, unarguable boundaries around the kingdom of heaven. It is fair to have doubts, fair to explore what we believe and what we have trouble believing; but it is not fair for us to gather on Sunday and say, "Jesus Christ is Lord!" while at the same time behaving as if Jesus were dispensable—just a nice guy living in the first century who went about doing good.

In the church, we want to be able to define what fits within it and what does not. So naturally, there are important formulaic things that we say. We have Scripture. We have creeds. We have liturgy. We have tradition. We have convictions about baptism. We have boundaries—nice neat rows of carefully tended doctrine and practice.

Then, just to keep us honest, and just when we are least expecting it, we also have the voice of God whispering in our ear—pushing us beyond our boundaries, forcing us to discern whether they are in fact our boundaries or God's boundaries. In this sense, "the kingdom of heaven is like a mustard seed"—a tiny little symbol of how God is forever invading our orderly sense of things. It just hides there—in the sack, in the hand, in the church, in the mind of God—like a mustard seed, like a treasure

2. Ben Witherington III, *Matthew* (Macon, GA: Smyth & Helwys, 2006), 257ff., emphasis added.

Matthew 13:31-33, 44-52

Theological Perspective

so in some ages and places than in others, is to form disciples who value the contemporary equivalents of weeds, yeast, thieves, and merchants.

In the final segment of this lection, Matthew returns to the topic of "understanding": "Have you understood all this?" (v. 51), he asks the inner group of disciples. They reply that they have understood. Matthew then expresses what many commentators see as his self-understanding: a scribe trained for the empire of the heavens is like a householder who brings out of his treasure "what is new and what is old" (v. 52). What might this mean? If we take "scribe" to refer to those who interpret the Torah, then scribes trained for the empire of the heavens have a revised and more extensive treasure upon which to draw, one that includes the Scriptures, a tradition of interpretation, and the teachings of Jesus.

To bring out the old is to take the witness of tradition—the Hebrew Scriptures and the tradition of commentary thereon—seriously. To bring out the new is to engage in conversation, to keep continuity at points, and to change how we receive tradition, based on the teachings of Jesus. The teachings of Jesus are themselves of two kinds: the teachings as received through traditions, and the teachings of the living Lord speaking to the community through contemporary scribes trained for the empire of the heavens. Tradition can never be separated from the processes of transmission and reception, conversation and argument.

Matthew's self-description could serve as a mirror in which all of us who teach and preach the gospel might look and reflect on what we see. I cannot recall knowing preachers or teachers who explicitly understand themselves as scribes trained for the empire of the heavens, but Matthew's text invites us to do just that. What do we think we are doing when we preach and teach? With the traditions of both the Hebrew Bible and the New Testament as our "old," what constitutes the "new" we are also to bring forth from the treasure? Matthew's self-understanding, as expressed in verse 52, is a fine place to grapple with that question.

GARY PELUSO-VERDEND

Pastoral Perspective

corrupt leaven to bread enough to feed the multitudes. God's kingdom is like that, according to Jesus.

No wonder the next two parables tell of people who gladly give up everything for that treasure. The extravagant response of the tenant farmer and the pearl merchant is matched only by the extravagant mustard bush and loaves of bread of the preceding parables.

Of course, the paradox is that a kingdom worth the price of the great pearl or the hidden treasure is not made of silver or gold, but of bushes and bread. Would you give up all you have for a crop of kudzu?

No simple moral fables, Jesus' parables demand such decisions. Like Moses's last words, the parables underscore our responsibility to choose God's way. Moses frames it as a choice between life or death, blessing or curse (Deut. 30:15). Jesus' parables posit the realm of God versus that of the evil one, good fish or bad fish. Like Moses, Jesus does not let us off the hook. The nearness of God's realm challenges us daily to choose that realm.

Ironically, because they are so rooted in his world, Jesus' parables may keep us from experiencing that realm in our world. For most in our congregations, mustard is found in plastic bottles on the supermarket shelf, bread comes in plastic bags, and pearls go for discount prices on the Home Shopping Network. These first-century Palestinian parables can be as foreign to us as any otherworldly vision of God's realm.

So find new parables. What in your world produces the abundance of a mustard seed? In our time, what is like leaven, disdained as corrupt, but actually an agent of God's transforming power? Like the man plowing a field or the merchant searching for the pearl, what would your congregation give up everything to possess?

Like Jesus, tell new stories to speak timeless truths. Look at the world around you through his eyes. Then open the eyes and ears of your congregation to his vision of heaven close at hand.

TALITHA J. ARNOLD

Exegetical Perspective

The final section of parables, found in verses 44–50, is unique to Matthew. Unlike the prior parables in this sermon collection, these three are neither about Jesus nor about the listener's receptivity. Rather, they are about the ultimate value of the kingdom. The first two, the parables of the Hidden Treasure and the Pearl of Great Price, speak directly to the life situation of the struggling Christians at Antioch. Whether they have found the gift of the kingdom by accident or as the result of a long search, they have found in the gospel something of such supreme value that it has been worth their having given up everything else to make it their own.

The apocalyptic nature of the parable of the Dragnet reiterates the value of kingdom. As in the parable of the Weeds, there will come a time of separation. At the end of the age, judgment will come and with judgment, consequences—for good or ill—that are decided in the present. As in the parable of the Sower, the promise of the kingdom is widely cast, but the decision as to which of the "catch" is good and which is not will be made by the angels at God's behest and not by us.

The final parable comes as a closing statement to the disciples; it too is unique to Matthew's Gospel. Like Jesus, the disciples will be scribes. Those with whom the secrets of the kingdom have been shared now become teachers of those secrets after appropriating a final lesson. Challenges similar to those faced by Matthew's contemporaries continue to present themselves. So the discourse ends with a reminder: the truly wise teacher will recognize that there is value to be found in the old as well as the new, and wisdom honors truth as found in either.

With this final group of parables, Matthew punctuates the message that the kingdom is embraced by the marginalized, the unclean, and the left out; demonstrates that the rules of ritual (as in regard to leaven) do not apply to the eschaton; and says that response to the future actualization of the kingdom merits giving all that one has in the present. Those who do so discover Jesus' true family. Those who have ears to hear listen and understand.

J. DAVID WAUGH

Homiletical Perspective

hidden in a field, like a pearl of great value hidden amid the rest, like the tasty fish hidden amid the whole catch.

Sometime in the early 1980s, I remember watching a wonderful interview with Archbishop Desmond Tutu on public television. It is hard to believe now, but that was back when apartheid was very strong and there was no outward sign that it would end any time soon. Tutu said this curious thing: "When the white people arrived, we had the land and they had the Bible. They said, 'Let us pray.' When we opened our eyes, they had the land and we had the Bible. And we got the better of the deal."[1]

The kingdom of heaven, like the mustard seed, invades the cultivated soil of our certainties and our boundaries and creates out of it all something new—"the better of the deal." Hidden within what we think we see so clearly, it is subversive and grows up in unexpected ways until what we thought we knew is transformed and redeemed by our surprising, invasive God.

The story is told of a man who had been on the outs with the church ever since his adolescent days. The church, he said, was too concerned about the rules, so he left and said he was finished with it. His father worked on him, begging him to give the church another chance, and finally the man agreed that he would. He got up the nerve one Sunday and wandered into a church. The congregation was in the middle of the prayer of confession. "We have done those things which we ought not to have done and we have left undone those things which we ought to have done, and there is no health in us."

The man heard that and smiled to himself. "Good!" he said. "This sounds like my kind of crowd."[2]

THEODORE J. WARDLAW

1. Greg Jones, "Africa and the Bible," www.episcopalcafe.com, July 28, 2007.
2. William H. Willimon, "Our Kind of Crowd," preached at Duke University Chapel, September 15, 1996.

Isaiah 55:1-5

> ¹Ho, everyone who thirsts,
>   come to the waters;
> and you that have no money,
>   come, buy and eat!
> Come, buy wine and milk
>   without money and without price.
> ²Why do you spend your money for that which is not bread,
>   and your labor for that which does not satisfy?
> Listen carefully to me, and eat what is good,
>   and delight yourselves in rich food.

Theological Perspective

Few preachers still connect this reading from Isaiah to today's Gospel reading from Matthew incorrectly—but it is tempting to do so. How easy, especially during the season after Pentecost, to identify a Hebrew Scripture reading about an invitation to feast without cost as a prediction of the Matthean account of the loaves and fishes! This misses the rich complexity of both readings, especially that of Isaiah.

Chapters 40–55 of Isaiah are grouped together as the Book of Consolation. This Book of Consolation had a significant place in the life of the Israelite community because it developed during the exilic period, speaking words of hope and consolation to people cut off from their homes and caught in political situations. This consolation defies the oppressive situations of their lives. This section of Isaiah then represents a theology of history that places the experience of the exiled within the plan of God and as sign of the continued covenantal relationship.[1]

The Book of Consolation opens with the prophetic directive, "Comfort, O comfort my people" (40:1). Chapter 55 is the last in this Book of Consolation, and today's reading comes from it. The chapter begins with a vibrant invitation: "Ho, everyone who

Pastoral Perspective

Most of us resent invitations to meals with strings attached. Thanks, but no thanks! Invitations to meals or banquets occur several times in the Bible, and always come with a hitch. The good news is that all are invited; the bad news is that you have to bring a dish or do something. Adam and Eve got the whole garden for their pleasure, except for one fruit tree they could not resist, but they also were named caretakers of the garden. Jesus broke bread and poured wine, inviting all to a heavenly banquet, but followers were instructed to feed his sheep.

Today's text is no exception. All are invited to the water, but God reminds followers to eat the good things that matter. Isaiah is speaking to Judean exiles in Babylon, the intelligentsia and wealthy who were deemed important enough to deport from Judah to the empire of Babylon. Several generations later, many of these exiles have surely prospered in their captivity, even if in limited ways. Thinking of returning home might be a challenge for them. ("How can I possibly fit all this stuff in one shoddy oxcart?") They have accumulated goodies in Babylon. Isaiah is reminding them where they came from. The God who was apparently absent all this time is now inviting them back to rebuild that project of abundant life—and the new Judah will look nothing like the flamboyant Babylon to which they have become accustomed.

---

1. Cf. Elsie Stern, "Transforming Comfort: Hermeneutics and Theology in the Haftarot of Consolation," *Prooftexts* 23 (2003): 150–81.

³Incline your ear, and come to me;
   listen, so that you may live.
 I will make with you an everlasting covenant,
   my steadfast, sure love for David.
⁴See, I made him a witness to the peoples,
   a leader and commander for the peoples.
⁵See, you shall call nations that you do not know,
   and nations that do not know you shall run to you,
 because of the LORD your God, the Holy One of Israel,
   for he has glorified you.

Exegetical Perspective

Literary-Historical Context. Isaiah contains diverse prophetic materials spanning a long historical trajectory. Texts reflecting the Assyrian crisis (eighth century BCE), when the prophet Isaiah lived, are interspersed with texts reflecting the Babylonian crisis (sixth century) and texts reflecting the Persian restoration (ca. fifth century). The entire book is Isaianic in the sense that patterns of divine activity discerned by Isaiah himself in his own time are typologically projected onto later historical situations. Although some texts are evidently linked with particular events, and although some units have explicit rhetorical connections with neighboring units, it is difficult to read the entire book in any particular chronological or literary sequence. The book instead invites readers to connect texts that thematically echo one another, and to relate them typologically with the historical contexts described in the book.

Isaiah 55:1–5 belongs to a section defined in terms of marked rhetorical affinities extending from chapter 40 to chapter 55 (often called Second Isaiah). Within this section there are several texts that explicitly reflect the historical situation of Babylonian exile. It is therefore possible to read this pericope in relation to this particular historical context, as a prophecy of restoration. Affinities with the chapter's concluding pericope (55:12–13), which envisions a

Homiletical Perspective

One of the most provocative aspects of this lesson is how we envision the tone of the speaker. What is the timbre of God's call in this marvelous string of imperatives? The way in which preachers imagine and engage that tone of voice can have a dramatic impact on the way that we hear it, the way we approach the meaning of it, and the way we break it open to present it to the congregation.

The passage begins with an arresting expletive, "Ho," which sounds for all practical purposes like a "Hey you" or "Attention shoppers!" One scholar has suggested that the tone of the speaker in this passage is similar to that of a merchant in a crowded Middle Eastern bazaar, struggling to get the attention of the passing crowds, hawking his wares with enthusiasm and excitement. A classic American version might be the image of a barker in the carnival midway, calling out to the crowds to come and see the astonishing realities that lie just beyond the open tent flap behind him.

Whatever image you choose to employ, the concept beneath it is one of a God who seeks ardently and zealously to get the attention of the milling crowd, beseeching them to come, accept, and delight in the wondrous goods that are being so graciously offered to them.

This divine vendor, however, is inviting the crowd to engage in a very unusual and mysterious

Isaiah 55:1-5

Theological Perspective

thirsts, come to the waters; and you that have no money, come, buy and eat!" (v. 1a).

The language of these verses has been compared to that of Middle Eastern market vendors, but the sales pitch builds in intensity through these two verses.[2] Water, bread, wine, and milk are available, provisions beyond the capabilities of any single vendor. This lavish spread would have special appeal to those who were in exile: God had not abandoned them, despite their oppressive political situation.

Reflections on the cost of these basic human needs are woven through these two verses: come and feast "without money and without price" (v. 1b). The plentiful feast is yet more attractive to those in exile, recognizing their economic needs as part of their human needs. "Listen carefully to me, and eat what is good, and delight yourselves in rich food" (v. 2b).

However, the prophetic writer upends the prevailing economic system by inviting reflection on what is valuable: "Why would you spend your money for that which is not bread?" (v. 2a) and again "[why spend] your labor for that which does not satisfy?"

In this context, labor and money have great value, but bread is not all that satisfies. By asking, "What will truly satisfy you?" the author poses a difficult question for a marginalized people to answer. Their answer might come in pragmatic terms of food and money, but the truest satisfaction comes from something more. The prophetic voice in Isaiah comforts, even as it calls for deeper reflection on human valuation beyond such things as social class, wealth, and education.

Verses 3–5 present a new cost analysis, one based on a mutual relationship with God. Verse 3 calls the exiled community to "come to me; listen, so that you may live." This exiled community then is not damned but blessed, because their status as a chosen people is affirmed. The covenant to which they are invited is one of mutuality, as was that of God's with David. "I will make with you an everlasting covenant, my steadfast, sure love for David" (v. 3b). David remained a singular figure, humanly flawed but still loved by and in relationship with God. "See, I made him a witness to the peoples, a leader and commander for the peoples" (v. 4).

With David as a basis of comparison, the prophetic vision pivots to encompass the exiled community becoming a beacon to call unknown nations, reflecting the vendor's call to feast in verse

2. John Goldingay, *The Message of Isaiah 40–55* (London: T. & T. Clark, 2005), 544–45.

Pastoral Perspective

Scattered and exiled communities abound in our world today. The United States receives refugees from all over the world, whether they come at the invitation of our government or slip over the borders. Many describe their situation as one of exile. They are far from home in a land where consumerist gods of greed reign. Despite their many hardships and loneliness in this foreign land, however, many begin to prosper. They send money home to relatives in need.

Many talk about losing their cultural values here. Back home they knew their neighbors, took care of one another's children, helped each other out in hard times, and found enjoyment in simple things like walking in a warm rain or watching the sunset. They remark that the consumerism of Babylon, the USA, consumes them.

No doubt the same occurred with exiles in Babylon. They had reason to wonder if their god YHWH was even still around. After all, had not God's temple home been destroyed? Had YHWH's chosen people not been raped, destroyed, humiliated, and exiled? YHWH had lost. The flashy gods of Babylon were obviously stronger and worth homage. Why not live a little and consume as everyone else did? Eat those fast foods, buy Golden Calf Lotto tickets, get sucked into the television set, and watch another ballgame. Ignore your neighbors. They probably just want something. Take care of number one.

Isaiah's invitation in verses 1 and 2 today is good news for the poor. It is not necessarily bad news for others, but it is a wake-up call to put down the gadgets that pull our attention away from God's project of life in abundance for all. Those who strive, thrive, and adapt to Babylon's consumerist culture should hear words of warning, reminding them that their return to Judah means putting back the iToys they got in Babylon in order to focus on much more important matters.

These concluding verses of Second Isaiah provide for rich summer vacation reflections, as many have time to evaluate how our energies are spent. Are we so caught up in Babylon's gadgets and spiderweb of information overload that we are left empty inside, or are we spending our money and energies on the life project God calls us to join?

The banquet God invites us to is an uncomfortable one in one sense. Those without money (who sometimes smell, talk, and behave differently from us) and those with money are both invited. There is no A list or B list—just an invitation to show up and eat with others. While most of us prefer to eat and

return to the land, reinforce this possibility. In light of the book's overall design, however, readers are also invited to ask whether this prophecy of restoration might not recapitulate patterns of divine activity discerned in preexilic prophecies of deliverance from the time of Isaiah, and whether the same patterns might still be discernible even after the restoration has been accomplished. The book imagines that the return to the land, in fulfillment of its prophecies of restoration, is also a return to the threat of exile and the need of restoration all over again.

Invitation to Feast on the Word (vv. 1–3a). The pericope begins with an extended call to attention, preparing the audience to hear verses 3b–5. The call is metaphorically described as the invitation to a banquet (cf. Prov. 9:1–6). It is addressed to "all who are thirsty" and "those who have no money," urging them to come where water is plentiful and the basic stuff of food and drink—grain, wine, and milk, and so forth—is freely available. The rhetorical question that follows (v. 2a) shows that this would entail a major change, because the invitees are splurging on things that neither nourish nor satisfy. The heart of this introduction (vv. 2b–3a) invites them to turn away from such behavior and to listen carefully to the host. The word that he gives them will nourish and satisfy them, body and soul (cf. Deut. 8:3). The motivation to accept this invitation is life (cf. Deut. 30:19).

Promise of a New Future (vv. 3b–5). The word that the audience now hears is life giving, because it promises the creation of a new living arrangement in which the people of YHWH can flourish. This is allusively described in terms of one of the mythic traditions about the golden age of the Davidic empire. Just as the hegemony of the Davidic dynasty was international in scope (e.g., Pss. 2:8; 18:45; 72:8), so that David could bear witness to the nations of YHWH's purposes for them, this new earthly manifestation of YHWH's heavenly kingdom will be part of a world order in which YHWH's people can play the same role. They can seek to initiate relations with other nations, and vice versa. In comparison with their present situation, which precludes any such geopolitical prominence, this new arrangement will be "glorious" (v. 5bß).

Reading in Context. Considered in isolation, this pericope could be read as a prophecy addressed to the exiles, promising the restoration of the Davidic monarchy. However, the text itself is not specific

transaction. The normal rules of commerce do not seem to apply, and in truth they seem to have been completely overturned. One need not bring goods to barter or money to pay, because water, bread, wine, and rich food will all be provided "without money and without price" (v. 1b). All we must bring to the exchange is our thirst and hunger, our deep desire for the gifts that are being offered.

In verse 3, we are told what lies behind these gifts: no less than life itself, a life that is not dependent on money, bread, or labor, but is the fruit of a committed relationship with Almighty God. To enter into that everlasting covenant is to become in turn part of a divine sales force, offering to others gracefully and gratefully that which has been so generously given, a life anchored in the love and mercy of a living God.

The themes that arise from this passage are focused on (1) the giver, (2) the gift, and (3) the recipient. What strikes one about the giver, this divine merchant, is the sheer magnitude of the appeal. This sales pitch is made not to those with certain resources, qualifications, or religious credentials, but to "everyone who thirsts," to those "that have no money," and to those who are simply not satisfied. Like the sower in Jesus' parable, the seeds of this generous offering are scattered wildly and indiscriminately across the width and breadth of a diverse crowd. The proffered gift is eating and drinking with the Lord, who is the source of all life and delight. The only quality one must possess to join the rich banquet is a passionate yearning to be part of it.

From a slightly different angle, we see in the second half of the lesson (vv. 3b–5) that the love God lavished on his servant David is now offered to all people. The promise of the everlasting covenant is no longer relegated to the distant past but is now a present reality, freely offered to all who wish to lay claim to it. God's covenant with David is now available to all, and those who enter into it will become vessels of the glory of God, beacons that will attract the nations.

This Davidic heritage presents a preacher with a wonderful opportunity to talk to the congregation about the need and power of evangelism, not as an oppressive obligation but as a natural way through which we continue to experience and share the glorious gifts that have been so generously given to us. To sit at the banquet table of God's glory—to partake of wine and rich food without money and without price—is to be satisfied, filled with new life. This inestimable gift of new life is something that is realized only when it is recklessly shared with

Isaiah 55:1-5

Theological Perspective

1. There is nothing specific in this call, no promise of evangelizing the world. Instead, God glorifies the Israelite community—in exile at the time of this section of Isaiah—even in the midst of their troubles. These people will become witnesses to the power of God. "See, you shall call nations that you do not know, and nations that do not know you shall run to you, because of the LORD your God, the Holy One of Israel, for he has glorified you" (v. 5).

This theology of history places God's covenant as valuable for all people. The generosity of God to an exiled people signals true power, a beacon for other nations. This is not a call for other nations to convert, but "constitute[s] the community's fulfillment of its destiny to be YHWH's witness to the nations."[3]

As part of a theology of history, then, this reading from Isaiah considers the past, not in terms of the failure that led to exile, but in terms of the figure of David. The covenant of God with the chosen people is highlighted in their present moment of exile: rejoicing becomes emblematic of God's fulfilling and fruitful power through history. As is stated in verse 3, "Listen, so that you may live." The abundance of life beyond water and bread is given to this covenanted people, even when they are exiled and oppressed by political powers; indeed, God makes a way out of no way. Believing and trusting God's power and love are integral to a genuine faith for individuals and communities.

God's power, love, and generosity, then, underline the hope for the future where the exiled community stood as witness to these things. The cost for the community was not money but a loving commitment to a covenant with God. This covenant is the true feast, the full satisfaction to which the Israelite community is invited.

STEPHANIE Y. MITCHEM

Pastoral Perspective

worship with those whose income and status are similar to our own, this is hardly God's vision of life.

Verse 3 must have stung the exiled community. "Incline your ear, and come to me; listen, so that you may live." They had heard that Babylon's ruler was about to let them go back and rebuild their cities. Who was this YHWH, who had seemingly abandoned them for generations, to show up now and say these words!? "What do you mean, come to you? *You* come to *us*! Where have *you* been, YHWH?"

Often, when we suffer injustice or illness, God seems nowhere to be found. We conclude that God has jumped ship or was merely a fantasy we created when times were good. We move on to other gods. In these verses God reminds us that we are part of something much bigger and that God is very much involved. We learn yet again that God's recovery methods involve working alongside those who suffer, promising presence but not doing all the work alone. Victims who participate in their own recovery are usually better able to succeed than those who do not.

The final verses of the text (vv. 3b–5) remind the captives that the project begun so long ago continues. This insignificant, humiliated people will not just survive; they will be a light to others. Surrounded by more powerful and richer countries, YHWH's people will be looked to by many other nations for the kind of society they create in covenant with God. This covenant will be based on protecting the weakest members of society, controlling greed and usury among the more powerful, and breaking down the walls that divide rich and poor. Those with money and those without money will sit together and worship the same God who created them. It is the way they live and treat one another—not how many oxcarts they can fill—that makes them a light to others. That is God's definition of life in abundance.

DAVID MAXWELL

3. Ibid., 550.

Exegetical Perspective

enough to require this, and its ambiguities are open to alternative readings made possible by the overall design of the book. The introduction (vv. 1–3a) suggests that the audience is invested in unrealistic hopes, and that they need to see other possibilities. Perhaps they are expecting a return to the preexilic status quo ante, but against the extended historical background of Isaiah as a whole, this is practically impossible. What, then, are some other possibilities?

Isaiah viewed the Assyrian conquest of Judah in the late eighth century as YHWH's means of judging the nation for its infidelity, and Jerusalem's miraculous deliverance from Assyrian siege in 701 BCE as an expression of YHWH's mercy "for the sake of my servant David" (Isa. 37:35; see 29:1–8). The book also makes the Babylonian destruction of Jerusalem in the late sixth century a means of judgment, corresponding typologically to the earlier Assyrian intervention (chap. 39). The Persian restoration was thus similarly analogous to Jerusalem's rescue from the Assyrian siege, and Isaiah 55:1–5 emphasizes that YHWH is again motivated by the promises to David (2 Sam. 23:5; Pss. 89 passim; 132:13–18).

From this perspective Judah's restoration as a province of the Persian Empire was the fulfillment of this prophecy. The governor's authority was legitimated by his patronage of the temple of YHWH in Jerusalem and by his affiliation with its high priest (Zech. 6:9–15). The restored temple was a reincarnation of the Davidic dynasty's royal sanctuary, enabling the imperial province to represent theologically what the monarchy itself once represented. This divine legitimization of the provincial structure, in fulfillment of YHWH's promises to David, does not mean that Judah is exempt from YHWH's judgment. Now that the people of YHWH are again a geopolitical entity, they have the same problems that Israel experienced in its preexilic forms. Just as YHWH held the monarchy accountable (2 Sam. 7:14; Ps. 89:30–32), even to the point of its overthrow (Ps. 89:38–51), he also holds accountable this new temple-centered version of his kingdom (e.g., Isa. 58:1–2; 59:1–15).

Conclusion. This reading invites contemporary readers to similar typological reflection. In the context of the present changing world order, does the church need to be persuaded that God will give it a new form, fulfilling again the same promises to David once fulfilled in the coming of Christ?

MICHAEL H. FLOYD

Homiletical Perspective

others—when *we* become the hawkers of God's transforming grace.

A final distinction that seems to arise from a consideration of this passage has to do with the juxtaposition of the material and the spiritual, biological existence and divinely inspired life. This is not to say that the two are somehow opposed to each other, but that they really should not be separated. The material and the spiritual are two sides of the same coin, each informing the perception and experience of the other. Without divine inspiration (which is the divine "word" as we see in verse 11 of this chapter), biological existence becomes unfulfilling and unsatisfying. It is about eating for sustenance, not feasting with joy. It is about laboring for what is transient and barren, rather than about striving for what is eternal and filled with new life.

How much of our time and energy are spent sustaining existence, rather than celebrating a divinely inspired life? Remember, however, that a divinely inspired life can be experienced only through the reality of biological existence. If we do not find a way to express the divine word of God in the relationships that sustain us and in the reality that envelops us, we are living with a mental concept, not a living faith. Isaiah's divine vendor calls us to infuse our material lives with the divine word of God's redemptive love, which will change the daily fare of our ordinary lives into a rich banquet of God's transforming and redeeming grace.

WENDEL W. MEYER

Psalm 145:8-9, 14-21

> [8]The LORD is gracious and merciful,
>   slow to anger and abounding in steadfast love.
> [9]The LORD is good to all,
>   and his compassion is over all that he has made.
> . . . .
> [14]The LORD upholds all who are falling,
>   and raises up all who are bowed down.
> [15]The eyes of all look to you,
>   and you give them their food in due season.
> [16]You open your hand,
>   satisfying the desire of every living thing.

Theological Perspective

Psalm 145 beautifully demonstrates the *lex orandi lex credendi* rule of the Christian tradition. This classical phrase in Christian theology means that as the church prays, so it believes. Psalm 145 is an extended prayer of praise that has been used in the worship life of the people of God. It is very carefully constructed in an acrostic form, each letter of the Hebrew alphabet forming the first letter of successive verses. An acrostic pattern was a common structural device that aided in memory. The gathered people of ancient Israel prayed this psalm by heart, possibly with musical instruments accompanying them, and thus their communal belief and faith was formed. Some ancient manuscripts include a congregational refrain after each verse, "Blessed be YHWH, and blessed be his name forever!" that they may have sung.

This is a much-loved psalm in both the Jewish and the Christian traditions. It is the only psalm that is identified in the superscription (not included above) as a song of praise by David. This psalm "is the overture to the final movement of the Psalter," says one commentator.[1] It sets the tone for the last five psalms of the Psalter, which all begin with "Praise the LORD!" The Talmud, an ancient rabbinic

1. James L. Mays, *Psalms,* Interpretation series (Louisville, KY: John Knox Press, 1994), 439.

Pastoral Perspective

The table blessings of my childhood were rather solemn affairs. This is not so for my young nieces and nephew. As you read this commentary preparing for a summer sermon, they are at church camp, learning lively table blessings that, if history is any indicator, they soon will be teaching to their parents, grandparents, aunts, uncles, and cousins.

I get a kick out of singing "God is great; God is good" to the Jeopardy jingle or "Thank you, God, for giving us food!" to the Superman theme song. Even though I have never attended the church camp where my nieces and nephew learned these blessings, I experience some of the joy of that camp experience—the light, air, and freedom of God's great outdoor tent, Bible study that connects with tender hearts untethered for a week from Facebook and iPods, the sharing of secrets with a new friend in the inky darkness after lights out—when we sing our thanks together.

Psalm 145 sparkles with the joy of God's grace and mercy. So it is no surprise to learn that it is a traditional Jewish table blessing. In his Small Catechism, Martin Luther suggested that when it is mealtime, "the children and the members of the household are to come devoutly to the table, fold their hands, and recite: 'The eyes of all look to you, and you give them food in due season. You

¹⁷The L<small>ORD</small> is just in all his ways,
  and kind in all his doings.
¹⁸The L<small>ORD</small> is near to all who call on him,
  to all who call on him in truth.
¹⁹He fulfills the desire of all who fear him;
  he also hears their cry, and saves them.
²⁰The L<small>ORD</small> watches over all who love him,
  but all the wicked he will destroy.

²¹My mouth will speak the praise of the L<small>ORD</small>,
  and all flesh will bless his holy name forever and ever.

Exegetical Perspective

This is the only psalm in the book of Psalms (*tehillim*) that is entitled "Praise" (*tehillah*). Examination of the psalm's structure reveals that "praise" encompasses both the vow to praise God and the content of that praise. The psalm is structured as follows: there is an alternation of (a) the psalmist's declaration that "I" and/or others will praise God and (b) statements specifying the content of that praise (usually speaking of the Lord in the third person). The following analysis of the psalm, using the incipits of each section (and with our lectionary verses in italics), shows how this pattern occurs three times in the psalm:

(a) "I will extol you . . . ," vv. 1–2;
  (b) *"Great is the* L<small>ORD</small>, *and greatly to be praised . . . ,"* v. 3;
(a) "One generation shall laud your works to another . . . ," vv. 4–7;
  (b) *"The* L<small>ORD</small> *is gracious and merciful . . . ,"* vv. 8–9;
(a) "All your works shall give thanks to you, O L<small>ORD</small> . . . ," 10–13a;
  (b) *"The* L<small>ORD</small> *is faithful in all his words . . . ,"* vv. 13–20;

The vow is itself part of the praise. As one's commitment to give praise is made public, that public commitment becomes an act of blessing God's name.

Homiletical Perspective

The lectionary excerpts from Psalm 145 allow the first verse to proclaim the theme of the psalm and indeed the entire Hebrew Bible: the great goodness and trustworthiness of the God of Israel. The familiar language of verses 8 and 9 feels as steadfast and good as the love it describes.

Some teachers of preaching advocate the homiletical method of reading a Scripture passage several times, then closing one's Bible, and without peeking, writing down all the words and phrases that stick in one's memory. In the case of this passage, the inclusive words "every" and "all" would surely be prominent words for most preachers; no surprise, since they appear more than sixteen times throughout this praise hymn of David. Above all else, the psalmist points to the impossible breadth and comprehensive range of God's love and mercy, beyond even the furthest reaches of human imagination.

There is, however, a pivot point and a balance to God's love of "every" and "all." If verse 8 is the theme of the passage, then verse 17 is the central hinge. Before verse 17, the mercy of God is unconditional and inclusive; after verse 17, God is more nuanced and discerning, more conditional and exclusive in the showering of salvific love. Rather than God's compassion reigning "over all he has made," now it is for those who call on God "in

Psalm 145:8-9, 14-21

Theological Perspective

commentary on Hebrew Scripture, instructs the worshipers to repeat this psalm three times every day. Clearly the people of Israel were formed in their faith by the repetition of their hymns of praise.

The theological emphasis of this psalm is the greatness and graciousness of God. These theological themes are deeply integrated in the worship language and practices of the people. The structure of the psalm illustrates this; there are alternating statements of praise ("I will extol you, my God and King," v. 1; "My mouth will speak the praise of the LORD," v. 21) and attribute declarations ("The LORD is gracious and merciful," v. 8; "The LORD upholds all who are falling," v. 14).

The theological emphasis of God's greatness is magnified and expanded in this psalm. Because God's greatness is unlimited and comprehensive, praise is unlimited and comprehensive. There is an appropriate symmetry of who God is in matchless splendor and how we are called to give voice to that reality. This is illustrated by a frequent repetition of "every" or "all." In verse 9, God is "good to all," and his compassion is "over all." In verse 14, the Lord "upholds all" and "raises up all." Verse 15 declares that the "eyes of all" look to God. Verse 16 confesses that God satisfies the desire of "every living thing." Verse 17 states that God is "just in all his ways" and is "kind in all his doings." The steady emphasis of "all" and "every" continues: Verses 18–21 affirm that the Lord is "near to all," that God "watches over all," that "all the wicked" will be destroyed by God's judgment, and finally that "all flesh will bless" God's holy name.

Christian philosopher and theologian Nicholas Wolterstorff has said that the Christian faith has an "each and every principle." This principle is that God is concerned with *each* and *every* living being. It is a vision of the faith that is both expansive and particular. These verses of Psalm 145 express in poetic form that "each and every principle." God "is good to all," says verse 9, expressing God's providence in expansive form. God also "upholds all who are falling, and raises up all who are bowed down," in verse 14, expressing God's particular attention to individuals who struggle, who fail, who mourn.

The combination of expansive love and particular concern is important both theologically and pastorally. The Christian faith is seriously narrowed if God's care for the individual or the particular is the only note sounded. The individualism that marks some Christian traditions shows evidence of how the sweep and scope of the faith can be dramatically reduced if the "each" dominates or even eclipses the

Pastoral Perspective

open your hand, satisfying the desire of every living thing.'"[1]

Praise for "the LORD [who] is good to all [and whose] compassion is over all that he has made" (v. 9) is not limited to mealtime. Psalm 145 is an acrostic poem; its praise proceeds from A to Z, as it were. The word "every/all" is repeated sixteen times in its twenty-one verses. "*All* flesh will bless [God's] holy name forever and ever" (v. 21) is the psalm's final joyful exclamation point. Thus Psalm 145 becomes a comprehensive expression of praise for all occasions when human beings experience God's grace in their lives.

Perhaps you are a person who works twelve hours a day, six days a week. You know that you do not have to do it. You are financially secure. You could easily spend less time at work and more time in activities or in relationships that refresh your spirit. Why do you work so hard? In your more honest moments, you admit that you know the reason. You are working for the day when you hear your father say, "You do not have to be perfect. I am proud of you just as you are. You are as good as I ever was." You are working for the day that you will hear that compliment, but you know you never will, because your father has been dead for ten years.[2]

Then, one day you come to church. You slide into a pew. The liturgist stands and intones, "Come to me, all you that are weary and are carrying heavy burdens, and I will give you rest" (Matt. 11:28). In one tiny moment, you no longer feel like your father's imperfect child. You feel loved. You feel accepted.

What can you say, but "the LORD is gracious and merciful. . . . his compassion is over all that he has made"?

Perhaps you have hurt terribly someone you love. You turned your back on a friend when she really needed you; or you belittled your own child in scathing, undeserved tones in front of his friends; or you had an affair. You have done something so terribly wrong, and even though you feel sorry and have apologized, you harbor doubts that the strain and the pain in the relationship will ever be set right again.

Then one night the two of you are having pizza, and one of you shares something funny that happened at work or at school that day. The other one tells a joke. Before you know it, the atmosphere of

---

1. James Limburg, *Psalms* (Louisville, KY: Westminster John Knox Press, 2000), 490.
2. Harold S. Kushner, *How Good Do We Have to Be? A New Understanding of Guilt and Forgiveness* (New York: Little, Brown, 1996), 73–74.

Exegetical Perspective

A sense of comprehensiveness pervades this psalm, conveyed in multiple ways. The psalm is one of several acrostic or alphabetic psalms (e.g., Pss. 25, 34, 119), wherein the opening verse begins with *'aleph*, the first letter of the Hebrew alphabet, and each successive verse begins with the following letters of the alphabet in order. (The Hebrew Masoretic Text of Ps. 145 lacks the "n" [*nun*] verse, but the LXX and the Psalms scroll from Qumran include an "n" verse, which now appears in the NRSV translation as the final two lines of v. 13.) The use of the entire alphabet conveys a sense of the completeness or total development of this praise of God.

Several times in the psalm the poet declares that God's praise and dominion shall extend throughout the generations (vv. 4, 13) or "forever and ever" (vv. 1, 2, 21)—representing chronological or *temporal* comprehensiveness. The praise of God expands *spatially* outward from the "I" of the psalmist (vv. 1, 21a) to all the faithful (v. 10) and finally to "all creatures" (NIV, v. 21). This comprehensiveness is reinforced by the use of virtually every available synonym for "praise": extol, bless, laud, declare, proclaim, celebrate, sing aloud, give thanks, speak, tell, make known (using the NRSV translations).

Finally and most obviously, the sense of comprehensiveness is conveyed by the recurrence of "all" and "every" (both of these representing the Hebrew *kol,* which occurs seventeen times in the psalm). "Every day" (v. 2) God will receive thanks and blessing, which will come from "all" (vv. 10–12, 21). This thanks from all is most appropriate and fitting because, as the psalmist proclaims, the Lord upholds and raises up *all* who are falling or bowed down (v. 14), the Lord is the one to whom *all* look with their needs and desires (vv. 15–16), and the Lord cares for "*all* who call on him," "*all* who fear him," "*all* who love him" (vv. 18–20a).

The first two verses of today's lectionary selection (vv. 8–9) hark back to an affirmation about God that, according to the biblical tradition, was first revealed to Moses as a self-affirmation by God: "The LORD [is] a God merciful and gracious, slow to anger, and abounding in steadfast love" (Exod. 34:6). With minor variations this affirmation appears in the mouth of Moses (Num. 14:18), Nehemiah (Neh. 9:17), Jonah (Jonah 4:2), as well as in several other psalms (Pss. 86:15; 103:8). God is *slow to anger*, but the fact that the Lord is just (v. 17) means that the divine anger at wickedness cannot be ignored. It is noteworthy that in verses 14–21 the only negative note within a litany celebrating God's grace and

Homiletical Perspective

truth," those who fear God, those who love God, and not for the wicked.

The meting out of God's favor and protection, the corralling of the chosen and the not-chosen, the discernment of who is faithful and who is wicked—these are familiar themes to any reader of the Psalms in any era or region. Rich exploration with a congregation opens up around the honest and human reactions we have to the idea of some being chosen and others not, about how this does (or does not) line up with our Christian understanding of God, and about how the Hebrew understanding of the God of Israel is never complete without wrestling with the question of God's justice.

Echoes of verse 8 elsewhere in the Old Testament are noteworthy. The language originates from God's mouth in Exodus 34:6, just after YHWH exposes the divine backside to Moses and gives him a second set of commandment tablets. In Numbers 14:18, Moses parrots back God's words, reminding God of the divine covenant with Israel and beseeching God for mercy and strength. In Nehemiah 9:17 and 31, we hear the words again in a national remembering of God's character and Israel's story.

Concerning the question of God's justice, perhaps most interesting is the way these words pop up in Jonah 4:2. In petulant anger, we hear Jonah spitting to God that his mercy upon a repenting Nineveh is exactly why Jonah fled his prophetic assignment in the first place—why bother preaching about God's impending judgment upon the wicked if mercy and "steadfast love" are the real end results? In fact, Jonah rages, why even bother to live in a world where the wicked win and justice is a joke?

Jonah's frustration reminds the preacher that not every person in the pew will receive with joy Psalm 145's news of God's endless mercy and boundless love. Like Jonah, we want to know that the right get their reward and the wrong do not. Our feelings complicate matters, of course, in those life moments when *our* fallen natures seem so utterly inescapable, and when God's mercy seems the only light saving us from dark despair and wretched sin.

Such dark despair, such hungering, wanting, and needing—though this psalm focuses on the saving that God does, the shadow side of this psalm (like so many others) is the desperate, needy shadow place in which humanity so often finds itself. It is valuable to contemplate and explore not only just how good a God we have, but also just how badly we need a good God to save us from the shadowy places.

Psalm 145:8-9, 14-21

Theological Perspective

"every." Some churches that peddle the gospel as a product to "meet your needs" give way to this modern tendency. Psalm 145 holds together the dual affirmations of God's expansive care and God's particular care.

It must also be said that the Christian faith is seriously narrowed if the emphasis falls only in the other direction. God is the God of all creation, of all creatures, of all cosmic forces, to be sure. However, pastorally it is important to affirm God's very particular care. When a believer is sick or lonely or frightened, the clear affirmation of the faith is that God attends not only to the grand scheme of the universe, but also to all the details and circumstances of an individual life. Although Psalm 145 was used as a communal worship hymn in ancient Israel, it can certainly be used as a hospital-bed comfort for those who need to hear that "the LORD is near to all who call on him" (v. 18).

The comprehensive claim of Psalm 145, then, is that God is the God of all things great and small. The psalm then illustrates this comprehensive claim by listing the scope of God's care and the reach of God's actions. This is a psalm that paints in some of the details of God's overarching providence. The doctrine of providence traditionally includes both God's sustaining and upholding the created world and God's governing and directing the created world. This psalm illustrates both these aspects of providence. God upholds and sustains those who are faltering (v. 14). God governs seasons and climates so that all creatures are fed (v. 15).

An additional feature of providence is displayed as well. Not only does God uphold and sustain, not only does God govern, but God also watches with kindness (v. 17) and concern (v. 19). In other words, God is attentive; God notices. This characteristic of God expands the classical affirmations of providence by underlining God's deep connection with all the details. God knows the details, cares about them, and includes them in all divine actions and intentions.

LEANNE VAN DYK

Pastoral Perspective

polite, strained silence that has defined your relationship in recent days is being punctuated by relieved laughter. And you realize suddenly that you do not feel imperfect and sinful. You feel forgiven, accepted, loved, and loving.

What can you say, but "the LORD is gracious and merciful. . . . his compassion is over all that he has made"?

Perhaps your son has told you that he is gay. You do not tell your friends, even your best friends, for fear that they would judge you. You have to admit that though you love your son, this is not what you would have chosen for him. You spend sleepless nights reliving your years of parenting, asking yourself the question, "What did I do wrong?" You frame in your mind things that you might have done differently to shape a more perfect outcome.

Then you read about a support group of parents and friends of those who are gay or lesbian. You find out where they are meeting, and you go. Over time, in the embrace of a community of people who live the same struggle that you do, you lay aside the image of the person whom you wanted your child to be; and your real child, with whom you can have a real relationship, comes to life for you. You no longer judge yourself. You feel blessed to be the parent of a very special child whom God created and deemed "very good."

What can you say, but "the LORD is gracious and merciful. . . . his compassion is over all that he has made"?

At mealtime, or at any time, when we are filled to overflowing with the light and air and freedom and blessing of God, Psalm 145 provides words of praise for our mouths to speak and sing, "The LORD is gracious and merciful, . . . and all flesh will bless [God's] holy name forever and ever" (vv. 8, 21).

ELIZABETH MCGREGOR SIMMONS

Exegetical Perspective

kindness is the latter part of verse 20, "but all the wicked he will destroy." This half-verse, considered along with the affirmation that God is slow to anger, embeds in this psalm a warning not to presume on God's goodness, compassion, and patience.

The blessing of God or God's name is a structural motif featured at the beginning, middle, and end of the psalm (vv. 1–2, 10, 21). We read frequently in the Bible of God blessing people; in the OT such blessing is associated especially with prosperity, fertility, general material well-being (e.g., Gen. 12:1–7; 24:35–36; Deut. 28:1–14). We also read of God's blessing being invoked upon other people by such individuals as the patriarchs in Genesis (Gen. 27:27–29; 48:9–22; 49:1–28) and by the Aaronic priests (Num. 6:24–26).

What exactly is the purport of worshipers blessing God? What exactly does the psalmist intend when saying that "I will . . . bless [Heb. root *brk*] you/your name"(vv. 1–2), that "all your faithful shall bless you" (v. 10), and that eventually all creatures will "bless his holy name forever and ever" (v. 21)? In what way may *God's creatures* bless *God*? We may find a clue to an answer by noting that the LXX commonly uses the Greek word *eulogein* (lit. "to speak well") to translate the Hebrew *brk*.

Because of the power inherent in the divine word, when God "speaks well" of a person or a people, the divine word has a dynamic potency that brings about what God speaks (Isa. 55:10–11; Pss. 107:17–20; 147:15–18; Wis. 16:12). In a similar fashion, when an individual blesses or "speaks well" of God (NIV regularly translates *brk* by "praise"), this can indeed have a power of its own, a performative or kerygmatic power, evoking trust and praise from others of God's creatures. Such seems to be envisioned in Psalm 145: the closing verse of the psalm forms an *inclusio* (bookend) with the opening verse, but makes an advance on verse 1 by affirming in the second line that not just the psalmist, but (conceivably in response to the psalmist's praise) "*all flesh* will bless [God's] holy name forever and ever."

GEORGE W. RAMSEY

Homiletical Perspective

Chances are great that at least one creature listening on Sunday morning hungers to know how exactly God promises to help with our deepest shadows. God does not obliterate the shadow side of our lives and our selves. Rather, Walter Brueggemann suggests, the darkness itself is "strangely transformed, not by the power of easy light, but by the power of relentless solidarity."[1] Perhaps one task facing the preacher of this psalm is to show how this text is more than easy light. The darkness does not disappear.

Perhaps hungering for the darkness to disappear is not the right appetite. Most psychological schools of thought agree that one of the most difficult tasks facing the human psyche is integration: the holding of opposites, the bearing of contradicting truths. It is hard work to face the difficult fact that we can feel opposing feelings and hold conflicting values; growing up means learning to *both* love and let go of a person, to see *both* the yes and the no of a situation. When we fail to own our own shadow, admit the darkness exists, embrace it for the good and curious gifts it provides, Jungian analysts warn that we miss the opportunity for holy and whole-making transformation.

What about our appetites, our desires, our burning needs? According to this psalm, through God's mercy, all hungers are fed and all desires are fulfilled; but this psalm's alignment of human appetite and God's fulfillment is interestingly nuanced in verse 15 with the condition "in due season." Ask any parishioner who grows his or her own food or who shops intentionally from local farmers: there is spiritual fulfillment in aligning one's appetites with the seasons of God's creation. Of course, the broad scope of human appetite stretches beyond our growling stomachs. Much of ministry is helping folks manage mortal desires: hunger for meaningful work, hunger for real relationship, hunger for financial freedom, hunger for less loneliness.

No fruit is sweeter and more fulfilling than knowing the holy and graceful truth of this psalm: we are not prisoners to our appetites, no matter how virtuous or profane our hungers might be.

KATIE GIVENS KIME

1. Walter Brueggemann, *Spirituality of the Psalms* (Minneapolis: Fortress Press, 2002), xiii.

Romans 9:1-5

¹I am speaking the truth in Christ—I am not lying; my conscience confirms it by the Holy Spirit— ²I have great sorrow and unceasing anguish in my heart. ³For I could wish that I myself were accursed and cut off from Christ for the sake of my own people, my kindred according to the flesh. ⁴They are Israelites, and to them belong the adoption, the glory, the covenants, the giving of the law, the worship, and the promises; ⁵to them belong the patriarchs, and from them, according to the flesh, comes the Messiah, who is over all, God blessed forever. Amen.

Theological Perspective

Today's lectionary text introduces Paul's theological and existential struggle in Romans 9–11 with the apparent failure of most Jews to accept Jesus as the Christ. Contrary to popular belief, the overriding concern of Romans 9–11 is not *anthropo*logy, that is, which humans (Gk. *anthrōpoi*) get saved and which humans are damned. No. The theme is *theology*. Paul's message is about God, in particular, the steadfast mercy of God.

Many commentators throughout history, especially those in the Reformed tradition, have used sections from Romans 9–11 as evidence for double predestination, invoking Romans 9:19–21, in particular. Calvin himself cites Romans 9–11 in his defense of double predestination.[1] Misreadings of Romans 9–11 have also spurred a good deal of anti-Semitism, with many ancient and modern Christians taking a kind of perverse delight in the idea of God rejecting the Jews. Paul's attitude is the exact opposite. He anguishes over the perplexing failure of his fellow Jews to accept the reconciliation with God offered through Christ.

In a parallel manner, many modern Christians seem to find schadenfreude over the destruction of

Pastoral Perspective

It is a rare congregation that gathers on Sunday morning without someone bearing a broken heart. Life is full of heartbreak, big and small, from daily disappointments to life-altering destruction. People are touched by death, divorce, conflict, job loss, financial woes, wayward children, elderly parents, illness, and aging. Undoubtedly, there are some who might want to respond to the customary "How are you?" with Paul's words: "I have great sorrow and unceasing anguish in my heart" (v. 2). However, the norms of polite behavior, governing even (especially?) our worship services, dictate that people keep silent about their deepest distress.

Paul will have none of that. In a letter that might have been read in a Roman worship service, he speaks of his own despair. After some of the most inspiring testimony in all of Christian Scripture (chap. 8), he seems to break down, fall apart, with grief over the failings of his own people to receive God's gift of the gospel. He is so distressed that he is willing even to surrender his own relationship with Christ, if only the Israelites could see what they have. These are members of the family who have excused themselves from the dinner table, and he will give up the most precious thing he has in order to get them back.

In congregations with any history of conflict, especially if it is recent, this ancient grief will be

---

1. John Calvin, *Institutes of the Christian Religion*, 3.22.4–6, ed. John T. McNeill, trans. Ford Lewis Battles, Library of Christian Classics (Philadelphia: Westminster Press, 1960).

Exegetical Perspective

With Romans 9:1–5, the reader embarks upon one of the most exegetically confounding passages in all of Paul's writings. In the past, the consensus has viewed chapters 9–11 as essentially a digression, an afterthought to a theological crescendo that peaks in chapter 8. More recently, however, some have taken these infamous chapters to be not only integral to Paul's prior discussion, but culminating. There are exegetical reasons for assuming a deliberate connection on Paul's part, but perhaps the most important indication of the continuity between chapters 8 and 9 is nothing less than Paul's raw emotion. His sentiments beginning in 9:1 are merely the opposite side of the same coin that has led him to a rousing, almost poetic celebration of God's love at the end of the previous chapter.

Emotion, then, is the hallmark of today's reading; the nuances of Paul's argument concerning the status of Israel are saved for the verses that follow. Paul's words here come from the heart, where he is experiencing an unshakable anguish due to Israel's waywardness. His emphatic tone, expressed in a series of doublets, reverberates as if in an echo chamber. Compounded grief leads to compounded statements.

I Am Speaking the Truth; I Am Not Lying (v. 1). Typical of his forceful style (2 Cor. 11:21; Gal. 1:20;

Homiletical Perspective

Paul opens the ninth chapter of Romans with his own intensely personal lament. In these verses, he expresses unfathomable grief and sorrow that his own people have not come to faith in Jesus Christ. Paul's lament echoes through the centuries into our present age and congregations. What might we say to Paul and to those in our midst who grieve for those who do not follow Christ?

In order to put Paul's depth of feeling in context, we must reflect back upon Paul's journey of Christian discipleship. On the road to Damascus from Jerusalem, Saul of Tarsus dramatically encountered the living Christ. Because of his personal meeting with the risen Christ, Saul's life changed forever. Only such a profound experience could possibly explain his dramatic transformation from the zealot, holding the cloaks of Stephen's murderers, to the passionate missionary for Christ. Paul has spent his life traveling the Roman Empire, teaching and preaching the good news of Christ, primarily to the Gentiles but also to his own family. The constant grace, love, and mercy he experienced in his life with Christ enabled and empowered his life's work, even in the face of beatings, harsh imprisonment, and church conflict.

Paul's passionate faith pours through the words directly preceding this particular lection: "Who will

Theological Perspective

people with different beliefs and ways of life. One example is the success of the hyperviolent *Left Behind* series, with its nearly pornographic delight over the destruction of those who are left behind. In contrast, Paul is absolutely devastated over the idea that his fellow Jews might be rejecting the gift of "justification leading to eternal life through Jesus Christ our Lord" (5:21). Having experienced the "rescue from the body of death" (7:24) and the joy of life in Christ, he now experiences "sorrow and unceasing anguish" (9:2) over the people of Israel.

In contrast to all those Christians, both ancient and modern, who take a kind of self-righteous pleasure in the idea of the destruction of the outsider, the foreigner or the nonbeliever, Paul is willing once again to be "accursed and cut off from Christ for the sake" (9:3) of his fellow Israelites who are "stumbling over the stumbling stone"—that is the free gift of grace in Christ (9:32). In this sense Paul is like the Christ he worships, willing to take the punishment upon himself so that others might be saved.

Romans 9–11, which is introduced in this week's lectionary text, should be read and must be read as a continuation of what immediately proceeds it, namely, Paul's stirring proclamation regarding the invincible power of God's love. Romans 9–11, far from introducing the notion of exclusivity and rejection, is in fact a continuation of the previous chapter, where Paul announces, "For I am convinced that neither death, nor life, nor angels, nor rulers, nor things present, nor things to come, nor powers, nor height, nor depth, nor anything else in all creation, will be able to separate us from the love of God in Christ Jesus our Lord" (8:38–39).

As Karl Barth notes, "Paul, therefore (as a true Israelite) cannot lament over Israel without rejoicing . . . for Israel's sake—in the steadfastness and faithfulness of Israel's God."[2] Furthermore, it should be noted that Paul is not struggling here with the fate of individuals but with the fate of entire peoples.

Romans 9–11 is an assurance that God can fulfill God's covenant with humanity despite human unfaithfulness. It is about expansion, not exclusion. "The passage is therefore about the enlargement of God's mercy to include Gentiles, not about the narrow and predetermined fate of each individual."[3] The entire thrust of chapter 9 is an expansion of the covenant, from Jewish believers to Gentile nonbelievers. A microcosm of this message is found in

Pastoral Perspective

immediately understandable. When close friends and even family members have left a church or a denomination, or given up on faith altogether, those who remain will miss and mourn them. For these, it is essential that this brief pericope of the lectionary be read in the larger context of God's sovereign love. Even when the faithful separate themselves from one another, nothing can separate any of us from the unfailing love of God (Rom. 8:38–39), not even, apparently, our own foolish rejection of that love.

Ours is a self-help culture, though, and it is easy to believe that fixing things is all up to us. Paul himself appears to fall into this trap, offering up his own soul to be cursed in exchange for the enlightenment of his fellow Jews, as though God would be persuaded by such a swap. For some in our churches, this holy hubris will play out as a conviction that the problems of the church can be cured by better preaching, stronger outreach, more fervent prayer, increased giving, or (God help us!) new carpet in the sanctuary. Others, equally self-centered, will despair that anything can be done and, instead of staying around to turn off the lights, will quietly slip out the back door. For type A church members, a reminder that God is in charge—that the fate of Christianity does not rest entirely on their shoulders—can be a strong pastoral message. For the disillusioned, the same reassurance of the reach of God's power can help to restore hope.

We also encounter a kind of division among the faithful that is not limited to the church but spills over into the social and political arenas. Conservative/evangelical Christians bemoan the lack of attention to the basics of Scripture, while progressive/liberal Christians bristle at being considered less than faithful or being lumped together with the evangelicals.

Unlike Paul, though, we have for the most part tended to write each other off, ignoring the gracious fact of God's irrevocable gifts and calling (Rom. 11:29), which extends beyond our own specific circles. We might do better to feel some of the sorrow of the apostle at the divisions we have created among ourselves. Paul has not had an easy time of it (2 Cor. 11:24–28), and part of that stems from his anxiety for all the churches (2 Cor. 11:28). How many of us could say the same, either from the pulpit or the pew?

While we may not look on the state of Christianity today with the same acuteness of grief that Paul felt, still we have our own *lypē* and *odynē* (v. 2), words translated as "sorrow" and "unceasing anguish," both with a meaning something like

---

2. Karl Barth, *Church Dogmatics*, II/2 (Edinburgh: T.&T. Clark, 1942), 214.
3. Paul J. Achtemeier, *Romans* (Louisville, KY: Westminster/John Knox Press, 1985), 165. Quote at end of commentary is from p. 154.

Exegetical Perspective

1 Tim. 2:7), Paul on occasion trumpets his own truthfulness explicitly. That his own "conscience" corroborates his conviction need not signal a complex Pauline Stoicism. Josephus can also speak of the "conscience" as a witness (*Ant.* 4.286), and it is to this popular notion that Paul adds his own Christian overlay. His declarations are "in Christ," and the testimony of his conscience is "in the Holy Spirit."

Great Sorrow; Unceasing Anguish (v. 2). Paul's use of two seemingly redundant phrases expressing the profound grief "in his heart" is intentional. In Isaiah 35:10 (cf. 51:11) the LXX uses two words in succession to translate the single Hebrew word for "sorrow" (*yagon*). Paul cites the same two words here, implying that his distress has deep roots in Israel's history.

Accursed; Cut Off from Christ (v. 3). The gravity of Paul's tone is nowhere more evident than in his willingness to have Israel's guilt rest upon his own shoulders. In the entirety of the Pauline corpus, it is only here that he dares apply the term "accursed" (*anathema*) to himself. Doing so evokes the horrible fate of Jericho (Josh. 6:17), but the rhetorical move is reminiscent of Moses's anguished plea on behalf of the Hebrews who had gone astray at Sinai (Exod. 32:32). Paul is willing to suffer such a fate himself, even going to the extreme of being separated "from Christ," a stark statement against the background of 8:38–39.

The Adoption, the Glory, the Covenants; the Giving of the Law, the Worship, the Promises (v. 4). In this recounting of Israel's role in covenant history, Paul's deep conviction leads him once again to wax eloquent. Though difficult to see in English translation, this series of terms divides neatly into two parallel lists of three, showing intentional structure and balanced composition. Some of these concepts have multiple applications in Paul's thought (cf., e.g., "glory" in 4:20 and 8:18), but here they are all linked specifically to Israel's heritage and should be understood in that context. Using the terms "Israel" and "Israelites" (preferred Jewish self-designations) throughout chapters 9–11 shows that Paul is speaking as an insider (11:1).

Fittingly, the "adoption" and the "giving of the law" (*huiothesia* and *nomothesia*) are ideas replete in the Hebrew Scriptures, even if the specific terms are not. In the case of the "glory" and the "worship" (*doxa* and *latreia*), the implied possessives are key: Paul alludes here to the manifest "glory" of God's presence and the sacrificial "worship" of the temple.

Homiletical Perspective

separate us from the love of Christ? . . . For I am convinced that neither death, nor life . . . nor anything else in all creation will be able to separate us from the love of God in Christ Jesus our Lord" (8:35, 38–39). Paul's words mirror his experience of the living Christ, reflecting the love of God that has nourished and sustained Paul as he has taken the gospel from place to place. God's love also nourishes and sustains us as we have sought to live as Christ's disciples. Who has not turned to Paul's words seeking comfort and hope in the midst of pain and despair?

Then, following this beautiful passage of faith and hope, Paul confesses to the great sorrow of his life that causes unceasing anguish in his heart (9:2): *His own people have not accepted Jesus as the Messiah.* His grief is such that, with Moses of old (Exod. 32:32), Paul wishes that God would curse him and cut him off from the love of Christ, if only his own people could experience the risen Lord as he himself has experienced him—not only on the Damascus road but in the years since.

Perhaps in our day and time we do not grieve for Paul's people. Instead, we mourn for those known to us, those whom we love and care for, who for whatever reasons have not chosen to follow Christ and live as his disciples. Because we experience joy and fulfillment as Christ's followers, we hope and pray that our loved ones will join us on this journey.

As parents of two adolescents, my husband and I daily seek to guide our children in the way of the faith of Christ by example, teaching, and much prayer. We presented them as infants for baptism. In the water and the Word, Christ claimed them as his own beloved son and daughter, adopting them into his family. The promise and the inheritance are theirs. We have involved them in the life of the church. We have encouraged their faith. We profoundly desire that they experience the love of Jesus as we have, and choose a life of discipleship; but we cannot control their choice. They alone must choose. So at times we worry. We know others in the fellowship of believers who grieve for a son or daughter, a parent, a sibling, or a friend who has not chosen to follow Christ.

What might we say to Paul or to those in our church whose hearts are broken and filled with sorrow? Paul provides comfort and hope for us that he seems to miss for himself. He writes that to his people "belong the adoption, the glory, the covenants, the giving of the law, the worship, and the promises" (v. 4). His beloved people are recipients of great treasure, treasure that is valuable because of the one who gives it. It is God who is the adopter. It is from

Romans 9:1-5

Theological Perspective

verses 4–6, where Paul moves from those gifts specific to Israel in verse 4 to the gift that is available to all in verse 5a (Christ) and ends with a kind of doxology to God's omnipotence and omnipresence in verse 5b.

The key to today's lectionary text is 9:6, which is really just a restatement of 8:38–39. Indeed, this verse is the key to Romans 9–11: "It is not as though the word of God had failed." It is important to see the logic of Paul's thinking here. Paul begins with what he knows and then tries to make sense of what is less clear. (This is a useful hermeneutical tool, as well—reading the less clear passages of Scripture in light of those that are more clear.) He does not begin with a belief that some people are damned and some people are saved, and then try to construct a theology upon that presupposition.

Paul's approach, to which the Reformed tradition adheres (Calvin, Karl Barth, Jürgen Moltmann, etc.), is to begin with what we know about God, and use that knowledge as the basis for our understanding of sin, humans, evil, salvation, and so forth. What does Paul know as a certainty? He knows the cross. He knows Christ crucified. He knows that the crucifixion of Christ represents the "love of God in Christ Jesus our Lord" (8:39). What Paul knows without a doubt, what stands as the cornerstone of all other knowledge, is that the one who was crucified, the one "whom God put forward as a sacrifice of atonement" (3:25) in our place, has been raised. He knows that "Christ was raised from the dead by the glory of the Father" (6:4).

In fact, an alternative reading of Romans 9:5 is "to them belong the patriarchs, and of their race, according to the flesh is the Christ *who is God* over all, blessed forever." Paul is sure not only that Christ has been raised from the dead but that, as equal with God the Father (see Phil. 2:6), he gave himself willingly out of absolute love for humanity.

So whatever conclusion Paul reaches regarding the salvation of Israel must begin and end with his absolute assurance of God's steadfast love, as revealed in the cross of Christ. "What is at issue is the surety of God's grace for anyone who trusts him, because what is at issue is nothing less than the reliability of God's word and its ability to bring God's plans to fruition."

KYLE D. FEDLER

Pastoral Perspective

unspeakable pain. Brokenness in the world, in the church, in our own lives, when it is deeply felt, wounds us that way: it breaks our hearts. In an irony of faith, it may be that this is the way we come to know the strange workings of God in our lives.

The rabbis note that God writes the word, the law, on the heart rather than in it (Jer. 31:33). They say this is so that, when the heart breaks, the word falls into it. Absent the heartbreak, the word is never internalized as completely. Maybe this is how we come to know God, when God enters our hearts as fully as we have entered God's, and we share some of the pain of God's love rejected. Because surely God, embodied in the Messiah (v. 5), grieves at our refusal to be part of the blessed community (Matt. 23:37; Luke 13:34).

Just as the preacher who takes this text must be sensitive to the effect of division and loss within the congregation, so also she needs to be aware of her own sorrows related to the church. Every pastor who is honest about it will admit to some failure of ministry. Despite our best efforts, members of our faith community turn away. Even when we give it our all, there are some who will refuse to receive that gift of ourselves. While it will likely not be helpful to be as direct as Paul about how this feels, it is important for the preacher to speak from a position of authenticity, implicitly acknowledging personal disappointment and grief, but doing so in a way that always points to the grace and love of God.

For preacher and parishioner alike, the last words of the pericope are perhaps the most important, when Paul turns from his own despair to proclaim again the power of the Messiah "who is over all, God blessed forever. Amen" (v. 5b). It is that hope that puts our own losses and failures in the right context.

MARTHA C. HIGHSMITH

The final terms in each list, the "covenants" and the "promises" (*diathēkai* and *epangeliai*), are somewhat rare in the plural, but against the background of multiple patriarchs (v. 5) the plural forms easily hold sway over the singulars found in some manuscripts.

The Patriarchs; the Messiah according to the Flesh (v. 5a). Given that all the terms in verse 4 appear in a single relative clause, it is significant that the next two concepts, while linked thematically by the broader concept of genealogy, are divided grammatically. Like the previous list, "the patriarchs" also belong to the Israelites, but Paul stops short of saying the same thing of Christ. The Messiah descends from Israel, but Israel does not own him. It is Christ that does the claiming, and he claims as his own not only Israel but the nations as well (cf. 1:3–5).

Messiah . . . over All; God Be Blessed Forever (v. 5b). The finale of Paul's emotional outpouring is doxological, and in this case the translator has multiple options. Those who prefer to view the entire phrase as referring to Christ ("who is God over all, blessed forever") face a theological problem: the explicit equating of the titles Christ and God would be unique in Paul's writings; given the strongly traditional flavor of the passage, this would be a less than ideal place to break such theological ground. Those who do not see it as referring to Christ ("God who is over all be blessed forever") are forced to grapple with a variety of minor grammatical conundrums. Many translators therefore have opted for a middle ground, a dual statement which links only the first part of the clause with Christ ("who is over all, God be blessed forever") and minimizes both theological and grammatical difficulties.

In this passage, even as Paul wears his grief on his sleeve, it is important to keep in mind the larger message of chapters 9–11. With Israel's rich heritage and celebrated history squarely in view, Paul has faith that "the ransomed of the Lord shall return" (Isa. 35:10; see comments on v. 2 above) and that as Israel regains its covenantal footing, his great sorrow and unceasing anguish will turn to joy and gladness.

JOHN M. VONDERBRUEGGE

God's presence with the people that glory is realized. It is God who establishes the covenant. It is God who gives the law. It is God who is the focus of worship. It is God who is the promise maker and promise keeper. God will not abandon those to whom God has entrusted God's gifts.

It is God who called the patriarchs and matriarchs. It is God who sent the Messiah. It is God who called Saul on the road to Damascus. God alone calls each of us by name. All of this is a result of God's great love for the world, love that finally culminated in the sending of God's only Son. Nothing can separate us from this love. We, along with Paul, must trust the love of God. Finally, Paul must place his people into the hands of God. So must we.

For those in our congregation who worry, who anguish, or who bear great sorrow for those living outside of the community of Christ, we must remind them that God is the source and giver of life. We must place our trust in God and *entrust* to God those for whom we are anxious. What burden do we then bear? What might our role be in sharing God's love for the world? We must seek to live out our calling in Christ. Day by day, week after week, we witness to the life of the one whose love redeems, sustains, and shapes us. In our words and in our actions, we must seek to live as Christ commands, follow his way, and share the love and hope that is in us. Finally, at the end of the day, we must entrust all to God, who so graciously loves and cares for all of us.

MARY BETH ANTON

Matthew 14:13-21

¹³Now when Jesus heard this, he withdrew from there in a boat to a deserted place by himself. But when the crowds heard it, they followed him on foot from the towns. ¹⁴When he went ashore, he saw a great crowd; and he had compassion for them and cured their sick. ¹⁵When it was evening, the disciples came to him and said, "This is a deserted place, and the hour is now late; send the crowds away so that they may go into the villages and buy food for themselves." ¹⁶Jesus said to them, "They need not go away; you give them something to eat." ¹⁷They replied, "We have nothing here but five loaves and two fish." ¹⁸And he said, "Bring them here to me." ¹⁹Then he ordered the crowds to sit down on the grass. Taking the five loaves and the two fish, he looked up to heaven, and blessed and broke the loaves, and gave them to the disciples, and the disciples gave them to the crowds. ²⁰And all ate and were filled; and they took up what was left over of the broken pieces, twelve baskets full. ²¹And those who ate were about five thousand men, besides women and children.

Theological Perspective

On the face of it, it is a miracle to gladden the devil's heart—a trick with bread, an act of spiritual power with endless political potential. All it takes is a hungry crowd, stranded in a lonely, desolate place, fed with food from nowhere by Jesus. The public, at this point in his life, at least, cannot get enough of him, and because of their craving for his words, his touch, and his presence, they find themselves starving in the desert. Faced with their need, he produces a meal for the masses.

Is this not the same man who, only a short time ago, refused to feed himself by similar means when he was famished (Matt. 4:2–4)? Has he finally succumbed to the devil by, in effect, turning stones into bread?

The setting for Matthew's narrative provides the clue to its main theological themes. In Hebrew thought, the wilderness/desert is connected with wandering and uncertainty. It is the place of rebellion against the God who freed Israel from slavery in Egypt (Deut. 9:7). For Matthew's readers, it is also the place of temptation, the testing ground for Jesus at the outset of his public ministry (Matt. 4:1–11).

The desert raises profound questions about the source of human meaning and identity, security and sustenance. Fundamentally it challenges the very idea of God's faithfulness and provision for human life. In Psalm 78—an important text for understanding

Pastoral Perspective

The account of the feeding of five thousand in Matthew 14:13–21 has been an inspiration to Christians in many diverse situations. It occurs immediately after Jesus and the disciples learn of the brutal murder of John the Baptist and after a long day with large and desperate crowds. The disciples understandably were seeking to get away. They were grief stricken. So the disciples—as we would likely do— tell the crowds to go away.

We read, however, that Jesus had compassion, and he invited the multitudes to eat. The disciples were shocked, for they could locate only two fish and five loaves, hardly enough to feed themselves, much less a crowd of thousands. Nevertheless, Jesus instructed them to feed the crowd, and not only did all get enough to eat, but there were also twelve baskets left over. The disciples were in for surprise that evening—as they were often—at the miraculous power of God's love.

This is the only miracle story found in all four Gospels. It obviously was of great importance to the early church. Some suggest it was read regularly when early Christians gathered at the Eucharist. Others suggest that it shows a parallel to God's provision of manna from heaven for the children of Israel. More important than any of these reasons, this account of the feeding of the five thousand was treasured by the

Exegetical Perspective

At first glance, any connection between the feeding of the five thousand and the following two incidents seems an awkward fit: (1) Jesus' visit to Nazareth (13:53–58) and (2) the execution of John the Baptist by Herod Antipas (14:1–12). However, both incidents have something to do with *location*, as does today's reading.

In the first, Jesus comes to his *patris* (13:54), translated by the NSRV as "hometown," but also meaning "homeland." In spite of his wisdom and power, the people are scandalized because Jesus, a carpenter's son, is acting above his social status. So when Jesus claims his actions analogous to a prophet's and the scandal analogous to the rejection of a prophet, he must withdraw to a deserted place (14:13), thus choosing an alternative location to his *patris*.

In today's text, Jesus chooses an alternative location to the brutal world of Herod Antipas. This brutal world is an arm of the Roman Empire, wherein Roman rule is exercised indirectly through governors (Pontius Pilate), client kings (Herod Antipas, though he never had the title "king"), and local elites. Consequently, in the face of these imperial dynamics, a ruler like Herod had to collaborate with Rome or be dismissed. He also had to keep order among his people, or he would be dismissed. Matthew 14:5 says clearly that Herod *wanted* to put John to death, but

Homiletical Perspective

Maybe it was the size of the crowd on hand to see; maybe it was the "wow" factor; maybe it was the importance of the event for the ministry of Jesus. Whatever it was, none of the Gospel writers missed it. This is the only miracle of Jesus included in all four Gospels. There is no sermon in this story, nor is there a parable in words; this is a story filled with activity. Perhaps one of the lessons embedded in this story is that meeting human need has its own lasting impact. Preachers do not always need to elaborate on the facts.

Preachers might also note the size and scale of this story. While many of the biblical scenes of Jesus' ministry could easily be acted out at the local theater with a handful of actors, this scene is too large for a small stage. There are five thousand men plus the women and children. Furthermore, there is action! Consider the verbs ascribed to Jesus. Jesus *saw;* he *had compassion;* he *ordered;* he *took;* he *looked, blessed, broke,* and *gave.* This story is full of activity; yet, for all of its grandeur and activity, it begins with Jesus trying to find time alone.

Jesus retreats, as he often does in Matthew's Gospel. When this feeding miracle is over, he retreats again; however, as Jesus tries to retreat to a deserted place, his followers are literally following behind him. The crowds follow on foot, apparently following

Matthew 14:13‑21

Theological Perspective

Matthew's account—rebellious, unbelieving hearts speak against God, saying, "Can God spread a table in the wilderness?" (Ps. 78:19).

In many ways this miracle is very much in keeping with a recurring theme in Matthew: Jesus' action flows out of compassion (v. 14). Here and elsewhere in the Gospel he sees the people's need—for health, for truth, for nourishment, for peace of mind—and is deeply moved. He has compassion on them because they are "harassed and helpless, like sheep without a shepherd" (Matt. 9:36).

Jesus is gripped by the words of Hosea 6:6, "I desire mercy, not sacrifice," and uses this text on more than one occasion to define and defend his ministry in the face of religious criticism (Matt. 9:13; 12:7). It seems as though his understanding of his entire mission with respect to the coming of God's kingdom is shaped by compassion. Late in the evening, in a place far from fast-food outlets and shopping opportunities, mercy takes the form of bread.

The Scriptures are reserved about the details of the miracle itself. How does it happen? What is there to see? We are told only that at first there is little food—the five loaves and two fish that are all the disciples have to offer—and then there is an abundance, enough to satisfy everyone, with plenty to spare.

In Pasolini's great film *The Gospel according to St. Matthew*, the incident has a joyful quality—almost as explosive and unexpected as his depiction of the resurrection itself. Jesus prays over the disciples' meager supplies, and suddenly, without warning or explanation, there are baskets full of food.

The crucial details in Matthew's account have nothing to do with the mechanics of the miracle—about which we know nothing—and everything to do with the prayer of Jesus.

Jesus looks up to heaven (v. 19). This is a physical statement of faith and humility. Heaven is the dwelling place of God, "the Most High" (Luke 1:32, 35; 6:35), "the Father," the source of life and all goodness. In looking up to heaven, Jesus is hallowing God's name—honoring it, giving it first place—just as he has taught his disciples to do (Matt. 6:9).

The first temptation that Jesus faced in the wilderness was to declare independence from God, to assert his autonomy. In the Scriptures this is the central sin, the primary act of rebellion, and Jesus refuses to participate in it. He insists that we are utterly dependent on God: "One does not live by bread alone, but by every word that comes from the mouth of God" (Matt. 4:4; Deut. 8:3). Human existence rests on the word of God.

Pastoral Perspective

early church because it taught Christians the very heart of the gospel message and was a deep source of hope and inspiration for Christians who were seeking to be faithful against great odds.

In so many parts of the world we see the resurrection power of the story of the loaves and fishes coming alive in our midst today. It is a story of great power because it demonstrates that God is love, teaches what it means to follow Christ, and assures us of God's power for good in the world.

First and foremost, this story teaches us that God is love. The key reality is that Jesus had compassion. In spite of incredible pressures to the contrary, compassion for people was his prime motivation. It is not compassion in the abstract. It is a compassion that cares deeply about the most basic needs of all of us. In this event, it was concern that there be food for the hungry. This story confirms what so many in Latin America have helped us see as Jesus' basic orientation, that of an "option for the poor." God, who is the ultimate power of the universe, intends peace in the world, an end to hunger, the well-being of families, and spiritual wholeness for all people.

The second lesson we learn from this account is about being disciples—about the awesome responsibility that God has entrusted to us. Jesus did not feed five thousand. He told the disciples to do it. God has entrusted us to be the body of Christ—the hands and feet through which God's work is done in the world. God does not work alone, but through people, you and me. To follow Jesus is to express our faith in concrete acts of love, justice, and compassion toward others. It is no accident that Matthew tells us that we will meet Jesus in reaching out to the "least" of our brothers and sisters—the hungry, the thirsty, the imprisoned.

Third, this Gospel story reminds us that when we need it most, God will give us the power to work for good in the world, a reality many of us have discovered when faced with situations we were not sure we could manage. When Jesus told the disciples to feed the five thousand, the disciples thought it was impossible. The needs were so great, and the resources were so few. Have not we felt the same? However, when the disciples worked together and followed Jesus, they had more than enough.

This is not the only time that disciples have discovered the power of the Holy Spirit to do great things when Christians join together in unity and faithfulness to God's good purposes for the world. The promise of the story of the feeding of the five thousand is that if we join together in unity and

he feared the crowd and had to maintain order. Thus, when Salome asked for the head of John the Baptist on a platter (14:8), she had him in a bind, because the execution could cause uproar, disrupting the order he was to maintain.

Thus, when Jesus goes to a deserted location, he is choosing an alternative to the tentacles of Rome. Crowds follow him, choosing the same alternative (14:13). They forsake their towns, which are caught up in (1) domination by the status quo, and (2) domination by the empire through local collaborators. However, caution is in order. John the Baptist also chose a deserted location as an alternative to the tentacles of Rome represented by Herod. As was the case with John, Jesus' choice of an alternative will ultimately cause him to clash with Rome (Matt. 21–27).

Jesus offers the crowds an alternative world where compassion overturns status and stands in stark contrast to imperial brutality. While the Herodian imperial banquet results in the killing of a local prophet, Jesus of Nazareth attends to the daily life and needs of the crowds and feeds them. Matthew describes Jesus' alternative with sheer brevity: he served the weak (v. 14). Although the translation in the NRSV says that he cured the sick, the translation refers also to serving those who are of lower social status, like the son of a carpenter, and this should not be overlooked.

This alternative world, however, runs into a major problem. There is nothing to eat. The disciples come to Jesus and propose a return to the other world, where there is food, saying, "Send the crowds away." Jesus responds with an imperative to the disciples: "Give them something to eat." There is no need for them to go away if the disciples give them something to eat.

This presents another social reality of ancient Palestine. In the exchange of goods, the larger society presumed patron/client relationships, which involved unequal reciprocity between the elite patrons and the peasant clients. For example, in times of hunger, clients would appeal to patrons for food. In return, clients worked for or supported their patrons. In the alternative location of a deserted place there is no possibility of this kind of unequal reciprocity. Jesus asks his disciples to distribute food regardless of social status or reciprocity. The motivation for the relationship here is need and compassion.

Furthermore, Rome considered itself to be the world's bread basket. A coin minted under Nero had the emperor's image on one side and on the other side Ceres, the goddess of agriculture, with words meaning "the annual harvest of the emperor." This

longer and farther than they expected, because when mealtime comes, they discover that no one has packed a sandwich. What kind of person forgets to bring food on a trip that might last past mealtime?

Perhaps there is some hunger of the soul that causes people to continue to pursue Jesus even after their stomachs start growling. The disciples become concerned about the late hour and the need for the crowd to go buy food, but there is no mention of the crowd's grumbling about a physical hunger. It seems that they are satisfied to continue following the one who represents for them a different kind of fullness.

The disciples may be genuinely concerned with dinner, but "send the crowds away" (v. 15) makes it sound as if they are not concerned enough to get terribly involved. There is an ongoing tension here: big crowds of unmet needs tend to overwhelm our sense of agency. If there had been six people following Jesus when it came time to eat, then a disciple might have thought there was something he could do, but a whole crowd of unmet need is overwhelming. "Send the crowds away" may be a way of confessing powerlessness in the face of large-scale need, as well as getting the obvious need out of sight.

Jesus' response is a call to action. "They need not go away; you give them something to eat," he says (v. 16). The disciples are responsible for feeding the hungry, even if the size of the task is daunting to them. Too often, they want unmet need to go away, while their Lord responds by drawing nearer to it.

Most Bibles give a heading to this story that reads something like "Jesus Feeds Five Thousand." Actually, Jesus gives food only to the disciples, who then feed the others. While it is clearly the miracle of Jesus that feeds the multitude, this does not reduce the call to discipleship to a call of passive piety. Our call is to active ministry that meets human need. Jesus feeds the Twelve; the Twelve feed the five thousand.

For the preacher, this raises an obvious question: "In what ways have we been given blessed nourishment and failed to pass it along to people in need?" At first the disciples in this story do not respond to Jesus' command to give the crowd something to eat, but after the miracle they do give away what has been given to them.

There is another possible reason why the disciples may have been reluctant to act: they clearly thought that what they had was not enough. When Jesus ordered them to feed the crowd, they replied, "We have *nothing* here but five loaves and two fish" (v. 17, emphasis added). While it is true that what they had was meager, they described it as nothing. Commonly,

Matthew 14:13-21

Theological Perspective

Jesus blesses the loaves (v. 19). This is not some kind of magic ritual in which Jesus imparts to the bread a quality it did not previously have. The blessing of the loaves is an expression of praise and thanksgiving to God, the ruler of the universe, who "bring[s] forth food from the earth" (Ps. 104:14). It is not so much the bread that is being blessed here, as God, the giver of bread. Jesus is acknowledging that God is the one who provides all that is necessary for human life. His blessing is an expression of trust in God. He has already taught his disciples to pray, "Give us this day our daily bread" (Matt. 6:11), and now he is offering that prayer on behalf of five thousand hungry people.

Jesus recognizes that, while we may not live on bread *alone*, "without bread we cannot live."[1] John Chrysostom, the fourth-century theologian, suggests that one of Jesus' intentions in this miracle is "stopping the mouth of Marcion"[2]—in other words, affirming what Marcion and other superspiritualists deny, namely, the goodness of the material world. If that is so, it should be said that Jesus also intends to affirm what atheistic materialism and vacuous consumerism both deny, namely, the claim of God's word upon us. This is equally a miracle for Marcionites and Marxists and the devotees of mammon.

When manna rained down on the people of Israel in the wilderness, it was said that "mortals ate of the bread of angels" (Ps. 78:25). There is a very real sense in which all bread is the bread of heaven. Jesus bears witness to the fact that "while it is a fruit of the earth, bread really comes down from above as the gift of God alone."[3]

IWAN RUSSELL-JONES

Pastoral Perspective

faithfulness, God will be with us. It is not a promise of the absence of struggle and pain—Jesus even had to go the way of the cross—but a promise that God will be with us and that God's intention for love, peace, and justice in the world will ultimately prevail.

This is a promise that we badly need if we are even to dream about being faithful in carrying out the call of Christ to join Jesus in offering "life in fullness" to a world gripped by the forces of evil, which are driving millions of people and the planet itself into the most desperate of situations. We know that it is a promise the Lord kept with the disciples on that hillside in Galilee and has kept with God's faithful people over the centuries—and will keep with us!

The story of the feeding of the five thousand is very familiar to most Christians, but its message is always new:

—That God loves and cares for every person on earth and that the promise of "life in fullness" extends to every creature and to the creation itself

—That God calls us to be disciples—to be the means through which God's work is done in our world today

—That God promises us in the Holy Spirit that the power of the love of God can break through even in the most unlikely places when we join together as faithful disciples seeking God's good intentions for our world

The events that took place on that hillside in Galilee two thousand years ago were a miracle to the five thousand people assembled that day. However, the deeper message is the miracle of God's love for the six billion people on our planet today and the miracle that we are called to be partners with God in making fullness of life become a reality today for the world that God loves.

CLIFTON KIRKPATRICK

---

1. Augustine, Sermon VI "On the Lord's Prayer," in *Nicene and Post-Nicene Fathers of the Christian Church*, first series, vol. 6 (Grand Rapids: Eerdmans, 1974), 276.
2. John Chrysostom, Homily 49, in *Nicene and Post-Nicene Fathers*, first series, 14 vols. (Peabody, MA: Hendrickson, 1994), 10:305.
3. Dietrich Bonhoeffer, *The Cost of Discipleship* (New York: Touchstone, 1995), 167.

gave the provision of food a theological interpretation in terms of Roman religion: the emperor is Ceres's agent for providing food.

The feeding of the five thousand also has theological meaning. In this context, Jesus proclaims the arrival of God's ruling activity by performing acts that manifest God's ruling activity (see 12:28). When Jesus looks up to heaven and blesses the five loaves and two fish, he is serving the weak on the basis of compassion and this manifests God's ruling activity; his feeding of the hungry on the basis of need without hope of reciprocity manifests God's ruling activity.

Interpretations of this feeding of the five thousand usually emphasize the enormous number of people who are fed. There is another interpretation that is theological. The traditional expectation of God's final rule at the culmination of the ages is that it will be universal and all inclusive. Against this expectation, Jesus' acts of casting out demons, serving the weak, curing the sick, and feeding the hungry seem minuscule; but in the context of Matthew 13, such acts make sense theologically.

In Matthew 13 Jesus makes two kinds of proclamations using parables: one is public proclamation for the crowds (13:2), and the other is private for the disciples (13:36). At the end of the first section of chapter 13 are two parables that have to do with small beginnings. First, God's ruling activity is compared to a mustard seed that grows into a large plant (13:31–32); second, God's ruling activity is described as being like yeast that a woman kneads into a large amount of flour until it all becomes leavened (13:33).

From this perspective, Jesus' alternative world is a deserted place where he serves the weak, asks his disciples to give people food on the basis of need and compassion, and feeds more than five thousand with a small amount of food—five loaves and two fish. This feeding is best characterized as being like a mustard seed that grows and like yeast that leavens. Serving the weak and feeding the hungry on the basis of need and compassion show the way things are when God rules.

JAE WON LEE

sermons on this passage will emphasize how our meagerness, in the hands of Jesus, becomes bounty. This is certainly true. However, Jesus' first command to the disciples was, "You give them something to eat." Jesus transforms our humble offerings into more than we could have dreamed, but it is also true that Jesus is calling upon us to dream bigger. Jesus did not say, "Give me those fish and that bread, and I will feed them." His first call was for the disciples to change their ideas about their own power in the world.

For disciples who think they have "nothing," the possibilities are necessarily small. What might have happened if one of the disciples had "looked up to heaven, and blessed and broke the loaves"? Of course we will not know. The more daunting question is, how many times have we heard our Lord say, "Give them something to eat," and because of our sense of powerlessness turned away? If we think our baskets contain "nothing," when in fact we have a few loaves and fish, then Jesus has "nothing" with which to feed the hungry.

When Jesus does take the five loaves and two fish, he blesses, breaks, and gives in a way that foreshadows the Lord's Supper. While the emphasis has thus far been placed on a social gospel call to action, it is important to note that this story is also tied to holy mystery. The foreshadowing of the Lord's Supper reminds us that Jesus was not just sponsoring dinner. Holy Communion should attend this sermon. This story, along with the rest of the teaching and miracles, is part of the great redemptive drama of God's activity in the world. God is reconciling the world, and the ministry of Jesus is always actively taking part in that grand story.

DOCK HOLLINGSWORTH

1 Kings 19:9-18

⁹At that place he came to a cave, and spent the night there.

Then the word of the LORD came to him, saying, "What are you doing here, Elijah?" ¹⁰He answered, "I have been very zealous for the LORD, the God of hosts; for the Israelites have forsaken your covenant, thrown down your altars, and killed your prophets with the sword. I alone am left, and they are seeking my life, to take it away."

¹¹He said, "Go out and stand on the mountain before the LORD, for the LORD is about to pass by." Now there was a great wind, so strong that it was splitting mountains and breaking rocks in pieces before the LORD, but the LORD was not in the wind; and after the wind an earthquake, but the LORD was not in the earthquake; ¹²and after the earthquake a fire, but the LORD was not in the fire; and after the fire a sound of sheer silence. ¹³When Elijah heard it, he wrapped his face in his mantle and went out and stood at the entrance of the cave. Then

Theological Perspective

Verses 9–18 of this nineteenth chapter of 1 Kings can best be understood in the larger context of Elijah's prophetic ministry and calling at the moment of the story. In the previous chapter, Elijah seemed a different person. He commandingly ordered the people of Israel around. He called upon the Lord to accept a sacrifice dramatically. He challenged the prophets of Baal to prove the existence of their god. After their failure, Elijah had Baal's prophets killed.

At the beginning of chapter 19, Queen Jezebel was in a fury because of Elijah's killing of her prophets. She sent Elijah a message that she would retaliate and kill him. In terror, Elijah ran from Jezreel to Beer-sheba (about one hundred miles) and then fled farther into the desert. He lay down and prayed for death, stating that he was no "better than [his] ancestors" (v. 4). A messenger of God came to him, telling him to eat and drink; strengthened, Elijah was led to Horeb, to Mount Sinai. This location is significant, as the place where Moses communed with God. The verses of today's reading begin here.

When Elijah came to Horeb, he went into a cave. God questioned him: "What are you doing here, Elijah?" (v. 9). Elijah responded that he had been zealous as God's prophet, but that he was the last one, all others having been killed. "I alone am left, and they are seeking my life, to take it away" (v. 10b). While

Pastoral Perspective

The book of Kings was surely a *Babylonian Times* bestseller, placed in the Historic Action section of the local scrollstores. The book is filled with the scoop of recently known leaders. While the stories seem fantastic to today's reader, 2,500 years ago listeners sat glued to their seats as their recent history was told and explained.

The book retells the history of Israel's demise to an audience of scattered, exiled, humiliated Jews. How did that happen to a nation that once occupied such a bright spot on the world map? There are lessons to learn from the events that led up to their destruction. Past leaders are largely blamed. The sordid stories of those corrupt political and religious leaders (with a smattering of good ones) remind listeners to question authority. As rumors of a return to Israel grow, the historical lessons from the book of Kings are clear:

—Center your life on the covenant established with God, not on blind obedience to a political or religious leader.

—Your God does not reflect a consumerist image, flashy though it may be, but is rather a moving force of justice love.

—God's still small voice is very much alive and moving through those attentive and courageous enough to follow, despite the overwhelming odds against the movement.

there came a voice to him that said, "What are you doing here, Elijah?" [14]He answered, "I have been very zealous for the LORD, the God of hosts; for the Israelites have forsaken your covenant, thrown down your altars, and killed your prophets with the sword. I alone am left, and they are seeking my life, to take it away." [15]Then the LORD said to him, "Go, return on your way to the wilderness of Damascus; when you arrive, you shall anoint Hazael as king over Aram. [16]Also you shall anoint Jehu son of Nimshi as king over Israel; and you shall anoint Elisha son of Shaphat of Abel-meholah as prophet in your place. [17]Whoever escapes from the sword of Hazael, Jehu shall kill; and whoever escapes from the sword of Jehu, Elisha shall kill. [18]Yet I will leave seven thousand in Israel, all the knees that have not bowed to Baal, and every mouth that has not kissed him."

Exegetical Perspective

Literary-Historical Context. This pericope is part of the historical narrative extending from Joshua to 2 Kings, written as a sequel to Deuteronomy sometime after the beginning of the exile. This history compares the existence of Israel in two different sociopolitical forms—tribal league and monarchy—in changing circumstances. The narrative critiques the successes and failures of both, in light of the Deuteronomic criterion of covenant fidelity.

The sections concerning the tribal league (Deuteronomy–Judges) and the monarchy (1 Samuel–2 Kings) have a similar structure: (1) Each begins with an extensive account of how Israel came to exist in that form, featuring the particular prophetic leader and the particular political leader who were mainly responsible. (2) Then follows a relatively brief account of the political leaders who followed in succession, with each evaluated—often explicitly but sometimes implicitly—in terms of how well they fit the definitive pattern.

Thus in Deuteronomy and Joshua we have narrative portraits of Moses the prophet and Joshua the prototypical judge, who defined the pattern of Israel's existence as a tribal league. Then in Judges comes a brief account of each judge who followed Joshua. In 1 and 2 Samuel we have narrative portraits of Samuel the prophet and David the prototypical king (drawn

Homiletical Perspective

At the beginning of the nineteenth chapter in 1 Kings, Jezebel sends a messenger to Elijah telling him that she intends to kill him that very day, just as he killed all the prophets of Baal at Mount Carmel. Understandably, such news frightens Elijah, and he sets out on a journey "to save his life."

By the time he gets to Beer-sheba, however, his lust for life seems to have faded and almost completely disappeared. Leaving his servant behind, he journeys for a day into the wilderness, finally collapsing beneath a desert shrub. There he prays that God will take his life, since he feels as worthless as his ancestors. He is dejected and despondent, fearful that his life is not worth saving. God responds to his plea by sending an angelic messenger who feeds and cares for him and then sets him out on the long road to Mount Horeb, where he will experience his theophany.

In dealing with what follows, the preacher may follow a couple of approaches both worthy of exploration. One may focus on the story of Elijah and how this incident fits into the narrative of his life and ministry. Despite his fear and self-denigration, Elijah is actually at the pinnacle of his prophetic career, a status that is clearly reflected by the numerous parallels between this account and the story of Moses and his divine revelation on Mount Sinai.

1 Kings 19:9-18

Theological Perspective

this statement does not exactly match the way the story was told in the last chapter, it explains much about the prophet's state of mind. The interaction between human thought, action, and limitation on the one hand, and God's direction on the other can become a place for theological reflection and development. In Elijah's story, the self-reflection on his ministry's success or failure holds significance for the community on many levels. The next verses bring the process of theological reflection to the forefront.

God instructed Elijah, "Go out and stand on the mountain before the LORD, for the LORD is about to pass by" (v. 11a). As Elijah had called upon God to demonstrate power before the Baal prophets, he was now witness to that power in a new way. An earthquake and a fire did not contain God. But after the fire, "a sound of sheer silence" (v. 12b) caused Elijah to hide his face in awareness of God's presence.

This self-revelation of God in the sound of silence is in sharp contrast to the movie-produced images of, say, God delivering the Ten Commandments. One author discusses the significance of this "silent" revelation, comparing Elijah's experience to that of Moses receiving the Ten Commandments: "While 1 Kings 19:11–13 contains the Bible's strongest statement of this model of revelation, intimation of similar ideas appear in other biblical passages. . . . How much of the Ten Commandments did the nation [of Israel] hear? They heard no words, just as they saw no form. . . . The revelation was no more and no less than a signification of divine communication, an intimation of something beyond words and shapes, a trace that discloses a real and commanding presence."[1]

As Elijah had returned to Sinai, the site of God's revelation to Israel, so he experienced as profound a sound of silence as did the Israelites. In both cases, God intended to craft the community of believers in the covenant. In Elijah's case, though, his prophetic ministry was tied to calling the people back to the original covenant. The moments on the mountain and the sounds of silence with God's revealing of self were intended to rejuvenate Elijah, but for the greater purpose of the community.

In verse 9, God had asked Elijah, "What are you doing here?" After Elijah heard God in the silence, the question was repeated: "Then there came a voice to him that said, 'What are you doing here, Elijah?'" (v. 13b). Elijah answered with the same words he had earlier: "I have been very zealous for the LORD, the

1. Benjamin D. Sommer, "Revelation at Sinai in the Hebrew Bible and in Jewish Theology," *The Journal of Religion* 79, no. 3 (July 1999): 444–45.

Pastoral Perspective

—God has not abandoned you, despite your current tragic situation.
—God will ultimately prevail.
These are timely and practical lessons for many exiles scattered throughout the world today.

It is in this context that we meet Elijah, defender of God and the covenant, enemy of corrupt leaders of his own community and other nations who have abandoned the one true God. Saying Elijah's name back then might have been like telling stories of Che Guevara or Fidel Castro in a sermon today. Considered murderers and terrorists by the rich and powerful, these are real folk heroes, almost saints, to many of today's exiled and abandoned poor throughout Latin America.

While neither Che nor Fidel claimed to be a prophet of God, the revolutionary project they promoted—envisioning a world where widows, orphans, and strangers were protected against the cruel demands of a market economy gone wild—resonates with many who understand the divine connection. Elijah's picture certainly hung on the walls of many of the original hearers of today's text, much as pictures of Jesus and Che hang in the living rooms of today's shantytowns throughout Latin America, giving hope that God's justice will ultimately prevail.

Through stories of heroes we learn important lessons about God and ourselves. Elijah's courage to slay the 450 prophets of Baal made him legendary. However, most of us identify more with his panic attack, after Queen Jezebel pronounced his death sentence for killing her prophets. His moment of glory ended as abruptly as it began.

Elijah fled. We flee as well. For many, this text will be used in the summer months when those with resources flee to vacation spots or at least a local park, to escape from the frantic pace at which we live. There, in our caves, we anxiously await a word from God. This may take a while. Like Elijah, we may feel exhausted, alone, self-righteous, and under attack, as we look for new signs of God's presence and direction.

God's rather insensitive first remark to Elijah, "What are you doing here, Elijah?" is akin to a long-absent parishioner getting the plastic "we have missed you" phone call. "What do you mean, 'We have missed you'? Do you not know the hell that I have been going through? Where have *you* been?!"

Most of us can relate to Elijah's whiny, self-righteous tirade. When we have served on too many committees, been the lone prophetic voice while

Exegetical Perspective

in contrast with the dysfunctional king Saul), who defined the pattern of Israel's existence as a monarchy. Then in 1 and 2 Kings comes a brief account of each king who followed David.

The main complication in the narrative of the monarchy is the rise and fall of the northern kingdom. This is presented as a development that was tragically flawed from the outset. On the one hand, it began as a legitimate response to the Davidic dynasty's abuse of power (1 Kgs. 12:1–19). On the other hand, it was ideologically based on a form of Yahwism contrary to the covenant's prohibition of idolatrous images—the golden bulls that King Jeroboam installed in the royal sanctuaries at Dan and Bethel (1 Kgs. 12:26–30). Because this "sin of Jeroboam" was continued by every king, the northern kingdom could finally come to no good, despite the occasionally heroic episodes in its history.

To portray the emergence of the northern kingdom from this ambivalent perspective, the narrative of its origins (1 Kgs. 12–2 Kgs. 13) ironically mimics the origins of the tribal league and the Davidic monarchy. Instead of a single great prophetic advocate like Moses or Samuel, there are two prophets—Elijah and Elisha—who are more often adversaries. Instead of a single effective political leader like Joshua or David, there are several kings—Jeroboam, Baasha, Zimri, and Omri—who unsuccessfully attempt to found lasting dynasties. Elijah is a heroic example of fidelity to the covenant, but he is caught up in the botched attempts to establish the northern kingdom.

Anti-Theophany and Ambiguity. Because of Elijah's opposition to Queen Jezebel's attempts to establish the worship of Baal in Israel (1 Kgs. 18:1–19:3), he has been placed on her most-wanted list. To evade capture he flees south and takes refuge in a cave at Mount Horeb (1 Kgs. 19:4–9a). There he has an encounter with YHWH (1 Kgs. 19:9b–18): (1) The "word of YHWH" asks why he has come and, after he explains, advises him to await a direct manifestation of YHWH's presence on the mountain. (2) Elijah goes out and witnesses dramatic demonstrations of wind, earthquake, and fire—conventional elements of theophanies (Judg. 5:4–5; Pss. 18:7–15; 68:7–8; Hab. 3:1–15)—but YHWH is not present in any of them.

All that is left is *qwl dmmh dqh,* a difficult phrase that NRSV translates "a sound of sheer silence" but in this context is perhaps better rendered "a softly whispering voice" (cf. other recent translations). (3) Elijah goes back to the cave, where this same voice (*qwl*) again asks him why he has come, and he

Homiletical Perspective

Despite these evident signs of divine favor, Elijah continues to feel worthless, dejected, and fearful. Even after he has encountered the presence of God in "the sound of sheer silence" (v. 12), when God asks him for the second time what he is doing there, Elijah answers with the same complaint and explanation that he gave before his moment of revelation. In response to this spirit of fear and reticence, the Lord in effect relieves Elijah of his prophetic ministry, commanding him to appoint and anoint others to carry out the divine plan.

On one level, this dramatic exchange invites us to explore the relationship between awe and fear. Elijah remains shackled by his fear, instead of being moved by the awe of God's revelation. His encounter with the unveiled power of God is bracketed by the same question, "What are you doing here?" Nevertheless, his experience of the powerful presence of Almighty God does not move or change him; his heart remains anchored in feelings of desolation and self-denigration.

An experience of the power and presence of God, however mundane or majestic, is designed to inspire transformation and growth. God reveals God's self in order to foster new understanding and self-awareness. Awe may provoke a feeling of holy terror in us, but ironically it should release us from our fears, not reinforce them. To be struck by awe is to find that one's perception of reality has been swept away, creating an opportunity to rethink both self and reality, inviting and embracing transformation.

Alternatively, the preacher may decide to focus on the theophany itself. Many preachers have chosen to contrast the great wind, earthquake, and fire with the deafening sound of sheer silence. Here is an ideal opportunity to remind the congregation of the importance of creating prayerful times and spaces filled with silence, set apart from the din and confusion of the earthquakes of our lives.

From a related perspective, this passage addresses the enormous influence that our expectations have on our ability to discern and experience divine activity. Elijah's experience calls us to be sensitive to the power of our confining projections, our well-entrenched notions of how God's presence is made manifest in the convoluted patterns of our everyday lives.

I have been a birdwatcher for a number of years; so my attention is trained to focus on birds as they fly into my field of vision. Part of my brain has been shaped over the years to pay attention to birds, so that I notice their presence, even if I am not consciously searching for them. What often amazes me is

1 Kings 19:9-18

Theological Perspective

God of hosts; for the Israelites have forsaken your covenant, thrown down your altars, and killed your prophets with the sword. I alone am left, and they are seeking my life, to take it away" (v. 14). Some commentators find this repetition questionable on Elijah's part. Since Elijah had demonstrated the impotence of Baal's priests, these complaints seem to make no sense. Some commentators wonder if, ultimately, Elijah is making excuses to avoid his prophetic ministry.

Missed in such comments is the nature of prayer. Prayer is the base of theological reflection, a conversation between finite human beings and an infinite God. Prayer's dialogical nature becomes clear in God's answers to Elijah. Instead of a chastisement, God presented a plan of action to assuage Elijah's deepest fears of Israel's abandonment of the covenant and their desire to kill all prophets.

Elijah was directed by God to make three appointments: two kings and his own prophetic replacement. The three would be anointed by Elijah and together they would kill those Israelites who had broken with their covenant: "Whoever escapes from the sword of Hazeal, Jehu shall kill; and whoever escapes from the sword of Jehu, Elisha shall kill" (v. 17). God's most important statement answered the deepest of Elijah's fears: "Yet I will leave seven thousand in Israel, all the knees that have not bowed to Baal, and every mouth that has not kissed him" (v. 18).

This promise is a continuation of others wherein God vowed to remain with the faithful, some of whom would survive any destruction. The measure for exclusion from the destruction was refusal to worship Baal. For Elijah, knowing that there would be "seven thousand" left was also a message that he was not alone. Prayer's deepest answer might be that we are not alone, whatever the circumstances. It was not magic that demonstrated power over Baal's priests. Instead, God's love revealed a commitment to the covenant that demanded a true response.

STEPHANIE Y. MITCHEM

Pastoral Perspective

others have said nothing, certain we are the only ones who really walk the talk, it is probably best for us to go to a cave. No one wants to see or hear us anyway. As God listens to Elijah vent, we learn that Elijah has lost perspective and needs direction.

The earthquake, wind, and fire are distractions. God is not in any of them. Perhaps this is a way of reminding us that when we are desperate, we are tempted to succumb to any powerful force that may distract us, such as the flashy preacher promising riches or false happiness in some other world beyond. Perhaps the lesson for those first hearing this story was that God was definitely not in the golden temples and flashy idols of the empire's religion, despite the overwhelming power shown in their gaudiness.

Then comes the still small voice (NRSV "sound of sheer silence"), which does not sound very compassionate here but which is very clear. Elijah is not the only one left. There are thousands of others who have not abandoned the covenant. Has the prophet forgotten his grassroots base? Prophets and their followers should never forget that they are part of a community. At this point in the story, our perspective may switch from that of Elijah to that of the seven thousand others—who are, after all, the community of faithful exiles to whom the story is directed.

The still small voice gives Elijah instructions that will be played out in Israel's salvific history. Go, it says, return. Elijah surely felt strangely comforted to receive these detailed instructions. He was on the right path. Life had overwhelmed him and he had temporarily lost perspective. So do we. For many, Sunday worship is the time we gather with others on the same path, practicing Sabbath and listening for the still small voice that reminds us of the project of life we are constructing together.

The most important lesson in this text is the twofold message of hope and challenge. God will prevail, but our knees must not bow to Baal. Defining Baal in our consumerist baalistic culture is very easy. Resisting and not bending has always been the challenge.

DAVID MAXWELL

Exegetical Perspective

again answers in the same way. YHWH then commissions him to anoint Hazael as king of Aram, Jehu as king of Israel, and Elisha as his successor, in order to purge Israel of its Baal worshipers.

Elijah's encounter with YHWH ironically mimics what happens to Moses atop the holy mountain (Exod. 19:16–19). The stormy and fiery manifestation of YHWH's presence is the source of the divine word mediated by Moses to the people (Exod. 20:18–21). Elijah instead finds its source to be the inner voice with which he is already acquainted. The commission given to Elijah similarly mimics the commissions given to Samuel to anoint Saul and David as king of all Israel (1 Sam. 9:15–16; 16:1–3). Samuel is to anoint Israelites who can provide stable leadership and effectively protect the people against foreigners, but Elijah is to anoint a foreigner who will attack Israel and an Israelite who will foment rebellion. This encounter confirms the authenticity of the prophetic revelations given through Elijah, but also locates them within a turbulent historical situation in which the purposes of YHWH are not always readily evident.

The ambiguities of this context are shown by the way in which this prophecy comes true. Elijah himself does not accomplish everything. He immediately designates Elisha as his successor (19:19–21), and after Elijah's death (2 Kgs. 2:1–18) Elisha carries out the other two tasks. He urges Hazael to assassinate the king of Aram and take his place, realizing that this would result in great harm to Israel (2 Kgs. 8:7–15). As the Aramean threat grows, Elisha also instigates the rebellion of Jehu against King Joram, resulting in the bloody massacre of Joram's relatives and all worshipers of Baal (2 Kgs. 10:1–28). YHWH's promise to Elijah is thus fulfilled, but at a cost that even YHWH realizes is dubious (see Hos. 1:4–5).

Conclusion. The prophetic word continued to be authentically spoken and fulfilled during the time of the northern kingdom, but with muddled consequences because of the negative forces set in motion by its overall history of infidelity. Thus even the most heroic attempts to be faithful are subject to the limitations of their historical context. Because such limitations are discerned in retrospect, we are largely unaware of the ways and extent to which they affect our efforts. The only way to deal with them in the present is to learn from the mixed successes and failures of our forebears in faith—like Elijah.

MICHAEL H. FLOYD

Homiletical Perspective

how many people do not see birds, because, of course, they are not looking for them. However, they may see things that I do not see, because their patterns of attention are triggered by other expectations.

How do our expectations of how the Divine will manifest itself in our lives promote or inhibit our ability to perceive it? What have we done through prayer and study to shape those patterns of attention? Do we fail to see God's hand at work in our lives because we believe that God's presence is always made manifest in wind, earthquake, and fire? Have we taken the time and expended the energy to train our vision to be open, receptive, and vigilant, capable of focusing our attention on any flight of the Holy Spirit that happens to appear in our spiritual field of vision? How do our expectations and projections enable us to be open and attentive—or prevent us from being open and attentive—to the awesome presence of a living and loving God?

Despite Elijah's fears and failings, God does not give up on him. Elijah continues to prophesy to the rulers and people of Israel, demonstrating and exercising the power and will of Almighty God. It is heartening and inspiring to see that this favored one of God was so human in his character and career, susceptible to dejection, fear, self-doubt, and insecurity. For those who seek to minister in God's name, whether lay and ordained, Elijah's humanity is both encouraging and comforting, assuring us that God is indeed faithful, even in the face of our fear and depression, our worries and weariness, our blindness to God's revelations and our resistance to growth and change.

WENDEL W. MEYER

Psalm 85:8-13

⁸Let me hear what God the LORD will speak,
   for he will speak peace to his people,
   to his faithful, to those who turn to him in their hearts.
⁹Surely his salvation is at hand for those who fear him,
   that his glory may dwell in our land.

¹⁰Steadfast love and faithfulness will meet;
   righteousness and peace will kiss each other.
¹¹Faithfulness will spring up from the ground,
   and righteousness will look down from the sky.
¹²The LORD will give what is good,
   and our land will yield its increase.
¹³Righteousness will go before him,
   and will make a path for his steps.

Theological Perspective

Commentators suggest that Psalm 85 is a postexilic psalm of thanksgiving for deliverance from oppression. The tone of the psalm, however, takes into full account both thanksgiving and the realities of ongoing challenge, failure, and loss for the people of God. Both praise and lament characterize the first half of the psalm, a juxtaposition that may reflect a postexilic context.

The second half of the psalm is voiced by a single singer, reflecting on these mixed realities and declaring the character and intent of God. It is a voice that understands well the painful circumstances that are surrounding the people of God, yet expresses a stubborn and expectant faith. In this, the single singer is very much like a pastor who takes care to learn the struggles of the community of faith and speaks into those struggles a word of hope.

That single singer begins with an affirmation of God's peace. The Hebrew word *shalom* is so rich and full that a single English equivalent is not sufficient. *Shalom* means wholeness, completeness, fullness, balance, as well as peace in the sense of an absence of hostility or brokenness. A peace like this in our context today means not only that guns and bombs will fall silent, but also that gardens will be planted, houses rebuilt, and schools repaired. "God will speak peace to his people," says the singer in verse 8, a

Pastoral Perspective

The superscription (not printed above) to Psalm 85 reads, "To the leader. Of the Korahites. A Psalm." Thus, Psalm 85 is dedicated to the choir director (see 2 Chr. 20:19). Who could be more deserving of this choral dedication?

Once upon a time, a musically challenged pastor was invited to come to choir rehearsal by the generous choir director of the church she served. "Would you be willing to spend five or ten minutes with the choir each week, sharing with the singers a short synopsis of the biblical text for next Sunday? You and I can speak with them about how the hymns, anthems, and musical responses reinforce the text. We will close by praying together as we prepare to lead worship next Sunday."

The minister's life has never been the same. She had always thought that she appreciated choirs and the enormous contribution they make as leaders of worship. Listening to the hymns and anthems at Thursday rehearsals improved her sermons, as connections between the music and the biblical texts became apparent to her in ways that otherwise they would not have. At choir practice, she saw with her eyes and heard with her ears a visible, audible manifestation of the psalmist's affirmation, "Steadfast love and faithfulness will meet; righteousness and peace will kiss each other" (v. 10).

Exegetical Perspective

Postexilic Disappointments. Numerous commentators suggest that Psalm 85 reflects the circumstances of the Jerusalem community following the return from Babylonian exile in the sixth century BCE. The prophet of the exile, Second Isaiah, imbued the exiles with hope and expectancy. However, upon the return to Jerusalem there ensued a number of disappointments, and the spirit of the restoration community was deflated. One of the tribulations of that postexilic community was a series of disappointing agricultural seasons (Hag, 1:6, 9–11; 2:15–17). Psalm 85 may well be a response to that situation, expressing the sense of a restoration that was incomplete and a fear that perhaps Jerusalem had not in fact served her term and paid her penalty for past transgressions (see Isa. 40:2). So the poet of Psalm 85 pleads that God will "restore us again" (v. 4), "revive us again" (v. 6).

Recollection and Supplication. The words that the psalmist in verses 8–13 hears (spoken probably by a temple prophet) need to be understood against the backdrop of verses 1–7. The recollection of the Lord's favor in verses 1–3 of the psalm remind the Lord (and the community of God's people) that there is a precedent for the Lord to exhibit forgiveness and accomplish restoration. It is not uncommon for psalms of lament to recall past mercies of

Homiletical Perspective

Psalm 85 casts as beautiful a vision of salvation as any we find in the Psalms. The speaker relays God's promise of good and just times to a gathered congregation with powerful allegory and rich language, echoing the prophecy of Isaiah. In one sense, perhaps the preacher's only task is to repeat that vision to today's gathered congregation. After all, what do people seek in a sermon, if not to be told the good news of God's promise to bring about goodness and rightness in their lives and in the world around them?

However, there is more here than tomorrow's promises. This psalm is a prime instance of Hebrew verbs being vague on time and tense. In verse 10, it seems poetically unclear if love and faithfulness have met, are meeting, or will meet. In the next verse, have righteousness and peace kissed, or is it a kiss that we are still anticipating? Alter observes that the psalmist is "either remembering a time in the past when God forgave His people and favored the land as a precedent for the present plight, or he is imagining what he is about to pray for as though it were already an accomplished fact."[1]

Either way, this ambiguity makes this psalm an easy choice for Advent anticipation (living between

1. Robert Alter, *The Book of Psalms: A Translation with Commentary* (New York: W. W. Norton, 2007), 300.

Psalm 85:8-13

Theological Perspective

peace that extends to all places of brokenness, loss, and grief.

The confident affirmations of the singer continue. God's salvation is at hand, declares verse 9. The word for "salvation" in verse 9 has the same root as "righteousness" in verse 10. It is the root *hesed*, a Hebrew word as expansive and comprehensive as *shalom*. *Hesed* is the summative word of all of God's activities and goals, for they are just, right, saving, and healing. This confident declaration that "God's salvation is at hand for those who fear him" is one reason why Psalm 85 is often read out in Advent season. These words of the psalm are echoed in the chorus of angels, when they sing, "On earth peace among those whom God favors" (Luke 2:14).

The singer then identifies the qualities of God that will usher in the completeness of shalom. Verse 10 is a central verse in the psalm, because it gives a concise yet complete statement of God's goals and intentions for the world, a short summary of God's mission. Using poetic and vivid language, the psalmist declares that, "Steadfast love and faithfulness will meet; righteousness and peace will kiss each other."

The second part of Psalm 85, verses 8–13, gives an outline of a vigorous and comprehensive doctrine of God. These verses portray God as mighty in power, just in judgment, and worthy of the highest honor and praise. Verse 10 heightens and intensifies this portrayal of God; the "vintage" attributes of steadfast love (*hesed*), faithfulness (*'emet*), righteousness (*sedeq*), and peace (*shalom*) are combined to give the highest possible depiction of God. In this verse, God's attributes relate to each other in ways that increase their dynamic energy. Not only are these attributes convincingly combined in verse 10, they are also personified, given their own will and activity. "Steadfast love and faithfulness will meet" and "righteousness and peace will kiss each other."

The theological point of this verse is not simply to list important divine attributes but to give expression to their dynamic relationship. Salvation is a dynamic process in which the character of God in all its fullness is at work. Colossians 1:19 confirms this deep instinct of Psalm 85 when it identifies Jesus Christ as the agent of God's fullness of salvation, "For in him all the fullness of God was pleased to dwell." Salvation in all its completeness is the promised result of God's steadfast love, faithfulness, righteousness, and *shalom*.

Continuing the vivid imagery that gives energy and action to central divine characteristics, the

Pastoral Perspective

The most moving times for her are when she watches as the choir director melds the voices of teachers, computer programmers, nurses, secretaries, and carpenters into a unified choral voice calling the people of God back to praise and thanksgiving when things are not going well.

Such was the condition of the people when Psalm 85 was written. "Will you be angry with us forever?" the psalmist pleads in verses 5–6. "Will you prolong your anger to all generations? Will you not revive us again, so that your people may rejoice in you?" When things are not going well, the psalmist/choir director's technique in Psalm 85 is to impress upon the singers and the listeners—that is, the worshipers—that human faith is an echo of God's prior steadfast love and faithfulness; human righteousness and peace is a response to God's righteousness and peace, which is first directed toward them. Thus the psalm is both an expression of God's grace to people standing in need of salvation and a calling forth of a human response that extends the good news of God's salvific grace to others.

In one church that the aforementioned pastor served, a stunning quilt of messages of love, joy, and thanks was pieced together and presented to a retiring choir director. One of the quilt squares had been carefully created by a member of the middle school choir. On the quilt square were these words: "You have brought music into my life. Before you, I was ashamed of my voice."

This young woman was no stranger to steadfast love and faithfulness, to righteousness and peace. She had received the grace of God's love and faithfulness in her baptism and from a loving family who had given her roots and wings. She had received much love, but she was ashamed of her voice. She needed a teacher, someone who could save her from her shame and help her to learn, very specifically, that her voice was a gift from God's own hand to be used for the sake of others. God's grace, mediated through a gifted choir director, proved to be her salvation.

On another occasion, the minister was invited to a choral performance in a lovely basilica. High expectations pulsed within her as she anticipated the glorious music to be performed by the symphony chorus that was being joined that evening by young choristers from several area public schools. She handed her ticket to the usher and took her seat in the beautiful, holy space.

A family was seated in front of her. Later she would say, "Do not ask me about the concert. I heard

the Lord as a preliminary to calling upon the Lord for fresh demonstrations of power, forgiveness, or restoration (e.g., Ps. 22:3–5, 9–10; 77:11–15; 80:8–11). This motif has the dual purpose of motivating God to fresh deeds of pardon and revival and of arousing the worshipers' confidence that their God is indeed willing and able to restore their fortunes, even in the face of the people's iniquity.

Verses 4–7 proceed then to a plea that God will "revive us again" (v. 6). These verses appeal to the Lord's character as "God of our salvation" and remind the Lord of the divine reputation for "steadfast love," which is equated with "salvation" (v. 7). These verses also display at least an implicit acknowledgment that any such forthcoming act of revival and restoration by the Lord will be the act of a merciful God who is justifiably angry.

Two-Sided Relationship. God's steadfast love and faithfulness (v. 10) are qualities characteristic of the bonds of the covenant. Steadfast love (*hesed*) is God's covenant (*berit*) nature; these two Hebrew terms are frequently used synonymously (Deut. 7:9, 12; Ps. 89:28; Isa. 54:10). The covenant, of course, is two-sided: the "peace" that the psalmist anticipates coming from God (v. 8) and the salvation which is "at hand" (v. 9) come to those who in their turn are "faithful" (v. 8; Heb. *hasidim*; NIV "saints") and who "fear [God]" (v. 9).

The psalm makes repeated use of the Hebrew term *shuv* (turn, return, restore). We read of God's "restoring" the fortunes of Jacob, which is celebrated in verse 1 and sought in verse 4, and God's "turning" from anger in verse 3. In verse 8 it is the *people's* "turning" that is at issue. Translators debate the proper translation of the last clause in verse 8. NIV (along with numerous other English versions) renders the clause "but let them not *return* to folly." NRSV, following the Septuagint and seeking a suitable term in apposition to "his faithful," translates "to those who *turn* to [God] in their hearts." The NRSV alternative is more satisfying in a psalm that utilizes poetic parallelism consistently elsewhere. Whichever of these alternative translations one chooses to follow, the resumption of the *shuv* terminology in verse 8 recognizes that God's turning and God's practice of *hesed* must be met by a like response on the part of God's people.

Poetic Figures. The psalmist recruits a host of figurative devices to convey the dynamic of God's salvific work. *Personification* is employed to celebrate God's

"already" and "not yet"), but also promising in Ordinary Time. One homiletical challenge of Ordinary Time is to inspire fellow worshipers with the spirit of the special promise that God grants us in every moment of living (including the ordinary moments), while also gesturing to the path behind us and before us.

So what of these classically psalm-type words: "steadfast love and faithfulness," "righteousness and peace"? While the vision is captivating, the vocabulary is utterly psalm-ish, and the preacher must translate this vision into the language of the gathered worshiping community. What would it look like for all the godly forces in the universe finally to triumph? Would debt disappear? Would teenage grandchildren be safe from harm? Would addiction release its deathly grip, or impossible questions be answered and long-standing problems be solved?

It seems worth naming the longings of the hearts before you, without suggesting that God promises to tie up our long lists of requests with neat bows. While we do not fully grasp what God's arrangement of the kiss of justice and peace will look like—we know it may not be our vision—surely we have tasted that meal, and want more. Unpacking that desire might be a first move.

We should resist picking apart precise definitions for these salvific psalm words (steadfast love, faithfulness, righteousness, peace). Chasing down the Hebrew nuances of these well-worn words is not likely to bear much fruit. Walter Brueggemann suggests instead that we pay attention to the imaginative use of the words and the single theological reality to which they all gesture.[2]

Perhaps the most exceptional aspect of this psalm arrives at the end, in a theological twist. In the last verse, righteousness is making a path for God, setting out footsteps in which God may follow. Since when was God the follower of another leader? One common understanding is that these "leaders" (divine attributes of righteousness, faithfulness, etc.) are like heralds marching ahead of a king or like angelic messengers appearing elsewhere in Scripture. This image works, though it seems more rich and interesting to play with the idea of how God's own forces go before God's own self, and perhaps how this interacts with our Trinitarian understanding God as three persons. The preacher might consider how the playful use of these divine attributes as allegory brings to mind our

---

2. Walter Brueggemann, *The Psalms and the Life of Faith* (Minneapolis: Fortress Press, 1995), 44.

Psalm 85:8-13

Theological Perspective

psalm portrays God's faithfulness as springing up from the ground and God's righteousness as looking down from the sky in verse 11. This is a comprehensive image; all of creation, from ground to sky, is the stage of God's goodness. The final verse 13 extends the imagery even more, as righteousness marches on ahead of God, making a path for God to act.

Christian theology can learn from the dynamism of divine attributes in Psalm 85:8–13. Attribute theology has traditionally attempted to portray the fullness of God's divine self in a long list of descriptors or attributes. The Westminster Confession of Faith of the 1640s lists at least thirty divine attributes, including eternality, wisdom, lovingness, graciousness, holiness, immensity, and perfection. It is a noble list. Other statements of faith have attribute lists as well. The great strength of attribute lists is that they attempt to maximize God's greatness. The possible weakness of attribute lists is that they portray God in abstractions rather than from God's own self-revelation. Theologian Hendrikus Berkhof reminds us that our "experience of God in history" is the better way to begin to think about God.[1]

Divine attributes in Scripture function in a liturgical, historical, and dynamic way, rather than in an abstract way. The Psalms, of course, are filled with expressions of divine attributes in the context of worship and praise. The prophetic writings of the Old Testament confess the attributes of God in the context of covenant faithfulness and righteous judgment. Central divine attributes clearly became part of Israel's liturgical life in hymnic phrases. When the prophet Jonah cried out in frustration to God, "I knew that you are a gracious God and merciful, slow to anger, and abounding in steadfast love" (Jonah 4:2), he voiced, in a moment of striking irony, a hymn of praise that was deep in his bones.

This refrain echoes throughout Scripture (Neh. 9:17; Pss. 103:8; 145:8). Similarly, God's steadfast love (hesed), faithfulness ('emet), righteousness (sedeq), and peace (shalom), so vividly portrayed in Psalm 85, are deep in the bones of the believing community in all its challenges and opportunities today.

LEANNE VAN DYK

Pastoral Perspective

enough of it to know that it was lovely, but that is about all that I can tell you. Ask me about the family." There was a daughter, about ten years old, and a son who was thirteen or fourteen. They talked. They pinched. She kissed him on the cheek. He tugged on her hair ribbon. The father constantly shifted around in his seat and generally made it clear that, all things considered, he would rather have been at home watching the NBA playoffs on TV. The mother really did want to be there. She was as proud as she could be of her daughter, who was a singer in one of the school choirs, and to demonstrate how much she wanted to be there, she stage-whispered "Shhhh . . ." twenty times or more over the course of the evening.

Later that evening, the minister popped off an irate e-mail about people who do not know how to act during concerts to her friend, the director of the symphony chorus. He responded by first acknowledging that there is a trade-off in such matters. Then he continued, "One of the *great* success stories tonight is about those kids who had this actual life-changing experience. . . . Some were singing the excerpts long after the crowd was gone. A parent drove up to me in her pickup truck as I walked to my car in the parking lot. She had her son with her. . . . She was so grateful for this experience, and he was beaming. The kids coming off the risers were on a visible high, and it was caused by the music and the effort they put into getting it as absolutely as right as we could. They do not know about all that yet, but some of them will get it."

Salvation is at hand when children rehearse a musical piece under the baton of a gifted director who inspires them to get it as absolutely right as they can. Salvation is at hand when a minister who is a little too full of herself is gently chastened by a musical friend to see the larger picture of God's grace.

It is to such salvation, both gift and response, that Psalm 85—dedicated to an unnamed choir director—bears witness.

ELIZABETH MCGREGOR SIMMONS

---

1. Hendrikus Berkhof, *Christian Faith: An Introduction to the Study of the Faith*, rev. ed., trans. S. Woudstra (Grand Rapids: Eerdmans, 1986), 122.

Exegetical Perspective

characteristics: God's "steadfast love" and "faithfulness" meet; "righteousness" and "peace" kiss (v. 10). One can imagine an army of God's attendant attributes coming to the care of God's people, joining their powers to foster the salvation of those who revere the Lord. The images of "meeting" and "kissing" convey accord (or, in the case of separation caused by iniquity, reunion). Where there has been separation created by human sinfulness, God's saving work creates wholeness and unity.

Verse 11 utilizes a *merismus* (a figure in which two contrasting or complementary parts of an entity are cited to imply the whole) to convey the sense that God's saving work will encompass all creation: faithfulness will "spring up" (an agricultural term: cf. Gen. 2:5) from the ground, and righteousness looks down from the sky. Verses 11–12 seem to use a *chiastic* construction to exhibit a metaphorical comparison of God's saving work to the life-giving processes of nature: faithfulness from the *ground* and righteousness from the *sky* (v. 11) are echoed by the "good" (possibly the rain[1]) that God "gives" (root *ntn*) from *heaven* and the harvest that the *land* yields or "gives" (root *ntn*) in response. This life-giving movement is God's response to the plea (v. 6) that God should "revive" or "quicken" (ASV) the people.

Second Isaiah called for the preparation of a way (*derek*) for the Lord through the wilderness (Isa. 40:3) as emblematic of the return from exile. The closing verse of Psalm 85 anticipates that this way is about to be made. The restoration that the psalmist anticipates involves God's glory (*kabod*) taking up residence in "our land" (v. 9). According to the prophecy of Ezekiel, God's *kabod* (God's radiant splendor or effulgent presence) departed from the promised land at the time of Jerusalem's destruction (note the stages of the departure in Ezek. 9:3; 10:4, 18–19; 11:22–23), with the return not envisioned until Ezekiel 43:1–5 (cf. also Isa. 40:5; 46:13; 60:1). Our postexilic psalmist would seem to be yet waiting for God's way to be cleared and for the *kabod* to return to "our land."

GEORGE W. RAMSEY

Homiletical Perspective

attraction to superheroes, where goodness or strength are embodied in mythical beings, working for justice.

Of course, through the lens of Christian tradition we cannot help but see this imagery as possible prophecy for the arrival of God's ultimate herald in Jesus Christ. Laying down the flagstones of justice and mercy, of love and righteousness, creating a smooth and right path so that God's own self might trod triumphantly for the world—the possibilities for telling a congregation the good news with this imagery are rich.

Richer still might be the very image of path. Almost any worshiper can find himself or herself within the metaphor of journey, no matter what high or low, what beginning or what end, what clarity or obscurity, or with what swiftness or slowness we find ourselves on the path. The path is not yet complete, and in this psalm not even God sees the entire way. Though this may be a frightening prospect, it can also be freeing. To imagine that God is so linked to us, so locked in step with our lives as to be making the path along with us—some comfort and hope might be found here.

Anne Lamott points at the partially hidden path in describing her struggles with addiction, single parenthood, and the death of her father. The mantra she hears from her Alcoholics Anonymous friends is that "more will be revealed," meaning that she will know what to do when the time comes.

We cannot see the entire path, or how God's grace will intervene and make good from the pain of our lives; but even in our unknowing, God is with us on that path, and when we need to see the bend in the road ahead, the mist will clear enough for our visibility. The same goes for God's promise about the most impossible obstacles in our lives. Whether the issue is the dying parent or the lost job or the frightening teenager or the scary news, Lamott observes that the impossible is much more possible than we think: "It turns out that you've already gone ahead and done it before you realize you couldn't possibly do it, not in a million years."[3]

Such is the nature of God's promise, and of God's salvation: the impossible becoming possible, the path becoming clear.

KATIE GIVENS KIME

---

1. G. Rendsburg, "Hebrew *RHM* = 'Rain,'" *Vetus Testamentum* 33 (1983): 357–62, with reference to M. Dahood's suggestion that Hebrew *tob* may have the meaning "rain" in Ps. 85 and elsewhere.

3. Anne Lamott, *Operating Instructions: A Journal of My Son's First Year* (New York: Anchor Books, 1993), 103.

Romans 10:5-15

[5]Moses writes concerning the righteousness that comes from the law, that "the person who does these things will live by them." [6]But the righteousness that comes from faith says, "Do not say in your heart, 'Who will ascend into heaven?'" (that is, to bring Christ down) [7]"or 'Who will descend into the abyss?'" (that is, to bring Christ up from the dead). [8]But what does it say?

"The word is near you,
  on your lips and in your heart"

(that is, the word of faith that we proclaim); [9]because if you confess with your lips that Jesus is Lord and believe in your heart that God raised him from the

Theological Perspective

Today's lectionary text is in the middle of Paul's extended theological wrestling with the fate of his fellow Jews. (See commentaries in this volume on Rom. 9:1–5 and Rom. 11:1–2a, 29–32.) Paul anguishes over the fact that most Jews continue to seek righteousness through the law rather than through faith in Christ. Therefore, it is not surprising that we should find, here in the middle of Paul's explanation of the salvation of Israel, a treatment of the relationship between Christ and the law.

Romans 10:5–15 is an expansion of Romans 10:4, where Paul states that Christ is the "end of the law." Let us briefly explore what Paul means by looking at several ways in which Christ is the "end of the law" (Gk. *telos nomou*). The word *telos* can mean "termination," but it can also means fulfillment or purpose, as in the first article of the Westminster Shorter Catechism (Question: "What is the chief end of man?" Answer: "To glorify God, and to enjoy him forever."[1]) These are the different ways in which Christ is the end of the law. First, he terminates the law as a means of salvation. Second, Christ is the culmination of the law by doing what we were incapable of doing, reconciling us to God and to one another. Moreover, the

1. *The Book of Confessions* (Louisville, KY: Office of the General Assembly, 1999), 175.

Pastoral Perspective

It is unfortunate, and odd, that evangelism has come to be a kind of dirty word in some churches. People in these churches know it exists, but they are vaguely embarrassed by it. It is somehow not seemly to go around airing one's personal faith to others, especially those who might not share that faith. It is uncomfortable, not the kind of thing one would want to do, not something to talk about in polite company. Evangelism is one of those ideas that has somehow lost its way, at least in some religious circles; it has come to be associated with itinerant preachers, tent revivals, and fundamentalists— expressions of faith and ministry that seem out of place in our modern world, even offensive to some.

This is odd because, in its broadest sense, evangelism is the work of those who are messengers of good news. The word itself has the same roots as "angel." No matter what the times are like, we could all use a little good news; we could all benefit from more angels around us. Why then should it be so difficult for some churches to engage in evangelism and to support those who would talk about their own faith?

Evangelism is something that must always happen in context; there is no one-size-fits-all approach. For example, lots of New England Christians consider mission to be the most acceptable form of evangelism, while Southerners are more comfortable going

dead, you will be saved. [10]For one believes with the heart and so is justified, and one confesses with the mouth and so is saved. [11]The scripture says, "No one who believes in him will be put to shame." [12]For there is no distinction between Jew and Greek; the same Lord is Lord of all and is generous to all who call on him. [13]For, "Everyone who calls on the name of the Lord shall be saved."

[14]But how are they to call on one in whom they have not believed? And how are they to believe in one of whom they have never heard? And how are they to hear without someone to proclaim him? [15]And how are they to proclaim him unless they are sent? As it is written, "How beautiful are the feet of those who bring good news!"

Exegetical Perspective

"How beautiful are the feet of those who bring good news." With this citation of Isaiah 52:7 (cf. Nah. 1:15) Paul discloses to the Romans his goal in this passage. Given the complexities of his argument, it is good for the modern reader to keep this in mind and not lose sight of Paul's end point. Today's reading is indeed part of a larger unit, but verse 15 is a logical place to pause and reflect on what has come before; Paul noticeably changes directions, as indicated by the strong adversative "but" leading off verse 16. His concern in verse 15 is not solely the gospel message, however, but its presentation—its verbal, oral character as good news *proclaimed*. For Paul, this aspect of the gospel is inseparable from its content.

Despite its lack in the NRSV, the proper way to begin verse 5 is with the conjunction "for," a word frequently used by Paul to link what he is about to say with what he has just said. Historically, a tectonic shift is taking place, and based on 9:30–10:4, Paul seems to be well aware of this. His message about Jesus, the Messiah of Israel, has been rejected by Israel and accepted by Gentiles. Israel has always pursued a righteousness that comes from obeying the Torah, a righteousness uniquely their own, but they have not embraced the righteousness that comes from God through faith in Christ, a righteousness that is for everyone (10:3–4).

Homiletical Perspective

Most would agree that the mainline church in the United States is in decline. Many would point fingers and make accusations over who and what are responsible for this situation. Frankly, this does little to help any of us who are seeking what it means to be the church at this particular time and in our own particular situations. The lection before us offers clarity and vision for our mission. Paul continues to struggle with the "righteousness that comes from the law" and the "righteousness that comes from faith" (vv. 5–6), but he comes to a profound conclusion that is important for us: "if you confess with your lips that Jesus is Lord and believe in your heart that God raised him from the dead, you will be saved" (v. 9). Salvation is found in Jesus. Confessing with our lips and believing in our hearts implies deep and inner trust, beyond mere intellectual assent.

To confess, "Jesus is Lord," is difficult when one is an heir to discrimination, injustice, and oppression at the hands of an abusive power. To say, "Jesus is Lord," is to trust in one who came to serve rather than to be served and who offers freedom rather than bondage and chains. To have Jesus as one's Lord is to give allegiance to the one who has loved us before the dawn of time, who calls us each by name, and who desires that each of us be a full son or daughter. When we believe in our hearts that God

Romans 10:5-15

Theological Perspective

incarnation represents the very purpose of the law, namely, uniting us with God.

First, with the coming of Christ, the function of the law as the means of reconciliation with God has come to an end. In its place is Jesus Christ. In today's lectionary passage, Paul demonstrates this by weaving Christ into Old Testament passages about the law. In verse 5, Paul quotes Leviticus 18:5, which places the burden of salvation on human fulfillment of the law. Then in verses 6–8 Paul quotes Deuteronomy 30:11–12, which says: "Surely, this commandment that I am commanding you today is not too hard for you, nor is to too far away. It is not in heaven, that you should say, 'Who will go up to heaven for us, and get it for us so that we may hear it and observe it?'"

In Paul's creative use of these passages, where the law/commandment once stood, Christ now stands. The Deuteronomic passage above ends with the declaration that "the word is very near to you; it is in your mouth and in your heart for you to observe" (Deut. 30:14). When Moses talks about "the word" he is referring to the commandments—the law. In place of the law, Paul inserts Christ. We do not need to go to heaven to know God, God has come to us in the form of Christ who is near—as close as our hearts and mouths. Christ has replaced the law as the way to salvation.

With the coming of Christ, the law no longer serves the function of reconciling humans with God. In fact, the law has become an obstacle to salvation. "The very commandment that promised life proved to be death to me" (Rom. 7:10). Martin Luther knew this as well. He too tried to achieve salvation, not by strict adherence to torah, but by strict adherence to the medieval pillars of sacraments and cooperating grace. Like Paul, Luther found that what had once promised life brought only more doubt, despair, and death. So both men understood that, in one sense, the coming of Jesus represents the termination of the law as the primary means of reconciliation and righteousness.

Jesus is the end of the law in that he has fulfilled the very function of the law; he has reconciled humans to their Lord. As John Calvin says, Christ is the "meaning, the authority, the fulfiller, and the way to the fulfillment of the Law. He is Himself the righteousness before God, the divine justification that everyone is to receive and can receive through faith."[2]

2. Karl Barth, *Church Dogmatics*, II/2 (Edinburgh: T. & T. Clark, 1957), 245.

Pastoral Perspective

out and talking about faith, even in public, nonchurch, places. Perhaps there is something about the warmer climate that loosens the lips and softens the heart so that one can speak of personal faith in an open and unselfconscious way. Maybe Yankee ingenuity influences the northern faithful to take a more hands-on, problem-solving approach. Even though they are different, both forms of evangelism—social justice in the North and witnessing to one's faith in the South—are equally valid.

The tension around evangelism is not from the methods employed but rather from the motive; the tension is between doing and believing. Those who feel that, by their actions, they can "save" others, whether by goods works or persuasive words, have missed the mark. Paul offers a gentle correction to those who would bring Christ to others. He reminds us that Christ is already present. It is not up to us to save the world. God has already done that. It is up to us to believe that this is true and live as though we believe. We cannot save others by our actions alone. We cannot even save ourselves (vv. 5–7).

Some people will be comforted by this. They will see it as permission to sit back and let God do the work of salvation. It will feel like an easy way out. Others will find the whole discussion of salvation to be old-fashioned and not especially relevant for the complex issues facing the church and the world in the twenty-first century. They will skip over this to get to what they see as the substance of making a difference in practical ways. For many Christians, though, a thoughtful consideration of Paul's teaching will raise big questions: If God in Christ has already done it all, then what are we supposed to do? What is our purpose in the world? What does it mean to "confess with our lips" and "believe in our hearts"?

For these questioning Christians, it is important to understand that neither private piety nor streetcorner sermons will do. What the apostle is urging is a life of interior and exterior authenticity, a life based on faith. We may not be able to change anything, but faith can change everything.

This Christian faith creates an entirely new geometry. The circle of believers that was once defined by its boundaries, the law, is now defined by its center, Christ. The attention to who is in and who is out is no longer the focus. Rather the focus is on the One who calls and claims, redeems and loves. We are called to start in the center and live as though the circle is infinite—which, of course, it is.

This radical inclusion incorporates all who believe, however they express that belief (v. 10). The

Exegetical Perspective

Paul picks up on this dichotomy in verse 5 and offers a scriptural proof for the assertions he has just made. What follows is a catena of quotations, citations, and deliberate paraphrases culled from a host of scriptural witnesses. While some of his rhetoric in these verses carries a Greek flavor, his overall method resembles Jewish *pesher* (lit. "interpretation"), best represented in parallel literature by the Dead Sea Scrolls. Fundamental to this approach is the notion that Scripture can be read on multiple levels, and that a fuller understanding of its meaning grows out of its interpretation over time. The method is often applied to important historical figures. In *Pesher Habakkuk* (1QpHab), for example, the book of Habakkuk is reinterpreted as referring to the Teacher of Righteousness (among others), a key figure in the history of the Qumran community. Paul uses a similar approach in Romans, but for him the historical figure in question is Christ.

He begins where he left off in 10:3–4 with a contrast. There is an obvious distinction between two kinds of righteousness, that which is "from the law" (v. 5) and that which is "from faith" (v. 6). Along with this explicit contrast, however, is one that is more subtle but probably no less important in light of Paul's ultimate goal in this passage. The righteousness from the law is *written* ("Moses writes . . ."), but the righteousness from faith *speaks.*

One reason for the change in verbs may be the fact that Paul does not feel bound to the written word at this point. The first question, "Who will ascend into heaven?" is taken directly from Deuteronomy 30:12, but his second question, "Who will descend into the abyss?" is an extremely loose paraphrase of Deuteronomy 30:13, "who will cross to the other side of the sea?" There is no reason to assume Paul is dealing with a different version of the Deuteronomy passage; the changes are his own. A play on words is at work—the "sea" was also called the "abyss" (Gen. 1:2; Job 38:30; Ps. 33:7; Isa. 51:10)—but he is far more interested, as his explanatory ("that is . . .") remarks show, in explaining how the passage points to the reality of Christ.

A second reason for the change in verbs is the emphasis he wishes to place on the spoken word, so "near" that it can be found "on your lips" (lit. "in your mouth") and "in your heart" (v. 8; cf. Deut. 30:14). This word, Paul continues, is in fact "the word of faith that we proclaim." This is more than just a parenthetical statement; Paul makes the audacious claim that his newly proclaimed message is a new word for a new era (cf. Rom. 7:6). It is now clear

Homiletical Perspective

raised Jesus from the dead, we participate and share in resurrection life. In an age of uncertainty and shaky foundations, resurrection life brings meaning, hope, and purpose. Our confession and our belief begin and end with Jesus. From this foundation a life of faith and discipleship flows.

A second part to this lection that is central to our mission is found in Paul's rallying cry: "But how are they to call on one in whom they have not believed? And how are they to believe in one of whom they have never heard? And how are they to hear without someone to proclaim him?" (v. 14). In our day and time, "evangelism" is a loaded word. Evangelism often conjures up images of a door-to-door salesman asking the poor soul who mistakenly opens her door, "If you were to die tonight, where would you go?" We shudder at the thought of the advertising campaign on the side of London buses that asks, "When the son of man comes, will he find faith on earth?" and then offers the address of a Web site. At the site a warning is given to anyone who will not "accept the word of Jesus on the cross: You will be condemned to everlasting separation from God and then you spend all eternity in torment in hell."[1]

Despite these poor efforts at evangelism, we are called to go out into the world and proclaim Jesus. Because if we do not, how will those who are lost hear and have the opportunity to call on his name? Many in our day and time struggle with uncertainty and doubt. They search for something or someone in whom they can trust. Our job is to share the one who we know is trustworthy, the one who welcomes our questions and doubts. We are sent out to share Jesus, who offers certainty and hope regardless of circumstances.

Evangelism is about introducing others to Jesus. It is not our job to convert someone to our doctrine, to our style of liturgy or worship, or to our particular agendas. We are not responsible for the outcome of the introduction; this task belongs to Jesus. The introduction we make comes from our own experience with him. It begins with listening; it continues in conversation. This kind of evangelism requires that we live as Jesus calls us to live: with love, honesty, and humility.

A woman in our church turned fifty and in an effort to celebrate the occasion her husband offered to give her a grand party. She began making plans but was troubled by the expense and the fuss dedicated to

---

1. Ariane Sherine, "Atheists—gimme five," *The Guardian* (London), June 20, 2008, http://www.guardian.co.uk/commentisfree/2008/jun/20/transport.religion.

Romans 10:5-15

Theological Perspective

So how does the law function after Christ? Lutheran theologians see a twofold function of the law. The law serves to condemn us of our sinfulness (theological use) and the law functions to restrain evildoers (civil function). Where Luther saw a dichotomy between grace and law, Calvin saw greater continuity. Calvin and most Reformed theologians have emphasized greater continuity between law and gospel and therefore have posited a third use—pedagogical. It not only restrains evildoers and reveals human sinfulness; it "serves as the best instrument for enabling them [believers] daily to learn with greater truth and certainty what that will of the Lord is which they aspire to follow."[3]

In other words, the law is still good, as Paul says in Romans 7:12: "the law is holy, and the commandment is holy and just and good." Because we have a God who is faithful and constant, those moral laws that pleased God in the time of the Israelites continue to guide us in God's will, even with the coming of Christ. In this sense, the law does not terminate with Christ; it still has a role in Christian life.

In fact, Christ himself was the only human being who was capable of upholding and obeying the deeper meaning of the law. With a few exceptions, all torah commands had to do with one of these two primary relationships: human-human, God-human. Christ showed us what the law was intended to do and be. He was in harmony with God the Father, and he showed pure *agapē* love to his fellow human beings. He lived the life the torah was designed to create.

Finally, Christ is the very purpose of the law. The law was given in order to join humans and God. With the incarnation of God in Jesus Christ, the purpose of the law has been achieved; God and humanity have been united.

Because Christ is the termination of the function of the law, fulfillment of the function of the law, and the perfect adherent to the law, human beings need only believe in our hearts and confess with our lips that Jesus is Lord and believe in our hearts that God raised him from the dead, in order to be united eternally with the triune community.

KYLE D. FEDLER

Pastoral Perspective

infinite circle wraps around those who speak and witness, showing their faith with their lips, and those who pray and ponder, practicing their faith in their hearts. Jews and Greeks alike are in, because no one is out. God's generosity extends to all.

We who are made in the image of God are to be generous, as well. So here is the catch, the seeming paradox of being versus doing. Where faith is concerned, these are not polarities; instead, they are opposite sides of the same coin. Just as no one has a monopoly on the gracious abundance of the Lord's love, so those who know that love in their very being are to ensure that others do too.

Faith is an embodied reality. In this brief passage alone, Paul speaks of lips (vv. 8, 9), mouth (v. 10), heart (v. 8, 9, 10), and feet (v. 15). The way for believers to explain God to those who have not heard is not through theological brilliance, scriptural proofs, or doctrine and dogma. Instead, it is living out the word that is within (v. 8), and doing that in a way that makes sense in context. Even God, according to John Calvin, accommodates God's unknowable majesty to our finitude; "God is wont to in a measure to 'lisp' in speaking to us."[1]

We are to do the same, framing our message so it can be understood—human to human, somebody to another body. Depending on the context, this could mean witnessing to one's own faith by speaking about it, or by engaging in actions that proclaim that faith in concrete ways. In any case, the instruction of Scripture is clear: those who believe are to be messengers of the good news of faith. The pastoral challenge is also clear: Evangelism is not optional.

MARTHA C. HIGHSMITH

3. Ibid., 2.7.12.

1. John Calvin, *Institutes of the Christian Religion*, 1.13.1, ed. John T. McNeill, trans. Ford Lewis Battles, Library of Christian Classics (Philadelphia: Westminster Press, 1960).

that the voice of "the righteousness . . . from faith" (v. 6) is none other than Paul's own.

What Paul sets up with his quotation in verse 8 becomes programmatic for verses 9–13. His masterful summary of the gospel in verse 9 derives from Deuteronomy 30:14 directly: that which is "on your lips" is the early church's creedal confession "Jesus is Lord" (cf. 1 Cor. 12:3; Phil. 2:11); that which is "in your heart" is the belief that "God has raised him from the dead" (cf. 1 Cor. 15:14). He reverses the order in verse 10 to place belief in its more natural position before confession (as in v. 14).

With verses 11–13, Paul brings his scriptural proof to a close. As he asserted in verse 4, this new word is for everyone, Jew and Greek (v. 12). The word "every" is present in the LXX of Joel 2:32 (v. 13, "everyone"), but when it is not to be found in Isaiah 28:16, Paul adds it for the sake of his argument (v. 11, lit. "everyone who . . . will not . . ."). That this is his deliberate focus here is made even clearer by the absence of any such interpolation when he cites the same passage just a few verses earlier (9:33).

Paul's final flurry of rhetorical questions traces the confession of the believer back to the proclamation of the one who has been sent. The second question is more accurately rendered "How are they to believe in one whom they have never heard?" despite the KJV, NIV, and NRSV, which all add the word "of" before "whom." The change may seem subtle, but the implication is profound. The voice of the proclaimer is in fact the voice of Christ himself coming through the one whom he has sent. For today's proclaimer, this is both sobering and comforting. These are big shoes to fill indeed, but "how beautiful are the feet of those who bring good news!" (v. 15).

JOHN M. VONDERBRUEGGE

her birthday. So instead of a party for herself, she and her family threw a Thanksgiving feast for the members of the church and its neighbors, including the community who gather nightly to share their meals at the local soup kitchen. She hired the best country-western band in West Texas.

On the night of the party, all were welcomed, both neighbors who had never darkened the doors of the church and lifelong members. Everyone sat around tables eating and listening together as the band played old-time gospel hymns. Following dinner, Jody Nix and his Texas Cowboys cranked it up. Before long the wooden dance floor at the front of the fellowship hall was full of dancing couples young and old, members and neighbors dancing and laughing together.

I do not know if anyone was converted that night, but Jesus was present and introduced all around. I do know that several who had never been to church before are attending worship regularly on Sunday mornings. Because of the party, the members of the church have renewed their efforts to welcome visitors into their midst. *How are they to believe in one of whom they have never heard?* How are they to become acquainted with, get to know, believe in, and confess one whom they have never had the chance to really meet?

If we are to be the church of Jesus Christ, we must return to the foundation of our faith: Jesus, the one who was born, lived, died, and rose for us. We must be honest about what we attach to Jesus and require for inclusion in his church. With Paul, we must commit ourselves to evangelism. *How beautiful are the feet of those who bring good news!*

MARY BETH ANTON

Matthew 14:22‑33

²²Immediately he made the disciples get into the boat and go on ahead to the other side, while he dismissed the crowds. ²³And after he had dismissed the crowds, he went up the mountain by himself to pray. When evening came, he was there alone, ²⁴but by this time the boat, battered by the waves, was far from the land, for the wind was against them. ²⁵And early in the morning he came walking toward them on the sea. ²⁶But when the disciples saw him walking on the sea, they were terrified, saying, "It is a ghost!" And they cried out in fear. ²⁷But immediately Jesus spoke to them and said, "Take heart, it is I; do not be afraid."

²⁸Peter answered him, "Lord, if it is you, command me to come to you on the water." ²⁹He said, "Come." So Peter got out of the boat, started walking on the water, and came toward Jesus. ³⁰But when he noticed the strong wind, he became frightened, and beginning to sink, he cried out, "Lord, save me!" ³¹Jesus immediately reached out his hand and caught him, saying to him, "You of little faith, why did you doubt?" ³²When they got into the boat, the wind ceased. ³³And those in the boat worshiped him, saying, "Truly you are the Son of God."

Theological Perspective

After the feeding of the five thousand, the focus shifts from the wilderness to the sea—from God's provision in the desert to God's deliverance through the waters. Here too the echoes of Israel's story are strong. If the previous narrative presents Jesus as a prayerful and obedient servant utterly dependent on the word of God, this one puts him in an altogether more troubling light. The christological implications of this passage are immense.

Jesus sends his disciples away in their boat while he dismisses the crowds and spends time alone in prayer. In the early hours of the morning, when they are still far from land and being battered by the wind and waves, he appears to them.

He Came Walking toward Them on the Sea (v. 25). Even before he arrives, their situation is perilous, though presumably not unfamiliar to the fishermen among them; but it is the appearance of Jesus, not the storm, that terrifies them. They think it is "a ghost" (v. 26). According to the parallel passage in John, they recognize him immediately, but are still afraid (John 6:19). This may well be Jesus approaching them—but Jesus as they have never seen or known or understood him before.

What manner of being does such things? A trickster? A magician? A malignant spirit? The answer

Pastoral Perspective

Matthew 14:22–33 is a text filled with vivid imagery. The picture of the disciples sent on their own across troubled seas and of Jesus walking on water to save them and to calm the waters is a picture that has given comfort, encouragement, and challenge to Christians over the generations. This text and its parallel texts in Mark 6:45–52 and John 6:16–21 have been used over the centuries to remind us that Jesus often calls us to go into uncharted waters, but when we go in faithfulness, he never abandons us.

There is a variety of rich images in this text that bring to life important dimensions of God's call and God's assurance to us:

—The image of Jesus taking time to pray, even in a very uncertain situation, is a reminder that things are never so turbulent or so urgent as to take us away from the necessity of prayer.

—The image of Jesus sending out the disciples on a mission just as he sends us in mission today.

—The image of choppy seas and the reality that when we set out on Christ's mission, though we will often be in troubled waters, Jesus does not abandon us but rather comes to us, as he came to the disciples, when we need him most.

—The image that Jesus and the reign of God that he inaugurates have power even over the forces of

Exegetical Perspective

In keeping with the exegetical notes on Matthew 14:13–21 (pp. 309–13), the context of Jesus' visit to his homeland with negative results (13:54–58) and Herod's execution of John the Baptist (14:1–12) needs to be kept in mind. As in the case of serving the weak and feeding the hungry in a deserted place, Jesus' isolation on a mountain presents an alternative to the unbelief in his homeland and to the brutal imperial world of Herod Antipas.

The structure of the passage is simple. Jesus is alone on the mountain. At the same time, the disciples are in a boat on rough waters, separated from Jesus. Jesus comes to them walking on the sea, and this is connected with a question of Jesus' identity. In turn, the question of Jesus' identity is connected with Peter's ill-fated attempt to walk on the water; this requires Jesus to save him and results in an exhortation to trust.

Mountains were regarded in antiquity as places of contact between heaven and earth (e.g., Sinai, the Temple Mount). Matthew 14:23 is the first time Matthew refers to Jesus himself at prayer. In contrast to the Sermon on the Mount, which is full of instructions on prayer, this mountain experience is a brief literary summary, expressed with one word in Greek ("to pray"). Because the content of Jesus' prayer is missing, the passage functions almost

Homiletical Perspective

Like most preachers, Jesus keeps trying to get away. This story follows the account of the feeding of the multitude, which began with Jesus trying to get away to pray alone and the crowd persisting. Now that the crowd has been fed and dismissed, Jesus tries again. In the earlier story, Jesus gets away to pray, and then feeds the multitudes. In this story, Jesus gets away to pray, then walks on water. Matthew does not want us to miss the clear parallel between the prayer life of Jesus and the mighty things he does. Later in the story, Peter cries out in the storm, "Lord, save me!" (v. 30). His cry to Jesus may look like the prayers of many of Jesus' disciples, then and now. Jesus, however, prays *before* the storm, not in the storm. Matthew does not want us to miss this, either: it is the prayer before the storm that informs a sure-footed, "do not be afraid" presence when the winds pick up.

How many characters are in this story? It is a trick question. Of course, if all disciples are present, there are thirteen. For preaching, however, there are three characters. Jesus speaks and acts; Peter speaks and acts; and the disciples speak and act as one. The eleven disciples are treated with one voice in Matthew's account. This is significant for preaching, because it highlights the effect that one person's risk can mean for the rest of a community. When Jesus begins walking toward the boat, the disciples are

Matthew 14:22-33

Theological Perspective

suggested by Matthew's account is even more disturbing than that.

In Hebraic thought, water represents much more than a mere physical reality. Whether it is the sea with its unfathomable depths, the relentless river in full flood, or the all-consuming deluge, there is something metaphysical about the threat water poses to human life. According to Karl Barth, water, in the first biblical creation story, is "'the principle which, in its abundance and power is absolutely opposed to God's creation;' "it is a representative of all the evil powers which oppress and resist the salvation intended for the people of Israel."[1]

Throughout the Old Testament it is precisely this reality over which God's lordship is continuously demonstrated and God's victory affirmed. In the creation of the world (Gen. 1:2), in the covenant with Noah (Gen. 9:8–17), in the mighty act of deliverance from Pharaoh's army at the Red Sea (Exod. 14:21), and in the miraculous entry into the land of promise through the swollen River Jordan (Josh. 3:14–17), the Lord triumphs over the waters.

The God of Israel tramples on the waves (Job 9:8, Hab. 3:15) and walks "in the recesses of the deep" (Job 38:16). These are very specific signs of God's sovereign and transcendent power over all that would threaten and thwart God's purposes (cf. Ps. 93:4).

So when Jesus approaches the disciples in their boat as they battle with the elements, the prospect is, naturally, terrifying. Who can walk here with such authority and freedom? The act and its associations are unmistakable. Jesus is exercising a prerogative that belongs to God alone. When he speaks to them, his words serve only to reinforce the sense that this is a divine revelation.

Take Heart, It Is I; Do Not Be Afraid (v. 27). Jesus says *egō eimi,* which can mean simply "it is i"; but more is being suggested here. For Matthew's audience, this Greek phrase is packed with significance. These are the words that the Septuagint uses to translate the Hebrew name of God revealed to Moses at the burning bush (Exod. 3:14).

Jesus is using the divine name to announce his presence. I AM is here, trampling victoriously over the waves. In these brief but charged words and in the awesome vision that unfolds before the disciples, Jesus is identifying himself with God, the liberator and redeemer of Israel, who is at the same time the creator of the world and the victor over chaos.

1. Karl Barth, *Church Dogmatics,* III/1 (Edinburgh: T. & T. Clark, 1958), 105, 147.

Pastoral Perspective

nature and can conquer our fears and the evil that causes them.
—The image of the disciples who, because of their fear, could not recognize Jesus when he came to them in ways they never expected (walking on the water).
—The image of Jesus calming the troubled waters for the disciples and the reality that he can calm our troubled waters as well.
—The image of the disciples responding to Jesus' saving grace through worship and through the confession "Truly you are the Son of God" (v. 33).

All of these images have rich power for interpreting the love of God, the saving grace of Jesus Christ, our calling to be in mission, and the assurance of Christ's love and companionship when we need it most. However, what is unique to the Gospel of Matthew's version of these events, and not found in Mark and John's accounts, are the dialogue with Peter and Peter's attempt to step out of the boat and walk on water to Jesus, in response to the command of his Lord. It is this encounter that may have the richest imagery to enable the word of God to speak to us through this passage.

Like the other disciples, Peter is panicked both by the turbulent waters and by this figure walking toward them on the water in the very early morning hours. Even after Jesus speaks to the disciples, they are still not sure if it is Jesus. Peter, knowing that the call to discipleship is unique to his relationship with Jesus, responds, "Lord, if it is you, command me to come to you on the water" (v. 28). When Jesus issues the command, "Come," Peter steps out of the boat in faith and in faithfulness. Having embarked on his journey across the sea in faith, he then becomes frightened, but the strong arm of Jesus lifts him up and returns him to the boat.

What is so clear from this passage is that we are called to step out in faith, even in the midst of troubled waters, if we are to be faithful to the call of Christ. Stepping out in faith is not a guarantee that we will not face troubled waters or be filled with fear, but it is always accompanied by the assurance that Jesus will not abandon us, that when we need it most, he will extend his arm to lift us up and get us back in the boat.

Years ago, I attended an ecumenical gathering at which Ernest Campbell, then the pastor of Riverside Church in New York, was addressing a group of pastors on the crisis in our churches. I will always remember his assertion that "the reason that we seem to lack faith in our time is that we are not

exclusively to emphasize Jesus' isolation from others: "He was there alone" (v. 23).

Jesus' isolation emphasizes in turn the situation of the disciples. In keeping with the theme of an alternative to the world of Jesus' homeland and to the imperial world of Herod Antipas, the wind and waves show that there are perils even in the alternative world Jesus offers his followers. Significantly, the perils for the disciples are connected with Jesus' absence from them. As in cases like the storm at sea in the story of Jonah, calamity on the sea could be understood as divine punishment for something evil or deficient in those in the boat, and this is apparently the case here.

The perils of the sea are first described without any reference to the response of the disciples: the boat is far from land, battered by waves, and the wind is against them. At this point Matthew has Jesus come to them walking on water; like the feeding of the crowds, his action is miraculous. Walking on the water undoubtedly implies divine power over the elements of nature; thus this action is described as a "nature miracle."

Since the Enlightenment, interpreters have had difficulty with what are called nature miracles. Technically, because of the multiplication of food, the feeding of the crowds earlier in chapter 14 could also be called a nature miracle, but inasmuch as Jesus provides for the needs of hungry people, it is more often thought of as a "gift miracle." It is possible to understand Jesus' walking on the water as confirmation of his relationship with God, but it also has aspects of benevolent concern for others, for the well-being of the disciples. In this sense, walking on water is no less a gift miracle than the feeding of the crowds.

Interpreters almost universally conclude that Matthew has a more positive presentation of Jesus' disciples than does Mark. Still, they are flawed. At the end of Jesus' teaching in parables in Matthew 13:51, he asks them, "Have you understood all this?" They answer, "Yes." Nevertheless, when Jesus comes to them walking on the water while they are in peril on the sea, the disciples, who claim that they have understood Jesus' proclamation of God's ruling activity in the parables, are terrified.

Their terror is the result of a misinterpretation of Jesus' approach to them. They think he is a ghost. The cultural commonplace behind this incident is the belief in a cosmic battle going on between God and the powers of evil. As indicated above, the perilous sea could be understood as a manifestation of this battle.

terrified. At the end of the story, when they are all back on the boat and the wind has ceased, they worship Jesus. Between their fear and worship is one disciple's risk and security in the arms of grace. The trust and risk of one follower of Jesus has an effect on the whole community of followers. Individuals who risk boldly and move toward the call of Jesus can make a difference in the lives of other believers.

Fear is the recurring theme in this story. The phrases "terrified," "cried in fear," "do not be afraid," and "became frightened" all occur in just eleven verses, an appeal from the author that this theme not get overlooked. Fear plays many roles in this story. If this were a Greek tragedy and fear was a character, the character would leave several times to change masks. The first mask would display sheer terror as the disciples see Jesus walking toward them. This may be fear of the unknown, or it may be the fear that is present during challenges in our lives. A change of masks would then reveal fear in the guise of motivator, moving Peter to risk going toward Jesus in the storm. A final mask would show fear mingled with distraction as Peter's attention is drawn from Jesus to the waves that crash around him. When Peter notices the wind, fear of his situation diminishes his faith. So, when we fear Jesus moving toward us, or our fear moves us toward Jesus, or our fear distracts us, Jesus remains the constant enemy of all the faces of fear. "Take heart, it is I; do not be afraid" (v. 27). Focusing on the presence of Jesus dispels the fear.

Some teachers treat Peter's going under the violent waters as a baptismal image and preach this story through the lens of baptism. There are rich contrasts between this image of baptism and most baptisms today. Most current church baptisms, even in traditions that immerse, are rather risk free. The baptizer and the person being baptized walk down steps into a heat-controlled, fiberglass pool. Often, the baptizer will wear fishing waders to keep from getting wet. Then, after the baptism, the candidate is greeted by baptism committee members who offer warm towels and a hair dryer. Our current baptismal practices stand in stark contrast to the risky steps that Peter takes as he approaches his Lord across a raging sea. His feet do not land on a fiberglass bottom. This baptismal image is filled with risk and trust and commitment. Fierce storms, compelling risk, and real danger may be better images for the life that follows baptism.

After Peter cried out, "Lord, save me!" and Jesus reached out his hand and caught him, Jesus said,

Matthew 14:22-33

Theological Perspective

His words, instilling courage and banishing fear, assure the disciples that this awesome vision in the midst of the storm is intended as good news. A similar formula is to be found in a number of places in Isaiah, where God's self-revelation is accompanied by the injunction not to be afraid (e.g., Isa. 41:10, 13; 43:5; and esp. 43:1, 2, where it is explicitly linked with God's triumph over the waters).

Given its utterance at important moments throughout Scripture, especially at the birth and resurrection of Jesus, "Do not be afraid" is a keynote of the gospel itself. The unveiling of God's majesty is not intended to terrorize or diminish, but to save, uphold, and establish the creature.

This epiphany in the storm certainly contains a message of grace and mercy, but in the Bible, authentic revelation is never academic or self-indulgent. There is always a personal cost to be paid, a radical summons to faith to be heard and answered. Spirituality must take the form of discipleship.

Command Me to Come to You (v. 28). Peter recognizes his Lord and wants to accompany him in his royal walk on the sea. "Come," says Jesus (v. 29), and Peter boldly steps out of his comfort zone. Then he takes his eyes off Jesus and focuses on the elements instead. Soon he can only cry out for salvation from the waters, and Jesus reaches out his hand and catches him (vv. 30–31, cf. Ps. 69:1–2).

Peter calls him "Lord" without understanding that title's full significance. The lordship of Jesus is given specific content and meaning in this incident: he is lord over the deep, over the wind and the waves and all the destructive forces that threaten to overwhelm human life. Jesus' actions here hold out the promise of a new exodus for his followers, a new entry into the land of promise, a new future. "When they got into the boat, the wind ceased" (v. 32).

This is one of those moments, like the transfiguration, where the disciples gain some understanding and insight into Jesus' identity and mission. The whole event leads up to a mighty confession of faith: "Truly you are the Son of God" (v. 33). It is likely that this is primarily a recognition of Jesus as Messiah, the coming king, but there is no doubt that more is hinted at in this passage. According to Matthew, even before the resurrection, the disciples catch a glimpse of Jesus' unique relationship with the God of Israel.

IWAN RUSSELL-JONES

Pastoral Perspective

doing anything that requires it." He was right. The key to faith and fullness of life in Christ is to follow Peter's example and be willing to step out of the comfort and security of the boat and head into the troubled waters of the world to proclaim the love, mercy, and justice of God that we find in Jesus Christ. Being a disciple is a risky and exciting business, but that is exactly what God calls us to do and to be, and God assures us that if we "get out of the boat," we can count on the accompaniment of our Lord and Savior, Jesus Christ.

William H. Willimon may have put it best in a sermon entitled "How Will You Know If It's Jesus?":

> If Peter had not ventured forth, had not obeyed the call to walk on the water, then Peter would never have had this great opportunity for recognition of Jesus and rescue by Jesus. I wonder if too many of us are merely splashing about in the safe shallows and therefore have too few opportunities to test and deepen our faith. The story today implies if you want to be close to Jesus, you have to venture forth out on the sea, you have to prove his promises through trusting his promises, through risk and venture.[1]

Getting out of the boat with Jesus is the most risky, most exciting, and most fulfilling way to live life to the fullest. Matthew 14:22–33 invites us to do just that!

CLIFTON KIRKPATRICK

---

1. William H. Willimon, *How Will You Know If It's Jesus*, August 7, 2005, http://day1.org/950-how_you_will_know_if_its_jesus.

Exegetical Perspective

Without Jesus, the disciples are afraid of the battle and cry out in fear, because they are uncertain which way the struggle between God and evil will turn out. So when they see Jesus walking toward them on the water, his presence is at best ambiguous. Actually, it is worse. They think he is a ghost, a deception. Is he actually an agent of the powers of evil? A part of their problem is uncertainty as to whether they can know the presence of Jesus when he comes to them in their peril. The first part of the resolution of their problem is found in the words of Jesus: "Take heart, it is I; do not be afraid" (v. 27). Jesus tells his disciples that he is God's agent, so as to assure them that God's rule overcomes the power of evil.

Is that enough? For Peter, apparently it is not. Peter's request to walk on the water is still tied to the question of Jesus' identity: "If it is you, command me to come to you on the water" (v. 28). The ambiguity of Jesus' presence for the disciples thus has two outcomes. First, Peter's test to prove the identity of Jesus fails. He is afraid and sinks in the water. He still does not trust that Jesus is God's agent for God's rule, as Jesus has proclaimed in the parables. Second, Jesus saves them in spite of the deficiency of faith of Peter and the other disciples. The positive identity of Jesus as God's agent for overcoming the powers of evil is therefore confirmed.

Notably, walking on the water *itself* does not establish Jesus' identity as God's agent, as much popular interpretation of this passage claims. Indeed, walking on the water is ambiguous. What is decisive is Jesus' word and his saving act.

JAE WON LEE

Homiletical Perspective

"You of little faith, why did you doubt?" (v. 31). This may not be a rhetorical question. Why did Peter doubt? Why do we doubt in the presence of the one who constantly conquers the storms? Peter stepped toward Jesus because of an informed trust. Jesus had never failed him. Still, the strong wind scared him. His risk, however, created a deeper trust in the steadfast grace that continues to save.

Because we do not know the tone of voice Jesus used, there is a homiletical choice that must be made in delivering the question, "You of little faith, why did you doubt?" While commentaries can inform some of the questions about the historical background of a text, the preacher must choose the voice inflections that interpret the story for the listener. If the preacher imagines Jesus angry and scolding Peter for his "little faith," the sermon will go in a much different direction than if the preacher imagines Jesus amused and playful.

In a similar way, the preacher must also interpret "little faith." The sermon may demean "little faith" and challenge listeners to big faith, but Matthew offers another preaching possibility. In Matthew 17:20 the evangelist says, "If you have faith the size of a mustard seed, you will say to this mountain, 'Move from here to there,' and it will move." In the story that precedes this one, five thousand people are fed out of one lunch pail. Peter had only a little faith, but nobody else got out of that boat. A little faith may be all that is needed to transform a story that starts in terror into a story that ends in worship.

DOCK HOLLINGSWORTH

Isaiah 56:1, 6-8

¹Thus says the LORD:
  Maintain justice, and do what is right,
 for soon my salvation will come,
  and my deliverance be revealed.
. . . .
⁶And the foreigners who join themselves to the LORD,
  to minister to him, to love the name of the LORD,
  and to be his servants,
 all who keep the sabbath, and do not profane it,
  and hold fast my covenant—

Theological Perspective

Chapter 56 of Isaiah begins what is sometimes called Third Isaiah, with a third writer (or set of writers) with a focus somewhat different from the first two sections of the book. There are some continuing themes, however, one of which is implied in today's reading and will be discussed later.

The final chapters of Isaiah speak to a community returning from exile. The first verse signals the positions these former exiles should take—not to seek revenge but to "maintain justice and do what is right" (v. 1a). For the returning exiles, the idea of justice might seem to point only to the restoration of their freed status—God working on their behalf, so to speak. Instead, the call to justice is a call to look for God's salvific action: "Soon my salvation will come, and my deliverance be revealed" (v. 1b). Salvation and deliverance are not isolationist or retaliatory. The next verses demonstrate new directions that deepen God's covenantal relationship with the people.

The next verses point out that the former exiles are to open the door for foreigners to "join themselves to the LORD" (v. 6a). These new servants, the foreigners, will "minister to him" and "love the name of the LORD." Most importantly, they will "keep the sabbath, and . . . not profane it, and hold fast my covenant" (v. 6b).

Pastoral Perspective

If Second Isaiah (chaps. 40–55) is a cohesive, single-authored motivational message of comfort to exiles preparing to return home and rebuild, then Third Isaiah (chaps. 56–66) reflects the confused, ugly reality of that community returning home. Sometimes it is hard to tell why chapters 56–66 are considered a single section, given the mixed messages and different authors contained therein.

Nevertheless, chapter 56 does connect the themes of comfort and hope from Second Isaiah. The shift is in the widening circle of *who* receives comfort and hope.

Those who first heard these verses of Isaiah 56 included:

—*Exiles from Babylon and beyond* who had returned to their cities and towns, only to find others living in their homes, a disaster economy, a mix of cultures and religions, and a lack of the order they had known in exile. However bad it was in Babylon, there were stability and plenty of bread and water there.

—*Those Jews left behind* who were not considered important or wealthy enough to have been exiled. After scavenging a living for decades, watching other people come and rule their land, they now experienced the uppity exiles coming back, whining about the disarray while

⁷these I will bring to my holy mountain,
  and make them joyful in my house of prayer;
their burnt offerings and their sacrifices
  will be accepted on my altar;
for my house shall be called a house of prayer
  for all peoples.
⁸Thus says the Lord GOD,
  who gathers the outcasts of Israel,
I will gather others to them
  besides those already gathered.

Exegetical Perspective

Literary-Historical Context. Isaiah contains diverse prophetic materials spanning a long historical trajectory. Texts reflecting the Assyrian crisis (eighth century BCE), when the prophet Isaiah lived, are interspersed with texts reflecting the Babylonian crisis (sixth century) and texts reflecting the Persian restoration (ca. fifth century). The entire book is Isaianic in the sense that patterns of divine activity discerned by Isaiah himself in his own time are typologically projected onto later historical situations. Although some texts are evidently linked with particular events, and although some units have explicit rhetorical connections with neighboring units, it is difficult to read the entire book in any particular chronological or literary sequence. The book, instead, invites readers to connect texts that thematically echo one another, and to relate them typologically with the historical contexts described in the book.

Isaiah 56:1–8 belongs to a section defined by marked rhetorical affinities extending from chapter 56 to chapter 66 (often called Third Isaiah). Within this section are several texts that explicitly reflect the historical situation of the Persian restoration. This text seems to do so in its concluding reference to YHWH's "gathering" of Israel's "outcasts" (v. 8), but it also seems to envision restoration as an ongoing process that will finally include Jews excluded

Homiletical Perspective

The scholarly debates that swirl around the proper interpretation of the writings of Second and Third Isaiah are truly dizzying. It is easy to get caught up in the vortex of these exegetical and form-critical theories. In one sense, it would be far easier simply to ignore that whole hermeneutical layer, particularly given the fact that the perspective of this essay is homiletical; but to come to grips with the theme and intent of this passage, one has to dip into those turbulent waters. While preachers will find greater detail in the exegetical and theological perspectives on this text, they need to be aware of a couple of thematic generalizations.

Whatever the nuances of the relationship between the authors and material of Second and Third Isaiah, most scholars seem to agree that there is considerable narrative continuity between the two prophetic traditions. One primary thread of continuity is that both traditions emphasize that God is doing "new things" and that "former things" are passing away, soon to be forgotten.

Another common thread is that both prophetic traditions believe that God is bringing salvation to the people, delivering them from captivity and oppression. Having recognized these two general themes, we can now turn to the passage at hand to see what sort of "new thing" this particular passage

Isaiah 56:1, 6-8

Theological Perspective

This acceptance is new, even though there is a tradition of welcoming strangers throughout Hebrew Scripture (such as stated in Gen. 18). This remarkable desert hospitality was constitutive of those faithful to covenant living and defined one aspect of "justice." As the exiles return, however, they are instructed to go beyond caring for strangers: they must now prepare to welcome those who hold fast to the Sabbath. Such acceptance by God will bring foreigners into the covenantal relationship with the Israelites: "these I will bring to my holy mountain, and make them joyful in my house of prayer; their burnt offerings and their sacrifices will be accepted on my altar" (v. 7).

Not included in the excerpt this week are verses 2–5. These missing verses again underline the point of the widened invitation; in addition to foreigners, eunuchs who hold fast to the covenant will also be accepted as members of the chosen. The recognition of both eunuchs and foreigners who keep the Sabbath is a clear departure from past practices. This postexilic, more inclusive invitation is highlighted in verse 8: "Thus says the Lord GOD, who gathers the outcasts of Israel, I will gather others to them besides those already gathered." These words broaden the vision of the covenant, as two groups who have been excluded from the community of the faithful are welcomed to the altar.

At the same time, this passage implicitly reflects God's rejection of Israel's leaders who have not kept the covenantal law. Rejection is a consistent theme through all the book of Isaiah. "Yes," one commentator remarks, "Israel's latest generation of leaders, the class so frequently threatened and condemned in Isaiah 1–39, continues to transgress, despite the forgiveness proffered in Isaiah 40–55."[1] Opening the covenant to foreigners and eunuchs was not a method of punishing those who had broken faith with it, although the welcome of the formerly shunned may have stung those who took their "chosen" status for granted.

The political situation of the returning exiles emphasized again the broader vision of the covenant. One author, after studying the official records of the time, has noted that there were many foreigners living in the area when the exiles returned. "Jewish, Edomite, Arab, Phoenician, and Aramaean names are identifiable."[2] Accepting the

Pastoral Perspective

showing off the gadgets they had obtained in fancy Babylon.

—*Other powerless non-Jews and foreigners* who had landed in this politically unstable country and were now unsure of their own future as the Jews figured out how to reorganize both as a religion and as a society.

Disaster recovery is messy business, as we have seen in the United States and other countries devastated by war, natural disasters, and forced migration. Who makes decisions? How are land grabbers and those who profit from disaster recovery controlled? Whom can you trust when a ruptured social network is not yet repaired? You no longer know the people next door, because the ex-neighbors stayed with their uncle in another town and did not return. Instead, they gave the keys to their strange-looking nephew who is now occupying the house next door and playing loud music. Perhaps most importantly, who belongs and who does not? Can there be justice for all, and can community be re-created after such tragedy?

The author of today's passage states a vision of community that will include all these groups. A radical new definition of who is in and who is out is planted here. Membership will be based not on genetics or cultural customs, or even religion, but rather on behavior. Those previously excluded from the covenant may now belong. All may fit under YHWH's umbrella.

The requirement for membership is to keep the Sabbath and obey the covenant (vv. 6–7). This does not mean that if you go to church on Sunday and recite a few spiritual laws, you are in. It means living in a certain way. It requires one to "do good, seek justice, rescue the oppressed, defend the orphan, plead for the widow" (Isa. 1:17).

An extremely controversial part of this vision, then and today, is the idea that God's house of prayer might entertain, even accept other religions. Many denominations today in the growing multiethnic United States see evangelism possibilities with new immigrant groups, especially those of other religions. It does not appear, however, that Isaiah's vision calls for people to change their religion. Instead, it invites everyone to gather under a covenant based on justice and doing what is right.

Certainly Isaiah's message opens the religious door to those previously excluded based on their sexual condition (eunuchs), nationality, or religious practice. Read carefully, it does not require (or even ask) them to change their sexual condition, nationality, or religious practice. Their strange-smelling

---

1. Katheryn Pfisterer Darr, *Isaiah's Vision and the Family of God* (Louisville, KY: Westminster John Knox Press, 1994), 69.
2. Bernard Gosse, "Sabbath, Identity and Universalism Go Together after the Return from Exile," *Journal for the Study of the Old Testament* 29, no. 3 (2005): 369.

("eunuchs," vv. 4–5) as well as non-Jews ("foreigners," v. 6). This passage thus reflects the principle of typological recapitulation informing the book as a whole, imagining that the return to the land, in fulfillment of its prophecies of restoration, is also a return to impending exile and the need for further restoration.

Defining the Pericope. Limiting the pericope to verses 1 and 6–8, so as to foreground the text's concern with foreigners and efface its concern with eunuchs, is in line with the central theme of the NT lessons, the inclusion of the Gentiles. Such focusing is appropriate, but could have been achieved in a less disfiguring way by including verses 2–3a. Whether additional verses are read liturgically, exegesis will miss key points if the entire text is not taken into account.

The Whole Covenant for the Whole World. This oracular speech of YHWH takes the form of an exhortation beginning with the command, "Maintain justice and do what is right" (v. 1a). The approach of a critical time of judgment and deliverance (v. 1b) makes this urgent. The rest of the speech (vv. 2–8) elaborates on the benefit of heeding this command, the delimitation of those to whom it is addressed, and what is involved in "maintaining justice/doing right." The approaching crisis can result in being "blessed" (*'aher*, NRSV "happy," cf. Pss. 1:1; 32:2; 112:1; Matt. 5:3–12, etc.). This possibility is open to everyone who upholds both dimensions of the covenant, each of which is emphatically described both positively and negatively: duty to God ("keep sabbath"/"not profane it") and duty to neighbor ("do right"/"not do evil").

The all-inclusiveness of this invitation to uphold the covenant is emphasized by considering the polar extremes of all who might theoretically be "separated" (*bdl*, v. 3a) or "cut off" (*krt*, v. 5b): eunuchs even if they are Jews (Deut. 23:1), and foreigners (Exod. 12:43; Deut. 23:3; Neh. 13:3; Ezek. 44:9, etc.). Progress toward full participation is indicated by the transition from Sabbath keeping—a noncultic form of duty to God that became a sign of Jewish identity from the exile on—to taking part in the prayers and sacrifices offered in YHWH's "house." In the case of foreigners, Sabbath keeping shows a desire to relate to YHWH more completely (v. 6), and their coming into the temple recapitulates the exodus ("these I will bring to my holy mountain," v. 7; cf. Exod. 15:17; Ps. 78:54). As YHWH's temple becomes "a house of prayer for all peoples" (v. 7), this signals the full incorporation of persons from all nations into

holds out to us and what dynamic of deliverance is now to be expected.

The first verse brings a new level of understanding to God's promise of salvation. The promise articulated by Second Isaiah requires a response. It is not simply a matter of acknowledging that divine salvation is being graciously offered, for it is now paramount that such an acknowledgment bears fruit through a change in belief and character, a response of consent and obedience. It is difficult to discern whether the prophet is suggesting that a response of maintaining justice and doing what is right is a precondition for the advent of salvation or a necessary outcome of God's deliverance.

Either way, the prophet is saying that the two are inextricably tied together. To be an aspirant to or a recipient of God's salvation is to discover new expectations about what it means to be righteous and just. Verses 2–5, which are omitted in this lectionary scheme, spell out in a bit more detail what those expectations entail: keeping the Sabbath, refraining from evil, and holding fast to the covenant. In verses 6–8 the radical breadth and depth of this promise of salvation is presented to the people.

One of the astonishing new things that the Lord is doing is redefining Israel's relationship with foreign nations, widely expanding the purview of God's deliverance and salvation. Such salvation should no longer be seen as the byproduct of ethnicity, nationality, race, or cultic membership. It is, instead, open to all who respond with justice and righteousness, who join themselves to God by keeping the Sabbath and holding fast to God's promises.

Here the notion of who is a "servant" of God is drastically enlarged to include foreigners and outcasts, all who align themselves with the promise of God's deliverance and salvation, and all who respond with love and justice. God will bring all such people to the holy mountain, where they will experience the joy of worship as their prayers and offerings are accepted by the God who has gathered them together. God's house will be called a house of prayer, a gathering of all peoples, foreigners, outcasts, and Israelites.

The challenge for any preacher is to discover ways to make the radical character of this prophetic vision accessible to the congregation. This gathering of God's people on the holy mountain can so easily become a comforting caricature that simply makes people smile and think, "Oh, wouldn't that be nice." The real challenge for the preacher is to find images and illustrations that will expand the congregation's

Isaiah 56:1, 6-8

Theological Perspective	Pastoral Perspective

Theological Perspective

foreigners who live by the covenant accentuates how justice shall be maintained by the returning exiles: not with violence, but by "doing what is right."

The key to understanding this new inclusivity is the Sabbath. "Respect for the Sabbath now permits entrance into the house of the Lord in the same way that profanation of the Sabbath demands exclusion. After their arrival into the land, the first generations had not respected the Sabbath. . . . It is now the main law that permits the chosen and the servants to enter. . . . The cosmic signification of the Sabbath makes its universality easier."[3]

For Christians, this reading offers another level of theological reflection. This is particularly true since quite a few churches have the final verse of this selection emblazoned over their entrances. Liturgically, the days after Pentecost offer a season for communal theological reflection about relationships with those who do not have the same faith convictions. This reading from Isaiah might even challenge some Christian missiologies. The season of Pentecost brings images of evangelization, welcoming strangers, and new memberships. The reading from Isaiah invites new consideration of these words: "My house shall be called a house of prayer for all peoples" (v. 7). The invitation to all people is from God, and the community is called to respond as a matter of justice. Theological connections between inviting new members and justice become constitutive of Christian identity.

Upon their return, the former exiles are reminded of God's immeasurable generosity through the divine invitation to others. At the same time, they are called to do what is right, acting in justice, and—implicitly—remaining faithful to the covenant. The demands placed upon idol worshipers, which they witnessed during exile, are contrasted with the hallmark of God's loving-kindness. The former exiles themselves are challenged to remain open, reflecting God's own loving-kindness. This the how they will "maintain justice and do what is right," as stated in the first verse. This is the true "return" of the exiles.

STEPHANIE Y. MITCHEM

Pastoral Perspective

burnt offerings and sacrifices will be accepted, says God. "My house shall be called a house of prayer for all peoples" (v. 7).

Perhaps the challenge of the text is to those who think they are in the "in" group based simply on their religious affiliation. Like them, we can get blinded by believing that the house of prayer for all peoples is *our* house because we recognize the familiar religious objects and smells of the particular church where we burn our offerings each week.

Jesus will later drive the "in" group out of this house (Mark 11:15–17), angrily accusing respected members of being robbers because they sold the house, which was not even theirs, for personal gain.

What defines a faithful person is not his or her sexual condition, nationality, or religion, says Isaiah. The faithful person is the one who loves the name of the Lord, keeps the Sabbath, and holds fast God's covenant. These things do not have to do with church affiliation but with a way of life that honors and protects every single creature created by God. This is the Lord who rescued a people enslaved in Egypt, teaching them how to be a nation very different from their flashy, consumerist neighbors—some of whom wore gaudy religious jewelry made from diamonds dug up by starving children somewhere out of sight.

This God is different. This God refuses to be worshiped as an image. No golden calves or crystal cathedrals, please. This God recognizes the commitment and love of those who take care of one another—along with the widow, the orphan, and the stranger.

This text is great news for the hurricane or tsunami survivors who never left, scavenging a living while slowly rebuilding their home and community. It is good news for the Mexican day laborer who moved into the abandoned house next door with his wife and children. It is good news for the Palestinian Muslim refugee who was just placed in an apartment across the street. It is good news for the neighbor who is a drag-queen performer in the tourist district downtown.

All these are gathered by the God who gathers the outcasts of Israel. Given an equal opportunity to embody goodness, justice, and caring for one another, they will be joyful in God's house of prayer.

DAVID MAXWELL

---

3. Ibid., 367.

God's covenant with Israel ("others . . . gathered," v. 8), in its cultic as well as its ethical dimensions.

Reading in Context. From the book's perspective, being a eunuch is typical of the disqualifications that result from exile (Isa. 39:7). If eunuchs are excluded from full participation in the covenant, as they apparently were from the cult of the Second Temple, then exile is not over. This text assumes that even though Isaianic prophecies of restoration have been fulfilled, the covenant community defined in relation to the Second Temple is again, in effect, in exile. They are on the verge of a crisis in which YHWH can again act to restore them more fully. The text gives no specific reference to particular historical events, which allows it to be imagined in relation to, for example, the Ptolemaic takeover of Jerusalem (ca. 305 BCE), the desecration of the temple by the Seleucid Antiochus IV (ca. 165 BCE), or some similar calamity.

Prophetic descriptions of restoration generally envision it as an event with cosmic implications, in which YHWH's universal sovereignty is manifest so dramatically that other nations are drawn to acknowledge it. These descriptions vary with regard to whether foreigners who acknowledge YHWH remain within their own people (the pluralistic model; e.g., Isa. 2:2–3; Zeph. 3:9–10; Zech. 14:16), or become related to the people of Israel as subjects/slaves (the imperial/colonial model).

Isaianic prophecies mostly fall into the latter category (e.g., Isa. 14:2; 60:10, 12, 14; 61:5–6). This text is incomplete in the sense that it does not spell out what social status goes along with full participation. Scripture contains both models of how the blessing promised to all nations through Israel (Gen. 12:3b) is mediated, suggesting that each might be appropriate in particular historical circumstances.

Conclusion. According to the principle of typological recapitulation that informs this prophecy, its fulfillment will entail the need for it to be fulfilled again in a different way. If Christians imagine it to have been fulfilled in the new covenant established by Jesus Christ, we now have to ask how it needs to be fulfilled again. If, since the time of Constantine, Christians have imagined it to have been fulfilled in terms of the imperial/colonial model, we have to ask whether this is still appropriate under present historical circumstances. The people of God will have a particular demographic boundary at any given moment in history, but God is always redefining it to include those left out.

MICHAEL H. FLOYD

understanding of what it means to be a foreigner or an outcast.

Within each congregational culture, there are myriad ways in which people are excluded or simply ignored. One of these can be as innocent as the way in which the members of a parish group or guild have become so comfortable with one another that they no longer feel the need to invite or encourage new faces. Any person who naively wanders into their fold immediately feels a sense of exclusion when confronted with the depth of the group's familiarity and intimacy. Any number of parish groups may have become "exclusive," not by intention, but simply because they have lost their desire to reach out and gather in the foreigners and outcasts.

On a more insidious level, many congregations have become intentionally exclusive, responding out of fear and prejudice to foreign elements without or within their boundaries. Anyone with congregational experience knows that churches harbor myriad ways of making some people feel "out" and others "in." The vision of Third Isaiah can be used to identify and challenge such assumptions, inviting the congregation to look courageously into their projections and prejudice—all the ways they exclude those that they perceive are foreign or "other."

God calls us boldly and relentlessly to respond to the reality of salvation and the dynamic of deliverance by embracing justice and walking in righteousness. A just and righteous response demands that we look deeply into the inner workings of our minds and hearts to identify and dismantle those internal mechanisms that cause us to demean and dismiss others, the means by which we create foreigners and outcasts.

Isaiah's vision of God's holy mountain invites us all to celebrate with joy the delight that God takes in the great diversity of folk who love the Lord and are united in their common worship and by their commitment to God's justice and righteousness.

WENDEL W. MEYER

Psalm 67

¹May God be gracious to us and bless us
    and make his face to shine upon us,   *Selah*
²that your way may be known upon earth,
    your saving power among all nations.
³Let the peoples praise you, O God;
    let all the peoples praise you.

⁴Let the nations be glad and sing for joy,
    for you judge the peoples with equity
    and guide the nations upon earth.   *Selah*
⁵Let the peoples praise you, O God;
    let all the peoples praise you.

⁶The earth has yielded its increase;
    God, our God, has blessed us.
⁷May God continue to bless us;
    let all the ends of the earth revere him.

Theological Perspective

Psalm 67, perhaps a harvest psalm, exudes a quiet confidence in the gracious goodness of God. One can imagine the people of God bringing in a bountiful harvest and singing this song. The lovely repetition of the Aaronic blessing (Num. 6:24–26) at the beginning of the psalm sets the tone of deep satisfaction and rest in the care and keeping of God. So often, the life of Christian faith is portrayed as struggle and effort. In Scripture, the life of Christian faith is even portrayed as a battle, which requires the belt of truth, the shield of faith, the helmet of salvation, and the breastplate of righteousness (Eph. 6:10–17). These biblical admonitions for courage and strength connect deeply with our experiences in life. Struggles and battles are, in fact, a feature of living the gospel truthfully and faithfully.

Other scriptural voices fill in a more complete picture of Christian living. One of the most lovely statements of the calm confidence and joy of the believer is found in the familiar text, Philippians 4:4–7, that ends, "And the peace of God, which surpasses all understanding, will guard your hearts and your minds in Christ Jesus." In a similar tone, Psalm 67 paints a picture of faith as gratitude and peace. "May God be gracious to us and bless us," it begins. "The earth has yielded its increase; God, our God, has blessed us," it ends. The psalm is one confident

Pastoral Perspective

Words of blessing are so important. Surely the psalmist was drawn by this knowledge into caressing the ancient Aaronic blessing ("The LORD bless you and keep you; the LORD make his face to shine upon you, and be gracious to you; the LORD lift up his countenance upon you, and give you peace," Num. 6:24–26) into a blessing for his own worshiping community. The psalmist lovingly cradled the benediction that had been passed on to him as treasure from preceding generations and contemporized it. He wrapped language of old around his present experience of a bountiful harvest. The occasion of bringing in a good crop became an occasion both to praise the sovereign God from whom all goodness flowed and to impress upon worshipers that their mission was to extend divine blessing to all the ends of the earth.

Psalm 67 challenges modern communities of faith to apply ancient words of blessing in contemporary settings, as the psalmist did. In a culture where sharp lines are often drawn between "sacred" and "secular," rituals that are both ancient and new serve to unmask this division, revealing it as a false distinction. Wrapping language of worship and blessing around experiences such as returning to school in the fall, caring for a pet, and earning a driver's license can serve to draw people into a deepened

Exegetical Perspective

A song of thanksgiving for a good harvest? A prayer beseeching blessing from the Lord? A summons to "the nations" to honor the Lord? Much of the ambiguity regarding the genre of Psalm 67 arises from different ways of understanding some of the verb forms in the psalm. Fourteen of the Hebrew verbs are in the imperfect (*yqtl*) form, which is most commonly translated as a future indicative tense. However, the *yqtl* form can also represent the Hebrew jussive (or subjunctive), expressing a command, desire, or supplication. Owing to this ambiguity, we find that some translations render Psalm 67:7, "God will bless us, and all the ends of the earth will fear him" (NIV), whereas others render the verse "May God continue to bless us; let all the ends of the earth revere him" (NRSV).

So, should the *yqtl* forms be rendered by English future, or should they be represented by a subjunctive ("Let/May X do so-and-so")? Some Hebrew verbs have a distinctive form for the jussive; within Psalm 67 there is one such verb where the distinctive jussive form is used: *ya'er* in verse 1. This verb form prompts a translation of "[May God] make his face shine." Extrapolating from that instance, it is reasonable to consider that many of the other *yqtl* forms in the psalm should similarly be translated as entreaties or petitions. Especially prominent in the psalm is the

Homiletical Perspective

Just as most preachers can experience Sundays whipping past as fast as telephone poles on a highway, so can we experience Psalms and psalm language breezing past us in a lovely garble of predictable praise and high words. Psalm 67 presents some of that challenge. At first glance, it seems to end in the same place where it begins, coloring within the lines the whole way through. It is no stretch to imagine this psalm being sung; in the repeated chorus of verses 3 and 5, one can see the lyrics on the screen, the bouncing dot, the easily sung phrases.

As so often is the case with ancient, well-loved words from Scripture, deeper study leads to richer layers lying beneath the surface. In the Aaronic blessing sung in the first two verses, we hear the familiar call that God may "make his face to shine upon us." More than a poetic way of saying, "May God look at us," or "May God smile at us," the suggestion here is that God show us favor and even give protection.

One homiletical hook of this psalm might be the probing of what it means to feel the shining of God's face in our lives. To make one's face "shine" is really to glow and to focus one's entire countenance, along with one's total attention. On what, in our world today and in our daily lives, does God's face shine? Those in the pew could hear this differently: what does God see in my life about which it is worth

Psalm 67

Theological Perspective

affirmation after another. There are no enemies in this psalm. There are no calamities. Instead, God is gracious, God is blessing, and the people are praising.

John Calvin, in spite of living in a tumultuous time in the sixteenth century, understood the quiet rest and confidence a believer has in God. He liked to use the word "repose" to indicate the deep rest that comes from being created and loved by God. Whenever he lectured on the Bible to his students in Geneva, he began with a prayer. He prayed on one occasion, "May we repose in peace under that guardianship which You have promised us."[1] This prayer echoes what the psalmist expressed as well, so many years earlier. "May God continue to bless us" (v. 7). Rest and repose and peace are the colors of the palette of Psalm 67.

These colors of rest and repose are rooted in a fundamental orientation of this psalm to the God of all the universe. This psalm affirms a simple, yet profound, Christian principle: All good gifts come from God. All beauty, all love, all art, all deeds of kindness and mercy, all efforts toward justice, all halting steps toward reconciliation, all impressive achievements, all good gifts come from God. This means, quite simply, that God is the source of everything that is good, wherever that goodness is displayed. Calvin remarked in his commentary on the Psalms that Psalm 67 affirms that "we owe our happiness, our success, and prosperity, entirely to the same cause,"[2] namely, God alone.

This simple, yet profound, Christian principle gives us a perspective or framework for life. In modern cultures that vigorously propose alternate frameworks, the affirmation that all good gifts come from God steadies and orients the believer to the true source of life and being. No, the stock market is not the source of all good things; the marketplace is not the source of all good things; human ingenuity and will is not the source of all good things; certainly human power and control is not the source of all good things. It is God who is the source of all that is good.

However, the Christian faith does not stop with this principle. If God is the fountain of all that is good, then the people respond with joy and gratitude. Psalm 67 repeats in two verses the refrain, "Let the peoples praise you, O God; let all the peoples praise you" (vv. 3, 5). When God's face, the source of

1. John Calvin, *Commentary on Daniel*, 11:5.
2. John Calvin, *Commentary on the Book of Psalms*, 67:1.

Pastoral Perspective

recognition of their dependence upon and relationship with the Creator God, and into discernment of specific acts of responsive discipleship as well.

A church in Maryland begins each school year with a *Blessing of the Backpacks*. On a Sunday in early September, the children and teens of the church bring their backpacks to worship. They are invited to come forward and to sit on the floor of the chancel. Each student is given a prayer pull that has been lovingly crafted by an adult member of the congregation. This prayer pull can be attached to a zipper on a backpack, a computer case, or a coat. The students are told, "The zipper pull is a reminder of God's presence with you at all times. God walks beside you when things are going well; God walks with you when you are facing the most challenging of situations. God is your strength when you are joyful and when you are grieving. Each zip is a prayer— God is with me. God is with you." The service of blessing concludes with a prayer for students, teachers, aides, bus drivers, administrators, custodians, and cafeteria workers.

A church in North Carolina observes the feast day of Francis of Assisi (October 4) by holding a *Blessing of the Animals*. Attendance at the Sunday morning service rivals attendance on Christmas and Easter. The numbers are so large that the congregation has outgrown the sanctuary. Congregants, along with their pet dogs, cats, hamsters, and assorted reptiles, vacate their usual worship space and gather on a nearby hillside under the canopy of an azure sky. They confess in prayer their failure to respond in awe to nature's wonders, their abuse of the human power of dominion over creation, and the ways in which they have participated in the needless suffering of the animal kingdom.

They give thanks to a gracious God who teaches them to love and to cry through the companionship of their pets. They express prayerful gratitude for service animals that guide the blind and rescue the lost, and for animals who have given their lives for research that has led to new discoveries that enhance the quality of human life. They pledge themselves to care for their pets tenderly, as faithful and responsible stewards of God's good creation.

A church in Texas holds a *Driver's License Blessing* for teenagers and their parents when this most anticipated of adolescent landmarks is reached. Youth group members gather as these words are spoken, "This week, you have reached one of the most important milestones in a person's life. You have obtained your driver's license. We celebrate this

verb *brk*, "bless": there are three occurrences of *yebarekenu* in the psalm (vv. 1, 6, and 7). In line with what has just been said about rendering the *yqtl* verb forms as entreaty, a translation of *yebarekenu* in all three instances as "May God bless us" (or "continue to bless us") seems apt.

Companion Piece to Aaronic Blessing. The psalm may be considered as a companion piece to the Aaronic blessing in Numbers 6:24–26. Psalm 67 constitutes an appeal for God to do what the Aaronic benediction then bestows. When we lay the two passages alongside each other, we note that this psalmic entreaty asks for God's blessing to be upon the corporate "us," whereas the Aaronic benediction is specifically addressed to the individual—"the Lord bless *thee* and keep *thee*" (KJV)—even as the word following the Aaronic blessing declares, "So they [the priests] shall put my name on the Israelites, and I will bless *them*" (Num. 6:27). Blessing is experienced in the individual life, but that individual life is bound up with the blessed community.

Theocentric Orientation and Universal Horizon. Although Psalm 67 seeks blessing for "us," the psalm throughout is theocentric in its orientation, and its horizon is universal. The psalm acknowledges that it is God's role to bestow blessing: verse 1 begins with the petition for God's blessing, and the final verse of the psalm begins similarly. At the center of the psalm (v. 4) is an affirmation of God's constant activity: God judges "the peoples" (not just Israel) with equity and guides "the nations" of the earth. The two *yqtl* verbs in the psalm that do not lend themselves to a subjunctive or jussive interpretation (*tishpot* and *tankhem* in that central v. 4) affirm actions of God which provide the motivation for summoning "the peoples" to gladness and joy.

Although the psalmist beseeches God to bestow grace and blessing on "us," the ultimate objective of the blessing is stated at the opening and closing of the psalm: that those beyond "us" will know (v. 2) and revere (v. 7) God. Moreover, the central section of the psalm (vv. 3–5) seeks praise and rejoicing from "all peoples" (vv. 3, 5) and "the nations" (v. 4). The psalm recognizes God's chosen people as the medium through whose experience those *beyond* the ranks of the chosen people will be enabled to gain saving knowledge of the God of Israel.

Earth's Bounty, God's Blessing. The one perfect (*qtl*) verb in the psalm occurs in verse 6: "the earth *has*

smiling? When the shine of God's face hits my broken life, what is the dark corner that is revealed?

Another theme of Psalm 67 is evident in the first two verses: may God bless the people, so that the people, *all* the people, may praise God. In proposing this direct cause and effect, a particular approach to spreading the faith is suggested. Elsewhere, the psalmist is quick to ask that unbelievers and evildoers (though not always one and the same) be punished for failure to follow the God of Israel. Here, the suggestion is that the nations be so impressed with God's magnanimous blessings as to be wooed into the faith.

This method of evangelism is nothing new, but many occupants of this Sunday's pews may be refreshed in hearing about the power of presenting to the world the joy of our faith rather than our superiority, our intellect, or our power. Dietrich Bonhoeffer directed preachers to be tangible and enticing with their sermons: "[Preaching] must be like offering a child a fine red apple . . . and then saying, 'Do you want it?'"[1] Peel the fruit of our faith, let the juice run down your fingers. Take a bite in view of others, and marvel aloud about the taste, the texture, the utter fruity perfection. For Christians, the suggestion is that the good news is an easy sell; so why beat others over the head with it? It is far better to entice and invite, and let God do the rest.

Of course, we must always step cautiously when overlaying a Christian lens on Hebrew Scriptures; faithful exploration of any psalm cannot sidestep its decisively Jewish character. For the people of Israel, intentions to convert took a back seat to intentions to determine which peoples were blessed and which were cursed, whose god was holiest and mightiest, and whose god panned out to be a false idol. Far more than a source of domesticated spirituality, Walter Brueggemann points to the Psalms as a key crossword where issues of theodicy are chewed on: "Religious hungers in Israel never preclude justice questions."[2] The Psalms are nothing if not the story of the oppressed struggling against the unjust.

In verse 4, we hear good news about the questions of who is in and who is out, and where fairness may be found in an upside-down world. With wide inclusion, the God of Israel judges *all* peoples with equity. This suggests that other gods would not be so equitable, and that the nations—indeed, all the ends of

---

1. *Eberhard Bethge, Dietrich Bonhoeffer: Theologian, Christian, Man for his Times; a Biography* (Minneapolis: Fortress Press, 2000), 234.
2. Walter Brueggemann, *The Message of the Psalms* (Minneapolis: Augsburg Publishing House, 1984), 169.

Psalm 67

Theological Perspective

all good, shines upon humanity, the people spring up with gladness. Gracious love calls forth glad response.

From a theological perspective, this means that the revelation of God changes people. Revelation is not wasted; it is not mute. It calls, and the response follows. Karl Barth once said, "Knowledge of God's ways always implies a new human action corresponding to the divine."[3] Psalm 67 states that God's ways are known upon the earth (v. 2) and immediately the peoples break forth in praise (v. 3). In verse 4, the nations are glad and sing with joy because of God's revelation. God's self-disclosure has a true and right response. This theme is repeated once more in verse 7, where God continues to bless the nations of the earth, who then revere God. The pattern of revelation and response is a repeated pattern in Psalm 67.

The scope of God's gracious blessing extends to the wide world of "the nations" in this psalm. Similarly, the response to God's blessing extends to "the nations." Psalm 67 underscores the important theological emphasis of the covenant God formed with the people of Israel. When God spoke to Abram and said, "I will make of you a great nation, and I will bless you, and make your name great, so that you will be a blessing" (Gen. 12:2), the reach of God's gracious intent was clear. It covers and surrounds the people of God, but it also extends to the ends of the earth, to all peoples and tribes and nations. They too will join in the praise of God. "Let the peoples praise you, O God; let all the people praise you," says verse 3. "Let all the ends of the earth revere him," repeats verse 7.

No one is left out in this vision of global worship. Everyone is included. The prophecy of Isaiah joins in this wide covenant imagination: "Nations shall come to your light, and kings to the brightness of your dawn" (Isa. 60:3). Psalm 67 underlines an important theological theme seen throughout Scripture, that the blessing of God's people is for the salvation of the nations.

LEANNE VAN DYK

Pastoral Perspective

special day and pray that God will be with you, guiding and protecting you as you travel the streets and highways." Psalm 121 is read. A time of sharing behind-the-wheel safety tips follows.

The parents of the new driver pray, "Holy God, you are the beginning and end of every road we take. At every moment and in every place, you are near to your children. Keep this, your treasured child, in your care. Lead her as you led the children of Israel through the wilderness. Guide her as you guided the magi to your Son. Protect her as you protected Abraham and Sarah when they left their own land and set out on a journey. Enable her to travel safely, with care for the safety of others. May Christ always be a companion on her journeys." The gift of a keychain is presented. Finally, the youth group, their leaders, and the new driver's parents encircle the new driver for a closing blessing, "May the Lord remain constantly at your side, and guide your journey. Amen."

A parent reflected on how the experience blessed her: "For me, this was an incredibly touching experience, one that drew from me a well of tears as I read the prayer. As I listened to my sixteen-year-old son read his portion, the tears that came forth during the ceremony were tears of healing and letting go. No one gathered that day had known how tender I was about my son driving on his own, as my own brother was completely paralyzed from an automobile accident that took place in the 1970s."

Words of blessing are as important today as they were in the psalmist's day. The ever-ancient, ever-new language of Psalm 67 is a gift for contemporary folk, as it was for those in the psalmist's circle. It is language for joyful song, for healing tears, for bold commissioning.

ELIZABETH MCGREGOR SIMMONS

---

3. Karl Barth, *Church Dogmatics*, IV/3 (Edinburgh: T&T Clark, 1961), 184.

Exegetical Perspective

yielded [lit. "given"] its harvest/increase." (Some interpret this as a prophetic perfect, referring to a future event whose occurrence is so certain that it can be described as a completed event; KJV and NIV translate "shall/will yield.") From this clause we infer that Psalm 67 was composed in a mood of gratitude. It is not only in times of distress that the worshiper cries to God for blessing. Recent studies in Hebrew poetic parallelism have concluded that frequently the second line of a poetic parallel structure intensifies in some way the meaning of the first line.[1] The second line of our verse 6 correlates the earth's bounty with God's blessing and, further, seeks continuation of the same. The first part of verse 6 looks back; the second line looks forward. God's experienced favor is precedent, and indeed motivation, for entreating God's future favor.

While acknowledging God's blessing as an accomplished fact epitomized in the earth's bounty, the psalmist petitions for God's ongoing goodwill. The entreaty is grounded (pun intended) in material evidence of God's prior favor. The harvest is an earnest that emboldens the community to petition for God's continued blessing (note NRSV trans. of v. 7).

Aspects of God's Blessing. Verse 6 is a reminder that God's "blessing" has a decidedly *material* dimension. The Lord's "blessing" refers usually to God's ongoing *day-to-day work* of preserving the community and its well-being, as distinct from those occasional extraordinary mighty acts when the Lord's saving power is manifested in a striking fashion.[2] We note that the earth's bounty from "our God" is *not finally just for "our" benefit and enjoyment*, but is a visible token of God's grace to evoke the reverence of "all the ends of the earth." In sum, it appears that all of the possibilities for understanding Psalm 67 that were enumerated in the opening paragraph of this essay coalesce within the psalm.

GEORGE W. RAMSEY

Homiletical Perspective

the earth—may revere *this* God, knowing they are in the hands of one who will give them a fair shake.

Residents of the Sunday pews may not find this news so immediately startling. We expect nothing less from God than fairness and justice. If we take ourselves back to the words of the psalmist, however, we remember that ours is a modern assumption. In ancient Israel, to be close to God was to be close to judgment. The question is, What kind of judgment does God hand down? Are evildoers always punished, and are good people always rewarded? Is God all-powerful, or is God all-loving? Outside of the Psalms, one needs only look as far as Job to see the Old Testament struggle with these questions of theodicy.

But even these singular and ancient questions do not fully encompass the way the people of Psalms wrestled with theodicy. Instead, Brueggemann suggests that theodicy in the Psalms is an exploration about the distribution of power in the world, about how justice is meted out socially and materially, and about whether or not we can trust the character of God to be just. "What emerges . . . is that Israel is not interested in spirituality or communion with God that tries to deny or obscure the important issue of theodicy. An unjust relation with God is no relation at all."[3] In the world of the Psalms, the people's relationship with God must be strong enough to withstand critique.

KATIE GIVENS KIME

---

1. E.g., James Kugel, *The Idea of Biblical Poetry* (New Haven: Yale University Press, 1981); Robert Alter, *The Art of Biblical Poetry* (New York: Basic Books, 1985).

2. See esp. Claus Westermann, *Blessing in the Bible and the Church* (Philadelphia: Fortress Press, 1978).

3 Ibid., 173.

Romans 11:1-2a, 29-32

¹I ask, then, has God rejected his people? By no means! I myself am an Israelite, a descendant of Abraham, a member of the tribe of Benjamin. ²God has not rejected his people whom he foreknew, . . . ²⁹for the gifts and the calling of God are irrevocable. ³⁰Just as you were once disobedient to God but have now received mercy because of their disobedience, ³¹so they have now been disobedient in order that, by the mercy shown to you, they too may now receive mercy. ³²For God has imprisoned all in disobedience so that he may be merciful to all.

Theological Perspective

The theological journey Paul began in Romans 8:38–39 is brought to culmination here. Has God, from whom no power or principality can separate us, actually rejected his chosen people, the Israelites? Paul responds by using the most powerful phrase in his rhetorical arsenal: "By no means" (Gk. *mē genoito*). (See his use of this phrase in 6:2 and 11:11.) Paul could not be any clearer; God's covenant with the nation of Israel remains intact. So how does Paul explain the status of the nation of Israel, keeping in mind that Romans 9–11 is about groups of people, not individuals?

First, let us understand what Paul is not saying. Paul rejects supersessionism, the most basic version of which says that the new covenant in Christ "supersedes" the old Mosaic and Abrahamic covenants and that those who reject Christ are damned. The notion that Christianity simply replaces Judaism has a long history within the Christian church. Church fathers such as Justin Martyr and Origen taught variations on supersessionism and Augustine's understanding of election led him to a similar conclusion.

As Phillip Cary notes, "The Gentile church of his [Augustine's] time . . . could not imagine itself as other than the elect, which meant that the Jews must no longer be the chosen people, having been

Pastoral Perspective

One of the treasured tenets of American life is the conviction that, if you work hard, you will be rewarded; effort will pay off. Similarly, those who are lazy and ineffective will find themselves at the bottom of the heap or out the door. Either way, people get what they deserve, and they deserve what they get.

Some modern-day preachers convert this view into their own good news and insist that God wants us to be well-to-do. All we have to do is believe, attend church on Sunday, and pony up when the plate is passed. Then, so this version of the good news goes, God will be pleased with us and will reward us with our own riches. Unfortunately for the preachers of the prosperity gospel, there is little, if anything, in Christian Scripture to support this view. The gospel truth is much more complex.

Our relationship with God is not transactional, based on our being rewarded for our goodness. In the scandal of grace, we receive God's good gifts in spite of ourselves. Even disobedience to God's way becomes an avenue of mercy. We never get what we really deserve; we would perish if we did. We can never deserve what we do get, because God seems to love us, no matter what.

God has a long history of this irrational love. From "in the beginning," humans have been determined to go their own way, rather than following

Exegetical Perspective

A large portion of Romans 11 is not included in today's reading, but it contains important information for understanding Paul's message. Romans as a whole has instructions for both Jewish and Gentile Christians, but in this section Paul directs his remarks more specifically to the latter (v. 13). He is not as explicit about his reasons, but some can be deduced by reading carefully between the lines and by looking at the situation facing the church in Rome at the time.

Paul's prohibitions in verse 18 ("do not boast") and verse 20 ("do not become proud") are telling. The present tense of both verbs indicates that these actions may have already begun and that Paul is calling on the Gentiles to cease and desist (i.e., "stop boasting," "quit your pride"). The implication is that the Gentiles have taken to boasting about their newly found position of favor in God's family, and they are doing so over and against what they perceive as a loss of status by the Jews.

Exacerbating this problem may have been the recently repealed edict of Emperor Claudius, who a few years before had banned all the Jews from Rome.[1] During the period of Jewish absence, the Gentiles in the Roman church likely grew in numbers, influence,

1. Suetonius, *Claudius* 25.4.

Homiletical Perspective

My father-in-law Dean recently died at the age of eighty-nine within twenty miles of the place of his birth. At his funeral the congregation sang a nineteenth-century hymn that he and his wife of sixty-three years had chosen for the occasion, "O Love that Wilt Not Let Me Go."

> O Love that wilt not let me go,
> I rest my weary soul in thee;
> I give thee back the life I owe,
> that in thine ocean depths its flow
> may richer, fuller be.[1]

Dean lived through the Great Depression, taught school in a one-room schoolhouse when he was sixteen, briefly played minor league baseball for the Brooklyn Dodgers, flew for the Navy in World War II, and during the war married the love of his life. With her, he buried their firstborn child, worked and raised a family of two children, sang at pie suppers, churches, and community events with his siblings, all of whom he outlived and mourned.

Throughout those eighty-nine years of a life well lived, Dean never forgot the Love that would not let him go. He lived out his Love and shared it with his

1. George Matheson, "O Love That Wilt Not Let Me Go," in *The Presbyterian Hymnal* (Louisville, KY: Westminster/John Knox Press, 1990).

Romans 11:1-2a, 29-32

Theological Perspective

superceded in that role by the church."[1] Martin Luther's sharp distinction between law and grace and his vehement attacks on Judaism during the Reformation follow in this tradition of supersessionism. Calvin did not view law and grace as diametrically opposed, nor did he view the Old and New Testaments as standing in such stark opposition; therefore he was much less supersessionist than Luther. This explains the general, but by no means universal, tendency of Reformed theologians to seek alternatives to supersessionism.

Those who historically and presently maintain this version of supersessionism must explain away Paul's seemingly unambiguous denial of the rejection of Israel in Romans 11. To do so, they often claim that the "Israel" that is not rejected is the "new Israel," that is, those who confess Christ. This argument fails on two grounds: First, if the "Israel" to which Paul is referring is synonymous with believers, then he is basically saying that all the elect are elect and has uncharacteristically wasted a great deal of theological energy in simply proving a truism.

Second, there is nothing in Romans 9–11 that would lead one to believe that Paul is using the term "Israel" in a metaphorical sense to mean those who believe. Of the ten uses of "Israel" in Romans 9–11, nearly all refer to an ethnic group, not a combination of Gentile and Jewish believers. Repeatedly, he references Old Testament figures in the argument and cites the promises that were given to a specific, identifiable (and chosen) people: patriarchs, glory, worship, covenants, and so forth (9:4–5), those who are "descendants of Abraham" (11:2).

If Paul is not a supersessionist, then what is the answer to the question, "has God rejected his people?" (11:1)? Paul is making one or both of the following claims: first, all Jews are saved, because some of them (a remnant) have indeed believed; second, Jews are saved, because all people are saved.

The key to the first exegesis is Paul's reference to Elijah and an accompanying statement from God found between the two portions of today's lectionary text. In answering the question whether God has rejected Israel, Paul points to the story of Elijah after the contest on Mount Carmel. Elijah pleads with God to destroy Israel because of its wickedness: God replies, "I have kept for myself seven thousand who have not bowed the knee to Baal" (v. 4, adapting 1 Kgs. 19:18). Paul adds, "So too at the present time there is a remnant, chosen by grace" (v. 5).

1. Phillip Cary, *Inner Grace: Augustine in the Traditions of Plato and Paul* (New York: Oxford University Press, 2008), 124.

Pastoral Perspective

God's way. The biblical record is full of accounts of God's willful children and God's never-ending mercy, what the Hebrew Scripture calls *hesed*, often translated as "steadfast love." The Greek word for mercy, *eleos*, gives us our word "eleemosynary," or charity. This is where it gets hard for a lot of Christians, those who work hard to be independent and self-sufficient. Many of us, part of the "pray, pay, and obey" generation that has dominated many mainline denominations, are more used to giving charity than receiving it. It is very difficult for us to feel indebted to anyone.

That God's mercy is integral to God's sovereignty, not linked to our good or bad behavior, is hard to accept. Paul struggles to understand how Israel, God's own chosen people, can remain in the circle of God's love after rejecting God's Messiah. He concludes that the people's rejection of God does not lead to God's rejection of the people. We may violate our own integrity, but God's integrity, God's steadfast love, remains constant. Even more counterintuitive is the notion that God works through, and perhaps even creates, our disobedience.

The Hebrew Scripture from the semicontinuous track for this Sunday of the lectionary tells the story of Joseph and his brothers. Joseph eventually explains to his brothers their own actions: "Even though you intended to do harm to me, God intended it for good, in order to preserve a numerous people, as he is doing today" (Gen. 50:20). Joseph, and Paul after him, have a clear sense of God's freedom to redeem any human sinfulness, and an understanding that God takes the long view, always working in human history toward the fulfillment of God's will and way.

Some modern-day groups have taken as their cause the conversion of the Jews to Christianity, which seems a distortion of Paul's concern for his people. This concern applies as much to us as it does to the ancient Jews, because we too have been disobedient. We too have not fully embraced God's new way of life in Christ. We too have received mercy. God's wide horizon puts our present failures to be God's people in context: If the people God created and chose for God's own can disobey and still be part of God's plan, then so can we.

In a sweeping declaration, Paul proclaims that "the gifts and the calling of God are irrevocable" (v. 29)—once given, forever ours. Nothing we do can convince God to let go of us (cf. Rom. 8:38–39). We are the beneficiaries of an eternal love—but so is everyone else God claims. We get no special treatment; rather, God extends the special treatment to

Exegetical Perspective

and to some extent their sense of privilege, but by the time Paul writes (57–58 CE), the Jews have returned.

Thus, Romans 11 has the subtle but unmistakable tone of correction. Paul wants to reveal something to the Gentiles of which they are yet unaware, a mystery (v. 25) that is nothing less than God's sweeping, redemptive plan for history. The new era ushered in by Christ will not end with a church peopled only by Gentiles. Israel will not remain outside God's fold forever.

To this end, Paul takes a defensive posture on behalf of Israel, despite the fact that their covenantal missteps (discussed throughout chaps. 9–10) have left them in an unenviable position. To those who might assume that the era of Israel's special covenant with God is over, Paul responds emphatically. He begins in verse 1a with a solemn "I ask, then . . ." and continues with the very question that no doubt many Gentiles in Rome had been posing: "Has God rejected his people?"

The verb evokes language from numerous lament psalms (e.g., Pss. 43:2; 44:9; 60:1), but his primary inspiration is Psalm 94:14, which emphatically denies such a possibility. Paul does change the psalmist's blunt statement into a question, but it is hardly an "honest" question. The Greek construction (using the particle *mē*) always implies a negative response. To punctuate his point, Paul offers his trademark "by no means!" (cf. 3:4, 6, 31; 6:2, 15; 7:7, 13; 9:14; 11:11), followed by a straightforward statement in verse 2a.

Another defense of Israel comes in the way Paul identifies himself in verse 1b, as "an Israelite" (a preferred self-designation among Jews; cf. John 1:47; Acts 5:35; 2 Cor. 11:22), "a descendant of Abraham" (another favorite self-identification, cf. Luke 3:8; John 8:33; Acts 13:26; 4 Macc. 6:17), and "a member of the tribe of Benjamin" (a tribe with special status, according to Deut. 33:12). If anyone is tempted to think God has rejected Israel, they must first grapple with the identity of Paul himself.

A hint of God's master plan comes as early as verse 2a. Here, "his people whom he foreknew" is a reference not to all Christians but to Israel specifically, and God's foreknowing (Paul uses the verb only here and 8:29) emphasizes Israel's special role in redemptive history. The cosmic plan of God, then, is presented as a necessary corrective to a Gentile Christian overconfidence that was marginalizing Jewish brothers and sisters. Against this backdrop, today's reading moves rather seamlessly from verse

Homiletical Perspective

family and neighbors, only rarely leaving the small Kansas town that was his home. Dean understood the nature and character of God: faithful, gracious, and merciful. He knew true Love in the love of his Savior.

God does not let any of us go. In Romans, Paul struggles to understand why his brother and sister Jews have failed to turn to Christ as he has. In Jesus he has found redemption and reconciliation with his creator. Why not they? If they have not followed Christ, what is to become of the chosen people? Will God reject God's own?

In chapter 11, Paul concludes that it is impossible for God to reject God's own beloved, those whom God has created and called, "for the gifts and the calling of God are irrevocable" (v. 29b). God did not let Paul go, God did not let the Gentiles go, and neither will God let God's chosen people go.

It is difficult for Paul to comprehend fully the love, plans, and purposes of God. Paul's comprehension is limited by the scope of his humanity. God's plans and ways are often beyond human discernment and understanding. As the prophet Isaiah wrote, "For my thoughts are not your thoughts, nor are your ways my ways, says the LORD. For as the heavens are higher than the earth, so are my ways higher than your ways and my thoughts than your thoughts" (Isa. 55:8–9). Paul himself quotes Isaiah at the end of chapter 11 when he asserts that God's ways are just even if God does not disclose God's mind to us (vv. 33–34). What Paul knows for sure is that *the gifts and the calling of God are irrevocable.* He may not understand why everything is unfolding as it is with his Jewish brothers and sisters, but he trusts God with their present and with their future.

While we, with Paul, are unable to comprehend God's ways and plans, we may trust that God is faithful and good. God never lets us go. Who understands the way in which God has chosen to redeem the world? What kind of vehicles for divinity are a manger in Bethlehem, a cross, and an empty tomb on the outskirts of Jerusalem? A hymn text, perhaps by Thomas à Kempis, expresses not only the profound love of God, but God's mysterious way of offering salvation in Christ for all of humankind:

> O love, how deep, how broad, how high,
> How passing thought and fantasy,
> That God, the Son of God, should take
> Our mortal form for mortal's sake.[2]

---

2. "O Love, How Deep, How Broad, How High," in *The Presbyterian Hymnal.*

Romans 11:1-2a, 29-32

Theological Perspective

Paul's argument seems to be that all Israel will be saved, due to the faithfulness of some Jews who have accepted Christ. Just as God once saved Israel because there were some "who have not bowed the knee to Baal," God will once again save all the nation of Israel because of the righteous remnant of Jews who have believed with their hearts and confessed with their mouths. "Paul is showing that God's purpose of blessing all humanity through an elect people cannot be frustrated when some of those who belong physically to that people reject the purposes."[2]

There is a second, more radical possibility: all Jews are saved because all people are saved. Known as universalism or *apokatastasis*, this is not as foreign to Paul's thinking as one might believe. For example, in 1 Corinthians 15:22, Paul writes that "For as all die in Adam, so all will be made alive in Christ." Adam's sin led to the death of all human beings; Christ's sacrifice leads to the salvation of all human beings. Those who would deny that "all" (Gk. *pantes*) means "every single person" in terms of salvation must also deny that "all" means everyone in relation to Adam's sin. Paul's comparison of Jesus with Adam in Romans 5:12–21 is grounded on the notion that everyone partakes of the sin of Adam. "Therefore, just as one man's trespass led to condemnation *for all*, so one man's act of righteousness leads to justification and life *for all*" (Rom. 5:18, emphasis added). This seems supported by the final verse of today's passage, "For God has imprisoned *all* in disobedience so that he may be merciful to *all*."

This universalist claim and the remnant argument are not mutually exclusive. Israel may be saved because a remnant believes, or it may be the case that Israel is saved because everyone is saved because the *true* remnant believes, namely, Christ. This is essentially what Karl Barth argues, namely, that all Israel may be saved because all people are saved and all people are saved because there is one true remnant, the elected one, Jesus Christ, who becomes rejected for our sakes. So Paul ends where he began, with the fact that nothing can separate us (and hopefully anyone else) from the love of God.

KYLE D. FEDLER

Pastoral Perspective

all God's children. Many will welcome this inclusivity and take comfort in what may seem an unending string of second chances. Others, who work hard in the church and hope for a heavenly reward, may find this difficult, even offensive. What is the point of living obedient lives if the disobedient are pardoned without condition?

We are all among the disobedient, however, even the best of us. To be "imprisoned . . . in disobedience" (v. 32) is to claim the freedom to act as we will. God grants us that freedom so that we may choose to love as freely and gracefully as God does, but too often we convert our freedom into what Dietrich Bonhoeffer called cheap grace, "the grace we bestow upon ourselves."[1]

Costly grace, by contrast, "confronts us with a gracious call to follow Jesus, it comes as a word of forgiveness to the broken spirit and the contrite heart."[2] We cannot bless ourselves with God's grace, nor can we withhold blessing from others. God's gifts are freely given—by God who acts in sovereign love—not something we can give to, or even claim for, ourselves. Grace is God's alone to offer, and God offers it, it seems, to all people—the Jew and the Gentile, the ins and the outs, the faithful and the disobedient.

There is no one beyond the reach of grace. God's call is also inescapable. Those who have received the gift of grace are also to accept the call of the Giver. Grace, then, is a call to discipleship. God no more rescinds the call than God revokes the grace.

These twin constants, gift and call, are signs of God's unbounded faithfulness, which is unaffected by anything we do and, at the same time, never ceases to call us back to our own faithfulness. The gift, the grace, is irrevocable, and so is the call.

MARTHA C. HIGHSMITH

---

2. Paul J. Achtemeier, *Romans* (Louisville, KY: Westminster/John Knox Press, 1985), 157.

1. Dietrich Bonhoeffer, *The Cost of Discipleship* (New York: Macmillan, 1949), 47.
2. Ibid., 48.

Exegetical Perspective

2a to verse 29 where Paul features that plan once again. The "gifts" and "the calling," in this context, are again specifically Israel's. When Paul says that they are "irrevocable," the sense is not that God is confined and duty bound, but that for God to go back on the covenant would be simply unthinkable.

In verses 30–31, with a succinctness that he rarely approaches elsewhere in his writings, Paul summarizes God's entire cosmic plan in a single sentence. Whether Paul intended these verses to be read as structurally parallel (A-B-A-B), chiastic (A-B-B-A), or an elaborate combination of both, is open to debate. Regardless, Paul's overall message is clear, and in light of God's broad plan for history, an alternative structure seems possible: A-B-B-C.

Paul counters the commonly held assumption that history can be divided merely into two great stages: (a) that of Israel's inclusion, characterized by Gentile disobedience; and (b) that of the Gentiles' inclusion, characterized by Israel's disobedience. There is in fact a mysterious (see v. 25) final stage that God will see to fruition: (c) that of both Israel and the nations, characterized by God's mercy to both. Just as the Gentiles were formerly disobedient (a; v. 30a) yet now have been shown mercy (b, v. 30b), so also Israel is presently exhibiting disobedience (b, v. 31a), so that they might be positioned to receive God's mercy as well (c, v. 31b).

As if verses 30–31 were not succinct enough, Paul distills his historical summary to its most concentrated essence in verse 32. Though the theological challenge is undeniable, the force of the verb "imprisoned" (cf. Gal. 3:22–23) should not be minimized, as in the NAB's "delivered" or the RSV's "consigned." The word has a range of applications in the LXX, but the sense of "enclose" or "shut up/in" is common to all (see, e.g., Josh. 6:1 and 1 Sam. 1:6). Nevertheless, the emphasis in this verse is on the two key concepts from Paul's previous summary, disobedience and mercy, each of which is then linked to "all" of humanity (lit. "the all," the definite article perhaps indicating that Paul is thinking in holistic rather than universalistic terms).

In God's divine plan, even disobedience plays its assigned role as the precursor to God's ministry of mercy.

JOHN M. VONDERBRUEGGE

Homiletical Perspective

The image of the father in the story of the prodigal in Luke 15 is helpful when preaching this text. The father waits on his front porch, eyeing the road for a sign of his lost son. We are not told how long he waits. We know only that he faithfully watches for as long as it takes. When the prodigal returns, the father embraces the one who comes home, rejoices, and celebrates. The older brother is angry and refuses to attend the extravagant party underway for the prodigal. The older brother is not able to understand the Love that will not let the younger son go, or that the same Love embraces him. This Love is unconditional, not based upon our obedience, faith, or love. God offers this Love freely, now and always.

Three and a half months before his death, my father-in-law's doctor told him that the cancer had spread throughout his body and nothing else could be done. He and my mother-in-law listened to the news, spoke with the doctor for a while longer, and then drove home. Tired from the outing, Dean went into his room to rest. The pastor of their church arrived for one of his regular visits and went in to speak with him. Dean did not choose to say anything. Instead he sang all four stanzas of a hymn he had learned as a child that expressed his faith and trust in Christ. He followed this with the refrain of "God Will Take Care of You."[3]

> God will take care of you,
> Through every day, o'er all the way;
> He will take care of you,
> God will take care of you.

This man clearly understood, and wished to share with his pastor and family, that God is lovingly in charge of this world and all who are in it. "For from him and through him and to him are all things. To him be the glory forever. Amen" (v. 36).

MARY BETH ANTON

---

3. Civilla D. Martin, "God Will Take Care of You," in *The Hymnal* (Waco, TX: Word Music, 1986), #47.

Matthew 15:(10-20) 21-28

¹⁰Then he called the crowd to him and said to them, "Listen and understand: ¹¹it is not what goes into the mouth that defiles a person, but it is what comes out of the mouth that defiles." ¹²Then the disciples approached and said to him, "Do you know that the Pharisees took offense when they heard what you said?" ¹³He answered, "Every plant that my heavenly Father has not planted will be uprooted. ¹⁴Let them alone; they are blind guides of the blind. And if one blind person guides another, both will fall into a pit." ¹⁵But Peter said to him, "Explain this parable to us." ¹⁶Then he said, "Are you also still without understanding? ¹⁷Do you not see that whatever goes into the mouth enters the stomach, and goes out into the sewer? ¹⁸But what comes out of the mouth proceeds from the heart, and this is what defiles. ¹⁹For out of the heart come evil intentions, murder, adultery, fornication, theft, false witness,

Theological Perspective

When Dorothy L. Sayers's radio-play cycle *The Man Born to Be King* was first broadcast in 1941, some members of the public complained that it was vulgar and irreverent. She later recalled that one correspondent laughably objected to Herod telling his court, "Keep your mouths shut," on the grounds that such rough language was "jarring" on the lips of anyone "so closely connected with our Lord."[1] Such sensitive souls clearly had not read their Bibles.

Jesus' attitude and language in his encounter with the Canaanite woman is shocking. She is simply seeking deliverance for her demon-possessed daughter, and yet he calls her a dog—a name that his fellow Jews routinely gave to Gentile pagans. First, he is silent in the face of her cries, refusing even to acknowledge her (v. 23); then, he says that his mission is "only to the lost sheep of the house of Israel" (v. 24); finally, he tells her that the "food" for the children should not be thrown to the "dogs" (v. 26)—non-Israelites like her. The incident raises deep questions about prejudice, divine election, and the limits of God's mercy.

The very word "Canaanite" is charged with theological significance. It stirs up memories of ancient foes—idol-worshiping enemies over against whom

Pastoral Perspective

Thank God the lectionary adds a set of parenthetical verses to the Gospel lection for the day. One could only wish that they would have also included the first ten verses of chapter 15, because Matthew has taken great care to weave together tightly this theologically pregnant chapter from start to finish.

One theme running through this chapter is the role that tradition should play in religious life. Anyone involved in pastoral ministry knows of church battles fought "for God" in the name of "tradition." Tradition can mean anything from a worship practice that occurs more than once to a liturgical rite that the church has practiced for generations. Tradition can provide a solid, yet flexible, foundation for faithfulness, but it can also function in the opposite way. In this text, Jesus chastises the official keepers of Jewish tradition for having squeezed the life and liveliness out of their tradition until it has calcified into an irrelevant religious relic or worse.

For those who commit their lives to worship and serve God within the Christian community, today's Gospel lection has anything but the ring of ancient history. Matthew recalls the encounter between Jesus and the Jerusalem authorities, not just to record this memorable exchange. Matthew is writing to the church of his day, a church that is an increasing blend of Jew and Gentile, of those who were raised

---

1. Dorothy L. Sayers, *The Man Born to Be King* (San Francisco: Ignatius Press, 1990), 16.

slander. [20]These are what defile a person, but to eat with unwashed hands does not defile."

[21]Jesus left that place and went away to the district of Tyre and Sidon. [22]Just then a Canaanite woman from that region came out and started shouting, "Have mercy on me, Lord, Son of David; my daughter is tormented by a demon." [23]But he did not answer her at all. And his disciples came and urged him, saying, "Send her away, for she keeps shouting after us." [24]He answered, "I was sent only to the lost sheep of the house of Israel." [25]But she came and knelt before him, saying, "Lord, help me." [26]He answered, "It is not fair to take the children's food and throw it to the dogs." [27]She said, "Yes, Lord, yet even the dogs eat the crumbs that fall from their masters' table." [28]Then Jesus answered her, "Woman, great is your faith! Let it be done for you as you wish." And her daughter was healed instantly.

Exegetical Perspective

Matthew's story of a Canaanite woman follows a controversy with some Pharisees and scribes (Matt. 15:1–9), inviting comparison between the two incidents. Care should be taken not to stereotype these Pharisees and scribes. They should be treated as raising their own questions and not as representing Judaism or even all Pharisees or scribes.

Nevertheless, two points of comparison are significant. In the first incident, people who are socially accepted emphasize external differences and miss matters of the heart, whereas in the second, a woman who is socially marginalized breaks through external differences to claim God's mercy. The comparison produces a startling surprise. In the first incident, Jesus has the punch lines that enlighten his questioners, whereas in the second, the woman has the punch line that alters the way Jesus responds to her.

Likewise, there is another interesting twist in the passage. Although Jesus goes toward the Gentile cities of Tyre and Sidon (v. 21), whether this is a deliberate move toward the Gentiles is uncertain, because there were also Jewish towns in the district. After all, in 10:5 Jesus instructs his disciples not to go to the Gentiles, and he challenges the Canaanite woman similarly in 15:24. This story is not about Jesus taking the initiative for a mission to Gentiles; it is, rather, about a Gentile woman taking the

Homiletical Perspective

Long lists of instructions about what and when things could be touched or eaten dominate much of the first-century Jewish religious teaching. These dietary laws placed a high premium on the purity of the individual, and in today's passage, Jesus is turning expectations on their head. While most of the religious community was preoccupied with what would defile and hurt the body, Jesus was more concerned with what comes out of our bodies that can defile and hurt the world.

Yesterday's lunch is gone forever. Jesus asks, "Do you not see that whatever goes into the mouth enters the stomach, and goes out into the sewer?" (v. 17). It is a crude image. The sewer has carried away any mistakes we may have made by putting into our body things that the dietary laws call unclean. However, the careless words, the evil, the lies, and the fornication continue to be harmful. Our words and actions have the power to defile and hurt, and the pain of those choices is not washed down the sewer like yesterday's lunch.

If the dietary laws of ancient Israel seem distant, the principles on which they were based are still active in our culture today. Many in our culture were raised with a similar ethic. We were taught that good children kept their bodies clean of those things that could defile. While this is still true, Matthew's text

Matthew 15:(10-20) 21-28

Theological Perspective

the people of Israel defined themselves. In Matthew, it also carries rather more positive associations because of women like Tamar, Rahab, and Ruth, who are part of Jesus' family story (Matt. 1:3–5).

Some recent commentators see this as a moment where Jesus is "caught with his compassion down," and forced to confront his own prejudice; in a reversal of the usual roles, the respected teacher learns from an outsider "the need to broaden his ministry of hospitality to those outside the house of Israel."[2]

The key to this passage is the *mercy* that the woman seeks for herself and her daughter. Although she is not an Israelite, she clearly knows a good deal about Jesus and his reputation as a healer. She knows that his exorcisms in particular are being talked about in messianic terms (Matt. 12:23), and she cries out for mercy from this "Son of David" (15:22).

Kyrie eleison—"*Lord, have mercy.*" The prayer rings down through the centuries, chanted in cloisters, whispered in hospitals, screamed out on battlefields. It is the cry of the soul in extremis, a raw witness to the depth and the misery of the human condition. On this occasion, Jesus is silent in the face of it. Remarkably, the woman is undeterred by Jesus' indifference. Still she keeps shouting.

Her confidence does have solid grounds, for mercy, which is what she craves, is, according to Matthew, absolutely central to Jesus' ministry. Twice, in previous clashes with the Pharisees over questions of ritual purity and obedience to the law of God, Jesus quotes Hosea 6:6: "I desire mercy not sacrifice" (Matt. 9:13; 12:7). Mercy is the cornerstone of his critique of their religion and lifestyle.

Just before the story of the Canaanite, there is a further clash with the Pharisees on these very same issues, but this time there is no quotation from Hosea. It is as if the woman herself is now making the prophetic point: mercy, not sacrifice!

However, there is one major obstacle in the way of her quest for mercy, and it is Jesus who seems to put it there. The "food" he brings is intended for the children, not the dogs. He is saying that the doctrine of the election of Israel—a doctrine that, in the

2. Sharon Ringe, quoted in Elisabeth Schüssler Fiorenza, *But She Said* (Boston: Beacon Press, 1993), 98. Schüssler Fiorenza suggests that this woman, whom Mark calls a Greek-speaking Syro-Phoenician (7:26), is "a triple outsider" on account of her gender, her ethnicity, and her cultural-religious affiliations (12); Letty M. Russell, *Church in the Round* (Louisville, KY: Westminster John Knox Press, 1993), 163. An older school of interpretation, while stressing the woman's humility, tenacity, and insight, argues that Jesus intentionally draws this response from her. See, e.g., Augustine, "Sermons on New Testament Lessons," *Nicene and Post-Nicene Fathers of the Christian Church*, vol. 6, first series ed. (Grand Rapids: Eerdmans, 1974), 342–47; Martin Luther, *The Sermons of Martin Luther*, vol. 2 (Grand Rapids: Baker Book House, 2000), 148–54.

Pastoral Perspective

within the strictures of Jewish written and oral tradition and those who were excluded on the basis of the same tradition. Those new Christians who were raised in the Hebrew tradition are sorting through which of those written and oral traditions to carry forward into the church's life and why. In verses 1–10, Jesus mocks how religious leaders have used tradition in perverse ways to contravene the will of God, and echoes of this exchange are still nearly deafening in the twenty-first-century church.

In this lection's parenthetical verses (vv. 10–20), the evangelist recounts a sermon from Jesus that hit hard in its original setting and in Matthew's day, and even centuries later. Purity or religious faithfulness to God, says Jesus, is not about worshiping tradition uncritically. "It is not what goes into the mouth that defiles a person, but it is what comes out of the mouth that defiles" (v. 11). This is not just a curious aphorism that Jesus tosses into the conversation to baffle believers; it is a prophetic statement by the one who refused to allow "tradition" and traditions to be used as a "holy" reason for claiming that God's grace and eternal affection are reserved only for the ritually pure, that is, the people of Israel. For those in and out of the church who lament that the Bible has no relevance, invite them to spend time in the company of Jesus in verses 10–20.

While this encounter between Jesus and the Jerusalem religious authorities is good news for most Christians who come from Gentile stock, its warning carries over to church authorities. It serves as a dominical warning to the church to take great care in how it understands hospitality and faithfulness. What preacher has not heard—or, sadly, implied—that "they" would not be comfortable worshiping here? What church has not paid far more attention to "washing hands" than to cleansing hearts? What Christian has not claimed religious tradition as an excuse to act in a way far from the heart of Christ?

The argument between Jesus and the religious authorities is no obscure theological fight over how many angels can dance on the head of a needle. For Jesus, religious purity and faithful discipleship are not measured ultimately by how many perfect attendance badges one earns for Sunday school or worship, how often one has read the Bible from cover to cover, or how much money one contributes to the church treasury. Purity and faithfulness are shown ultimately by how the church speaks and lives out the radical hospitality and love of Christ.

As one reads this chapter in its entirety, Jesus moves from one intense encounter with the keepers

Proper 15 (Sunday between August 14 and August 20 inclusive)

initiative to encounter Jesus. In doing so, she dramatizes what faith is.

What cultural presumptions would Matthew's readers have had about this woman? The Canaanites were the inhabitants of the land that Israel came into at the time of the conquest under Joshua, so one could assume distance between Judeans and Canaanites. Differences of ethnicity, heritage, religion, and gender separate her from Judean social norms. Further, demon possession marginalizes her daughter.

In addition, the woman's behavior is unacceptable. Her culture expects women to be reserved in public. When she not only takes the initiative but also shouts her demand at Jesus, she violates social norms. Social affronts do not merit consideration, so Jesus seems to be playing by the social rules of his time when he does not even respond to her (v. 23). Further, his disciples recognize the social offense of her shouting and implore Jesus to send her away.

In agreement with his instruction to the disciples in 10:5 not to go to the Gentiles, Jesus tells this woman that his mission is only to Israel. Because more metaphorical language comes up later, it is worth noting here that Jesus uses metaphors to describe his mission as only for the "lost sheep of the house of Israel" (v. 24).

At this point the woman's manners change. She falls down at Jesus' feet in a gesture of reverence and pleads, "Help me" (v. 25). On the affective level, this causes a dramatic shift for Matthew's readers, from social affront to sympathy. Jesus still defends his mission to Israel: "It is not fair to take the children's food and throw it to the dogs" (v. 26). Again Jesus uses metaphors, and these metaphors cannot be reduced to literal language. Nevertheless, the metaphors imply that God's blessings are for Israel, and to share them with others would be to misappropriate them. Still, does the metaphor "little dogs" imply that Jesus degrades the woman and her daughter?

Nevertheless, the woman will not be deterred. Even though the metaphorical language of "little dogs" is dehumanizing, the Canaanite woman identifies with them to claim the crumbs under the table (v. 27). With this the story moves away from social affront to affirmation. None other than Jesus identifies her actions as manifesting great faith, and the healing of her daughter confirms God's mercy upon them (v. 28).

The incident begins with the woman's shout for mercy. Though the translation "have mercy" (v. 22) suggests that mercy is a noun, in Greek the request is purely a verb: *eleēson*. The same verb is used to

may help listeners shift from a purely individualist theology to a broader Christian citizenship. Jesus calls us from a self-centered consideration of what might harm our bodies to a broader concern of how our actions and attitudes hurt others.

Matthew connects this discussion of defilement with Jesus' encounter with the Canaanite woman, a difficult passage for preaching, raising questions that are difficult to answer in a single homily. This passage has a demon, Jesus ignoring the cries of a desperate mother, annoyed disciples, a restrictive mission of Jesus, and the apparent insult of Jesus calling this woman a dog—too much to raise and satisfy in one sermon or even a few sermons. Nevertheless, preaching the difficult texts reminds us all that life is messy and that not every issue of significance is neatly tied up in three points. Preacher and listener have a chance to struggle together.

Jesus is in the Gentile region of Tyre and Sidon, where prudent Israelites do not walk alone. Racial stereotypes and bigotry inform all encounters between Israelites and Canaanites. The disciples walk with full attention, informed by the stories of animosity and violence. Then one of *them*, a resident of this alien territory, shouts at Jesus. These are not the expected shouts of bigotry that characterize the relationship of mutual disdain. Instead, this is the earnest plea of a mother.

Some roles trump all others. Yes, she is a Gentile. Yes, as a citizen of Tyre or Sidon she probably worships Herod. Yes, she is a Canaanite. However, she is also a mother with a troubled child, and in the desperate cry of a concerned parent, she petitions the one who has a reputation for healing the sick. Her appeal is a compelling one. She calls him "Lord" and appeals respectfully and cross-culturally to the "Son of David" with her petition on behalf of her daughter who is tormented by a demon.

The trouble for preaching begins here. Jesus does not answer her, and the disciples are even more offensive. They appeal for Jesus, "Send her away, for she keeps shouting after us" (v. 23). In terms of civility, Jesus' silence is the high moment of this pericope. He answers her petition with the explanation of a limited mission: "I was sent only to the lost sheep of the house of Israel" (v. 24). While this is a restrictive mission, it is important to note that Jesus clearly understands his mission. Matthew's Gospel highlights the time Jesus spends away in prayer. Through prayerful relationship with God, Jesus understands his mission in the world. He is not deterred from his ultimate and redemptive purpose.

Matthew 15:(10-20) 21-28

Theological Perspective

hands of the religious leaders who are so critical of him, has become one of favoritism, exclusion, and contempt—means that she cannot receive mercy.

Again the Canaanite is undeterred. She does not object to God's having mercy on the chosen people. To the contrary, she seizes on it as the grounds of her own hope: "even the dogs eat the crumbs that fall from their masters' table" (v. 27). She grasps the fact that the fundamental basis of election is God's decision to be a merciful God: "I will have mercy on whom I have mercy, and I will have compassion on whom I have compassion" (Exod. 33:19; Rom. 9:15). This is the way that God has determined to be God—through mercy.[3]

She understands what Jesus revealed in his conversation with another "outsider," that "salvation is from the Jews" (John 4:22). While mercy may begin with Israel, she knows it cannot end there, because of the very nature of Israel's God. It overflows to others in the house—even to "the dogs."

The woman comes to Jesus with a crystal, unshakable conviction that God's mercy is enough for her daughter and for herself. Jesus has witnessed faith like this in a Gentile before, prompting him to foresee a time when "many will come from east and west and will eat with Abraham and Isaac and Jacob in the kingdom of heaven" (Matt. 8:11). With obvious delight he commends her "great faith" and grants her request.

IWAN RUSSELL-JONES

Pastoral Perspective

of tradition to an equally intense encounter with two anonymous women for whom tradition has proven to be a "holy" fence, keeping them on the outside. In good prophetic tradition, Jesus enacts the parable of what he has just argued. He travels into "unwashed" territory that tradition considers a "toxic waste area." What church and what Christian has not pointed to a territory that is considered an unclean, miry, dangerous place where discipleship may well be polluted?

Matthew tells this story to stimulate the pastoral imagination and to ask questions that common sense would quickly quell. What would it mean for the church to follow Jesus into the "toxic waste areas" of the world? What would it mean for the faithful to fret less about how "we have always done it this way" and listen more to the cries of those that tradition considers "unclean" or "unwanted"? On behalf of her anonymous, Gentile daughter, this anonymous, Gentile woman refuses to allow even Jesus to let "tradition" become an external barrier, blocking access to the grace of God. As Karoline Lewis observes, "The woman, aware of her location and the limitations placed on her, does not succumb to them but brings them into the light and calls them into question: 'Yes, Lord, yet even the dogs eat the crumbs that fall from their master's table.'"[1]

Matthew weaves together these verses to foreshadow the closing charge from the risen Jesus: "Go therefore and make disciples of all nations" (Matt. 28:19). Yes, Jesus has come to fulfill God's promise to the people of Israel, "I was sent only to the lost sheep of the house of Israel" (15:24). Whatever Jesus meant by these sharp words, Matthew cites them to remind the church always to rejoice that God's love and promise for Israel is fulfilled in the life, death, and resurrection of Jesus. Those of Gentile stock, adopted into this covenant tradition, need never forget this and never tire in giving thanks that, in Jesus, God's covenant promises stretch the length of the cross for *all* nations.

GARY W. CHARLES

---

3. See Karl Barth, *Church Dogmatics*, II/2 (Edinburgh: T. & T. Clark, 1957), 218f.

1. Karoline M. Lewis, "Living by the Word," *Christian Century*, August 12, 2008, 18.

describe the mercy that the merciful receive in the Beatitudes (5:7). It is also what others seeking healing ask for (9:27; 17:15; 20:30–31), and it is what the unforgiving servant lacks in 18:33.

Perhaps the clearest clue to its meaning in Matthew is Jesus' own explanation of casting out demons: "If it is by the Spirit of God that I cast out demons, then the kingdom of God has come to you" (12:28). In the grand view of Matthew, the woman's cry for mercy is a positive challenge for her to benefit from God's ruling activity. Furthermore, when she pleads, "Help me" (v. 25), she is virtually repeating Peter's plea when he was sinking in the water (14:30). Both Peter and the woman are pleading for the realization of God's ruling activity in Jesus' actions.

What constitutes the woman's faith that Jesus affirms so strongly? Though the woman calls Jesus "Lord" (vv. 22, 25), this may not be a "confessional" use of the word "Lord," since the same word can mean "sir." She also calls Jesus "Son of David" (v. 22), which is a christological title in Matthew. Significantly, when she calls Jesus Lord and Son of David, there is no response from Jesus that recognizes her faith. Rather, there is something more.

Again and again she violates boundaries, boundaries set up because of ethnicity, heritage, religion, gender, and demon possession. She must even contend with Jesus' reluctance to violate the ethnic boundary; but contend she does. In the grand scheme of Matthew, she believes that she and her daughter are people who should benefit from God's ruling activity (God's kingdom). So she is willing to break through the barriers, and breaking through the barriers dramatizes her faith. When the Canaanite believes that she and her daughter should receive mercy from the ruling activity of God, this is what Jesus calls faith.

In spite of his perspicacity, Jesus listens to and asks for information from others throughout the Gospel of Matthew. In this case, Matthew's Jesus is big enough not to be ashamed to learn something from a Gentile Canaanite woman. We cannot be certain whether or not Jesus enlarges his mission because of his encounter with this woman, but at the end of Matthew, the gospel is for all nations (28:19).

JAE WON LEE

Saying yes to great things means saying no to good things. The limitations of time and space, for everyone who walks this planet, mean choosing to leave some things not done.

Although Jesus remains undeterred, the mother continues her appeal on behalf of her tormented daughter, "Lord, help me" (v. 25). As already noted, the silence of Jesus is his most civil response. This time, Jesus refers to her as a dog, "It is not fair to take the children's food and throw it to the dogs" (v. 26). Referring to Canaanites as dogs was a familiar and favorite insult of the Israelites. Calling a woman a female dog had the same tone as if it were shouted today in a high-school hallway.

This language is not what the more sensitive of us expect. We expect Jesus to respond differently. Some homiletical attempts have been made to soften the response of Jesus. Some suggest that Jesus' talking with a Canaanite woman at all is a radical affirmation of her personhood. Some point to the fact that Jesus finally grants her plea, as an example of Jesus' radical inclusion of a Gentile, making an appeal for the broad reach of the gospel. The response of Jesus may have been tongue-in-cheek irony, using conventional language to make the opposite point. After all, it does follow the admonition about what comes out of our mouths.

It is possible for this text to be preached in a way that explains the behavior of Jesus in a way that we can easily grasp. However, the preacher may also stand squarely in front of the reality that Jesus does not always come through for us as we expect. Inside this story and inside our own stories, Jesus does not always conform to what we hope for. How do we respond honestly and reengage our faith when Jesus does not come through for us as we expect? Honest engagement with difficult texts validates the questions of sincere disciples.

DOCK HOLLINGSWORTH

Isaiah 51:1-6

¹Listen to me, you that pursue righteousness,
  you that seek the LORD.
 Look to the rock from which you were hewn,
  and to the quarry from which you were dug.
²Look to Abraham your father
  and to Sarah who bore you;
 for he was but one when I called him,
  but I blessed him and made him many.
³For the LORD will comfort Zion;
  he will comfort all her waste places,
 and will make her wilderness like Eden,
  her desert like the garden of the LORD;
 joy and gladness will be found in her,
  thanksgiving and the voice of song.

Theological Perspective

Western Christian eschatology has frequently inter-preted biblical time in terms of linear movement. In this view, progress characterizes the unfolding of God's activity in history. The modern human being sees the past as an unfolding collection of events from which one may learn in order to avoid repeat-ing past mistakes. In the best possible cases, the past serves as an important source of information to aid discernment in the present, so that a new, different future becomes possible.

   During comprehensive examinations in the mid–1990s, historians in my graduate school would ask degree candidates for an assessment of the last five hundred years in history—a very Protestant peri-odization. They received two distinctive answers to their inquiry. Those whose work focused on Chris-tian history and the history of Christian thought emphasized discoveries, achievements, and positive turning points in the advancement of the human condition. Those whose work focused on the history of the ecumenical and missionary movements of Christianity, the history of Christianity's encounters with other religions, and the history of Christianity in the third world emphasized a whole different list. Their answers included colonialism, imperialism, complexities of economic development, wars, and dramatic changes in geopolitics. Thus peers who

Pastoral Perspective

Even if the person speaking is sitting right next to us at the game, trying to discern what she or he is saying can be a chore amid stadium or arena noise: yelling, clapping, cheering of the favorite team, hawking ven-dors pacing about, and ongoing announcements coming full blast from huge speakers all around. Moreover, one need not be physically at the game. One can become so involved in its televised action at home that all other conversation in the room is virtu-ally muted from consciousness. How often in life does a situation become so all consuming that its pervasiveness literally drowns out all other sounds and voices around us, leaving only the unrelenting chatter of the *one* reality claiming our attention?

   Unlike the renewed energy that results from the joyful respite of a recreational event, preoccupation with the weight of disappointment or failure can exhaust even the most upbeat personality, drowning out all other sounds except the noise of its own sad-ness. Whether the overwhelming reality is a natural disaster, such as Hurricane Katrina or the 2008 earthquake that killed some 50,000 people in China, the unexpected loss of a job, a bleak diagnosis from the physician, or the death of a loved one, some cir-cumstances in life are so traumatic that they can numb and render us deaf to all but the sound of our own pain.

⁴Listen to me, my people,
  and give heed to me, my nation;
for a teaching will go out from me,
  and my justice for a light to the peoples.
⁵I will bring near my deliverance swiftly,
  my salvation has gone out
  and my arms will rule the peoples;
the coastlands wait for me,
  and for my arm they hope.
⁶Lift up your eyes to the heavens,
  and look at the earth beneath;
for the heavens will vanish like smoke,
  the earth will wear out like a garment,
  and those who live on it will die like gnats;
but my salvation will be forever,
  and my deliverance will never be ended.

Exegetical Perspective

"The LORD will comfort Zion; he will comfort" (v. 3). In keeping with the thrust of all of Second Isaiah (Isa. 40–55), our poem proclaims God's wondrous comfort. Cyrus the Great of Persia, on the move since 550 BCE, will soon defeat Babylonia and allow the exiles to return to Judah. This is just the beginning. The real news of comfort, far transcending political repatriation, is the announcement of Zion in luxuriant bloom.

A Theme of Fecundity. Our passage envisions Zion renewed as a garden paradise. It speaks of God's making "her wilderness like Eden, her desert like the garden of the LORD" (v. 3). The parallelism of verse 3's initial line declares fecundity to form the definitive content of God's good news of comfort. "Waste places" lie depopulated, barren, arid. To comfort Zion is to infuse these "waste places" with verdant new life. It is to water and fructify them.

Across the passages of Second Isaiah, Zion's "waste places" spring with growth, teem with life (see Isa. 44:26; 49:19; 52:9; 58:12; 61:4). In Isaiah 49:19–21, for example, waste places explode with new inhabitants. Zion had been bereaved and barren (49:21), in mourning and sterile as a salt flat. Suddenly, she finds herself so blessed with progeny that she is too cramped for comfort. "The place is too crowded for me," her children cry (49:20).

Homiletical Perspective

No fewer than seven times in these six verses listeners are invited to participate, joining the prophet in remembering the past and imagining the future. A sermon on Isaiah 51:1–6 might do the same, both by the occasional use of direct address ("Listen!") and by the use of vivid, visceral language in describing the past and future the text envisions. The lection overflows with imperative and imaginative zeal. Listen. Look. Give heed.

A preacher would do well to ask early in the interpretative process: why would anyone want to look, listen, or heed these ancient words in the first place?

The passage is initially addressed to "you that pursue righteousness," that is, the persecuted remnant from among the returning exiles who continue to "seek God," even as they stand in the rubble, wondering how they will ever rebuild, replant, and restore all that was lost. Those who seek God, then and now, are the ones with the most at stake when God's promises to bless appear to be in jeopardy. The skeptics gave up on the whole enterprise long ago.

A preacher could explore ways that the discouragement of the returning exiles may resonate with congregations who know the anxiety that comes with declining numbers and dwindling budgets in the midst of larger communities rife with physical, emotional, and spiritual needs.

Isaiah 51:1-6

Theological Perspective

shared mentors, readings, and courses gave two very different interpretations of the last five hundred years in human history.

Both interpretations are accurate. There is little doubt that our biographies shape our historical understandings and our current daily life practices—whether or not we are aware where they come from. Progress and wars, economic development and oppression, scientific achievements and destructive weapons, new nations and new structures of colonialism, new cultural and linguistic sciences and new forms of cultural superiority have complex interplay in the historical interpretation of the last five hundred years of global history. The past is much more than just a discovery of mistakes not to be repeated or a source of information for a better future; it is also much more than simply the history of colonialism or of low-conflict warfare as a result of the cold war. So what is the past? Is there a purpose for history?

The first verses of our text invite the righteous and those who seek the Lord to "look" at their past, and to "look" hard and intensely to their ancestors. The imagery that connects the people of Israel with their ancestors is powerful: we all come from the same rock, from the same quarry of Sarah and Abraham. Breaking a rock does not change its chemical or mineral composition. The rocky ground, "the quarry from which you were dug" (v. 1), is the source of our grounding today. The image offers continuity. Our ancestors and their history are connected to our hope; our hope is the foundation of our future. God's promises to Sarah and Abraham *flow to* and *infuse hope in* the exile.

The faith of the ancestors *flows through* and *nourishes* a new beginning for the people of Israel. An intense "look" at our ancestors' voices reveals God's transformation. Rediscovering our past provides energy for our present and future lives, transforming "waste places and wilderness" into Eden, so that the desert will be "like the garden of the LORD" (v. 3), and joy will be the song of the people.

To "look" hard at our ancestors is a generative reminder that God's deliverance is swift and extends to the ends of creation. Heaven and earth will vanish, but salvation is forever. For Isaiah, the past is agency and energy; it is memory that shapes the current experience of the exile and generates new expectations for renewal and salvation.

The underlying meanings of the terms "past," "present," and "future" are legacies of Western Christian thought and the modern worldview. As Christian communities in Africa, Asia, and Latin

Pastoral Perspective

Isaiah 51:1–6 begins with words drawn from the voice of God, saying, *"Listen to me"* (and not to all the other chatter swirling around in your life). These words were addressed to people who had experienced more than a generation of pain and disgrace in exile after Judah and its capital city were overrun by ruthless Babylonian conquerors in 587 BCE. The exiles recalled the burning of Jerusalem, the capture, torture, and death of their king, Zedekiah, the slaughter of their leading citizens, and their ignominious trek into Babylonian captivity (Jer. 52:4–27).

No wonder the prayer at the end of the book of Lamentations recalling these events says, "Remember, O LORD, what has befallen us; look, and see our disgrace! . . . Women are raped in Zion, virgins in the towns of Judah. Princes are hung up by their hands; no respect is shown to the elders"(Lam. 5:1, 11–12). The dirge in Psalm 137:1 also betrays profound grief: "By the waters of Babylon—there we sat down and there we wept when we remembered Zion." These verses were clearly uttered by people who had lost all hope. All they could hear was the sound of their own sadness.

Whether they are expected, deserved, or thrust into one's life without warrant, depressing realities can foster all manner of self-doubt, prompting investigative noises: Why this? Why me? What could or should I have done differently? Where is God in all this? Is there a God? Does God care? In the midst of confusing noises of stress or crisis, it is not unusual to lose a clear sense of perspective. The struggle for basic physical and/or emotional survival can become so pressing that it is difficult to understand situations in their proper context. In such times, it is not unusual for the noise of discouragement, anger, frustration, or bitterness to become the only audible sounds the anguished spirit hears.

It was against this type of spiritual chaos and noise that God, through the prophet, challenged people: "Listen to me" (vv. 1, 4). In 539 BCE, the Persian general Cyrus defeated the Babylonians and envisioned an opportunity for Jewish exiles to return to their homeland. As a new era of opportunity was perceived on the horizon, the prophet spoke in the elevated language of hope as he sought to remind beleaguered exiles who they were and whence they had come: "Listen to me, you that pursue righteousness, you that seek the LORD. Look to the rock from which you were hewn, and to the quarry from which you were dug" (v. 1). Just as God had called their ancestors Abraham and Sarah and blessed

Exegetical Perspective

Beyond demographic expansion, God's fecundity yields spiritual invigoration. The poetry of Isaiah 44:3–5 correlates the promise of "water" on a "thirsty land" with an infusion of God's presence. "I will pour my spirit upon your descendents," God declares (44:3). Fecundity from God makes salvation spring up; it causes communities of goodness to bud forth. Isaiah declares that by soaking up God's deliverance (Heb. *sedeq*), poured out in buckets by God, earth will sprout harmony, bloom right living (Isa. 45:8).

Channeling wondrous fecundity to earth has always been God's plan. Consider Abraham and Sarah as verse 2 presents them. Our poem roots Zion's coming blessing in the wonder that overcame these barren ancestors of Israel. God's intention to overturn sterility, God's ability to shower us with new life, is obvious in the miraculous beginnings of God's people. Verse 2 reminds us that all the masses of Israel stemmed from one solitary infertile couple, whom God "blessed" (see Gen. 17:16) and "made many" (see Gen. 17:2).[1]

The Spirituality of Eden. What spirituality lies behind the poem's emphasis on luxuriant growth, primordial fecundity? The question plunges us to the heart of our text's witness about life lived as God intends. To live ideally in "Eden . . . the garden of the LORD" (v. 3) is to live in tune with the verdant energy of a teeming landscape. It is to let go of the sweaty work of justifying yourself. One relaxes, instead, buoyed by the unforced rhythms of the landscape, reveling in the freedom and ease of its gratuitous gift of abounding life.

Henri Nouwen captures the spiritual meaning of fecundity well: "The great mystery of fecundity is that it becomes visible where we have given up our attempts to control life and take the risk to let life reveal its own inner movements. Whenever we trust and surrender ourselves to the God of love, fruits will grow."[2]

Verses 1b and 2a of our poem ask the reader to "look" to God's flowing new life in believing amazement, just as Abraham, in sacred wonder, took in God's starscape. (Our poem echoes Gen. 15:5–6, repeating the Hebrew of God's command.) Abraham reveled in God's mystery and God counted it as "righteousness," "deliverance," and "victory." *Tsedaqah*, the Hebrew term in Genesis 15:6, means all three.

1. On the importance of Gen. 17 for Second Isaiah, see Stephen L. Cook, *Conversations with Scripture: 2 Isaiah* (Harrisburg, PA: Morehouse, 2008), 107–29.
2. Henri J. M. Nouwen, *Lifesigns: Intimacy, Fecundity, and Ecstasy in Christian Perspective* (Garden City, NY: Doubleday, 1986), 65.

Homiletical Perspective

The lection itself does not linger here with present troubles, however, but summons hearers almost immediately to consider the unexpected parenthood of Abraham and Sarah, when it seemed all hope for their future was lost. God's gracious intervention in their lives long ago becomes the basis for a present promise of blessing, even amid ruins. God planted a garden in the desert before, the prophet assures us, and God can be trusted to do so again. We are told to remember the story of God's way with our distant parents, not as an exercise in nostalgia or as a matter of historical curiosity, but as a lifeline. Whatever God announces here and now about what will be is intimately bound up with what has come before, in all its particulars.

A sermon shaped by the dynamics of this "back to the future" motif might take the opportunity to revisit Abraham and Sarah and their baby called Laughter, especially if the story has not been considered from the pulpit in recent memory. There might also be benefit in following the trajectory of the text by offering snapshots of other times in Israel's history when God transformed a seeming wilderness into a place of growth, gratitude, and song: the Spirit taming the chaos, the abundance of Eden, Noah's deliverance, Moses drawn out of the water, slaves set free from their Egyptian prison, Hannah with her little son Samuel, maybe even all the way to the empty tomb—there are many possibilities.

The sermon might also explore the way that these transformations are ultimately not just for Israel's sake but for the blessing of all, as the broadening of the prophet's vision to include the hopes of a wider world in verses 4 and 5 indicates. While the text began by speaking particularly to those who "seek the LORD" in Israel, it becomes clear that the promised deliverance will be a light to any who long with Israel for a just and fruitful world.

A preacher might ask, is this visit back to the times when grace blossomed in Israel's past enough to "sustain the weary" (Isa. 50:4) of today? Can we trust the promise that God will act "swiftly" (v. 5) to make a garden out of our present wilderness?

The wise preacher will not neglect the fact that most hearers know of many barren situations, both intimate and sweeping, that have not been transformed into sites of joy and thanksgiving, though the hope and longing for such transformation has been great indeed. Looking back at God's promises fulfilled in the past and looking forward to fresh scenes of deliverance in a distant future does not entail the denial of the frustrated hopes here and

Isaiah 51:1-6

Theological Perspective

America—with no prior bureaucratic Western Christian structures—appropriate and contextualize the Christian religion, theological questions and debates about eschatology emerge. Can African Christians, with a religious and cultural worldview connected to the "past," understand Christian eschatology with its future connotations?

Can the mysterious world of the ancestors be a "model" for the future reign of God? Can Asian Christians, with their cyclical view of time, see the forthcoming reign of God as a future end on a linear timetable? Can the memory of the dead among Latin American and Caribbean Christians contribute to an understanding of a future of justice, peace, and reconciliation?

John S. Mbiti, a distinguished African theologian, raises some of these questions in his book *New Testament Eschatology in an African Background*. He recognizes the contextual complexities that arise when Western interpretations of Christian eschatology clash with traditional African worldviews. Regretfully, his deep and insightful analysis falls short when he concludes that "if African Theology . . . concentrates upon anthropology, it loses its perspective and can no longer be regarded as Theology."[1] Today we know that good theology is frequently informed by good anthropology.

Rather than seeking to fit non-Western worldviews of time (and therefore of eschatology) into a Western/Christian/modern framework, it is possible to see how this text creates an organic web that links memory, experience, and expectation at mutually enriching rather than progressive/linear points. The intertwining of these three keeps the meaning of life and the restoration of faith connected to the multifaceted journey of a communal faith. In other words, the faith of my ancestors and the promises of God to my ancestors belong not to me, but to those who share the same ancestry and embrace the same hope.

The Western/modern theological constructs of past, present, and future collapse in this wonderful text as God's promises *flow* through any human concept of time. God's salvation for all creation *flows* through us as we "do" memory, as we experience hope, and as we expect divine deliverance that never ends.

CARLOS F. CARDOZA-ORLANDI

Pastoral Perspective

them, God was now calling the beleaguered descendants of this faith heritage to put things in proper perspective.

Although circumstances looked discouraging, the prophet reminded people that God could bring amazing realities from ugly situations: "The LORD will comfort Zion, . . . comfort all her waste places, and will make her wilderness like Eden, her desert like the garden of the LORD" (v. 3).

Listening to God, rather than to the transitory noises of fear, disillusionment, and cynicism, not only clarifies the perspective of the believer, but ultimately enlightens all people, even those unaware of God's involvement in their lives: "Give heed to me, my nation; for a teaching will go out from me, and my justice for a light to the peoples" (v. 4). It is not surprising that several New Testament passages draw upon the reassuring and comforting language of Isaiah (e.g., Isa. 40:3; 53; 61:1–2) to clarify God's revelation to the world in Jesus Christ.

It is this type of *listening* for God's voice that enables today's believers to get a sense of God's presence with us amid all the noisy challenges of our time. Today's clamor from war; a withering economy; the leadership crisis of confidence in business, government, and religious institutions; and the politics of division that has become standard procedure in our time cannot drown out the good news that God still speaks to us, saying, "Listen to me, you that pursue righteousness."

Loud sounds of gun violence, lost jobs, defrauded pensions, ruptured relationships, poor educational systems, unaffordable health care, homelessness, and injustice will not have the last word. The perceptive ear of faith will still hear God's voice in spite of screaming cynicism and doubt, reminding us that God's salvation is sure and eternal, even outlasting all creation: "the heavens will vanish like smoke, the earth will wear out like a garment, . . . but my salvation will be forever, and my deliverance will never be ended" (v. 6).

RONALD E. PETERS

---

1. John S. Mbiti, *New Testament Eschatology in an African Background* (New York: Oxford University Press, 1971), 186.

Exegetical Perspective

Finding tsedeq. The addressees of Isaiah 51 are deeply familiar with the "righteousness," "deliverance," and "victory" of Abraham. They "know" the true value of *tsedeq* (v. 7); *sedeq* is what they "pursue" (v. 1). Satisfying their desire, the poem unleashes *sedeq* in abundance.

Look to Sarah and Abraham, verse 2 insists. These stone-sterile ancestors saw a closed womb open, saw birth water flow forth. Verse 1b helps us live the miracle for ourselves. The words "rock" and "hewn" in Hebrew make harsh cutting sounds: *kh* and *ts*. As we pronounce this verse, we hear God hewing out a cistern, boring through our encrusted doubts. As we reach the verse's end, Hebrew *r*, *m*, and *n* sounds murmur like water. Effortless life drenches us. God has tapped a font of joy for us, opened a "cistern's mouth" (NRSV "quarry").

Finding *tsedeq* requires breaking through our hardness of heart, aligning ourselves with God's natural rhythms. That takes concentration. Attending to the poem's rhetoric, we must refocus. Urgent calls to "listen" begin the initial stanzas of Isaiah 51 (vv. 1, 4, 7).

We need to listen anew, as our poem commends, because *sedeq* is not about victory as normally understood. Far from the victory of assertion, it is the triumph of what is right and selfless. Verses 4 and 5 specifically link *tsedeq* with God's revelations, with God's decisions that set things right. *Tsedeq* is about a divine harmony that blesses us, that shoots up kindness from God's garden soil (Isa. 45:8). There will be no power plays in God's paradise, no grasping for security in Eden. Vitality flows freely there, relieving us of fear. Drenched with life, we will find that selfless love comes easy in this landscape. As Henri Nouwen rightly affirms, "Fecundity brings forth . . . new, fresh, and unique ways: . . . a kind word, a gentle embrace, a caring hand, . . . a new communion among the nations."[3]

When selfless love awakens in the garden of Zion, it spreads inexorably throughout earth. God brings near God's *tsedeq* swiftly. It hits the ground running and speeds to all peoples, even to the remotest of islands (v. 5 NIV; KJV "isles," NRSV "coastlands"). Taking hold globally, it reveals its staying power. Whereas self-righteousness unravels like a moth-eaten sweater, the *tsedaqah* that God provides is permanent (v. 8). Even heaven and earth will wear out some day, but not God's *tsedaqah* (v. 6)!

STEPHEN L. COOK

Homiletical Perspective

now; but it does invite hearers of this text to put them in broader, even eschatological, perspective, as the final verse of the passage illustrates.

While congregations of previous generations may have had a hard time believing the assertion of verse 6 that the heavens will "vanish like smoke" and the earth will "wear out like a garment," today's hearers are likely to consider this an obvious conclusion. Land, sea, atmosphere, and ecosystem are precarious in our sight, and portrayals of the steady or dramatic disintegration of the natural world abound in contemporary art, literature, and film. We can see by the light of each new cataclysm and global climate change the evidence that humans beings will eventually "die like gnats," one way or another. A preacher might find verse 6 a productive place of meeting between the vision of the text and contemporary awareness of the transience of life.

The text does not visit the distant apocalypse for the purpose of scaring hearers with grim ecological news. Instead, the ending of this world is affirmed in order to contrast its inevitable disintegration with the unending reality of the promises of God. Yes, this world will evaporate, but those whom God delivers will not. The garden of joy, gladness, thanksgiving, and song that has been prepared for the redeemed *will* endure. Hearers pressing forward through barren, wasted lands can indeed find strength in the temporary gardens God planted in the deserts of our forebears, but even more in the expansive horizon of the garden that will finally, unshakably, perennially thrive.

What do we do here in between?

Listen. Look. Give heed. Remind one another of what has been and what will be when present circumstances look hopeless. The sermon might invite these ongoing practices of listening, looking, and reminding indirectly, by imagining or naming a contemporary situation in which the pattern of looking back to the stories of God's faithfulness and leaning forward toward the consummation of all things *has* become a lifeline for a community or individual—like bread in the desert, like water in the wilderness.

ANGELA DIENHART HANCOCK

---

3. Ibid., 81.

Isaiah 51:1–6   367

Psalm 138

[1]I give you thanks, O LORD, with my whole heart;
   before the gods I sing your praise;
[2]I bow down toward your holy temple
   and give thanks to your name for your steadfast love and your faithfulness;
   for you have exalted your name and your word
   above everything.
[3]On the day I called, you answered me,
   you increased my strength of soul.

[4]All the kings of the earth shall praise you, O LORD,
   for they have heard the words of your mouth.

Theological Perspective

Psalm 138 is one of the happiest psalms in the Hebrew Bible, but it is not only a song of endless praise to God. It also teaches who God is, what God does, and how humans should respond to God. Many Christian hymns proclaim God as immortal, invisible, wise, holy, light, power, and hope. Theologians use philosophically inspired words such as "omnipotent" (all-powerful), "omnipresent" (present everywhere), and "omniscient" (all-knowing) to describe God. In Psalm 119, the author portrays God as holy, great, high, and eternal (forever). However, a careful reading reveals that in this text the psalmist primarily describes God in terms of what God *does*, not who God *is*. The author praises God for steadfast love, faithfulness, answering humans, increasing strength, speaking, regarding the lowly, preserving, reaching out, delivering, and fulfilling God's purpose for humans.

One of the main themes flowing through this psalm is what Christian theologians call the doctrine of God's providence. When theologians reflect on God's providence, they—like the psalmist—are inquiring about God's ordering of creation and exploring how God acts in the world. The author of this psalm had no doubt that God is the creator who intervenes in the world, the history of Israel, and the lives of individuals.

Pastoral Perspective

To come face to face with authentic gratitude can be a humbling experience. An encounter with another's thanks-giving often evokes personal reflection: Have we given thanks lately? Have we expressed our gratitude to God and to significant others in our lives? Have we overlooked the many reasons we have to offer our thanks?

Terry's clothes told of hard work, paint, dirt, and overuse. He needed a long hot shower, but that would have to wait. He beheld in his hands the check from the church, the small amount that would still be enough to forestall eviction from his apartment. He turned it over and over, searching for words of gratitude for the church that had come to his family's aid. Unlike some who asked for help and then scoffed at the limits of what could be offered, Terry was deeply grateful. As he turned to walk up the sidewalk and head for the bus stop, he mumbled his hosannas: "Thank you, Lord. Thank you, Jesus. Yes, Lord. Thank you, Lord." It was his own version of the psalmist's hymn, "On the day I called, you answered."

Some experiences renew our souls; other experiences diminish them. The list of potential soul-shrinkers is without end: lack of a living wage, prolonged illness or disability, a failed relationship, physical or mental abuse. The psalmist has such a list, indeed has lived such a list. Living on the margins?

⁵They shall sing of the ways of the Lord,
 for great is the glory of the Lord.
⁶For though the Lord is high, he regards the lowly;
 but the haughty he perceives from far away.

⁷Though I walk in the midst of trouble,
 you preserve me against the wrath of my enemies;
 you stretch out your hand,
 and your right hand delivers me.
⁸The Lord will fulfill his purpose for me;
 your steadfast love, O Lord, endures forever.
 Do not forsake the work of your hands.

Exegetical Perspective

Identified in its superscription (not printed above) as "of David" or "to David," Psalm 138 is classified by most commentators as an individual song of thanksgiving. The psalm appears in the fifth and final section of the canonical book of Psalms, where songs of thanksgiving and praise predominate, leading to the crescendo of praise in Psalm 150. Psalm 138, moving from individual thanks to collective recognition and praise by both heavenly beings and earthly kings, recognizes YHWH's saving action, expands the praise to include the entire world, and asks for the continued protection and blessing of YHWH.

As with most biblical psalms, the precise historical location and social context of Psalm 138 is impossible to identify. The references to the "gods" in verse 1 and to the "kings of the earth" in verse 4 suggest a postexilic context in which the psalmist, in the midst of various nations and cults, gives thanks for YHWH's deliverance of Israel and offers a prayer for continued deliverance and restoration (vv. 7–8). This late dating is reinforced by elements of Deuteronomistic theology found in the psalm. What may originally have been an individual prayer has been adapted for use in the context of the cult for collective worship and praise.

The psalm begins with a clear and complete statement of praise in language typical of thanksgiving: "I

Homiletical Perspective

The psalm is not usually the focus of the sermon, and yet the homilist who pays attention to the psalm while preparing to preach may find unexpected help, or even buried treasure. Since in many traditions the psalm is sung or recited by the congregation, the words enter the consciousness of the hearers on a different level from that of the lessons they hear more passively. The psalm creates a new listening context for the hearers and enriches their response to the Gospel and the sermon. The preacher who has explored the psalm may be more aware of the unexpected, even unconscious resonance it can set off in the minds and hearts of the hearers, and may be able to discover, with those hearers, deeper, more surprising insights.

Two themes in today's psalm, though they appear to have no direct relevance to the Gospel passage, the confession of Peter (Matt. 16:13–20), remind the hearers and the preacher of some of the great themes and stories of Hebrew Scripture, which form a foundation for our hearing of the Gospel and our preaching. First among these is God's *hesed*, or "steadfast love," in a phrase that has become a hallmark of the RSV and NRSV.

Steadfast love (*hesed*), often linked, as here, with faithfulness (v. 2), is the loving commitment of God to act on our behalf at every moment in the history

Psalm 138

Theological Perspective

This is an amazing claim—that the Creator of the universe has a specific purpose for each facet of creation. If this is so, what is this purpose? How does God govern? Did God merely plan everything out at the beginning of time and let creation follow that plan? If so, perhaps we are not as free as we think. If God micromanages everything, perhaps we have no choice. This seems to contradict the intimate, loving relationship between God, creation, and free creatures that is described elsewhere in the psalm, where the author joyously thanks God for answering, increasing, and preserving her or him.

Christian theologian Paul Tillich wrote insightfully about God's active relationship with creation and described how God continually works through history in a way that preserves human freedom. "Providence is a permanent activity of God. He is never a spectator; he always directs everything toward its fulfillment . . . through the freedom of man and through the spontaneity and structural wholeness of all creatures."[1]

Perhaps Tillich and the psalmist are trying to say the same thing about the Divine. God *is* holy, high, and eternal, but God is also responsive, loving, and intimately involved with creation and its creatures. Numerous contrasts in the psalm communicate this paradox of grandeur and intimacy. Humans experience the love of God on a personal level, yet God is so vast that all the kings of the earth will praise God. The name of God is above everything, yet God has a specific vocation for individual humans. God is forever, yet God will stretch out God's hand for the sake of the believer.

What holds these divergent claims together is that they are all expressions of God's loving faithfulness. The Hebrew word *hesed* (v. 2) has been translated as "steadfast love," "amazing grace," or "loyal love," and in this psalm—as elsewhere—it tries to express God's passionate, faithful love for creation.[2] The God who is beyond time intervenes in history on account of this amazing grace.

How can we respond to this loyal love? The actions of the psalmist serve as a model. He or she begins with thanksgiving from the whole heart. Praise is not merely intellectual agreement with a faith claim, nor is it based on an isolated emotional experience. "Whole heart" expresses the psalmist's joy that all of whom she or he is has been grasped by God.

Pastoral Perspective

Dwelling in the very midst of one's enemies? Being separated from the places that keep life centered and grounded? The psalmist knows, has lived through and with, and has come out on the other side of suffering. Gratitude rises up from the marrow of his being: "On the day I called, you answered" (v. 3).

The Holy One of Israel did not merely acknowledge the plea for help, but according to the grateful one, "increased my strength of soul" (v. 3). What a gift it is, to come through trials and tribulations to discover a deeper peace, a new sense of strength within one's own being. There will be more trials, no doubt, but the soul is made stronger, more resilient and sure. Thank you, Lord. As individuals, as a community, we have a deep-seated need to give thanks. When we find a way to allow it to pour forth, we discover that a space opens up in us where grace can flow even more freely.

Such gratitude can rearrange one's perspective, or that of a whole congregation. Such a depth of thanks-giving can reorient, turn hearts back to God as the source, the redeemer, the center. "You know my soul look back and wonder how did I make it over?" asks the old gospel hymn.[1] The soul-shrinkers have done their worst. The damage, seen or unseen, cannot be denied. Nevertheless, in the midst of trouble we called, and YHWH stretched out an arm of strength, a steadying hand, and somehow, praise God, we made it over. The needed money was found, the surgery got all the cancer, the ones breathing threats faded away.

Perhaps they did not. As many other psalms remind us and as life teaches us, the answer does not always come in the form expected. What is given is not always the easy cure, the miraculous windfall, or the dawning of peace dispelling all conflict. What is given, Psalm 138 reminds us, is strength of soul.

A congregation struggles for survival, facing dwindling numbers and an aging facility. The church down the road is tied up in knots over the agenda of a few. The faith community across town wrestles with decisions that will significantly impact its future. How do we turn aside from the soul-shrinking ways we so easily slide into?

The psalmist names one trap to avoid: be watchful of haughty attitudes that create distance. Participate in God's mindfulness of the lowly. How does a congregation engage in the soul-strengthening action of God? Practice gratitude. Seek to serve, not to be served. Watch carefully for that steadying hand.

1. Paul Tillich, *Systematic Theology* (Chicago: University of Chicago Press, 1951), 1:266–67; quoted in Peter C. Hodgson and Robert H. King, *Readings in Christian Theology* (Minneapolis: Fortress Press, 1985), 146.
2. James Limburg, *Psalms*, Westminster Bible Companion Series (Louisville, KY: Westminster John Knox, 2008), 463.

1. Clara Ward, "How I Got Over" (New York: Mastership Music, 1951).

Exegetical Perspective

praise you [*'odeka*] with my whole heart." The latter phrase, "with my whole heart," emphasizes the exclusive nature of the praise and worship of YHWH, as opposed to the inclusion of YHWH along with other gods of other nations who might be worshiped (Ps. 119:2, 10, 34, 58, 69, 145; Jer. 3:10; 24:7). This monotheistic tendency is emphasized by verse 1b, where the awkward structure of the Hebrew is translated by the NRSV as "before the gods I sing your praise." The context for the phrase is the ancient Near Eastern understanding of a council of the gods in which YHWH is recognized as supreme.

The psalmist continues the exaltation of YHWH in verse 2 by affirming the "holy temple" as the center and focus of worship. This focus connects the psalmist to the Deuteronomistic emphasis on the temple in Jerusalem as the legitimate place where the worship of YHWH can occur and where the "glory" (*kabod*, v. 5) of YHWH resides. The psalmist also brings into the mix the Deuteronomic name theology (Deut. 12:5, 11), focusing worship on the "name" of YHWH that resides in the temple.

The psalmist thanks YHWH for "your steadfast love [*hesed*] and your faithfulness [*'emet*]." The term *hesed*—usually translated as "steadfast love"—appears 245 times in the Old Testament, with 127 of those occurrences in Psalms. The term is frequently paired with *'emet*, which is most often translated "faithfulness," as it is here (e.g., Gen. 24:49; Exod. 34:6; Josh. 2:14).

The terms describe fundamental characteristics of YHWH and are used in appealing to YHWH for help (e.g., Pss. 40:11–12; 115:1–2) or as a statement of trust in YHWH (e.g., Pss. 57:3; 85:10–13). The use of the terms together in this phrase is generally considered a hendiadys, with *'emet* reinforcing the stability and constancy of the divine *hesed*.[1] Verse 3 concludes the first segment of the hymn by referring—in a general and undefined way—to a time when the psalmist called on YHWH, who answered and strengthened the psalmist in a time of crisis.

The second section of the hymn, verses 4–6, moves the praise from a personal thanksgiving and worship to a corporate, universal level. Now it is "all the kings of the earth" who recognize YHWH as worthy of praise. These kings have "heard the words of your mouth," recognizing in those words the loving kindness and faithfulness of verse 2, but even more the glory (*kabod*) of verse 5. The recognition

1. H.-J. Zobel, "Hesed," in *The Theological Dictionary of the Old Testament*, ed. Johannes Botterweck and Helmer Ringgren, trans. David E. Green (Grand Rapids: Eerdmans, 1978), 5:44–64.

Homiletical Perspective

of salvation. It is God's *hesed* that is with Joseph in prison (Gen. 39:21) and that leads Israel out of Egypt (Exod. 15:13). It is the source of confidence for the psalmist who sings, "Surely [*hesed*] shall follow me all the days of my life" (Ps. 23:6), and for the prophets who know that God's *hesed* will bring restoration to ruined Israel (Isa. 54:8, 10). It is not only a divine action; Ruth seeks *hesed* from someone as yet unknown when she goes to the fields to glean (Ruth 2:2) and shows *hesed* to Boaz when she goes to him on the threshing floor at harvest time (Ruth 3:10).

Hesed may function for a preacher as a touchstone, a sign of the history and promise in which we place our trust. The word may never show up in the text of the sermon, but it informs the theology of the preacher and shapes all that individual proclaims. A preacher for whom God's *hesed* is a central component of history and faith will be inclined to speak a word that honors our grounding in the tradition of Israel and looks to the future in hope and confidence.

God's regard for the lowly, whether individuals or communities, is an essential element of OT theology, and becomes central to the message and healing work of Jesus. Those who hear the phrase "[God] regards the lowly" (v. 6) will almost certainly think of the Song of Mary (Luke 1:46–55), and then many of them will remember as well Hannah's song (1 Sam. 2:1–10). God cares for and vindicates those who are accounted valueless and shameful: a childless woman whose husband has children by another woman, an unmarried pregnant teenager. God values those who seem to have nothing, and chastens those who have much. A preacher who keeps this in mind will look differently at the power and authority granted to Peter when Jesus gives him the keys of the kingdom (Matt. 16:19).

Three minor aspects of the psalm may enrich the reflections of a homilist preparing to focus, in the sermon, on the confession of Peter. Though it is unlikely that any of this work will find its way into the actual text of the sermon, these reflections may add depth and complexity to the preacher's questions, and shape the final outcome in subtle ways.

In the opening stanza, the psalmist repeatedly invokes the power of the holy name, which carries the force of the divine self. Though the name YHWH is itself too holy to be uttered, reference to the holy name is a way of evoking the awesome nature of the Divine. Naming is a creative act that belongs to God. In this context, Jesus' naming of Simon as Peter goes far beyond giving a nickname and making a pun. Jesus, in giving Simon a name, is participating in the

Psalm 138

Theological Perspective

The psalmist's response to God is not a private one. Look at the dramatic shift between verses 3 and 4. God answers the call of the believer, which seems like a personal experience of God's steadfast love. Then in the next verse, "All the kings of the earth shall praise you." The intimate relationship between God and the author has now become global. Like the psalmist, we can respond to our encounter with God by telling others of God's amazing grace.

The last verse of the psalm also offers insight into how we can respond to God's faithfulness. We can use our talents and gifts and work in harmony with God's purposes for creation. Christians have long used the term "vocation" to talk about the human response to God. Prior to the Reformation, having a vocation meant becoming a monk, priest, or nun. Martin Luther believed, however, that all Christians have a purpose in life that can be lived out in the world in any occupation. The purpose of each individual's vocation is to serve the neighbor as a way of expressing wholehearted love for God.

Luther wrote, "The same is true for shoemaker, tailor, scribe, or reader. If he is a Christian tailor, he will say: I make these clothes because God has bidden me do so, so that I can earn a living, so that I can help and serve my neighbor. When a Christian does not serve the other, God is not present."[3] The work of our hands mirrors the praise we feel in our hearts. The joyful tone and thankfulness of Psalm 138 helps us realize that we ought to respond to God with praise, tell others about God, and live out God's purpose in loving service to the neighbor. This is how we give wholehearted thanks to God.

MARY ELISE LOWE

Pastoral Perspective

When the prayers are not being answered as hoped, uncover the ways they are being answered as needed.

Where is there new strength of soul, a swelling of energy, new light breaking forth? How have challenging times in the past served to usher in unexpected blessings? Can we see God's hand sustaining, guiding us through to a better day? As individuals and as communities of faith, when we look back, we are amazed at the clear signs of YHWH's help, signs we could not detect when the suffering was at its worst. "We called you, and you answered us, you increased our strength of soul" (v. 3, adapted).

The one in great need cries out, the One in love responds; but the story does not end there. There are promises yet to fulfill, a purpose to unfold and complete. This work too is ultimately in God's outstretched hands. God will not leave unfinished what God has begun. "I am confident of this, that the one who began a good work among you will bring it to completion by the day of Jesus Christ" (Phil. 1:6).

We are not made whole simply so that we can feel better. We are restored, renewed, and lifted up so that we may rejoin God's great design and give thanks. A grateful, redeemed community is one that can face anything in trust. A grateful, redeemed community is charged to be a living witness to the steadfast care of the Almighty. In time, even the halls of power will recognize and give thanks to the one true Power.

Check still in hand, Terry made his purposeful way up the street, his lips continuing to pour forth his praise. Thank you, Lord. Thank you, Jesus. Yes, Lord. "Oh thank my God how he kept me. I'm gonna thank him 'cause he never left me . . . my soul look back and wonder how did I make it over?"[2]

JULIE PEEPLES

---

3. Martin Luther, "Sermon in the Castle Church at Weimar" (25 October 1522, Saturday after the Eighteenth Sunday after Trinity), in *D. Martin Luthers Werke: Kritische Gesamtausgabe*, 60 vols. (Weimar: Herman Böhlaus Nachfolger, 1883–1980) 10/3:382; quoted in and translated by Fred Gaiser, "What Luther Didn't Say about Vocation," *Word and World* 25, no. 4 (Fall 2005): 361.

2. Ibid.

and worship of YHWH in his "words" may refer to the formative stages of the Torah that were present in exilic and postexilic Israel.

Thus the kindness and faithfulness of YHWH is expressed in the words of the Law and Prophets as they are being gathered in the traditions of the people of Israel. The acknowledgment from "all the kings of the earth" echoes the language of Second Isaiah with eschatological overtones, echoing the prophetic promise that all nations will recognize the glory of YHWH and be gathered in praise (Isa. 60:1–3). The parallelism of the psalm equates the "glory of YHWH" with the "ways of YHWH."

Ironically, in the words of the psalmist, this glory and way of YHWH is manifested not in the splendor and magnificence of earthly kings, but in regard for the "lowly" (v. 6); indeed, the "haughty" are regarded by YHWH from "far away." The reference gathers up both the personal and the corporate references present in the psalm. The psalmist, threatened by "trouble" and "the wrath of . . . enemies" (v. 7), is connected to YHWH in spite of any illness or oppression. Likewise, Israel is recognized and lifted up even in the midst of exile and loss. As the kings of the earth recognize the glory of YHWH, they will also recognize the true nature of YHWH's chosen ones, whether the individual or the nation in exile.

In verses 7–8 the hymn returns to a mix of individual praise and petition. In a form typical of the Psalms, the psalmist mixes recognition of YHWH's dependable presence in a time of trouble, the assurance that YHWH's protection and love will continue, and a petition for continued help. The recognition of YHWH's present help is once again described using the term "steadfast love" (*hesed*), this time in a typical phrase asserting that this love "endures forever."

RICHARD A. PUCKETT

divine work of making a new, transformed human being. His naming is more powerful than Peter's identification of Jesus by the title "Messiah."

The psalmist praises God "before the gods" (v. 1) of a foreign land. The preacher preparing to focus on Peter's confession, "You are the Messiah, the Son of the living God" (Matt. 16:16), might wonder, "Who or what are the gods in our foreign land? Who is competing to take the place of God? In a world so full of other gods, how do we affirm what Peter saw and proclaimed? How can we proclaim the God who is really God, give thanks for our relationship with that God, and acknowledge what God has done and will continue to do for us, especially in the person of Jesus the Messiah?"

Finally, the psalmist, though far away from Jerusalem, takes care in praising God to turn toward the temple, the place where God lives (v. 2) and also, perhaps, acknowledges that God, though dwelling far away, can see and care for the faithful wherever they are.[1] This psalmist goes on to praise the God whose power extends over all kings and places, who will be known and worshiped everywhere (v. 4). The preacher, reflecting on this evolving understanding of God, may see the drama unfolding in the Gospel passage in a new light. "But who do you say that I am?" (Matt. 16:15) Jesus asks. Peter makes one confession. Another response, for some preachers and some hearers, might be, "You are the home of God, the God whose glory and holy name have come to dwell in the person and presence of Jesus."

ELIZABETH P. RANDALL

1. See the alternate reading of verse 6 proposed in the Anchor Bible commentary, "though [YHWH is] the Lofty, he [*sic*] heeds even from a distance" (Mitchell Dahood, *Psalms III* [Garden City, NY: Doubleday, 1970], 274, 279f.).

Romans 12:1-8

¹I appeal to you therefore, brothers and sisters, by the mercies of God, to present your bodies as a living sacrifice, holy and acceptable to God, which is your spiritual worship. ²Do not be conformed to this world, but be transformed by the renewing of your minds, so that you may discern what is the will of God—what is good and acceptable and perfect.

³For by the grace given to me I say to everyone among you not to think of yourself more highly than you ought to think, but to think with sober judgment, each according to the measure of faith that God has assigned. ⁴For as in one body we have many members, and not all the members have the same function, ⁵so we, who are many, are one body in Christ, and individually we are members one of another. ⁶We have gifts that differ according to the grace given to us: prophecy, in proportion to faith; ⁷ministry, in ministering; the teacher, in teaching; ⁸the exhorter, in exhortation; the giver, in generosity; the leader, in diligence; the compassionate, in cheerfulness.

Theological Perspective

How can one think of an apostle, like Paul, writing a comprehensive theological treatise under no pressure at a serene location in what can be described as a confessional situation (*status confessionis*)?[1] Such thinking involves several distortions or pitfalls, and they are serious. To continue reading the apostle Paul as a theologian writing theological treatises out of a serene and comfortable location is to misunderstand Paul and the life-and-death challenges that he and the early Christian communities faced.

There is something more at stake that is properly theological. What is involved here is a failure to understand the nature of theology and the relationship of theology to ethics and to context. To fail to relate theology to ethics and context is to misunderstand theology: Theology is an expression of faith communities seeking understanding in relation to their lives (*fides quaerens intellectum*—Anselm) or a reflection on the praxis of faith communities. Theology is to inform the faith praxis of believing communities. The paraenetic (exhortatory) character of our lectionary text is not to contrast theology and moral action, but only a shift in emphasis.

1. Neill Elliot, *Liberating Paul: The Justice of God and the Politics of the Apostle* (Minneapolis: Fortress Press, 2006), 73–75.

Pastoral Perspective

The variety and complexity of Paul's use of the concept of "body" offers the preacher the opportunity to explore the metaphor with reference to individuals, the congregation, and the church as a whole. In this text, as in others in which he uses the metaphor, various meanings emerge as one pushes the boundaries of the metaphor from literal and specific to broader possibilities.

"Present your bodies as a living sacrifice." Most worshipers in the twenty-first century have no point of reference for presenting a dead sacrifice to God. Sacrificing animals by way of atonement for sin or as a gift of thanksgiving is so removed from our experience that a redefinition of the term seems required.

Sacrifice in popular usage usually connotes something negative. Parents of Olympic athletes make economic sacrifices for the training of their children. Employees are asked to sacrifice raises or benefits when a company falls on hard times. A heroic soldier sacrifices his life to save his comrades. That last example is one of the few involving a physical body, and in that case sacrifice means death or severe injury.

Paul calls on believers to present our bodies as *living* sacrifices. This does not seem to indicate a "take up your cross" expectation that we will need to die physically in the course of our discipleship, though it does not rule it out. Paul ties bodily, living

Exegetical Perspective

Literary Context. "Therefore" (12:1) indicates that the moral exhortations to follow are based on the theological foundation laid in chapters 1–11. In the larger context, these chapters promote a life defined by God's righteousness (1:17; 3:21). In the immediate context, they illustrate the lifestyle expected of "all Israel" (11:26), Jews and Gentiles. How will this new people live together, and how will they be related to the outside world?

Chapters 12–13 are framed by appeals to apocalyptic eschatology, "this age" (12:2 NRSV, alternative trans.), and "know the time" (13:11–14), all describing a life oriented toward God's future (see the exegetical essay on Rom. 13:8–14 in *Feasting on the Word*, Year A, vol. 4). After the opening statement (12:1–2), Paul discusses various aspects of relations with other believers and with nonbelievers. (Regarding the shift from one to the other, see the exegetical essay on 12:9–21 in *Feasting on the Word*, Year A, vol. 4.) Verses 3–8 discuss relations among believers, though one might logically extend the pericope as far as verse 16.

Not Conformed . . . Transformed (vv. 1–2). The main theme of chapters 12–13 is sounded here, where Paul exhorts his readers, "Do not be conformed to this age, but be transformed by the renewing of your minds." Here is a call for a new way of thinking.

Homiletical Perspective

Today's preacher is living in a culture in which sound bites are used to communicate complex ideas. Imagine, for a moment, the sound bites that might be generated by this text: "Loving one another is easier said than done"; "Doing love transcends merely speaking of love." Of course sound bites are not the way that we want the gospel preached, but we certainly need to capture our congregants' attention with the kind of lingering impact that the media generate. Like Paul in this text, we must deliver sermons that convey the complex truth of the gospel faithfully, forcefully, and succinctly.

In Romans 12:1–8, Paul articulates a practical theology that details ways and means for practicing love in households of faith and toward the public at large. In just eight verses Paul communicates weighty, useful truth about what the faithful must do in order not to be conformed to this world but transformed by the renewing of their minds: godly sacrifice, radical commitment, sacred mindfulness, transformative grace (vv. 1–2); intentionality, communal unity, and vocational awareness (vv. 3–8).

Moreover, transformation is a result of God's gracious activity alongside human initiative throughout the text. Transformed individuals become the transformed community ("we, who are many, are *one body in Christ*") when we recognize that we need one

Romans 12:1-8

Theological Perspective

We are living in a confessional situation (*status confessionis*), and this situation must inform the way we think, dwell, and act. If imperial Rome was the empire in Paul's time, our contemporary empire is more powerful, pervasive, and cunning. If imperial Rome was able to claim devotion and demand sacrifice, the empire of our time (a global domination system) has greater uncanny power to make idolatrous claims. This is even more so if we think that we not only live in a "market economy," we also live in a "market society" or, broadly, the global domination system of which the market is one expression. Its more ubiquitous and beguiling presence gives validity to its claim: "outside of the market there is no salvation" (*extra mercatum nulla salus*). Nations have claimed imperial status, but they all bow down and serve this god—an idol. Modern rulers have passed draconian measures both to perpetuate themselves in power and in the defense of this idol.

It is in light of this confessional situation that we must see what true worship of God is. Failure to read and name this context, to paraphrase Thomas Aquinas (*Summa contra gentiles*), is failure to understand and worship God. In the face of idols that demand devotion and sacrifice, worship of the true God can be no other than the giving of one's total self as a "living sacrifice." This is the "true worship" (TEV) or the "spiritual worship" (NRSV) that one must offer. The offering of one's whole self is the only holy and acceptable worship. It is noteworthy that, even as Paul calls believers to "present their *bodies* as a living sacrifice," he names it as "*spiritual* worship" (NRSV, v. 1).

This emphasis means that the spirit is not opposed to the bodily or, to state it positively, that "spiritual" worship is bodily worship. Moreover, "spiritual" worship is the offering of one's body or the whole self (head, heart, and bankbook) as a daily "living sacrifice." There is more, however, to this exhortation of presenting one's body as a "living sacrifice" that our therapeutic society would rather want to remain muted because of its subversive character. True/spiritual worship is a sacrifice, not because sacrifice itself is good, but because it does not offer "cheap grace." True worship is a sacrifice because that is the only way one can truly worship in a world tyrannized by the idols of death. Many have been nipped in the bud because of their commitment to worship and obey the true God.

The call to offer oneself as "living sacrifice" in a confessional situation not only tells us about what true/spiritual worship is; it gives us an understanding

Pastoral Perspective

sacrifice to discerning and living into the will of God. Connecting the body in this way forces us to go beyond esoteric, emotional, or intellectual assent to God's will in order to consider what implications there might be for our very bodies as we live out our discipleship to God. Paul indicates that this may mean we need actually to *do* things that will put us outside the norms of behavior for our society, wrapping our minds around what we do day to day in our lives that expresses God's will.

He spells out some of these things as the text continues. We are called, each according to our gifts, to use our bodies as prophets, ministers, teachers, exhorters, givers, leaders, and in acts of cheerful compassion. Verse 3 may indicate that one "sacrifice" involved in all of this comes when we admit to ourselves, and then live out in our lives, the reality that the world does not revolve around us as individuals. "It is not about you," Paul seems to be saying, "and that includes your body."

This does not mean that some other person can control our bodies, or that following God means letting another human being abuse our bodies. The church has taught this to women in particular over the centuries. For Paul, "sacrifice" is a positive term of consecration—of dedication to the will and the work of God that results in the use of gifts through the body—not the abuse of the body as a sign of submission to God or anyone else.

Paul then expands the body metaphor to describe the church, in a passage reminiscent of 1 Corinthians 12. Now the metaphor becomes less literal, as he asks us to consider ourselves parts of a human body in which each part has different functions, each part has value, and each part is as intimately connected to the other as the head, neck, and torso of a human body are. Each part of the body works, not to bring glory to itself or to meet only its needs, but to ensure the healthy functioning of the whole system. The gifts of each member are to be used for the common good.

Although this reminder of our common need for one another—and of the way in which our gifts are to be used not for our own glory but for the health of the community—is good for any church to remember, this text speaks directly to congregations where there is division or conflict. The sacrifice of the first part of the reading is still operative as the metaphor shifts. Indeed the instruction not to think of oneself more highly than one ought helps foster an atmosphere where communities may work together harmoniously and productively.

Exegetical Perspective

The transformed life will be one of bodily sacrifice that will constitute the believer's *logikē latreia,* a difficult phrase sometimes translated "spiritual service." *Logikē* connotes rationality ("logical"). In ancient Stoic philosophy, the *logikos* distinguished humans from animals and related them to deity.[1] *Latreia* refers to acts of pious devotion or worship (John 16:2; Heb 9:1, 6). The idea in verses 1–2 is that one's whole life—body and mind—becomes an expression of devotion to God.

In verse 2 Paul exhorts his readers to "prove [KJV, RSV; NRSV "discern"] . . . the *teleios* will of God." The noun *telos* is a common designation for the end time in apocalyptic contexts (Mark 13:7, par.; 1 Cor. 15:24; 1 Thess. 2:16; Rev. 2:26), and the related adjective *teleios* here suggests that the will of God is "end times oriented" (Matt. 5:48: 19:21; 1 Cor. 2:6; 14:20; Phil. 3:15), which is another way of saying "not conformed to this age."

Overview of 12:3–8. Paul's target readers ("all of you," NRSV "everyone") are Gentile converts (1:5–6, 13; 11:12), and the "grace given" to him is his apostolic commission to preach to Gentiles (1:5–6; 15:15–16). So we should expect his arguments to resonate with Gentiles.

This paragraph asserts the necessity of good thinking (v. 3). Paul elaborates the content of good thinking beginning in verse 9, but two supporting arguments undergird the need for good thinking in verses 4–5 and 6–8.

Good Thinking (v. 3). It is impossible to represent in English Paul's fourfold use of the verb root *phronein* ("to think"). Paul exhorts his readers "not to think of yourself more highly [*hyperphronein*] than you ought to think [*phronein*], but to think [*phronein*]" (and here the translation gets tricky) "about being modest" (*eis to sōphronein*; NRSV "with sober judgment").

It is easy to see what Paul says *not* to do—do not get the big head. What Paul says to *do* is harder to follow in many translations. In Greco-Roman philosophy, however, *sōphrosynē* was one of the four cardinal virtues. Usually translated "temperance" or "moderation," this word group represented composure and lack of excess (e.g., Mark 5:15). The translation "being modest" strikes the right contrast against egotism (*hyperphronein*).

One Body (vv. 4–5). Why should one not have a big ego? Because all are members of one body, and each

1. Epictetus, *Discourses* 1.16.15–21.

Homiletical Perspective

another ("and *individually* we are members one of another," v. 5). There is an ongoing process of divine-human interaction. By God's grace, we are given gifts; when we accept that individuals receive *different* gifts from God, we become a vibrant sacred (transformed) community. "We have gifts that differ according to the grace given to us: prophecy, in proportion to faith; ministry, in ministering; the teacher, in teaching; the exhorter, in exhortation; the giver, in generosity; the leader, in diligence; the compassionate, in cheerfulness" (vv. 6–8).

Maintaining a balance between God's grace and human initiative in understanding the spiritual transformation of persons and communities is vital. Too much emphasis on grace may leave persons apathetic about what it means not to be conformed to this world. If we place too much emphasis on human initiative, we forget that we are transformed in order to "discern what is the will of God—what is good and acceptable and perfect" (v. 2b).

When Martin Luther King Jr. led a nonviolent movement to transform the soul and laws of the United States, he grasped something about maintaining this balance while seeking to discern the will of God. His words are illustrative and instructive:

> Human progress never rolls in on wheels of inevitability; it comes through the tireless efforts of men [*sic*] willing to be co-workers with God, and without this hard work, time itself becomes an ally of the forces of social stagnation. We must use time creatively in the knowledge that the time is always ripe to do right.[1]

Indeed, human effort is always divinely—albeit mysteriously—inspired and energized because our transformation is a reorientation to time. We are transformed to live oriented to God's future.

A sermon on authentic Christian discipleship and community may flow naturally from this text. The imperatives of verses 1–2 call us to be and do as Christ's disciples according to the gifts God has given each of us, in order to be fully "one body in Christ" (v. 5). The words of legendary dancer Judith Jamison about the relationship between dance and the spirit may help us think about coming into the fullness of community. "Dance," she said, "is bigger than the physical body. Think bigger than that. When you extend your arm, it doesn't stop at the end of your fingers, because you're dancing bigger than that; you're

1. Martin Luther King Jr., *Why We Can't Wait* (New York: Signet Classics, 2000), 74.
2. See http://www.nutquote.com/quote/Judith_Jamison; accessed March 10, 2010.

Romans 12:1-8

Theological Perspective

of what a church is or what it means to be a church. In other words, it leads us to the matter of ecclesiology. The gestalt of this church begins to take shape when we juxtapose "living sacrifice" and "nonconformity" in relation to the world. True/spiritual worship is a "living sacrifice" because it demands that believers not be "*conformed* to this world" (v. 2). Conversely, worship as "living sacrifice" is an expression of a nonconformist community of believers. What we have then is a view of the church as a "countercultural community." Nonconformity in relation to the world is the stance that the community of believers must take in light of the life and ministry of Jesus and of the coming new age ("Do not be conformed to this age," v. 2 NRSV alternative trans.). The community of believers must live differently, as if the future (new age) were already present. Unfortunately, in an effort to be acceptable to the world, the church's message has become indistinguishable from mainstream culture. Experiencing threats to its survival, such as declining membership, resources, and influence, the church is suffering from goal displacement and spiritual drought.

How can the church reclaim and embody an identity as an alternative/contrast community in a confessional situation without becoming a fortress community? If a free flow of air is needed to make a fire, likewise a free flow of the Spirit (air) is needed to form a church with a "burning center and porous borders."[2] Without the Spirit, we will not only have conformist churches, we will also have churches suffering from respiratory failures. If churches are not *inspired* by the Spirit, they will eventually *expire*. So we must pray the prayer of the early church, *Veni Creator Spiritus* (Come, Holy Spirit). When the Spirit dwells in the community of believers, a new vitality will be its expression and various charisms will be its gift. Then a new way of thinking, dwelling, relating, and acting will reign in the community that stands in contrast to the ways of the world—to the ways of the global domination system and its myriad expressions.

ELEAZAR S. FERNANDEZ

Pastoral Perspective

Again, however, a caveat is in order. While there are certainly church members who may think *too* highly of themselves, there are also those with obvious gifts or skills who may not think highly *enough* of themselves, assuming they are not "good enough" to contribute. Paul's body metaphor challenges that group of people to consider that *everyone*—every member of the body of Christ in the church—has a gift to contribute to the functioning of that body. This implies that everyone's gifts are not only present, but *needed* for the living body of Christ to function in the world, as it seeks to discern and live out the will of God. In this case, the "transformation of the mind" back in verse 2 may mean that someone ceases to deny her or his gifts and steps out in faith, taking a risk to serve.

Stretching the body metaphor a bit further calls us to consider not just an individual or an individual congregation but the church of Jesus Christ as a whole. From the beginning of its existence, the church has manifested the body of Christ in a great variety of ways. It is fallacious, for example, to talk about "the early church," as though all the Christian communities of the first century looked exactly alike. From the beginning, different communities have structured their worship life, their governance, their teaching, and their theologies in various ways.

Too often this has meant competition, conflict, and even hatred between Christians. To apply the words of Paul throughout this passage to each of us in our individual roles in the body of Christ brings us to a sobering reflection on the dysfunctional body that may impede the enactment of God's will in the world today. Reflecting on ecumenism within Paul's framework of body metaphor brings hope and possibility to what too often seems an enterprise fraught with struggle.

ROCHELLE A. STACKHOUSE

---

2. Eleazar S. Fernandex, *"Critical Presence" as Good News: Meeting God's People and Creation at the Point of Deepest Need*, http://www.globalministries .org/resources/mission-study/college-of-mission/critical-presence-as-good .html, accessed August 4, 2010.

part has its function. Paul develops this image more fully in 1 Corinthians 12:12–27. Here he keeps it simple: the body parts are "each one members of one another" (cf. Marcus Aurelius, *Meditations* 2.1; Livy, *From the Founding of the City* 2.32.9–11).

Many Gifts (vv. 6–8). As in 1 Corinthians 12, Paul relates the body metaphor to the distribution of spiritual gifts. Similar lists appear in 1 Corinthians 12:4–11, 28–30 and Ephesians 4:11. Since no two lists are identical, we should not read any of them as definitive of rank, which could become an exercise in egotism. Each list is illustrative. This list may appear to be random, depending on translation choices, but in my opinion it falls into two groups.

The first four gifts are teaching functions: prophecy, ministry, teaching, and exhortation. The second of these, "ministry" (*diakonia*), is ambiguous in that the root carries two connotations in the NT. The literal meaning is table service, referring to those who cook and serve (Luke 8:3; 10:40; 17:8; Acts 6:1) or who administer funds for food (Acts 6:2; 11:29; 12:25), including Paul's famine relief fund (Rom. 15:31). The root is also a metaphor for "service of the word" (Acts 6:4; cf. Acts 1:17, 25; 20:24; 21:19). Given its placement between prophecy and teaching, it seems that here Paul has in mind teaching ministry.

The last three gifts are financial support functions exercised by donors, patrons, and almsgivers. The second of these is usually translated "leader," but the location between donor and almsgiver suggests a connotation of financial backer ("who gives aid," RSV). The word *proïstamenos* is literally "being in front." Ancient writers used it with many connotations, depending on what one was in front of and why.[2]

In Roman culture, the related noun *prostatēs* meant "patron," one who had oversight and/or responsibility to protect and support financially, as a father "provides for" children (1 Tim. 3:4–5, 12; cf. Epictetus, *Discourses* 3.24.3). So Paul refers to Phoebe as a "patroness" (*prostatis*) of the church (Rom. 16:2), suggesting that she was a socially prominent financial supporter of the congregation.

Distinctions among the teaching and giving functions should not be pressed too far in this illustrative list, but since teachers and financial supporters tend to be prominent, the admonitions of verses 3–5 are important for keeping these gifts in perspective.

CHRISTOPHER R. HUTSON

dancing spirit."[2] Surely we are dancing spirit when we practice our differing gifts as a way to connect as "members one of another."

Moreover, in order to practice our gifts as a way to connect with one another, we must not be arrogant. The text admonishes both preacher and her or his congregants with these words: "For by the grace given to me I say to everyone among you not to think of yourself more highly than you ought to think, but to think with sober judgment, each according to the measure of faith that God has assigned" (v. 3).

Finally, we come full circle to Paul's opening appeal to be transformed by the renewing of our minds. Good thinking (i.e., renewed minds) is prerequisite for sober judgment. Good thinking is a sign of faithfulness. Perhaps, then, the preaching task is one of guiding the community in discernment of God's will and its gifts. In order to be a faithful community, congregants will need to hear sermons that open their minds so as to prepare them to be God's nonconformists in the world and the church.

In the world, the faithful will need to engage as those who seek what is good and acceptable to God, and this will surely mean witnessing with their whole selves (presenting their bodies as a living sacrifice) against injustice and advocating for anyone who is marginalized because of matters such as the color of their skin, their gender, their sexual orientation, their poverty, and/or their immigrant status. In the church, the faithful will need to let go of value systems that order relationships hierarchically and embrace instead a value system that honors diversity without destroying distinctly and equally valuable persons ("many members, and not all the members have the same function," v. 4).

The preacher will have to plead with his or her congregants like Paul ("I appeal to you therefore, brothers and sisters, by the mercies of God," v. 1a) in order to guide them. The congregation must hear in the sermon's delivery and content that the preacher is with them in this process of becoming the body of Christ, wherein each person practices fully her or his gift. The sermon will definitely not be a sound bite, for the preached word must nurture and sustain the community as they journey together toward God's future.

KIRK BYRON JONES

2. *Theological Dictionary of the New Testament* (Grand Rapids: Eerdmans, 1964–1976), 6.700–703.

Matthew 16:13-20

¹³Now when Jesus came into the district of Caesarea Philippi, he asked his disciples, "Who do people say that the Son of Man is?" ¹⁴And they said, "Some say John the Baptist, but others Elijah, and still others Jeremiah or one of the prophets." ¹⁵He said to them, "But who do you say that I am?" ¹⁶Simon Peter answered, "You are the Messiah, the Son of the living God." ¹⁷And Jesus answered him, "Blessed are you, Simon son of Jonah! For flesh and blood has not revealed this to you, but my Father in heaven. ¹⁸And I tell you, you are Peter, and on this rock I will build my church, and the gates of Hades will not prevail against it. ¹⁹I will give you the keys of the kingdom of heaven, and whatever you bind on earth will be bound in heaven, and whatever you loose on earth will be loosed in heaven." ²⁰Then he sternly ordered the disciples not to tell anyone that he was the Messiah.

Theological Perspective

Peter's historic confession of faith at Caesarea Philippi stands as one of the great christological affirmations in the Gospels. Matthew presents it almost as a blurt—unanticipated, not overtly foreshadowed in the preceding narrative. People are saying various things about Jesus, trying to understand what is going on in their encounters with him, identifying him with one great prophet or another come back to life. Jesus asks Peter about all of this, then looks at him directly: "But who do *you* say that I am?" Peter is somehow able to respond, "You are the Messiah, the Son of the living God." Mark's version, as usual, is more curt: "You are the Messiah" (Mark 8:29). Like Mark, Matthew includes Jesus' order to keep the "messianic secret," charging his disciples to keep quiet about what they know.

Peter's flash of insight may be compared with other moments in the Gospels when there are early glimpses—deeper than deferential addresses of "Lord," "Teacher," or even "Son of David" (Matt. 9:27)—of Jesus' unique identity:

—"I know who you are, the Holy One of God" (Mark 1:24, a disruptive man with an unclean spirit)

—"You are the Son of God!" (Luke 4:41, demons shouting as they come out of many afflicted persons)

Pastoral Perspective

The Roman Catholic Church stands on this passage. In their understanding, the apostolic authority passed on from generation to generation, beginning with Peter receiving the "keys of the kingdom" from Jesus, is what makes the church *the church*. Pope Benedict XVI receives his authority from Pope John Paul II who received his authority from those popes before him all the way back to the apostle Peter. While Protestants may not affirm this particular interpretation, we can agree that the authority Jesus gives to Peter must also be central to our understanding of our authority as a part of the global church. What, though, is the nature of that authority?

Many of us are nervous when our children are first given keys to drive a vehicle capable of going 100 mph at the age of sixteen. Do they have the maturity to handle such responsibility? We might ask the same about Jesus' giving Peter the keys of the kingdom. If we look at Peter's track record prior to and after this event, could we claim that he has the maturity of even a sixteen-year-old? He is constantly missing the point and often talks before he thinks. A few verses later Jesus calls him "Satan" for setting his mind on human instead of divine things (v. 23)! Then Peter later denies Jesus three times (Matt. 26:69–75). How does one give the keys to the kingdom of heaven and build the church upon someone

Exegetical Perspective

Matthew has borrowed this pericope from Mark (8:27–30) but has made several significant changes to Mark's version. In Mark, this episode (along with vv. 31–33) serves as a further example of the failure of Simon Peter (and thus all the disciples) to understand the identity and purpose of Jesus. Peter's "confession" initially sounds laudatory—"You are the Messiah"—but his unwillingness to accept that Jesus' mission (and ultimately that of the disciples) involves suffering and death receives a stern rebuke from Jesus. Rather than serving as a role model in Mark's Gospel, Peter has become an example of an "outsider," one who is on the side of Satan rather than of God.

Matthew, however, rehabilitates Peter in this scene by inserting Jesus' praise of Peter after Peter's identification of Jesus, an identification that Matthew views positively (Matthew's version provides a fuller identification: "You are the Messiah, the Son of the living God," v. 16). Rather than serving as a negative character at this point, Peter represents the true disciple who has accurately understood the significance of Jesus. The titles that are used for Jesus in this section—Son of Man, Messiah, Son of God—are all important for Matthew's Christology. (Only "Messiah" is in the Markan source; Matthew adds the other two.)

Homiletical Perspective

The overall structure of this passage itself offers an almost Socratic dialectic for the preacher to follow. Jesus begins the session with a setup. First, he questions the disciples about the public perception of his ministry and identity. Then, Jesus turns the questioning to the disciples' own perceptions. Simon Peter steps forward to affirm what has already been revealed to the disciples (14:33): Jesus is "the Messiah, the Son of the living God" (v.16). The revelation of Jesus' identity and authority is the foundational authority of the Christian community and the church. Preachers may follow this Q and A development to help congregations understand their own ecclesial traditions in the context of faith and public dialogue.

The matter of ecclesiology is pivotal to this passage. Preachers may wish to explore the formation of this ecclesial fulcrum in the larger section expanding across chapters 14–18. This text illumines the formation of a new community in response to the rejection of Jesus' ministry and divine identity. This exchange between Jesus and his disciples follows a direct challenge by the Pharisees and Sadducees, who insist upon a sign from Jesus (vv. 1–4). Not only does Jesus refuse to perform on demand, but he warns the disciples to exercise caution over teachings from the temple leaders. The formation of this new faith community is

Matthew 16:13-20

Theological Perspective

—"Here is the Lamb of God who takes away the sin of the world" (John 1:29, John the Baptist, saying more than he does in the Synoptics, and more than he knows in Matt. 11:3)

—"We know that this is truly the Savior of the world" (John 4:42, Samaritan villagers, after being introduced to Jesus by the woman who had met him at the well)

Peter's confession is distinctive in that Jesus presses him for it and then rewards him with a powerful blessing. This suggests that there is urgency in the theological enterprise; doctrine is not an add-on to what is essentially spiritual, but integral to religious experience itself. Theology and spirituality are two sides of the same divine encounter.

Jesus makes this a teaching moment to explain that such theological understanding is not the product of human reasoning ("flesh and blood has not revealed this to you") but is the gift of "my Father in heaven" (v. 17). One must not artificially read the church's later theological developments back into biblical texts. An explicit doctrine of the triune God—Father, Son, and Holy Spirit in perichoretic unity—and of the second person of this Trinity possessed with fully divine and fully human natures are not developed or even posited in the Synoptic Gospels. Nevertheless, these essential Christian understandings of God and Christ do resonate profoundly with Matthew's account of Peter's confession that Jesus is Messiah (the Christ, the Anointed One, the Savior) and in an absolutely unique way "the Son of the living God" (v. 16).

Jesus' play on Simon bar Jonah's nickname Peter, with his promise that "on this rock I will build my church" (v. 18), is historically one of the Bible's most contested verses. From about the fourth century, the Catholic Church has interpreted the verse as a basis for the primacy of the bishop of Rome. Protestants have argued that it is Peter's faith in Jesus Christ that is the foundation of the church. Whatever one may think about specific theories of apostolic succession, the text does provide an image of the continuity of God's people over time. Simon first could have earned the nickname due to his stolid character or rocky hardheadedness, but with this christological confession Jesus tells him it has new significance, that now he is going to live up to the highest meaning of "Peter." He becomes a rock upon which God will place other stones as, over time, Christ builds a people for himself.

Jesus may have had Isaiah 51 in mind, where those who "pursue righteousness" and "seek the

Pastoral Perspective

so unstable? Clearly Peter's authority is not based on his rightness or righteousness. Then what is its basis?

Back at the beginning of this passage, Jesus asks his disciples, "Who do people say that the Son of Man is?" (v. 13). Their response seems to depend on what particular faction they are a part of—whether they are partial to John the Baptist, Elijah, Jeremiah, or another prophet. In the Protestant church today, people might respond by interpreting Jesus through the lens of Luther, Calvin, Wesley, Darby, Barth, Aimee Semple McPherson, or Billy Graham. The tendency, in other words, is for people to project onto Jesus their particular cultural, theological, and denominational allegiances.

In the next verse, however, Jesus responds by making the question to his disciples more pointed: "But who do *you* say that I am?" (v. 15). Simon Peter, as he often does, speaks first and replies, "You are the Messiah, the Son of the living God" (v. 16). Jesus responds, "Blessed are you, Simon son of Jonah! For flesh and blood has not revealed this to you, but my Father in heaven. And I tell you, you are Peter (*Petros*), and on this rock (*petra*) I will build my church, and the gates of Hades will not prevail against it" (vv. 17–18).

By the sound of it, Peter got a serious promotion; if there was any doubt about his supremacy among the other disciples, surely this cleared it up! Notice, however, that Jesus was responding not to Peter's particular strengths and accomplishments as a disciple (which left much to be desired) but to his *testimony*—"What I have experienced in you, Jesus, is that you are the Messiah, the one that has been sent to us as a gateway into the kingdom of God."

The temptation of the church has always been to attempt to shore up its authority through external means, the doctrine of apostolic succession being but one example. For centuries the Western church has attempted to prove the existence of God through natural theology, logic, metaphysics, and, more recently, science. Furthermore, the authority of ministers has become rooted in seminary education and ordination certified in a particular denominational tradition. Jesus is a very mercurial figure, though, who cannot be boxed in and used in these ways. The foundation of the church is not Peter, the original bishop, who passes on his regal authority from pope to pope as in the Roman Church; but neither is it the ability to memorize, assent to, and repackage the "hallowed" confessions of the Protestant Reformation.

The church is not founded on Peter, just as it is not founded on John the Baptist or Elijah, Luther or

Exegetical Perspective

That Simon Peter has expressed a correct understanding of Jesus is confirmed by Jesus' statement that Peter's confession is not based on Peter's own insight, but is a revelation given to him by God. Consequently, Jesus gives Simon a new title or nickname, "the Rock" (*petros* in Greek and *kefa* in Aramaic [transliterated into Greek as *Cephas*], neither of which is used at this time in Palestine as a person's name). In a play on words, Jesus says to Simon, "You are 'Rock,' and upon this 'rock' I will build my church." (In John 1:42 explicitly and in Mark 3:16 implicitly, Jesus bestows this nickname on Simon earlier.)

Most scholars consider that this section comes from Matthew (or pre-Matthean material), rather than from Jesus himself. Here and in Matthew 18:17 are the only two occurrences of the word "church" (*ekklēsia*) in the Gospels. For Matthew, then, the church is not simply an institution that arises after the resurrection of Jesus to promote his teachings; rather, the church is founded, or at least its blueprints drawn, by the earthly Jesus to be a continuation of the work that he has begun.

"Hades" (not "hell," as in KJV) in verse 18 is the Greek equivalent of the Hebrew Sheol, the place of the dead. The statement that "the gates of Hades will not prevail" against the church serves as a promise and as words of encouragement; no power in the world, not even humanity's greatest enemy, death itself, will be able to thwart or overcome the work of the church. Such words would have been welcomed by Matthew's community, caught in the sometimes reciprocally caustic struggles to define itself over against the Jewish synagogue. These words, likewise, are potent reminders for the church of all ages when confronted with internal strife and divisions, as well as external assaults or claims of irrelevance.

Peter is given special prominence in this passage, likely reflecting the lofty estimation of Peter in the Matthean community as well as the historical role of Peter as the spokesperson for the disciples and the early leader of the Jerusalem church. Not only does Jesus declare that he will build his church upon Peter, but he also promises him "the keys of the kingdom" (v. 19), which is further explained as the power to "bind and loose," rabbinic terminology for doctrinal and disciplinary authority. In spite of the attempt by some interpreters (frequently Protestant) to play down the role of Peter and argue that it is Peter's faith, not Peter himself, upon which the church is built, this passage clearly recognizes Peter's leadership role among the disciples.

Homiletical Perspective

contextualized in the struggle to understand divine identity and the authority of Christ.

The term used for this community, *ekklēsia*, means to be "called out" but does not indicate a rejection of Israel; instead, ecclesial identity takes shape in the revelation of Christ's identity and mission.[1] Peter's affirmation of faith roots even our questions concerning divine revelation in Christ.

Some scholars consider the rejection of the Pharisees and Sadducees and the resultant break in communication exercised by Jesus to indicate a paradigm of rejection, new identity, and mission facing the emergent church.[2] This argument suggests a form of debate that may demand special attention in our sermons. To what end does the larger section move intently to Peter's affirmation of faith in demonstrating the authority and ministry of the church community facing rejection as did Jesus?

Preaching through questions of rejection and potential responses of faith can offer a pastoral paradigm of care for our own faith identity or formation of faith undergirded by divine revelation and care. Alternatively, a significant risk exists in treating rejection as the evidence or inspiration of our faith responses. The church often faces challenges to our claims of divine revelation or authority to interpret faithful living. Preaching from this passage should exercise caution against criminalizing all challenges to our faith claims. "How" we confess or affirm our faith and divine authority in revelation becomes critical in our sermons.

Perhaps the most prevalent reference to this passage is to Jesus' blessing and naming Peter as the rock upon which the church is to be built (vv. 17–19). Many claims have been made upon the nature of Simon Peter's "renaming" and the formation of a new community of faith. Does Jesus' naming Peter as the rock reflect the anointing or of Abram, his renaming as Abraham, and the formation of the people of God? Others speculate that Peter stands under the shadow cast by Jesus' authority, as Aaron might have under the shadow of Moses. Much has been made of the Catholic and Protestant debates over apostolic succession and the authority of the church.

Agreement can be claimed among scholars insofar as Peter is the central figure for the Gospel writer in the formation of the new church. Still, this passage remains a central piece in the arguments between the

---

1. M. Eugene Boring, "The Gospel of Matthew," in *The New Interpreter's Bible* (Nashville: Abingdon Press, 1995), 8:342–47.
2. Donald J. Verseput, "Faith of the Reader and the Narrative of Matthew 13:53–16:20," *Journal for the Study of the New Testament* 46 (1992): 3–24.

Matthew 16:13-20

Theological Perspective

Lord" are admonished: "Look to the rock from which you were hewn, and to the quarry from which you were dug." The prophet identifies Abraham and Sarah as the first "rocks" dug from the quarry of faithfulness (Isa. 51:1–2). In the NT, 1 Peter picks up the image, as Christ is called "a living stone, though rejected by mortals yet chosen and precious in God's sight" (1 Pet. 2:4). Now we are called to be like Jesus himself and like Peter and others down the generations who have confessed Jesus as Son of God and Savior: "Like living stones, let yourselves be built into a spiritual house" (1 Pet. 2:5).

Preachers of various ecclesial traditions today should be able, from this text, to explore a theology of the church positively and without the old polemics. For example, we can know that the church is essential to Christian faith and theology. The Apostles' Creed is right ("I believe in . . . the holy catholic church, the communion of saints") and American utilitarianism is wrong when it comes to ecclesiology. The church is not merely a means to achieve a greater goal, nor is it just a voluntary association of like-minded individuals. It is an article of faith. Jesus promises that *he* will build *his* church. He will protect the church he is building so that, while the force of sin and death will do its worst to destroy, the church nevertheless will prevail.

Jesus connects his church and his kingdom. It is not just that the church announces the kingdom that is to come or prepares people for that day. When Jesus gives "the keys of the kingdom of heaven" and grants authority to "bind" and "loose," he is creating the church as the epicenter of the Father's answer to Jesus' prayer that God's kingdom will come, that his will may be done, "on earth as it is in heaven" (Matt. 6:10). The text, therefore, suggests a high ecclesiology to go with its Christology—a missional theology in which the church continues the *missio Dei* that Peter recognized in the person of Jesus.

Jesus "sternly ordered the disciples not to tell anyone that he was the Messiah" (v. 20) during those dangerous days before going to Jerusalem. After Pentecost, proclaiming that gospel became the primary work of his church.

CHARLES E. HAMBRICK-STOWE

Pastoral Perspective

Calvin. The rock is not Peter, but Peter's *testimony*. Therefore, while this passage has been interpreted to give the church empirical power and permanence, the underlying lesson is that the church is as resilient or fragile as each of us in our own faith. The church exists daily in this tension of power and powerlessness. Jesus' question to each of us is, "Who do *you* say that I am? What is *your* testimony of me? What is *your* experience of the living God through my witness and presence?"

This is the rock on which the church is founded and the source of the Christian's authority. This is what grants us the keys of the kingdom of heaven, to bind and to loose on earth. God relates to the church not as a coercive ruler but as a loving parent who entrusts to a fragile and immature child the power to do right and to do wrong, to be faithful and to drift away.

The history of Christianity, of course, attests to how vulnerable we are to complacency as Christians, and how easy it is for us to slip into idolatry by resting on and reifying someone else's confession of Christ. This passage calls us to move beyond our particular political and denominational factions, our various theological emphases, and our respective ethnic loyalties by speaking truthfully to one another in and through our differences about the impact of Jesus Christ in our own lives.

As the apostle Paul understood, it is in our weakness that Christ's strength is made apparent (2 Cor. 12:9–10). We become not only individual testifiers within a community, but a community that testifies to the life-giving gospel of Jesus Christ. By liberating the "priesthood of all believers" in this way, the body of Christ realizes its own authority as living witness that overcomes the power of death and despair.

JIN S. KIM

Exegetical Perspective

Contrary to traditional Roman Catholic exegesis, however, the passage does not support any claim to apostolic or Petrine succession. In fact, the authority of binding and loosing that is here bestowed upon Peter is in verse 19 given explicitly to the disciples and implicitly to the whole church. (In 18:19 binding and loosing refer more to the disciplinary than the teaching authority of the church, but the two ideas are related.)

Throughout his Gospel, Matthew portrays Jesus as "binding and loosing" the teachings of the Torah; that is, Jesus declares certain actions to be necessary and others not to be required. Jesus does this because he operates with the authority of God (see, e.g., 5:21–48). Matthew also presents Jesus as granting that teaching authority to Peter and the disciples (and the church) because Jesus continues to be present in the community of believers he has called into being. From the birth narrative (1:23) to the final commission to the disciples (28:20), Matthew emphasizes the abiding presence of God in the world. Thus the church operates with the authority to teach in the name of Jesus, to interpret the kingdom of God to the world.

In the words of Mark Allan Powell, Matthew is convinced that "the church has the authority to declare God's will not because it exhibits more insight or greater faithfulness to God than others but because Jesus Christ, God's Son, has chosen to be present in the church and to exercise his authority on earth through this community."[1] The church has been given a daunting task—to interpret the will of God to the world. In Matthew's Gospel, the manner in which Jesus declares what is "binding" and what is "loosed" becomes a model for how the church is to practice its task. Scripture is not static; it must be reapplied to new situations. Just as Jesus applies the teachings of the Torah in fresh and creative ways, the church must be emboldened to interpret the teachings of Jesus in new and inspired ways, attempting both to be faithful to the teachings of Jesus as found in Matthew's Gospel (and the rest of the New Testament) and to be open to the voice of Jesus that speaks through the church to new situations and problems.

MITCHELL G. REDDISH

Homiletical Perspective

authority *of* the church and authority *over* the church. It seems particularly important here to keep in mind that Matthew is addressing the formation of this new community of faith amid the context of rejection. Matthew is concerned with addressing questions of the identity and authority of this church community through the revelation of Christ himself.

The identity and authority of Jesus translates into the identity and therefore the authority of the church; Christology is the revelation forming ecclesiology. It is the substance and nature of revelation in the formation of the church that preoccupies Matthew's attention here. Still, what kind of rock is Peter? How much of these verses refers to the person or to the event of revelation?

While this event in Matthew builds directly from the Gospel of Mark, verses 17–19 have no corollary in the Markan source. This addition, in the context of Matthew's focus on ecclesial identity and authority, therefore informs how we may treat these verses in preaching. While Peter is clearly named with the event and therefore his role in the early church does not become irrelevant, the focus of this passage is upon divine revelation through Christ as the source of our identity and authority to interpret revelation for the community of faith.[3]

The keys to binding and loosing are keys for interpretation of revelation. We gather more insight into this point from its parallel in 18:15–20. While further review of this correlation with the latter passage can be found in the study for Proper 18 Sunday in *Feasting on the Word* Year 1, vol. 4, here one may draw from those verses to understand that the authority to interpret revelation—that is, to bind and to loose—relates to the identity and work of the church.

Interpretation of revelation concerns how we live in historical context and in faith. Our theology of preaching, the preaching event in the church, and thus the sermon under consideration for this week all wrestle with the identity and authority of the church within the community of faith and the world. Even the closing charge of the passage, to tell no one yet that Jesus is the Messiah (v. 20), points back to deciphering the nature and authority of revelation to root the emerging formation of the church.

DALE P. ANDREWS

1. Mark Allan Powell, *Fortress Introduction to the Gospels* (Minneapolis: Augsburg Fortress, 1998), 80.

3. M. Jack Suggs, "Matthew 16:13–20," *Interpretation* 39, no. 3 (July 1985): 291–95.

Contributors

Charles L. Aaron Jr., Pastor, First United Methodist Church, Farmsville, Texas

O. Wesley Allen Jr., Associate Professor of Homiletics and Worship, Lexington Theological Seminary, Lexington, Kentucky

Herbert Anderson, Research Professor in Practical Theology, Pacific Lutheran Theological Seminary, Berkeley, California

Dale P. Andrews, Martin Luther King Jr. Professor of Homiletics and Pastoral Theology, Boston University School of Theology, Boston, Massachusetts

Mary Beth Anton, Chaplain, Trinity School of Midland, and Parish Associate, First Presbyterian Church, Midland, Texas

Talitha J. Arnold, Senior Minister, United Church of Santa Fe, New Mexico

Rachel Sophia Baard, Lawrence C. Gallen Postdoctoral Fellow, Villanova University, Villanova, Pennsylvania

Douglass M. Bailey, President, Center for Urban Ministry, Inc., and Assistant Professor of Urban Ministry, Wake Forest University School of Divinity, Winston-Salem, North Carolina

David L. Bartlett, Professor of New Testament, Columbia Theological Seminary, Decatur, Georgia

David M. Bender, Pastor, Faith Presbyterian Church, Indian Land, South Carolina

Thomas W. Blair, Pastor, Second Presbyterian Church, Baltimore, Maryland

Dave Bland, Professor of Homiletics, Harding University Graduate School of Religion, Memphis, Tennessee

Richard Boyce, Associate Professor of Preaching and Pastoral Leadership, Union Presbyterian Seminary, Charlotte, North Carolina

Stephen B. Boyd, Chair and Professor, Department of Religion, Wake Forest University, Winston-Salem, North Carolina

James T. Butler, Associate Professor of Old Testament, Fuller Theological Seminary, Pasadena, California

Carlos F. Cardoza-Orlandi, Professor of Global Christianities and Mission Studies, Perkins School of Theology, Southern Methodist University, Dallas, Texas

Robert A. Cathey, Professor of Theology, McCormick Theological Seminary, Chicago, Illinois

Karen Chakoian, Pastor, First Presbyterian Church, Granville, Ohio

Gary W. Charles, Pastor, Central Presbyterian Church, Atlanta, Georgia

Emily R. Cheney, Research Scholar, Athens, Georgia

Jana Childers, Professor of Homiletics and Speech-Communication, San Francisco Theological Seminary, San Anselmo, California

Kate Colussy-Estes, Julia Thompson Smith Chaplain, Agnes Scott College, Decatur, Georgia

Stephen L. Cook, Catherine N. McBurney Professor of Old Testament Language and Literature, Virginia Theological Seminary, Alexandria, Virginia

Stephen A. Cooper, Professor of Religious Studies, Franklin and Marshall College, Lancaster, Pennsylvania

Carole A. Crumley, Senior Program Director, Shalem Institute for Spiritual Formation, Washington, D.C.

David S. Cunningham, Professor of Religion and Director, The Crossroads Project, Hope College, Holland, Michigan

Steed Vernyl Davidson, Assistant Professor of Old Testament, Pacific Lutheran Theological Seminary, Berkeley, California

Steven P. Eason, Senior Pastor, Myers Park Presbyterian Church, Charlotte, North Carolina

Heather Murray Elkins, Professor of Worship, Preaching, and the Arts, Drew University, Madison, New Jersey

Kyle D. Fedler, Vice President and Dean of Faculty, Huntingdon College, Montgomery, Alabama

Eleazar S. Fernandez, Professor of Constructive Theology, United Theological Seminary of the Twin Cities, New Brighton, Minnesota

Michael H. Floyd, Professor of Old Testament, Centro de Estudios Teológicos, Santo Domingo, Dominican Republic

William Goettler, Co-Pastor, First Presbyterian Church, and Assistant Dean of Ministry Studies, Yale Divinity School, New Haven, Connecticut

Barbara Green, Professor of Biblical Studies, Dominican School of Philosophy and Theology, Berkeley, California

Garrett Green, Professor Emeritus of Religious Studies, Connecticut College, New London, Connecticut

David M. Greenhaw, President and Professor of Preaching and Worship, Eden Theological Seminary, St. Louis, Missouri

David P. Gushee, Distinguished University Professor of Christian Ethics, Mercer University, Atlanta, Georgia

Charles E. Hambrick-Stowe, Pastor, First Congregational Church of Ridgefield, Connecticut

Angela Dienhart Hancock, PhD Candidate, Princeton Theological Seminary, Princeton, New Jersey

Walter J. Harrelson, Professor Emeritus of Vanderbilt University, residing in Winston-Salem, North Carolina

James Henry Harris, Professor of Homiletics and Pastoral Theology, Virginia Union University, School of Theology, Richmond, Virginia

Trace Haythorn, President, The Fund for Theological Education, Atlanta, Georgia

Martha C. Highsmith, Deputy Secretary of the University and Lecturer in Divinity, Yale Divinity School, New Haven, Connecticut

Dock Hollingsworth, Assistant Dean and Assistant Professor of Supervised Ministry, McAfee School of Theology, Mercer University, Atlanta, Georgia

H. James Hopkins, Pastor, Lakeshore Avenue Baptist Church, Oakland, California

Christopher R. Hutson, Associate Professor of New Testament, Hood Theological Seminary, Salisbury, North Carolina

Earl S. Johnson, Jr., Pastor, First Presbyterian Church, Johnstown, New York, and Adjunct Professor of Religious Studies, Siena College, Loudonville, New York

Kirk Byron Jones, Adjunct Faculty in Ethics, Andover Newton Theological School, Newton Centre, Massachusetts

Jin S. Kim, Senior Pastor, Church of All Nations, Minneapolis, Minnesota

Katie Givens Kime, Associate Pastor for Adult Ministries, Trinity Presbyterian Church, Atlanta, Georgia

Clifton Kirkpatrick, Visiting Professor of Ecumenical Studies and Global Ministries, Louisville Presbyterian Theological Seminary, Louisville, Kentucky

Constance M. Koch, OP, Dominican Sisters of Hope, Dobbs Ferry, New York

Jae Won Lee, Assistant Professor of New Testament, McCormick Theological Seminary, Chicago, Illinois

John R. Levison, Professor of New Testament, Seattle Pacific University, Seattle, Washington

Thomas G. Long, Bandy Professor of Preaching, Candler School of Theology, Emory University, Atlanta, Georgia

Mary Elise Lowe, Assistant Professor of Religion, Augsburg College, Minneapolis, Minnesota

Harold E. Masback III, Senior Minister, The Congregational Church of New Canaan, Connecticut

David Maxwell, Executive Editor, Geneva Press and The Thoughtful Christian, Louisville, Kentucky

Wendel W. Meyer, Retired Rector, St. John's Episcopal Church, North Berwick, Maine

Steven D. Miller, Pastor, Community United Methodist Church, Westcliffe, Colorado

Stephanie Y. Mitchem, Professor and Chair, Department of Religious Studies, University of South Carolina, Columbia, South Carolina

Diane Givens Moffett, Senior Pastor, St. James Presbyterian Church, Greensboro, North Carolina

Shawnthea Monroe, Senior Minister, Plymouth United Church of Christ, Shaker Heights, Ohio

Mary Alice Mulligan, Affiliate Professor of Homiletics and Ethics, Christian Theological Seminary, Indianapolis, Indiana

Debra J. Mumford, Frank H. Caldwell Assistant Professor of Homiletics, Louisville Presbyterian Theological Seminary, Louisville, Kentucky

D. Cameron Murchison, Dean of Faculty and Executive Vice President, Columbia Theological Seminary, Decatur, Georgia

Stephen Butler Murray, Senior Pastor, The First Baptist Church of Boston, Massachusetts, and College Chaplain and Associate Professor of Religion, Endicott College, Beverly, Massachusetts

Guy D. Nave Jr., Associate Professor of Religion, Luther College, Decorah, Iowa

Lance Pape, Assistant Professor of Homiletics, Brite Divinity School, Fort Worth, Texas

Eugene Eung-Chun Park, Dornsife Professor of New Testament, San Francisco Theological Seminary, San Anselmo, California

V. Steven Parrish, Professor of Old Testament, Memphis Theological Seminary, Memphis, Tennessee

Steven D. Paulson, Professor of Theology, Luther Seminary, St. Paul, Minnesota

Julie Peeples, Senior Minister, Congregational United Church of Christ, Greensboro, North Carolina

Gary Peluso-Verdend, President and Associate Professor of Practical Theology, Phillips Theological Seminary, Tulsa, Oklahoma

Ronald E. Peters, President, Interdenominational Theological Center, Atlanta, Georgia

Blair Alison Pogue, Rector, St. Matthew's Episcopal Church, St. Paul, Minnesota

Luke A. Powery, Perry and Georgia Engle Assistant Professor of Homiletics, Princeton Theological Seminary, Princeton, New Jersey

Richard A. Puckett, Director of Public Relations and Development, United Methodist Children's Home, Decatur, Georgia

Melinda Quivik, Associate Professor of Christian Assembly, Lutheran Theological Seminary at Philadelphia, Pennsylvania

George W. Ramsey, Kristen Herrington Professor of Religion Emeritus, Presbyterian College, Clinton, South Carolina

Elizabeth P. Randall, Cathedral Spiritual Director, St. John's Cathedral, Denver, Colorado

Mitchell G. Reddish, Professor and Chair of Religious Studies, Stetson University, DeLand, Florida

Iwan Russell-Jones, Television Producer, Cardiff, United Kingdom

Elizabeth McGregor Simmons, Pastor, Davidson College Presbyterian Church, Davidson, North Carolina

Ted A. Smith, Assistant Professor of Ethics and Society, Vanderbilt Divinity School, Nashville, Tennessee

Rochelle A. Stackhouse, Senior Minister, Church of the Redeemer United Church of Christ, New Haven, Connecticut

Meda A. A. Stamper, Minister, Anstey United Reformed Church, and Visiting Lecturer, St. John's College, Nottingham, England

Nibs Stroupe, Pastor, Oakhurst Presbyterian Church, Decatur, Georgia

John L. Thomas Jr., Assistant Professor of Practical Theology, Phillips Theological Seminary, Tulsa, Oklahoma

Emilie M. Townes, Associate Dean of Academic Affairs, Andrew W. Mellon Professor of African American Religion and Theology, Yale Divinity School, New Haven, Connecticut

David G. Trickett, President and Henry Warren Professor of Ethics and Leadership, The Iliff School of Theology, Denver, Colorado

Diane Turner-Sharazz, Director, Course of Study School of Ohio, Methodist Theological School in Ohio, Delaware, Ohio, and Pastor, McKinley United Methodist Church, Dayton, Ohio

Leanne Van Dyk, Dean and Vice President of Academic Affairs, Western Theological Seminary, Holland, Michigan

John M. VonderBruegge, Instructor in Religion, Northwestern College, Orange City, Iowa

Robert W. Wall, Paul T. Walls Professor of Scripture and Wesleyan Studies, Seattle Pacific University, Seattle, Washington

Theodore J. Wardlaw, President, Austin Presbyterian Theological Seminary, Austin, Texas

J. David Waugh, Interim Pastor, Madison Baptist Fellowship, Madison, Mississippi

Jo Bailey Wells, Associate Professor of the Practice of Christian Ministry and Bible and Director of Anglican Studies, Duke University Divinity School, Durham, North Carolina

Barbara G. Wheeler, Director, Center for the Study of Theological Education, Auburn Theological Seminary, New York, New York

Alexander Wimberly, Minister, McCracken Memorial Presbyterian Church, Belfast, Northern Ireland

Scripture Index

Author Index

Abbreviations

E	Epistle	PP	Pastoral Perspective
EP	Exegetical Perspective	PS	Psalm
G	Gospel	OT	Old Testament
HP	Homiletical Perspective	TP	Theological Perspective
NT	New Testament		

Numerals indicate numbered Sundays of a season; for example, "Lent 1" represents the First Sunday in Lent, and "Easter 2" the Second Sunday of Easter.

Contributors and entries

Charles L. Aaron Jr.	Proper 12 PS EP	Richard Boyce	Day of Pentecost OT EP, Trinity Sunday OT EP, Proper 3 OT EP
O. Wesley Allen Jr.	Proper 10 PS HP, Proper 11 PS HP		
Herbert Anderson	Proper 10 PS PP, Proper 11 PS PP	Stephen B. Boyd	Day of Pentecost G TP, Trinity Sunday G TP, Proper 3 G TP
Dale P. Andrews	Proper 16 G HP	James T. Butler	Proper 7 OT EP, Proper 8 OT EP, Proper 9 OT EP
Mary Beth Anton	Proper 13 E HP, Proper 14 E HP, Proper 15 E HP		
		Carlos F. Cardoza-Orlandi	Proper 16 OT TP
Talitha J. Arnold	Proper 10 G PP, Proper 11 G PP, Proper 12 G PP	Robert A. Cathey	Proper 7 PS TP, Proper 8 PS TP, Proper 9 PS TP
Rachel Sophia Baard	Proper 7 OT TP, Proper 8 OT TP, Proper 9 OT TP	Karen Chakoian	Proper 10 E EP, Proper 11 E EP, Proper 12 E EP
Douglass M. Bailey	Proper 7 OT HP, Proper 8 OT HP, Proper 9 OT HP	Gary W. Charles	Proper 12 PS PP, Proper 15 G PP
David L. Bartlett	Proper 12 PS HP	Emily R. Cheney	Proper 7 PS EP, Proper 8 PS EP, Proper 9 PS EP
David M. Bender	Day of Pentecost NT PP, Trinity Sunday E PP, Proper 3 E PP		
		Jana Childers	Day of Pentecost NT HP, Trinity Sunday E HP, Proper 3 E HP
Thomas W. Blair	Proper 10 OT PP, Proper 11 OT PP, Proper 12 OT PP	Kate Colussy-Estes	Proper 7 PS PP, Proper 8 PS PP, Proper 9 PS PP
Dave Bland	Day of Pentecost OT HP, Trinity Sunday OT HP, Proper 3 OT HP	Stephen L. Cook	Proper 16 OT EP

David Maxwell	Proper 13 OT PP, Proper 14 OT PP, Proper 15 OT PP	Julie Peeples	Proper 16 PS PP
		Gary Peluso-Verdend	Proper 10 G TP, Proper 11 G TP, Proper 12 G TP
Wendel W. Meyer	Proper 13 OT HP, Proper 14 OT HP, Proper 15 OT HP		
		Ronald E. Peters	Proper 16 OT PP
Steven D. Miller	Proper 4 PS PP, Proper 5 PS PP, Proper 6 PS PP	Blair Alison Pogue	Proper 10 E HP, Proper 11 E HP, Proper 12 E HP
Stephanie Y. Mitchem	Proper 13 OT TP, Proper 14 OT TP, Proper 15 OT TP	Luke A. Powery	Proper 4 G HP, Proper 5 G HP, Proper 6 G HP
Diane Givens Moffett	Proper 4 E PP, Proper 5 E PP, Proper 6 E PP	Richard A. Puckett	Proper 16 PS EP
		Melinda Quivik	Day of Pentecost OT TP, Trinity Sunday OT TP, Proper 3 OT TP
Shawnthea Monroe	Proper 7 E PP, Proper 8 E PP, Proper 9 E PP	George W. Ramsey	Proper 13 PS EP, Proper 14 PS EP, Proper 15 PS EP
Mary Alice Mulligan	Proper 4 OT HP, Proper 5 OT HP, Proper 6 OT HP	Elizabeth P. Randall	Proper 16 PS HP
Debra J. Mumford	Proper 4 PS HP, Proper 5 PS HP, Proper 6 PS HP	Mitchell G. Reddish	Proper 16 G EP
		Iwan Russell-Jones	Proper 13 G TP, Proper 14 G TP, Proper 15 G TP
D. Cameron Murchison	Proper 12 PS TP		
Stephen Butler Murray	Proper 4 G TP, Proper 5 G TP, Proper 6 G TP	Elizabeth McGregor Simmons	Proper 13 PS PP, Proper 14 PS PP, Proper 15 PS PP
Guy D. Nave Jr.	Proper 4 G EP, Proper 5 G EP, Proper 6 G EP	Ted A. Smith	Proper 7 E TP, Proper 8 E TP, Proper 9 E TP
Lance Pape	Proper 7 G HP, Proper 8 G HP, Proper 9 G HP	Rochelle A. Stackhouse	Proper 16 E PP
		Meda A. A. Stamper	Day of Pentecost G EP, Trinity Sunday G EP, Proper 3 G EP
Eugene Eung-Chun Park	Proper 7 G EP, Proper 8 G EP, Proper 9 G EP	Nibs Stroupe	Day of Pentecost PS PP, Trinity Sunday PS PP, Proper 3 PS PP
V. Steven Parrish	Day of Pentecost PS EP, Trinity Sunday PS EP, Proper 3 PS EP	John L. Thomas Jr.	Proper 10 OT TP, Proper 11 OT TP, Proper 12 OT TP
Steven D. Paulson	Proper 10 E TP, Proper 11 E TP, Proper 12 E TP	Emilie M. Townes	Proper 7 G TP, Proper 8 G TP, Proper 9 G TP

David G. Trickett	Day of Pentecost PS TP, Trinity Sunday PS TP, Proper 3 PS TP	Theodore J. Wardlaw	Proper 10 G HP, Proper 11 G HP, Proper 12 G HP
Diane Turner-Sharazz	Proper 4 E HP, Proper 5 E HP, Proper 6 E HP	J. David Waugh	Proper 10 G EP, Proper 11 G EP, Proper 12 G EP
Leanne Van Dyk	Proper 13 PS TP, Proper 14 PS TP, Proper 15 PS TP	Jo Bailey Wells	Proper 10 PS TP, Proper 11 PS TP
John M. VonderBruegge	Proper 13 E EP, Proper 14 E EP, Proper 15 E EP	Barbara G. Wheeler	Proper 4 OT TP, Proper 5 OT TP, Proper 6 OT TP
Robert W. Wall	Proper 4 E EP, Proper 5 E EP, Proper 6 E EP	Alexander Wimberly	Proper 4 G PP, Proper 5 G PP, Proper 6 G PP

green
press
INITIATIVE

Westminster John Knox Press is committed to preserving ancient forests and natural resources. We elected to print this title on 30% post consumer recycled paper, processed chlorine free. As a result, for this printing, we have saved:

97 Trees (40' tall and 6-8" diameter)
31 Million BTUs of Total Energy
9,210 Pounds of Greenhouse Gases
44,358 Gallons of Wastewater
2,693 Pounds of Solid Waste

Westminster John Knox Press made this paper choice because our printer, Thomson-Shore, Inc., is a member of Green Press Initiative, a nonprofit program dedicated to supporting authors, publishers, and suppliers in their efforts to reduce their use of fiber obtained from endangered forests.

For more information, visit www.greenpressinitiative.org

Environmental impact estimates were made using the Environmental Defense Paper Calculator. For more information visit: www.edf.org/papercalculator